PROCEDURES IN

FEDERAL TAX

CONTROVERSIES

• Administrative and Trial Practice

MARVIN JOSEPH GARBIS
MEMBER OF THE MARYLAND, DISTRICT OF COLUMBIA,
AND FEDERAL BARS

ROBERT L. FROME
MEMBER OF THE NEW YORK AND FEDERAL BARS

THE RONALD PRESS COMPANY • NEW YORK

Library of Congress Catalog Card Number: 68-13003
PRINTED IN THE UNITED STATES OF AMERICA

To Phyllis and Pat

PREFACE

In the Federal tax system many procedures are available for the resolution of tax controversies. These procedures range from administrative practices before the Internal Revenue Service to litigation in the various Federal courts. Moreover, the judicial forums given jurisdiction over tax controversies—the Tax Court of the United States, the United States Court of Claims, and the United States district courts—provide distinctly different litigation procedures. This book is intended as a guide to these procedures for the tax practitioner—whether attorney or accountant. It should also be of interest to the attorney in general practice and to the accountant whose clients may become involved in tax controversies.

The authors have attempted to present the material in a manner comprehensible to the non-specialist and to cover all of the many options and alternatives available, both on the administrative level before the Internal Revenue Service and in the courts. The procedures discussed are applicable to controversies regarding the correct amount of a taxpayer's liability for all internal revenue taxes.

In practice most tax cases are closed by a settlement rather than by judicial determination. Accordingly, settlement procedures are as important as trial procedures in handling tax controversies. Thus, the subject of settlement of a case prior to the various review levels of the Internal Revenue Service is discussed throughout the chapter on prelitigation administrative procedures, and separate chapters are devoted to settlement of Tax Court cases and tax refund suits. The discussion of tax practice before the courts encompasses the entire course of a case from commencement to conclusion. Particularly detailed discussions of the pleadings and pretrial procedures in the tax forums have been included.

The authors wish to make it clear that the views expressed in this book are their own and do not necessarily reflect the policies of any department or agency of the United States government.

Throughout their work on the book the authors have concentrated on producing a *practical* and comprehensive guide to the handling of federal tax controversies. If those who use it in any phase of a tax dispute find it helpful, the authors' purpose will have been achieved.

Marvin Joseph Garbis
Robert L. Frome

Baltimore, Md.
New York City
January, 1968

v

ACKNOWLEDGMENT

This book was written with the aid of Kurt L. Kamm, Esq., to whom the authors are most grateful for excellent writing and thorough research in the areas of Internal Revenue Service administrative procedures and Tax Court practice. His hard work, talent, and constructive thinking were an invaluable contribution to this book.

The authors would also like to thank Mr. David A. Wilson, Jr., Chief, Refund Trial Section No. 1, Tax Division, United States Department of Justice, and Mr. Benjamin Lewis, of the firm of Marlin, Lewis, and Green, for having read the manuscript and offered the benefit of their guidance.

The authors wish to state their appreciation to members of the judiciary, the Tax Division of the United States Department of Justice, the Internal Revenue Service, and the private tax bar who gave their encouragement, enthusiasm, and suggestions during the course of this work.

Finally, special acknowledgment is made to:

Chief Judge Norman O. Tietjens, Judge Craig S. Atkins, Judge C. Moxley Featherston, and Judge Howard A. Dawson, Jr., of the United States Tax Court;

The Honorable Mitchell Rogovin, Assistant United States Attorney General;

Messrs. Richard C. Pugh, First Assistant, Tax Division; and Arthur Biggins, Special Assistant, Tax Division—United States Department of Justice;

Messrs. Marvin Hagen, Regional Counsel (N.Y.); William Halloram, Assistant Regional Counsel (N.Y.), Tax Court Section; Paul Frankel, Trial Attorney, Regional Counsel Office (N.Y.); Arthur Zucker, Chief, Conference Staff, District Director's Office (N.Y.C.); Albert Fink, Audit Division, District Director's Office (N.Y.C.); and Paul Kavanaugh, Chief, Estate and Gift Tax Branch, District Director's Office (Cleveland)— United States Internal Revenue Service;

Messrs. Edwin H. Baker, of the New York City law firm of Willkie, Farr, Gallagher, Walton and FitzGibbon, and Richard Frome, member of the New York Bar, and Mrs. Fannie Cooper, of the firm of Cooper & Frome, New York City.

M. J. G.
R. L. F.

CONTENTS

APPENDIXES

TABLES AND INDEX

PROCEDURES IN FEDERAL TAX CONTROVERSIES

CHAPTER 1

PRELITIGATION ADMINISTRATIVE PROCEDURES

The internal revenue system of the United States is unique. Never have so many paid so much to support their government. The success of the United States tax system is primarily attributable to voluntary compliance by taxpayers, which is largely due to the fairness of the tax law both in substance and in application. To achieve such an even-handed application of the law, effective procedures are necessary for examining returns to assure their accuracy and to dispose fairly of disputes. This chapter provides a guide to the methods used in examining returns and the most advantageous procedures a taxpayer can employ for settling disputes without going to court.

PROCESSING THE RETURN

Recently the Internal Revenue Service began using a computerized Automatic Data Processing System, or A.D.P., for processing tax returns. Physically the system consists of seven regional service centers, corresponding to the seven Internal Revenue Service Regional Offices, and a National Computer Center in West Virginia. In 1966, A.D.P. processed 98 million documents.[1] When a return is filed, it is processed as follows:

1. After preliminary examination of the returns, the Service Center transcribes all relevant information to computer punch cards.
2. The transcription is verified, and data transferred to magnetic tape.
3. The mathematical computations and certain other information are checked by the computer. When an error is found, the return is sent to the error resolution branch for appropriate action.
4. The tapes with the data from each return are sent to the National Computer Center, which records the data on each taxpayer in its central files along with data recorded from prior years.
5. The filed data is then compared with data from past years to determine inconsistencies. Further comparison against predetermined audit standards produces those returns selected for audit. Tapes containing the data for such returns are prepared and forwarded to the Audit Division in the office of the appropriate District Director.
6. Tapes listing returns that require refunds are sent to the Treasury Department.

SELECTION OF CASES FOR AUDIT

The Service has two objectives in conducting audits: One is to encourage voluntary compliance with the revenue laws, and the second is to recoup the revenues lost as a result of errors and omissions in returns.

Insofar as criteria for the auditing process are concerned, the Service does not publicize the standards it employs. Furthermore, such standards may vary from year to year or even from month to month as well as from

[1] 24 Journal of Taxation 304 (1966).

region to region or district to district. Nonetheless, it is clear that every tax return filed cannot be thoroughly examined; hence certain criteria must be established to aid in selecting for audit those returns with the greatest potential for error. Some of these criteria are discussed below.

Gross Income: A Basic Audit Standard

In 1964 approximately 5% of all tax returns were audited.[2] The Service concedes that the percentage of 1040A forms audited is quite low. An audit of a 1040A form will usually disclose only blatant fraud, which is rare, or excessive exemptions, which will yield only minimal revenues. Thus, although some auditing of 1040A forms is necessary to encourage compliance, auditing 1040A forms does not yield substantial additional revenue.

As the amount of gross income reported increases, the percentage of returns audited increases.[3] Apparently most if not all returns reporting income over $30,000 are audited. Clearly such auditing is done as much to collect revenue as to encourage compliance.

National and Regional Criteria

Each year the national office at Washington requires that all district offices are to audit returns that exceed a specified amount of gross income or that report a specified amount of income from a particular source. Similarly, the national office may direct that deductions exceeding a particular amount or a specified portion of gross income, such as for travel, entertainment, or charity, are subject to an automatic audit.

In addition to the national standards, each Regional or District Office may have similar or additional standards that it applies to audits within its jurisdiction.

Industry and Occupational Criteria

Each year the Regional Office will determine that the returns filed by a particular industry or by members of a particular profession in a certain area in the region are to be audited. This is called the "Industry Compliance Program." Thus, in a particular year, the returns of all dentists or all chemical manufacturers may be subject to audit.

Other Criteria

There may be other causes for an audit besides the fact that the return happens to fall into one or another category requiring an automatic audit. Some audits occur because the itemization on the return raises some cause

[2] Annual Report of the Commissioner of Internal Revenue of the United States for the Fiscal Year Ended June 30, 1965, 16.
[3] *Ibid.*

for doubt. If the available information does not agree with the return or if the return on its face indicates an error or omission, an audit will be necessary.

Experience also shows that when a taxpayer has an excessively large income or when a previous audit has disclosed a substantial amount of additional tax due, his subsequent returns are often audited either periodically or for a consecutive number of years. The Service has stated that such auditing is not the result of an intentional policy of surveillance and that consecutive or periodic audits probably are a result of the fact that such a taxpayer is often caught up in one or another of the classes subject to national or regional audit.

Finally, an additional group of returns is selected for audit on the basis of a mathematical sample administered by the Statistical Division in Washington. This procedure brings a number of purely random returns within the scope of the audit.

Use of A.D.P. in Auditing

The service expects to pinpoint returns requiring audit more accurately through the use of the A.D.P. system. By use of the computer, each return can be automatically compared with the predetermined audit standards (which are changed from time to time), and large amounts of information relating to each return can be used to determine its correctness. The system also can be used to digest descriptive information concerning all returns filed, in order to determine future classifications for automatic audit. In addition to the accuracy with which the returns can be processed, use of A.D.P. enables returns to be processed at a speed heretofore thought impossible.

After a return has been reviewed, it will be classified as "closed on survey," "subject to office audit," or "subject to field audit." If a return is "closed on survey," it is acceptable as filed unless information acquired at a later date should cause it to be examined. If a return is so classified, the taxpayer will hear nothing about his return.

PREPARING FOR THE AUDIT

When a taxpayer's representative learns of a forthcoming audit he should have his client execute a power of attorney authorizing the representative to appear and act on his behalf before the Service.[4] Naturally, preparations for an audit will vary depending on the facts and circumstances of the particular case, such as the type of taxpayer, return, and audit involved. The following are general guidelines and procedures that may be

[4] See Administrative Practice Forms Nos. 1 and 2, pages **C**·3–6.

helpful in many cases although inappropriate in others. In considering the desirability of preparatory procedures, the effort and expense of preparation must be weighed against the likelihood that an item will be questioned and the amounts involved.

Generally an audit will be either a field audit on the taxpayer's premises or an office audit at the District Director's office. In the former the initial audit may be followed by a conference with the taxpayer or his representative to discuss the issues raised. In these cases the taxpayer may utilize the initial audit to delineate the issues and defer a substantial portion of the preparation for the period between the audit and the conference. Advance knowledge of the issues will permit efficient preparation, although experienced practitioners can often recognize most issues prior to the audit and prepare accordingly. In the case of an office audit the taxpayer will be advised of the issues prior to the audit. Consequently, thorough preparation can be completed in advance in the hope that the case can be disposed of at the initial meeting.

The first step in preparing for an audit is analysis of the return in question. In an office audit the taxpayer's representative should try, in reviewing the return, to anticipate any issues that may arise other than those indicated. In the case of a field audit the items that may be questioned should be anticipated to the greatest extent possible. Then, the factual information supporting the taxpayer's position should be assembled.

It will be helpful at this stage if the likelihood of an audit has been kept in mind during the preparation of the return. Being mindful of an eventual audit, the preparer of the return should reduce to writing all oral facts submitted by the taxpayer, maintain a written record indicating how all items on the return were determined, and retain records of all information that may be utilized to support the items on the return. Moreover, in the course of preparing the return the taxpayer should be advised of all items that may be questioned and, if necessary, cautioned against using his opinions rather than factual data in determining what to report on the return.

The task of gathering the proof necessary should generally be performed by the client under the supervision of his adviser. The organization and presentation of the proof should be done by the latter. In advising the taxpayer as to necessary proof, it is desirable that instructions be written, detailed, and specific. Thus in a case involving an entertainment deduction, a request for diaries, memoranda, bills, vouchers, receipts, and checks for each item of expense together with a statement naming the individual entertained, his occupation and/or title, the business relationship to the taxpayer, the date, duration, time, place, and nature of the business which preceded, followed, or accompanied the expense, etc., is much more useful than a request merely for all information supporting entertainment deductions.

After all the factual data has been gathered and organized, the taxpayer's representative should be in a position to furnish proof necessary to support the taxpayer's position on any item on the return that may be questioned by the agent.

At this point, a decision must be made as to whether there is any question of law involved. If a legal question is likely to arise, appropriate research should be done and legal authority for the taxpayer's position obtained. If the taxpayer's adviser is not a lawyer and the legal problem is significant, consideration should be given to obtaining counsel.

Finally, the likelihood that the taxpayer's position will be sustained and his overall vulnerability (including the effect on prior and subsequent years) should be estimated. After the foregoing is done, the taxpayer's representative will be in a position to represent the taxpayer effectively and decide what would constitute a desirable outcome of the audit.

CONDUCT OF THE AUDIT

Office Audit

In the audit of most nonbusiness returns, where the records to be examined are not extensive or only minor adjustments are necessary, a form letter will be forwarded to the taxpayer requesting that he furnish additional information by mail or that he appear at an office interview.[5] Generally, the letter requesting an office conference will also request proof to support certain items on the return. In these instances the taxpayer's representative will be able to prepare thoroughly for the interview. Proof as to any of the questioned items and favorable legal authority should be organized for effective presentation. Generally, the objective should be to dispose of the matter in a single interview.

Field Audit

In the field audit the agent will come to the taxpayer's place of business or, in some instances, to his representative's office—wherever he can obtain access to the necessary records. Field audits are generally performed in connection with a return filed by a business with extensive records to be examined. In these instances the taxpayer will not know which issues will be raised until the audit is completed. Accordingly, preparation of evidence and legal authority relevant to potential issues will be less extensive than in the case of an office audit. Some effort, however, should be made to anticipate the issues and to gather the necessary information and, where necessary, favorable legal authority for the field audit.

[5] Treas. Reg. § 601.105(b) (2).

Generally, notification of a field audit will be received by a phone call or letter from the agent. An appointment for the audit will then be arranged. When the agent arrives, his credentials should be requested. The taxpayer should ascertain whether the agent is from the Audit Division or a special agent from the Intelligence Division. If there are two agents, the taxpayer should be sure that neither is a special agent from the Intelligence Division. The presence of a special agent indicates that a criminal investigation is being made. In these cases the audit should not proceed until counsel has been consulted and the advisability of permitting an examination is considered in light of the taxpayer's right not to incriminate himself. Where it is ascertained that the audit is routine, it should proceed.

In conducting the audit the agent should be given a comfortable place to work—preferably a private office or semi-private work area. Only one person should be assigned to work with the agent. The agent should be provided with the information and records he requests. Answers to his questions should be candid and complete and be given by someone qualified to answer. If the agent detects an attempt to be devious or evasive or to conceal something, he is apt to extend his audit to be certain he is getting the full story. In providing the agent with the information he requests the taxpayer should, however, be mindful of the fact that it is neither necessary nor desirable to volunteer more than the information requested. After the agent has completed his examination of the taxpayer's records, the first phase of the audit is complete.

It is desirable to utilize this first phase to determine what items on the return the agent is questioning, to provide the agent with the information he needs, and to avoid any detailed discussion of the issues. From the taxpayer's standpoint it is desirable to discuss the issues in detail at a second conference. This will generally prevent the agent from extending his audit to find added issues or at least make it inconvenient for him to do so, although he may find at the second conference that certain issues are seriously disputed or that most issues are being resolved in the taxpayer's favor.

The taxpayer's representative may use the time between the first and second conferences and his knowledge of the items questioned by the agent to gather and organize additional proof and to research any technical legal questions involved.

Working with the Agent

Obviously, an important element in arriving at a successful disposition of the issues raised during an audit is the development of a sound relationship with the agent. Perhaps the first step in establishing this relationship is the adoption of the attitude that both the taxpayer's representative and the agent are professionals, and that neither of them is personally or emotionally involved in the case. Toward this end the taxpayer's representative should start with the assumption that the agent is doing a job and will be fair and open-minded. It is important also that the taxpayer's representative have the respect of the agent—respect not simply for his knowledgeability but more significantly for his integrity. The acknowledgment of the validity of the agent's points when they are clearly valid as well as the volunteering of information as to any obvious errors or omissions will help establish this respect. Of course general friendliness, cordiality, and consideration will help create the desired relationship with the agent. The creation of this relationship will also be fostered by providing the agent with favorable working conditions, assisting him effectively, and facilitating his conduct of the audit.

Scope of the Audit

The Internal Revenue Code authorizes the Internal Revenue Service (as a delegate of the Secretary of the Treasury) to examine any books, papers, records, or other data relevant or material to the determination of the tax liability of any person.[6] In order to enforce this authority the Service is empowered to summon the person liable for the tax or any other person deemed proper to appear and to produce such data.[7]

While a request for an examination usually results in voluntary compliance, if a taxpayer refuses to comply, a summons may be issued. If the summons is not obeyed, the Service can obtain enforcement by "appropriate process" in the United States District Court.[8] Generally the District Court will issue an order commanding appearance before the Service unless good cause is shown why such an appearance should not be required. Refusal to obey a summons may result in criminal punishment if bad faith or willfulness is shown.[9] The government does not, however, have an unlimited power to examine any person or his records.

The statute provides, in addition to the requirement that the inquiry be relevant and material to the determination of a tax, that the time and place of the examination must be reasonable [10] and that no taxpayer shall be subjected to unnecessary examinations.[11] The requirements of relevancy to

[6] IRC § 7602.

[7] IRC § 7602(2) ; Rev. Proc. 55–6, 1955–2 CUM. BULL. 903. See Administrative Practice Form No. 3, page C·7.

[8] IRC § 7604(a).

[9] United States v. Becker, 259 F.2d 869 (C.A.2d).

[10] IRC § 7605(a).

[11] IRC § 7605(b). This section also prohibits more than one examination for each taxable year unless the taxpayer consents to the additional examination or the Service, after investigation, notifies him in writing that it is necessary. Presumably this means a second audit will be sanctioned only if justified. See United States v. H. M. Reinman, 301 F.2d 267 (C.A.7th).

determination of a tax and the proscription of unnecessary examinations enable the taxpayer to resist a fishing expedition by the agent. Thus, the documents requested by the agent must be described with sufficient particularity so that the taxpayer can identify and produce them. The agent must also show that the records are relevant to a particular taxpayer. If this is demonstrated, the test becomes whether the document is relevant to the taxpayer's return being audited. Consequently, the Service is prohibited from examining the records of a bank in order to determine whether an unrelated taxpayer had certain transactions with the bank.[12] Generally, however, almost all of a taxpayer's own records will be relevant to an examination of his return.

In order to test in court whether the Service is within its rights in conducting any aspect of the audit, the taxpayer need only refuse to grant access to his records. If the Service feels justified in its requests, it will issue a summons, and if compliance is refused, the Service will institute appropriate process in the United States District Court where the taxpayer will have the opportunity to show the Court why the Service is not entitled to proceed. As an alternative the taxpayer may request that the United States District Court quash or modify the summons.[13]

PRESENTING PROOF TO THE SERVICE

Establishing a case before the Service is much like presenting a case to any other fact finding forum. Evidence is introduced by means of testimony or documents that support the taxpayer's conclusions. The major distinction between administrative proof and judicial proof is that the rules of evidence are not applicable in proceedings before the Service, and the proceedings themselves are informal.

The degree of formality increases as the taxpayer proceeds up the administrative ladder, but requirements as to evidence and admissible proof are flexible. Accordingly, the Service will accept as proof not only the taxpayer's business records, but documents, letters, contemporaneous memoranda, diaries, and similar items. Unlike a judicial proceeding, these items need not be sworn to or formally authenticated.

The presentation of proof at a settlement conference or office audit should be carefully planned. Thorough preparation is critical: all evidence must be collected and organized concisely and comprehensibly. In cases where the factual situation is complex, summaries and diagrams may be useful.

[12] United States v. Third Northwestern Nat'l Bank, 102 F. Supp. 879 (Minn.).
[13] Application of E. A. Colton, 291 F.2d 487 (C.A.2d).

STATUTE OF LIMITATIONS—THE 872 CONSENT FORM

The assessment of any tax more than three years after the tax return is due or filed, whichever is later,[14] is prohibited by the Internal Revenue Code.[15] Consequently, if an audit is to be performed, it must be completed and an assessment made during the three-year period. Frequently, the statutory period is about to lapse and the audit has just begun or is nowhere near completion. In such cases the Service will request that the taxpayer sign Form 872, known as a "Consent Fixing Period of Limitation upon Assessment of Income and Profits Tax" (see Fig. 1–1, page 1·11).[16] If the taxpayer executes this form, the expiration of the statute of limitations is extended to the date indicated on the form. The Audit Division keeps close check on matters pending before it, and a request to sign Form 872 will be made no later than 30 days before the expiration of the statutory period. If a taxpayer refuses to sign the consent form, a formal deficiency notice, which serves to stop the running of the statute of limitations,[17] will be issued immediately.[18]

No hard and fast rule can be stated as to the advisability of signing the consent form. The considerations in deciding whether or not to sign are similar to those used in deciding how to handle the administrative procedures and when to settle. In deciding whether to sign the consent form, the taxpayer should try to anticipate which items on his return will be questioned and how they can be disposed of. If such issues involve either questions of proof, which the taxpayer believes can be adequately resolved, or are of a routine nature and can be disposed of by agreement with the agent performing the audit or other Internal Revenue personnel, the waiver should be signed. In most cases, this is the best procedure to follow. If, however, the taxpayer anticipates that a particular item or items on the return involve legal or factual questions that preclude an amicable resolution with the Service, he should refuse to sign the consent.

His refusal to sign will result in the issuance of the deficiency notice and will enable him to obtain a judicial resolution of his liability at an earlier date. Since the deficiency notice in this case will be issued before the Service can complete its audit, the Service will resolve all doubts in its own favor, and the notice may include some deficiency items that cannot be

---

[14] IRC § 6501(a).

[15] IRC §§ 6501(c) and (e) provide for longer periods of assessment in fraud and certain other cases. See p. 4·10, *infra*.

[16] Note that similar forms are used for other taxes, i.e., Forms 872–B (miscellaneous and excise), 872–G (gift).

[17] IRC § 6503(a)(1).

[18] Treas. Reg. § 601.105(f).

FORM **872** (REV. JAN. 1965)	U.S. TREASURY DEPARTMENT - INTERNAL REVENUE SERVICE **CONSENT FIXING PERIOD OF LIMITATION UPON ASSESSMENT OF INCOME AND PROFITS TAX**	**To be executed in triplicate**

IN REPLY REFER TO:

Pursuant to existing Internal Revenue laws, ___Stephen and Joyce Solomon_____

_____, a taxpayer

(or taxpayers) of ___2775 E. 16th Street, Brooklyn, N. Y. 10675_____, and

(Number, street, city or town, State, ZIP code)

the District Director of Internal Revenue (or Assistant Regional Commissioner-Appellate) hereby consent and agree as follows:

That the amount of any Federal income or profits taxes due under any return (or returns) made by or on behalf of the above-named taxpayer (or taxpayers) for the taxable year ended ___·December 31, 1966_____,

under existing or prior revenue acts, may be assessed at any time on or before ___December 31, 1971_____,

except that if a notice of a deficiency in tax is sent to the taxpayer (or taxpayers) by certified or registered mail on or before such date, then the time for making any assessment as aforesaid shall be extended beyond such date by the number of days during which the making of an assessment is prohibited and for sixty days thereafter.

(Signature)		(Date)	
/s/ Stephen K. Solomon		Dec. 10, 1969	
(Signature)		(Date)	
/s/ Joyce G. Solomon		Dec. 10, 1969	
(Signature)	(Title)	(Date)	
By			Corporate Seal
District Director of Internal Revenue or Assistant Regional Commissioner - Appellate			
/s/ John J. Jones Assistant Regional Comm. Dec. 14, 1969			
(Signature)	(Title)	(Date)	
By			

If the consent is executed for a year for which a JOINT RE-TURN OF A HUSBAND AND WIFE was filed, it must be signed by both husband and wife unless one, acting under a power of attorney, signs as agent for the other.

If the taxpayer is a corporation, the consent must be signed with the corporate name followed by the signature and title of the officer(s) duly authorized to sign. It is not necessary that the corporate seal be affixed. The space provided for the seal is for the convenience of corporations required by charter or by the laws of the jurisdiction in which they are incorporated to affix their corporate seals in the execution of instruments.

The consent may be executed by the taxpayer's attorney or agent provided such action is specifically authorized by a power of attorney which, if not previously filed, must accompany the forms.

If the consent is executed by a person acting in a fiduciary capacity (such as executor, administrator, trustee, etc.), Form 56, "Notice of Fiduciary Relationship," should, unless previously filed, accompany this form.

FORM **872**(REV. 1-65)

FIG. 1–1.

substantiated by the Service but that it believes to be questionable. Since such items might not be included in the deficiency notice after a complete audit, the taxpayer should exercise some caution in refusing to sign the consent. However, if the taxpayer is certain that he has legally admissible evidence to substantiate his position on these issues, the risks of their inclusion in the deficiency notice are minimal.

The 872 Consent Form may also be used in situations in which the issue raised is the same as one already involved in a pending case or being studied by the Service. In such a case both parties may find it advantageous to hold the matter in abeyance pending resolution of the issue.

OUTLINE OF ALTERNATE ADMINISTRATIVE PROCEDURES

A number of general considerations should be kept in mind in discussing the administrative procedures designed to resolve disputes between a taxpayer and the Service. First, the procedures are relatively flexible and informal, and the extent to which the available settlement procedures are pursued usually is determined by the taxpayer.[19] The circumstances of each taxpayer's case will determine the extent to which he will go to settle and the steps he will take to do so. Generally, the taxpayer will use only some of the procedures available. Most frequently, only one of the post audit procedures (either District or Appellate Conference) is used, although the taxpayer if he wishes may utilize all procedures available.

Second, although the procedures may be flexible, the entire process may be interrupted in some cases by the imminent expiration of the statutory period for the assessment of the tax (see above). If this occurs, the taxpayer will be asked to sign a waiver of the statute of limitations, and if he does not comply, a notice of deficiency will be issued immediately, thus short-circuiting the settlement procedures.

Finally, unless either the taxpayer or the Service has an almost perfect case supported squarely by law and facts, the process will be essentially one of give and take, each side striving for a favorable disposition or settlement of its strongest points and willing to make concessions on those that are weakest.

For purposes of understanding the discussion, the following outline of the possible procedures may be helpful:

    I. Agreement with agent
        1. Agent's report

[19] It has been indicated that the prelitigation administrative procedures established by the regulations are permissive and not mandatory in nature. Luhring v. Glotzbach, 304 F.2d 560 (C.A.4th). See also Cleveland Trust Co. v. United States, 19 A.F.T.R.2d 1770 (N.D. Ohio) (alleged failure of Service to apply proper standard of review to recommendation of informal conferee held not to invalidate assessment).

    2. Review by Audit Division
    3. Execution of settlement form
    4. If settled, eventual issuance of bill or refund
    5. Possible post settlement review
  II. No agreement with agent
    1. Request for technical advice
    2. Informal District Conference (office audits only)
 III. Issuance of 30-day letter and protest
    1. Payment on receipt of letter
    2. Partial payment
    3. Filing of protest
      A. Request for District Conference
      B. Request for Appellate Division Conference
      C. Settlement at conference level
        a. Execution of settlement form
        b. Conferee's report
        c. Review
        d. Issuance of bill or refund
    4. No protest filed, deficiency notice issued
  IV. Filing of petition in tax court or payment followed by tax refund suit.

AGREEMENT WITH THE AGENT

When the audit is concluded, the taxpayer will have the opportunity to reach an agreement with the agent as to the amount of tax due. Agreement at this point may be the simplest and most desirable means of disposing of the dispute, particularly if the agent's approach indicates that he is willing to recognize the validity of the taxpayer's position to some extent and a compromise seems possible. Once the audit has been completed, the agent will prepare what is known as the Revenue Agent's Report. If the agent and the taxpayer have reached a tentative agreement, the report will outline the nature of the agreement and the reasons for making the agreement and will indicate the proposed computations. The taxpayer will eventually receive a copy of portions of this report. When the tentative agreement is reached, the taxpayer will be asked to sign a settlement form, Form 870.

If no agreement has been reached with the taxpayer, the agent's report will serve as a summary of the case and will be passed on for use by the agent's superiors at the next administrative level. If such is the case, the report will include a statement of the arguments advanced, the settlements proposed, the reasons for rejecting them, all facts, documents, and chronological events relating to the case, and a summary of the agent's own opinion of the case.[20]

[20] Treas. Reg. § 601.105(b)(4). *Cf.* Treas. Reg. § 601.105(c)(3).

Review of the Agreement

An agent's agreement with the taxpayer is only tentative pending a number of steps of review. When the agent submits his report, it will be reviewed first by his group supervisor and then forwarded to the Review Staff in the office of the Audit Division.[21] At either point the report may be returned to the agent with the request that he supply additional information or ask the taxpayer to supply additional information, or with instructions to continue the audit in order to resolve newly raised legal issues. If the Review Staff accepts the report, the settlement may proceed. If the report is not accepted, the taxpayer is left with the alternative of making a settlement satisfactory to the reviewers or proceeding to the next administrative level for further negotiations.

Processing the Settlement

Assuming that there is agreement between the taxpayer and the agent, and that the agreement has not been disturbed upon review, the settlement will be forwarded for processing. The Accounting Branch will perform a thorough check of the mathematics of the computations and will investigate whether any other taxes are owed or refunds are due, and what effect the settlement may have on any other matters affecting the taxpayer that are still pending. All deficiencies and overassessments will be offset against one another,[22] and the Collection Division will finally issue a bill for a deficiency, or a refund for overassessment will be made from Washington or through the local office. The above procedure may take anywhere from two months to over a year, depending on the complexity of the issues involved in the case. There may be an additional delay if the taxpayer's case has come up for postaudit review.

Post Audit Review Procedure

Each year, certain cases selected at random are subjected to what is known as a post audit review. The standards for choosing cases for such a review are established in Washington, but there is much discretion on the part of the Regional Commissioner, who carries out the review. Generally, the post audit review functions merely as a psychological deterrent to inappropriate activity by the agent as well as to insure uniformity in application of the provisions of the Code.[23]

---

[21] If the settlement calls for a refund of $100,000 or more, it will be reviewed by the Joint Congressional Committee on Internal Revenue Taxation before becoming final. Treas. Reg. § 601.108. See also p. **7·9** *infra*.

[22] IRC § 6402(a).

[23] Treas. Reg. § 601.105(b)(5).

ADDITIONAL PROCEDURES TO FACILITATE AGREEMENT PRIOR TO 30-DAY LETTER

If the taxpayer cannot reach an agreement with the agent, he may utilize several procedures to dispose of the disagreement without resort to litigation. Since the choice of using the various procedures is made by the taxpayer, he must consider the alternatives and then decide which, if any, are likely to produce the most desirable disposition of his dispute.

If an audit discloses issues that cannot be fairly resolved on the basis of existing law and precedents, either the agent or the taxpayer may request technical advice from the Assistant Commissioner (Technical) in the national office. The taxpayer may also request a conference or permission to submit a brief on the matter in order to assist the national office in formulating its decision. Obviously, a request for technical advice is desirable only in unusual cases. It is of little effect when there is simply a disagreement as to interpretation of legal principles; it is most useful when the Service concedes that there is a substantial doubt as to the existing law.

Unlike the other procedures available on request to the taxpayer, a request for technical advice will be granted only if the Chief of the Audit Division in the District Director's office consents.

After an office audit, the taxpayer may request a meeting with a member of the Conference Staff in the District Director's office. The conference can be useful if the taxpayer believes that the agent is completely and clearly wrong—especially if his error involves a question of law rather than fact or if a personality clash precludes an amicable disposition of the case with the agent. This conference may also be desirable if the taxpayer and the agent are close to an agreement and minor concessions can dispose of the case.

THE 30-DAY LETTER

If an agreement is not reached at the agent level, the case is forwarded for review and issuance of the 30-day letter. A number of other items will be delivered with the letter:

1. A copy of a portion of the Revenue Agent's Report, indicating the deficiency and showing the computations used and the adjustments made to reach the result,
2. A Form 870 should the taxpayer decide to accept the findings as reported,
3. A Form No. 5 (Rev. 8–64), which contains instructions for preparing a protest.[24]

[24] See Administrative Practice Form No. 6, page C·1.

U. S. TREASURY DEPÂRTMENT
INTERNAL REVENUE SERVICE
DISTRICT DIRECTOR
P. O. BOX 3100
NEW YORK, N. Y. 10015

IN REPLY REFER TO
Form L-191

January 15, 1967

Mr. John White
377 West Broadway
New York, New York 10023

Dear Mr. White

Enclosed is your copy of an examination report explaining adjustments to your tax liability for the years shown. We have carefully reviewed this report.

If you accept the findings, please sign and return the enclosed Waiver Form. If additional tax is due, you may prefer to make payment at this time. See paragraph 1 of the enclosed instructions for details.

If you do not accept the findings, we recommend that you request a conference to discuss the proposed adjustments with a member of our Conference Staff. Most cases considered at a conference are brought to a satisfactory conclusion. If you desire, you may send us a written statement outlining your position along with your conference request. See paragraphs 2 and 4 of the instructions for details concerning a District conference and representation.

If you do not desire a District conference, you may request a hearing with the Appellate Division of the Regional Commissioner's Office. Your request for a hearing must be ·accompanied by a written protest which we will forward to the Appellate Division. That Division will contact you to arrange a hearing. See paragraph 3 of the instructions for details concerning the preparation of a protest.

If you do not respond within 30 days from the date of this letter, we will process your case on the basis of the adjustments shown in the examination report.

Important: Please send all communications concerning your case to the above address using the symbols in the upper right corner of this letter.

Very truly yours,

District Director

Enclosures - 3:
Examination report
Waiver Form
Instructions - Unagreed Income, Estate, or Gift Tax Cases

FORM L-191 (8-64)

FIG. 1–2.

The 30-day letter itself, a form letter of which there are three types, will advise the taxpayer that if he does not agree with the proposed settlement he may file a written protest within thirty days and request a conference with either the District Director's office or the Appellate Division. The letter will request that the taxpayer inform the District Director of his contemplated action and will give notice that, if the taxpayer takes no action within thirty days, a deficiency notice will be issued. If the statute of limitations for collection of the tax expires before the end of the 30-day period, the deficiency notice will issue before the expiration date.[25]

Three Types of 30-Day Letter

Although the 30-day letter is a form letter, three different forms are used, depending on the nature of the dispute. If the amount in question is less than $2,500 and the issues involved are relatively simple, a type I letter (Form 191) will be issued (see Fig. 1–2, page 1 · 16). This letter encourages the taxpayer to seek the more informal type of meeting in the district office and advises him that, along with his request for such a conference, an informal written statement of his position may be submitted although it is not required.

If the amount in dispute is over $2,500 but it appears that the case can be settled at the district office, a type II (Form 191A) [26] letter will be issued. It suggests that the taxpayer attempt disposition at the district level and that if he does so, a written statement of his position will be required. In both of the above instances, the taxpayer may ignore the advice of the letter and seek a conference at the Appellate Division. In such a case, a formal statement of the taxpayer's position must accompany his request.

If the disputed amount is over $2,500 and the issues are such that agreement at the district office appears unlikely, a type III letter (Form 191B) [27] will recommend to the taxpayer that he bypass the district office and request a hearing with the Appellate Division. If the taxpayer ignores the 30-day letter, a notice of deficiency will be issued.

ALTERNATIVE RESPONSES TO 30-DAY LETTER

When a 30-day letter is received, the taxpayer has four alternatives: He can pay the deficiency asserted, make partial payment, ignore the letter, or protest it and request further administrative proceedings in the hope of disposing of or settling the case.

[25] Treas. Reg. § 601.105(d).
[26] See Administrative Practice Form No. 4, page C·9.
[27] See Administrative Practice Form No. 5, page C·10 Rev. Proc. 67–27, 1967–20 I.R.B. 45.

Payment

If payment of the deficiency asserted in the 30-day letter is made, such payment will be assessed and will, in effect, obviate the taxpayer's right to petition the Tax Court. He will be able, however, to file a claim for refund and institute suit for recovery of the refund in a United States District Court or Court of Claims if he wishes to contest the issues raised by the 30-day letter in one of those tribunals.

Partial Payment

Some taxpayers will make partial payment of the deficiency asserted in order to stop the running of interest. Yet, they will still be hopeful of utilizing further administrative procedures with respect to the balance of the asserted deficiency, or they may wish to file a petition in the Tax Court to contest all issues relative to the year in question. Payment with respect to some issues will generally impede subsequent administrative proceedings because the taxpayer, by such payment, gives up in advance concessions that might be of value in the give-and-take of a settlement conference. Unless the interest that can be saved is extremely significant, partial payment is inadvisable because it may result in a waiver of the taxpayer's right to petition the Tax Court. This waiver may occur because a Tax Court petition may be filed only during the 90 days following the issuance of a deficiency notice. If the Service accepts the taxpayer's payment and does not issue a deficiency notice, the taxpayer will not be able to petition the Tax Court.[28] If, however, a deficiency notice is issued with respect to the unpaid portion of the deficiency, the taxpayer can allege overpayment and collect any sums erroneously paid. Expectancy that a deficiency notice will issue despite the partial payment (enabling the filing of a Tax Court petition and litigation of all issues) encourages taxpayers to make partial payment and stop the running of interest.

No Protest

If the taxpayer chooses to ignore the 30-day letter, a statutory notice of deficiency will be issued. The taxpayer will then have 90 days to file a petition in the Tax Court. If a petition is filed, the deficiency may not be assessed or collected until the litigation is completed.[29] If no petition is filed, the deficiency asserted may be assessed and collected forthwith.[30]

[28] Assessment or collection of any deficiency is prohibited prior to the issuance of the deficiency notice, absent voluntary payment, or other special circumstances. IRC § 6213. If a Tax Court petition is filed, the prohibition continues until the final decision of the court, assuring the taxpayer's right to a judicial determination of his liability prior to payment of the tax.

[29] IRC § 6213(a).

[30] IRC § 6213(c).

Protest

If the taxpayer believes he can dispose of the case administratively, he can respond to the 30-day letter by filing a protest and requesting a meeting with the Conference Staff of the Audit Division in the District Director's Office or, if he wishes to omit the District Conference, with the Appellate Division in the Regional Commissioner's Office.

FACTORS INFLUENCING RESPONSE TO 30-DAY LETTER

If the taxpayer does not wish to concede that the agent's determinations set forth in the 30-day letter are correct, his basic decision is whether to litigate the issues or make further attempts to resolve them administratively by filing a protest. If litigation is being given serious consideration and the taxpayer's representative does not intend to prosecute the litigation himself, he should at this point suggest that the taxpayer retain counsel. Counsel will be able to determine the impact that continued settlement efforts before the Service may have on ultimate litigation and advise as to which of the three tax litigation tribunals would be most desirable for the taxpayer.[31]

If the decision to litigate is made, the taxpayer must decide whether to (1) ignore the 30-day letter or request a deficiency notice and litigate in the Tax Court, or (2) pay the asserted deficiency, file a claim for refund, and litigate in the appropriate United States District Court or the United States Court of Claims.

Current precedents, possibility of claims for increased liabilities in the Tax Court, available defenses, desire for a jury trial, and necessity of prompt decision are just a few of the many factors that will influence the choice of how to proceed.[32]

If the decision is to continue efforts to resolve the issues with the Service, the taxpayer must protest the 30-day letter and request a meeting with a district conferee (with the possible thought of a subsequent conference with the Appellate Division if it is necessary or desirable) or a conference with the Appellate Division.[33]

Naturally, the decision as to how to proceed will vary depending on the circumstances in each case. It may be helpful, however, to discuss some of the procedures used to arrive at the decision and the considerations influencing it.

---

[31] Chapter 2 is devoted to a discussion of which tribunal is most desirable for the taxpayer.

[32] *Ibid.*

[33] See p. 1 · 23 *infra* for a discussion of the considerations relevant to deciding whether to select district conference, appellate conference, or both.

The taxpayer's representative should analyze the return in question and the 30-day letter to determine the proof necessary to support the taxpayer's position, the extent to which the available proof provides the needed support, and the extent to which the relevant legal authorities favor the taxpayer. On the basis of this information, an estimate of a fair and desirable disposition, as well as a judgment as to the probable outcome of a lawsuit, can be made. With this in mind, the amount of the deficiency asserted by an agent or a conferee can be weighed against the expense and risks in continuing settlement efforts or proceeding to litigation and a choice can be made accordingly.

In deciding how to proceed, at least three other important factors must be considered. First is the impact of the disposition on years not involved in the audit. An issue resolved by litigation [34] or in certain settlements (depending on the settlement form used) [35] will be binding in other years. Second, the taxpayer's representative must be mindful of his client's vulnerability on doubtful items on the return that have not been raised by the agent or in the review of his report. While the Service professes that no intensive effort is made to find additional issues once the audit is completed, if an issue that has not been previously raised is evident to Appellate or District conferee, it will of course be explored. If the vulnerability on these issues is substantial, it may dictate an early and even an unfavorable disposition foregoing all post audit procedures. If the taxpayer wishes, he may reopen the conceded issues without vulnerability on undiscovered issues by making a claim for refund after the statute of limitations on assessment has expired. He may then sue for a refund on the claim if the likelihood of recovery and the amounts involved warrant the suit. The government in this case will then be able to raise new issues only to offset the claim. However, the government will not be able to create additional liability.[36]

Another consideration in deciding whether to continue in the administrative process or go directly to court is the likelihood of settlement and added proof available. Generally, any additional proof will not be significant, but in unusual cases the taxpayer may have information that will be valuable at trial and that the government has not inquired about and will not know about. This is more likely in a Tax Court case, where there are no discovery procedures. If effective presentation of his case before a conferee requires disclosure of such information (as it generally will), continuing in the administrative process may damage the taxpayer at trial. Accordingly, these circumstances may favor bypassing any conferences and proceeding directly to litigation.

[34] See p. 12·12 et seq. infra for a discussion of res judicata and collateral estoppel.
[35] See p. 1·24 et seq. infra.
[36] See p. 12·3 et seq. infra.

PROTEST AND SUBSEQUENT ADMINISTRATIVE PROCEEDINGS

Contents of the Protest

If the taxpayer decides that additional administrative proceedings will probably result in a desirable disposition of the dispute, he must file a protest in response to the 30-day letter.[37] No particular form is required for the protest that must be filed, but certain information is essential to presenting a clear and precise statement of the taxpayer's arguments. These requirements are set out in Form No. 5 (Rev. 8–64), which accompanies the 30-day letter. Basically, the protest should include

1. The name and address of the taxpayer.
2. Designation of the year or years involved and the type and amount of tax in dispute for each year.
3. A detailed list of each finding in the Revenue Agent's Report to which an exception is taken. Each exception should be followed by the taxpayer's own contentions. Excessive length should be avoided, but the material facts should be presented and, if unfavorable, explained, not deleted.
4. In conclusion, a request for the appropriate conference.

All protests must be executed by the taxpayer. The execution must contain a statement that the taxpayer is subject to the penalties of perjury for any false statement in the protest.

District Conference and Settlement

The District Conference is conducted by a member of the Conference Staff of the Audit Division in the District Director's office. The taxpayer or his counsel will be given an opportunity to present the taxpayer's position. There are no formal procedures or rules of evidence. The Conference Staff is aware of and successful in performing its function of disposing of as many cases as possible in a manner satisfactory to the taxpayer yet consistent with governing law and policy.

The conferee will prepare a report of the conference indicating results of the conference, his findings and conclusions. Dispositions are approved by the Chief of the Conference Staff or his designee, who is usually a reviewer or the conferee's Section Chief.[37a]

---

[37] For instances where it is not necessary to file a protest, and for the effect of failure to protest when it is required, see pp. 1·17 and 1·18 *infra.*

[37a] Despite the foregoing procedure outlined in Rev. Proc. 64–38, 1964–2 CUM. BULL. 965, the Conference Staff in many districts will forward many matters to the Review Staff for approval before reversing a position taken by the Agent performing the audit. See Katten, "I.R.S. Expands Procedures," 27 J. TAXATION 6,7(1967).

Appellate Conference and Settlement

Settlement negotiations with the Appellate Division constitute the last stop before the Tax Court. There is an Appellate Division located in each of the Internal Revenue regions, and the officers of the Division have authority to settle regional cases that have come to them on protest.

Proceedings before the Appellate Division are not formal, and testimony is not taken under oath. The taxpayer may appear in person or through his representative. The Appellate Division conferee will be well acquainted with the case. If, after the first conference, the taxpayer needs additional time to produce additional information, permission will be granted. If necessary, a matter may be referred back to the District Director's office for further audit and clarification.[38]

Once the case has been discussed at the conference, the taxpayer or his representative will be expected to submit an offer of settlement for consideration by the conferee. The conferee will not initiate settlement, but some prompting on his part at the appropriate time may facilitate agreement. Both sides will usually have strong and weak points, and the settlement will involve compromise on both sides. Either side may attempt to interject new issues merely to enhance its bargaining position, but the practice is not generally fruitful.

It is the Conferee's job to consider the settlement proposal taking into account the Service's position and to recommend whether the settlement offer should be accepted. Obviously the concessions the Service is willing to make will be limited by the necessity of consistent policy to avoid discrimination between taxpayers.

If a settlement is reached, the taxpayer will be asked to execute a settlement form, and the officer who has conducted the conference will prepare what is known as an action memorandum, similar to the Revenue Agent's Report. The settlement will be reviewed, in cases involving less than $50,000, by the conferee's immediate superior or, in cases involving more than $50,000, by the Chief of the Appellate Division Branch Office. Usually a settlement reached at the conference will not be overturned upon review. After completion of the review the file will be returned to the district office and the refund or bill for the deficiency will be processed.

If a settlement cannot be reached—that is, if the taxpayer's proposal is deemed unacceptable or if the conferee's superior does not accept the proposal—and no further compromise is made—the case will go unsettled and a deficiency notice will be issued to the taxpayer. The taxpayer may have a subsequent conference with the Appellate Division once his case is docketed in the Tax Court.[39]

---

[38] Treas. Reg. § 601.106(**F**).
[39] See p. **7 · 3** *infra*.

Considerations in Choosing District or Appellate Conference or Both

The choice of which conference to select will depend, of course, on the amounts involved and on an analysis of the nature of the dispute in light of the differences between the two conferences. While they are similar in many respects, the differences are significant. The conference staff in the District Director's office generally handles cases involving smaller amounts and less complicated issues. Taxpayers frequently appear before the conference staff without accountant or attorney, procedures and proof being informal, and dispose successfully of a large portion of their cases.

The Appellate Division, in addition to having somewhat more formal procedures and evidentiary requirements, is experienced in handling larger and more complex cases. Moreover, the Appellate Division is authorized to settle cases. The agent and the district conference staff can dispose of a case only if the taxpayer satisfies them that his position is valid.[39a] Appellate, however, can consider the expense and hazards of litigation, the admissibility of evidence, and credibility of witnesses, and then decide to settle; he can "split the difference" on an issue, while a district conferee may not.

The district conference should nonetheless be considered seriously—not only for its informal settlement procedures and good record of disposing of cases, but also because it can frequently be arranged at an earlier date. In Appellate, which also deals with settlement of cases pending in the Tax Court, prelitigation cases are often delayed, while cases *in* litigation are expedited so that the Tax Court and Regional Counsel will know whether they will be settled or tried.[40]

Another factor making a district conference desirable is the form used to effect a disposition of the case. A taxpayer may dispose of the case at the district conference and then make a claim and sue for a refund, whereas the form for an appellate conference case may preclude refund suit.[41]

Some taxpayers secure a district conference and go on to Appellate only if unsuccessful in the first instance. While this may be useful when minor concessions, compromise, or settlement will dispose of the case, the taxpayer is ill advised to approach the appellate conference in the hope that it will completely reverse the decisions of the agent and district conferee, for the appellate conferee may be reluctant to decide that two of his colleagues are wrong. In fact, the affirmance by the district conferee will add stature to the agent's report and will make it difficult to reverse. Accordingly, it is usually desirable to decide which conference is best in view

---

[39a] However, in certain cases involving less than $2,500 in tax for any year, the Chief of the Conference Staff may settle selected issues on a basis similar to a disposition of a substantially identical "pattern" case by the Appellate Division in the same region. Rev. Proc. 67–27, 1967–20 I.R.B. 45.

[40] See generally Treas. Reg. § 601.106.

[41] See p. 1·24 *et seq. infra.*

of all the circumstances and select that conference on the assumption that no further appeals will be made.

SETTLEMENT FORMS AND THEIR EFFECTS

Form 870

If the taxpayer and the Service are able to effect an agreement at any stage in the settlement procedure prior to the Appellate Division conference, the taxpayer will be asked to sign a Form 870 (Waiver of Restrictions on Assessment and Collection of Deficiency in Tax and Acceptance of Over-assessment; see Fig. 1–3, page 1·25).

Form 870 is also used when the government makes no concession in reaching agreement as to the tax due at an Appellate Division conference. By executing Form 870, the taxpayer waives the statutory requirement that the Service formally notify him that it has determined, and intends to assess, a deficiency at least 90 days prior to actual assessment. Since a petition may be filed with the Tax Court only after a formal notice has been received by the taxpayer, the execution of Form 870 results in relinquishment of the taxpayer's right to file a petition in the Tax Court.[42] Signing the waiver, in addition to allowing immediate assessment, stops the running of interest on the 31st day after its effective date.

Although the execution of Form 870 usually results in final disposition of the case, it does not (as the form itself indicates) prevent the assertion of an additional deficiency by the government, nor does it prevent a suit for a refund by the taxpayer.

Form 870–AD

When settlement of a case is arrived at after an Appellate Division conference in which concessions are made by the Service, the taxpayer will be asked to execute a Form 870–AD (see Fig. 1–4, page 1·26). This form is often used rather than the statutory closing agreement. In the past, the procedures within the Internal Revenue Service necessary to obtain execution of a statutory closing agreement were arduous and complicated.[43] The Service has recently simplified the procedures for execution of the statutory closing agreement, evidently in order to encourage more frequent use of the closing agreement.[43a]

In effect, the Form 870–AD is an offer by the taxpayer to waive the re-

---

[42] See p. 3·4 *infra.*

[43] Unlike Form 870, which is only signed by the taxpayer, Form 870–AD must be executed by both the government and the taxpayer.

[43a] See p. 1·28 *infra.*

FORM 870 (REV. MAR. 1963)	U. S. TREASURY DEPARTMENT · INTERNAL REVENUE SERVICE WAIVER OF RESTRICTIONS ON ASSESSMENT AND COLLECTION OF DEFICIENCY IN TAX AND ACCEPTANCE OF OVERASSESSMENT	DATE RECEIVED BY INTERNAL REVENUE SERVICE

Pursuant to section 6213(d) of the Internal Revenue Code of 1954 or corresponding provisions of prior internal revenue laws, the restrictions provided in section 6213(a) of the Internal Revenue Code of 1954 or corresponding provisions of prior internal revenue laws are hereby waived and consent is given to the assessment and collection of the following deficiencies, together with interest on the tax as provided by law; and the following overassessments are accepted as correct:

DEFICIENCIES

TYPE OF TAX	YEAR ENDED	TAX	PENALTY		TOTAL
Income	12/31/64	$14,129.50	none		$14,129.50
Income	12/31/65	$22,500.74	none		$22,500.74

OVERASSESSMENTS

TYPE OF TAX	YEAR ENDED	TAX	PENALTY		TOTAL

SIGNATURE(S) OF TAXPAYER(S)

/s/ Mr. George Butland

(SEAL)	ADDRESS OF TAXPAYER 6779 Sunshine Lane Beverly Hills, California, 88112
	BY DATE

Note.—The execution and filing of this form at the address shown in the accompanying letter will expedite the adjustment of your tax liability as indicated above. It is not, however, a final closing agreement under section 7121 of the Internal Revenue Code of 1954, and does not, therefore, preclude the assertion of a deficiency or a further deficiency in the manner provided by law should it subsequently be determined that additional tax is due, nor does it extend the statutory period of limitation for refund, assessment, or collection of the tax.

If executed with respect to a year for which a JOINT RETURN OF A HUSBAND AND WIFE was filed, this form must be signed by both spouses unless one spouse, acting under a power of attorney, signs as agent for the other.

Where the taxpayer is a corporation, the form shall be signed with the corporate name, followed by the signature and title of such officer or officers of the corporation as are empowered to sign for the corporation, in addition to which the seal of the corporation must be affixed.

643 · 16 · 77938 · 1 GPO

FORM 870 (REV. 3-63)

Fig 1–3.

FORM **870-AD** (REV. MAY 1966)	U. S. TREASURY DEPARTMENT · INTERNAL REVENUE SERVICE **OFFER OF WAIVER OF RESTRICTIONS ON ASSESSMENT AND COLLECTION OF DEFICIENCY IN TAX AND OF ACCEPTANCE OF OVERASSESSMENT**

SYMBOLS	NAME OF TAXPAYER Mr. Charles Burden
	ADDRESS *(Number, street, city, State, Zip code)* 477 West 65th Street New York, New York 10021

FOR INTERNAL REVENUE USE ONLY	DATE ACCEPTED FOR COMMISSIONER	SIGNATURE
	OFFICE	TITLE

Pursuant to the provisions of section 6213(d) of the Internal Revenue Code of 1954, or corresponding provisions of prior internal revenue laws, the undersigned offers to waive the restrictions provided in section 6213(a) of the Internal Revenue Code of 1954, or corresponding provisions of prior internal revenue laws, and to consent to the assessment and collection of the following deficiencies with interest as provided by law. The undersigned offers also to accept the following over-assessments as correct:

DEFICIENCIES

YEAR ENDED	TYPE OF TAX	TAX			
12/31/62	Income	$12,000.42	$4,000.78		

OVERASSESSMENTS

YEAR ENDED	TYPE OF TAX	TAX			

This offer is subject to acceptance by or on behalf of the Commissioner of Internal Revenue. It shall take effect as a waiver of restrictions on the date it is accepted. Unless and until it is accepted, it shall have no force or effect.

If this offer is accepted by or on behalf of the Commissioner, the case shall not be reopened in the absence of fraud, malfeasance, concealment or misrepresentation of material fact, an important mistake in mathematical calculation, or an excessive tentative allowance of a net operating loss carryback, and no claim for refund or credit shall be filed or prosecuted for the year(s) above stated other than for the amounts of overassessment shown above and amounts attributed to a claimed deduction for a net operating loss carryback or an investment credit carryback as provided by law.

SIGNATURE OF TAXPAYER /s/ Charles Burden	DATE 3/15/67	
SIGNATURE OF TAXPAYER	DATE	CORPORATE SEAL
BY	DATE	

NOTE.—The execution and filing of this offer will expedite the adjustment of your tax liability. It is not, however, a final closing agreement under section 7121 of the Internal Revenue Code of 1954, nor does it extend the statutory period of limitation for refund, assessment, or collection of the tax.

If this offer is executed with respect to a year for which a **JOINT RETURN OF A HUSBAND AND WIFE** was filed, it must be signed by both spouses unless one spouse, acting under a power of attorney, signs as agent for the other.

Where the taxpayer is a corporation the offer shall be signed with the corporate name followed by the signature and title of the officer(s) duly authorized to sign the offer. It is not necessary that the corporate seal be affixed to the offer. The space provided for the corporate seal is for convenience of corporations required by charter or by the laws of the jurisdiction in which they are incorporated to affix their corporate seals in the execution of instruments.

This offer may be executed by the taxpayer's attorney or agent provided such action is specifically authorized by a power of attorney which, if not previously filed, must accompany the form.

FORM **870-AD** (REV. 5-66)

FIG. 1–4.

strictions on assessments and collection. The form indicates that, if the offer is accepted by the Internal Revenue Service, "the case shall not be re-opened nor shall any claim for refund be filed or prosecuted in the absence of fraud."

In keeping with this language, the government does not assert additional deficiencies (absent fraud or other malfeasance by the taxpayer) once a Form 870–AD "settlement" has been consummated. In a number of instances, however, taxpayers have sought to violate the terms of the Form 870–AD. Typically, these taxpayers have waited until the statute of limitations on further assessments expired and then filed claims for refund. The discussion of government defenses in tax refund suits covers, in detail, the government's attempts to bar taxpayers from refund suits once a Form 870–AD agreement has been reached.[44] At this point, however, a few general observations regarding this matter are appropriate. First, it is established that a Form 870–AD "settlement" is not a closing agreement pursuant to the Internal Revenue Code.[45] Accordingly, the Form 870–AD *per se* would not bar a subsequent claim for refund or tax refund suit in spite of its provisions. However, some courts have determined that taxpayers who have executed Form 870–AD agreements, waited out the period of limitations on assessments, and then prosecuted refund claims should be estopped from bringing suit on their claims.[46] Other courts, however, have concluded that estoppel is not appropriate.[47] Such tribunals, in sum, have concluded that the parties, by not executing a statutory closing agreement, cannot be said to have made an effective "settlement." Accordingly, these courts conclude, the taxpayer may file claims for refund and the Government may use, as offsets, any issues conceded in the Form 870–AD "settlement." [48]

Notwithstanding the fact that some courts will permit a taxpayer to sue for a refund even though a Form 870–AD "settlement" has been reached, this course of action cannot be recommended. Not only does a Form 870–AD give the government a possible defense to suit, it also amounts to a representation, by the taxpayer (and his representative), that no claims will be filed. It is far better for a taxpayer, looking toward the possibility of a tax refund suit, to modify a Form 870–AD expressly reserving the right to file claims for refund. By so doing no procedural defense can be raised by the government, and taxpayer's representative will not appear to have made any misrepresentation to the Service during the course of settlement procedures.

---

[44] See p. **12**·10 *et seq. infra.*
[45] IRC § 7121.
[46] *E.g.,* Daugette v. Patterson, 250 F.2d 753 (C.A.5th), *cert. denied,* 356 U.S. 902.
[47] *E.g.,* Uinta Livestock Corp. v. United States, 355 F.2d 761 (C.A.10th).
[48] See p. **12**·3 *et seq. infra* for a discussion of offsets in tax refund suits.

Forms 866 and 906

Forms 866 [49] and 906 [50] are the closing agreements that comply with § 7121 of the Internal Revenue Code. The Code states, with respect to the finality of these agreements:

(b) FINALITY.—If such agreement is approved by the Secretary or his delegate (within such time as may be stated in such agreement, or later agreed to) such agreement shall be final and conclusive, and, except upon a showing of fraud or malfeasance, or misrepresentation of a material fact—

(1) the case shall not be reopened as to the matters agreed upon or the agreement modified by any officer, employee, or agent of the United States, and

(2) in any suit, action, or proceeding, such agreement, or any determination, assessment, collection, payment, abatement, refund, or credit made in accordance therewith, shall not be annulled, modified, set aside or disregarded.

Thus, execution of these forms results in a final settlement or closing which may not be disturbed by the government or the taxpayer.

Form 866 (agreement as to final determination of the liability) is used to effect the final closing of the total tax liability of the taxpayer. Form 906 (closing agreement as to final determination covering specific matters) is used to effect the final closing as to one or more separate issues affecting the tax liability of a taxpayer.

Thus, Form 866 is used to close conclusively the total tax liability for a period ending prior to the date of the agreement. This is not only useful in resolving disputes, but may also be desirable for a fiduciary seeking discharge of his obligations, or in making final distributions, or in the case of a corporate liquidation or sale of a corporate business. Form 906 may be used not only as to prior but also with respect to subsequent taxable periods. With respect to prior years' items, such as the amount of gross income, a particular deduction or valuation may be agreed upon; and with respect to future years, matters such as basis and depreciation may be agreed upon.

Closing agreements may be approved and entered into by the Regional Commissioner (Appellate), his assistant, or the Chief or Associate Chief of an Appellate Division Branch Office.[51]

[49] See Administrative Practice Form No. 7, page **C**·12–13.
[50] See Administrative Practice Form No. 8, page **C**·14–15.
[51] Del. Order 97 (Rev. 4), 1967–15 I.R.B. 28.

CHAPTER 2

TAXPAYER'S SELECTION OF FORUM

THE TAX LITIGATION TRIBUNALS

When a private citizen is engaged in a tax dispute with the Internal Revenue Service he is entitled to select the court that will determine his correct tax liability. The taxpayer is usually able to select his forum from among the Tax Court of the United States, the United States Court of Claims, or the United States District Court in his home district. Each of these courts utilizes a different type of litigation procedure. Moreover, in some instances the respective tribunals have different bodies of precedent applicable to the issues in the taxpayer's case.

The taxpayer's selection of the forum for litigating his tax controversy is the single most important decision he must make during the entire course of the controversy. The choice will significantly affect his ability to close his case successfully with either a favorable adjudication or a satisfactory settlement. It has been noted that

A recovery which results from the careful choice of a favorable court to decide the case may at first seem difficult to justify, but such pre-trial strategy is an everyday occurrence. In the tax area, [forum] shopping appears to be a natural consequence of the court system established by Congress. . . . The taxpayer's notorious exercise of this choice without objection suggests that it is not an accidental characteristic of the system.[1]

Given the opportunity to maximize his litigation chances through a careful selection of tribunal, the taxpayer should seek to take full advantage of the forum shopping built into our system of tax litigation.

Tax Court of the United States

The Tax Court of the United States is a specialized national tribunal [2] which hears only cases requiring a determination of taxpayers' liabilities for income, estate, gift, and excess profits taxes.[3] It was created to provide a forum in which a taxpayer could, at his option, secure a redetermination of his tax liability without first paying a deficiency asserted against him.[4] While the Tax Court has limited jurisdiction insofar as subject matter is concerned, its geographical jurisdiction is restricted only by the scope of application of the income, estate, gift, and excess profits tax laws of the United States.

The sixteen Tax Court judges are based in Washington, D.C., where the court's files are maintained. However, trial and motion hearings are held in a number of cities throughout the United States for the convenience of the parties and witnesses. The effective handling of a Tax Court case does not require a trip to Washington, D.C., at any time during the proceedings.

Although the Tax Court Rules do not provide for formal discovery procedures as do the procedural rules of the tax refund tribunals, a trial in the Tax Court is conducted in much the same manner as any civil case presented to a judge sitting without a jury in a United States District Court. However, the decisional process in the Tax Court is different from that utilized in the district courts. The ultimate decision in a Tax Court case is the action of the Tax Court and not that of the individual judge who presided at trial. The Tax Court judge who heard a case will, after con-

---

[1] Note, *"Mistake" and Forum Shopping in Suits for Refund of Federal Tax,* 114 U. PA. L. REV. 1244, 1248 (1966).

[2] The Tax Court, originally the Board of Tax Appeals, is "an independent agency in the Executive Branch of the Government." IRC § 7441. Its function is judicial, however. As stated by the United States Commission on Organization of the Executive Branch of the Government, Task Force Report on Legal Services and Procedures, 255 (1955), "The Tax Court, as its name implies, is in fact a court which exercises only judicial functions, and not administrative, regulatory, investigative, or policy making authority. . . . It functions in the same manner as a Federal District Court. . . ."

[3] IRC § 7442. And see, for a discussion of the jurisdiction and authority of the Tax Court, Chapter 3 *infra.*

[4] Martin v. Commissioner, 358 F.2d 63 (C.A.7th).

sidering the evidence and submissions of the parties, write an opinion. The trial judge's opinion is referred to the Chief Judge for his consideration. The Chief Judge will either permit the trial judge's opinion to constitute the decision of the Tax Court or will refer the case to the full court which will decide the suit *en banc*.

The losing party in a Tax Court case has the right to appeal the decision to a United States Court of Appeals. While it is subject to review by the Courts of Appeals, the Tax Court does not consider itself bound to follow their precedents. Rather, it will follow its own decisions and those of the United States Supreme Court.[5] However, the Courts of Appeals tend to disagree with the Tax Court's attitude on this point.[6]

In Tax Court litigation the government is represented by members of the staff of Regional Counsel, Internal Revenue Service. Regional Counsel's office is a part of the Service operating under the supervision of the Chief Counsel. However, the Regional Counsel operates with a large measure of autonomy. Settlement of Tax Court cases is negotiated with the Appellate Division and Regional Counsel. Authority to settle Tax Court cases is vested jointly in the Regional Counsel and the Appellate Division until the time of trial. Thereafter, settlement authority is vested in Regional Counsel alone.

United States District Courts

The United States District Courts are the general trial courts of the federal judicial system. The judges are not judicial specialists but hear cases arising under all aspects of federal and frequently of state law. However, in view of the impact that tax law has had on legal practice in recent years, it is safe to assume that a United States District Judge will be familiar, at least in a general way, with the substantive law of taxation.

The procedural rules followed in the district courts provide for a full range of discovery devices such as depositions of prospective witnesses to discover their testimony before trial, written interrogatories to parties to obtain detailed information, and other procedures. Trials in the district courts proceed in the traditional manner, more or less as they do in state courts of general jurisdiction. The district courts are the only tax forums in which a jury trial may be had—on demand of either the taxpayer or the Government.

In character the United States District Courts are the only "local" forums for tax suits. Unlike litigation in the two national courts having

[5] Lawrence v. Commissioner, 27 T.C. 713, 716–720; *rev'd on other grounds*, 258 F.2d 562 (C.A.9th).
[6] *E.g.*, Stacy v. Commissioner, 237 F.2d 605, 606 (C.A.6th).

jurisdiction over tax matters, cases in the district courts will be heard and decided by a judge (or jury) from the district in which the case is pending (usually the taxpayer's residence).

The district courts consider themselves bound by the decisions of the Supreme Court and those of the United States Court of Appeals for the circuit in which they are located. Appellate review of an adverse district court judgment is a matter of right for the losing party.

In most district court tax refund suits the government is represented by attorneys from the Tax Division of the United States Department of Justice. In some instances the government is represented by an Assistant United States Attorney who, for all practical purposes, acts as a Tax Division trial attorney in the case. Settlement negotiations are handled by the Justice Department, and ultimate authority to compromise refund suits is vested in the Attorney General of the United States or an official of the Tax Division designated by him.

United States Court of Claims

The United States Court of Claims is a national tribunal, located in Washington, D.C., which has jurisdiction to hear claims against the government including those for tax refunds. The court has a degree of tax specialization approximately midway between that of the Tax Court and that of the typical United States District Judge.

The Court of Claims Rules provide for the use of discovery proceedings prior to trial to almost the same extent as the Federal Rules of Civil Procedure followed in the district courts. However, the procedure for presenting a case to the Court of Claims is unique among the tax forums. In substance, a Court of Claims case consists of a trial and an appellate stage. Pretrial proceedings and the hearing of evidence are handled by a trial commissioner. Trial hearings in a case are set at one location (or more) for the convenience of the parties and witnesses, and, where appropriate, the trial sessions of a case can be separated by several weeks or more.

The commissioner, after the evidence is closed, will submit to the court a report containing his findings of fact and, where the court so directs, his recommendations for conclusions of law. Thereafter, the parties submit briefs and present arguments to the court itself which, in effect, reviews the commissioner's determination. Final decision (on the facts and the law) is then rendered by the Court of Claims.

The Court of Claims will follow its own decisions and those of the United States Supreme Court. Opinions of other courts, while possibly persuasive, are not considered to be binding on the court. Appeal from an adverse judgment of the United States Court of Claims is possible only upon the granting of a writ of certiorari by the United States Supreme Court. In view of the rarity with which certiorari is granted (in about one tax case per year), the Court of Claims, for practical purposes, is thought of as a court of last resort.[7]

In the view of some writers the Court of Claims is the best forum available for the presentation of tax cases and should be selected by the taxpayer in the absence of a more favorable body of precedent elsewhere.[8] The particular advantages of the Court of Claims urged by its practitioners include

1. The probability that its decision will not be reviewed
2. The opportunity to present evidence at several locations so as to permit the trier to see and hear witnesses
3. The opportunity to have several separated trial sessions so as to permit time for reflection during the course of trial
4. The system of presenting a case first to a commissioner and thereafter a court, which, it is asserted, permits a more thorough presentation of the case.

Some commentators feel that the Court of Claims has a tendency to disregard technical rules and evidentiary restrictions where the equities favor the taxpayer.[9] Others disagree.[10] In the authors' view it is safer to rely on specific precedents in the area under consideration than on any overall feeling about the "attitude" of the Court of Claims.[11]

In all Court of Claims tax refund suits the government is represented by trial attorneys from the Court of Claims Section of the Tax Division of the Justice Department. Settlement authority is vested in the Attorney General of the United States or an official of the Tax Division designated by him.

CONSIDERATIONS IN SELECTING A FORUM FOR TAX LITIGATION

Restrictions on Taxpayer's Choice

While three forums exist for tax litigation, every taxpayer does not have the ability to choose among the three courts in every case. There can be unavoidable restrictions on his choice.

In order to be within the subject matter jurisdiction of the Tax Court, a taxpayer's dispute, first of all, must involve income, estate, gift, or excess

[7] Pavenstedt, *The United States Court of Claims as a Forum for Tax Cases,* 15 TAX L. REV. 1 & 201, 20–21 (1959–60) ; Miller, *Tax Refund Litigation in the United States Court of Claims,* 55 GEO. L.J. 454, 457–58 (1966–67).

[8] Miller, *op. cit., supra* note 7, at 468–70; Pavenstedt, *op. cit., supra* note 7 at 228; Ferguson, *Jurisdictional Problems in Tax Controversies,* 48 IOWA L. REV. 312, 349 (1962–63).

[9] *E.g.,* Pavenstedt, *op. cit., supra* note 7, at 28–33.

[10] *E.g.,* Miller, *op. cit., supra* note 7, at 477.

[11] For a discussion of the actions of the Court of Claims in specific types of tax cases, see Miller, *op. cit., supra* note 7, at 479–94, and Pavenstedt, *op. cit., supra* note 7, at 8 (note 27), 201–28.

profits taxes.[12] Disputes regarding other taxes must be litigated, after payment, in a tax refund suit. Secondly, the Tax Court will have jurisdiction of the dispute only where a timely petition has been filed, usually within 90 days after the issuance of a deficiency notice ("90 day letter").[13] Where the taxpayer has chosen to waive his right to a deficiency notice or contends he overpaid his taxes even though no deficiency was assessed (for example, if he erred in the Government's favor on his tax return) he cannot elect the Tax Court as his forum.

The principal obstacle to the bringing of a tax refund suit is the full-payment rule [14] which makes the payment of the deficiency asserted by the Internal Revenue Service for a taxable period a prerequisite. For those tax deficiencies that can be reviewed by the Tax Court the payment burden can be heavy and may, as a practical matter, force the taxpayer to litigate in the Tax Court. The taxes beyond the subject matter jurisdiction of the Tax Court (*e.g.*, excise taxes) have been classified as "divisible taxes" for which the jurisdictionally required prepayment will normally be quite small.[15] Thus, congruously, the taxpayer who is jurisdictionally barred from the Tax Court will not be financially prohibited from testing his liability through a tax refund suit.

Factors in Selecting Forum

Whenever the Internal Revenue Service indicates that an adjustment may be made of a taxpayer's reported liability, a potential tax suit is in existence. While every effort should be made to resolve controversies during the Service's administrative process, the taxpayer should act with a view toward possible litigation. Early in the course of any dispute he should, at least tentatively, elect the forum in which he wishes to test his liability should litigation become necessary. Thereafter, his actions before the Service should be guided so as to protect his ability to litigate his case in the most advantageous tribunal if he cannot obtain a satisfactory settlement administratively.

The election of the most advantageous forum for a taxpayer requires a consideration of his particular dispute and the nature of the courts available to him. We shall discuss here the most important factors bearing upon the taxpayer's choice.[16]

---

[12] See Chapter 3 *infra.*
[13] See p. **5**·3 *infra.*
[14] See p. **10**·2 *et seq. infra.*
[15] See p. **10**·4 *et seq. infra.*
[16] There are a number of articles that deal with the various factors to be considered by the taxpayer who is selecting his forum for tax litigation. *E.g.*, Gannet, *Pretrial Strategy in a Tax Case: Choice of Forum: A Checklist of Points to Consider,* 22ND N.Y.U. TAX INST. 75 (1964) ; Ash, *Factors in Selecting the Forum in Which To Litigate,* 12TH N.Y.U. TAX INST. 935 (1954).

THE PRECEDENTS. As illustrated by the following chart, each of the tax tribunals considers itself bound by a different body of precedents:

	Tax Court	District Court	Court of Claims
Precedents considered binding in addition to its own decisions	Supreme Court	Court of Appeals for its circuit and Supreme Court	Supreme Court

Unless a point has completely been resolved by the United States Supreme Court there may be a difference in the pertinent law as applied by the courts available for tax litigation. The first step, then, in the taxpayer's selection of a forum should be the analysis of the precedents with a view toward selecting the most favorable legal climate for his controversy. Where there is a significant difference in the body of precedents applicable, this factor should be given almost conclusive weight in the taxpayer's choice of a tribunal.

The authors do not consider the overall percentages of taxpayers' recoveries in the three tax forums to be of any significance in the choice of forum. Nor do they consider the manner in which case dispositions are recorded (*i.e.,* government wins, government losses, "partials") a reliable or consistent measure of the results in tax cases.[17]

APPELLATE REVIEW. The perfect forum for the taxpayer's suit is one in which a favorable decision will be reached by the trial court and will not be appealed by the Government. While this ideal cannot always be achieved, the taxpayer should seek a forum in which the odds are in his favor in the event any appellate review is necessary.

With regard to the district courts, there are no unusual problems with respect to appellate review of tax cases since the trial court is bound by the decision of the Court of Appeals that can review its decision. Accordingly, the same favorable precedents that made the district court an advantageous forum for trial will minimize the taxpayer's problems in the event of an appeal. With respect to the Court of Claims, appellate review may be had only on a writ of certiorari. The writ is so rarely granted that, for planning purposes, the taxpayer can virtually ignore the possibility that an appeal will be necessary. Moreover, as in the district courts, the Court of Claims will consider itself bound by any precedents in the court to which appeal may be made (*i.e.,* the Supreme Court).

The Tax Court presents an extraordinary problem with respect to appellate review because it does not consider itself bound by the precedents in the courts of appeals that review its decisions. Therefore, a taxpayer could conclude that, as to his case, a decision by the Tax Court is very

[17] See Miller, *op. cit., supra* note 7, at 473–74; Walston, *The Use of Juries in Federal Civil Income Tax Cases,* 39 TAXES 144, 147, note 14 (1961).

likely to be reversed on appeal. In this event, it is unlikely that the Tax Court will be a desirable forum. If the Tax Court precedents are favorable to the taxpayer then he faces the distinct possibility that the Government would appeal from, and obtain reversal of, a decision for him. On the other hand if the taxpayer's chance to win rests in the court of appeals he must sustain the burden of an appeal in addition to a trial in order ultimately to prevail. A case in point is *Estate of deGuebriant v. Commissioner*.[18] There, the Tax Court stated,

> We are aware that our decision was reversed by the Court of Appeals for the Second Circuit in Jandorf v. Commissioner, 171 Fed. (2d) 464, but, with due deference to its views, we remain convinced of the soundness of our position as expressed in our decision therein and adhere to it in this proceeding.[19]

In view of the Tax Court's action the taxpayer had to bear the expense of an appeal to the Second Circuit in order to secure a *per curiam* reversal.

BURDEN OF PREPAYMENT AND RUNNING OF INTEREST. As previously noted, there can be cases in which the taxpayer simply cannot make the prepayment of taxes prerequisite to the bringing of a tax refund suit. In this event, only the Tax Court is available to him as a forum to test his tax liability. Most taxpayers can, with varying degrees of difficulty, "stake" themselves to a tax refund suit. The advantages, if any, of a tax refund forum for a particular case must be weighed against any hardship the taxpayer will suffer in satisfying the full-payment rule.

The running of interest has a bearing on the financial effects of a prepayment of taxes. If the taxpayer should proceed in the Tax Court without a prepayment he runs the risk of having to pay interest at 6% per annum on any deficiency that may be found.[20] Since the interest payment will be deductible,[21] the effective rate will be somewhat lower than 6%. On the other hand if the taxpayer makes a prepayment of taxes he is entitled to interest at 6% per annum on the amount of any overpayment of his taxes.[22] This interest, when received, is taxable income.[23] The interest situation provides an opportunity for effective tax planning. The taxpayer can consider the possibility of arranging for the payment of interest in the taxable year in which it will have the most beneficial effect as a deduction. Similarly, he can seek to time the receipt of interest in a year in which its inclusion in income will generate the least amount of additional income tax.

---

[18] 14 T.C. 611, *rev'd sub nom.* Claflin v. Commissioner 186 F.2d 307 (C.A.2d).

[19] *Id.* at 620.

[20] IRC § 6601. A taxpayer may proceed in the Tax Court even though he makes a prepayment of taxes. See p. **3·4–5** *infra*. See also Giljum, *Federal Tax Problems Encountered in Advance Tax Payment Transactions,* 21 TAX L. REV. 495 (1966).

[21] IRC § 163.

[22] IRC § 6611.

[23] IRC § 61.

POSSIBILITY OF ADDITIONAL DEFICIENCIES. On occasion, in the course of Internal Revenue Service administrative procedures, the Service, through oversight, will assert only some of the tax deficiencies that it, at least arguably, could contend exist. Where there exists the possibility that, in the course of preparation for litigation, the government may discover grounds upon which it could contend that there are substantial additional deficiencies in tax, the taxpayer should seriously consider avoiding the Tax Court and taking any litigation to a refund tribunal. As noted by one writer,[24] when a taxpayer has filed a complicated return containing many controversial items he should seriously consider the wisdom of "letting sleeping dogs lie."

Once a Tax Court petition is filed (after a deficiency notice has been issued) the statute of limitations on assessments is in suspense for the duration of the proceedings.[25] Should the government discover and assert a new deficiency and satisfy the Tax Court that it is correct, the taxpayer may be required to pay an even greater tax deficiency than he chose to contest.

A classic case in point provides an example of the hazards in electing the Tax Court as a forum.[26] A taxpayer filed a petition with the Tax Court in order to contest a proposed deficiency assessment of $15,977.61. The Commissioner, in the course of preparation for trial, discovered a new issue and raised it by an amendment to his original answer. Ultimately the Commissioner was sustained on the new issue, and the taxpayer's total deficiency was increased by $1,026,340.40, more than one million dollars in excess of the amount he originally chose to contest in the Tax Court.

Tax refund litigation can be handled so as to avoid the possibility that the taxpayer will have to pay more than the deficiency asserted during the administrative process. By virtue of the statutes of limitations relating to the filing of refund claims and refund suits it is almost always possible to commence a refund suit *after* the time for additional assessments has expired.[27] Therefore, any new deficiencies discovered in the course of preparation for trial can be used by the government only to reduce the amount of the taxpayer's recovery on his refund claims.[28] Regardless of the size of an offsetting adjustment successfully raised by the government, the taxpayer's net loss [29] is limited to the deficiencies that were timely assessed.

OPPORTUNITY TO HAVE TRIAL BY JURY. A taxpayer's tax liability can be contested in a jury trial only in a United States District Court. How-

[24] Ash, *op. cit., supra* note 16, at 941.
[25] IRC § 6503(a).
[26] Raskob v. Commissioner 37 B.T.A. 1283, *aff'd sub nom.* duPont v. Commissioner, 118 F.2d 544 (C.A.2d), *cert. denied,* 314 U.S. 623.
[27] See p. **10·20** *et seq. infra.*
[28] See p. **12·3** *et seq. infra.*
[29] For the taxable periods in suit.

ever, the right to a jury determination is a two-edged sword, available to the government as well as the taxpayer once a refund suit is filed in a district court.[30]

We have discussed elsewhere the factors that must be taken into account in deciding whether or not a trial by jury would be advantageous to the taxpayer.[31] This consideration should precede the selection of a forum, for it is at this stage that the taxpayer has the power to block the government from obtaining a jury by selecting a court in which no jury trials are available.

AVAILABILITY OF FORMAL DISCOVERY PROCEDURE. In the Tax Court there is no formal discovery while in the other two tax forums extensive formal discovery procedures are available. In tax controversies the existence of discovery procedures generally works to the advantage of the government since the taxpayer usually is aware of the pertinent facts prior to the time he brings suit. Accordingly, in a tax refund suit the taxpayer can expect to be subjected to extensive discovery. Only in exceptional circumstances, for example in fraud cases, could the taxpayer get as much direct benefit from discovery as the government. While normally a "light" factor, the existence of discovery procedures in the tax refund tribunals usually tends to make them less desirable for a taxpayer than the Tax Court.

SPECIALIZATION OF THE TRIBUNAL. As to specialization and experience in deciding controversies under the internal revenue laws, the available tax forums are vastly different. At the two extremes of the spectrum are the Tax Court and the United States District Courts with the Court of Claims in the middle, having, according to some writers, a greater tendency than either of the other tribunals to apply the spirit rather than the strict letter of the tax law.[32] In weighing this factor the taxpayer should ask himself whether his particular case will best be presented to a tax specialist who may tend to view the matter solely within the four corners of the Internal Revenue Code or to a judge of more varied background who may approach the problem from a more generalized point of view.

SETTLEMENT POSSIBILITIES. Settlement negotiations in a Tax Court case are conducted for the Government jointly by the staffs of the Appellate Division and Regional Counsel's office. Hence there is some participation in the settlement process of the agency that initially set up the controversy. On the other hand, a tax refund suit is totally divorced from the Internal Revenue Service's administrative process. The Government is represented by attorneys of the Tax Division of the Department of Justice, and ultimate settlement authority is vested in that Department.

---

[30] 28 U.S.C. § 2402.
[31] See p. **15**·6 *et seq. infra.*
[32] See notes 8 and 9 *supra.*

Costs and Duration of Litigation.   Every taxpayer, in electing a forum, will want to consider the amount it will cost him to litigate and the amount of time he will have to wait for a final decision in each of the tribunals. Unfortunately, it is impossible to predict these matters with any reasonable degree of accuracy.

With respect to expenses, a given case can usually be litigated in the Tax Court at less cost than in the other two forums available. Next in order of usual cost would be a district court suit in which the major additional expenses would relate to the costs of discovery procedures (primarily in attorney's and witnesses' time) and the possibility that a longer trial (particularly in jury cases) would be necessary. Usually most expensive would be a Court of Claims case. In addition to the expenses incurred in a district court case a Court of Claims case requires the printing of many documents, the presentation of a post-trial "appeal," and an argument in Washington. However, in Tax Court and District Court litigation it may be necessary to add the expenses of an appeal to those incurred at trial, while in Court of Claims litigation the expense of an appeal need only rarely be incurred.

In most tax cases the relative time required for resolution is not a significant factor in the taxpayer's forum selection. First of all, most cases (in all three courts) are resolved by means of a settlement. Hence the speed of resolution depends primarily upon the rapidity with which serious settlement negotiations can be commenced. This, of course, is largely dependent upon the taxpayer's approach to settlement. Secondly, it is virtually impossible to predict which of the three tribunals is most likely to provide the fastest final conclusion of the particular case. The speed with which the respective courts can act depends upon (1) the extent to which the case can be submitted on a dispositive motion or stipulation and (2) the state of the particular docket on which the case is pending.

In the Tax Court one can usually expect a case to be called for trial within from a year to a year and a half after it is commenced. However, the time for decision can be considerable. It is not uncommon for a decision to be handed down more than a year after a case has been tried and briefed. On the other hand, it should be noted that a Tax Court case can be commenced earlier in the Internal Revenue Service administrative proceedings than a refund suit—*i.e.,* as soon as a deficiency notice has issued. Accordingly, there is no need for the taxpayer to file a claim for refund and wait six months before commencing his action.

In the district courts there is no uniformity regarding the time that will elapse between the filing of a complaint and the commencement of trial. In some districts trial can be held within six months after suit is brought. On the other hand, some districts have dockets so crowded that several years will expire before a civil case can be reached. Experience in the district court in which taxpayer is contemplating bringing a refund suit is more important than an overall national average [33] in determining the probable time required to dispose of a case.

The presentation of a case to the United States Court of Claims requires, in effect, a trial plus an appeal. Hence the time consumed by a Court of Claims case will always be considerable. While the precise time required for a particular case will depend largely upon the nature of the controversy and the schedule of the trial commissioner to whom it is assigned, one can safely predict that most cases will require at least two years for conclusion. Many can be expected to consume in excess of three years.[34] In most instances this would make the Court of Claims the slowest of the tax refund forums. However, unlike Tax Court or district court cases, a Court of Claims case is almost never reviewed by an appellate court. Accordingly, the likelihood that an additional year or more [35] will be consumed in appellate proceedings is remote in a Court of Claims case. However, this possibility must always be taken into account when considering the likely time required for prosecuting a Tax Court or district court case.

DIFFERENCE IN TAXPAYER'S BURDEN OF PROOF.   There is a difference between the legal theory of a Tax Court case and that of a tax refund suit. As a consequence of this difference the taxpayer's burden of proof will depend upon his choice of forum. In most instances, however, the subtle difference in the burden of proof will have little effect on the selection of a forum.

A Tax Court case is, in essence, an action brought by a taxpayer for the review of an administrative determination, *i.e.,* the Commissioner of Internal Revenue's determination that additional taxes are owed as expressed in a deficiency notice. In the Tax Court the taxpayer's burden is simply to prove that the Commissioner was wrong with regard to the tax adjustments stated in the deficiency notice.[36] If the Government wishes to contend that additional tax adjustments should be made then it must bear the burden of proof as to the new issues raised.[37] However, if the government should prevail on the newly raised adjustments, the taxpayer may have to pay an even greater tax deficiency than the one proposed by the deficiency notice.[38]

A tax refund suit is an action brought by a taxpayer for a refund of an overpayment of his taxes for the period in issue. In such a suit the tax-

[33] Approximately one year and eleven months from initiation to disposition (including settlements) in the five years ending June 30, 1965. Miller, *op. cit., supra* note 7, at 471.

[34] The average time from commencement to decision in a Court of Claims case for the five years ending June 30, 1965, was two years and ten months. Miller, *op. cit., supra* note 7, at 471.

[35] The average time consumed by an appeal in a tax case for the five years ending June 30, 1965, was one year and four months. Miller, *op. cit., supra* note 7, at 471.

[36] Helvering v. Taylor, 293 U.S. 507, *affirming* Taylor v. Commissioner, 70 F.2d 619, 620–21 (C.A.2d).

[37] Tax Ct. R. 32.

[38] See p. **3 · 6** *infra*.

payer does not sustain his burden of proof merely by showing that the Commissioner was wrong with respect to the specific tax adjustments placed in issue by the claims for refund.[39] He must go further and establish his correct tax liability for the period in issue so that the court can determine that he, in fact, overpaid his taxes.[40] The practical effect of this "double burden of proof" is to place on the taxpayer the burden of proof with regard to new issues raised by the government.[41] However, if the taxpayer has been careful about his timing the government will be able to use the new issues defensively only.[42]

In some special circumstances the choice of a forum can directly affect the burden of proof on the principal issue in a tax controversy. For example, consider an accumulated earnings tax [43] case. The Internal Revenue Code provides that, in the Tax Court, a taxpayer can shift the burden of proof on the accumulated earnings tax issue to the government by filing an adequate statement of the grounds on which he relies in contending that the accumulation of earnings was proper.[44] There are, of course, practical problems inherent in the use of this statutory provision. For example, many Tax Court Judges will not rule upon the adequacy of a Section 534 statement until after trial. Accordingly, the taxpayer is forced to assume that he has the burden in order to avoid losing due to a failure of proof. The burden of proof on this issue cannot be shifted in the refund tribunals even though discovery procedures in these forums ensure that the government will have access to at least as much information from the taxpayer as would be sufficient to shift the burden of proof in the Tax Court.

ADDITIONAL FACTORS. In addition to the foregoing a case may present other circumstances worthy of weight in the taxpayer's selection of a forum. For example, the possibility that publicity could result from a trial in a local district court may indicate that the relative anonymity of Tax Court or Court of Claims litigation is desirable. Or, the local aspects of a case may influence the decision whether to present the case to a local judge and/or jury or to a national tribunal.

WHEN CHOICE MUST BE MADE

During the course of a tax controversy the critical decision on choice of forum will have to be made within one of two time limitations. First, if a

[39] Compton v. United States, 334 F.2d 212, 216 (C.A.4th).

[40] *Ibid.* Taylor v. Commissioner, 70 F.2d 619 (C.A.2d), *aff'd sub nom.* Helvering v. Taylor, 293 U.S. 507.

[41] Missouri Pac. R.R. v. United States, 337 F.2d 637 (Ct. Cl.); duPont v. United States, 13 A.F.T.R.2d 824 (Del.).

[42] See p. **10·20** *et seq. infra.*

[43] IRC § 531.

[44] IRC § 534.

deficiency notice is issued, the taxpayer has only a short time (normally ninety days) to decide, once and for all, whether he wishes to elect the Tax Court or a tax refund forum. Second, if he has not selected the Tax Court he must elect definitely the tax refund tribunal he wishes to hear his case before the commencement of his action.

Effect of Issuance of Deficiency Notice on Choice of Forum

In controversies within the jurisdiction of the Tax Court a taxpayer who receives a deficiency notice has a specified time, usually ninety days, within which to file a petition with the Tax Court.[45] Should the taxpayer allow the statutorily provided period to expire without commencing an action in the Tax Court he is barred from the tribunal.[46] Thereafter, he may contest his tax liability only in a tax refund forum.

If a taxpayer receives a deficiency notice in an income, estate, or gift tax controversy and files a timely petition with the Tax Court he gives the Tax Court exclusive jurisdiction over his controversy.[47] Thereafter a tax refund suit is barred.[48] It should be noted that it is the taxpayer's action in electing the Tax Court, and not any action taken by the court, that bars a subsequent refund suit.[49] Hence, any petition that serves to give the Tax Court jurisdiction of the controversy, even one that was dismissed[50] or raised totally different issues from those sought to be presented in a refund action,[51] will serve to bar a subsequent suit. However, the document filed with the Tax Court must amount to a petition, or a refund suit will not be barred.[52] The scope of the prohibition against a tax refund suit is co-extensive with the jurisdiction conferred upon the Tax Court by the taxpayer's petition. For income and gift taxes refund suits are barred with respect to the taxable years before the Tax Court. For estate taxes the prohibition is total inasmuch as there is only a single taxable period for estate tax purposes.[53]

Three specific exceptions to the prohibition against refund suits are provided by statute, *i.e.,* suits for refund of (1) overpayments determined by

---

[45] IRC § 6213(a).
[46] See p. **5·3** *infra.*
[47] IRC § 6512(a).
[48] *Ibid.*
[49] Elbert v. Johnson, 164 F.2d 421, 424 (C.A.2d); Holzer v. United States, 250 F. Supp. 875 (E.D. Wis.), *aff'd* 367 F.2d 822 (C.A.7th).
[50] Fiorentino v. United States, 226 F.2d 619 (C.A.3d).
[51] United States v. Wolf, 238 F.2d 447 (C.A.9th); Moir v. United States, 149 F.2d 455 (C.A.1st).
[52] Cutling v. United States, 26 F. Supp. 586, 592–93 (E.D.N.Y.).
[53] Guettel v. United States, 95 F.2d 229 (C.A.8th), *cert. denied,* 305 U.S. 603. In the case of an estate, the commencement of a Tax Court action by one executor on behalf of the estate will bar a later refund suit by the estate even if it is brought by a different executor. Irwin v. Larson, 94 F.2d 187 (C.A.5th).

a final decision of the Tax Court, (2) amounts collected in excess of a tax deficiency computed in accordance with a final decision of the Tax Court, and (3) amounts collected after pertinent periods of limitations have expired.[54] None of these exceptions is of aid to a taxpayer who wishes to revoke his election to contest his tax liability in the Tax Court.

When a deficiency notice is issued with regard to the taxes in issue in a pending tax refund suit the taxpayer is given an additional choice of forum.[55] He can elect to have the deficiency notice issues litigated in the Tax Court. In this event the refund forum will lose jurisdiction over the case before it to the extent jurisdiction over the deficiency notice issues is acquired by the Tax Court. Alternatively, he can elect to have the deficiency notice issues litigated in the refund suit. In that case the government can amend its answer to assert a counterclaim based upon the deficiency notice.

Effect of Commencement of Tax Refund Suit on Choice of Forum

A taxpayer bringing a tax refund action has the right to elect to commence his action either in a United States District Court or in the United States Court of Claims. These tribunals have concurrent jurisdiction over tax refund suits.[56] However, as a practical matter, once the taxpayer has elected one tax refund forum he may not change his election in order to engage in further forum shopping.

In both tax refund forums the taxpayer has the right to take a voluntary dismissal of his action without prejudice until the government files its answer or a summary judgment motion.[57] Accordingly, up to that point the taxpayer may change tax refund forums provided the statute of limitations will permit the filing of a new action. Thereafter, however, the taxpayer has no right to a dismissal without prejudice. A dismissal without prejudice (leaving the taxpayer free to commence a new refund suit elsewhere) can be obtained either by agreement of the government or by order of the court.[58] While there are a number of reasons for which a court may permit a voluntary dismissal after issue has been joined, a desire for further forum shopping is not normally among them.[59]

If a tax refund suit is pending in one tax refund forum it is not permissible to commence a new suit on the same cause of action in another tax refund forum. The second action is subject to dismissal.[60]

---

[54] IRC § 6512(a).
[55] IRC § 7422(e). See pp. **13·**29–30 *infra*.
[56] 28 U.S.C. § 1346(a)(1).
[57] Fed. R. Civ. P. 41(a)(1); Ct. Cl. R. 67(a)(1).
[58] Fed. R. Civ. P. 41(a)(2); Ct. Cl. R. 67(a)(2).
[59] See generally 5 Moore's Federal Practice ¶ 41.05 (2d ed., 1966).
[60] 28 U.S.C. § 1500. Tecon Engineers, Inc. v. United States, 343 F.2d 943 (Ct. Cl.), *cert. denied,* 382 U.S. 976; Tecon Engineers, Inc. v. United States, 15 A.F.T.R.2d 467 (E.D. Ky.).

CHAPTER 3

JURISDICTION AND AUTHORITY OF
THE TAX COURT

THE TAX COURT

Description of the Court

The Tax Court's sole function is to determine a taxpayer's liabilities in income, estate, gift, and excess profits tax cases.[1] While the Court's jurisdiction over subject matter is limited in scope, its geographic jurisdiction is nationwide. In interpreting the Internal Revenue Code, the Court, because of its national nature, is required to follow only those precedents that have been promulgated by the Supreme Court of the United States and those embodied in its own earlier decisions. Appeal may be made to the Circuit Court of Appeals having jurisdiction over the place where the taxpayer resides.[2]

[1] IRC § 7442.
[2] IRC § 7482.

Two of the principal differences between the Tax Court and other forums are that all Tax Court cases are tried to a judge sitting without a jury and discovery proceedings are not available.[3] The time it takes to litigate a case in the Tax Court, from the filing of the petition to the decision, will vary from case to case and cannot be stated exactly. Generally, however, the process takes from 18 to 32 months.

JURISDICTION

The Prerequisites

The jurisdiction of the Tax Court, in addition to being confined to income, estate, gift, and excess profits taxes,[4] is limited to hearing cases involving these taxes only when other prerequisites are fulfilled. The other prerequisites to Tax Court jurisdiction are that

1. The government determine that a deficiency exists,
2. The government formally notify the taxpayer, in keeping with the statutory requirements, that it intends to assess the deficiency,
3. The taxpayer file a timely petition with the Court requesting a redetermination of the deficiency.[5]

Generally stated, a deficiency means the difference between the amount of tax reported as due by the taxpayer and the amount the government asserts is due. The government is prohibited from assessing or collecting the additional tax asserted by it until the taxpayer's time for filing a petition in the Tax Court expires.[6] If the taxpayer files a petition, the prohibition continues until the decision of the Court becomes final. Consequently, filing a petition in the Tax Court enables the taxpayer to obtain an independent judicial determination of his tax liability prior to the time he is required to pay the tax the government asserts is due.

Once a petition is properly filed in the Tax Court, however, the Court's authority is not confined to determining the correctness of the deficiency asserted by the government. It has the authority to increase the amount of the deficiency on the same grounds asserted by the Commissioner prior to the filing of the petition or on other grounds if they are properly raised during the litigation.[7] Moreover, once the Tax Court has jurisdiction, it is empowered to determine that the taxpayer has overpaid his taxes.[8]

---

[3] See p. **6·14** *infra.*
[4] IRC § 7442.
[5] See pp. **5·1–23** *infra.*
[6] IRC § 6213(a).
[7] IRC § 6214(a).
[8] IRC § 6512(b) ; Treas. Reg. § 301.6512–1(b).

Deficiency

The term "deficiency" has a dual significance. First, the Commissioner may assess only taxes shown on a return or a deficiency.[9] Second, Tax Court jurisdiction pertains only to deficiencies.[10]

DEFINITION. A deficiency is defined as the amount by which the correct tax exceeds the tax shown by the taxpayer on his return,[11] increased by any rebates [12] (any abatement, credit, or other repayment made to the taxpayer on the ground that correct tax is *less* than the tax shown by the taxpayer on his return [13]) and reduced by any amount previously assessed or collected (not simply paid) without assessment.[14] For purposes of determining the amount of a deficiency, the payments on account of estimated tax and credits for taxes withheld are disregarded.[15] Thus, a deficiency equals correct tax minus tax on return minus prior assessments plus rebates.[16]

Accordingly, the existence of a deficiency does not depend on amounts paid or amounts owing but on a disagreement between the government (asserting the "correct tax") and the taxpayer (showing tax due on his return) as to the proper amount of tax that should be paid.

TAX SHOWN ON "RETURN." In harmony with the policy that a deficiency is the difference between the tax the Commissioner asserts as correct and the tax the taxpayer asserts as correct, the courts have held that the tax shown on the return is not determinative when accompanied by a clear statement by the taxpayer that such tax is not legally due.[17]

In these cases the amount the taxpayer asserts as the correct amount legally due has been considered "the amount shown on the return." [18] Similarly, when the taxpayer does not file a return and the Commissioner files a return on his behalf showing a tax in excess of the amount the taxpayer concedes is due, the amount the taxpayer concedes is due is considered tax shown on the return and the excess is a deficiency.[19]

In cases involving amended returns, however, it has been held that the amount of tax shown on the original return is the "amount . . . shown as the tax" referred to in the statute. Thus, where the amended return

[9] IRC § 6201(a), (d).
[10] IRC § 6213.
[11] IRC § 6211(a).
[12] IRC § 6211(a)(2).
[13] IRC § 6211(b)(2) ; Treas. Reg. § 301.6211–1(f).
[14] IRC § 6211(a)(1)(B).
[15] IRC § 6211(b)(1).
[16] See the computations in Kurtzon v. Commissioner, 17 T.C. 1542.
[17] Penn Mutual Indemnity Co. v. Commissioner, 277 F.2d 16 (C.A.3d).
[18] John A. Gebelein, Inc. v. Commissioner, 37 B.T.A. 605.
[19] Taylor v. Commissioner, 36 B.T.A. 427.

showed a greater amount of tax than the original, it was held that the deficiency based on the original return was correct [20] and, where the tax on the amended return was less than the tax on the original return (which the Commissioner had accepted as correct), that no deficiency existed.[21]

PENALTIES. While penalties are generally treated as tax [22] and required to be assessed and collected in the same way as taxes, an exception is provided for penalties resulting from failure to file tax returns promptly or to pay estimated taxes [23] which may be assessed forthwith. In cases, however, where penalty for failure to file a return is attributable to a deficiency or, if no return is filed, to a penalty for underpayment of estimated taxes, such penalties are subject to the same deficiency procedures as taxes.[24]

Effect of Waiving Notice of Deficiency

An essential element of Tax Court jurisdiction is the existence of a deficiency and statutory notice thereof. The taxpayer is assured of receiving the statutory notice of a deficiency [25] because assessment or collection of any tax prior to the mailing of such a notice and for 90 days thereafter is prohibited.[26] If, however, the taxpayer waives his right to a statutory notice,[27] the Commissioner is relieved of the prohibition and may make an immediate assessment and collection of the tax.[28] Thus, no statutory notice will be mailed and the Tax Court will have no jurisdiction.

Effect of Payment

PAYMENT PRIOR TO ISSUANCE OF DEFICIENCY NOTICE. The Commissioner is authorized to assess any tax paid upon receipt of payment.[29] Consequently, if payment is made, no 90-day letter, as the statutory notice of deficiency is commonly called, will be issued and the Tax Court will not have jurisdiction. Moreover, such a voluntary payment of a proposed deficiency constitutes a tax "collected without assessment," [30] eliminating the deficiency and another prerequisite to Tax Court jurisdiction.[31]

[20] Powell Coal Co. v. Commissioner, 12 B.T.A. 492.
[21] Shanley v. Commissioner, 7 B.T.A. 521.
[22] IRC § 6659(a).
[23] IRC § 6659(b).
[24] IRC § 6659(b)(2); see also S. REP. No. 1098, 86th Cong., 2d Sess. 3 (1960), U.S. Code Cong. & Adm. News, 86th Cong., 2d Sess. 1960, vol. 2, at 2025–27.
[25] Described in IRC § 6212.
[26] IRC § 6213.
[27] By executing a Form 870 or 870–AD.
[28] IRC § 6213(d).
[29] IRC § 6213(b)(3).
[30] IRC § 6211(a)(1)(B).
[31] Bendheim v. Commissioner, 214 F.2d 26 (C.A.2d).

PAYMENT SUBSEQUENT TO ISSUANCE OF DEFICIENCY NOTICE. In order to enable a taxpayer to stop the running of interest without foregoing the right to litigate his tax liability before the Tax Court, the Code was amended in 1954 to state, "In any case where such amount is paid after the mailing of a notice of deficiency . . . such payment shall not deprive the Tax Court of jurisdiction." [32]

Thus, it is clear that a taxpayer may pay the asserted deficiency at any time after the mailing of the statutory notice without depriving the Tax Court of jurisdiction.

Effect of Jeopardy Assessment

The Tax Court has jurisdiction although the full amount of tax the government asserts is due has been collected pursuant to a jeopardy assessment. A deficiency exists, since the deficiency does not depend on amounts collected,[33] and the Commissioner is, in the case of a jeopardy assessment, required to send a statutory notice of deficiency within 60 days after he has assessed the tax unless he did so prior to assessment.[34]

However, despite the fact that the Tax Court has jurisdiction to redetermine the amount of tax due, it may not interfere in the purely administrative decisions made by the Commissioner in regard to the necessity for the jeopardy assessment.

POWER OF TAX COURT TO ADJUST THE TAX

Power To Redetermine the Deficiency

The Tax Court is authorized to redetermine the correct amount of the deficiency in any case within its jurisdiction.[35] Obviously, the Court may reduce the deficiency asserted by the Commissioner in the 90-day letter and find the taxpayer liable for the reduced amount [36] or find that no deficiency exists. The Court may also find that the correct amount of the deficiency exceeds the amount asserted, and the taxpayer will be required to pay this amount if the Commissioner asserts the increased deficiency prior to the hearing or a rehearing.[37]

While the Court may, in redetermining the deficiency, consider such facts about taxes in other years as may be relevant to the year set forth in

[32] IRC § 6213(b)(3).
[33] See p. **3·3** *supra.*
[34] IRC § 6861(b).
[35] IRC § 6214(a).
[36] Commissioner v. Meldrum & Fewsmith, Inc., 230 F.2d 283 (C.A.6th).
[37] IRC § 6214(a).

the deficiency notice, the Court will not and does not have jurisdiction to determine the correct amount of taxes due for other years.[38]

When the Deficiency May Be Increased

The Commissioner is generally permitted to send more than one statutory notice to a taxpayer,[39] provided such notices are within the statute of limitations.[40] However, he is prohibited from sending additional notices if the taxpayer files a petition to the Tax Court with respect to the first notice sent to him.[41]

In order to assess a larger deficiency than that set forth in the statutory notice, the Commissioner is required to make a timely assertion of the increased deficiency before the Tax Court. The statute requires that the assertion must be made prior to the hearing, or a rehearing, in order for the Tax Court to determine an increased deficiency.[42]

Normally, the claim for an increased deficiency will be included in the Commissioner's answer. If, however, the assertion is not made in the answer, the taxpayer may oppose a subsequent attempt to amend the answer to include such a claim because it is not timely. The statutory purpose of requiring that the claim be asserted prior to the hearing is to prevent prejudice that may result from the taxpayer's inability to prepare his case against the newly interposed claim. Accordingly, it has been held that permitting an amendment to an answer increasing the deficiency is a decision within the discretion of the Tax Court which must be made in light of the facts in each case and in view of the prejudice that may accrue to the taxpayer due to the Commissioner's delay in asserting the increased deficiency.[43] Thus, where the Court found facts supporting a deficiency larger than that asserted by the Commissioner, it refused to redetermine a deficiency in an amount larger than that asserted by the Commissioner prior to the hearing.[44]

Grounds Supporting the Deficiency

If the grounds asserted by the Commissioner do not support a deficiency determination, the Court will refuse to determine that a deficiency exists although it may be supported on other grounds.[45] This is not to say that the Commissioner is confined to the theories supporting the deficiency that

---

[38] IRC § 6214(b).
[39] Smoot v. Commissioner, 25 B.T.A. 1038.
[40] Ruud v. Commissioner, 15 T.C. 374.
[41] IRC § 6212(c) ; McCue v. Commissioner, 1 T.C. 986.
[42] IRC § 6214(a).
[43] Commissioner v. Long, 304 F.2d 136 (C.A.9th).
[44] Pitman v. Commissioner, 24 B.T.A. 244.
[45] Commissioner v. Fifth Ave. Bank, 84 F.2d 787 (C.A.3d).

he set forth in the 90-day letter,[46] but merely that the taxpayer is entitled to know the grounds in advance of the hearing so that he may prepare to oppose them. Thus, the Commissioner may be able to get a rehearing when he asserts an increased deficiency based on a theory that, at the time of the original hearing, could not be advanced [47] or when the original case was tried on an incorrect theory.[48]

Overassessment and Overpayment; Power To Require a Refund

If the government mails a statutory notice of deficiency with respect to income, estate, or gift taxes and the taxpayer files a timely petition, the Tax Court's jurisdiction is established. If the Court has jurisdiction it may find there has been an overpayment.[49] Such a finding requires that the overpayment be refunded or credited to the taxpayer when the Tax Court's decision becomes final.[50]

A refund or credit will be allowed, however, only when the Court finds that the payment was made within the time allowed for making a claim for refund.[51] In determining that there has been an overpayment, the Court's jurisdiction is limited to consideration of those kinds of taxes for which a deficiency has been determined.

[46] Blansett v. United States, 283 F.2d 474, 478 (C.A.8th).

[47] Commissioner v. Wells, 132 F.2d 405 (C.A.6th).

[48] Helvering v. Edison Securities Corp., 78 F.2d 85 (C.A.4th).

[49] IRC § 6512(b)(1).

[50] *Ibid.* While a refund is required by virtue of an appropriate Tax Court determination, the Tax Court does not have jurisdiction to order the government to pay over a refund. Theoretically, a taxpayer would have to sue for a refund on the basis of the Tax Court determination in order to have payment compelled. United States v. Rochelle, 363 F.2d 225, 231, 232 (C.A.5th).

[51] See p. **10·21** *et seq. infra.*

CHAPTER 4

THE DEFICIENCY NOTICE

FUNCTION AND EFFECT OF DEFICIENCY NOTICE

A taxpayer is entitled to have his income, estate, gift, or excess profits tax determined by an independent judicial body prior to the assessment of any deficiency asserted by the Internal Revenue Service. If the taxpayer wishes to utilize this right, the statutory notice of deficiency is of critical importance. This notice not only safeguards the right to petition the Tax Court for a judicial determination, but is actually a prerequisite to the filing of the petition. Failure to file a petition promptly after the receipt of the notice deprives the taxpayer of his right to petition the Tax Court. If this occurs, the taxpayer will be required to pay the tax as determined by the Service and then make a claim for a refund. If the refund is denied, the taxpayer will have to sue in the District Court or Court of Claims if he wishes to have his tax liability determined by a judicial tribunal.

The taxpayer's right to a Tax Court determination prior to payment is insured by § 6213(a) of the Internal Revenue Code, which prohibits the assessment of any tax prior to the expiration of 90 days after the mailing of a notice of deficiency (150 days if the taxpayer lives or is traveling outside the country when the notice is mailed).[1] Subject to six strictly con-

[1] IRC § 6213(a).

strued exceptions, the deficiency notice is a prerequisite to assessment in every case. Issuance of a notice is not necessary if any of the following is true:

1. The taxpayer has filed a written waiver of the deficiency notice.[2]
2. The taxpayer has made a mathematical error in his return.[3]
3. The taxpayer has voluntarily paid the tax without assessment.[4]
4. The taxpayer has been adjudicated bankrupt.[5]
5. The taxpayer has failed to file a bond pending appeal of an adverse Tax Court decision.[6]
6. A jeopardy assessment is required.[7]

An attempt to assess or collect a tax prior to the issuance of a proper and timely deficiency notice may be enjoined in any but the foregoing cases.[8]

If the taxpayer wishes to petition the Tax Court, he may do so only within the 90 days following the mailing of the deficiency notice, hence the informal name of the deficiency notice is the 90-day letter.[9] This period for filing is fixed by statute and cannot be extended by stipulation with the Service. Any petition filed before the mailing of the notice will be dismissed as premature, and any petition filed after the expiration of 90 days from the mailing of the notice will be dismissed as late. Once a timely petition is filed with the Tax Court, the prohibition on assessment or collection of the tax will continue until the entry of a final decision of the Tax Court.[10]

The mailing of the 90-day letter also has the effect of suspending the running of the statute of limitations on assessment or collection of any tax.[11] The statute is suspended for the 90-day period and for 60 days thereafter. If a petition is filed with the Tax Court, the running of the statute remains in suspense until 60 days after the final decision of the Court.[12]

THE CUSTOMARY DEFICIENCY NOTICE

If an additional tax is deemed due but the Service and the taxpayer are in disagreement on the amount, the Service will send a 90-day letter to the taxpayer by certified or registered mail so that it will be in a position to

---

[2] IRC § 6213(d) ; Moore v. Cleveland Ry., 108 F.2d 656 (C.A.6th).

[3] IRC § 6213(b)(1) ; Denton v. United States, 132 F. Supp. 741 (N.J.), aff'd 235 F.2d 733 (C.A.3d).

[4] IRC § 6213(b)(3) ; Bendheim v. Commissioner, 214 F.2d 26 (C.A.2d).

[5] IRC § 6871(a).

[6] IRC § 7485. Cf. IRC § 6863. Tomlinson v. Poller, 220 F.2d 308 (C.A.5th), cert. denied sub nom. Pace v. Tomlinson, 350 U.S. 832.

[7] IRC § 6861(a) ; Berry v. Westover, 70 F. Supp. 537 (S.D. Cal.).

[8] Salven v. United States, 45 A.F.T.R. 1256 (S.D. Cal.) ; Ventura Consol. Oil Fields v. Rogan, 86 F.2d 149 (C.A.9th), cert. denied, 300 U.S. 672.

[9] IRC § 6213(a).

[10] Ibid.

[11] IRC § 6503(a)(1).

[12] Ibid.

U. S. TREASURY DEPARTMENT
INTERNAL REVENUE SERVICE
DISTRICT DIRECTOR
P. O. BOX 3100
NEW YORK, N. Y. 10015

September 12, 1966

IN REPLY REFER TO
Form L-21
AU:R:90D

Excelsior Construction Company, Inc.
1970 Third Avenue
New York, New York 10066

TAXABLE YEAR ENDED	DEFICIENCY
12/31/60	$13,309.34
12/31/61	$18,385.39

Gentlemen:

In accordance with the provisions of existing internal revenue laws, notice is given that the determination of your income tax liability discloses a deficiency or deficiencies in the amounts and for the taxable years shown above. The enclosed statement shows the computation of the deficiency or deficiencies.

If you do not intend to contest this determination in the Tax Court of the United States, please sign the enclosed Waiver, Form 870, and return it promptly in the enclosed envelope. This will permit early assessment of the deficiency or deficiencies and limit accumulation of interest.

If you do not sign and return the Waiver, the deficiency or deficiencies will be assessed for collection, as required by law, upon the expiration of 90 days (150 days if you are outside the States of the Union and the District of Columbia) from the date of this letter, unless within that time you contest this determination in the Tax Court of the United States by filing a petition with that Court in accordance with its rules. A copy of the rules of the Court may be obtained by writing to the Clerk, Tax Court of the United States, Box 70, Washington, D. C. 20044.

Very truly yours,

Commissioner

By

District Director

Enclosures - **3:**
Statement
Waiver, Form 870
Return envelope

FORM L-21 (REV. 12-65)

GPO 958-850

FIG. 4–1. NINETY-DAY LETTER (FORM L-21).

assess and collect the deficiency it has asserted. Generally, a printed form letter will be used (see Fig. 4–1, page **4·3**).

This letter will be accompanied by a Form 870 and a short statement setting forth the manner in which the deficiency was arrived at and the Service's computations. Thus, the customary letter will apprise the taxpayer of the amount of the deficiency asserted, and an accompanying statement [13] will indicate the items in the return that are objected to and the reasons for such objections.

DEFECTIVE DEFICIENCY NOTICE

While the Service takes every precaution to see that the 90-day letter is mailed to the taxpayer in its proper form, some unavoidable errors may be made: An improper form may be used, the form letter and the statement may become separated and only one may reach the taxpayer, an informal letter may be used, or an otherwise proper letter may be misaddressed. Thus, the question arises as to how far the deficiency notice may depart from the proper form and yet still be effective.

Irregularities of Form and Content

Section 6212 of the Code does not specify that the deficiency notice be in any particular form, and notices have been held to be valid so long as the taxpayer is adequately apprised of the amount of the deficiency asserted and the fact that the Service intends to assess the stated deficiency.[14] If these minimal requirements are fulfilled, the notice accomplishes the statutory purpose and is effective, and no precise phrasing is required.[15] If these requirements are not fulfilled, the purported notice will not be valid, assessment by the Service is not permitted, and a petition based upon such a notice will not confer jurisdiction on the Tax Court. Thus, notices that fail to assert an actual deficiency or which merely express an intention to make an assessment will be ineffective. Such defective notices include those that merely state that an audit shows additional tax due or notification of the results of such an audit,[16] statements advising of liability for or requesting payment of assessed interest,[17] or statements rejecting a taxpayer's claim for refund.[18]

---

[13] See Administrative Practice Form No. 9, p. **C**·16–18. Another 90-day letter and its accompanying statement are given in Administrative Practice Form No. 10, p. **C**·19–21.

[14] Perlmutter v. Commissioner, 44 T.C. 382, *aff'd,* 373 F.2d 45 (C.A.10th) ; Olsen v. Helvering, 88 F.2d 650 (C.A.2d).

[15] Cooper Agency, Inc. v. McLeod, 235 F. Supp. 276 (E.D.S.C.), *aff'd per curiam,* 348 F.2d 919 (C.A.4th).

[16] Moyer v. Commissioner, 1 B.T.A. 75.

[17] Commissioner v. Kilpatrick's Estate, 140 F.2d 887 (C.A.6th).

[18] Shanley v. Commissioner, 7 B.T.A. 521, *aff'd* 28 F.2d 1018 (C.A.2d).

Attempts to vitiate the 90-day letter on grounds of other less basic irregularities in form or content have been unsuccessful. In cases in which the notice of deficiency is ambiguous as to the period involved, the courts have held that the notice pertains to the year intended by the Service although it is not clearly expressed.[19] Allegations that a notice is ineffective because it is ambiguous [20] or has not been signed by the proper person in the Service or has not been signed at all [21] have also been rejected by the courts. Similarly, notices attacked for arbitrary determinations of the elements of the deficiency [22] and notices challenged because they were inconsistent with those sent to other taxpayers [23] have been held to be valid.

Improper Mailing

Use of Regular Mail. The Service may send the notice of deficiency by certified or registered mail,[24] and a number of cases have held that mailing by certified or registered mail is mandatory.[25] There is, however, some authority that the use of registered or certified mail is not required and that regular mail may be used.[26] In any case, if the taxpayer wants to petition the Tax Court, he should not ignore a deficiency notice sent by ordinary mail, inasmuch as the receipt of such a notice accomplishes the statutory purpose of notification.

Incorrect Address. Unless the taxpayer has notified the Service of a change of address, the notice of deficiency will be deemed to be properly addressed if mailed to the "last known address" of the taxpayer.[27] As used in the statute, this phrase means the last address of the taxpayer available to the Service. Thus, the Service can safely rely on the address stated in the taxpayer's most recent return and is not expected to surmise that there has been a change of address unless the taxpayer has actually filed proper notification of such a change.[27a]

Since there is no standard form for a change of address, the taxpayer is best advised to send a statement of his change of address by certified or registered mail. The notification should clearly identify the taxpayer and

---

[19] Commissioner v. Forest Glen Creamery, 98 F.2d 968 (C.A.7th), *cert. denied,* 306 U.S. 639.

[20] A. Finkenburg's Sons v. Commissioner, 17 T.C. 973.

[21] Commissioner v. Oswego Falls Corp., 71 F.2d 673 (C.A.2d).

[22] Moriarty v. Commissioner, 18 T.C. 327, *aff'd,* 208 F.2d 43 (C.A.D.C.).

[23] Revell, Inc. v. Riddell, 273 F.2d 649 (C.A.9th).

[24] IRC § 6212(a).

[25] Oskar Block v. Commissioner, 2 T.C. 761.

[26] Boren v. Riddell, 241 F.2d 670 (C.A.9th). *But cf.* Rosewood Hotel, Inc. v. Commissioner, 275 F.2d 786 (C.A.9th).

[27] IRC § 6212(b), see Brown v. Lethert, 360 F.2d 560 (8 C.C.A.).

[27a] Compare De Welles v. United States 19 A.F.T.R.2d, 1390 (C.C.A.9th), where the Service was not required to use the address on a return filed after the return under audit.

set forth the following: the taxpayer identification number, the type of tax involved, the old address, the new address. Failure to notify the Service of a change of address will probably result in a notification being sent to an address no longer used by the taxpayer, a delay in actual receipt of the notice with a corresponding decrease in the time available for filing a petition, and, if the address used is challenged, a ruling that the Service properly relied on the last known address.

The matter of proper or improper address raises a number of possible problems. For example, if the taxpayer anticipates an audit of his return or if the return is in the process of audit and he wants to be assured that a notice of deficiency mailed to a former address will be ineffective, he must notify the Service of his new address. Where the taxpayer's address is not that shown on his most recent return, the change of address may be the result of the fact that the taxpayer has moved or died, or that, in the case of a legal entity such as a corporation or a trust, dissolution has terminated its existence. Under such circumstances, failure of the taxpayer or appropriate fiduciary or transferee to notify the Service of a change of address will result in a valid mailing to the address last known to the Service.[28] The above circumstances also raise the collateral problem of the proper person to whom the notice may be sent.[29]

It should also be noted that a change-of-address notice may be required for each possible kind of tax with which an individual is concerned. Thus, it has been held that a notice of deficiency of estate taxes sent to an executrix at the address shown on the estate tax return was effective even though the executrix, after filing the return, indicated a new address on letters relating to the audit of a connected gift tax return.[30] In fact, even notice that the executrix, as an individual, had moved did not compel the Internal Revenue Service to mail the deficiency notice (addressed to her as executrix) to her new address instead of the address shown on the subject return.[31]

A second typical problem relating to improper address arises when the Internal Revenue Service, having the correct and current address of the taxpayer, inadvertently uses a defective address or the wrong address. In the event the taxpayer receives the notice of deficiency, the statutory purpose of notification is satisfied and a fault in the address will not be sufficient to invalidate the notice if the taxpayer is able to file a timely petition.[32] If the taxpayer is unable to file a timely petition due to an untimely deficiency notice which has been improperly addressed, the notice is not valid.[33]

[28] IRC § 6212(b)(1); Treas. Reg. § 301.6212–1(b).
[29] See p. **4·7** infra.
[30] Estate of Clark v. Commissioner, 10 T.C. 1107, aff'd, 173 F.2d 13 (C.A.2d).
[31] Ibid.
[32] Wright v. Commissioner, 101 F.2d 309 (C.A.4th).
[33] Heaberlin v. Commissioner, 34 T.C. 58.

NOTICE DIRECTED TO WRONG PERSON.   Generally, a notice of deficiency will be directed to the taxpayer unless the Service has notice that someone other than the taxpayer is the appropriate person to receive the mailing. A fiduciary or transferee should therefore notify the Service of such status so that the notice may properly be directed. Such notification should follow the form outlined above and should also include a clear indication of the fiduciary or transferee status. In the absence of notification, a deficiency notice directed to a decedent, incompetent, or beneficiary will be valid, as would be a notice directed to a dissolved corporation.[34] In each of these cases, however, the fiduciary [35] or transferee [36] will be the appropriate person to petition the Court.

In cases in which a deficiency notice is erroneously directed to a third party but is received by the taxpayer for whom it was intended, the notice will be deemed effective since it accomplishes the statutory purpose of notification.[37] Thus, it has been held that notices directed to the taxpayer's attorney are effective notifications to the taxpayer himself.[38] In cases in which the taxpayer for whom the notice was intended does receive it and is able to file a timely petition, such filing usually constitutes a waiver of any defect in the notice.[39]

TAXPAYER'S RESPONSE TO DEFECTIVE NOTICE

Attacking the 90-Day Letter

Receipt of a notice of deficiency that does not contain proper information or is sent to the wrong address, directed to the wrong person, or improperly mailed raises the problem of what the taxpayer should do about the defect. In a situation where the taxpayer has a strong defense on the merits of his case, there is probably no cause to delay by raising objections based on minor defects in the deficiency notice. This is especially true if, by raising such objections, there is the risk that a subsequent hearing on the merits may be precluded because the time to file a petition has expired. There are cases, however, in which the taxpayer may wish to compel the Service to fulfill all the statutory requirements for an effective deficiency notice. When the merits of the taxpayer's case are not particularly strong and the Service has failed to fulfill all the statutory prerequisites for a statu-

---

[34] IRC § 6212(b)(1) ; Treas. Reg. § 301.6212–1(b).

[35] New York Trust Co. v. Commissioner, 20 B.T.A. 162, *rev'd,* 54 F.2d 463 (C.A. 2d), *cert. denied,* 285 U.S. 556.

[36] Burnet v. San Joaquin Fruit and Investment Co., 16 B.T.A. 1290, *modified,* 52 F.2d 123 (C.A.9th).

[37] Olsen v. Helvering, 88 F.2d 650 (C.A.2d).

[38] Commissioner v. Stewart, 186 F.2d 239 (C.A.6th).

[39] *Ibid.*

tory notice, the taxpayer may delay the ultimate determination of his liability or altogether prevent the collection of any tax whatsoever by proving such defects.

There are two possible means of attacking the notice of deficiency, both of which are hazardous. The first is to ignore the deficiency notice altogether and seek to enjoin the Commissioner when he attempts to assess the tax on the ground that he has failed to give the statutory notice of deficiency required prior to assessment.[40] In the event that a deficiency notice is held to be a nullity, the Service will simply send a second notice that is proper. If, however, the statute of limitations on the assessment of the tax has run, or if a second notice of deficiency is not issued before the statute does run, the Service will be precluded from issuing a second notice and the taxpayer will have accomplished his objective. If, however, the original notice is held effective, the taxpayer will have foregone his right to petition the Court, since the 90-day period for filing a petition will have expired. The risk involved in adopting the aforementioned procedure is increased because precedents stating what constitutes effective notice are not uniform and hence a prediction as to the result of an attempt to enjoin assessment cannot be made with any degree of certainty.

An alternative means of challenging the Service's failure to send a proper notice is to petition the Tax Court. Using this method, the taxpayer will file a routine petition and make a motion to dismiss on the ground that the Court is without jurisdiction because no effective statutory notice has been given. In this way, the taxpayer preserves his right to a Tax Court adjudication on the merits if the notice is found to be effective. Unhappily for the taxpayer, filing a petition in answer to a deficiency notice suspends the running of the statute of limitations, thus giving the Service additional time to issue a corrected notice if the petition is dismissed for lack of jurisdiction due to a defect in the original notice.[41] Furthermore, if a timely petition is addressed to the merits of a case and not simply to any defects in the notice, such defects may be deemed to have been waived.[42] If a notice is received after the 90-day period has expired, due to defective address or mailing to the wrong person, the subsequent filing of a petition going to the merits will not preclude a motion for dismissal based on a defective notice.[43]

Since the filing of a petition may operate as a waiver of defects in the deficiency notice and will suspend the statute of limitations as described above, the most that can be accomplished by this procedure is delay. Con-

---

[40] Salven v. United States, *supra* note 8; Whitmer v. Lucas, 53 F.2d 1006 (C.A. 7th), *action abated,* 285 U.S. 529.

[41] Sanborn v. Commissioner, 39 B.T.A. 721, *aff'd,* 108 F.2d 311 (C.A.8th).

[42] Commissioner v. Rosenheim, 132 F.2d 677 (C.A.3d), *reversing* 45 B.T.A. 1018.

[43] Heaberlin v. Commissioner, *supra* note 33.

sequently, if a taxpayer decides seriously to contest a deficiency notice, his best procedure is probably to ignore the notice and subsequently attempt to enjoin the assessment at the risk of losing his right to petition the Tax Court. In deciding whether to ignore the deficiency notice, the taxpayer will have to consider two factors: first, the extent to which the deficiency notice is faulty and, second, his desire to have his tax determined by the Tax Court rather than a refund tribunal. If, after a careful examination of the precedents, the taxpayer is certain that the communication from the Service is not an effective deficiency notice, he should ignore it. If there is a serious question in the taxpayer's mind as to whether the communication is an effective deficiency notice, he must consider the risk that an injunction proceeding after the 90-day period has expired is very likely to be unsuccessful.

Timely Receipt of 90-Day Letter

Generally, where the timeliness of the petition is challenged, the 90-day period for filing a Tax Court petition will be held to be extended to compensate for any delay due to improper address or direction to the wrong person so long as such delay is not a result of the taxpayer's own lack of diligence.[44]

When a second notice has been sent due to a defect in the first notice, and such defect was not caused by the taxpayer, the 90-day period is deemed to run from the day of actual receipt of the defective notice or from the date of mailing of the corrected notice, whichever period expires later.[45] Since both notices may be received at approximately the same time and the validity of the first notice is not immediately ascertainable, the safest procedure is to consider the 90-day period as having begun with the mailing of the first notice. It should be noted, of course, that when the Service remails the notice to a newly discovered address, the new mailing will not extend the 90-day period for filing when the first notice has been sent to the last known address.[46]

Receipt of More than One 90-Day Letter

While there is generally no restriction on the number of deficiency notices the Service may send to a single taxpayer within the period for assessment,[47] the filing of a petition in the Tax Court precludes the mailing of further deficiency notices for the same tax.[48] Not only are notices mailed after the filing of the petition barred, but, assuming that the first notice

[44] Arlington Corp. v. Commissioner, 183 F.2d 448 (C.A.5th).
[45] Eppler v. Commissioner, 188 F.2d 95 (C.A.7th).
[46] Block v. Commissioner, 2 T.C. 761.
[47] Ruud Mfg. Co. v. Commissioner, 15 T.C. 374.
[48] IRC § 6212(c).

is not defective, filing renders invalid any notice respecting the same tax issued within 90 days after the mailing of the first notice.[49]

STATUTE OF LIMITATIONS ON ASSESSING A DEFICIENCY

Subject to specified exceptions, the assessment of any tax more than three years after the return is filed or the date it is due, whichever is later, is prohibited by the statute of limitations.[50] The taxpayer must plead and prove this defense, which is strictly enforced. The Service has the burden of proving that one of the exceptions exists once the taxpayer shows that the normal period of limitations has expired.[51] The exceptions apply in the following instances:

1. In the case of a false or fraudulent return with intent to evade tax, the tax may be assessed at any time.[52]
2. In the case of a willful attempt to evade tax, assessment may be made at any time.[53]
3. In the case of failure to file a return, the tax may be assessed at any time.[54]
4. In the case of an agreement in writing executed prior to the expiration of the statute of limitations between the taxpayer and the Service, the expiration of the statute is extended to the date fixed in the agreement.[55]
5. If the taxpayer omits from gross income an amount in excess of 25% of the gross income actually reported in the return, the tax may be assessed at any time within six years from the date the return is filed.[56]

As previously indicated,[57] mailing of a deficiency notice suspends the running of the three-year period at the date of mailing. This suspension continues until 60 days after the taxpayer's time to file a petition has expired or, if he has filed a petition, until 60 days after the Tax Court's decision becomes final.

An estate or corporation contemplating dissolution may shorten the three-year period for assessment to 18 months by properly making a request for prompt assessment.[58]

---

[49] Ruud Mfg. Co. v. Commissioner, *supra* note 47; Harvey Coal Co. v. Commissioner, 12 T.C. 596.
[50] IRC § 6501(a).
[51] Reis v. Commissioner, 1 T.C. 9
[52] IRC § 6501(c)(1).
[53] IRC § 6501(c)(2).
[54] IRC § 6501(c)(3).
[55] IRC § 6501(c)(4).
[56] IRC § 6501(e).
[57] See p. **4·2** *supra*.
[58] IRC § 6501(d).

PLEADINGS IN THE TAX COURT

THE PETITION

Function and Content of the Petition

FUNCTION. The petition is the first document to be examined by the Court. Prior to reading the petition, the Court will have no knowledge of the dispute.

Thus, it is generally advisable for the petitioner not only to satisfy Tax Court Rule 7(c)(2), requiring that the petition "be complete in itself so as to fully state the issues," [1] but to submit a petition that adequately informs the Court of all facts and allegations upon which the petitioner relies.

[1] Pleadings in the Tax Court serve to set forth the facts in the case to a greater extent than they do in the tax refund forums. Compare p. **5**·10 *et seq.* and p. **11**·8 *et seq. infra.*

A petitioner who has submitted an inadequate petition may find little help from the Court or the Service in presenting necessary matters that have been omitted. In this respect, the Tax Court has commented that

> It behooves counsel for a petitioner to state his case at least so that it can be understood and to prove and call attention to sufficient facts to support his theory. He may not safely rely upon the Tax Court to dig out and develop a case for him. That is not the function of the court. . . . Furthermore, it would not be fair to the Commissioner if the Court surprised him by developing in its opinion a case against the Commissioner which he had no way of anticipating or contesting . . . the point is that the parties have the primary duty of presenting their cases, and they cannot shift that duty to the Commissioner or complain if the Court does not exceed its proper function to make up for counsel's shortcomings.[2]

GENERAL FORM AND CONTENT. In deciding on the form and content of the petition, some general rules are helpful.

1. *The petition should demonstrate to the Court that the petitioner has a just cause for complaint.* Among other things this means that all issues that the taxpayer believes relevant to the case must be included in the petition. Compliance with this rule will avoid the possibility that the Court will refuse to consider an issue because it is not raised in the petition.

2. *The petition should place the case properly within the Court's jurisdiction so that a motion to dismiss will be unsuccessful.* Satisfaction of this rule means an adequate statement of the necessary jurisdictional allegations. This is discussed in detail in the subsequent section on jurisdictional allegations.

3. *The petition should lay a foundation for the introduction of evidence.* A well-prepared counsel will have coordinated his pleadings and proof in advance so that upon reading the petition the Court will be able to anticipate and realize the significance of the evidence as it is introduced. Careful planning of this sort will alleviate the necessity of moving to amend the pleading to conform to the proof and avoid the risk that the motion will be denied.

4. *The petition should demonstrate that the taxpayer is competently represented.* Since the petition is the first and foremost opportunity to impress the Court and the Regional Counsel with the taxpayer's case, a competent petition will undoubtedly command more respect for the petitioner's case as well as for his counsel. The value of a good impression in obtaining stipulations and in settlement negotiations should not be underestimated. To this end, the best indication of competency is scrupulous adherence to the rules of the Tax Court as they relate to the petition, for that matter, all subsequent papers submitted to the court.

[2] Producers Crop Improvement Ass'n v. Commissioner, 7 T.C. 562, 565.

APPLICABLE RULES OF THE TAX COURT. Since an improperly drafted petition is subject to a motion to dismiss,[3] the Rules of the Court should be examined in detail and should be followed in any Tax Court litigation.

The Court has statutory authority to promulgate rules of practice and procedure for the conduct of its proceedings.[4] These Rules have the force and effect of law [5] but are purely procedural. Although certain procedural requirements such as timely payment of the filing fee have been known to be waived by the Court, adherence to the Rules is a necessity, and counsel should not rely on the possibility of a waiver. Particular Rules will be referred to as various aspects of the petition are discussed later in this chapter, but it is helpful here to note that Rules 4, 6, and 7 are those most directly concerned with the petition. A familiarity with Rule 4 is essential since it sets out the rules for the form and style of all papers submitted to the Court. This includes such matters as the typing or printing process to be used, the form of citations, and the number of copies to be submitted. Rules 6 and 7 are more directly related to the petition. Rule 6 governs the parties who may properly file a petition, and Rule 7 governs the actual contents of the petition.

Filing the Petition—The 90-Day Rule

PROPER TIME TO FILE. A petition must be filed with the Tax Court within 90 days after the mailing of the deficiency notice.[6] If the petition is not filed during this period, the taxpayer forfeits his right to petition the Court. The only exception to this Rule is made for certain taxpayers who are not in the United States when the deficiency notice is mailed.[7] The 90-day period is prescribed by § 6213(a) of the Internal Revenue Code and may not be waived by the Service or by the Court.

Computing the 90 Days. In determining when the 90-day period has begun, the date of the notice itself is not proof of the mailing date, and the notice is not deemed to have been mailed until it is delivered to the post office or deposited in a mail box. In computing the 90-day period based on the postmark of the notice, the actual day of mailing is excluded from the computation, and the 90-day period is said to begin on midnight of the day on which the notice was mailed and postmarked.[8]

[3] Tax Ct. R. 7(a)(2). The Rules of Practice of the Tax Court of the United States are available from the Superintendent of Documents, Washington, D.C.

[4] IRC § 7453.

[5] Banker's Pocahontas Coal Co. v. Burnet, 287 U.S. 308, 313, *affirming* 55 F.2d 626, *affirming* 18 B.T.A. 901.

[6] IRC § 6213(a).

[7] In this case, the time for filing the petition is extended to the 150 days following the mailing of the notice. IRC § 6213(a).

[8] Burnet v. Willingham Loan and Tr. Co., 282 U.S. 437, *reversing* 36 F.2d 49 (C.A.5th), which reversed 15 B.T.A. 931. See also Frank E. Moffat v. Commissioner, 46 T.C. 499.

For purposes of filing, a Saturday, Sunday, or legal holiday in the District of Columbia will not count as the 90th day. Prudent counsel, however, should never wait until the last moment to file the petition. Since numerous unexpected events may occur to delay the drafting of the petition, counsel should allow a safe margin of time before the expiration of the 90 days so that necessary work is not sacrificed in order to meet the deadline.

Date When Petition Is Considered Filed. When a petition is filed, the Court will note on the face of the petition the postmark on the envelope and whether the petition came by regular, registered, or certified mail. The general rule [9] is that the date of the postmark of the envelope containing the petition will be deemed its date of filing. Thus, a timely mailing constitutes a timely filing, but this rule must be qualified by the fact that along with timely mailing the petition must be sent to the Tax Court at its proper address.

Since the postmark can be so crucial, some of the problems relating to a timely or untimely postmark should be noted. If the postmark is illegible or if a properly postmarked petition is received after such time as it would ordinarily be received, the taxpayer may be required to prove a timely mailing.[9a] A petition received after the expiration date and bearing no postmark is not timely.[10] If the postmark has been made by a private postal meter, all the same rules apply and the petition must be received in the ordinary course of the mail when the postmark shows a date close to or on the 90th day of the filing period. Most of the problems inherent in timely mailing and an adequate postmark can be avoided by sending the petition by registered or certified mail. The receipt from such a mailing is deemed prima facie evidence of delivery.[11]

EXCEPTIONS TO 90-DAY RULE. *Taxpayers Outside United States— 150-Day Rule.* If the taxpayer resides outside the United States, an additional 60 days are allowed for filing, bringing the total time allowed to 150 days. Aside from the different filing period allowed, all of the above rules are applicable to the filing of the petition. A more difficult situation is presented when the notice is directed to an address within the United States, but the taxpayer is outside the United States when the notice is sent. The early decisions of the Tax Court held that the 150-day period applied only when the taxpayer actually resided outside the country,[12] but the most recent holding of the Court, in acquiescence to a Court of Appeals decision,[13] has held that the 150-day period also applies to a taxpayer temporarily

---

[9] IRC § 7502(a).
[9a] See Alexander Molosh v. Commissioner, 45 T.C. 320.
[10] Bloch v. Commissioner, 254 F.2d 277 (C.A.9th).
[11] Treas. Reg. § 301.7502–1.
[12] Hamilton v. Commissioner, 13 T.C. 747.
[13] Mindell v. Commissioner, 200 F.2d 38 (C.A.2d).

away from his United States residence at the time the deficiency notice is mailed.[14]

Special Rule for Armed Forces. If the taxpayer happens to be serving in the armed forces in a combat zone or is in a hospital outside the country as a result of such service, the filing period extends for 180 days after the end of the service or incapacitation.[15]

Improperly Addressed or Misdirected Notice. The only other cases in which the 90-day rule has been relaxed are those in which questions have been raised as to the proper mailing of the deficiency notice. Generally, if the Commissioner is responsible for a substantial delay in receipt of the notice (e.g., if the notice is received by the taxpayer 80 days after mailing because the Commissioner put the wrong address on the envelope), the date of receipt may be treated as the date of mailing.[16]

FILING FOR MORE THAN ONE DEFICIENCY. When the taxpayer receives a single deficiency notice that includes deficiencies for either separate years or separate kinds of taxes, a timely petition must include all contested deficiencies. Thus, if a petition concerning one deficiency or year is timely, a subsequent amendment to include a plea concerning a second deficiency or year will not relate back to the filing of the original petition,[17] and the amendment with the additional plea may be dismissed for not having been filed within the 90-day period.[18]

FILING EMERGENCY PETITION. Generally, an emergency petition in the form of a letter sent at the last moment to avoid the expiration of the filing period will be invalid. Usually this type of petition will contain only a skeleton appeal or a mere request for redetermination of the deficiency and will fail to contain the necessary assignments of error and jurisdictional allegations. Although the Court, at its discretion, might accept the letter as a petition, it would more likely be dismissed for lack of proper jurisdiction upon proper motion by the Commissioner. In this respect the Tax Court Rules provide that "no telegram, cablegram, radiogram, telephone call, or similar communication will be recognized as a petition." [19] Furthermore, a petition that is actually a motion for extension of time will not qualify as a petition. Clearly, the best method is to plan ahead in order to obviate the necessity of an emergency petition. Nonetheless, if an emergency petition is unavoidable, it should consist of the appeal itself rather than a statement of future intent to appeal, a motion for extended time, or a request that col-

---

[14] Estate of William Krueger v. Commissioner, 33 T.C. 667.
[15] IRC § 7508.
[16] For details as to the application of this exception see p. **4·9** *supra.*
[17] Estate of Archer v. Commissioner, 47 B.T.A. 228.
[18] W. H. Krome, P-H Memo TC, ¶¶48, 118.
[19] Tax Ct. R. 7(c)(3).

lection be suspended. An emergency petition should conform as closely as possible to a regular petition.

WHERE AND HOW TO FILE. The Tax Court has only one office and mailing address. The petition and all other correspondence and documents should be addressed to "Tax Court of the United States, Box 70, Washington, D.C. 20044." [20] At the time of filing, a fee of $10 must be paid, all checks and money orders being made payable to the Treasurer of the United States and delivered with the petition. If the petition is to be filed in person, the business hours of the Clerk of the Court are 8:15 a.m. to 5:15 p.m. on all days except Saturdays, Sundays, and legal holidays in the District of Columbia.[21]

Who May Petition the Court

WHICH TAXPAYERS MAY PETITION. A taxpayer may petition the Court for a redetermination of a deficiency if he is (1) a citizen residing in the United States or abroad, (2) an alien residing in the United States or a nonresident alien if he has a source of income in the United States, or (3) a domestic corporation or a foreign corporation with a source of revenue in the United States.[22] Almost every taxpayer will be in one of these three categories, thereby fulfilling the first prerequisite to filing a valid petition. The second requirement is that the Tax Court have jurisdiction over the taxpayer based upon the facts set forth by the petition.

Tax Court jurisdiction is confined to cases where (1) the Commissioner has determined that a deficiency exists and (2) has notified the taxpayer of the existing deficiency and the impending assessment thereof by proper mailing of a statutory notice of deficiency.[23] Consequently, in normal circumstances, the taxpayer to whom the notice of deficiency is addressed will be the only proper party to file the petition. In cases where the proper taxpayer is deceased or no longer in existence the petition may be filed on his behalf only by a qualified fiduciary or successor. When a deficiency notice is directed to the proper party and a petition is filed by a person not qualified to do so, the Tax Court will dismiss the petition for lack of jurisdiction. If the proper party or someone qualified to act for him does not file a petition within the 90-day period, an adjudication in the Tax Court will be precluded.

This situation should be distinguished from the one in which the notice is erroneously directed to the wrong person and that person petitions the Court. In such a case, the Court will dismiss the petition for lack of jurisdiction, and a new deficiency notice may be issued to the proper person.

[20] The judge presiding at a case may permit filing of documents at that session, but this exception will not apply to a petition. Tax Ct. R. 5.

[21] Tax Court Rule 1 sets forth the telephone number and location of the Court.

[22] CASEY, FEDERAL TAX PRACTICE, § 6.29 (1955).

[23] See p. **3·2** *supra.*

In a situation where there is a minor variance in the name or address, but the notice of deficiency is received by the proper person and that person petitions the Court, Rule 6 of the Court requires that "a statement of the reasons for such variance shall be set forth in the petition." Failure to comply with this rule may result in the Commissioner moving to dismiss for lack of proper jurisdiction.

WHO MAY PETITION FOR TAXPAYER.   When a Tax Court case is not filed by and in the name of the taxpayer against whom the deficiency has been asserted, it may be brought "by and in the full descriptive name of the fiduciary legally entitled to institute a case on behalf of such person." [24] There are a number of standard situations in which a person other than the taxpayer has attempted either to bring a case in the taxpayer's name or to act on his behalf.

Husbands and Wives.   One spouse has no authority to file a petition for the redetermination of a deficiency that has been determined against the other on the basis of an individual tax return.[25] Where a joint return has been filed, the situation is somewhat different since the spouses are jointly and severally liable under § 6013(d)(3) of the Internal Revenue Code. Where a joint return has been filed, the Commissioner may issue a single joint deficiency notice, and a joint petition would be acceptable although the taxpayers would not be precluded from filing separate petitions.[26] Where both have filed separate returns and have received separate notices of deficiency a joint petition is not permissible.[27]

Fiduciaries.   Where a person is appointed to act in a fiduciary capacity for a taxpayer, an independent formal notice of the exercise of fiduciary functions must be sent to the Commissioner.[28] Once this has been done the fiduciary may properly file a petition based upon a deficiency notice sent to the taxpayer for whom he acts.

Similarly, a fiduciary may act for a taxpayer until formal notice of the termination of his function is filed with the Commissioner. Thus, presumably a discharged fiduciary might still file a petition on behalf of the taxpayer where no notice of termination is sent to the Commissioner.[29]

Deceased Taxpayers.   If a deficiency notice is sent to the estate of a taxpayer, it is clear that the executor or administrator of the estate could file a petition. If, however, the notice is directed to the deceased taxpayer

---

[24] Tax Ct. R. 6.
[25] Davison v. Commissioner, 13 T.C. 554.
[26] Howell v. Commissioner, 10 T.C. 859, *aff'd*, 175 F.2d 240 (C.A.6th).
[27] Melczer v. Commissioner, 23 B.T.A. 124, 127.
[28] IRC § 6903.
[29] Estate of Botts v. Commissioner, 42 B.T.A. 977, *rev'd on other grounds sub nom.* Tooley v. Commissioner, 121 F.2d 350 (C.A.9th).

himself, an executor or administrator could file a petition only if the Commissioner was notified of the fiduciary capacity. In the situation where the taxpayer has filed the petition but dies before the hearing, no subsequent substitution of parties is needed, and the Tax Court's jurisdiction is not impaired.[30]

Joint Tenants.   A person who has owned property jointly with a now deceased taxpayer is not authorized by virtue of such ownership to file a petition on behalf of the decedent. As is the rule with all other deceased taxpayers only the authorized fiduciary may file the petition.[31]

Dissolved Corporations.   The Commissioner may issue a deficiency notice for a corporate taxpayer even if it has terminated its existence.[32] The main problem raised in these circumstances is whether the Court has jurisdiction over a petition from an entity whose existence has been legally terminated. Generally the Court has required in these circumstances that the corporate life continue through the date of the filing of the petition and that the petition be brought in the name of the corporate taxpayer by someone authorized to do so. An example of such a person would be a former officer of the corporation. The petition must clearly indicate the authority of the person to act for the corporation.

In cases of this sort, the corporation law of the state will play a decisive role,[33] and no all-inclusive rule can be formulated as to when the corporate existence has been adequately perpetuated. In deciding the issue of proper jurisdiction, the Court will follow the precedents applicable in the appropriate state.[34]

In the case of national banks, it has been held that after voluntary liquidation the bank continues to exist as a corporation until such time as its affairs are completely settled.[35]

Corporations Whose Powers Are Suspended.   Generally, suspension of power does not terminate corporate existence and does not deprive the Court of jurisdiction,[36] although an exceptional state law to the contrary may be determinative.

Successor Corporations.   The Court has been reversed on its stand that a successor to the assets and business of a predecessor corporation has

---

[30] Yeoman v. Commissioner, 25 T.C. 589.

[31] Dombrowski v. Commissioner, 35 B.T.A. 1028.

[32] IRC § 6212(b)(1).

[33] See, *e.g.*, Falls City Pontiac Co. v. Commissioner, 15 T.C. 977, *aff'd* 194 F.2d 536 (C.A.6th).

[34] See the partial summaries of the precedents in leading states set out in 1 CASEY, FEDERAL TAX PRACTICE, § 6.36 (1955), and WHEN YOU GO TO TAX COURT, ¶ 115 (1967).

[35] Central Nat'l Bank of Lincoln, Neb. v. Commissioner, 29 B.T.A. 719.

[36] California Iron Yards Co. v. Commissioner, 15 B.T.A. 25, *aff'd,* 47 F.2d 514 (C.A.9th).

no standing to file a petition on behalf of its predecessor.[37] Often in these situations the Commissioner may send the notice of deficiency in care of the successor, thus facilitating the filing.

Merged and Consolidated Corporations. Whenever the state law controlling mergers and consolidations between corporations provides that the constituent corporation is dissolved, the surviving consolidated corporation is not the proper party to file a petition. Unless the statute under which the consolidation takes place clearly provides for continued existence of a constituent corporation, it may be deemed dissolved, and the consolidated corporation may have no liability for the deficiency.[38] In determining whether or not a merged corporation will be liable for the deficiency of one of its constituents, and whether the corporation is the proper party to file a petition, the law of the appropriate state is controlling. Under the law of many states, a deficiency may properly be determined against a merged corporation.[39]

Affiliated Corporations. Where a group of corporations files a consolidated tax return, notices of deficiency will be mailed only to the common parent corporation. Under these circumstances only the common parent may file a petition. Notice to one or more of the affiliates is not notice to the others, and the petition may be filed only on behalf of those to whom the notice was directed.[40]

Partnerships. When a deficiency is determined against taxpayers who are partners, the partnership may not file a petition with the Court.[41] When such petitions are filed they are amended to constitute separate petitions from each taxpayer. It is possible that, for convenience and efficiency, separate petitions by partners would be consolidated for trial.

Transferees. The Commissioner may determine that a transferee is liable for a deficiency determined against a transferor. For the purpose of these cases, the statutory definition of a "transferee" includes heirs, legatees, devisees, and distributees.[42] The Commissioner has expanded the scope of this rule to include shareholders of dissolved corporations and parties to reorganization.[43] For purposes of appeal to the Court, the transferee becomes the "taxpayer" named in the deficiency notice.

SUBSTITUTION AND MISJOINDER OF PARTIES. A substitution of proper parties may be made on the motion of a party or upon the Court's own

---

[37] Nichols & Cox Lumber Co. v. Commissioner, 24 B.T.A. 54, 65 F.2d 1009 (C.A. 6th).
[38] Grange Nat'l Bank v. Commissioner, 22 B.T.A. 1209.
[39] *E.g.*, Alaska Salmon Co. v. Commissioner, 39 B.T.A. 455.
[40] Central Market St. Co. v. Commissioner, 25 B.T.A. 499.
[41] Taylor Bros. v. Commissioner, 9 B.T.A. 877.
[42] IRC § 6901(h).
[43] Treas. Reg. § 301.6901–1(b).

motion.[44] Generally, such a motion can be made upon the death of a petitioner, where a mistake in name or address of a party appears, or where a fiduciary or successor fiduciary is appointed.

In the case of erroneously joined parties, a timely petition filed jointly has been held to be sufficient to invoke the jurisdiction of the Tax Court.[45]

PREPARING PETITIONS WHEN UNCERTAIN AS TO PROPER PETITIONER. A petition filed by the improper person may be dismissed and a subsequent petition by the proper person precluded due to the expiration of 90 days from the issuance of the deficiency notice. In view of this hazard, when serious doubt as to the proper petitioner exists, consideration should be given to filing petitions in the name of each person who may be the proper person to petition the court [46] and then letting the court decide which petitions should be dismissed.

Drafting the Petition

PRELIMINARY STEPS. In preparing to write a petition, counsel for the taxpayer should remember that his main purpose is to obtain a redetermination of a tax, resulting in a dollar amount. In this respect, it is crucial that the petition contain every fact and figure that will be necessary to sustain the taxpayer's position.

Before writing the petition, a thorough job of primary research ought to be done. This preparation will be doubly important if counsel for the taxpayer has not represented the taxpayer in all of the events leading up to the issuance of the deficiency notice. Ideally, counsel should prepare for his case in the Tax Court in the following fashion. First, he should examine all records, documents, and papers including the tax return, the 30-day letter, and protest, if any. Interviews with prospective witnesses shall also help. After becoming fully apprised of the taxpayer's situation, counsel should make a list of each error to be disputed and correlate it with the proper part of the deficiency notice. Next, counsel should prepare a list of all facts that will be needed to support each finding of error. At this point, preparing a list of all the facts upon which the Service is likely to rely for its defense will help bring the issues into focus and point up the facts that the taxpayer will need. The next step is to consider the law that both supports and detracts from the taxpayer's case. In this respect the precise facts upon which recent decisions turned may be crucial. Remember, the Court will be persuaded by the similarity or dissimilarity of facts in previous cases.

[44] See p. **6·2** *et seq. infra.*

[45] Sparrow v. Commissioner, 20 B.T.A. 865.

[46] *E.g.,* a corporation whose existence is terminated may file petitions in its own name, by its officers, directors, shareholders, its successor by consolidation, and combinations thereof.

At this stage counsel should have a good idea of his own case and the case the Service will make to defend its adjustments. Counsel should now be in a position to prepare an outline of his brief and proposed findings of fact so that he may be sure that the petition will include all matters that may be raised later in the case.

In drafting the petition, a few basic rules ought to be kept in mind:

1. The petition should be clear, concise, and understandable but also complete.
2. The petition should not be written in an argumentative style.
3. The rules of the Tax Court should be complied with.
4. The essential parts of the petition should be set out under separate headings so that the general structure of the petition can be seen at a glance.

If counsel has progressed in the manner described above and has complied with the provisions of Tax Court Rule 7 which emphasizes adequate differentiation through the use of clear and concise separate paragraphs for setting out jurisdictional allegations, assignments of error, and statements of fact, the petition will be well drafted. Again it should be emphasized that Rule 4, setting out the requirements as to the form of the pleadings and other documents, should be followed.

CAPTION. The caption should leave a three-inch margin at the top of the page to allow space for Court stamps. Rule 7(c)(4)(A) of the Court provides for a caption in the following form:

TAX COURT OF THE UNITED STATES

FREDERICK R. BELTER,

    Petitioner,

       v.   Docket No.

COMMISSIONER OF INTERNAL REVENUE,

    Respondent.

PETITION

After the petition has been filed, both parties will be notified of the docket number and, according to Rule 11, all subsequent papers and correspondence must include a reference to the number. In preparing the petition "[t]he full name and surname of each individual petitioner shall be set forth in the caption, but without any prefix or title, such as 'Mrs.,' 'Dr.,' etc." [47] If an action is not brought by and in the name of the person against whom the deficiency has been determined, it may be brought by a qualified fiduciary.[48]

[47] Tax Ct. R. 4(e).
[48] See p. **5·7** *supra*.

If such is the case the caption should include the name of the person, estate, or trust on whose behalf the petition is filed, followed by the name of the fiduciary and his title, as follows: [49]

Estate of Frederick R. Belter, deceased,
John R. Gossett, Executor,
Petitioner,

Where there is a variation between the name of the taxpayer as set out in the notice of deficiency and the correct name as set out in the caption, the reason for such variation must be explained in the petition in the Allegations of Jurisdictional Facts.[50] In all cases, the Commissioner of Internal Revenue will be the defendant in a suit brought in the Tax Court.

OPENING STATEMENT. The opening statement, which serves as an introduction to the taxpayer's petition, should read as follows:

The above-named petitioner hereby petitions for a redetermination of the deficiency set forth by the Commissioner of Internal Revenue in his notice of deficiency (Internal Revenue Service symbols _____) dated August 1, 1967, and as a basis for his proceeding alleges as follows:

Following this standard statement the petitioner presents his allegations.

JURISDICTIONAL ALLEGATIONS. Since a petition that lacks the basic jurisdictional allegations may be subject to a motion for dismissal, counsel for the petitioner must see to it that all jurisdictional requirements are alleged. These allegations will be divided into three paragraphs.[51]

Allegations as to Petitioner. Rule 7(c)(4)(B)(1) of the Tax Court Rules requires a paragraph that includes "petitioner's name and principal office or residence, and the office of the director or district director of internal revenue in which the tax return for the period in controversy was filed." In this paragraph the petition should clarify the taxpayer's status, *e.g.,* as an individual, an estate, a corporation, etc. This is also the appropriate place for any explanation as to variation in name. Any and all information such as corporate resolutions or other instruments conferring authority upon a person to act for the taxpayer should also be included.[52]

Allegations as to Deficiency Notice. The Tax Court Rules [53] require that a second paragraph be included in the jurisdictional allegations indicating "the date of mailing of the notice of deficiency on which the petition is based or other proper allegations showing jurisdiction in the court." In-

[49] Tax Ct. R. 4(e).
[50] Tax Ct. R. 6.
[51] Tax Ct. R. 7(c)(4)(B).
[52] Tax Ct. R. 7, 23.
[53] Tax Ct. R. 7(c)(4)(B).

cluded in this paragraph should be a statement as to the date that the deficiency notice was mailed. The purpose here is to indicate that the petition has been filed within 90 days from the mailing of the notice of deficiency. It must also be stated in this paragraph that the notice of deficiency is attached and marked as an exhibit.[54] Any statements accompanying the notice should also be referred to and appended. The deficiency notice is best copied by some sort of photostat process, since a typing error may result in the service's denial that the petition contains a true copy of the notice.

Allegations as to Tax. In the third paragraph, "the amount of the deficiency (or liability, as the case may be), determined by the Commissioner, the nature of the tax, the year or other period for which the determination was made, and, if different from the determination, the approximate amount of taxes in controversy" should be included.[55] As regards the statement as to the amount of tax in dispute, the entire deficiency adjustment is almost never in dispute, and a statement of the deficiency should be followed by the phrase "substantially all of which is in dispute" unless the petitioner actually does wish to controvert the entire deficiency.

Sample Jurisdictional Allegations. For an individual:

1. The petitioner, Samuel S. Ross, is an individual residing at number 43 East 80th Street, New York, N. Y. (former address and address appearing on return: 39 East 10th Street, New York, N. Y.). The return for the period here involved was filed with the District Director of Internal Revenue, Manhattan District, New York.

2. The Notice of Deficiency (a copy of which is attached and marked EXHIBIT A) was mailed to the petitioner on June 12, 1966.

3. The deficiency, as determined by the Commissioner, is for income tax for the calendar year 1962 in the amount of five thousand six hundred and 81/100 dollars ($5,600.81), substantially all of which is in dispute.

If the petitioner is a corporation, the first paragraph would be as follows:

1. The petitioner is a corporation organized and existing under the laws of the State of New York, with its principal office at 4200 Western Boulevard, Troy, New York. The corporation's income tax returns for the period here involved were filed with the District Director of Internal Revenue for the Albany District, New York.

Since the jurisdiction of the Court, "is strictly statutory in nature and is not subject to equitable enlargement," [56] counsel for the petitioner must see to it that the Court's jurisdictional requirements are satisfied and pleaded.

[54] Tax Ct. R. 7(c) (4) (E).
[55] Tax Ct. R. 7(c) (4) (B) (3).
[56] Estate of Barnhart v. Commissioner, P-H Memo TC, ¶¶ 59, 042.

ASSIGNMENTS OF ERROR. The purpose of the Assignments of Error is to set forth all the reasons why the taxpayer has petitioned the Tax Court for a redetermination. This must be done by the use of lettered paragraphs that indicate by "clear and concise assignments . . . each and every error which the petitioner alleges to have been committed by the Commissioner in the determination of the deficiency." [57] Since the Court knows nothing about the case until the petition is filed, it will rely on the petitioner's Assignments of Error as the controlling statement of his case.

What Should Be Included. The Assignment must be complete. Issues not pleaded will not be considered by the Court.[58] If the petitioner alleges facts that would result in conclusions not embodied in the Assignment, the Assignment is inadequate. The Assignment should allege each matter in the deficiency notice that petitioner believes to be erroneous. In drafting the Assignment of Error, counsel should remember that the Court's jurisdiction is related to deficiencies and that Assignments related solely to overassessments will be stricken. This does not mean, however, that an overpayment should not be claimed if there are also adjustments in the deficiency computations.

If the petitioner intends to assert alternative Assignments of Error, this is permissible, regardless of inconsistency.[59] Since all the necessary facts must be presented in the petition, counsel may have to make use of alternative allegations with the hope that some if not all of his theories will be accepted by the Court. Furthermore, since it may be difficult to anticipate whether certain secondary issues can be solved by mere mathematical adjustment or whether they will require the introduction of evidence, the Assignment should be as complete as possible. Since counsel cannot wait for the Court to pass on some issues before deciding whether other issues ought to be raised, the safest rule to follow is to plead all the possible issues whose determination will require the introduction of evidence. Obviously the petitioner will be better off if the Court grants a motion to strike a superfluous pleading than if it denies his own motion to amend his pleading to conform to his proof.

Amending Inadequate Petition. Unless an issue is raised by an Assignment of Error, the Court will consider it only if leave to amend the petition is granted. Although Rule 17(d) provides that "the Court may at any time during the course of the trial grant a motion of either party to amend its pleadings to conform to the proof . . . ," leave to amend is at the discretion of the Court, and undue surprise to the Service or lack of diligence

---

[57] Tax Ct. R. 7(c)(4)(B).
[58] Gregg v. Commissioner, 18 T.C. 291, 303, *aff'd,* 203 F.2d 954 (C.A.3d).
[59] McEnaney v. Commissioner, 3 T.C. 552, 560–61.

on the part of petitioner's counsel may result in a denial of the motion.[60] Where there is no amendment, an insufficient pleading may be stricken or the Court may refuse to pass on issues not raised therein. Thus, where the issue is not raised in the petition, it will not be sufficient for counsel to touch upon it in an opening statement,[61] by introduction of related evidence,[62] or in the brief filed after trial.[63] An issue not raised in the petition will not be considered even if there has been a stipulation of the facts involved.[64]

How To Write Assignments of Error. The starting point in drafting Assignments of Error is the notice of deficiency. Assignments must be directed to specific adjustments in the notice. General allegations are insufficient. Each disputed adjustment in the notice should be identified by amount and page number. Where more than one year is involved, the Assignments may be organized into separate years. Generally, each Assignment should consist of an averment that a particular adjustment is wrong or is in error. This really amounts to a rewording of the matters set out in the notice, thus forming Assignments of Error. Where a reference to the Code is appropriate, it may be included.

Sample Assignment. A typical Assignment of Error might read as follows:

4. The determination of taxes set forth in said notice of deficiency is based upon the following errors:

(a) In determining the taxable income of the petitioner for the year 1962, the Commissioner erroneously included, in the determination of the said taxable income, realized capital gain in the total amount of $105,515.00 (before capital gain deductions).

(b) In determining the taxable income of the petitioner for the year 1962, the Commissioner erroneously eliminated from taxable income the sum reported by the taxpayer as a capital gain (before capital gain deduction) of the amount realized, on the installment method, from the sale of the stock of the Ross Engineering Company.

(c) In determining the taxable income of the petitioner for the year 1962, the Commissioner erroneously disallowed deductible interest expense in the total amount of $2,389.00.

(d) In determining the taxable income of petitioner for the year 1963, the Commissioner erroneously excluded from the determination of the said taxable

---

[60] Sicanoff Vegetable Oil Corp. v. Commissioner, 27 T.C. 1056, *rev'd on other grounds,* 251 F.2d 764 (C.A.7th).

[61] C. D. Johnson Lumber Corp. v. Commissioner, 12 T.C. 348, 362.

[62] Rissman v. Commissioner, 6 T.C. 1105, 1117–18.

[63] Gregg v. Commissioner, *supra* note 58.

[64] Arnold v. Commissioner, P-H Memo TC, ¶¶ 43, 248, at 798, *aff'd,* 147 F.2d 23 (C.A.1st).

income, reportable as a long-term capital gain, the total sum of $15,918.00 (before capital gain deductions).

(e) In determining the taxable income of the petitioner for the year 1963, the Commissioner erroneously excluded from the determination of the said taxable income, earned interest income in the sum of $337.00.

(f) In determining the taxable income of the petitioner for the year 1963, the Commissioner erroneously disallowed deductible interest expense in the sum of $2,187.00.[65]

Assignments Where Burden of Proof Is on Commissioner. The Rules of the Court provide that "issues in respect of which the burden of proof is by statute placed upon the Commissioner will not be deemed to be raised by the petitioner in the absence of assignments of error in respect thereof." [66] This means, for example, that if the notice of deficiency includes a fraud penalty, the petitioner must include in his petition as an Assignment of Error the fraud penalty. After the petitioner makes the Assignment, it is up to the Commissioner to affirmatively plead the facts of the fraud.

Sample Fraud Penalty Assignment. An Assignment of Error in determining a fraud penalty would be in the following form:

The determination of liability for Fraud Penalty under the provisions of Section 6653(b) of the Internal Revenue Code of 1954 is based upon the following errors:

a. The erroneous and illegal findings that fraud was present in the alleged transaction with the Hercules Building Company, Inc., which are the basis for the assessment of additional income taxes herein;

b. The erroneous and illegal finding that fraud, as a matter of law, was present in the instant case.

STATEMENT OF FACTS. *What Should Be Included.* The pleading of facts is an important part of the petitioner's case.[67] A concise but complete Statement of Facts setting out the facts upon which the petitioner rests his case and laying the foundation for the introduction of the evidence can be impressive. The difficulty lies, however, in determining what should and what should not be included in the statement. The purpose of the Statement of Facts is to substantiate each Assignment of Error, but the detail in which the facts must be alleged is a matter that will vary from case to case. In this respect (other than Rule 7 which provides that the allegations should be "clear and concise lettered statements of the facts upon which the petitioner relies as sustaining the assignments of error . . ."), there are no specific rules governing the Statement of Facts. Nonetheless,

[65] See also Tax Court Form No. 1, page **C**·23–26.

[66] Tax Ct. R. 7(c)(4)(B)4.

[67] Failure to allege a clear and concise statement of facts may result in dismissal of the petition. See Martin v. Commissioner, 358 F.2d 63 (C.A.7th).

a few guidelines can be set out. The statement should not include lengthy allegations covering each detail and each event relating to the disputed adjustments. There should also be no allegations concerning proceedings before the Service at any administrative level. These matters have no bearing on the case. The statement must contain, however, all allegations that, if proved, will constitute an adequate basis for the petitioner's case. No fact necessary to prove the assigned errors ought to be omitted.[68] Counsel is thus left with a difficult job of including what are commonly called the "ultimate facts" of the case, but excluding the evidentiary detail that will be introduced as proof.

When in doubt, it is probably better practice to include a matter in the statement than to exclude it. In contrast to the pleadings submitted in other courts, the purpose of a Tax Court petition is to convey as much information as possible to the Court. In deficiency cases most of the facts are overt, and a complete presentation of the facts upon which the petitioner relies cannot harm his case. Although there is some opinion that where a disputed deficiency turns on facts rather than upon law, full disclosure of the factual support for the petitioner's position will give undue aid to the Service in preparing the defense and may tend to commit the petitioner to a single position, such a situation is probably exceptional. Furthermore, the Court has been increasingly insistent that the pleadings be specific and complete. Detailed pleadings are also required of the Service, and in the fraud case of *Peter Licavoli* failure of the Commissioner to comply with a Court order for more specific pleadings resulted in a decision for the petitioner.[69]

Consequences of Inadequate Statement. Since the Court may not consider issues of fact not raised in the pleadings, all issues and the facts necessary to substantiate them must be pleaded.[70] Failure to plead a fact necessary to substantiate an Assignment of Error can generally be remedied by filing an amendment setting out additional facts, but failure to do so will be deemed a failure to properly raise the issue. In some cases the Court may deny the amendment with the result that the evidence concerning the issue is precluded.[71]

How To Write the Statement of Facts. Basically, it is a simple matter to go paragraph by paragraph through the notice of deficiency and write the Assignments of Error. Following up with allegations of fact that will substantiate a cause of action based on those errors is somewhat more diffi-

---

[68] The petitioner does *not* have the burden of proving all the items on his return. He must simply prove that the asserted deficiencies are incorrect. Wallis v. Commissioner, 357 F.2d 313, 314 note 1 (C.A.10th).

[69] Licavoli v. Commissioner, 252 F.2d 268 (C.A.6th), *affirming* P-H Memo TC, ¶¶ 56, 187.

[70] Nicholson v. Commissioner, 3 T.C. 596.

[71] See p. **5 · 25** *infra*.

cult. The facts should match the Assignments of Error, and a good test of whether they are adequate is to ask whether, given the Assignments of Error, proof of the facts as alleged will result in a decision that the Commissioner's determination was incorrect.

Since the burden of proof is on the petitioner in most cases brought before the Court, he should seek to obtain as many admissions of factual allegations by the Commissioner as possible; this will serve to eliminate the time and expense of proving what may in reality be mere background facts or other matters not actually controverted. Therefore, the factual allegations should be set out in separate statements which the Commissioner can easily admit (or deny) in his Answer. The paragraphs and sentences should be short, and non-controversial facts should be isolated to facilitate an admission as to them by the Commissioner. To this end, the Rules of the Court require that the Statement of Facts be set out in separately lettered paragraphs.[72] An orderly presentation of facts with each material fact set out separately will aid the Court in understanding the factual background as well as allow the Commissioner to make at least a minimal number of admissions on undisputed issues. Facts organized according to the issue to which they relate or in chronological order will be helpful. Statements of Fact should not be phrased in argumentative fashion thus compelling the Commissioner to deny them. Similarly, inferences and conclusory statements should be avoided.

Sample Statements and Typical Answer by Commissioner. The following is a modified portion of a petition and the related portion of the Commissioner's answer.

5. The facts upon which the petitioners rely as the basis of this case are as follows:

(a) The taxpayer Samuel S. Ross filed his tax return for the calendar years 1962 and 1963, and later filed amended tax returns for 1962 and 1963.

(b) On September 1, 1955, a Certificate of Incorporation of the Ross Engineering Company was filed with the Department of State of the State of New York.

(c) On December 31, 1955, Samuel S. Ross was issued five (5) shares of the capital stock of the aforesaid corporation, represented by certificates numbered 1, 2, 3, 4, 5.

(d) Samuel S. Ross subscribed to the aforesaid five shares at a price of of $1,000 each, which sum was paid to the corporation.

(e) On January 9, 1962, Samuel S. Ross sold his five shares, representing a 100% interest in the stock of the Ross Engineering Company, to Morton Ross.

(f) Samuel S. Ross sold his stock interest, as aforesaid, at a gross selling price of $170,000.00

---

[72] Tax Ct. R. 7(c)(4)(B)(5).

(g) The purchase price was payable as follows: the sum of $6,000.00 in the year of sale (1962), and the balance of $164,000.00 represented by a series of ten (10) promissory notes, each in the amount of $16,400.00, the first note payable on January 9, 1963, and the remaining notes annually thereafter, with the final note due January 9, 1972.

(h) The ten (10) notes referred to above bore interest at the rate of 4¼% per annum.

(i) Taxpayer has elected, in proper fashion, to report the gain on the installment basis and so reported such gain on the installment basis.

(j) Taxpayer has a son, born Morton Ross, who was and is married to one Sarah Howard Ross.

(k) During 1962, Samuel S. Ross received from Morton Ross moneys in the sum of $129,500.00 (see the statutory notice on page 2, adjustment (b)).

(l) The said sum of $129,500.00 was a loan made to Samuel S. Ross by Morton Ross.

(m) Of the said sum of $129,500.00, Samuel S. Ross repaid $3,600.00 to Morton Ross in 1962.

(n) During 1962, the taxpayer made payments in the sum of $2,389.00 to Morton Ross and another (see the statutory notice on page 3, adjustment (d)).

(o) The sum of $1,354.80 was interest paid by Samuel S. Ross for the use of money loaned to him in 1962 by Morton Ross.

(p) The sum of $133.33 was interest paid by Samuel S. Ross for the use of money loaned to him in 1960 by one Jerome Davids, which loan was repaid by Samuel S. Ross in 1962.

(q) During 1963, Samuel S. Ross made payments to Morton Ross in the sum of $42,000.00.

(r) The said sum of $42,000.00 was in partial repayment of amounts due to Morton Ross on account of an indebtedness originating in 1962 (see 5(1), *supra*).

(s) During 1963, Samuel S. Ross made payments in the sum of $2,187.00 to Morton Ross (see the statutory notice on page 4, adjustment (c), explained at page 3, adjustment (d)).

(t) The said sum of $2,187.00 was interest paid by Samuel S. Ross to Morton Ross for the use of money.

(u) During 1963, Samuel S. Ross received the sum of $13,000.00 from Morton Ross.

(v) The said sum of $13,000.00 was in partial repayment of an amount due to Samuel S. Ross on account of an indebtedness arising from the sale of stock effected in 1962 (see 5(g), *supra*).

(w) During 1963, Samuel S. Ross received the sum of $337.00 from Morton Ross (see the statutory notice on page 4, adjustment (e)).

(x) The said sum of $337.00 was interest received from Morton Ross, and was in payment for the use of money.[73]

That part of the Commissioner's answer directed to the above Statements of Fact would be as follows:

[73] See also Tax Court Forms No. 1, p. C·23–26; No. 3, p. C·29–33; and No. 6, p. C·37–40.

The Respondent, in answer to the petition filed in the above-entitled case, admits, denies and alleges as follows:

.   .   .   .

5. (a) Admits the allegations of subparagraphs (a) of paragraph 5 of the petition.

(b) Denies the allegations of subparagraph (b) of paragraph 5 of the petition.

(c) Admits that Samuel S. Ross was issued five (5) shares of the capital stock of Ross Engineering Company, represented by certificate numbered 1, 2, 3, 4, 5. Denies the remaining allegations of subparagraph (c) of paragraph 5 of the petition.

(d) Admits that Samuel S. Ross paid $1,000 for each of the aforesaid shares. Denies the remaining allegations of subparagraph (d) of paragraph 5 of the petition.

(e) to (i), inclusive. Denies the allegations of subparagraphs (e) to (i), inclusive, of paragraph 5 of the petition.

(j) and (k) Admits the allegations of subparagraphs (j) and (k) of paragraph 5 of the petition.

(l) to (x), inclusive. Denies the allegations of subparagraphs (l) to (x), inclusive, of paragraph 5 of the petition.

6. Denies generally each and every allegation of the petition not hereinbefore specifically admitted, qualified or denied.

In the above example, a careful job of drafting the Statement of Fact resulted in a number of admissions on the part of the Commissioner, thus reducing the number of facts to be proven by the petitioner.

In comparison with the above sample Statement of Facts, consider the one set out below:

5. The facts upon which petitioner relies as a basis of this proceeding are as follows:

(a) *General Statement.*

On August 7, 1961, while returning from a business trip by car, petitioner was involved in a head-on collision with a heavy truck-trailer. He was removed to a hospital at Denver, Colorado. His principal complaint was neck pains. The x-rays of the injured area taken at that time were deemed negative, and, because petitioner continued to complain, petitioner was kept at the hospital for one week. Prior to his discharge, petitioner was fitted with a neck collar or brace.

When petitioner returned to Chicago, he found that he could not attend to his business because of the continuing and persisting pains in the neck and arms even though he continued to wear the neck brace. On or about October 19th on the recommendation of his personal physician, petitioner consulted an orthopedic specialist to determine whether it would be safe and advisable to discard the neck brace and also for advice and consultation regarding his persistent neck and arm pains. As part of the examination the orthopedist x-rayed the affected areas. The following day, petitioner was instructed to enter the

West Side Hospital, Chicago, Illinois, as the x-ray plates revealed a forward subluxation of the fourth cervical vertebra on the fifth cervical vertebra.

Petitioner remained at said hospital until February 18, 1962. During the period December 31, 1961, until his discharge on February 18, 1962, petitioner was in traction, had Crutchfield tongs applied and was the subject of an operation for the fusion of his spine. As the course of treatment required the utmost relaxation on the part of the patient (petitioner herein) and resulted in substantial and practically continuous pain, massive amounts of drugs and narcotics were administered to petitioner.

During all of the year 1962, and for a substantial period thereafter, and at all times herein pertinent, petitioner's medical advisers and doctors continued to prescribe drugs and narcotics as part of petitioner's post-operative care, and petitioner continued to consume large quantities of drugs and narcotics.

(b) During all of the period and at all times that the alleged diversion of funds from Lesser Drug Company occurred, the petitioner was under the influence of drugs and narcotics.

(c) At the time petitioner's income tax return for the year 1962 was prepared and filed, petitioner was under the influence of drugs and narcotics.

(d) Upon information and belief, during all of the year 1962 and during all of the period that petitioner's income tax return for the year 1962 was prepared, petitioner was incapacitated and not in full possession of all of his faculties by reason of the quantities of drugs and narcotics then consumed by him.

(e) Upon information and belief, during all of the year 1962 and during the period that petitioner's income tax return for 1962 was prepared, petitioner was not capable of having the necessary intent to commit fraud or of knowing that he was perpetrating fraud.

(f) Upon information and belief, during all of the year 1962 and during the period that petitioner's income tax return for 1962 was prepared, petitioner, as a matter of law, was not capable of having the necessary intent to commit fraud.

(g) That petitioner reimbursed Lesser Drug Company in the sum of Eighteen Thousand Dollars ($18,000.00) during 1963 upon being informed by counsel that he had no legal right to retain said sum.

The above example, modified from an actual statement of facts submitted to the Tax Court, illustrates how such a statement should not be drafted. Taking into account that the case involved fraud and the petitioner may have had to grasp at extraneous facts to support his petition, the statement is nonetheless faulty. The paragraphs are extremely long and are full of details that do not belong in a Statement of Facts. The statement not only includes much that should not be included, but is drafted in such a form so as to make it highly unlikely that the Commissioner would be able to admit any particular facts without admitting substantially all of them. In fact, the Commissioner, in his answer, denied all but a single sentence of the actual Statement.

PRAYER FOR RELIEF. The taxpayer concludes his petition with a Prayer for Relief.[74] The prayer for relief should be a simple request for the type of relief to which he is entitled, but in no case may the relief granted exceed the statutory powers of the Court. The Prayer may also include a standard clause requesting any other general relief. A typical clause is as follows:

WHEREFORE, the petitioner prays that this Court may hear the proceeding; determine that there are no deficiencies in income tax due from the petitioner for the calendar years 1960 and 1961; and grant petitioner such other and further relief to which it may be entitled.

SIGNATURE AND VERIFICATION. Every petition must be signed and verified by the taxpayer.[75] In the case where the taxpayer is sojourning outside the United States or is a nonresident alien the petition may be signed and verified by an attorney in fact.[76] The purpose of the signature and verification, as stated in the Rule is to certify ". . . that there is good ground for the petition, the case has not been instituted merely for delay, and it is not frivolous." [77] When a petition is filed by the taxpayer solely for purposes of delay the Court may, under its statutory powers, award the United States damages up to an amount of $500.[78] A fiduciary or agent may verify a petition when authorized to do so, but must state in the verification that he has the power to act for the taxpayer. The authority of such a person is open to challenge as is any other allegation in the petition.

The requirement of verification is a procedural rule which the Court may waive at its discretion. Although the Court has been known to waive the verification, counsel for the taxpayer should not fail to have the petition properly verified, since the Court has also been known to deny a petitioner the right to amend his petition by adding a verification on the ground that the amendment would result in a new petition by someone who had failed previously to invoke the Court's jurisdiction at the appropriate time.[79]

In addition to verification of the petition by the taxpayer, the signature of the taxpayer or his counsel is required.[80] Since a law firm may not be admitted to practice before the Court, counsel should sign in his individual capacity, indicating also his mailing address and firm name where appropriate.

Although an original and four copies of the petition must be filed, only the original need be signed.

---

[74] Required by Tax Ct. R. 7(c)(4)(B)6.
[75] Required by Tax Ct. R. 7(c)(4)(D).
[76] *Ibid.*
[77] *Ibid.*
[78] IRC § 6673. Treas. Reg. § 301.6673–1.
[79] Greenan v. Commissioner, 145 F.2d 134 (C.A.9th), *cert. denied,* 324 U.S. 848.
[80] Tax Ct. R. 4(f), 7(c)(4)(C).

The verification and signatures should follow the Prayer for Relief in the petition and should be set out in the following form: [81]

Geoffrey P. Wharton
Attorney for Petitioner
Wharton and Price
63 Wall Street
New York, New York

State of New York } ss.:
County of New York

Judith Ann Lesser, duly sworn, says that she is the President of the Lesser Laundries, Inc., the petitioner above named; that she is duly authorized to verify the foregoing petition; that she has read the foregoing petition, or has had the same read to her, and is familiar with the statements contained therein, and that the statements contained therein are true, except as to those stated upon information and belief, and those she believes to be true.

Judith Ann Lesser

Notary Seal and
Signature

Requesting Place for Trial

At the time the taxpayer files his petition he should also file a request indicating his preference for a place of trial.[82] Any such request must be in the form of a separate document filed in triplicate. If the taxpayer files no request, the Service may do so. The Court will fix the place for trial to afford the taxpayer reasonable opportunity to try his case with as little inconvenience and expense as practicable. The taxpayer's request is likely to be granted so long as it is for a site at which sessions of the Court are conducted. A partial list of cities in which sessions of the Court are held is set out in Fig. 5–1, page **5**·24. A trial may be requested in any place where adequate facilities will be available and where a sufficient number of cases are ready for trial. Where facilities are not available or there is not a sufficient number of cases, the Court may calendar the case in a city within reasonable proximity to the location requested by the taxpayer.

A motion may be filed to change the place of trial at any time before the notice of the time of trial is mailed. The Clerk of the Court will notify the parties of the place, date, and time of the trial not less than 90 days in advance.[83]

[81] For an individual verification, see Tax Court Form No. 1, p. **C**·25.
[82] Tax Ct. R. 26.
[83] Tax Ct. R. 27.

ALABAMA:
  Birmingham.
  Mobile.
ARIZONA: Phoenix.
ARKANSAS: Little Rock, or Memphis, Tenn.
CALIFORNIA:
  Los Angeles.
  San Francisco.
COLORADO: Denver.
DISTRICT OF COLUMBIA: Washington.
FLORIDA:
  Jacksonville.
  Miami.
  Tampa.
GEORGIA: Atlanta
HAWAII: Honolulu, or Los Angeles or San Francisco, Calif.
ILLINOIS: Chicago
INDIANA: Indianapolis.
IOWA: Des Moines.
KENTUCKY: Louisville.
LOUISIANA: New Orleans.
MASSACHUSETTS: Boston.
MICHIGAN: Detroit.
MINNESOTA: St. Paul.
MISSISSIPPI: Jackson.
MISSOURI:
  Kansas City.
  St. Louis.
MONTANA: Helena.
NEBRASKA: Omaha.

NEW JERSEY: Newark.
  (New York City courtroom usually used.)
NEW YORK:
  Buffalo.
  New York City.
NORTH CAROLINA: Greensboro.
OHIO:
  Cleveland.
  Cincinnati.
  Columbus.
OKLAHOMA: Oklahoma City or Tulsa.
OREGON: Portland.
PENNSYLVANIA:
  Philadelphia.
  Pittsburgh.
SOUTH CAROLINA: Columbia.
TENNESSEE:
  Knoxville.
  Memphis.
  Nashville.
TEXAS:
  Dallas.
  Houston, or Galveston, or San Antonio.
UTAH: Salt Lake City.
WASHINGTON:
  Seattle.
  Spokane.
WEST VIRGINIA:
  Charleston.
  Huntington.
WISCONSIN:
  Milwaukee, or Chicago Ill.

FIG. 5–1. CITIES IN WHICH SESSIONS OF THE TAX COURT ARE REGULARLY HELD.[84]

Amending and Withdrawing Petition

AMENDING THE PETITION. A petitioner may amend his petition without leave of the Court at any time before an Answer is filed by the Commissioner.[85] Between the time the Commissioner files an Answer and the beginning of the trial, the petitioner may amend only on consent of the Commissioner or by leave of the Court. Any motion to amend before the

[84] Appendix II to Tax Court Rules.
[85] Tax Ct. R. 17(b)(1).

trial must be accompanied by the proposed amendment itself. The danger of waiting until after trial has begun before moving to amend has been referred to previously. Although the Rules provide that "the Court may at any time during the course of the trial grant a motion of either party to amend its pleadings to conform to the proof . . . ," [86] the Court may act at its discretion and may deny the motion where the other party, usually the Commissioner, is unduly prejudiced or surprised by the amendment.

Since Rule 17 provides that an amendment to conform the petition to the proof is allowed at any time before the conclusion of the hearing but not thereafter, [87] the issue arises as to what constitutes the conclusion of the hearing. On this issue it has been held that the hearing constitutes the entire period of time up to the entry of a decision. [88] Thus, in the exceptional situation where the petitioner discovers new evidence and acts diligently in seeking to amend his petition at the hearing, such an amendment will generally be allowed. [89] Excepting the aforementioned situation, the Court will not permit a petitioner to amend his petition and then seek to offer proof to substantiate the amendment.

In passing on a petitioner's motion to amend at the hearing, the Court will consider not only whether the Commissioner is unfairly surprised but whether the petitioner has been diligent in requesting such leave to amend. The Court may not arbitrarily deny the motion, but the petitioner should have a good reason for his motion. For example, where the petitioner is unable to produce an expected witness, or when the Court rules that certain disputed evidence is admissible or inadmissible, the result may be that the original Assignments of Error or Statements of Fact do not conform with the proof as adduced at trial. In such circumstances the petitioner will be justified in making a motion to amend. When a motion to amend at the hearing is granted, the amendment must be filed either at the hearing itself or with the Clerk of the Tax Court within such a period of time as the Court may determine.

When a taxpayer's petition is vague or incomplete, either the Court or the Service may move to cause the petitioner to file a further and better statement of his allegations or claim or, alternatively, may move to dismiss for failure to prosecute. In cases where the petition was not filed within ninety days or the tax is asserted for a year over which the Court has no jurisdiction, no amendment will cure the petition. Conversely, a mere error of form or failure to state sufficient facts are matters that can be properly cured by an amendment to the petition.

---

[86] Tax Ct. R. 17(d).
[87] Bennett v. Commissioner, 139 F.2d 961 (C.A.8th).
[88] Edison Securities Corp. v. Helvering, 78 F.2d 85 (C.A.4th).
[89] *Cf., e.g.,* M. C. Parrish & Co. v. Commissioner, 3 T.C. 119, *aff'd,* 147 F.2d 284 (C.A.8th).

WITHDRAWING THE PETITION. In some instances the taxpayer may want to withdraw his petition, especially when the Commissioner's answer increases the amount of the deficiency beyond what it was in the deficiency notice. Unfortunately, once a petition is filed with the Tax Court, it cannot be withdrawn without the consent of the Service. The Tax Court has ruled that once a petition is filed, either party has the right to a determination, either on the merits or on a default,[90] and counsel for the taxpayer must answer the question "should this petition be filed with the Tax Court" before and not after filing.

THE ANSWER

Procedure After Filing Petition

After the petition has been filed and the Clerk of the Court has served a copy on the Service by delivering it to the Office of the Chief Counsel, the copy will be forwarded to the Regional Counsel of the area in which the petitioner is located. The Regional Counsel will assign the case to an attorney on his staff for preparation of an answer. Along with the copy of the petition, the staff attorney will receive from the Appellate Division an administrative file containing assorted background material for the case such as the Revenue Agent's Report and the taxpayer's protest. If the petition is not defective and does not require a motion for clarification or dismissal, the staff attorney will prepare the Commissioner's answer.

Content of Answer

FORMAT. In general, the format of the answer will be identical to that of the petition.[91] Defects in the form of answer will be disregarded unless the defect is such that it affects the substantive content.

THE DENIALS AND ADMISSIONS. The Commissioner's answer should advise the petitioner and Court fully of the nature of the defense.[92] It shall contain "a specific admission or denial of each material allegation of fact contained in the petition." [93] The first part of the answer will do exactly that.

Usually the answer will contain a standard phrase that each and every allegation of the petition not specifically admitted or qualified is to be denied. If such a clause is not included in the answer, Rule 18(a) provides that "every material allegation of fact set out in the petition and not expressly admitted or denied in the answer shall be deemed to be admitted."

[90] Capital Bldg. & Loan Ass'n v. Commissioner, 12 B.T.A. 349.
[91] See Tax Court Forms No. 2, p. C·27–28, and No. 4, p. C·34–35.
[92] Tax Ct. R. 14(b).
[93] *Ibid.*

At this point it should again be emphasized that admissions to factual allegations are much more likely to be made when the allegations are simply stated and well differentiated so that the Commissioner is not forced to admit either more than he wishes or nothing at all.

THE AFFIRMATIVE STATEMENTS OF FACT. Tax Court Rule 14 further requires that the answer contain "a statement of any facts upon which the Commissioner relies for defense or for affirmative relief or to sustain any issue raised in the petition in respect of which issue the burden of proof is, by statute, placed upon him." [94] Generally, the answer will be a simple statement of admissions and denials, but in some typical situations, set out below, the answer will contain an affirmative pleading of facts.

Civil Fraud Cases. In cases in which the Service determines a penalty for fraudulent intent to evade taxes is due (this is to be distinguished from a criminal fraud prosecution) the Commissioner affirmatively pleads the facts upon which he bases his allegations of fraud.[95] Such fraud allegations may properly be raised for the first time in the answer. To the extent that the Service can reasonably be assumed to have knowledge of material facts, the answer should be definite and specific. *A fortiori*, specificity will be required in the answer where the factual data upon which the Service relies has been made available to it or is within its control. In instances where the Commissioner's allegations are vague or are written in general terms, the Court may grant a motion by the petitioner for a more specific answer. In the *Licavoli* case, the Commissioner's answer was stricken by the Court after repeated motions for a more specific answer were not complied with to the satisfaction of the Court.[96]

Increased Deficiencies; Deficiencies Based on New Issues. When an increased deficiency is asserted by the Commissioner in his answer, it must be substantiated by a formal claim and an adequate statement of the facts giving rise to the deficiency. If the deficiency claim is not accompanied by specific facts to substantiate it, the Court will not consider the claim. These requirements of specificity have been held not to be satisfied by a general provision at the end of the Commissioner's answer claiming any increased deficiency that may subsequently arise from any subsequent redetermination.

To be distinguished from allegations concerning an increased deficiency is the situation in which the answer alleges the same deficiency but raises entirely new facts to support the determination. Where the new facts are inconsistent with those relied upon in the notice of deficiency and where the petitioner would be unfairly surprised at the trial because of the newly

[94] *Ibid.*; see p. **8**·4 *et seq. infra* for a discussion of the situations in which the Commissioner has the burden of proof.
[95] IRC § 6501(c).
[96] Licavoli v. Commissioner, *supra* note 69.

raised factual issues, these matters must be affirmatively pleaded in the answer.[97] This situation can often cause some amount of confusion since it may be questionable whether the new facts constitute new issues to be pleaded or whether they are merely new facts that substantiate the issues originally raised in the deficiency notice.

Other Situations Requiring Affirmative Pleading. There are certain other somewhat common situations in which the Commissioner must affirmatively plead facts in the answer. In cases where the petitioner has raised the issue of the three-year statute of limitations as a bar on assessment of the tax, the answer must contain affirmative allegations that the taxpayer has signed a consent for the extension of time for assessment, or that there has been an omission from gross income of an amount in excess of 25 per cent of the amount actually reported in the return, or that no return has been filed if the Service wishes to assert that a longer statute of limitations applies.[98]

In cases of accumulated earnings taxes the burden of proof may be upon the Commissioner.[99] If this is the case the answer will affirmatively plead all facts necessary to establish that earnings and profits have been permitted to accumulate beyond the reasonable needs of the taxpayer's business.

Finally, the answer may contain affirmative pleadings in certain transferee cases governed by § 6901 of the Internal Revenue Code, in which the Commissioner will allege that a certain transferee stands in the place of the taxpayer.

Filing the Answer

Upon service of a copy of the taxpayer's petition the attorney preparing the Commissioner's answer is allowed 45 days in which to file a motion or 60 days in which to file an answer.[100] If a motion is filed, then the filing date of the answer will be extended to 60 days from the date when final action on the motion is taken by the Court. In contrast to the statutory period for filing the petition, the Court may exercise its discretion in the case of the answer and waive the 60-day filing period, thus allowing an answer to be filed at a later date.[101]

After the answer has been filed, the Clerk of the Court will serve a copy of the answer upon the taxpayer or upon his attorney of record.[102]

---

[97] *Cf.* Commissioner v. Chelsea Prods., Inc., 197 F.2d 620 (C.A.3d) ; see also p. **8 · 5** *infra.*

[98] IRC §§ 6501(c), (e) ; see Tax Court Form No. 4, p. **C · 34–35**.

[99] See p. **8 · 6** *infra.*

[100] Tax Ct. R. 14(a).

[101] Brooklyn Union Gas Co. v. Commissioner, 22 B.T.A. 507, *aff'd,* 62 F. 2d 505 (C.A.2d).

[102] Tax Ct. R. 22(a).

Amending the Answer

There are no specific provisions in the Tax Court Rules controlling amendments to the answer, and the Court has allowed amendments at the trial [103] at any time up to the day the Court's decision is entered, or at an even later date in case of a retrial.[104]

A motion to amend may be scheduled for argument [105] but is often granted *ex parte* without notice to the petitioner.

Sample Answer

Although the content of the answer will vary with the nature of the affirmative allegations, the form of the answer remains the same. The sample below would be a typical answer in a civil fraud case:

TAX COURT OF THE UNITED STATES

RICHARD W. PERRY,

    Petitioner,

     v.   Docket No. 8723–66

COMMISSIONER OF INTERNAL REVENUE,

    Respondent.

ANSWER

THE RESPONDENT, in answer to the petition filed in the above-entitled case, admits, denies and alleges as follows:

1. and 2. Admits the allegations of paragraphs 1 and 2 of the petition.

3. (a) and (b) Admits the allegations of subparagraphs (a) and (b) of paragraph 3 of the petition.

4. (a) (i), (ii) and (iii) Denies the allegations of error of subparts (i), (ii) and (iii) of subparagraph (a) of paragraph 4 of the petition.

(b) (i), (ii) and (iii) Denies the allegations of error of subparts (i), (ii) and (iii) of subparagraph (b) of paragraph 4 of the petition.

5. (a) GENERAL STATEMENT Denies the allegations of the four subparagraphs under the heading "(a) GENERAL STATEMENT", of paragraph 5 of the petition.

(b), (c), (d), (e) and (f) Denies the allegations of subparagraphs (b), (c), (d), (e) and (f) of paragraph 5 of the petition.

6. Denies generally each and every allegation of the petition not hereinbefore specifically admitted, qualified or denied.

[103] See California Brewing Ass'n v. Commissioner, 43 B.T.A. 721, 725–26, in which it is noted that amendment at trial will be permitted only where the hearing can proceed without prejudice.

[104] Henningsen v. Commissioner, 243 F.2d 954 (C.A.4th).

[105] Tax Ct. R. 19(b).

7. FURTHER ANSWERING the petition and in support of the determination that all or a part of the underpayment of tax required to be shown on the petitioner's 1965 return is due to fraud, the respondent alleges:

(a) That for the taxable year 1965 the petitioner filed an individual income tax return in which he reported taxable income in the amount of $21,134.72; whereas, his true taxable income for said year was at least $33,134.72.

(b) That during 1965 the petitioner, with the intent to evade and defeat tax, failed to keep adequate and complete books and records of his income-producing activities as required by the applicable provisions of the Internal Revenue Code of 1954 and the regulations promulgated thereunder.

(c) That during 1965 the petitioner was the president of Perry Drug Company; the owner of all of its stock after April 25, 1965; and the owner of 75 per cent of its stock prior to April 25, 1965.

(d) That during 1965 the petitioner received $12,000.00 from Perry Drug Company which the petitioner did not include in his reported taxable income for that year.

(e) That the accumulated earnings and profits of Perry Drug Company exceeded $12,000.00 during 1965.

(f) That the $12,000.00 which the petitioner received during 1965 from Perry Drug Company and did not include in his reported taxable income for that year was a dividend.

(g) That the petitioner knew that said $12,000.00 should have been included in his reported taxable income for 1965.

(h) That the petitioner willfully and fraudulently failed to report said $12,000.00 as income for 1965.

(i) By virtue of his willful and fraudulent failure to report said $12,000.00 as income for 1965, the petitioner's 1965 income tax return was false and fraudulent.

WHEREFORE, it is prayed:

1. That the relief sought in the petition be denied;

2. That the deficiency in income tax for the taxable year 1965, as set forth in the statutory notice, be in all respects approved; and

3. That the addition to the tax for the taxable year 1965 under the provisions of §6653(b) of the 1954 Code, as set forth in the statutory notice, be in all respects approved.

LESTER R. URETZ
Chief Counsel
Internal Revenue Service

OF COUNSEL:
   MARVIN E. HAGEN
   Regional Counsel
   PAUL H. FRANKEL
   Attorney
Internal Revenue Service
30 Church Street, New York, New York 10007

Joinder of Issue

As is true in all litigation the function of the answer is to put the case at issue. In this respect, Rule 16 of the Court provides that, unless a reply is required, "(a) case shall be deemed at issue upon the filing of the answer . . ."

THE REPLY

When Reply Is Necessary

When a petition and answer are filed, the issues of fact are raised by allegations and denials, and issues of law are raised as to the meaning of the facts. When an answer is filed that raises new issues, the better practice is for the petitioner to file a reply which should "contain a specific admission or denial of each material allegation of fact contained in the answer and shall set forth any facts upon which the *petitioner* relies for defense." [106] Every material allegation not expressly denied is deemed admitted. Thus, Rule 16 provides that in the case where a reply is necessary there is no joinder of issue until a reply is filed or the newly raised issues are ruled to be admitted upon a motion by the Commissioner.

Thus, whenever the answer asks for affirmative relief (other than a request that the deficiency set out in the 90-day notice be approved) or alleges facts in support of issues in which the Commissioner has the burden of proof, a reply should be made.

Any new material the petitioner includes in the reply will be deemed denied.

Failure To File Reply

When a reply is filed "every material allegation of fact set out in the answer and not expressly admitted or denied in the reply . . . shall be deemed to be admitted." [107] When a reply is not filed, however, the affirmative allegations of the answer will be deemed denied unless the Commissioner files a motion seeking an admission of the allegations within 45 days after the expiration of the period for filing such a reply.[108] This motion will recite that a reply was required but was not entered and will request an order that specified allegations in the answer be deemed admitted. A copy of the motion will be served upon the petitioner along with notice of a

---

[106] Tax Ct. R. 15(b).
[107] Tax Ct. R. 18(b).
[108] Tax Ct. R. 18(c)(1).

hearing. Rule 18(c)(2) provides that "the Court may grant the motion unless the required reply is filed on or before the day fixed for such hearing."

Since those parts of the answer requiring a reply will be allegations as to fraud, an increased deficiency, the statute of limitations, or transferee liability, and since such allegations pertain to issues as to which the Commissioner has the burden of proof, an order granting the Commissioner's motion for an admission will relieve him of the burden of proving these issues raised by the allegations.[109] Thus, failure to file a reply can cause the petitioner to lose his case.

Timeliness of Reply

When a reply is required, Rule 15(a) provides that the petitioner has a period of 45 days from the date of mailing of the answer in which to file a reply or a period of 30 days in which to file a motion with respect to the answer.[110]

In cases where neither a reply nor a Motion for Admission has been filed, the Court may exercise its discretion and extend the period for filing a reply.[111] Such replies have even been received by the Court after the close of the hearing.

Sample Reply

The form of the reply is the same as that of the petition. No verification is required, but the Court, on its own motion or on that of the Commissioner, may require verification.[112]

The sample set out below would be filed in reply to the sample answer beginning on page **5 · 29**, *supra*.[113]

THE TAX COURT OF THE UNITED STATES

RICHARD W. PERRY, *Petitioner,* —*against*— COMMISSIONER OF INTERNAL REVENUE, *Respondent.*	Docket No. 8723–66 REPLY

The PETITIONER, in reply to the answer filed in the above-entitled case, admits, denies and alleges as follows:

---

[109] Mauch v. Commissioner, 35 B.T.A. 617, *aff'd*, 113 F.2d 555 (C.A.3d).
[110] Tax Ct. R. 15(a).
[111] Nicholson v. Commissioner, 32 B.T.A. 977, *aff'd*, 90 F.2d 978 (C.A.8th).
[112] Tax Ct. R. 15(d).
[113] See also Tax Court Form No. 5, p. **C · 36**.

7. (a) Admits that Petitioner filed an individual income tax return for the year 1965 in which he reported taxable income in the sum of $21,134.72. Denies the remaining allegations of said Subparagraph (a) of Paragraph 7 of the Answer.

(b) Denies each and every allegation contained in Subparagraph (b) of Paragraph 7 of the Answer.

(c) Admits that he was the president of Perry Drug Company during 1965.

(d) Admits the allegations contained in Subparagraph (d) of Paragraph 7 of the Answer.

(e) Denies knowledge or information sufficient to form a belief as to the allegations contained in Subparagraph (e) of Paragraph 7 of the answer.

(f), (g), (h) and (i) Denies each and every allegation contained in Subparagraphs (f), (g), (h) and (i) of Paragraph 7 of the Answer. Petitioner repeats and realleges the allegations contained in Subparagraphs (a), (b), (c), (d), (e) and (f) of Paragraph 5 of the Petition herein and incorporates the same by reference as if fully set forth at length herein.

8. Denies each and every allegation of the answer not hereinbefore specifically admitted, qualified, or denied.

WHEREFORE, the PETITIONER prays the Court for the relief prayed for in the Petition.

HAROLD P. EYRING
Attorney for Petitioner
189 Broadway
New York, N.Y.

CHAPTER **6**

PROCEEDINGS BEFORE TRIAL IN THE TAX COURT

MOTION PROCEDURE

A motion is a request for some action or ruling by the Court. For example, a party may move that the petition be dismissed, that the answer be stricken, or that parties be substituted. The Court's action on such motions may result in an ultimate decision on the case or may change its basic form. The subject of motions can also be procedural, such as motions to substitute counsel, postpone the hearing, or obtain a subpoena.

In the Tax Court various actions taken by the Court on its own initiative are also described as motions. For example, the Court, on its own initiative, may move to dismiss for lack of jurisdiction. In addition to motions by the parties and by the Court, other persons whose rights may be affected by the decision of the Court may also move to intervene.[1]

Proper Time for Motions

The appropriate time for making a motion will vary with the nature of the motion. In this respect, the Rules of the Tax Court merely provide that "motions must be timely." [2] Some motions, such as a motion to dismiss for lack of jurisdiction, may be made at any time. Others, such as a motion to amend a pleading or for a continuance, are not required to be made at any specific time, yet the Court may refuse to consider such motions if the moving party appears responsible for undue delay or for lack of diligence. Finally, the Tax Court Rules establish specific times during which certain motions must be made. Thus, a motion to take a deposition that is not filed more than 30 days prior to the date of trial will be denied by the Court because it is not timely.[3]

Unless the Rules of the Court or the applicable case law firmly establish that a motion will be timely whenever counsel makes it, all motions should be made at the earliest possible time. If this policy is not adhered to, counsel may have the added burden of demonstrating that the motion is timely as well as persuading the Court that the motion is sound on the merits.

Motion Timetable

Figure 6–1 provides a list of commonly made motions and the proper time for making them. Motions that may be made "anytime" must none-

---

[1] Central Union Trust Co. v. Commissioner, 18 B.T.A. 300.
[2] Tax Ct. R. 19(a).
[3] Tax Ct. R. 45(b).

theless be filed as soon as possible.[4] The postopinion motions listed here are discussed in a subsequent chapter.[5]

Motions Before and During Hearing	Appropriate Time
1. Motion to dismiss for lack of jurisdiction, for lack of prosecution, as a matter of law	Anytime,* Rule 21
2. Motion for more specific answer or to strike the answer	Anytime*
3. Motion to consolidate	
4. Motion to amend the petition	Before or after answer is filed —see Rule 17 (b), (c), (d)
5. Motion for a subpoena	Anytime,* Rule 44
6. Motion to take a deposition	30 days prior to trial, Rule 45 (b)
7. Motion for substitution of parties	Anytime,* Rule 23
8. Motion for submission of case without hearing or appearance	Anytime,* Rule 30
9. Motion for extension of time to file brief	Anytime,* Rule 20 (a)
10. Motion for substitution of counsel	Anytime,* Rule 24 (b), (c)
11. Motion for continuance	Anytime,* Rule 27 (d) (1)
Motions After Trial	
1. Motion for retrial	Within 30 days after opinion served, later with leave of Court, Rule 19 (e)
2. Motion for further trial	
3. Motion for reconsideration	
4. Motion to vacate decision	Within 30 days after decision entered, later with leave of Court, Rule 19 (f)
5. Motion to revive decision	

* See note 4, this page.

Fig. 6–1. Motion Timetable.

Preparing the Moving Papers

All motions, except certain motions made at the hearing relating to the receipt of evidence, must be in writing.[6] The form and style of the motion must conform to the general requirements of Rule 4, which is applicable

---

[4] "Anytime" used in this context means that the rules do not specify a time at which the motion can be made. However, the Court may, nonetheless, refuse to consider the motion because it is made too late, if the lateness is due to a lack of diligence or is prejudicial to the adverse party.
[5] See p. 9·14 et seq. infra.
[6] Tax Ct. R. 19(d) ; see also Whittaker v. Commissioner, P-H Memo TC, ¶51,085.

to all papers filed with the Court. Set out below is a typical "Motion To Dismiss for Lack of Jurisdiction" made by the Service.[7]

RICHARD W. WELLS,

    Petitioner,

      v.   Docket No. 34,657

COMMISSIONER OF INTERNAL REVENUE,

    Respondent.

MOTION TO DISMISS FOR LACK OF JURISDICTION

THE RESPONDENT MOVES that the above-entitled case be dismissed for lack of jurisdiction for the year 1966 where the statutory notice of deficiency has not asserted a deficiency for that year.

IN SUPPORT THEREOF, the respondent respectfully states:

1. The petitioners allege in subparagraph (b) of paragraph 3 of the petition that the year 1966 is in dispute.

2. The petitioners allege error by the respondent for 1966 in subparagraphs (d), (e) and (f) of paragraph 4 of the petition.

3. The statutory notice of deficiency sets forth an overassessment for the taxable year 1966 in the amount of $8,087.88 and not a deficiency. Thus a deficiency as provided in § 6211 and § 6212 of the Internal Revenue Code of 1954 has not been determined.

4. The petitioner is prohibited from filing a petition under § 6213(a) of the Internal Revenue Code of 1954 for the year 1966 because no deficiency has been determined by the respondent (*Rosemary Manufacturing Co.,* 9 T.C. 851, 856 (1947); *Charles E. Myers, Sr.,* 28 T.C. 12 (1957); *Paccon, Inc.,* 45 T.C. No. 36 (1966).

WHEREFORE, it is respectfully requested that the petition be dismissed.

           LESTER R. URETZ
           Chief Counsel
           Internal Revenue Service

OF COUNSEL:
  MARVIN E. HAGEN
    Regional Counsel
  PAUL H. FRANKEL
    Attorney
  Internal Revenue Service
  30 Church Street
  New York, New York 10007

The heading—in this case, "Motion To Dismiss for Lack of Jurisdiction"—should be a brief description of the nature of the motion. The heading is followed by a concise introductory statement, which should set forth, in summary fashion, the purpose of the motion and the relief sought.

[7] For other sample motions, see Tax Court Forms Nos. 8 through 11, pp. C·42–48.

The body of the motion papers should apprise the Court of the facts that form the basis of the motion and the legal conclusions supporting the relief requested. Where the facts and law involved are fairly simple, as in the specimen above, and counsel does not anticipate submission of briefs or oral argument, citations or brief excerpts from the rules or statutes relied upon are often desirable. In all cases the motion papers should be brief. Consequently, if complicated factual or legal questions are involved, the basic job of persuading the Court should be reserved for oral argument or accomplished by submitting a brief.

The motion should conclude with a "wherefore" clause. This clause should specify the relief requested and, if counsel desires, should also request that the Court order a hearing for argument on the motion. The motion should be signed by counsel. Endorsements in the name of the Chief Counsel are signed on his behalf by Regional Counsel or Assistant Regional Counsel.

Procedure for Making Motion

"No-Objection" Motions. There are two courses of conduct that the taxpayer's counsel may take after he has drafted the motion papers. He may attempt to get an endorsement of "no objection" from the Regional Counsel and then file the motion with the Clerk of the Court or he may ignore the "no-objection" procedure and file directly. The Court's policy of encouraging parties to obtain the endorsement is expressed in its Rules, which provide that "Disposition of motions will be expedited if the party filing the same, after consultation with his adversary, is able to note on the motion that there is no objection thereto." [8]

When a "no objection" is obtained, the endorsement is noted on the moving papers as follows:

WHEREFORE, the petitioner respectfully requests that the Court order that the hearing fixed for September 15, 1967, be continued until November 1967 or thereafter.

GEOFFREY P. WHARTEN
Wharten and Price
60 Broad Street
New York, New York 10005

NO OBJECTION

LESTER R. URETZ
Chief Counsel
Internal Revenue Service

Counsel is well advised to make an effort to obtain the "no-objection" endorsement unless it is obvious that there is no chance it will be given by

[8] Tax Ct. R. 19(b).

the Regional Counsel or he is certain that the motion will be granted. Once the endorsement is obtained, the motion can be filed with reasonable assurance that it will be granted, although on rare occasions the Court may deny a motion despite the endorsement. The "no-objection" endorsement is obviously more valuable in borderline cases in which the Regional Counsel can be persuaded that no objection is warranted than in instances where the petitioner is obviously right. Even if the endorsement is not obtained, the effort of seeking it may not be wasted, since counsel may in this manner discover the basis for the Regional Counsel's opposition, thereby improving his position when he argues his motion or submits his supporting brief. Furthermore, if counsel's motion is of a procedural nature, he can frequently work out a satisfactory compromise when he seeks the endorsement. For example, the Regional Counsel may agree to a continuance although it may not be for as long a period as counsel might wish. It is usually better to thus obtain a fair compromise which suffices to accomplish part of the objective than to fail to get a "no-objection" endorsement and risk an all-or-nothing decision by the Court.

Filing Without "No-Objection" Endorsement. When a motion without a "no-objection" endorsement is filed, the Court will examine it, and the motion "will be acted upon as justice may require and may, in the discretion of the Court, be placed upon the motion calendar for argument." [9] In exercising the broad discretion vested in it by Rule 19, the Court has adopted three procedures for dealing with motions filed directly. In some cases, the Court may act on the motion *ex parte* and issue an appropriate order that will notify the parties of the action it has taken. In other instances, the Court will serve copies of the moving papers on the adverse party together with a notice stating that the motion will be granted unless the Court receives an objection to the motion by a specified date. If no objection is filed, the motion will be granted. If an objection is filed, a date will be fixed for hearing argument of the motion. The third course of action the Court may take after examining the moving papers is to set the motion on the calendar for argument without waiting for an objection from the adverse party.

Although it is not possible to state a definite rule regarding the action the Court will take with respect to any particular type of motion, the Court's decision as to whether a hearing or inquiry for objection is necessary will generally depend on two factors. The first factor is the certainty with which the moving party is entitled to the relief requested, based on previous decisions and precedents. The second is the effect that granting the motion will have on the rights of the adverse party. Thus, if it is evident from the moving papers that a motion should be granted, the Court may act upon it

[9] *Ibid.*

ex parte. For example, if a witness is critically ill, the Court may grant *ex parte* a motion to take his deposition. *Ex parte* decisions, however, are not confined to procedural matters. Thus, if the Commissioner moves to dismiss a petition filed on May 1, in response to a 90-day letter dated December 30, the Court may grant the motion *ex parte* because it is evident that the petition was filed too late. The Court will also be inclined to grant a motion *ex parte* if it will not adversely affect the rights of the other party. Thus, a motion to substitute counsel, assuring the Court that the substitution will not cause delay, will probably be granted *ex parte.*

If a taxpayer is adversely affected by a motion that has been granted *ex parte,* he should make a prompt motion for reconsideration and request that a hearing on the motion be held. The taxpayer should assert that the deprivation of his opportunity to contest the motion and be heard by the Court is a violation of his constitutional rights. Although there is no authority directly supporting such a constitutional claim, the Court will generally give the taxpayer an opportunity to be heard in every case where the adverse effect of the motion is substantial and there is relevant authority supporting his right to be heard.[9a] In seeking to protect the taxpayer's rights, it has even been held that a taxpayer was entitled to argue a motion to dismiss for lack of jurisdiction at a location reasonably convenient for his appearance.[10]

PROCEDURE ON MOTIONS CALENDARED FOR HEARING. Motions set on the calendar for a hearing will be argued orally before the Court. The Court, in its discretion, may fix the place for argument in Washington or in a city where a division of the Court sits regularly. Tax Court Rule 27(a)(2) provides that

If a party fails to appear at the call of the motion calendar, the Court will hear the proceeding *ex parte.* However, a memorandum or brief stating the position of the petitioner upon the pending motion will be accepted, when the failure of the petitioner to appear is justified by distance, shortness of time, or other good reason stated in such memorandum or brief.

Thus, if the petitioner and his counsel are from New York City and the hearing for argument of the motion is calendared for Washington, counsel may submit a brief in lieu of making a personal appearance to argue the motion. The brief, in addition to setting forth the petitioner's argument in support of the motion, should explain counsel's failure to appear.

The desirability of submitting a brief in support of a motion depends on the nature of the motion. If counsel is relying on a number of decisions and authorities to support his motion or if the factual background of the

---

[9a] See Schildhaus v. Commissioner 370 F.2d 549 (C.R.2d) holding that the petition cannot be dismissed in the taxpayer's absence when no advance notice of such action was given.

[10] Maxfield v. Commissioner, 153 F.2d 325 (C.A.9th).

motion is very complex, a brief supporting the motion may be quite desirable.

ARGUING THE MOTION.   When both parties appear at the oral argument, each will be heard. The party making the motion will present his argument first; then the opposing party will answer. The practice as to oral argument is informal and to some extent dependent on the presiding judge. Generally, if counsel wishes to rebut the answering argument he will be allowed to do so. The practice is designed to give each party every opportunity to be heard, and even the right to surrebuttal will not generally be foreclosed.

DISPOSITIVE MOTIONS—MOTIONS TO DISMISS

Jurisdictional Grounds

The Court will grant a motion to dismiss a petition for lack of jurisdiction unless the petition demonstrates that a deficiency has been determined and that a notice of deficiency was mailed.[11] A dismissal for lack of jurisdiction will also be granted if it appears that the petition was not filed within 90 days of the mailing of the deficiency notice [12] or that the petitioner is not the proper person to file the petition.[13] A motion to dismiss for lack of jurisdiction is usually made by the Service, but can be made by either party or the Court at any time. In fact, this motion has been granted when made by the service in its brief submitted after the hearing.[14] If the motion to dismiss for lack of jurisdiction is granted, the Court is in effect deciding that it has no authority to hear the case. Obviously this motion will generally be made by the service, but in some circumstances the taxpayer may also wish to make it since, if granted, a subsequent tax refund suit is not barred. If there is a serious question regarding the jurisdiction of the Court, counsel may feel it necessary to resolve the issue before the time for filing a refund claim expires. If he does not do this, a successful motion by the Service after the time for filing a claim for refund expires will prevent the taxpayer from obtaining an adjudication before any tribunal.

The Court will follow its general policy by hearing the motion for dismissal in Washington. However, if a taxpayer requests hearing of argument on the motion at a place convenient to him, it has been held that the Court must comply with his request.[15]

---

[11] *Cf.* Mutual Lumber Co. v. Commissioner, 16 T.C. 370.

[12] Drouin v. Commissioner, 203 F.2d 953 (C.A.3d).

[13] Falls City Pontiac Co. v. Commissionr, 15 T.C. 977, *aff'd*, 194 F.2d 536 (C.A. 6th).

[14] Goldstein v. Commissioner, 22 T.C. 1233.

[15] Maxfield v. Commissioner, *supra* note 10.

Motion To Dismiss as a Matter of Law

In order to succeed in getting the Court to grant a motion to dismiss a petition or strike an answer, the moving party must show that even if all factual allegations in the pleading are true, it cannot, as a matter of law, sustain the position of the party submitting the pleading. Thus, when such a motion is addressed to the petition, the Court will assume that the averments in the petition are true and, in effect, will apply the law to them as if they were findings of fact after a hearing. For example, if the petition alleges that the Service erred in disallowing, to the extent of $975, a business gift of $1,000, the Court will decide that, even if the taxpayer did make a gift of $1,000, as a matter of law $975 is not deductible, and the petition will be dismissed. Of course, if the petition fails to allege facts essential to his case, the petition will fail to state a claim as a matter of law.

Although the taxpayer is entitled to use the motion to dismiss as a matter of law, he seldom has the opportunity to do so because the answer will normally contain denials that create factual issues, thus making such a motion inappropriate. To refer again to the simple business gift illustration, if the taxpayer alleges 100 gifts of $25, the answer will usually deny this allegation. Thus, a question of fact as to whether the gifts were made will be raised and a dispositive motion will not be granted. When the taxpayer does make this motion, it is often called a motion to strike the answer. The opportunity to make such a motion arises when the answer contains affirmative pleadings, such as an allegation of fraud or the inclusion of a new deficiency. In this connection, it should be noted that the answer as well as the petition may be dismissed as a matter of law not only because the conclusory allegations, if taken as true, do not state a legally valid claim or defense but also because inadequate facts in support of a claim or defense are alleged.[16] Thus, when the Service alleges fraud, it must allege sufficient facts that, if proved, will support the claim. For example, an allegation by the Service that the taxpayer failed to report income with intent to commit fraud or even an allegation that the taxpayer's bank deposits exceeded reported income are too conclusory and do not state sufficient facts to support the claim of fraud. In order to support such a claim, the answer must allege the dates and places where deposits in excess of reported income were made. While the specificity required in a fraud claim is somewhat greater than the standard in other cases, in each instance where a motion to dismiss is made because the facts alleged do not constitute a valid claim or defense, it is the specific factual allegations and not the conclusory allegations that **are** considered.

[16] Commissioner v. Licavoli, 252 F.2d 268 (C.A.6th).

Often the motion to dismiss may be obviated by changing the form of the pleading or by adding new facts. If the taxpayer's counsel can do this, he should promptly request leave to file an amended petition and submit a copy of such a petition with his moving papers.[17] In such instances, leave to amend will usually be granted, and if the amended petition cures the defects, the motion to dismiss will be denied. If counsel fails to amend the pleading after a motion by the Service, the Court may issue an order directed to the defects that, if not complied with, will be grounds for dismissal.[18]

Motion To Dismiss for Failure To Prosecute

Failure to appear at a hearing may result in a dismissal of the petition for lack of prosecution, but the Court will exercise its discretion in so doing and may treat the case as being submitted by the absent party.[19] In this respect, Rule 27 (c) (3) provides

Attendance at trials.—The unexcused absence of a party or his counsel when a case is called for trial will not be the occasion for delay. The case may be dismissed for failure properly to prosecute or the trial may proceed and the case be regarded submitted on the part of the absent party or parties.

PROCEDURAL MOTIONS

There are numerous procedural motions made in the Tax Court. These are similar to procedural motions available in any other forum. The following is a discussion of those motions that have special significance in the Tax Court.

Motion To Amend the Pleading

A petition may be amended at any time before the answer is filed. Once the answer has been filed, the petition may be amended only upon consent of the Regional Counsel or by permission of the Court.[20] When the Court's permission to amend is sought, the moving papers should state the reasons for the amendment and should be accompanied by the proposed amendment. Generally, the Court is liberal in considering motions to amend, and such a motion will be granted unless the amendment will prejudice the adverse party, or the introduction of new matter or the tardiness of the motion is

---

[17] See California Brewing Ass'n v. Commissioner, 43 B.T.A. 721, where motion to amend petition was deemed too late when made when case called for hearing.

[18] Fisher v. Commissioner, 149 F.2d 540 (C.A.7th); see also Tax Ct. R. 18.

[19] Cf. Fisher v. Commissioner, 149 F.2d 540 (C.A.7th).

[20] Tax Ct. R. 17(b).

likely to disrupt the calendar. Thus, the earlier the motion is made, the greater its chances of being granted.[21]

Motions Addressed to Adversary's Pleading

A party may address a motion to the pleadings of his opponent. Rule 17(c)(1) of the Court states.

> The Court upon its own motion, or upon motion of either party showing good cause filed prior to the setting of the case for trial, may order a party to file a further and better statement of the nature of his claim, of his defense, or of any matter stated in any pleading. Such a motion filed by a party shall point out the defects complained of and the details desired.

The taxpayer's motion to obtain a proper answer will generally be in the form of a motion to strike the answer in its entirety or to strike specific paragraphs on the ground that it does not comply with Rule 14. The motion may also be labeled a motion for a further and better statement.[22] The Service's motion may also bear this label or may be in the form of a motion to dismiss the petition. Regardless of the labels of these motions, their purpose is the same—to obtain a better and further statement of a claim or defense or any other matter stated in a pleading.

When a motion for further and better statement is made, the party to whose pleadings the motion is addressed may immediately file an amended pleading that corrects the defects. Rule 27(a)(3) states that the prompt filing of a proper pleading correcting the defects "may obviate the necessity of a hearing on the motion." It is quite appropriate that the Court afford the party a fair chance to correct a defective pleading rather than strike it forthwith, since the purpose of the motion addressed to the pleading is to obtain a correct pleading.

When a proper pleading is not filed in response to the motion, the Court will make a decision on the motion *ex parte* upon notice and opportunity to object, or after a hearing on the motion. The Court is authorized to use its discretion either to calendar the motion for hearing or to make a decision *ex parte*.[23] If a motion addressed to the pleading is granted, the Court will order the party whose pleading is found defective to file a corrected pleading. If the party fails to comply with such an order,

> The Court may strike the pleadings to which the motion was directed or make such other order as it deems just, if an order of the Court to file amended pleadings hereunder is not obeyed within 15 days of the date of the service or said order or within such time as the Court may fix.[24]

---

[21] See Steele-Wedeles Co. v. Commissioner, 63 F.2d 541 (C.A.7th), *affirming* 11 B.T.A. 279, where motion to amend petition was denied when made one year after filing.

[22] See Marcia Silk Mills, Inc., P-H Memo TC, ¶ 54, 186.

[23] Tax Ct. R. 17(c)(2).

[24] Tax Ct. R. 17(c)(3).

Thus, if a party fails to utilize the opportunity promptly, the pleading to which the motion is addressed will be dismissed or stricken.[25]

Motion for Severance of Issues

A motion may be made to obtain a separate hearing on a single fact or group of facts at issue between the parties even though no provision for such a motion is made in the Rules of the Court. The Court has broad discretion in granting such a motion but uses it sparingly and only where adjudication of the severed issue will dispose of the entire case. The issue of the statute of limitations is a good example of the type of issue that may be severed.[26] If this issue is resolved in favor of the taxpayer, it will dispose of the entire case and the necessity of hearing the other issues will be avoided. Other issues that may be appropriate for severance are whether the petitioner is the transferee [27] or whether a closing agreement precluded further deficiency determinations.[28] On the whole, experience indicates that severance results in expediting relatively few cases and, if not limited, is used as a dilatory tactic. Thus, the Court grants such motions only when it is absolutely clear that time will be saved by severing the issues.

Motion for Consolidation

If a common issue is determinative of several cases and a uniform result is desirable, the Court will, upon motion of the various taxpayers, consolidate the cases to permit a common hearing. In this way shareholders of a dissolved corporation,[29] members of a partnership,[30] beneficiaries of a trust,[31] trustees of a single trust,[32] and similarly situated transferees [33] have obtained common trials even though they would not be permitted to file joint petitions.[34] In such cases, the Service will often have no objection to consolidation, and counsel should attempt to obtain endorsement to that effect on the moving papers.

A motion to consolidate stands a better chance of success if the positions of the various petitioners coincide. In addition, the Court may consider whether granting the motion will delay a particular case or disrupt the Court's calendar, and whether the petitioners are represented by the same

---

[25] *Cf.* Fisher v. Commissioner, *supra* note 19.
[26] *E.g.,* Central Paper Co. v. Commissioner, P-H Memo TC, ¶ 58,048.
[27] Gideon-Anderson Co. v. Commissioner, 20 B.T.A. 106.
[28] Phillips v. Commissioner, 8 T.C. 1286.
[29] Johnson v. Commissioner, 19 T.C. 465.
[30] Ford v. Commissioner, 19 T.C. 200.
[31] Clyde v. Commissioner, 32 B.T.A. 799.
[32] Pelton v. Commissioner, 32 B.T.A. 198, *aff'd*, 82 F.2d 473 (C.A.7th).
[33] Clovis v. Commissioner, 32 B.T.A. 646.
[34] Sparrow v. Commissioner, 20 B.T.A. 865.

or different counsel.[35] In cases in which the interests of the parties are different and each is represented by different counsel the motion has little chance of succeeding even though a common question of fact may be involved.[36] In such cases, a common trial would involve problems of cross proof, cross examination, and other controversies among the parties that would not arise at separate hearings.

Motion for Continuance

It is the Court's policy to refuse to grant postponements as a matter of course. This policy is embodied in the Rules which provide

> Court action on cases set for hearing on motions or trial will not be delayed by a motion for continuance unless it is timely, sets forth good and sufficient cause, and complies with all applicable Rules.[37]

The reasons for this policy, which is contrary to the practice in many state courts, are better understood when the nature of the Tax Court and its calendar are considered, A judge of the Court comes to a city to sit for a week or two, and such an appearance in the same city may occur only once a year. Thus, the judge's program in each city must be carefully arranged and followed to the greatest extent possible. Moreover, counsel is advised of the approximate date of the trial session six months in advance and is given an opportunity to object to the tentative date in response to the Trial Status Request. If counsel wants a continuance, he should make his request as early as possible. This will reduce the possibility that the request will be denied because it is not timely and enable him to have adequate time to prepare his case if the motion is denied. If counsel acts quickly enough he may be able to get a "no-objection" endorsement.

The motion for a continuance may be granted even though it is not made immediately after the issuance of the trial calendar if counsel can show good cause.[38] Thus, if the taxpayer or an important witness is taken ill, the motion will usually be granted.[39] In these circumstances it is desirable that a doctor's certificate accompany the moving papers submitted to the Court. The certificate should state that the illness exists, describe its nature briefly, and, if possible, estimate the period of disability.

If both parties advise the Court that they have agreed on a settlement and are in the process of reducing it to writing or getting the necessary

---

[35] Community Water Serv. Co. v. Commissioner, 32 B.T.A. 164.

[36] *Ibid.*

[37] Tax Ct. R. 27(d)(1). For a detailed discussion of motions for a continuance made at the calendar call, including citation of several significant cases, see p. **8·4** *infra.*

[38] See Szilagye v. Commissioner, P-H Memo TC, ¶ 50,231, *aff'd sub nom.* Silagye v. Commissioner, 192 F.2d 886 (C.A.2d), where two continuances were granted to allow the taxpayer to obtain counsel but a third was denied.

[39] *Cf.* Katz v. Commissioner, 188 F.2d 957 (C.A.2d).

approvals within the Service or that they are about to agree on a settlement, a continuance will usually be granted. With respect to conflicting engagements of counsel or the fact that new counsel is appearing as ground for a continuance, the Tax Court Rules state,

> Conflicting engagements of counsel or the employment of new counsel will never be regarded as good ground for continuance unless set forth in a motion filed promptly after the notice of hearing or trial has been mailed or unless extenuating circumstances are shown which the Court deems adequate.[40]

While there is a possibility that the Court, due to reluctance to deprive the taxpayer of an opportunity to be heard, may grant a continuance at the call of the calendar, counsel should not under any circumstances rely on the Court granting a continuance at that time.

TAX COURT "DISCOVERY"

No Discovery Mechanism for Taxpayer

There is no formal Tax Court procedure that a taxpayer can utilize to discover what testimony a witness will give at the hearing or what evidence is in the Service's possession.[41] While the taxpayer may take depositions of a witness, these may be taken for evidentiary purposes and only when the witness will not be available to testify at the trial or when the deposition is to be submitted in lieu of testimony at the trial.

It should be noted that the absence of taxpayer's discovery in the Tax Court stems from the Court's policy of refusing applications for the taking of depositions for discovery purposes. Hence, within the framework of the present Tax Court Rules discovery could be permitted. It is possible, therefore, that the Tax Court could change its practice and permit taxpayers discovery in appropriate cases without changing the Tax Court Rules. Moreover, the "Freedom of Information Act" [42] (effective July 4, 1967) may be interpreted to permit taxpayers access to some government materials of value to them in the course of a Tax Court case.

Discovery Mechanism Available to Service

While there is no formal discovery procedure available to the Service either, it can achieve discovery by use of the administrative subpoena, since

---

[40] Tax Ct. R. 27(d)(2).

[41] Starr v. Commissioner, 226 F.2d 721 (C.A.7th), cert. denied, 350 U.S. 993. Cf. Louisville Builders Supply Co. v. Commissioner, 294 F.2d 333 (C.A.6th). But see Robida v. Commissioner, 371 F.2d 518 (C.A.9th), in which the appellate court remanded the case to the Tax Court and expressly stated that discovery proceedings by the taxpayer would be appropriate.

[42] 5 U.S.C. § 1002 (as amended, July 4, 1966).

the Service is authorized to conduct investigations for the purpose of ascertaining the correctness of any tax return.[43] Toward this end, the Code empowers the Service to require the production of any books, papers, or records deemed relevant for examination and to summon any taxpayer, his agents, or any other person deemed proper to appear before the Service.[44] Persons so called may be required to testify under oath. Generally, taxpayers and witnesses cooperate during the administrative procedure that precedes the issuance of the 90-day letter, and the Service is seldom required to resort to its statutory powers to summon taxpayers or witnesses. In cases where a summons is required, it is usually issued and the necessary information obtained prior to the assertion of the deficiency in the 90-day letter. Consequently, the Service will seldom use its authority while a Tax Court case is pending, although the authority is available if circumstances require its use. Taxpayers have tried to restrict the examination of witnesses during the dependency of a Tax Court case but have been unsuccessful. It has been held that the right to inspection and examination continues notwithstanding the fact that a petition is pending before the Tax Court.[45] Thus, the Service effectively has a discovery procedure not available to the taxpayer.[46]

EVIDENTIARY DEPOSITIONS

Purpose and Use of Depositions

Either party to a Tax Court case may take the deposition of the taxpayer or witness for evidentiary but not discovery purposes.[47] The deposition is a sworn statement of the witness made in response to oral or written questions. The testimony of the witness contained in the deposition may be introduced at the hearing as evidence and will be considered by the Court in the same manner as testimony given at the hearing.[48] Depositions may be taken solely for the purpose of preserving testimony or obtaining testimony from witnesses who cannot testify at the hearing. Although the Rules are not explicit in this respect, depositions will not be permitted for the purpose of discovering the facts or evidence that an adverse party will use to support

[43] IRC § 7602.

[44] *Ibid.*

[45] Bolich v. Rubel, 67 F.2d 894 (C.A.2d). See also National Plate & Window Glass Co. v. United States, 254 F.2d 92 (C.A.2d), *cert. denied,* 358 U.S. 822, in which the Court noted that administrative subpoenas were available to ascertain the existence of additional deficiencies that could be raised in a pending Tax Court proceeding.

[46] In practice, the Service rarely uses its available discovery, however.

[47] See Tax Ct. R. 45.

[48] See Carey Salt Co. v. Commissioner, 26 B.T.A. 675, *rev'd on oher grounds sub nom.* Commissioner v. Emerson Carey Fibre Prods. Co., 70 F.2d 990 (C.A.10th), where depositions lodged with the Court but not offered in evidence were not considered. See also Tax Ct. R. 47.

his case.[49] In this respect, the practice in the Tax Court differs substantially from the practice in the district courts, the Court of Claims, and most state courts.

How To Obtain the Deposition

STIPULATION BY PARTIES.   Depositions may be taken either by leave of the Court or upon stipulation by the parties.   Rule 45(e) of the Court, which provides for the taking of a deposition by oral questions pursuant to stipulation of the parties, states: "At any time after issue is joined, the parties or their counsel may, by stipulation duly signed and filed, take depositions . . . In such cases, no order to take depositions will be issued, but they shall be taken and returned by the officer in accordance with the Rules of the Court." This method for arranging for the taking of a deposition is the simplest and most desirable, saving the time and effort of both parties as well as that of the Court. Under this procedure the parties may agree, for their own convenience and that of a witness, that the witness' testimony will be submitted by deposition rather than in person at the trial, even though the witness is available to testify at the trial. This procedure is also for the convenience of the witness, but it is contingent upon the agreement of both parties, and the convenience of the witness will not be a determining factor if either party insists that the witness testify at the hearing. In some instances the parties may be able to reach agreement that all testimony can be in the form of depositions, thereby obviating the necessity of a hearing.

When the parties agree to take a deposition, they execute a stipulation conforming to the requirements of the Court.[50]

DEPOSITION BY PERMISSION OF THE COURT.   If a deposition cannot be obtained by stipulation, the party wishing to take a deposition must file with the Court an original and two copies of a verified application to take a deposition.[51] The Court has promulgated an official form (Form 5–A) to be used for this purpose.[52] Copies of the form will be furnished by the Clerk of the Court upon request, and whenever possible the official form should be used. When the space furnished on the form is inadequate, "a substitute form may be used, but the substitute must contain all of the information called for on the Court's form." [53] Thus, when the Court's form is not used, the form used by the petitioner must parallel the official form as closely as possible; the numbering on the Court's form should be followed and the printed language copied verbatim.

[49] *Cf.* Louisville Buliders Supply Co. v. Commissioner, *supra* note 41.
[50] As set forth in Tax Ct. R. 45(e).
[51] Tax Ct. R. 45(a).
[52] See Tax Court Form No. 13, p. C·50–51.
[53] Tax Ct. R. 45(a).

When an application to take a deposition is filed, the Clerk will serve a copy on the other party and will allow a reasonable time for objection.[54] If no objection is made, the application will generally be granted. If objection is made, it will often be on the ground that the reasons for taking a deposition rather than using direct testimony are inadequate or because the date or place for taking the deposition are inconvenient. When objection is made on the latter ground, the Court may fix an alternate time and place for taking the deposition. When the objection is made because the grounds for taking the deposition are inadequate, a hearing for argument of the motion may be requested. If it appears probable that the witness will be unable to testify at the hearing because of age or illness, the motion will probably be granted. If the witness resides a great distance from the place of trial or expects to be out of the country for an extended time so that his appearance at the trial will work a great hardship or inconvenience, or cause a substantial expense, this may also be sufficient ground to allow a deposition to be taken. A deposition will not be permitted, however, merely because the witness is too busy to appear and testify at the hearing or because his appearance causes minor inconvenience.

If the motion for taking a desposition is granted, the Court will fix the time and place for taking the deposition.[55]

When Depositions May Be Taken

A deposition may be taken only after the petition has been filed in the Tax Court. Taxpayers have attempted to obtain depositions prior to the isuance of the 90-day letter but have not been successful.[56] The Tax Court has held that this procedure is not available even though the Federal Rules authorize the taking of a deposition for the purpose of preserving testimony prior to the commencement of an action in the District Courts. As to the latest time for taking a deposition, Rule 45(b) provides

> Applications to take depositions must be filed at least 30 days prior to the date set for the trial of the case, and such depositions must be completed and filed with the Court at least 10 days prior to the trial . . . *Provided, further,* That under special circumstances, and for good cause shown, the Court may otherwise order.

Procedure for Taking Deposition

When a deposition is taken in the Tax Court the procedure is quite similar to that in other federal courts. When the witness appears to have his deposition taken in response to oral questions, he will take an oath or

---

[54] Tax Ct. R. 45(d).
[55] *Ibid.*
[56] Louisville Builders Supply Co. v. Commissioner, *supra* note 41.

affirm that the answers he is about to give are true.[57] Representatives of both parties will be present as well as an officer authorized to administer the oath. Any person authorized to administer oaths under federal or state laws will suffice.[58] Rule 45(c) of the Court further provides that an employee or any person connected with either of the parties shall not administer the oath unless both parties consent and unless no one else is available.

Once the witness has been sworn, the party who sought the deposition will question the witness. Following the completion of this part of the deposition, the other party may conduct cross examination. Redirect examination may then be had if desired. The questions put to the witness as well as his answers are recorded verbatim.[59] Either party may exclude from the room during the taking of the deposition any person whom either expects to call as a witness at the hearing.[60] If such person remains despite the request, he will not be permitted to testify without the consent of the party who requested his exclusion.[61]

If a party wishes to object to "errors and irregularities in the manner of taking the deposition, in the form of any question or answer, in the oath or affirmation, or in the conduct of parties, and errors of any kind which might have been obviated, removed or cured," [62] such an objection must be made during the taking of the deposition.[63] If such an objection is not made at this time, the right to make objection will be waived and will not be considered at the hearing. Objections to the competency of a witness or objections based upon the competency, relevancy, or materiality of testimony may, however, be made at the hearing even though they are not raised at the taking of the deposition.[64] It is nonetheless the safest policy to make such objections during the taking of the deposition if possible, because an objection, even though it is based on competency, relevancy, or materiality, will be waived if "the ground for the objection is one which might have been obviated or removed if presented at or before the time of the taking of the deposition." [65] Thus, if a party has failed to elicit testimony showing that the witness had knowledge of the facts to which he has testified, an objection based on competency raised at the hearing might be precluded by arguing that the examining party could have laid a proper foundation had the objection been raised previously. Consequently, objections raised at or before the taking of the deposition will preclude any possibility that the objection is not timely.

[57] Tax Ct. R. 45(f).
[58] IRC § 7622.
[59] Tax Ct. R. 45(f).
[60] Tax Ct. R. 45(g).
[61] *Ibid.*
[62] Tax Ct. R. 47(a)(2).
[63] *Ibid.*
[64] Tax Ct. R. 47(a)(1).
[65] *Ibid.*

When an objection is raised, it is noted verbatim on the transcript. Lengthy comments or argument relative to the objection are unnecessary.[66] When an objection is made, the question put to the witness may be withdrawn or rephrased, or the witness may answer the question as it stands. If the question is answered over the objection, the Court will rule on the validity of the objection at the hearing.

Depositions upon Written Interrogatories

WHEN WRITTEN INTERROGATORIES ARE USED. The Tax Court will not permit depositions upon written interrogatories to be taken unless great expense or inconvenience must be incurred in order to take the testimony by deposition upon oral questions. Generally, the use of the deposition upon written interrogatory is confined to situations where a witness is in a foreign country, in which case such a deposition is required.[67] The Court, in its discretion, may dispense with the requirement that such a deposition be used, but this is not a likely occurrence.

Aside from a situation in which the witness is in a foreign country, the Court will not permit depositions upon written interrogatories unless the inconvenience is comparable to that when a witness is abroad. Thus, there might be sufficient inconvenience when a witness is in Alaska and the place of the hearing is in New York.

HOW TO OBTAIN DEPOSITION UPON WRITTEN INTERROGATORIES. Depositions upon written interrogatories are obtained in substantially the same manner as depositions upon oral questions. The application to take the deposition in either manner is submitted on the same form, the caption in this case indicating that it is an "Application To Take a Deposition upon Written Interrogatories." An original and five copies of the interrogatories must be filed along with the application.[68] Once filed, the application and a copy of the interrogatories will be served on the adverse party by the Clerk of the Court. The adverse party then has 15 days in which to object to the taking of the deposition, to object to specific questions in the interrogatory, or to file cross interrogatories.[69] If cross interrogatories are filed, they will be served on the moving party who will then have 15 days to object.[70] No objections to interrogatories or cross interrogatories will be permitted at the hearing unless they are previously raised during the appropriate 15-day period.[71]

---

[66] Tax Ct. R. 45(f).
[67] Tax Ct. R. 46(d).
[68] Tax Ct. R. 46(a).
[69] *Ibid.*
[70] *Ibid.*
[71] Tax Ct. R. 47(b).

The application to take a deposition upon written interrogatories must be filed sufficiently in advance of the trial to permit the entire process of serving interrogatories, cross interrogatories, the taking of the deposition, and the filing, which must be completed at least 10 days before the trial.[72] Thus, in order to be safe, the initial application for a deposition upon written interrogatories should be filed at least 3 months before the hearing is scheduled.

TAKING DEPOSITION UPON WRITTEN INTERROGATORIES.   The taking of the deposition upon written interrogatory proceeds in much the same manner as a deposition upon oral questions. The officer taking the deposition reads the interrogatories and cross interrogatories to the witness. After each question is read, the witness gives his answers which are stenographically transcribed.[73] No person is permitted to be present during the taking of the deposition except the witness, the officer taking the deposition, and the reporter.[74]

DESIRABILITY OF USING WRITTEN INTERROGATORIES.   Although situations in which counsel will have a choice of using oral questions or written interrogatories are limited, some discussion of their relative merits is warranted. The purpose and use of both depositions are the same, namely to obtain evidence that can be introduced at the trial in lieu of testimony. If counsel is completely familiar with the testimony the witness is going to give and is able to prepare questions to elicit this testimony, written interrogatories may be as effective as oral questions as well as being more convenient. Generally, however, the ability to follow up when the witness misunderstands a question, fails to give a clear answer, or opens a promising avenue of inquiry makes depositions on oral questions a more effective tool for obtaining testimony than written interrogatories.[75] Furthermore, the Court has indicated that it gives less weight to evidence obtained by written interrogatories, thus favoring that obtained by oral questions.

Cost of Depositions

The party at whose request the deposition of a witness is taken will be required to pay the costs of taking and preparing the deposition.[76] The fees and mileage paid to witnesses in Tax Court cases are the same as those paid in United States District Courts.[77]

---

[72] Tax Ct. R. 46(a).
[73] Tax Ct. R. 46(b).
[74] *Ibid.*
[75] See the Tax Court's comments in Roerich v. Commissioner, 38 B.T.A. 567, 578, *aff'd,* 115 F.2d 39 (C.A.D.C.), *cert. denied,* 312 U.S. 700.
[76] IRC § 7457(b).
[77] 28 U.S.C. § 1821.

USE OF NOTICE TO PRODUCE

Generally, a taxpayer will have possession of all documents he wishes to introduce as evidence at the hearing. In unusual circumstances, however, the Service may have obtained a document from a third party or from the taxpayer which the taxpayer does not have. If the taxpayer wishes to utilize such a document as evidence, he may compel the Service to produce it. Although there is no rule specifying the taxpayer's right to compel production or the procedure for doing so, the Tax Court has sanctioned this practice in a number of cases.[78]

In order to obtain the desired documents, the taxpayer's counsel should prepare a Notice to Produce and serve duplicate originals upon the Chief Counsel in Washington and upon the Regional Counsel at the local office. If the Notice is to be effective, it must specify the document or documents desired with sufficient clarity so that the Service can identify them. The Notice must also give the Service a reasonable time prior to the hearing to produce the documents. If the Service fails to produce the documents requested and can give no satisfactory explanation for such failure, an inference will arise that the evidence contained in such documents is unfavorable to the Service.[79]

STIPULATIONS IN THE TAX COURT

Use of Stipulations

In the majority of Tax Court cases a substantial part of the facts are stipulated, thus saving the time and effort of the parties and the Court.[80] In

---

[78] *E.g.*, Capento Securities Corp. v. Commissioner, 47 B.T.A. 691, 697–98, *aff'd,* 140 F.2d 382 (C.A.1st).

[79] *Ibid.*

[80] The Tax Court's "Special Notice for the Guidance of Tax Court Practitioners" (Feb., 1966) states, with respect to stipulations of facts,

"Rule 31 (*b*)(1) has been in effect since the earliest days of the establishment of this Court and recites that this Court 'expects the parties to stipulate evidence to the fullest extent to which complete or qualified agreement can be reached including all material facts that are not or fairly should not be in dispute.' Over the years other subparagraphs have been added designed to implement the workings of this general rule with respect to stipulating facts. It is compliance with this rule by the members of the tax bar that has been so effective in shortening the trial time and trial records in the trial of cases in this Court.

"Much of the evidence in Tax Court trials is in book or documentary form, where copies can be checked and agreed to. All documents that either party desires to introduce, the authenticity of which is not in dispute, and all undisputed facts should be the

order to facilitate stipulations, Rule 31(b)(1) of the Court provides

> The Court expects the parties to stipulate evidence to the fullest extent to which complete or qualified agreement can be reached including all material facts that are not or fairly should not be in dispute.

It behooves the taxpayer to stipulate as many facts in a case as is feasible. Since the taxpayer has the burden of proving the essential elements of his case, each time a fact is stipulated his burden is reduced. Thus, as between the parties, it is the taxpayer who derives the greatest benefit from stipulations.

Typical matters usually stipulated are facts necessary to establish the jurisdiction of the Court, the fact that the return was filed, the facts stated in the return, the dates on which various events occurred, the marital status of a party, the authenticity of a contract or other documents such as accounting statements and records, and similar items. The taxpayer will thus be relieved of the annoyance of establishing a foundation for and proving a myriad of simple facts.

Stipulated facts, however, are not confined to such routine matters as outlined above. Both parties should be willing to stipulate to facts that are unfavorable but cannot be controverted. For example, in a thin capitalization case, the Service may discover that the corporation to which the taxpayer has made a 'loan' had applied to a commercial lender prior to the taxpayer's loan and that the loan application was rejected by the lender. If the Service wishes to use this as evidence, counsel will accomplish nothing by refusing to stipulate that this had occurred although it may be unfavorable. In stipulating such facts, counsel is not only accepting the inevitable but engendering an atmosphere of fairness and cooperation which may enable him to secure a stipulation that may be unfavorable to the Service.

In seeking stipulations from the Service, counsel may be able to get the Service to stipulate to facts that, while true, may be expensive and difficult to prove and that could conceivably be controverted. Counsel may accomplish this if he can convince the trial attorney that his ability to contest a fact is weak and that the chances of offsetting the taxpayer's proof are minimal, thus making it not worthwhile for him to attempt to do so.

In addition to stipulating facts, the parties may also stipulate various

---

subject of stipulation. An objection on the ground of materiality or relevance, with respect to any documentary evidence or any other facts about which there is no dispute as to authenticity or truth, may be noted in the stipulation or at the time of trial, but such objection is not to be regarded as just cause for refusal to stipulate as to such documents or facts.

. . . .

"These rules with respect to stipulation are mandatory and the Court expects all practitioners before it to observe them, to the end that cases be quickly submitted, with only disputed facts the subject of testimony by witnesses."

procedural matters such as taking the testimony of certain witnesses by deposition rather than by producing them at the trial. The parties may also stipulate as to the area of the dispute, thereby narrowing the issues for trial.

Procedure for Obtaining Stipulations

It is in obtaining a stipulation that the exercise of skill by counsel is required. Generally, stipulations can be obtained either informally by consent or by a motion made to the Court. The second method, although described as a 'motion for an order to show cause why certain facts should not be stipulated,' is actually quite similar to a request for admissions used in many states and in the Federal courts. The procedure for obtaining this order will be dealt with subsequently. Its use in practice is an exception rather than a rule.

There is no formal procedure for procuring a stipulation. If taxpayer's counsel has not approached the Regional Counsel concerning stipulations by the time the case is calendered for trial, the Regional Counsel will contact counsel. It is almost always desirable for counsel to take the initiative in obtaining stipulations rather than wait for the Regional Counsel to contact him. When routine matters are the only facts to be stipulated, the ultimate stipulation will be the same regardless of how the stipulation process is handled. If, however, counsel wishes to maximize the facts to be stipulated, he should approach the Service. Counsel should be mindful that the process of obtaining stipulations is basically one of persuasion and negotiation. Approaching the Service in good faith and with a cooperative attitude will afford him a better basis for negotiation and persuasion and permit him to obtain stipulations at the earliest date.

It is desirable for taxpayer's counsel to prepare the stipulations. In selecting the facts to be stipulated, he should exercise his judgment. He should not request stipulation of facts that he cannot reasonably expect Regional Counsel to stipulate. Such a request would merely demonstrate that counsel intends to be unfair and might result in the failure of Regional Counsel to stipulate any facts that are the least bit doubtful. To obtain stipulations, counsel should request a conference at the office of the Regional Counsel. Prior to the conference, he should carefully prepare proposed stipulations and gather all possible evidence supporting the proposed stipulations. The proposals and the supporting evidence should be brought to the conference and should serve as the starting point for the negotiations. Although substantial work may be involved, this procedure is likely to result in the most favorable stipulations, thus reducing the taxpayer's burden at the trial.

It is sometimes difficult to obtain a stipulation as to the authenticity of a document without obtaining a stipulation as to its meaning, since quesions may arise as to which of these the parties have stipulated. If counsel is asked to stipulate a document, he should be extremely cautious; it is conceivable that significant evidence relating to the document may be precluded by an objection to admissability on the ground that the document speaks for itself. In these circumstances, counsel should attempt to obtain a stipulation to all of the related evidence or be ready to risk its exclusion. If he is willing to run this risk, he should see to it that the stipulation clearly indicates the intention to stipulate the authenticity of the document and not the meaning. Counsel should never stipulate the meaning when he intends to submit additional evidence on that matter.

All stipulations must be signed by counsel and by the Service in the name of the Chief Counsel. (The Regional Counsel and Associate Regional Counsel are authorized to sign a stipulation on behalf of the Chief Counsel.) Generally, stipulations will be negotiated with a trial attorney, and his recommendations will be accepted by Regional Counsel. In rare instances, however, Regional Counsel may refuse to accept the trial attorney's recommendations. This is an important reason for counsel to initiate the stipulation procedure at an early stage of the proceedings. When he waits to be contacted by the trial attorney, the hearing may be imminent by the time the contact is made. Any stipulations agreed upon must be forwarded to the Regional Counsel for signature and approval. If they are not forwarded until shortly before the hearing and the Regional Counsel does not accept the trial attorney's recommendations, counsel may learn on the eve of the hearing that he must prove facts he assumed would be stipulated.[81] Thus, until counsel has an executed stipulation, he must be prepared to offer proof of the stipulated matters. The problem of being ready to offer proof on all matters can easily be obviated if counsel attempts to obtain stipulations at an early stage of the litigation.

When a stipulation is signed, it is filed in duplicate with the Court. Exhibits are annexed to the original copy only.

Drafting the Stipulations

The stipulation should contain the same caption set forth at the head of all papers submitted to the Tax Court in connection with the same case. Immediately below the caption the stipulation should be marked *"Stipulation of Facts."* Following the caption and heading, a preamble will appear, which should state,

It is hereby stipulated that for the purposes of this case the following statements are accepted as facts and all exhibits referred to herein and attached hereto are incorporated and made a part of this stipulation subject to the right

---

[81] See Lantz Bros. v. Commissioner, 139 F.2d 192 (C.A.6th), in which the failure of the Service to expedite the approval of proposed stipulations was deemed an adequate ground for a postponement.

of either party to object to the admission in evidence of such facts or documents on the grounds of immateriality or relevancy, provided, however, that either party may introduce other and further evidence not inconsistent with the facts herein stipulated.[82]

Although signing a stipulation does not waive the right to introduce additional evidence, it is the better practice to reserve that right explicitly.[83] The same is true with respect to reserving the right to object to stipulated facts on the ground of admissibility. When a stipulation contains many facts that counsel believes are immaterial or irrelevant, he may consider requesting that they be placed in a separate stipulation in order to emphasize his objection to their admissibility. It should be remembered that objection to the admissibility of facts does not constitute a proper ground for refusing to stipulate.

The most important part of the stipulation is, of course, the statement of the stipulated facts. In preparing the stipulation, the language used to express the facts is extremely important, as disputes may arise as to just what the parties intended to stipulate.[84] By drafting the language of the stipulation with great care, such disputes can be eliminated or at least minimized. In this connection, it is obvious that it will be advantageous for counsel to prepare the stipulations if he wishes his own language to be used.

Set out below is an example of a portion of the facts stipulated in connection with a case involving an attempt by a taxpayer to deduct a partnership loss:

1. Morton Lieb and Marsha Lieb (hereinafter referred to as petitioners) are husband and wife. They reside at 1050 Fifth Avenue, New York, New York. They filed a joint 1965 income tax return (a copy of which is attached hereto as Exhibit 1) and a joint 1966 income tax return (a copy of which is attached hereto as Exhibit 2) with the District Director of Internal Revenue, New York, New York. Petitioners use the cash method of accounting.

2. From June 1, 1960 to date, Morton Lieb held the majority interest in the partnership of Morton Lieb & Company (hereinafter referred to as the partnership). Attached as Exhibit 3 is a copy of the 1966 form 1065, United States Partnership Return of Income for Morton Lieb & Company which was filed with the District Director of Internal Revenue, New York, New York

· · · · · · · · · · · · · ·

4. Attached as Exhibit 4 is a copy of Morton Lieb & Company's amended partnership agreement dated July 1, 1965. Pursuant to this agreement, the partnership was to commence, and it did in fact commence business on July 1, 1966 with an aggregate capital of $650,000.00.

---

[82] See Tax Court Forms Nos. 14–16, pp. **C**·52–58.

[83] See, *e.g.*, Russell Box Co. v. Commissioner, 208 F.2d 452 (C.A.1st), where the taxpayer tried unsuccessfully to prevent a challenge to the correctness of book entries that the parties stipulated were made.

[84] *E.g.*, Lane-Wells Co. v. Commissioner, 134 F.2d 977, 979–80 (C.A.9th), *rev'd*, 321 U.S. 219.

5. Capitalization of the partnership resulted from contributions to the capital of the partnership by each of the partners in the amount set forth opposite his name as follows:

Morton Lieb	—	$500,000.00.
John Morris	—	100,000.00.
Arthur Miles	—	50,000.00.

. . . .

14. The respondent determined that the partnership did not suffer a deductible loss as claimed.

15. By notice of deficiency dated July 24, 1967, the respondent determined a deficiency in the petitioners' 1966 income tax aggregating $34,000.00.

16. The only adjustment in that notice of deficiency which is in dispute in this case is the disallowance, as not deductible, of the $32,000.00 loss claimed by the petitioners for 1966 and carried back by them to 1963.

It can be seen from the foregoing sample that the stipulation consists of separately numbered paragraphs, each stating a fact or a related group of facts. The language is simple and concise. The sentences and paragraphs are short. By formulating the stipulation in this fashion it is clear to the parties and the Court what is being stipulated. Moreover, it can be seen that the stipulation summarizes certain facts that can be gleaned from a reading of the exhibits, such as in paragraph 4 above. While not essential, it is helpful to the Court to express the significant portions of exhibits in summary style. (It can be seen from paragraph 16 that the stipulation pinpoints the area of the dispute between the parties.) Exhibits should be marked serially and numbered 1, 2, 3, etc., if offered by the petitioner or lettered a, b, c, etc., if offered by the Service.[85]

Effect of Stipulations

Generally, the Court will not receive evidence tending to qualify, change, or contradict any fact properly introduced into the record by stipulation.[86] The Court may, however, according to Rule 31(b)(6), set aside a stipulation in whole or part where justice requires.[87] The widespread practice of entering into stipulations as previously described and their importance to the Court in managing its calendar obviously indicate that facts stipulated between parties will be taken to be true in all but unusual circumstances, such as cases in which evidence is introduced without objection and such evidence clearly and convincingly contravenes a stipulated fact. In such a case the stipulation may be disregarded. Generally, a timely objection interposed at the trial will prevent the introduction of evidence that contravenes a stipulation.

[85] Tax Ct. R. 31(d).
[86] Tax Ct. R. 31(b)(6).
[87] *Ibid.*

Stipulations may also be vitiated on the ground that there was mistake or fraud in inducing their execution.[88] Stipulated facts may not be effective when the parties disagree as to the meaning of the stipulation and each argues mistake and a different interpretation of the stipulation. For this reason stipulations must be carefully drafted in clear and indisputable language. This is also an important factor that weighs in favor of preparation of the stipulation by taxpayer's counsel.

Finally, it should be noted that stipulations entered into that contravene the revenue laws or other statutes will be deemed ineffective [89] as will be stipulations of law.[90]

Compulsory Stipulation upon Motion

If for some reason a party is unwilling to stipulate facts not genuinely in dispute or has failed to confer with his adversary for the purpose of obtaining stipulations, the party who wishes to obtain a stipulation can have the Court compel his adversary to stipulate. This procedure is similar to a request for admission in the federal courts, compelling the adversary to admit certain facts as true. It also relieves the moving party of proving facts that should not be disputed. In view of Regional Counsel's cooperative attitude toward stipulation, the taxpayer will rarely be in a position to make this motion, and it is most often made on behalf of the Service.

If no stipulation has been entered into at the time the trial calendar is issued and a party wants to compel stipulation, he may file a motion with the Court for an order to show cause.[91] This must be done within 50 days but not less than 35 days prior to the date set for the hearing.[92] The order will require the adverse party to show cause why the facts and evidence covered in the motion should not be accepted as established facts for purposes of the case.[93] This motion should contain adequate references to the sources of information that establish the facts sought to be stipulated as well as a statement as to whether such sources are in the control of the moving party and, if they are, that the opponent has had reasonable access thereto.[94]

The form of such a motion will generally conform to that of other motions made in the Court. When filed, it should be accompanied by proof of

---

[88] See Logan Lumber Co. v. Commissioner, 365 F.2d 846 (C.A.5th), abrogating a stipulation based on an erroneous interpretation of law which was clarified when the Supreme Court reversed a line of cases on which the stipulation was based. Hub Cloak & Suit Co. v. Commissioner, P-H Memo TC, ¶ 56, 196.

[89] Littauer v. Commissioner, 25 B.T.A. 21.

[90] Gaddy v. Commissioner, 38 T.C. 943.

[91] Tax Ct. R. 31(b)(5).

[92] Ibid.

[93] Ibid.

[94] Ibid.

service on the opposing party or his counsel. The proposed facts should be shown with particularity and set forth in separately numbered paragraphs. The basis for establishing the facts should be set forth in detail. In preparing the motion papers, counsel should be mindful that the Regional Counsel will be required to show why each paragraph should not be established as fact. Consequently, if the various facts or groups of facts are organized in separately numbered paragraphs, Regional Counsel will be compelled to controvert a number of paragraphs individually rather than address himself to one or two paragraphs containing a diverse collection of facts. Thus, the probability of having at least some, if not all, of the facts stipulated will be increased.

In acting on such motions, the Court will generally exercise its discretion by issuing an order to show cause. The exercise of discretion in granting such motions effectuates the Court's policy of obtaining stipulations whenever possible. Thus, when counsel submits motion papers adequately supported by the facts, the Court will usually grant the order.

The party against whom the order to show cause has been issued has 25 days from the date of such order to file a response listing by number the paragraphs to which there is no dispute.[95] If there is disagreement as to any paragraph in the proposed stipulation or to any part thereof, the response should so state. If the objection is to wording of a paragraph, it should show the basis for disagreement and set forth supporting sources of information. Objections as to relevancy may be noted but are not grounds for refusal to stipulate.

Generally, argument will be heard and rulings made upon the stipulations when the case is called on the trial calendar. Hence, the moving party must be prepared to prove the facts in the stipulation should the Court rule adversely on the motion. If practical, the Court may allow argument of the motion prior to the calenda; call. Appropriate action concerning stipulations should, therefore, be taken at the earliest possible date.

SUBMISSION OF A CASE WITHOUT TRIAL: RULE 30

From time to time there are cases that can be submitted to the Court without the testimony of any witnesses. The two most typical situations appropriate for such submissions are (1) when the parties have stipulated all of the facts and the sole issue for decision by the Court is a question of law and (2) when all of the evidence on an issue of fact is embodied in stipulations and depositions. In these situations, the parties may immediately submit the case to the Court for decision.[96] They need not wait for

---

[95] *Ibid.*
[96] Tax Ct. R. 30.

the case to be calendared, nor need they appear in person.[97] If the parties wish to proceed in this manner, they are required merely to submit a notice to the Court.

Upon receipt of the notice, the Court will assign the case to a judge for decision. If counsel wishes to make an oral argument and to submit a brief in support of his case, he must apply to the Court for leave to do so. It is desirable to make such an application, since this affords a good opportunity to persuade the Court that the taxpayer's position should prevail. After the application is granted, the Court will fix a time for oral argument and for filing briefs.

When Rule 30 procedure is followed, the case is treated much like cases brought before an Appellate Court. The parties submit a record, make oral arguments, and submit briefs supporting their decisions. The advantage of this procedure is twofold. First, the time and expense involved in a trial are eliminated. Second, the disposition of the case by the Court is substantially hastened by the elimination of the time that the parties must wait before the case is placed on the calendar and the time that elapses before the case is tried. If counsel believes that the live testimony of his witnesses will not measurably improve his chances, this procedure is desirable. Certainly, where much of the important evidence consists of documents or books and credibility is not a factor, there is usually no reason for a hearing.

In adopting Rule 30 procedure, the petitioner must be cautious. The fact that the case is substantially stipulated and that Regional Counsel has agreed that the appearance of witnesses and the necessity of a hearing are superfluous does not necessarily mean that the stipulated facts and other evidence submitted by the taxpayer constitute a *prima facie* case. In this respect, Rule 31(g) states, "The provisions of Rule 30 do not relieve the party upon whom rests the burden of proof of the necessity of properly producing evidence in support of issues joined on questions of fact." Consequently, prior to consenting to a Rule 30 submission, counsel must be certain that the stipulated facts and other evidence he is submitting are sufficiently strong to carry the burden of proof.

THE PRETRIAL CONFERENCE

Pretrial conferences are held by the Court solely for the purpose of narrowing issues, stipulating facts, and simplifying the presentation of evidence.[98] Toward this end the Court may assist the parties in negotiating appropriate stipulations of fact and by giving indications or advance rulings on how it will treat the admissibility of certain evidence and the burden of

[97] *Ibid.*
[98] Tax Ct. R. 28(a).

proof. Although the pretrial conference is not generally used to obtain stipulations where the parties themselves have failed to obtain such stipulations, Rule 28(d) does provide that

. . . a pretrial conference for the purpose of assisting the parties in entering into the stipulations called for by Rule 31(b)(1) will be held by the Court only where the party requesting such pretrial conference has in good faith attempted without success to obtain such stipulation from his adversary.

In cases in which stipulations have been prepared and are simply awaiting approval by the Regional or Assistant Regional Counsel, counsel may request a pretrial conference at which he can enlist the aid of the Court in facilitating the signing of the stipulations by the Service.

When a case is calendared for hearing, either party or the judge may request a pretrial conference. Generally, pretrial conferences will be held after the call of the trial calendar. If a party wishes a conference prior to the time the case is calendared for hearing, he may make a motion requesting such a conference or the Chief Judge may fix such a conference. Generally, conferences requested prior to the time a case is placed on the calendar will be set for the next sitting of the Court in the city where the hearing has been requested. The Court, in its discretion, may fix such a conference in another convenient city or in Washington. A request or motion for a pretrial conference must state the reasons for the conference. No conference will be held if the request is frivolous or made for the purpose of delay.[99]

[99] Tax Ct. R. 28(d).

SETTLEMENT OF TAX COURT CASES

Tax Court cases are usually resolved by settlement. In fact, approximately four-fifths of all Tax Court cases are settled by the parties.[1] The Tax Court is hard pressed to decide the cases that come before it now and would be totally overwhelmed should the number of cases reaching the Court increase substantially. Thus, if the taxpayer wishes to discuss settlement, Treasury Department policy is designed not only to facilitate it, but to encourage it. In the following pages, settlement procedures and tactics are discussed.[2]

STATUTORY AUTHORITY FOR SETTLEMENT

The Internal Revenue Code authorizes the Secretary of the Treasury or his delegate to compromise any civil tax case arising under the internal

[1] Annual Report of the Commissioner of Internal Revenue of the United States for the Fiscal Year Ended June 30, 1964, 18.

[2] See pp. 1·12–28 *supra* for a discussion of prelitigation settlement procedure.

revenue laws.[3] Generally, the reasons that may justify a compromise are doubt as to the liability of the taxpayer or doubt as to the collectibility of the tax.[4] The Code further requires that whenever a compromise is reached, the reasons for the compromise and the details concerning it shall be filed in the records of the Treasury or the Service.[5]

SETTLEMENT PROCEDURES

In settling a tax dispute, differing settlement procedures are followed depending on whether or not the taxpayer has utilized his right to have a formal settlement conference with the Appellate Division prior to the issuance of the 90-day letter.

Procedure in Absence of Pre-90-Day-Letter Conference

If no formal conference has been held with the Appellate Division prior to the issuance of the 90-day letter, the Regional Counsel will turn over the taxpayer's file to the Office of the Assistant Regional Commissioner, Appellate Division, as soon as issue has been joined in the Tax Court. The Appellate Division will then assign the case to a conferee who is required to analyze the factual data and promptly arrange a conference for the purpose of discussing settlement. This procedure is required in every case in which no formal conference is held during the period prior to issuance of the 90-day letter.[6]

The time and place of the settlement conference are arranged informally, at the convenience of the petitioner's counsel, Regional Counsel, and the conferee. Except in "unusual circumstances," Regional Counsel will be represented at the conference by a trial attorney. If the settlement discussions are not fruitful, the Appellate Division will bring settlement discussions to a conclusion following the issuance of the Trial Status Request. (The Request is usually issued 6 months after the petition is filed and 6 months prior to the opening date for the session at which the trial is calendared.) Thus, the file will usually be returned to Regional Counsel substantially in advance of the issuance of the trial calendar (this occurs 3 months after the issuance of the Trial Status Request), and, at the latest, by the time the calendar is issued. The negotiations may continue beyond this date only if the Regional Counsel consents in writing. The purpose of this policy is to afford Regional Counsel ample time for trial preparation. The

[3] IRC § 7122.

[4] Treas. Reg. § 301.7122–1. The following procedures relate to compromises based on questionable liability.

[5] IRC § 7122(b).

[6] See Rev. Proc. 60–18, 1960–2 CUM. BULL. 988, for a description of the settlement procedures applicable to cases pending in the Tax Court.

taxpayer will be advised in writing when the file has been returned. If it appears to the Appellate Division conferee at an earlier stage that settlement is not feasible, he will return the file immediately and advise the taxpayer in writing accordingly.

Procedure When Pre-90-Day-Letter Conference Has Been Held

If the taxpayer has had a formal conference with the Appellate Division prior to the issuance of the 90-day letter, the Service will take no action with respect to settlement of the case. In this instance, the taxpayer must take the initiative if he wishes to discuss settlement.

Once the taxpayer has filed his petition with the Tax Court, the Service will be receptive to settlement proposals even though such negotiations may involve reviewing matters already explored at the previous conference; the very fact that the petition was filed indicates that attempts to settle previously failed. There are no formal procedures that must be complied with to arrange a settlement conference. If the taxpayer's counsel has occasion to meet the trial attorney in the Regional Counsel's office, he will be happy to arrange a conference. If not, a letter or telephone call to the Regional Counsel or to the Assistant Regional Commissioner, Appellate Division, will be sufficient to initiate a conference.

Appropriate Time To Settle

Obviously, the sooner settlement is reached, the more satisfactory it will be to all concerned. In selecting the time for requesting settlement negotiations, taxpayer's counsel should be mindful of the practice of concluding negotiations, whenever possible, by the time the trial calendar is issued. It is the Service's stated policy to settle cases that can be settled as early as possible and in no event later than the time trial preparations are intensively commenced. When an early settlement can be effected, both parties are saved the time, effort, and expense involved in preparing a case for trial. It should be noted, however, that despite the efforts by the Service to obtain early settlement and particularly to avoid settlements on the courthouse steps, a number of cases are nonetheless settled just before the trial session or even after the session has begun. Even at this late date the Service may be willing to accept an offer of settlement that is fair and equitable, but there is some risk in this sort of strategy since once preparations have been made, the Service may prefer to proceed to trial.

No general rule stating the optimum time to settle can be formulated. The innumerable human factors, such as the attitudes of the Appellate conferee, the trial attorney, the taxpayer, and his counsel, as well as considerations as to the merits of the case, the available evidence, and the taxpayer's finances make such a formulation impossible. As stated before, the most definitive statement that can be made is that the sooner settlement is reached, the better, and the taxpayer has nothing to lose by an intensive effort to settle at the beginning of the negotiations. If the negotiaions are unsuccessful, the taxpayer will at least know where he stands early in the proceedings and have more time to prepare his case or to consider any alternative actions that may be available to him.

Conducting Negotiations

The settlement negotiations themselves are conducted in the same manner regardless of whether a formal conference has been held. The procedure is completely informal. The conferee from the Appellate Division will conduct the negotiations, and a trial attorney from the staff of the Regional Counsel will participate. In cases where a formal conference has been held previously, the same conferee will generally be assigned to the negotiations held after the filing of the petition in the Tax Court.

Although the taxpayer, his counsel, and the conferee may have had no success in reaching a settlement at the formal conference, many cases are nonetheless settled in the post-petition conference. A number of factors may contribute to this success. First, the parties are closer to trial and may thus be more eager to settle. Second, the emphasis at the formal conference and at the post-petition conference is somewhat different. In the former the conferee, while trying to compromise, is also reviewing the decision of the revenue agent. In the latter, the conferee is basically trying to reach a compromise that will be consistent with policy. The difference, while subtle, is not without some significance. The third, and often most important, factor is the participation of the trial attorney from the Regional Counsel's office. The trial attorney will not have participated in prior discussions and will usually provide a fresh and somewhat more trial-oriented approach. The trial attorney can function to some extent as a mediator and may persuade both the taxpayer and the conferee to adopt more moderate positions. Furthermore, he may be in a position to recognize certain weaknesses in the Service's case that the conferee has not noted. Since the trial attorney has the job of trying the case, he is in a better position to appreciate the problems concerning admissibility of evidence, burden of proof, probative value of evidence, and credibility of the witnesses. This, of course, can also work against the taxpayer where weaknesses in his own case become apparent to the trial attorney at the conference.

Should a situation arise in which the taxpayer's counsel believes he cannot, due to personality problems, make any progress toward settlement with the conferee assigned to him, he may request a meeting with the Assistant Regional Commissioner, Appellate, or with an Associate Chief of the Conference Staff of the Division. The granting of such a conference is within the discretion of the Chief of the Conference Staff. Such a meeting is most unusual and should be requested only if the conferee is extremely unreasonable or if a personality conflict with the conferee precludes a reasonable settlement.

Effectuating Settlement

When a settlement among the taxpayer, trial attorney and conferee is reached, the conferee prepares a memorandum setting forth the proposed settlement together with his analysis and recommendation. A detailed computation of the tax or refund due is then prepared and forwarded with the conferee's memo to the Assistant Regional Commissioner, Appellate, or his delegee for approval. If approval is granted the file is forwarded to the Regional Counsel's office where the trial attorney prepares a settlement decision which is sent to the taxpayer for execution subject to further approval and acceptance by the Service. The executed settlement decision is then generally forwarded to Regional Counsel or his delegee for final acceptance. If final acceptance is conferred, as it almost always is, all that remains is filing with the Court.

SETTLEMENT TACTICS AND CONSIDERATIONS

Desirability of Settlement

The first step the taxpayer and his counsel should take in considering settlement is evaluation of the case. They should consider the applicable law, the facts that must be established to succeed, and the evidence that can be adduced to prove the facts needed. If the evidence is in the form of oral testimony, the creditibility and effectiveness of the witness must be considered. After making an equivalent evaluation of the position to be taken by the Service, some estimate of the likelihood of winning or losing can be made.

Second, taxpayer and counsel must consider what can be gained or lost if the case is tried. They must consider whether the taxpayer is likely to get at least a partial victory or whether it will be an all-or-nothing decision. For example, if the issue concerns a deduction, such as travel expenses, a partial victory may be possible, whereas if the issue is one of a legal interpretation, such as whether an exchange is tax free or taxable, the decision may result in total victory or total loss. Consideration must also be given to what may be lost as a result of a trial in addition to the tax dollars at issue. Clearly the expenses of the trial and a possible appeal should be weighed. In addition, such diverse matters as unfavorable publicity and the taxpayer's health must be taken into consideration.

Finally, an extremely important element in some cases will be the effect a decision will have on related items of tax in future and prior years. This factor will arise in cases involving depreciation schedules, accounting methods, and other matters affecting taxes in more than one year. While at this stage the risk is small, consideration must be given to the possibility that the government will amend its answer to raise new issues, thereby increasing the deficiency and the taxpayer's liability.

Once these factors and others like them have been considered, a judgment as to the desirability of settlement can be made.

Tactics in Negotiating

Once counsel has assembled the supporting evidence and legal precedents, he must utilize them to persuade the trial attorney and conferee of the strength of his case. In order to accomplish this and achieve a favorable settlement, counsel must be well prepared when he arrives at the conference. He should have with him a list of the legal authorities supporting his position and excerpts from any authorities that may be particularly persuasive. He should also be prepared to summarize the evidence to be submitted in support of his case. Where such evidence can be documented (*e.g.,* checks, affidavits, contracts, etc.), he should have the documentation or be prepared to supply it. Submission of a written memorandum supporting the taxpayer's case is often quite helpful. An element that will influence the Service's desire to settle is the effectiveness of the taxpayer's counsel. A well-prepared and persuasive presentation at the conference will demonstrate that the taxpayer will be effectively represented at the trial.

One thing the taxpayer's representative should not have with him at the conference is his client. If counsel has properly prepared himself by eliciting all of the relevant facts from the client, the latter will have little to contribute to the conference and may say things better left unsaid. He may object to concessions that should be made and disrupt the rapport that counsel, the trial attorney, and the conferee can establish among themselves as professional people doing their job. An exception to this rule may be the case turning on the taxpayer's testimony and credibility. If, in a case like this, the taxpayer is a credible and persuasive witness, his presence at the conference may be desirable as it will demonstrate to the trial attorney what is in effect a strong point of the taxpayer's case.

In conducting the settlement negotiations, counsel must be mindful of the fact that there is no discovery procedure in the Tax Court. Consequently, he should utilize all of his evidentiary data only if there seems to be a genuine prospect of settlement. To this end, counsel should begin by making a generalized presentation of his case, stating the facts and law in a conclusory manner and indicating that he can support his statements with evidence. He should then try to get some indication of the Service's position on settlement. If the position of the Service makes settlement out of the question, it is best to terminate the negotiations without disclosing the details of the evidence. If ultimate settlement seems a realistic possibility, counsel should then present his case in detail, including full factual and legal documentation. The disclosure of any information during this process is usually worthwhile since in most cases it will facilitate a more advantageous settlement. Moreover, even if the case is not eventually settled, the trial attorney will usually feel constrained to rebut the taxpayer's facts and authorities, thereby affording an equal amount of disclosure of the Service's case.

Finally, it should be said that no settlement offer ought to be accepted without some reflection. The time that transpired between a tentative agreement reached at the conference and the final approval by the taxpayer should be used for thorough consideration as to the desirability of making the final committment.

Basis for Settlement

In most civil cases one party will be trying to recover a specific sum of damages from the other party as compensation for a specific act or transaction. In such a case, the claim can be settled by agreeing on a flat sum that the defendant is willing to pay, this amount being less than the plaintiff demanded. Tax cases may also be settled in this way regardless of whether one or several items are in issue. Because several issues are often in dispute, the means of arriving at a settlement are somewhat more variable than in the simple civil case. The flat cash settlement method may be applied on an issue-by-issue basis, or one party may concede entirely on some issues while the adversary concedes on the others. Another alternative is to concede completely on some issues and make a flat cash adjustment on the others. The taxpayer's representative should be mindful, however, of the government's strict policy of refusing to settle any case purely on the basis of nuisance value.

Another peculiarity of tax litigation is that settlement of an issue in dispute may affect the taxation of other items not in dispute. In these situations the settlement must spell out the agreement of the parties as to how the resolution of disputed items will affect items not in dispute.

As in other civil cases, the ability to pay may affect the settlement. The Treasury Regulations specifically authorize the Service to take collectability into account in compromising a claim.[7] These procedures are utilized by the collection division after the amount of liability has been agreed upon between the taxpayer and the representatives of Appellate and Regional

[7] Treas. Reg. § 301.7122–1.

Counsel outlined above. In connection with uncollectable claims the Service has adopted certain formal procedures. The taxpayer must execute Form 433, requiring him to make a sworn statement, under penalty of perjury, stating his assets, liabilities, income, and expenses in detail. The taxpayer is also required to execute Form 656, which sets forth in detail when the compromised amount will be paid.[8]

Desirability of Submitting Written Settlement Offer

As previously indicated, the taxpayer is not compelled to submit a written settlement offer. Nonetheless, except in the simplest cases, it is desirable to do so because the preparation of an offer will enable the taxpayer and his counsel to make sure of their understanding of the proposed settlement. Counsel will thus state precisely what the proposal is and cover in the settlement all related items for the year in question. Any misunderstandings will become apparent to the trial attorney and the conferee when they receive the written offer. Moreover, when the taxpayer reviews a written settlement proposal before it is forwarded to the Service, any misunderstanding on his part as to the terms of settlement will be avoided.

GOVERNMENT REVIEW OF PROPOSED SETTLEMENTS

When a settlement among the taxpayer, trial attorney and conferee is reached, the conferee prepares a memorandum setting forth the proposed settlement together with his analysis and recommendation. A detailed computation of the tax or refund due is then prepared and forwarded with the conferee's memo to the Assistant Regional Commissioner Appellate or his delegee for approval. If approval is granted the file is forwarded to the Regional Counsel's office where the trial attorney prepares a settlement decision which is sent to the taxpayer for execution subject to further approval and acceptance by the Service. The executed settlement decision is then generally forwarded to Regional Counsel or his delegee for final acceptance.[9]

The conferee and trial attorney have no authority to settle on their own, but their recommendations are usually accepted. If both the Regional Counsel and the Assistant Commissioner approve of the settlement, it is accepted by the Service. If only one of them accepts the settlement, the proposal is forwarded to the Chief Counsel in Washington for decision. His decision is final. Such disagreements between the Regional Counsel's office

---

[8] See Administrative Practice Form No. 11, page **C**·22.

[9] Authority to settle is vested in these two individuals or their delegates. Generally, the settlement function is delegated to the Chief of the Conference Staff—or his assistant, in cases involving less than $50,000—and to an Assistant Regional Counsel.

and the Appellate Division are very rare, and most cases are settled at the regional level.

The only other cases sent to the Chief Counsel are those involving refunds of an overpayment or overassessment in excess of $100,000. In these cases the Internal Revenue Code requires that the Chief Counsel send the proposal to the Congressional Joint Committee on Internal Revenue Taxation together with his recommendations.[10] The Joint Committee will return the offer with its comments to the Chief Counsel for final action.

The settlement procedure after the opening of the trial session for which hearing of the case is calendared is somewhat different. While settlements prior to the opening of the session require the joint approval of Regional Counsel and the Appellate Division, settlements after the opening of the trial can be made by the Regional Counsel alone since he has sole jurisdiction over the case at that point. Such settlements are thus final when the trial attorney obtains the approval of the Regional Counsel.

[10] IRC § 6405.

CHAPTER 8

TRIAL PROCEDURES IN TAX COURT CASES

CALENDAR PROCEDURE

The Trial Status Report and Report Calendar

Approximately six months before a case is expected to be reached for trial, the Court will issue to each party a request for a trial status report.[1] The request will specify a future date upon which it is anticipated that the case will be heard and will request information on the progress of the parties' preparations. A portion of the order will be in the following form,

[1] See Tax Court Form No. 17, p. C·59.

which is to be filled in by each of the parties and returned to the Court:

Response to this Order on behalf of petitioner is required to ascertain the status of this case for trial and must be made by use of the enclosed copy. The same information has been requested from respondent for that purpose.

1. It is expected that this case must be tried _____, or is it likely that it will be settled without trial? _____.

2. If this case must be tried, will it be ready for trial at the session indicated above? Yes_____. No_____. If the answer is No, or if trial at that session is not appropriate, state why. (If awaiting outcome of other litigation, state case and Court.)

---

3. Give the best present estimate of time required for the trial of this case assuming that all material facts which are not, or fairly should not be, in dispute are stipulated pursuant to the Court's Rule 31(b)._____hours.

Note Rule 31(b)(1) and the requirement for stipulation conference in Rule 31(b)(2) in connection with this item.

The order may also request further information as to other matters affecting the hearing, such as the number of witnesses to be called.

If the case is settled prior to the return of the response, it will be so indicated in Item 1, above, and stipulations of settlement will be filed. If it is indicated that a basis for settlement has been reached or is likely to be reached, the case will be calendared at a Washington Motions Session for settlement purposes. If the case is settled prior to that time the appropriate settlement documents are filed. If settlement has not been reached, both parties must be present to report their progress to the Court. At this stage, the Court will calendar the case for further report or for a hearing, depending on whether or not the parties indicate that a settlement is likely.

When one party reports in Washington that it is prepared for trial while the other reports that it is not, the case will be placed on the report calendar in the city where the trial is anticipated. By placing the case on a report calendar in the city designated for trial, the Court can often prod the unprepared party into readying his case. When both parties indicate that they will not be ready for trial on the date anticipated, the case will not be scheduled for hearing at the date suggested.

It should be remembered that the order for a trial status report is not a notice of trial and that a trial calendar will not be prepared until expiration of the 75-day period allowed for trial status responses.

Procedure at the Calendar Call

When the Court has collected the necessary information, a calendar of the cases to be reported and tried is made up, and a Notice of Trial will be sent to each party approximately 90 days prior to the first day of the session for which the case is calendared.[2]

[2] Tax Ct. R. 27(c)(1). See Tax Court Form No. 18, p. **C·60**.

The Court's trial sessions will generally last for two weeks. On the first day of the trial session the calendar will be called. Each case will be called in the order it appears on the docket for purposes of evaluating the case and assigning an order for trial. Briefly, the procedure of the calendar call is as follows:

1. As each case is called, the Court will hear statements by counsel concerning the readiness of the case and the estimated time for hearing. A request for a particular date during the session hearing may be entered.
2. Motions for continuance may be argued immediately or deferred until the call is completed.
3. Requests for pretrial conferences will be considered and conferences will be scheduled.
4. When the call is completed and motions for continuance have been heard, the Court will announce a tentative date and time for hearing each case.

As previously indicated, in addition to cases placed on the calendar for trial, a case may have been scheduled on the calendar merely for a report on the development of preparations for trial. During the calendar call these cases will be called prior to those for which a hearing is scheduled. This is the so-called calendar report specified in Rule 27(b), which provides that counsel must

. . . report as to whether the case is to be tried or otherwise disposed of, and if the latter, to report on its status, and second, if it is to be tried . . . report on the current status of preparations for trial. . . .

After the Court hears a report by counsel on the status of the case, it may set it down for a hearing or for further report at a subsequent session or for report at a motion term in Washington.

When a case is calendared for trial and not merely for report at the calendar call, counsel or the parties will state their estimate of time required for trial or file stipulations in lieu of trial.[3] Counsel will generally not be required to give more than a mere estimate of the number of hours required for the hearing, but if it is indicated that the trial may be lengthy, the Court may inquire as to the number of witnesses to be called and the nature of the issues.

Obtaining a Convenient Hearing Date. When counsel steps forward to estimate the time required for trial, he may also raise any problems relating to the availability of out-of-town witnesses and preferences for hearing dates. In this matter, counsel for the petitioner and the Service should meet in advance of the calendar call and agree on a mutually convenient date. This preference may then be made known to the Court, which will generally attempt to accommodate witnesses or counsel who are from out of town. Preferences as to hearing dates may be denied, how-

[3] Tax Ct. R. 27(c)(2).

ever, by some judges who make a practice of hearing cases in the order in which they appear on the calendar. Preferences may also be ignored when previously scheduled cases are disposed of sooner than expected. Since the latter situation is common, counsel and witnesses should be ready so that an appearance on short notice can be made when necessary.

MOTIONS FOR CONTINUANCE. Motions for continuance may be argued at the calendar call or, if contested, may be scheduled for argument after the other scheduled cases have been heard.[4] As previously indicated, unless good cause for delay is shown, continuances will not be granted. Conflicting commitments of counsel, witnesses, or the taxpayer do not constitute good cause for delay.[5] The Court has only limited time in each city, and the general attitude of the Tax Court judges is that matters before the Court should take precedence over conflicting commitments. Furthermore, since counsel are given 90 days' notice as to the date of the calendar call, the inconvenience is not too severe.

While the Court is reluctant to grant continuances, it has been known to do so where good cause, such as illness of counsel, the taxpayer, or a witness, is shown. In these circumstances it may be helpful to have a medical certificate to certify illness. When the taxpayer's reasons are less valid, the Court may nonetheless grant a continuance requested at the calendar call though it will rarely do so when the request is made a second time. Counsel, however, should not rely on receiving a continuance at the calendar call, as the willingness to grant such a motion will vary from judge to judge. Clearly, the safest policy is to be prepared to try the case when it is called, since cases can be disposed of rather suddenly either at the calendar call or shortly after being called for hearing.

BURDEN OF PROOF

The General Rule—Petitioner Has Burden of Proof

At a hearing in the Tax Court, the taxpayer has the burden of proving that the deficiency determined by the Commissioner is incorrect.[6] There

---

[4] See Tax Ct. R. 27(d) and Chiquita Mining Co. v. Commissioner, 148 F.2d 306 (C.A.9th), in which the Tax Court was upheld in refusing to grant a continuance owing to unavailability of two of taxpayer's witnesses. Compare Lantz Bros. v. Commissioner, 139 F.2d 192 (C.A.6th), in which the Tax Court's refusal to grant a continuance to allow the taxpayer to obtain the Service's agreement to a stipulation was deemed reversible error.

[5] Tax Ct. R. 27(d)(2). Compare United States v. Koplin, 227 F.2d 80 (C.A.7th) (criminal prosecution), in which taxpayer's counsel had been led to believe that complicated tax-fraud cases would not be called for trial and had made other commitments. Reviewing the refusal of a continuance, the Court of Appeals held that such refusal deprived the taxpayer of his constitutional right to counsel.

[6] Tax Ct. R. 32; Taylor v. Commissioner, 70 F.2d 619 (C.A.2d), aff'd, sub nom. Helvering v. Taylor, 293 U.S. 507.

are, however, several exceptions. These apply to new matter pleaded by the Commissioner and in specific circumstances set forth in the Internal Revenue Code.

New Matter in the Answer

The Commissioner has the burden of proving any new matter pleaded in his answer.[7] Consequently, the Commissioner has the burden with respect to proof of any additional deficiencies asserted in the answer [8] or of any affirmative defenses.[9] Similarly, the burden is on the Commissioner when he alleges new adjustments to support the deficiency or when he abandons the theory of his deficiency notice and adopts and alleges a new and inconsistent ground or theory to support his assertion.[10]

Thus, when the Commissioner asserted a deficiency on the ground that advances to a corporation were non-business bad debts, it was held that the Commissioner had the burden to prove that the advances were non-deductible contributions to capital.[11] However, the burden of proof remains with the taxpayer when the Commissioner simply alleges facts supporting the deficiency asserted in the 90-day letter [12] or where the grounds asserted are consistent with the 90-day letter,[13] unless the specification of the grounds comes at such a late stage of the proceeding (*e.g.,* at the hearing) that it results in surprise to the taxpayer.[14]

Specific Statutory Rules

FRAUD CASES.   In any case where the Commissioner alleges fraud or seeks to recover fraud penalties, he has the burden of proving fraud with intent to evade payment of tax.[15]

TRANSFEREE CASES.   When the Commissioner attempts to impose liability upon a person as a transferee of property of a person liable for taxes, he has the burden of proving that the petitioner is liable for payment of the tax as a transferee of property.[16]

[7] *Ibid.*
[8] Wineberg v. Commissioner, P-H Memo TC, ¶ 61, 336, *aff'd,* 326 F.2d 157 (C.A. 9th).
[9] Falck v. Commissioner, 26 B.T.A. 1359.
[10] Tauber v. Commissioner, 24 T.C. 179.
[11] Markle v. Commissioner, 17 T.C. 1593.
[12] Newhall v. Commissioner, 10 B.T.A. 656.
[13] Sorin v. Commissioner, 29 T.C. 959, *aff'd,* 271 F.2d 741 (C.A.2d). Compare Weaver v. Commissioner, 25 T.C. 1067, 1085.
[14] *Cf.* Wilson v. Commissioner, 25 T.C. 1058, holding that a new ground was presented but noting specifically that the Commissioner first raised the new ground at trial.
[15] IRC § 7454.
[16] IRC § 6902(a).

EXTENDED STATUTE OF LIMITATIONS.   When the taxpayer interposes the statute of limitations as a defense he must prove that its 3 years have expired prior to the mailing of the deficiency notice. If, however, the Commissioner asserts that the 6-year statute of limitations applies because the taxpayer omitted more than 25% of gross income, he then has the burden of proving the omission and the consequent applicability of the longer statute.[17]

ACCUMULATED-EARNINGS CASES.   The burden of proving that a corporation's earnings and profits have accumulated beyond the reasonable needs of the corporate business, subjecting it to the accumulated earnings tax, rests with the Commissioner unless, in advance of the formal deficiency notice, he notifies the taxpayer by certified or registered mail that he intends to determine a deficiency based in whole or part on the accumulated earnings tax.[18] If notice is given by the Commissioner, the burden shifts to the taxpayer.

The taxpayer may return the burden on the issue of reasonable needs of the business to the Commissioner by filing, within 60 days after the mailing of the Commissioner's notice, a statement setting forth the grounds on which it relies to show that earnings and profits have not been allowed to accumulate beyond the reasonable needs of the business.[19] In these cases, although the burden of proof as to unreasonable accumulations may be with the Commissioner, the ultimate burden of proving that the corporation was not utilized to avoid tax on the shareholders remains with the taxpayer.[20]

RULES OF EVIDENCE

The introduction of evidence in the Tax Court is governed by Rule 31 of the Court and § 7453 of the Internal Revenue Code which provides, in part, that "the proceedings of the Tax Court and its divisions shall be conducted in accordance with the rules of evidence applicable in trials without a jury in the United States District Court of the District of Columbia." Accordingly, the evidentiary provisions of the District of Columbia Code, the United States Code, and the Federal Rules of Civil Procedure apply. In conflicts, the rule favoring admissibility of evidence is controlling. The statutory provisions governing the rules of evidence in the Tax Court are set forth in Appendix A, *infra,* pp. **A** · 2–16.

---

[17] Reis v. Commissioner, 1 T.C. 9.

[18] IRC § 534(a), (b).

[19] IRC § 534(a) ; Treas. Reg. § 1.534–2.

[20] Pelton Steel Casting Co. v. Commissioner, 28 T.C. 153, 183, *aff'd,* 251 F.2d 278 (C.A.7th), *cert. denied,* 356 U.S. 958.

SUBPOENAS

If evidence necessary to a petitioner's case cannot be obtained from witnesses who are willing to appear voluntarily on behalf of the petitioner, the appearance of such witnesses at a trial hearing or at the taking of depositions can be compelled by issuance of a subpoena.[21]

While a subpoena may in some instances foster hostility of a witness and therefore be undesirable strategically, this is not usually the case. Not infrequently, cooperative witnesses feel more comfortable about testifying if they feel they must do so.

When Subpoenas Are Available

A subpoena may be obtained to compel the attendance of a person whose testimony is relevant to facts at issue. Subpoenas are also issued to require the production of documents or records at the hearing or taking of depositions.[22]

Limitations on Issuance of Subpoena

Generally, subpoenas will be issued to any person who can give relevant testimony. Despite the statutory provisions requiring the maintainence of secrecy, Treasury Department employees can be subpoenaed. The internal rules of the Treasury Department do require, however, that employees must obtain the express consent of the Commissioner of Internal Revenue himself before responding to the subpoena. Although appearance of Service employees can be compelled, the scope of the testimony they can be required to give or of the documents they can be compelled to produce is not entirely clear. Thus, it has been held that the Service cannot be compelled to produce a confidential report prepared by a revenue agent.[23] Presumably any document given to the government can be recovered, and copies of any documents sent to the taxpayers by the government can be obtained. Any facts about the petitioner's affairs within the knowledge of the government or other information such as the filing date and due receipt of returns can be obtained. The right to obtain information from the return of another taxpayer or the return itself is uncertain.

Witnesses may not be subpoenaed in order for a party to discover information but only to give evidence. While the line between obtaining evidence and discovering evidence may not always be obvious, if it appears

---

[21] Tax Ct. R. 44.
[22] Tax Ct. R. 44(c).
[23] O'Dwyer v. Commissioner, 28 T.C. 698.

that the taxpayer is conducting a fishing expedition the subpoena will be quashed.[24]

Subpoenas may also be withheld or quashed if they request the production of documents in such broad and general terms as to be unreasonable or if they ennumerate so many documents that they are unduly burdensome to the witness.[25]

How to Subpoena a Witness

A subpoena is obtained by requesting Form 4 from the clerk of the Court. The subpoena will then be forwarded to petitioner's counsel.[26] It will be duly signed by the clerk of the Court and will bear the Court's seal but will otherwise be entirely blank. Counsel should then fill in the form by inserting the appropriate caption and the name and last-known address of the witness. In proper blank spaces on the form the time, date, and place of appearance as well as whether the appearance is at a hearing or deposition and, if the latter, the person before whom the deposition will be taken should be inserted. The form requires that the party calling the witness be indicated and that the documents to be brought to the hearing or deposition be specified.

If the subpoena requires the testimony of a business firm or corporation by an individual, it should indicate whether another agent may appear in lieu of the individual subpoenaed. Thus, as the witness it may designate "J. Doe Corp. by John Doe, President, residing at _____, or by an officer, agent or employee of said Corporation having knowledge of the facts _____ in connection with _____."

When documents are required to be produced, they should be described and enumerated with sufficient particularity so that they can be identified by the witness. Specificity in identifying documents will avoid the claim that the purpose of the subpoena is discovery or that the witness could not discern what was to be produced. Moreover, as stated above, generalized demands for documents are quashed because they are unreasonable and unduly burdensome.[27] After the subpoena is prepared, a copy must be personally delivered to the witness by a person who is at least 18 years of age and not a party to the pending case.

Enforcement of Subpoena

The Tax Court has no power to enforce subpoenas issued by it except against a party to the action. If a party refuses to respond to a subpoena

---

[24] Hamilton Web Co. v. Commissioner, 10 B.T.A. 939.
[25] United States v. Union Trust Co., 13 F. Supp. 286 (W.D. Pa.).
[26] See Tax Court Form No. 12, p. C·49.
[27] See United States v. Union Trust Co., *supra* note 25.

by failing to appear or produce documents as required therein, the Court will resolve against him any issues to which the refused testimony is pertinent. As to witnesses who are not parties, enforcement of a Tax Court subpoena can be accomplished by obtaining an order of the United States District Court requiring compliance with the subpoena. If a witness is served with such an order made by the district court and fails to comply, he will be subject to punishment for contempt of the district court.

THE HEARING

Pretrial Brief

Pretrial briefs are not generally submitted in Tax Court cases. If, however, the taxpayer's representative believes that the facts are unusually complicated, a difficult question of law is presented, or a peculiar problem of evidence may arise, it may be desirable for him to prepare and submit a pretrial brief. Although the Court seldom requests a pretrial brief, it may do so when the situation warrants. More frequent use of the pretrial brief by Tax Court practitioners would enable them to represent the taxpayer and utilize the art of advocacy more effectively. Moreover, in many instances, the submission of a brief would be helpful to the Court.

If a pretrial brief is submitted, it should be concise and introductory in nature, rather than lengthy and exhaustive. Unless an unusual problem of law or evidence is anticipated, discussion in the pretrial memorandum should be confined to the general principles of law applicable, an outline of the evidence to be offered, and the conclusion to be established.

Opening Statement

Although some judges of the Court prefer to examine the deficiency notice and petition and then ask questions of counsel, an opening statement is often made. When an opening statement is permitted, counsel should state briefly the issues involved, the facts intended to be proved, and relevant principles of law.

In other words, the opening statement should serve to assist the Court in obtaining an initial understanding of the case. To this end, an effective opening statement will include the following:

1. An introduction naming the petitioner and indicating his status, the type of tax involved, the year for which the deficiency was determined, the amount of the deficiency asserted, and the amount in dispute
2. A concise statement of the issues involved including the Commissioner's determinations and the taxpayer's denials

3. A concise statement of the issues of law involved with reference to the applicable sections of the Internal Revenue Code and an enumeration of the witnesses, an indication of the nature of their testimony, and an outline of what the evidence will prove

On preparing the opening statement, a number of things should be kept in mind. First, it should be prepared carefully in advance. Second, any argument on the merits is generally reserved for the conclusion of the hearing and should be excluded from the opening statement. Third, any reference to the actions taken by the Service prior to the statutory notice should be omitted. Finally, excessive factual detail should be avoided in order to present a concise introduction.

Generally, unless the government has the burden of proof it will not make a substantial opening statement. The Service may state, however, that it affirms the correctness of the deficiency notice or seek to correct any misstatements of the facts or issues that it believes the taxpayer has made.

Introducing Proof Established Prior to Trial

Following the opening statement, stipulations may be submitted to the Court. The Court may ask for a short clarification of the exhibits attached to written stipulations or may allow counsel to summarize portions of the stipulations to assist the Court. Counsel should be prepared for this and have some sort of written statement that can be read into the record without error or omission.

After the stipulations have been introduced, any depositions and written interrogatories may be introduced, in accordance with the provisions of Rule 47 of the Court.

In submitting such documents to the Court, it should not be forgotten that, although stipulations need not be formally presented to the Court to be considered in evidence,[28] testimony in the form of deposition will not be considered unless offered and received in evidence.[29]

Order of Proof

The evidence in a Tax Court case will be presented in much the same order as in other civil trials. Except in a situation in which the Service has the burden of proof, the taxpayer will present his case first, followed by the testimony and evidence submitted on behalf of the government and then a rebuttal by the taxpayer when warranted. At the conclusion, the Court will announce whether it will accept briefs.

[28] Tax Ct. R. 31(b)(3) eliminates the need for introduction of stipulations that have been filed with the Court.

[29] Tax Ct. R. 31(c). See, *e.g.,* Carey Salt Co. v. Commissioner, 26 B.T.A. 675, *rev'd on other grounds sub nom.* Commissioner v. Emerson Carey Fibre Co., 70 F.2d 990 (C.A.10th).

Taxpayer's Case

The taxpayer must prove the allegations in his petition. If the pretrial procedures are effectively utilized, a substantial portion of the allegations will already be established, and after introducing this material taxpayer's counsel will be able to devote his attention to proving that the Commissioner erred with respect to the substantive tax issues involved. To prevent the omission of important evidence, it is desirable for counsel to have on paper a checklist of the evidence he feels is essential to his case.

The Government's Case

A portion (frequently a substantial portion) of the government's evidence will be presented by cross examination of the taxpayer's witnesses. As the circumstances may require, the government will present witnesses and exhibits to support its contentions.

Rebuttal

After the government's presentation, the taxpayer may present evidence to rebut the government's proof. In exceptional circumstances the taxpayer may, upon leave of the Court, present new evidence.

IMPORTANCE OF THE RECORD

Since the decision of the Court is usually not written until approximately six months after the hearing, and in some cases not until one or two years after the hearing, the importance of getting all necessary facts, testimony, and other information on the record in desirable form cannot be overemphasized. Although the judge of the Court will listen diligently to the proceeding before him and will in most cases take notes, at the time he prepares his decision he will rely heavily on the record before him. Under these circumstances, if a matter has not been placed in the record, either by the proper introduction of evidence or by eliciting the appropriate testimony, it is lost for purposes of the case.

Moreover, if the record contains digressions or irrelevant material or is disorderly, the judge may find it difficult to follow or may not focus on those matters that are important to the taxpayer's case. Thus, it is essential not only that the record contain all necessary evidence but that it exclude extraneous material.

CHAPTER 9

POSTTRIAL PROCEDURES IN THE TAX COURT

THE BRIEF

Importance of Brief

At the close of the presentation of the evidence, the parties will usually be given leave by the Court to file written briefs. The brief will probably be the only, and certainly the best, opportunity to argue the merits of the case. Although Rule 35(a) states that "The parties should be prepared to make oral argument at the conclusion of a trial . . ." such argument is seldom made. A written brief to which the Court can refer when it reviews the record will more effectively present the taxpayer's position than will an oral argument crowded in at the end of the presentation of evidence at the hearing. Moreover, since the decision of the Court may not be made until some months after the hearing itself, the persuasive effect of an oral argument may be largely lost whereas a statement of the taxpayer's position in the form of a brief is always available at such time as the Court chooses to prepare its decision.

Procedure for Filing Brief

Rule 35(a) provides that "The filing of briefs . . . shall be in accordance with the directions of the Judge presiding at the trial." When the hearing is concluded, the parties usually request permission of the Court to file briefs, and, if the Court is willing to accept them, it will specify the sort of briefs it desires and the order in which they may be filed. The Court may specify that it will accept only abbreviated or memorandum briefs relating to a particular issue or that it will accept only proposed findings of fact. When a case turns mainly on the interpretation of facts and does not involve many legal issues, the Court may prefer only proposed findings of fact. In some instances the Court will indicate that it will receive no briefs whatsoever. Counsel should not miss an opportunity to file a brief. Although there have been instances in which the Court allowed one party to file a brief while denying the opportunity to the other,[1] the Court will usually accept briefs from both parties whenever it indicates that it will accept them at all.

Assuming that a number of factual and legal issues are raised at the hearing and the Court has ruled that it will accept briefs from the parties, Rule 35 will govern the filing procedure. The parties will usually file simultaneous briefs and, according to the procedure outlined in Rule 35(b),

Each party shall file an original brief within 45 days after the day on which the trial was concluded and a reply brief within another 30 days thereafter unless the trial Judge directs otherwise. . . .

There is also an alternative procedure, not mentioned in the Rules, for filing seriatim briefs. If this procedure is used, the taxpayer submits a reply to the Service's brief if necessary. This procedure can be advantageous to one or both parties and may be granted, at the Court's discretion, upon request. In the taxpayer's case, seriatim filing gives him the first and last word in the argument. In the Service's case, it may be desirable to see what issues the taxpayer argues before preparing its own brief, thus avoiding the necessity of a lengthy reply brief. Rule 35(b) further provides that a party

---

[1] Dunn v. Commissioner, 220 F.2d 323 (C.A.9th).

failing to file an original brief may not file a reply brief except by permission of the Court. If a brief is submitted after the time prescribed for filing, permission to file should be requested in a motion accompanying the brief.

Since § 7459(a) of the Internal Revenue Code requires that a report shall be made by the Court on any proceeding instituted before it, failure to submit a brief would probably not result in a dismissal of the case. Nonetheless, issues not raised in a petitioner's brief are deemed abandoned [2] and failure to file a brief might be deemed tantamount to the abandonment of all issues.[3]

Service of the brief upon the opposing party is made by the Clerk of the Court.[4] Service will be made immediately after the time for filing has expired in the case of simultaneous briefs. In the case of seriatim briefs, service will be made immediately after each brief is filed.

Contents of Brief

In the subsections below, each part of the brief will be discussed, and samples, where helpful, will be set forth.[5]

COVER PAGE AND CAPTION. The caption of the brief will be the same as that used on the petition and all other documents and papers submitted to the Court. The following format should appear on the front page of the brief:

CHARLES LESSER

Petitioner,

v. Docket No. 38574

COMMISSIONER OF INTERNAL REVENUE,
Respondent.

BRIEF FOR THE PETITIONER

J. R. Rausch
85 Broad Street
New York, New York

Counsel for Petitioner

The same caption, excluding the name and address of the counsel, should again appear in the brief immediately following the table of contents and

---

[2] Green Spring Dairy, Inc. v. Commissioner, 19 T.C. 217, *aff'd* 208 F.2d 471 (C.A. 4th).

[3] Seserman v. Commissioner, P-H Memo TC, ¶¶ 55, 293.

[4] Tax Ct. R. 35(c).

[5] The style and format of the brief should comply with the provisions of Tax Ct. R. 4 and 35(e).

the case and statutory citations, and immediately preceding the body of the brief.

TABLE OF CONTENTS. Rule 35(e)(1) requires that the table of contents be the first page of the brief. The contents should contain page references to the main topic headings in the brief as follows:

CONTENTS   Page

The page following the table of contents must set forth an alphabetical list of case citations used in the brief and references to all statutes, regulations, and other authorities relied upon.[6] When appropriate, a further section setting forth the specific provisions of controlling statutes and regulations may be included. The brief for the Service will always include such a section.

PRELIMINARY STATEMENT. The preliminary statement should provide a simple outline of the case.[7] In all instances it should include the following:

1. The tax years involved
2. The nature of the tax
3. The amount of the deficiency
4. The nature of the proof
5. The name of the judge presiding at the hearing
6. The date and place of the hearing
7. The due date of the brief
8. The appropriate statement if an overpayment is claimed or if a Rule 50 decision should be entered

The following is a typical preliminary statement:

PRELIMINARY STATEMENT

This case involves an income tax deficiency for the taxable year ended December 31, 1963 in the amount of $616.52.

The case was heard before the Honorable Arnold Raum on October 6, 1967 in New York, New York. The evidence consists of a written stipulation of facts

[6] Tax Ct. R. 35(e)(1).
[7] Tax Ct. R. 35(e)(2).

with attached exhibits, testimony and exhibits introduced at trial, and a written supplemental stipulation of facts filed subsequent to trial by leave of the Court.

The Court directed the parties to file simultaneous briefs by November 26, 1967. The due date of the briefs was extended to December 8, 1967 by leave of the Court, based on respondent's motion for an extension of time.

A computation under Rule 50 will not be necessary.

QUESTIONS PRESENTED. This section, begun on a separate page of the brief, should clearly and concisely define the issues of the case for the Court.[8] Each issue should be set out in a separate paragraph. As mentioned previously, since any issue not raised in the brief will be deemed abandoned, it is crucial that all issues raised by the taxpayer be accounted for in this section. Any issue settled or abandoned should be referred to in this section in a separate paragraph. An excerpt of the questions presented would read as follows:

QUESTIONS PRESENTED

1. Whether the payment by the petitioner of $575.00 to the Brooklyn Committee for Urban Development, Inc., during the taxable year 1963 is deductible as a charitable contribution under Section 170 of the Internal Revenue Code of 1954.

REQUEST FOR FINDINGS OF FACT. Rule 35(e)(3) provides that

The party having the burden of proof shall set forth complete *statements of the facts* based upon the evidence. Each statement shall be numbered, shall be complete in itself, and shall consist of a concise statement of the essential fact and not a discussion or argument relating to the evidence or the law. Reference to the pages of the transcript or the exhibits relied upon in support thereof shall be inserted after each separate statement.

Although Rule 35(e)(3) seems to imply that only one party should submit a statement of the facts, this is not the case. In fact, both parties will submit their requests for factual findings. This portion of the brief is extremely important since it is here that each party will present and emphasize the facts upon which he bases his case. Before preparing the findings of fact, a preliminary step is to read the record thoroughly, picking out the testimony and supporting facts from which the requested findings will be derived. The proposed findings of fact should then be organized according to topics and phrased in the language of the record. Counsel should attempt to draw up proposed findings of fact that the Court can adopt as its own findings with little or no change.

In preparing the request for findings of fact, the evidence in the record and the exhibits should be fair and accurate. Evidence should not be pre-

[8] *Ibid.*

sented out of context, and unfavorable matters should not be distorted or avoided. The best approach is to meet unfavorable evidence directly, attempting to show that its significance is not great or is outweighed by other matters. The proposed findings should be numbered and correlated with the supporting parts of the record and exhibits.[9] Reference to the pages of the record and exhibits should be inserted after each proposed finding. Each group of findings should be set out in a separate paragraph. If desired, the ultimate facts can be organized at the end of the request. Fnally, it should be remembered that the factual findings are evidentiary, and although these facts can be argumentatively presented, extraneous argument of the law or evidence of the case in the requested findings is inappropriate.

Sample portions of the findings of fact might read as follows:

1. The petitioner Charles Lesser filed a federal income tax return for the taxable year 1963 with the District Director of Internal Revenue, Manhattan District, New York, New York (Stip. par. 1).

.   .   .   .

3. Petitioner Charles Lesser drafted the certificate of incorporation for the Brooklyn Committee for Urban Development, Inc. He also prepared the application for a charitable exemption for said corporation and performed other legal functions for it (Stip. par. 3; Tr. 16 and 27; Ex. B at p. 9).

.   .   .   .

17. The Internal Revenue Service on September 8, 1964, retroactively revoked the tax-exempt status of the Brooklyn Committee for Urban Development, Inc., on the ground that it was never intended to be operated for public charitable purposes (Ex. J).

18. The Brooklyn Committee for Urban Development, Inc., exists solely to assist persons of minority races in finding adequate housing within the New York metropolitan area (Tr. 5, 7, 8, 13; Stip. par. 3).

.   .   .   .

The petitioner respectfully requests the Court to find the following ultimate facts:

26. The Brooklyn Committee for Urban Development is a charitable corporation within the meaning of Section 501(c)(3) of the 1954 Internal Revenue Code.

27. The contributions made to the Committee by the public in general and by the petitioner Charles Lesser in particular were charitable contributions within the meaning of Section 170 of the 1954 Internal Revenue Code.

POINTS RELIED UPON.   This short section following the proposed findings of fact is required by Rule 35(e)(4). This section should be a concise summary of the facts and the petitioner's argument. It should point out the principal points to be developed in the ensuing argument and make clear the pivotal issues. In drafting this section and the following section containing the argument itself, repetition should be avoided. This section should be

[9] Tax Ct. R. 35(e)(3).

drafted so that if the section on issues presented and this section on points relied upon were read alone, the petitioner's case would be briefly but completely outlined. The following is a sample of the points relied upon:

POINTS RELIED UPON

The petitioner may deduct a contribution of $575.00 to the Brooklyn Committee for Urban Development, Inc., as a charitable contribution if he proves that the corporation meets the definition of a charitable corporation in Section 170 of the 1954 Internal Revenue Code.

The Brooklyn Committee for Urban Development was organized by public-spirited individuals to provide members of minorities in the City of New York with facilities through which they might obtain adequate housing at reasonable rates. The Committee assisted a total of 129 families in finding housing as of September 8, 1964, the date on which the Internal Revenue Service revoked the Committee's tax exempt status. The Committee has performed no other functions.

All of the facts in the case sustain the conclusion that the petitioner has proved that the Committee has functioned solely as a charitable organization and that the petitioner's donation to the Committee is a charitable contribution.

THE ARGUMENT.   The argument is another critical part of the brief since it is here that the petitioner presents his interpretation of the facts and law controlling his case. The presentation should be complete but concise. Long quotations should be avoided where possible, and lengthy statutes and regulations can be merely referred to in the argument and set out in their entirety in the appropriate part of the brief as mentioned previously.

Points in the argument should be organized in headings and subheadings, all presented in a positive and persuasive manner. Main headings can be indicated by roman numerals, subheadings by capital letters, and second subheadings, if any, by small letters.

Facts and evidence should be arranged and argued in the most logical and convincing order. All factual matters relied upon should be clearly indicated or summarized for the Court's benefit by reference to the appropriate evidence in the record, stipulations, etc. Unnecessary repetition of references to pages of the record and exhibits should, however, be avoided.

String citations should also be avoided. The cases cited and relied upon should be read and thoroughly checked. When citing, some sort of summary of the facts and holding of each case should be included for the Court's benefit. Those authorities contrary to the position taken should not be ignored. They should at least be mentioned, and, when possible, discussed and distinguished.

A portion of the argument would read as follows:

ARGUMENT

I.

The payment by the petitioner of $575.00 to the Brooklyn Committee for Urban Development during the taxable year of 1963 constitutes a charitable contribution pursuant to section 170 of the Internal Revenue Code of 1954.

.   .   .   .

The prohibited transactions for which a tax-exempt status can be revoked are limited to those enumerated in Section 503 of the Code and the regulations thereunder. Treas. Reg. § 1. 503(c)–1(a) is intended to deny the tax-exempt status only to those organizations that engage in transactions which inure to the private advantage of the contributors to the organization. It is clear that, in the instant case, no specific personal benefit inured to the contributors to the organization. . . .

.   .   .   .

Section 170(c)(2)(B) defines a charitable corporation as one "organized and operated exclusively for . . . charitable . . . purposes." The petitioner has clearly shown that the Committee has a charitable purpose and that contributions made to the Committee did not have the primary purpose of benefitting the contributors.

CONCLUSION.   The conclusion should read as follows:

It follows that the determination of a deficiency in the petitioner's tax return for the year ending December 31, 1963 in the amount of $616.52 was erroneous.

J. R. RAUSCH
Counsel for the Petitioner

THE REPLY BRIEF

Rule 35(e)(3) provides, in part, that

If the other party disagrees with any or all of the statements of fact, he shall set forth each correction which he believes the evidence requires and shall give the same numbers to his statements of fact as appear in his opponent's brief. . . .

In addition to providing an opportunity to dispute the other party's findings of fact, the reply brief provides an opportunity to answer the legal arguments and distinguish the authorities in the opponent's brief.

Since the rules do not specify a particular format for the reply brief, it may be drafted to suit its purpose. Nonetheless, it is recommended that the reply brief follow, as far as possible, the form of the original brief. Thus, a reply brief should contain the following:

1. A proper caption
2. A table of contents and list of authorities

3. A preliminary statement indicating when the original briefs were filed and the date when the reply briefs are due
4. Objections to the findings of fact
5. An argument, insofar as is necessary
6. A conclusion

OPINION OF THE COURT—RULE 50 COMPUTATIONS

Review by Chief Judge

After the judge hearing the case has written his opinion, it will be submitted for approval to the Chief Judge of the Tax Court. The opinion of the judge who heard the case will become the opinion of the Court 30 days after the opinion is filed with the Chief Judge unless he disagrees with the opinion and decides that it should be referred to the Court as a whole for consideration.[10]

The Chief Judge will usually order the review of only those cases that involve issues of law not previously passed upon by the Court. Cases involving only issues of fact are never submitted to the entire Court. The Chief Judge's power to submit a case for review by the entire Court is a matter of discretion and not subject to review.[11] The taxpayer will have no means of ascertaining who is actually deciding his case until the opinion is made available. If a case has been reviewed by the entire Court, the words "Reviewed by the Court" will appear at the end of the opinion. If a case has been reviewed by the entire Court, the findings of the judge who heard the case will not be a part of the record considered by the Court.[12]

Opinions Requiring Rule 50 Computations

When a deficiency is determined by the Service, it will usually involve a number of separate adjustments in the taxpayer's return, thus resulting in a number of separate issues. By the time the Court files its opinion, the taxpayer may have acquiesced in some of the Service's determinations, and the Court will have resolved the remaining issues, some in favor of the Service and some in favor of the taxpayer. In such a case, the Court will file its opinion ruling on the disputed issues and will conclude merely with a statement that "Decision will be entered under Rule 50." Generally, resolution of the issues of the case will have an effect on a number of collateral tax issues. Not only must recomputations based on the newly settled issues be made, but recomputations of such matters as medical and charitable de-

[10] This procedure is required by the Internal Revenue Code, § 7460(b).
[11] Sisto Financial Corp. v. Commissioner, 149 F.2d 268 (C.A.2d).
[12] IRC § 7460(b).

ductions must often be made since these will depend on such figures as adjusted gross income arrived at in compliance with the Court's resolution of the disputed issues. Since the Court itself is not equipped to make the required computations, Rule 50 provides the following procedure:

(a) . . . Where the Court has filed its opinion determining the issues in a case, it may withhold entry of its decision for the purpose of permitting the parties to submit computations pursuant to the Court's determination of the issues, showing the correct amount of the deficiency or overpayment to be entered as the decision. If the parties are in agreement as to the amount of the deficiency or overpayment to be entered as the decision pursuant to the report of the Court, they or either of them shall file . . . a computation showing the amount of the deficiency or overpayment. . . . The Court will then enter its decision.

(b) . . . If, however, the parties are not in agreement as to the amount of the deficiency or overpayment to be entered as the decision . . . either of them may file with the Court a computation of the deficiency or overpayment believed by him to be in accordance with the report of the Court. The Clerk will serve a copy thereof upon the opposite party, will place the matter upon a motion calendar for argument in due course, and will serve notice of the argument upon both parties . . . .

In other words, Rule 50 places the onus upon the parties to supply the Court with the correct amount of the deficiency or overpayment in accordance with the rationale of the Court's findings.

Rule 50 Procedure

WHO MAY SUBMIT THE COMPUTATION. After the Court indicates that a decision under Rule 50 is to be entered, the Audit Staff of the Appellate Division of the Service will usually prepare a tentative Rule 50 computation and submit it to the taxpayer's counsel. In preparing the computation, the starting point is the Service's determination in the deficiency notice. The computation may be predicted on only those facts ruled upon by the Court in its findings or agreed upon by the parties prior to trial.[13] The Court will, in some situations, instruct the parties to resolve an issue between themselves before submitting their computations.[14]

If the parties are able to agree on a mutually satisfactory computation, then an original and 2 copies of the computation along with a statement of agreement will be filed with the Court. The Court will then enter its decision accordingly. If the parties are unable to agree, the procedure is more complicated. In such a case, either party may file his own proposed computation and, after service of a copy of the proposed computation on the

[13] If an overpayment is involved, all the jurisdictional facts required by IRC§ 6512 (b) (2) must accompany the computation. See p. **10·**21 *et seq. infra* for a discussion of the limitations on amounts of overpayments refundable.

[14] Snyder v. Commissioner, P-H Memo TC, ¶¶ 62, 191.

opposing party by the clerk, the party served may submit an objection accompanied by an alternative computation.[15]

When the opposing computations have been filed, the case will be calendared for argument, usually in Washington, and, as a rule, the judge who wrote the opinion will hear the argument. Since it is possible that a new judge may hear the argument, the proposed computations should be as comprehensible as possible. When the computations involve issues that are extremely complicated, briefs may also be filed.

DRAFTING PAPERS ACCOMPANYING COMPUTATION. In a case in which both parties have agreed to a Rule 50 computation, the computation will be submitted to the Court along with the following statement, prepared by the Service and submitted to the taxpayer's counsel for signature prior to filing:

RESPONDENT'S COMPUTATION FOR ENTRY OF DECISION

The attached computation is submitted, on behalf of the respondent, in compliance with the Court's opinion determining the issues in this case.

This computation is submitted without prejudice to respondent's right to contest the correctness of the decision entered herein by the Court, pursuant to the statute in such cases made and provided.

> LESTER R. URETZ
> Chief Counsel
> Internal Revenue Service

OF COUNSEL:
> MARVIN E. HAGEN
> Regional Counsel
> PAUL H. FRANKEL
> Attorney
> Internal Revenue Service

Without prejudice to the right of appeal, it is agreed that the attached computation is in accordance with the opinion of the Tax Court in the above-entitled case.

> _____
> Counsel for Petitioner

When acquiescing to a computation prepared by the Service, it is customary, as indicated above, for the taxpayer to reserve his right to appeal.[16]

When there is no agreement and separate computations are submitted, each party will submit a statement similar to the one above, omitting, of course, the final paragraph containing the other party's acquiescence.

---

[15] It has been held that the computations submitted by the Service under Rule 50 may be considered even when not timely filed. Washburn Wire Co. v. Commissioner, 67 F.2d 658 (C.A.1st).

[16] See also Tax Court Form No. 22, p. C·66–70.

ARGUING THE RULE 50 COMPUTATION. Rule 50(c) provides that

Any argument under this Rule will be confined strictly to the consideration of the correct computation of the deficiency or overpayment resulting from the report already made, and no argument will be heard upon or consideration given to the issues or matters already disposed of by such report or of any new issues. This Rule is not to be regarded as affording an opportunity for retrial or reconsideration.

Thus, as the Rule indicates, the argument may raise no new issues and must be based solely on issues raised at the hearing and disposed of by the Court or reserved to the parties for settlement.[17] This Rule, as promulgated by the Court, has been upheld as a proper exercise of the Court's statutory rule-making power and is strictly construed.[18]

Much of the dispute in Rule 50 cases may center around whether or not an issue involved in the computation was raised at the hearing. Generally, an issue is deemed to have been raised when mentioned in the deficiency notice or set out in the pleadings and accompanied by proof. Issues are deemed not to have been raised for purposes of Rule 50 computation if they are raised for the first time in the brief, referred to in the petition but not accompanied by proof, or abandoned at the hearing. The distinction between a new issue and a mere computation to make matters conform to the Court's opinion is often difficult to make.[19] For example, when a deduction is involved that is geared to the amount of taxable income, such a deduction may be properly included in the Rule 50 computation even though only the amount of income and not the deduction was the issue at the hearing.[20] Certain matters are, however, clearly new issues. For example, the Court has, on numerous occasions, precluded one of the parties from introducing into the computation a matter not referred to in the petition, the deficiency notice, or the answer.[21] Furthermore, although Section 6214(a) of the Internal Revenue Code gives the Commissioner the power to claim an increased deficiency "at or before the rehearing," it has been held that no claim for an increased deficiency may be raised for the first time at the Rule 50 hearing.[22]

---

[17] Hartley v. Commissioner, 23 T.C. 353, 359, supplemented 23 T.C. 564.

[18] *Ibid.* Bankers Pocahontas Coal Co. v. Burnet, 287 U.S. 308.

[19] See the Court's approach in Welsh Homes, Inc. v. Commissioner, 279 F.2d 391 (C.A.4th). See also the distinctions made in CASEY, FEDERAL TAX PRACTICE, § 8.41 (1955).

[20] Zimmerman v. Commissioner, 36 B.T.A. 618, *rev'd on other grounds,* 100 F.2d 1023 (C.A.3d).

[21] *E.g.,* Myers v. Commissioner, 12 T.C. 648 (precluding introduction of new issues by the taxpayer); Baird v. Commissioner, 43 B.T.A. 415 (precluding same by the Service).

[22] Commissioner v. Sussman, 102 F.2d 919 (C.A.2d). *But cf.* the circumstances in Helvering v. Edison Securities Corp., 78 F.2d 85 (C.A.4th), where new issues were raised on rehearing.

When new evidence is found or there is some other adequate justification for the Court to hear argument on a new issue, the appropriate motion for a rehearing may be made pursuant to Rule 19, and the Court may grant a hearing. Such a hearing shall be held before the Rule 50 argument whenever possible.

ENTRY OF DECISION

When the necessary computations for determining a deficiency or overpayment are arrived at through the Rule 50 procedure, a decision on the case is then entered. In those situations in which the Rule 50 procedure is not invoked in the opinion, the decision can be entered without delay. Section 7459 of the Internal Revenue Code provides,

(c) Date of Decision—A decision of the Tax Court (except a decision dismissing a proceeding for lack of jurisdiction) shall be held to be rendered upon the date that an order specifying the amount of the deficiency is entered in the records of the Tax Court. If the Tax Court dismisses a proceeding for reasons other than lack of jurisdiction and is unable from the record to determine the amount of the deficiency . . . , or if the Tax Court dismisses a proceeding for lack of jurisdiction, an order to that effect shall be entered into the records of the Tax Court and the decision of the Tax Court shall be held to be rendered upon the date of such entry.

Report of Decision

Section 7459 of the Internal Revenue Code further provides, in respect to the report of the decision, that

(a) . . . A report upon any proceeding instituted before the Tax Court and a decision thereon shall be made as quickly as practicable. . . .
(b) . . . It shall be the duty of the Tax Court and of each division to include in its report upon any proceeding its findings of fact or opinion or memorandum opinion.

The Court will publish opinions of all cases that it considers to involve important principles of law. The other opinions, called memorandum opinions, usually involve factual issues or legal issues based on clearly established principles. These are published in the Tax Court Memorandum services of Commerce Clearing House and Prentice-Hall.

Finality of Decision

For purposes of determining when a timely petition for review may be filed, as well as for determining when deficiencies may be collected and refunds paid, § 7481 of the Internal Revenue Code has detailed provisions specifying when the decision of the Court will become final.[23] Generally, the decision is final in three months.[24] The most important provision of § 7481 is subsection (1) concerning timely petitions for review. Under subsection (1), the decision of the Court is final "upon the expiration of the time allowed for filing a petition for review, if no such petition has been duly filed within such time." Section 7483 of the Code provides that a petition for review may be filed within three months after the decision in the Tax Court is rendered. Once the decision is final, the Tax Court has no power to vacate or alter its decision.[25] Furthermore, a final decision cannot be affected by subsequent retroactive legislation [26] or by any subsequent decision of any court.[27] Even when the Court of Appeals which had issued a mandate to the Tax Court reversed its own view of the law a final decision of the Tax Court based upon the original mandate could not be altered.[28] The finality of a Tax Court decision can be postponed, however, by a timely post opinion motion for rehearing or for vacating a decision.[29]

POST OPINION MOTIONS

Procedure for Making Post Opinion Motions

When an adverse opinion is served on a party or an adverse decision is entered against him, a number of post opinion motions may be appropriate. Rule 19 of the Tax Court, which governs such motions, provides,

(e) No motion for retrial, further trial, or reconsideration may be filed more than 30 days after the opinion has been served, except by special leave.
(f) No motion to vacate or revive a decision may be filed more than 30 days after the decision has been entered, except by special leave. Motions covered by (e) and (f) shall be separate from each other and not joined to or made a part of any other motion.

When an adverse opinion has been served, a party may move for a reconsideration by the judge who heard the case and wrote the opinion or for a

---

[23] When a decision does become final, deficiencies must be assessed and paid according to IRC §§ 6215 and 6861, and refunds refunded according to IRC § 6512.

[24] IRC §§ 7481, 7483.

[25] Lasky v. Commissioner, 235 F.2d 97 (C.A.9th), aff'd per curiam, 352 U.S. 1027. Swall v. Commissioner, 122 F.2d 324 (C.A.9th). Compare Reo Motors, Inc. v. Commissioner, 219 F.2d 610 (C.A.6th) (criticized in Lasky v. Commissioner, *supra,* 235 F.2d at 99).

[26] White's Will v. Commissioner, 142 F.2d 746 (C.A.3d).

[27] Sweet v. Commissioner, 120 F.2d 77 (C.A.1st).

[28] Commissioner v. Hughes Tool Co., 160 F.2d 540 (C.A.5th).

[29] See p. **9·**16 *infra.*

review by the entire Court.[30] In instances where new evidence becomes available, a party may move for a further trial on the new evidence.

If an adverse decision has also been entered, a party may, in addition to the above motions available to him, move to vacate the decision.

If one of the above motions is contemplated, counsel can avoid difficulties and possible unnecessary litigation by filing the motion within the appropriate 30-day period as outlined in Rule 19. A filing within 30 days will serve both to bring the motion before the Court at the proper time and to extend the running of the period for appeal.[31]

If such a motion is filed after the prescribed 30-day period but within the 3-month period for appeal,[32] it is not clear whether the motion will be deemed timely. Such motions may be filed after the 30-day period with leave of the Court,[33] and affirmative action on such motions is deemed to be a matter of the Court's discretion.[34] Furthermore, it has also been suggested that such leave may be granted only by the entire Court.[35] One case has held that a motion filed after the 30-day period but within 3 months will serve to postpone the finality of the Tax Court's decision regardless of when the motion is acted upon,[36] while it has also been held that such a motion must have been acted upon by the Court within the appeal period to postpone finality.[37] Since the decisions on these matters are far from clear and far from uniform, the problems they raise are best avoided by filing postopinion motions within the 30-day period required by Rule 19.

In all postopinion motions the factual basis in support of the motion should be included in the motion. If alternative motions are submitted, they should be submitted separately.[38]

Motions for Retrial, Further Trial, or Reconsideration

Generally, a motion for a retrial or further trial will be prompted by newly discovered evidence or by evidence required but not submitted at the original hearing. In the case of such a motion, the exact evidence to be submitted should be specified in the motion and accompanied by a statement indicating the relevance of such evidence.[39] An explanation for the failure to introduce such evidence at the original hearing will also be appropriate.

[30] See Tax Court Form No. 21, p. **C**·64–65.
[31] *Cf.* Leishman v. Associated Wholesale Elec. Co., 318 U.S. 203.
[32] IRC § 7483.
[33] Tax Ct. R. 19(e).
[34] Entertaining such a motion is "entirely a matter of grace on the part of the Tax Court." Home Furniture Co. v. Commissioner, 168 F.2d 312, 314 (C.A.4th).
[35] Commissioner v. Realty Operators, Inc., 118 F.2d 286 (C.A.5th).
[36] Simon v. Commissioner, 176 F.2d 230 (C.A.2d).
[37] Denholm & McKay Co. v. Commissioner, 132 F.2d 243 (C.A.1st).
[38] Tax Ct. R. 19.
[39] Commissioner v. Erickson, 74 F.2d 327 (C.A.1st).

Retrials or further trials are solely within the discretion of the Tax Court [40] and will be granted only when justified by a substantial reason. Usually such motions will be granted when the moving party shows that there is new evidence that will produce a different result [41] or that it was not reasonable to expect that such evidence would be required at the original hearing.[42] On the other hand, evidence that is merely cumulative,[43] not relevant to the issues pleaded,[44] or merely additional testimony by a previous witness [45] will be insufficient to sustain such a motion.

Generally, a motion for reconsideration of an opinion without a rehearing will be appropriate when, prior to the time a decision becomes final, the rule of law upon which it is based is altered by an intervening decision.[46]

When the Tax Court denies any of the above motions, the Courts of Appeals are loath to disturb such decisions since they are in the discretion of the Tax Court.[47] Nonetheless, Section 7482(c) of the Internal Revenue Code does confer upon Courts of Appeals the power to modify or reverse decisions of the Court as justice may require. Thus, in some instances the Tax Court has been reversed, such as when it denied a rehearing as a result of a mistake of law and an erroneous assumption of fact.[48] Rehearings have also been granted to allow the Service to make a claim for an additional deficiency after intervening decisions affected the case.[49] Sometimes the Courts of Appeals order rehearing based on the finding that additional evidence should have been received by the Tax Court.[50]

Motions To Vacate Decision

The only common circumstance giving rise to a motion to vacate a decision occurs after a petition has been dismissed by the Court for lack of jurisdiction. If the taxpayer is able to discover facts that will establish the Court's jurisdiction within the time allowed for such a motion, the taxpayer may move to vacate the decision dismissing the petition.

---

[40] Bankers Pocahontas Coal Co. v. Burnet, *supra* note 18.

[41] See, *e.g.*, Ohio Valley Rock Asphalt Co. v. Helvering, 95 F.2d 87, 89 (C.A.D.C.), reversing denial of rehearing where witness not available at trial.

[42] *E.g.*, Estate of Guggenheim, 40 B.T.A. 181, *modifying* 39 B.T.A. 251, *modified*, 117 F.2d 469 (C.A.2d), *cert. denied*, 314 U.S. 621 (additional evidence presented by stipulation)

[43] Baltimore & Ohio R.R. v. Commissioner, 78 F.2d 460 (C.A.4th).

[44] Citizens Nat'l Tr. & Sav. Bank v. Commissioner, 34 B.T.A. 140, 144–45.

[45] Wise & Cooper Co. v. Commissioner, 53 F.2d 843 (C.A.1st).

[46] Clark v. Commissioner, 19 T.C. 48 (earlier opinion, Dec. 19, 1943, recalled by order).

[47] Mensik v. Commissioner, 328 F.2d 147 (C.A.7th).

[48] Harwell v. Commissioner, 170 F.2d 517 (C.A.10th).

[49] Commissioner v. Wells, 132 F.2d 405 (C.A.6th). *But cf.* Levy Trust v. Commissioner, 341 F.2d 93 (C.A.5th).

[50] Stock Yards Nat'l Bank v. Commissioner, 153 F.2d 708 (C.A.8th) ; Ohio Valley Rock Asphalt Co. v. Helvering, *supra* note 41.

APPEALING THE TAX COURT'S DECISION

Government's Decision To Appeal

The government's decision as to whether to seek appellate review of an adverse decision of the Tax Court is ultimately made by the Solicitor-General of the United States. Initially, the position of the Internal Revenue Service regarding appeal is formulated by Regional Counsel and Chief Counsel of the Internal Revenue Service. The Internal Revenue Service's recommendation regarding the advisability of taking an appeal is forwarded to the Appellate Section of the Tax Division of the Department of Justice (the office that would represent the government before the appellate court). Within the Tax Division the procedure used for considering appeal will depend upon the nature and importance of the case in question. One or more Appellate Section attorneys will study the case and make recommendations. Appropriate conferences will be held with representatives of the Service as well as the Solicitor-General's office, and the views of the senior officers of the Tax Division may be obtained. Finally, formal recommendations will be submitted to the Solicitor-General, who will make the decision regarding the government's appeal.

Taxpayer's Decision To Appeal

Upon receipt of an adverse decision in the Tax Court, the taxpayer must decide whether or not it is worthwhile for him to seek appellate review. The choice requires that he consider the amount he is likely to gain as a result of a favorable appeal, his chances of success on appeal, and the expenses that will be incurred in prosecuting his appeal and in engaging in any further proceedings before the Tax Court that may be directed by the Court of Appeals.

Should the Service have taken an appeal from all or part of the Tax Court's decision, the taxpayer should consider whether to file a cross-appeal as to any parts of the decision unfavorable to him. If there is a substantial chance for him to prevail he should consider a cross-appeal, since the Service has already forced him into the appellate tribunal.

Scope of Review

Each party to a case in the Tax Court is entitled to review by a Court of Appeals of the issues decided against him. Section 7482(c) of the Internal Revenue Code gives the Courts of Appeals broad powers to affirm, modify, or reverse decisions of the Tax Court. These are the same powers the

Courts of Appeals exercise in other civil cases and, in accord with Federal policy, only final decisions of the Tax Court will be reviewed.

Since a decision of the Tax Court is subject to appellate review in a Court of Appeals to the same extent as a decision of a district court, the Tax Court's findings of fact can be overturned only if they are, in the view of the appellate tribunal, "clearly erroneous." As to questions of law, the appellate court may reverse if it disagrees with the Tax Court's opinion of the law without regard to the need for finding that the Tax Court was clearly erroneous.

Venue

Section 7482(b) of the Internal Revenue Code of 1954 now provides that Tax Court decisions are subject to review

. . . by the United States Court of Appeals for the circuit in which is located"

(A) in the case of a petitioner seeking redetermintaion of tax liability other than a corporation, the legal residence of the petitioner,

(B) in the case of a corporation seeking redetermination of tax liability, the principal place of business or principal office or agency of the corporation, or, if it has no principal place of business or princial office or agency in any judicial circuit, then the office to which was made the return of the tax in respect of which the liability arises.

If for any reason neither subparagraph (A) nor (B) applies, then such decisions may be reviewed by the Court of Appeals for the District of Columbia. For purposes of this paragraph, the legal residence, principal place of business, or principal office or agency referred to herein shall be determined as of the time the petition seeking redetermination of tax liability was filed with the Tax Court.

Notwithstanding this generally applicable venue rule, Section 7482(b)-(2) permits the parties to agree, by stipulation, that appelate review of a case may be had in any mutually agreeable United States Court of Appeals. Typically, the parties will stipulate to a shift in appellate venue where connected cases are pending in different Circuits, or the taxpayer's change of residence or of principal place of business would make an appeal in the normally required Circuit unduly burdensome.

Procedure for Obtaining Review

Section 7483 of the Internal Revenue Code provides that

The decision of the Tax Court may be reviewed by a United States Court of Appeals as provided in section 7482 if a petition for such review is filed by either the Secretary (or his delegate) or the taxpayer within 3 months after the decision is rendered If, however, a petition for such review is so filed by one party to the proceeding, a petition for review of the decision of the Tax Court may be filed by any other party to the proceeding within 4 months after such decision is rendered.

When an appeal is taken from the Tax Court, the rules governing the contents of the petition, the timeliness of motions, and all other such matters will be the rules adopted by the particular Court of Appeals to which the appeal is taken. Since there is a great diversity in these rules, counsel should obtain the rules for the appropriate court before making the appeal. One rule, however, is uniform among all Courts of Appeals—review of a decision of the Tax Court is taken by filing a petition for review with the Clerk of the Tax Court.[51] The rules of the particular Court of Appeals will further require either that the party taking the appeal must serve a copy of his petition on the opposing party or that additional copies of the petition be submitted to the clerk of the Tax Court for service by him. The appeal must be taken within the 3-month period prescribed by § 7483. If the last day for filing the petition with the Clerk of the Tax Court falls on a Saturday, Sunday, or legal holiday, the next business day becomes the last day for filing.

When the taxpayer seeks appellate review, and he files with the Tax Court a bond not exceeding double the amount of the portion of the deficiency that is the subject of the appeal, the appeal operates as a stay of assessment or collection of the deficiency determined by the Tax Court.[52]

Finally, it should be remembered that the filing of a petition for appeal will result in the transfer of the case to the Appellate Section of the Tax Division of the United States Department of Justice. From that point on, Tax Division attorneys will be responsible for prosecuting the case and for handling any settlement proposals that might be made during the appellate process.[53]

[51] See Tax Court Form No. 23, p. **C**·71–72.
[52] IRC § 7485.
[53] See p. **14**·8 *et seq. infra.*

PREREQUISITES TO TAX REFUND SUITS

As particularly well put by one Tax Division trial attorney,

A tax refund suit . . . is a simple and effective way of litigating a taxpayer's liability. There are, however, a number of jurisdictional and procedural requirements peculiar to this type of action which must be satisfied. Much of the complex litigation in this area is the result of the failure to observe a fairly straightforward set of rules, rather than the rules themselves.[1]

In this chapter each step required of the taxpayer prior to his commencing a refund suit with a complaint in court will be considered.

Tax refund suits are actions in which the sovereign has waived its immunity and consented to be sued by taxpayers who wish to contest their tax liability.[2] This waiver of sovereign immunity has been conditioned

---

[1] Singer, *Filing a Tax Refund Suit*, Ariz. B.J., Sept., 1965, p. 17.
[2] United States v. Michel, 282 U.S. 656.

upon the taxpayer's complying with a number of prerequisites to the bring-
ing of his suit.[3] These jurisdictional prerequisites are strictly construed.
As stated by Justice Holmes, speaking for the Supreme Court of the United
States,

Men must turn square corners when they deal with the Government. If it
attaches even purely formal conditions to its consent to be sued, those conditions must be compiled with. *Lex non præcipit inutilia* (Co. Lit. 127b) ex-
presses rather an ideal than an accomplished fact.[4]

In order properly to bring his tax refund suit before a court, a taxpayer
must take all of the required steps in the required order. He must

1. Pay the tax of which refund is sought
2. File a proper and timely claim for refund
3. Wait until six months pass or the claim for refund is rejected by the
   Internal Revenue Service
4. File a timely and proper complaint with the court

PAYMENT OF CONTESTED TAX—THE FULL-PAYMENT RULE

As their name implies, tax refund suits are actions brought by taxpayers
to recover a refund of taxes allegedly overpaid. Thus, logically as well as
legally, the first step toward getting the controversy before a court is the
payment of the tax in question.

The law requires that a full payment of the tax sought to be refunded
must be made.[5] This "full-payment rule" means that the taxpayer is required to pay the full tax asserted to be due by the Internal Revenue
Service for a taxable period. However, depending upon the type of tax
concerned, payment need not necessarily be made in the full amount of the
tax assessment made against the taxpayer.

The full-payment rule usually is expressed in terms tending to indicate
that the payment of assessed interest is not jurisdictionally required.[6] There
is legal authority to this effect.[7] However, in the authors' view, the question
is not totally free from doubt.[8] The best course of action prior to a definitive
statement by the taxpayer's elected forum, is the payment of assessed interest as well as the underlying tax.

[3] United States v. Chicago Golf Club, 84 F.2d 914 (C.A.7th) ; Lipsett v. United
States, 37 F.R.D. 549 (S.D.N.Y.), *appeal dismissed,* 359 F.2d 956 (C.A.2d).

[4] Rock Island &c R.R. v. United States, 254 U.S. 141, 143.

[5] Flora v. United States, 357 U.S. 63, *rehearing denied,* 358 U.S. 871, *rehearing* 362
U.S. 145, *rehearing denied,* 362 U.S. 972. Citations to this case refer solely to the decision on rehearing, 362 U.S. 145, unless otherwise indicated.

[6] *E.g.,* Flora v. United States, *supra* note 5, 362 U.S. at 149–50.

[7] Kell-Strom Tool Co. v. United States, 205 F. Supp. 190 (Conn.).

[8] Treas. Reg. § 301.6201–1. See BALTER, TAX FRAUD AND EVASION 9.7, note 25 (3d
ed., 1963).

Payment Must Be on an Assessment

The payment jurisdictionally required is one made on a tax assessment.[9] It is not enough for a taxpayer voluntarily to advance a payment in the amount of an anticipated assessment. Hence, an attempt to create a tax refund suit in court prior to assessment will not succeed. This procedure is sometimes attempted by taxpayers seeking to obtain the benefits of civil discovery against the Government during the pendency of a criminal investigation or prosecution.[10]

Should a taxpayer wish to make an advance payment prior to assessment in order to stop the running of interest against him, he may do so without relinquishing his right ultimately to sue for a refund.[11] He should wait until after the anticipated assessment is made, however, before he files his claim for refund with respect to the advance payment.

Income Taxes

In case involving taxes that may be contested in the Tax Court (*i.e.* income, estate, and gift taxes) without payment, the full-payment rule is most burdensome. For income taxes, which are reported and paid on an annual basis, full payment must be made for the tax assessed for an entire year.[12]

In the planning stage there is some possible room for amelioration of the full-payment rule in income tax disputes where an assessment is proposed for several taxable years based upon a common issue. For example it is possible that the taxpayer can execute waivers extending the statute of limitations on assessments [13] for all but one of the taxable years concerned and ask for an assessment with regard to one year. Then, the taxpayer can pay the tax due for one single year and litigate the common issue while the remaining taxable years are kept in suspense. Use of this procedure depends upon the voluntary cooperation of the local District Director's office and would only be available where the taxpayer could persuade the Service that there are no expected collection problems should the taxpayer lose his case. One readily apparent disadvantage of this procedure is that interest on the unpaid years' taxes runs against the taxpayer during the entire course of litigation.

---

[9] Farnsworth & Chambers Co. v. Phinney, 279 F.2d 538 (C.A. 5th), *affirming* 178 F. Supp. 330 (S.D. Tex.).

[10] *E.g.,* Campbell v. Eastland, 307 F.2d 478, *cert. denied,* 371 U.S. 955.

[11] See generally 10 MERTENS, LAW OF FEDERAL INCOME TAXATION §§ 55.04, 58.44 (Zimet rev., 1964).

[12] Flora v. United States, *supra* note 5; Tracy v. United States, 226 F. Supp. 709 (S.D. Calif.).

[13] Treasury Form 872; see Fig. 1–1, page 1·11.

Another possible tactic, which does not require the cooperation of the Internal Revenue Service, is for the taxpayer to await a deficiency notice and then file a timely petition with the Tax Court for all but one of the years in dispute. As to the remaining year he can pay the full assessment and, ultimately, file a refund suit. The principal hazard of this procedure lies in the risk that the Tax Court case would be tried or decided prior to the refund suit brought in the forum of choice. Thus, the taxpayer's attempt to present his case to his elected tribunal could be frustrated to the extent that the Tax Court determination was adverse to him and could be utilized by the government as either (1) a highly persuasive precedent or (2) an adjudication collaterally estopping the taxpayer in his refund action.[14] Moreover, settlement negotiations of the two pending cases would normally be coordinated by the government. Thus, the process of compromise would be more formal and more time consuming than usual, requiring both a Tax Court and tax refund suit settlement.[15]

Estate and Gift Taxes

With regard to estate taxes the full-payment rule is most harsh in its application. Full payment must be made of the entire tax assessed against the estate since estate tax returns are filed, and estate taxes paid, only once per lifetime. With regard to gift taxes, which, like income taxes, are reported and paid annually, the rule requires payment of the tax assessed with regard to a single year even though the amount of tax due is determined from the lifetime gift history of the taxpayer.

There is little room for maneuvering to avoid the full impact of the *Flora,* or full-payment rule with regard to estate and gift taxes. However, with regard to gift taxes, it is possible that a case could present a common issue for several taxable years. In this unlikely event the tactic of paying for a single year of several in dispute, as with income taxes, might be considered.[16]

The "Divisible" Taxes

As has previously been noted, the Tax Court of the United States has jurisdiction to hear only income, estate, gift, and excess profits tax cases.[17] Taxpayers faced with assessments of other internal revenue taxes can only litigate a dispute with the Internal Revenue Service in a tax refund suit. Hence, they are forced to pay the assessed tax prior to litigation. Forced refund suit situations arise in cases involving all excise taxes, including

---

[14] See p. **12·**12 *et seq. infra.*
[15] See Chapters 7 and 14 for discussions of the two types of settlement procedures.
[16] See p. **10·**3 *supra.*
[17] See Chapter 3 *supra.*

manufacturer's and employer's taxes, as well as in controversies regarding penalties asserted against responsible persons for another taxpayer's failure to collect and pay over taxes.[18] In all these cases the full-payment rule of *Flora v. United States* [19] still governs. However, the aforementioned taxes are considered to be "divisible taxes," and the full-payment rule is satisfied if the taxpayer pays the tax assessed with regard to a single taxable transaction or event.[20]

EXCISE TAXES. In the case of excise taxes, the Supreme Court noted in the *Flora* case [21] "that excise tax deficiencies may be divisible into a tax on each transaction or event, so that the full payment rule would probably require no more than payment of a small amount."

For cabaret excise tax assessments, the full-payment rule certainly is satisfied by the payment of the assessment with respect to a single taxable period, *i.e.* a quarter.[22] In fact, there is authority indicating that the rule can be met by the payment of the assessment made with respect to a single day's taxable receipts or possibly by the payment of the tax due by virtue of a single allegedly taxable sale.[23] Analogously, the *Flora* rule can be met with regard to wagering excise taxes by paying the assessment with respect to a single taxable period (*i.e.* a month) and probably an even smaller amount.[24] Similarly, manufacturers facing an assessment of manufacturer's excise taxes with regard to an allegedly taxable product can satisfy the full payment requirement by a payment for a single taxable period or, if they wish to push the "divisible tax" concept to its limit, by paying the tax allegedly due with respect to a single sale.[25]

EMPLOYER'S TAXES AND "RESPONSIBLE OFFICER" ASSESSMENTS. Assessments of employer's (F.I.C.A.[26] and F.U.T.A.[27]) taxes and assessments made for failure of an employer or a "responsible person" to collect and pay over withholdings from employees' wages [28] are considered to be divisible assessments made with respect to each individual employee.[29] In other words, employers, or allegedly "responsible persons," can satisfy the

---

[18] IRC §§ 6671, 6672.
[19] *Supra* note 5.
[20] Flora v. United States, *supra* note 5, 362 U.S. at 171, note 37.
[21] *Ibid.*
[22] Christie v. United States, 179 F. Supp. 709 (Ore.).
[23] Jones v. Fox, 162 F. Supp. 449 (Md.) ; Geer v. Birmingham, 88 F. Supp. 189, *rev'd on other grounds,* 185 F.2d 82 (C.A.8th), *cert. denied,* 340 U.S. 951.
[24] Compton v. United States, 334 F.2d 212, 215, note 6 (C.A.4th) ; O'Neill v. United States, 172 F. Supp. 904 (E.D.N.Y.) ; Williams v. Wiseman, 333 F.2d 810 (C.A.10th) (dictum).
[25] Rosenberg v. United States, 327 F.2d 362, 363, note 1 (C.A.2d) (furs) ; Tysdale v. United States, 191 F. Supp. 442 (Minn.) (transportation tax).
[26] IRC § 3111.
[27] IRC § 3301.
[28] IRC §§ 6671, 6672.
[29] Steele v. United States, 280 F.2d 89 (C.A.8th).

full payment rule by paying the amount of the tax or penalty assessed with respect to the wages paid any one individual employee for a single taxable period (*i.e.* a quarter). [30] In the authors' view it would not be advisable to contend that the full-payment rule was satisfied by the payment of the tax (or penalty) with respect to a single individual for less than a full taxable period.

STAMP TAXES. Stamp taxes are divisible taxes separately imposed on each transaction or commodity subject to tax. Occupational taxes (such as the wagering stamp tax) [31] are separately imposed for each period in which the taxpayer engages in the pertinent occupation. For documentary and commodity stamp taxes the full-payment rule can be satisfied by the payment of the tax assessed with regard to a single transaction or commodity subject to tax.[32] For the occupational tax, the payment of the tax due with respect to a taxable period would be required.

Selection of Prepayment of Tax To Be Made

As has been seen, the full-payment rule can be satisfied for divisible taxes even though only a small part of the tax that the government alleges due is paid. Moreover, even as to income and gift taxes there is some possibility that a payment of less than the total amount in dispute can be adequate. However, a taxpayer seeking to take advantage of the opportunity to prosecute a refund suit with a minimal prepayment of taxes must be careful to consider the jurisdictional basis for his planned law suit.

When a taxpayer has paid the tax upon a single divisible transaction and has taken the subsequent required steps toward getting his case into court, his actions will serve to give the court jurisdiction *only* over his right to recover the amount of tax actually paid by him and claimed for refund and not over the correctness of the total assessment outstanding.[33] For the court to obtain jurisdiction over the unpaid balance of the total assessment, the government must file a counterclaim in the refund suit.[34] And it does not appear that the filing of the counterclaim is compulsory.[35] Therefore,

---

[30] Spivak v. United States, 17 A.F.T.R.2d 971 (S.D.N.Y.).

[31] IRC § 4411.

[32] Friebele v. United States, 20 F. Supp. 492 (N.J.).

[33] Etheridge v. United States, 300 F.2d 906 (C.A.D.C.); Poretto v. Usry, 295 F.2d 499 (C.A.9th), *cert. denied,* 369 U.S. 810.

[34] Etheridge v. United States, note 33 *supra;* Dowie v. United States, 15 A.F.T.R.2d 1475 (N.D.N.Y.).

[35] Fed. R. Civ. P. 13(a). This rule defines a compulsory counterclaim as one that "arises out of the transaction or occurrence that is the subject matter of the opposing party's claim." The "divisible tax" concept requires a consideration of the total assessment as being composed of individual and separate taxable events. It would appear inconsistent to hold that the "divisible taxes" all arose out of a single transaction or occurrence for purposes of characterizing the government's counterclaim for the unpaid balance of the total assessment as "compulsory." *Cf.* Flora v. United States, *supra* note 5.

if a minimal prepayment is to be made, the taxpayer should be sure that it is made with regard to a transaction or taxable event that is representative of his entire controversy. If this is done, a decision on his right to a refund of the amount paid would necessarily determine the correctness of the entire assessment even if the government decided not to counterclaim. For example, in a manufacturer's excise tax case [36] the taxpayer paid $589.54 of a total assessment of $41,342.67 based upon the government's assertion that a certain type of transaction was taxable. The small prepayment was made as to several allegedly taxable sales. The government did not assert a counterclaim for the unpaid balance of the total assessment. The court noted, in denying the government's motion to dismiss the complaint, that the small prepayment of the divisible tax was adequate to place the taxpayer's right to a refund of that amount before the court. Since a determination of the correctness of the total assessment depended upon the same decision as the determination of taxpayer's right to refund of the small amount prepaid, *i.e.* his liability for excise tax on a certain type of transaction, the court's decision on his refund claim would "likely be determinative of the validity of the remaining assessment"; [37] the minimal prepayment sufficed to get a characteristic transaction before the court for decision.

In the example discussed, it should be noted that the court did not obtain jurisdiction to determine the validity of the entire assessment. However, its determination of the small case properly before it would be conclusive as to any allegedly identical issues presented by the total assessment by virtue of the doctrine of collateral estoppel.[38]

With regard to minimal prepayments, jurisdictional brinksmanship is not recommended. It is far better to prepay perhaps more than the minimum required in order to insure that a refund suit will present a meaningful issue to a court and to avoid the possibility of facing a problem in proving that a small prepayment was actually paid with regard to an appropriate divisible taxable event or transaction.[39] Ordinarily, the payment of the full assessment with regard to a taxable period should be made so as to enable the taxpayer to give a court jurisdiction of the full range of issues presented by the total assessment in dispute if the government files no counterclaim.[40]

THE CLAIM FOR REFUND

The Internal Revenue Code of 1954 provides that no tax refund suit may be brought in any court until a claim for refund has been duly filed

[36] Tysdale v. United States, *supra* note 25.

[37] *Id.*, 191 F. Supp. at 443.

[38] See p. 12 · 12 *et seq. infra.*

[39] See Spivak v. United States, *supra* note 30, where plaintiffs failed to establish the jurisdictional basis for their refund suit when they failed to prove the amount of withholdings due as to one employee for one quarter.

[40] Customarily, full payment is made for the taxable period for which the smallest assessment was made.

with the Internal Revenue Service in accordance with the applicable law and regulations.[41]

What Constitutes a Claim for Refund

Basically, a claim for refund is a request by a taxpayer for a refund of taxes, interest, and/or penalties allegedly overpaid. The underlying requirement is that the document put the Commissioner of Internal Revenue on notice as to what the taxpayer contends and that he is claiming a refund.[42]

FORMAL CLAIMS. The Regulations provide that claims by the taxpayer for the refunding of overpayments of taxes, interest, penalties, and additions to tax shall be made on Treasury Form 843.[43] In some instances, the Regulations provide that claims for refund may also be made on other forms as well. For example, in the case of income tax, claims for refund may not only be made on Form 843 but also on any individual, fiduciary, or corporation income tax return, or on any amended income tax return.[44] In effect, the taxpayer, by reporting that he has prepaid more taxes than shown due on the return, is claiming a refund of the overpayment.

A claim for refund should always be made on either Treasury Form 843 or, where appropriate, another form expressly approved by the Treasury Regulations. A taxpayer should not invite possible trouble by putting what he wishes to have considered as a claim for refund in the form of a letter, a protest, or any other document not specifically designated in the Treasury Regulations as a permissible form.

INFORMAL CLAIMS. Should, for any reason, a taxpayer have failed to file a formal claim for refund during the pertinent statutory period, it is still possible that some other document timely submitted to the Internal Revenue Service would constitute a valid informal claim for refund. A claim for refund must be made in writing. Or, as the courts put it, a claim must have a "written component." [45]

As soon as a taxpayer is aware of the necessity for relying upon an informal claim a careful search should be made of the taxpayer's and counsel's correspondence and other communications with the Internal Revenue Service to find all documents that might constitute valid informal claims.

For a document to constitute a valid informal claim for refund it must advise the Internal Revenue Service of the nature and grounds of the tax-

[41] IRC § 7422(a).

[42] American Radiator & Standard Sanitary Corp. v. United States, 318 F.2d 915 (Ct. Cl.).

[43] Treas. Reg. § 301.6402–2(c). See Tax Refund Suit Form No. 1, page C·73–74.

[44] Treas. Reg. § 301.6402–3(a).

[45] American Radiator & Standard Sanitary Corp. v. United States, *supra* note 42; Benenson v. United States, 257 F. Supp. 101 (S.D.N.Y.); Hansen-Sturm v. United States, 201 F. Supp. 392 (S.D.N.Y.)

payer's claim and it must constitute a request for the refund of taxes paid.[46] Obviously, there is ample room for argument regarding whether a given document is or is not a valid informal claim for refund, and there is no universally reliable rule of thumb. Letters from taxpayers or counsel to the Service have in some cases been held to be valid informal claims and in others have been considered inadequate.[47] Notations or protests on tax returns have also been differently treated.[48] A taxpayer relying upon an allegedly valid informal claim can only prepare to litigate the question by marshaling the facts, looking for evidence of a waiver of defects by the Internal Revenue Service, and studying the precedents regarding informal claims with particular care prior to electing his forum.

Drafting Claims For Refund

The taxpayer's claim for refund will be the foundation for his planned tax refund suit. In drafting this document his counsel should "turn square corners" and seek to avoid all possible disputes regarding the validity of his claim. As one author graphically put it,

It would be hard to find a field of law in which careful draftsmanship is as vital as in the filing and prosecuting of income tax refund claims. Although much of the litigation has arisen in unfortunate cases where the ground [for] refund relied upon was not known when the claim was filed, most of the losing taxpayers have been the victims of carelessness on the part of themselves or their lawyers.

When a claim is prepared, it should be treated with the same respect as a pleading; more so in fact, because after the period of limitations has expired, it can almost never be satisfactorily amended.[49]

Generally, a claim for refund must advise the Commissioner of Internal Revenue of the identity of the taxpayer, state the fact that a refund is being requested, identify the payment sought to be refunded and the period with regard to which it was paid. And, it must state the grounds upon which it is based. As expressed in the Treasury Regulations:

The claim must set forth in detail each ground upon which a credit or refund is claimed and facts sufficient to apprise the Commissioner of the exact basis thereof.[50]

It is helpful to consider the subject of drafting a claim for refund in connection with an example. The discussion will deal with those portions

[46] American Radiator & Standard Sanitary Corp v. United States, *supra* note 42.

[47] *Compare* Tobin v. Tomlinson, 310 F.2d 648 (C.A.5th), *cert. denied* 375 U.S. 929, *with* Crenshaw v. Hrcka, 237 F.2d 372 (C.A.4th).

[48] *Compare* American Radiator & Standard Sanitary Corp. v. United States, *supra* note 42, *with* Mutual Trust Life Ins. Co. v. United States, 45 F.2d 288 (Ct. Cl.).

[49] Moser, *Effect of Variations Between Claim for Refund and Trial in Suits for Refund*, N.Y.U. 12TH INST. ON FED. TAX 949, 962 (1954).

[50] Treas. Reg. § 301.6402–2(b)(1).

FORM **843** (Rev. July 1965)	U.S. TREASURY DEPARTMENT - INTERNAL REVENUE SERVICE **CLAIM** TO BE FILED WITH THE DISTRICT DIRECTOR WHERE ASSESSMENT WAS MADE OR TAX PAID	District Director's Stamp (Date Received)

The District Director will indicate in the block below the kind of claim filed, and fill in, where required.

- [X] Refund of Taxes Illegally, Erroneously, or Excessively Collected.
- [ ] Refund of Amount Paid for Stamps Unused, or Used in Error or Excess.
- [ ] Abatement of Tax Assessed (not applicable to estate, gift, or income taxes).

PLEASE TYPE OR PRINT PLAINLY

Name of taxpayer or purchaser of stamps
> Kendall Marva

Number and street	City, town, State, Postal ZIP Code
2805 Terrace Drive	Chevy Chase, Maryland 20015

Fill in applicable items—Attach letter size sheets if space is not sufficient

a. Your social security number	Wife's number, if joint return	b. If an employer, enter employer identification number
017 : 32 :5147		

c. District in which return (if any) was filed	d. Name and address shown on return, if different from above
Baltimore	Same

e. Period—if for tax reported on annual basis, prepare separate form for each taxable year	f. Kind of tax
From January 1 19 65, To December 31 19 65	Personal Income Tax

g. Amount of assessment	Dates of payment
$ 5,615.00	June 14, 1967

h. Date stamps were purchased from Government	i. Amount to be refunded (If income tax, complete computation below) $ 5,615.00*	j. Amount to be abated (not applicable to income, estate, or gift taxes) $

k. The claimant believes that this claim should be allowed for the following reasons:

[See attached sheet]

*or such greater amount as is legally refundable

COMPUTATION OF INCOME TAX REFUND	Income Tax
1. Tax withheld..	$ 3,500.00
2. Estimated tax paid..	2,000.00
3. Tax paid with original return..	1,000.00
4. Any additional income tax paid.....................................	5,615.00
5. Total tax paid (Add lines 1–4)......................................	12,115.00
6. Less: Your computation of correct tax...............................	6,500.00
7. Amount of overpayment...	5,615.00
8. Amount previously refunded..	– –
9. Net overpayment (Enter in item i above).............................	5,615.00

Under penalties of perjury, I declare that this claim, including any accompanying schedules and statements, has been examined by me and to the best of my knowledge and belief it is true and correct.

Signed ....

Dated. July 15 , 19 67 ....

SEE INSTRUCTIONS ON REVERSE

FORM 843 (Rev. 7–65)

Fig. 10–1.

INSTRUCTIONS

1. The claim must set forth in detail each ground upon which it is made and facts sufficient to apprise the Service of the exact basis thereof.

2. If a joint income tax return was filed for the year for which this claim is filed, social security numbers, if any, of both husband and wife must be entered and each must sign this claim even though only one had income. If the taxpayer has been assigned an employer identification number, it must be entered on the form.

3. The claim may be executed by an agent of the taxpayer, but the original or a true copy of a power of attorney must accompany the claim.

4. If a return is filed by an individual and a refund claim is thereafter filed by a legal representative of the deceased, certified copies of the letters testamentary, letters of administration, or similar evidence must be annexed to the claim, to show the authority of the executor, administrator, or other fiduciary by whom the claim is filed. If an executor, administrator, guardian, trustee, receiver, or other fiduciary files a return and thereafter refund claim is filed by the same fiduciary, documentary evidence to establish the legal authority of the fiduciary need not accompany the claim, provided a statement is made on the claim showing that the return was filed by the fiduciary and that the latter is still acting.

5. Where the taxpayer is a corporation, the claim will be signed with the corporate name, followed by the signature and title of the officer having authority to sign for the corporation.

6. If claim is for excess social security (F.I.C.A.) tax withheld as a result of having had more than one employer during a calendar year, include the names and addresses of your employers, and the amount of wages received and F.I.C.A. employee tax withheld by each as part of your explanation in item k. Do not claim tax withheld if you have claimed the excess withholding on your individual income tax return.

Kendall Marva, Attachment Sheet To Claim For Refund for Calendar Year 1965

k. The claimant believes that this claim should be allowed for the following reasons:

The District Director of Internal Revenue erroneously disallowed taxpayer's claimed deduction for the 1965 loss from the operations of Crawness Farm. The aforementioned farm was in 1965, and since 1960 when acquired by the taxpayer, a bona fide beef cattle business operated for profit. Moreover, the expenditures made by taxpayer in operating Crawness Farm maintained and increased the value of the land on which the farm was operated. Accordingly, the taxpayer was entitled to deduct the loss arising from the operations of Crawness Farm in 1965 by virtue of Sections 162 and 212 of the Internal Revenue Code of 1954.

FIG. 10–1. (*Continued*).

of the Form 843 shown in Fig. 10–1 (page **10**·10–11) that are not self-explanatory.

IDENTIFICATION OF TAXPAYER.   The heading and questions "a" through "d" of the form require the draftsman to identify the taxpayer and the Internal Revenue District in which the subject return was filed. While normally the identity of the correct taxpayer is obvious, there are situations in which some question could arise.[51]

NUMBER OF CLAIMS REQUIRED.   The response to item "e" states the taxable year or other taxable period to which the claim relates. In cases in which a refund is sought for payments made with regard to more than a single taxable period, several separate claims for refund may be necessary. Thus, in the case of income, gift, and federal unemployment taxes, the regulations require that a separate claim for refund be filed as to each year or other applicable taxable period.[52] For estate taxes, with only one return being filed per lifetime, only one claim need be filed and the response to item (e) will indicate the date of the decedent's death. In the case of other taxes, such as excise taxes, a single form can properly serve to claim payments made with regard to several taxable periods provided the taxable periods involved are identified.

In response to item "f" the taxpayer should identify the one type of tax for which the payment in question was made. A separate claim for refund must be filed with regard to each type of tax for which a refund is being sought.[53] Thus, where a connected valuation question arises in a gift and an estate tax controversy, separate claims for refund should be filed.

AMOUNT REFUNDABLE.   The next item to be discussed [54] is item "i" relating to the amount to be refunded. The amount inserted is the amount refundable according to the taxpayer's computations. The phrase "or such greater amount as is legally refundable" is added as a precaution to avoid any possible contention that the amount refundable should be limited to the dollar amount stated on the claim for refund. Denney et al.[55] note that

It has sometimes happened that a taxpayer, through inadvertence or misunderstanding, has failed to claim the maximum amount refundable on a claim. To safeguard the full recovery, therefore, it is advisable to add the clause "or such greater amount as is legally refundable together with interest" after the insertion, in the space provided on the form, of the amount of tax to be refunded.

---

[51] See p. **10**·15 et seq. infra.

[52] Treas. Reg. § 301.6402–2(d).

[53] Ibid.

[54] Items "g" and "h" are self-explanatory. Item "g" refers to the assessment as to which the payments to be refunded were made. Item "h," of course, relates only to documentary stamp tax controversies.

[55] DENNY, RUA & SCHOEN, FEDERAL INCOME TAXATION OF INSURANCE COMPANIES at 2.18 (2d ed. 1966).

However, it is doubtful that the government would be able to succeed in limiting a taxpayer to the amount claimed where the evidence showed he was entitled to a larger refund.[56]

The response to item "j", asking for a specification of the amount of an assessment to be abated, is not applicable to income, estate, or gift taxes. In the case of the divisible taxes, where a taxpayer wishes the Commissioner not only to consider his rights to a refund but also to consider whether the unpaid portion of an assessment should be abated, he should insert the amount of the assessment he wishes abated. It should be noted that, even where a request for abatement has been made part of a refund claim, the taxpayer may bring suit only for the refund of taxes paid. A suit for abatement of an assessment is prohibited.[57]

STATEMENT OF GROUNDS FOR RECOVERY.   The response to item "k", setting forth the taxpayer's asserted grounds for recovery, is the heart of the claim for refund. The statement provides the basis for the contentions the taxpayer will assert at the trial of his refund suit. The key point to bear in mind is that grounds for recovery not raised in the claim for refund cannot be relied upon by the taxpayer. In other words, the special defense of "variance" is available to the government at trial if a taxpayer, at trial, seeks to urge a ground not set out in a claim to support his right to a refund of taxes.[58]

Therefore, in drafting the claim for refund, the taxpayer should attempt to set forth all reasonable grounds for recovery that may be available. Consideration should not be limited to the issues that the Internal Revenue Service raised in asserting the deficiency assessment. It is possible that there are grounds to contend that the taxpayer overpaid his taxes even before any deficiency was assessed. For example, it may be found that a questionable item on the subject return was reported, possibly erroneously, in the government's favor. Inasmuch as litigation is anticipated in any event, a taxpayer may feel that it would be worthwhile to assert this "new issue" in his claim for refund.

In stating the taxpayer's grounds for refund the draftsman should take care to express them as broadly as possible while giving the Internal Revenue Service fair notice of the taxpayer's precise contentions. It would not be adequate, for example, simply to state that "the taxpayer has overpaid his taxes." [59] On the other hand the statement of grounds need not be specific or comprehensive to an extreme. The statement need only be ade-

---

[56] Pink v. United States, 105 F.2d 183 (C.A.2d). *But see* Austin Nat'l Bank v. Scofield, 84 F. Supp. 483 (W.D. Tex.).

[57] Etheridge v. United States, *supra* note 33.

[58] United States v. Felt & Tarrant Mfg. Co., 283 U.S. 269. See p. **12**·**7** *et seq. infra* for a discussion of the defense of variance.

[59] See Leas v. United States, 248 F. Supp. 1014 (S.D. W. Va.).

quate to draw the attention of the Commissioner of Internal Revenue to the grounds for recovery upon which the taxpayer will rely in his refund suit.

In appropriate excise tax cases the claim for refund must establish that a "passing-on" defense is not available to the government. Hence, the claim must include a statement establishing that the taxpayer has neither included the tax in the price charged customers nor collected the tax from his customers. In the absence of such a statement the taxpayer must either establish that he has repaid the tax to his customers or has obtained the written consent of his customers to the allowance of a credit or refund to the taxpayer.[60]

Several sample statements of grounds for refund claims have been included to illustrate the degree of specificity found adequate in litigated tax refund suits.[61]

Finally, it should be noted that the taxpayer may properly assert several inconsistent grounds for recovery in his refund claim in order fully to protect his rights.[62]

An extreme example of ingenuity in finding alternative grounds for recovery in a relatively simple factual situation is found in the following statement:

The taxpayers are entitled to a refund of taxes because:

(1) Mr. W_____ who died in December, 1962, was the law partner of the taxpayer, F_____, under an oral agreement made shortly prior to the former's death. The Commissioner of Internal Revenue included in taxpayers' income and denied them deductions for the sums of $1,800.00, $2,800.00 and $3,600.00 paid, respectively, in the taxable years 1963, 1964 and 1965 to Mr. W_____'s widow. Taxpayers allege that such payments were includible in their income, being distributions of partnership income to the widow of a partner, paid in accordance with the terms of the oral partnership agreement.

(2) In the alternative, taxpayers allege that the amounts paid Mrs. W_____ were deductible from their income as referral fees to which the estate of Mr. W_____ was entitled.

(3) In the alternative, taxpayers allege that the amounts paid to Mrs. W_____ were profits from the law business of her late husband, after compensation to Mr. F_____ for his services in the amounts retained by him therefrom, and consequently not includible in taxpayers' income.

(4) In the alternative, taxpayers allege that the amounts paid to Mrs. W_____ were reasonable compensation for her services in taxpayer F_____'s law practice.

(5) Finally, in the alternative, taxpayers allege that the payments to Mrs. W_____ were payments on the purchase price of tangible personal property and a contractual right, the total value of which was $18,000.00, and the cost of which was depreciable over their useful life, which taxpayers allege

---

[60] Treas. Reg. § 48.6416(a)–1.
[61] See Tax Refund Suit Forms Nos. 1–5, pp. **C**·73–75.
[62] United States v. Pierotti, 154 F.2d 758 (C.A.9th).

to be not in excess of six years. Taxpayers, therefore, are entitled to a deduction of $3,000.00 for such depreciation in each of the years 1963, 1964 and 1965, as well as in later years until the cost of the assets has been exhausted.[63]

Who Should File Claims for Refund

The Internal Revenue Code requires a claim for refund to be filed by "the taxpayer." [64] And the Code defines the term "taxpayer" to include "any person subject to any internal revenue tax." [65] In the usual case it is simple to determine the identity of the party or parties who should file claims for refund. Where a tax return was filed, the person, persons, or taxable entity filing the return and paying the tax shown due will normally be the taxpayer or taxpayers who should file claims for refund. The Internal Revenue Service prescribes that, in the case of a joint income tax return, the claim for refund must be filed by both the husband and wife who signed the return even though only one of them may have had income during the taxable year in question.[66]

Where, either without a return having been filed or as a result of an audit, a deficiency assessment is made, the taxpayer or taxpayers against whom the assessment was made and who paid the taxes should file the claims for refund.

AGENTS AND FIDUCIARIES ACTING FOR TAXPAYER. When a taxpayer, for any reason, is unable to act for himself in connection with a claimed overpayment of taxes, a claim for refund may be filed in his behalf by an agent or fiduciary provided the formal requirements relating to representative claims for refund are followed.

In the case of an agent filing a claim on behalf of a taxpayer, the original or a true copy of a power of attorney authorizing the agent to act on behalf of the taxpayer in connection with the claim must be filed with the claim for refund.[67]

In the case of a fiduciary, such as an executor, administrator, guardian, trustee, or receiver filing claims for refund on behalf of a taxpayer, several formalities must be observed.[68] In filing the claim for refund the fiduciary must annex to the claim certified copies of the letters testamentary, letters of administration, or similar evidence showing the authority of the fiduciary

[63] From the claim for refund in Finkelmeier v. United States, 17 A.F.T.R.2d 112 (S.D. Ohio).

[64] IRC § 6511(a).

[65] IRC § 7701(a)(14).

[66] Treasury Form 843, Instructions, ¶ 2. *But see* Pettengill v. United States, 17 A.F.T.R.2d 598 (N.D. Ill.), permitting the spouse who paid taxes for the years in suit to sue alone for a refund.

[67] Treas. Reg. § 301.6402–2(e). It has been held that, where the required powers of attorney were filed after the claim for refund, the district director had authority to accept them. Estate of Oldham v. Campbell, 217 F. Supp. 819 (N.D. Tex.).

[68] Treas. Reg. § 301.6402–2(e).

to file the claim. The only exception to this requirement arises where the fiduciary is filing a claim for refund with respect to a return filed by the same fiduciary. In that case only, documentary evidence establishing the fiduciary's authority does not have to accompany the claim provided that, in the claim itself, there is a statement showing that the return was filed by the fiduciary who is still acting in that capacity on behalf of the taxpayer.

CORPORATIONS. Like individual taxpayers, corporate taxpayers normally file claims in their own names. The appropriate officer (or a fiduciary where necessary) can sign the claim on behalf of the corporation. Mergers, dissolutions, liquidations, and the like can raise questions regarding the correct party to file a claim for refund on behalf of a corporate entity.

Where consolidated tax returns have been filed by affiliated corporations, the parent corporation is the sole agent for members of the consolidated group of corporations.[69] Therefore, as agent, the parent corporation has authority to file claims for refund based upon alleged overpayment of the taxes shown due on the return or assessed with regard to the consolidated return.[70]

Where a corporation has been liquidated by merger with a successor corporation, a claim for refund of taxes overpaid by the liquidated corporation should be executed by the successor in the name of, and on behalf of, the liquidated corporation. The name of the original corporation should be followed by the name of the successor corporation. Filed with each claim for refund must be proper evidence establishing the liquidation and succession. As stated in a Revenue Ruling on this point:

> If the succession is a matter of public record, certificates of the secretaries of state or other public officials having custody of these records must be attached [to the claim for refund]. If the succession is not a matter of public record (and only in such event) then all pertinent documents pertaining to such succession, properly certified by a notary public or other qualified officers of the corporation, must be attached to the claim.[71]

Where a corporation has been dissolved, the identity of the proper party to file a claim for refund on behalf of the dissolved corporation is governed by applicable provisions of state law regarding the parties entitled to prosecute the claims, and wind up the affairs, of the dissolved corporation.[72]

PARTNERSHIPS. A partnership is not a taxable entity under the internal revenue laws. When a tax controversy arises in the context of part-

---

[69] Treas. Reg. § 1.1502–16.

[70] See 8A MERTENS, LAW OF FEDERAL INCOME TAXATION c. 46 (Zimet rev., 1964).

[71] Rev. Rul. 54–17. CUM. BULL. 1954–1 p. 160.

[72] H. M. O. Lumber Co. v. United States, 40 F.2d 544 (C.A.6th) ; Dayton Engineering Lab. Co. v. United States, 3 F. Supp. 351 (S.D. Ohio).

nership operations it is the individual partners whose tax liability is in question. The individual partners will be assessed deficiences and will pay the taxes at issue. Accordingly, it is the individual partners who, in their own names, should file claims for refund.

PERSONS PAYING TAXES OF ANOTHER—VOLUNTARY AND INVOLUNTARY PAYMENTS, SURETIES, WITHOLDING AGENTS. Where one person or legal entity pays the tax of another there can be a question regarding the proper party to file a claim for the refund of the taxes paid. Where a person has involuntarily paid the taxes of another he may seek to recover his payment on the grounds that (1) even though the taxpayer actually owed the taxes it was error to collect them from the payor and (2) all, or part, of the payment was a collection in excess of the taxpayer's true liability.[73] Accordingly, the involuntary payor is the proper person to file a claim for refund of the taxes paid.

Where a person has voluntarily paid the tax liability of another he is not entitled to recover the payment to the extent it represents the actual tax liability of the one on whose behalf the payment was made.[74] Under present law a difficult problem arises when a party voluntarily pays an assessment made against another and then seeks to recover all, or part, of the payment on the ground that there was an overpayment of the true tax liability. The 1939 Internal Revenue Code provisions [75] authorizing the Commissioner of Internal Revenue to make refunds to "taxpayers" was changed in the 1954 Code to authorize refunds to "the person who made the overpayment." [76] Accordingly, it appears that a "volunteer" may be the proper party to file and prosecute a claim for a refund of an overpayment of taxes that he made on behalf of another.[77] Nevertheless, until the issue is definitively determined, counsel handling a tax controversy involving a voluntary payment would be well advised to seek to have both the "volunteer" and the taxpayer file separate claims for refund in order to minimize the possibility that any rights to a refund may be lost.

A surety, which pays a taxpayer's tax liability pursuant to a bond, may seek to recover an overpayment of taxes, and the surety company is the proper party to file the claims for refund.[78]

[73] Stahmann v. Vidal, 305 U.S. 61; McMahon v. United States, 172 F. Supp. 490 (R.I.).

[74] Keith v. Woodworth, 115 F.2d 897 (C.A.6th); Wourdack v. Becker, 55 F.2d 840 (C.A.8th), *cert. denied,* 286 U.S. 548.

[75] Internal Revenue Code of 1939 §§ 322(a), 912, 1027(a), 3770(a)(1).

[76] IRC § 6402(a).

[77] See 3 CASEY, FEDERAL TAX PRACTICE § 10.19 (1955); 10 MERTENS, LAW OF FEDERAL INCOME TAXATION § 58.11 (Zimet rev., 1964).

[78] Maryland Casualty Co. v. United States, 32 F. Supp. 746 (Ct. Cl.). Compare Ceravolo & Comis, Inc., v. United States, 19 A.F.T.R.2d 895 (S.D.N.Y.), in which a prime contractor, which reimbursed a surety for the surety's payment of a subcontractor's taxes, was held to be an improper claimant.

A withholding agent, for purposes of this discussion, is one who withholds or collects taxes from others and pays them over to the government. For instance, an employer who withholds a portion of the wages of his employees can be considered a withholding agent. Similarly, a businessman who collects from his customers the excise tax due on a taxable product or service is a withholding agent. Normally, a withholding agent may not claim a refund of payments that he made to the government on the ground that the payments were in excess of the true tax liability of the persons from whom they were withheld or collected.

For example, in the case of an employer deducting and paying over withholdings from his employees' wages, it is the employee who has the right to file a claim for refund and collect any overpayment of his taxes. By statute, the employer is permitted to claim a refund "only to the extent that the amount of [an] overpayment of the employee's taxes was not deducted and withheld by the employer or withholding agent." [79] In other words, recovery is permissible only to the extent the withholding agent erroneously paid the government more than he withheld for a given employee.

In the case of excise taxes, the normal rule is that the party who bore the burden of the tax may claim its refund. Hence, a number of cases have turned upon whether or not a business that provided products or services to its customers "passed on" the burden of a tax to its customers. [80] If it did, the claimant has been held the wrong party to seek a refund. However, even where a business did pass on its tax liability the Internal Revenue Code will permit it to prosecute a claim for refund of certain excise taxes provided the claimant can establish that (1) the tax was repaid to the customers from whom it was collected or (2) the customers from whom the tax was collected have consented to the claimant's obtaining a refund or credit with respect to the tax. [81]

ASSIGNEES OF RIGHT TO FILE CLAIMS FOR REFUND. It sometimes occurs that, between the time an alleged overpayment of taxes was made and a claim for refund is filed, the taxpayer's assets (including the potential right to a refund of an overpayment of taxes) pass into the ownership of a transferee or assignee. As discussed more fully elsewhere, [82] the Antiassignment Statute [83] renders void an assignment of a claim against the United States (including a claim based upon an overpayment of taxes) unless the assignment occurred by operation of law. Where a transfer of the right to file a claim has passed by operation of law, *e.g.,* to the personal

---

[79] IRC § 6414.
[80] *E.g.,* Crown Zellerbach Corp. v. United States, 14 A.F.T.R.2d 6340 (N.D. Calif.) ; Deluxe Check Printers, Inc. v. United States, 99 F. Supp. 785 (Minn.).
[81] IRC § 6415.
[82] See p. **12·**9–10 *infra.*
[83] 31 U.S.C. § 203.

representative of a deceased taxpayer, the party owning the right at the time the claim for refund is due to be filed should file the claim for refund.[84] If the right to file a claim for refund has been assigned in violation of the Anti-assignment Statute the assignment is considered void as against the United States.

CLAIM FILED IN NAME OF INCORRECT PARTY. The filing of a claim for refund in the name of an incorrect party does not constitute a forfeiture of the correct party's right to file and prosecute his claims. If the error is discovered within the period permitted for filing new claims for refund, a new claim should be filed in the name of the correct party. If the error is discovered too late for a timely claim to be filed, the taxpayer and his counsel should consider whether it would be worthwhile to contend that the timely claim (even though it named an incorrect claimant) should be considered valid. This contention can succeed if, under all the circumstances of the case, it can be fairly said that when the District Director of Internal Revenue received the claim for refund[85] he was adequately advised of the identity of the taxpayer actually seeking the claim for refund.[86]

Time for Filing Claim for Refund

In order to be valid, a claim for refund must be timely filed. The claim must be filed prior to the expiration of the statutorily provided period for filing. Moreover, as will be seen, a claim filed too early may be legally insufficient or tactically unwise.

LEGALLY PREMATURELY FILED CLAIMS. Claims for refund should be made *after,* and not before, the taxpayer has made the payments he wishes to have refunded. A taxpayer who files a claim "prematurely," *i.e.* before he makes some or all of the payments he wants refunded, unnecessarily raises serious questions regarding the validity of his claim.

To cite as an example the most typical situation in which a premature claim is filed, consider a taxpayer who pays a tax assessment on an installment basis. Problems arise when the taxpayer files a claim after a few installments have been paid in which he asks for a refund of the amount paid, an abatement of the assessment, and, perhaps, a refund of the amounts to be paid in the future. If the taxpayer does not file a timely claim for refund of the subsequent installments after they are paid, his claim may be held invalid insofar as it relates to payments made after it was filed.[87] Thus, as one taxpayer found, his suit for refund was limited to a suit for the $469.68

---

[84] See Pettingill v. United States, 17 A.F.T.R.2d 598 (N.D. Ill.).

[85] Or at least prior to the time the limitation period for filing new claims for refund expired.

[86] Thompson v. United States, 332 F.2d 657 (C.A.5th).

[87] Rock Island R.R. v. United States, 254 U.S. 141; Stern v. United States, 40 F.2d 971 (W.D. Wash.).

paid before filing his claim for refund as opposed to an action for a refund of the $5,485.81 total paid on an assessment.[88]

Some courts have found that the Internal Revenue Service waived the defect of prematurity where it considered a prematurely filed claim on its merits after the payments in question had been made.[89] Other courts have considered the government's contention that a taxpayer's case should be dismissed due to a prematurely filed claim to be a "senseless technicality." [90] However, at the planning stage the technical rule should be followed, and any hazard that the claim would be held invalid in part should be avoided. Accordingly, the taxpayer should keep track of the payments he makes to the Internal Revenue Service on a tax assessment. Then, he should be certain that all payments made are "covered" by a claim for refund timely filed *after* the payment. If a claim for refund is filed within two years of the date of payment of the earliest installment "covered" by the claim, the statute of limitations will be met.[91]

TACTICALLY PREMATURELY FILED CLAIMS.   The law does not require that claims for refund be filed as soon as possible but only that they be filed before the expiration of the limitations period fixed by statute. Claims for refund will cause the Internal Revenue Service to examine the subject returns in order to ascertain whether the claims should be granted. With every such examination there is always a possibility that an issue or theory not recognizing upon a previous examination will come to the examining officer's mind. If the return was not previously audited the claim for refund may provoke an audit. If the time for assessing a tax deficiency, or an additional deficiency, has not expired the taxpayer may find himself in a larger tax dispute than he intended to enter. On the other hand, if the time for making assessments has passed, a newly discovered controversy cannot result in a tax deficiency. A new issue can only provide a ground for an offset against the claim for refund.[92] It cannot be used offensively by the Government.

Tactically, then, a number of matters should be considered in deciding when to file the claim for refund. The taxpayer must carefully scrutinize the subject tax return to ascertain whether there is any significant possibility that a new issue may be raised upon an examination of his claim for refund. The likelihood of an offensive contention by the Internal Revenue Service, the amount of taxes a proposed deficiency would probably

---

[88] DeNubilo v. United States, 343 F.2d 455 (C.A.2d) (appeal dismissed after partial dismissal of complaint by district court).

[89] Fidelity Trust Co. v. United States, 39 F. Supp. 451 (W.D. Pa.); Continental Ill. Nat'l Bank & Trust of Chicago v. United States, 39 F. Supp. 620 (Ct. Cl.).

[90] Crenshaw v. Hrcka, *supra* note 47; United States v. Fidelity & Deposit Co. of Md., 178 F.2d 753 (C.A.4th).

[91] IRC § 6511(a).

[92] See p. **12·3** *et seq. infra.*

involve, and the chance that the Government may be determined correct should be weighed against the taxpayer's need or desire to have his controversy terminated as soon as possible. If there appears to be a reasonable chance that the claim may stimulate a deficiency assessment of a size significant to the taxpayer, he should give serious consideration to delaying the filing of his claim or claims for refund until after the statutory period for making assessments against him has expired. Except for fraud and failure to file cases [93] it will almost always be possible for the taxpayer to delay filing his refund claims until the statute of limitations on further assessments has expired.

STATUTE OF LIMITATIONS ON FILING REFUND CLAIMS. *General Rules.* A claim for refund is timely filed if filing occurs within whichever of the following periods expires later:

1. Three years from the date the return in question was filed
2. Two years from the date the payments were made that are sought to be refunded [94]

In the event that no tax return was filed, the period for filing a claim expires two years after the payment in question was made.[95]

The limitations periods applicable to the filing of claims for refund are statutorily imposed and cannot be waived by the government.[96] Therefore, where a claim is not filed within three years of the time the subject return is filed but is filed within two years of the date some of the payments in question are made, the refund allowable on the claim is limited to the amount paid during the two years immediately preceding the filing of the claim.[97] Where the claim is filed within three years of the date the return was filed, the claim is effective only as to payments made during a period immediately preceding the filing of the claim for refund equal to three years plus the period of any extension or extensions of time granted for the filing of the subject return.[98] It should be noted that where a claim for refund is timely as to only a part of the payments made on the subject assessment it is not invalid. A refund suit can be based upon the claim. However, the taxpayer's recovery in the suit will be limited to the payments with respect to which the claim for refund was timely.[99]

[93] In which an assessment can be made "at any time." IRC § 6501(c) (1), (2), (3).

[94] IRC § 6511(a). For a stamp tax, the statute of limitations expires 3 years after the tax is paid. *Ibid.*

[95] *Ibid.*

[96] Garbutt Oil Co. v. United States, 302 U.S. 528.

[97] IRC § 6511(b)(2)(B).

[98] IRC § 6511(b)(2)(A). Note that advance payments of taxes are considered to have been paid on the date the return was due. IRC § 6513(a).

[99] Hutchens Metal Prods., Inc. v. Bookwalter, 174 F. Supp. 338 (W.D. Mo.), *rev'd on other grounds,* 281 F.2d 174 (C.A.8th); San Joacquin Light & Power Corp. v. McLaughlin, 65 F.2d 677 (C.A.9th).

The limitation on recovery relates only to the *amount* recoverable, not the grounds for refund that can be asserted.[100] Therefore, if the only payment "covered" by a claim was made on an assessment based upon the disallowance of travel expenses, a refund could still be claimed on the ground, for instance, that the taxpayer was entitled to a depreciation deduction larger than had been taken on the originally filed return. The following example illustrates operation within the limitation rules:

April 15, 1966	Return filed and reported taxes paid ($10,000.00) by prepaid estimated taxes.
May 1, 1968	Deficiency assessed ($5,000.00 plus interest)
June 1, 1968	First payment ($2,000.00 plus interest)
September 1, 1968	Second payment ($2,000.00 plus interest)
December 1, 1968	Final payment ($1,000.00 plus interest)

A claim filed before April 16, 1969 would be filed within three years of the date the return was filed. Thus, it would be timely and effective to support a claim for all payments made including a claim for a refund of a portion of the taxes shown due on the original return.

A claim filed on April 20, 1969 would be outside the three-year period. However, it would be timely with regard to all deficiency payments made. Hence, it would be effective only to the extent of the $5,000.00 plus interest paid within two years of the date it was filed.

A claim filed in August, 1970 would be timely only as to the second and final payments; the maximum allowable refund would be the $3,000.00 plus interest paid two years prior to the claim.

Finally, a claim filed after December 1, 1970 would be too late as to all payments and completely ineffective.

Extending Statute of Limitations on Assessments. As noted in the discussion of prelitigation administrative procedures,[101] there are occasions when the Internal Revenue Service requests a taxpayer to agree to extend the period during which assessments may be made. These agreements, or waivers, which are made on Treasury Form 872,[102] allow the Service extra time to make an assessment but also give the taxpayer the benefit of an extension of the period within which he must file claims for refund. The statute permitting the taxpayer and the government to agree to an extension of the time for assessment expressly excludes estate taxes.[103]

The Internal Revenue Code provides that where a Form 872 agreement has been made, the period for filing a claim for refund [104] shall not expire

[100] S.M. 3380 Cum. Bull. IV–1 p. 80 (1925) ; San Joacquin Light & Power Corp., *supra* note 99.

[101] See Chapter 1.

[102] See Fig. 1–1, p. 1·11 *supra*.

[103] IRC § 6501(c)(4).

[104] And the period within which the Service can make a refund or credit without a claim.

prior to six months after the expiration of the period within which an assessment could have been made pursuant to the agreement and any extension thereof.[105] Furthermore, as to any claim filed after the 872 agreement is made and prior to six months after the end of the extended assessment period, the normal rules limiting the amount refundable pursuant to the claim are also extended. The claim will be effective to obtain a refund of all amounts paid between the date the agreement is executed and the date the claim is filed, plus all amounts that would be refundable under the normal rules if a claim had been filed on the date the Form 872 agreement was executed.[106]

The limitations benefits given to a taxpayer who agrees to extend the assessment period do not shorten any longer period otherwise available to him. The statute providing for the extension states that where an agreement is made, the limitation period for filing claims "shall not expire prior to" the end of the extended period.[107] Therefore, the normal rule permitting a claim to be filed within two years after payment is made is still applicable. The following example illustrates operation within the extension rules:

April 15, 1964	Return filed and reported taxes paid by prepaid estimated taxes
April 1, 1967	Form 872 agreement extending statute of limitations for assessment to April 15, 1968
April 1, 1968	Deficiency assessment made
August 1, 1968	Deficiency assessment paid

By virtue of the Form 872 agreement a claim for refund filed not later than October 15, 1968 would be timely since it would have been filed within six months after the extended period for assessments expired. Moreover, the October 15, 1968 claim would be valid even if it sought a refund of all taxes paid by the taxpayer on the subject return, since a claim filed on the date the agreement was made would have been filed within three years of the date the return was filed. A claim filed on or before August 1, 1970 but after October 15, 1968 would still be valid insofar as it sought a refund of the amount paid on August 1, 1968. That is, the claim, which would be filed within two years of the date of the payment in question, would be timely (as to that payment only) under the normally applied limitations rules.

In order to be entitled to an extension of the normally applicable limitations period for filing claims a taxpayer must have duly entered into a proper agreement extending the limitations period for the Service to make an assessment. The Treasury Regulations provide that an agreement, to be effective, must be signed by the taxpayer and by a District Director of Internal Revenue or an Assistant Regional Commissioner.[108] Moreover,

---

[105] IRC § 6511(c)(1).
[106] IRC § 6511(c)(2).
[107] IRC § 6511(c)(1).
[108] Treas. Reg. § 301.6511(c)–1(d).

the agreement must extend the limitations period for making an assessment for the particular taxable periods as to which a refund is sought.[109] Finally, the agreement must constitute an extension of the time for *assessment;* an extension of the time for *collection* is not sufficient.[110]

In any questionable case the course of prudence is for the taxpayer to assume that an extension of the normally applicable limitations period is not available. While some courts may be liberal in finding a sufficient agreement to justify an extension of the limitations period, others may interpret the law more strictly.[111] The issue is best handled when it is avoided.

Special Circumstances. Recognizing that there are circumstances in which it would be difficult, or impossible, for a taxpayer to file his claims for refund within the normal limitations period, the Internal Revenue Code provides a lengthened period for filing claims based upon certain specified grounds. Whereas the general rule requires a claim to be filed within three years after the return in question is filed or within two years after the taxes in question have been paid, the special rules discussed herein lengthen the three-year period. In other words, the taxpayer retains the ability to file a claim within two years of a tax payment and receives also the right to file a timely claim within a period greater than three years after the subject tax return was filed. And, where a claim is filed within the lengthened period, the amount recoverable is not limited by the normally applicable rules to the extent the claim is based upon the special grounds for which the lengthened period is provided.

In the case of a claim for refund based upon a deduction for (1) a bad debt loss, (2) a security that became worthless, or (3) a carryback resulting from a bad-debt loss or worthless security, the limitations period that normally expires three years after the subject tax return is filed is lengthened to seven years from the date the subject return *was required to be filed.*[112] Moreover, with regard to claims based on a carryback resulting from a bad debt or worthless security loss the taxpayer is entitled to any additional time for filing a claim that may result from the special rule extending the limitations period for all claims based upon carrybacks.[113] It should be noted, however, that the Treasury Regulations provide that the

---

[109] Brad Foote Gear Works, Inc. v. United States, 288 F.2d 894 (Ct. Cl.) (agreement as to loss year did not operate to extend limitations period as to year to which the loss was carried back as a net operating loss).

[110] Hill v. United States, 52 A.F.T.R. 1462 (S.D. Fla.); Turnage v. United States, 45 A.F.T.R. 1152 (E.D. Ark.). Nor is an extension of time for filing a return adequate to extend the limitations period for filing claims. Stevens v. United States, 20 A.F.T.R.2d 5087 (S.D. Ohio).

[111] *Compare* Senger v. United States, 245 F. Supp. 109 (Del.), *with* Dubiske v. United States, 98 F.2d 361 (C.A.7th), *affirming* 21 A.F.T.R. 1258 (N.D. Ill.).

[112] IRC § 6511(d)(1).

[113] IRC §§ 6511(d)(1), (2).

lengthened limitations period is available only with regard to bad debts that became totally, as opposed to partially, worthless during the taxable year in question.[114]

In the case of a claim for refund based upon a net operating loss carryback, the period that normally expires three years after the subject return is filed is extended to the fifteenth day of the fortieth month (thirty-ninth month for corporations) following the end of the taxable year in which the net operating loss occurred.[115]

The limitations period is also lengthened for filing claims based on less frequently encountered grounds for refund, for example, foreign tax credits, investment credit carrybacks, self employment taxes under special circumstances, etc.[116]

In the case of remedial statutes retroactively enacted giving rise to an overpayment, some, but not all, courts hold that the tax is deemed to have been constructively paid on the date the statute was enacted. Hence, a judicial extension of the limitations period for filing claims may be available.[117]

In estate tax cases there are invariably additional administrative expenses (particularly attorney's fees) incurred in the estate's presentation of a tax refund action. In this situation a refund is allowable to the estate corresponding to the reduction of tax due to the additional deductions even though such refund was not claimed on a claim for refund.[118] To avoid problems the taxpayer should, however, make a claim based upon additional attorneys' fees etc. before judgment is entered in the tax refund suit.[119]

Commencement of Limitations Period. The limitations periods for filing claims for refund are measured from either (1) the date the tax return for the pertinent taxable period is filed or (2) the date of payment of the amount sought to be recovered. The fixing of these dates is, therefore, important in determining whether claims have been timely filed.

---

[114] Treas. Reg. § 301.6511(d)–(1)(c).

[115] IRC § 6511(d)(2). The statute provides an additional period for net operating loss carrybacks arising out of certification issued under Section 317 of the Trade Expansion Act of 1962—IRC § 6511(d)(2)(i)—and for net operating loss carrybacks arising out of the elimination of excess profits by a renegotiation. IRC § 6511(d)(2)(ii).

[116] IRC § 6511(d)(3), (4), (5).

[117] *Compare* Lorenz v. United States, 296 F.2d 746 (Ct. Cl.), *and* Zacks v. United States, 280 F.2d 829 (Ct. Cl.), *with* United States v. Dempster, 265 F.2d 666 (C.A. 6th), *cert. denied,* 361 U.S. 819, *and* Tobin v. United States, 264 F.2d 845 (C.A.5th). See also Smith v. United States, 304 F.2d 267 (C.A.3d), *cert. denied,* 375 U.S. 929; Canton v. United States, 19 A.F.T.R.2d 1132 (Minn.).

[118] Treas. Reg. § 20.2053–2(c)(2).

[119] See Frank v. Granger, 145 Supp. 370 (W.D. Pa.). See also Wells Fargo Bank v. United States, 18 A.F.T.R.2d 6316 (court held claim for refund arose when state court determined fee allowable—hence timely even though filed more than three years after tax paid).

For statute of limitations purposes the date of filing a tax return is the same as the actual date of filing whenever the return is filed (1) on the last day prescribed for filing it without an extension, (2) during an extension period granted for its filing, or (3) late. A tax return filed prior to the time it is due (without an extension) is deemed to be filed on the last day it could have been timely filed without an extension.[120] In other words, an early filed return will get the benefit of the latest possible timely filing date for purposes of commencing the limitations period for filing refund claims.

It appears that the return to which reference is made in the statute of limitations is the required tax return that sets forth the information prescribed by the pertinent Treasury Regulations.[121] If an original return is tentative or defective, the period will commence with the filing of an amended return.[122]

A tax payment made after assessment is considered as having been paid on the date it is received by the appropriate Internal Revenue Service official. Payment by a valid check is deemed made when the check (not the proceeds of the check) is received by the appropriate official.[123]

The date, for limitations purposes, of payments made prior to assessment is governed by special rules. Any payment with respect to a tax liability made prior to the time prescribed for filing the tax return reporting the tax is deemed to have been made on the last day prescribed for filing the return without an extension.[124] However, employer's taxes are subject to a special rule: "If a tax with respect to remuneration paid during any period ending with, or within, a calendar year is paid before April 15 of the succeeding calendar year, such tax shall be considered paid on April 15 of such succeeding calendar year." [125] Payments of estimated income taxes are deemed paid on the last day prescribed for filing the income tax return with respect to which they were made.[126]

Income tax withholdings are deemed to have been paid by the recipient of the income on the fifteenth day of the fourth month following the close

---

[120] IRC § 6513(a). For employer's taxes and withholdings, the statute provides that a return for any period ending with, or within, a calendar year and filed before April 15 of the succeeding calendar year is considered filed on April 15 of the succeeding calendar year. IRC § 6513(c).

[121] See 3 Casey, Federal Tax Practice, § 10.6, at 18 (1955).

[122] *But see* Kaltreider Constr., Inc. v. United States, 303 F.2d 366 (C.A.3d), *reversing* 192 F. Supp. 229 (M.D. Pa.) (subject return not tentative; suit barred).

[123] Second Nat'l Bank of Saginaw v. United States, 42 F.2d 344, *supplementing* 39 F.2d 759 (Ct. Cl.).

[124] IRC § 6513(a).

[125] IRC § 6513(c)(2).

[126] IRC § 6513(b). See United States v. Miller, 315 F.2d 354 (C.A.10th), considering estimated taxes as paid on the date the return was due, even though no timely return was filed. See also Chemical Bk. N.Y. Trust Co. v. United States, 19 A.F.T.R. 2d 1481 (S.D.N.Y.)

of his taxable year for which the withholdings were made.[127] However, as to the withholding agent (employer), the Code provides that the payment is considered made on April 15 of the year following the year in which the wages were paid.[128] Hence the employer's and the employee's respective dates of payment do not necessarily coincide.

When a taxpayer has "paid" a tax liability by means of a credit of an overpayment for another taxable period, the date of payment, for limitations purposes, is the date the credit was allowed.[129] This is the date on which the scheduling of an overassessment is first authorized.[130] However, where the credit for an overpayment of income taxes for one year is applied against the taxpayer's estimated tax [131] for the succeeding taxable year it is, in effect, a payment of estimated taxes for the succeeding year.[132] Accordingly, the limitations period with regard to the payment would not commence until the last day for filing an income tax return for the year as to which the credit was made.

There is some question regarding the precise date of payment when a taxpayer remits funds to the government for the purpose of paying an anticipated assessment.[133] There is authority indicating that payment does not occur until the assessment is made and the taxpayer's remittance is applied in satisfaction of the payment.[134] However, other authorities tend to indicate that payment may take place prior to the time of assessment under some circumstances.[135] For planning purposes it would be advisable for a taxpayer to to measure his limitations period for filing claims from the date of his remittance, thus insuring the timeliness of his claim.

Termination of Limitations Period. The statutory periods provided for filing claims for refund are triggered by either (1) the payment of a tax or (2) the filing of a return. For purposes of computing the last day on which a claim for refund could be filed the day on which the filing or payment occurred is excluded from the computation.[136] Thus, if a payment is made on June 30, 1966, the two year period of limitations does not com-

---

[127] IRC § 6513(b).

[128] IRC § 6513(c)(2).

[129] IRC § 7422(d).

[130] IRC § 6407.

[131] Pursuant to IRC § 6402(b).

[132] IRC § 6513(d). Once the overpayment has been used to "pay" an obligation of the taxpayer, it cannot be refunded.

[133] See generally 10 MERTENS, LAW OF FEDERAL INCOME TAXATION § 58.27, at 77–81 (Zimet rev., 1964). Giljum, *Federal Tax Problems Encountered in Advance Tax Payment Transactions,* 21 TAX L. REV. 495 (1966).

[134] United States v. Dubuque Packing Co., 233 F.2d 453 (C.A.8th); Thomas v. Mercantile Nat'l Bank, 204 F.2d 943 (C.A.5th). See also Rosenman v. United States, 323 U.S. 658.

[135] Northern Natural Gas Co. v. United States, 354 F.2d 310 (Ct. Cl.); Fortugno v. Commissioner, 353 F.2d 429 (C.A.3d).

[136] Burnet v. Willingham Loan & Trust Co., 282 U.S. 437.

mence running until July 1, 1966. Therefore, the period for filing a claim for refund does not expire until July 1, 1968 and any claim for refund filed on or before June 30, 1968 will be timely with respect to the payment.[137]

When the last day for filing a claim for refund falls on a Saturday, Sunday, or "legal holiday" the claim is considered timely if it is filed on the next day not a Saturday, Sunday, or "legal holiday." [138] The term "legal holiday" includes all legal holidays in the District of Columbia (listed in Treas. Reg. § 301.7503-1(b)) plus all state-wide legal holidays in the state in which the claim for refund must be filed.

When Claim Is Considered Filed. A claim for refund is considered to be filed on the day it is received by the correct Internal Revenue Service official.[139] However, if a claim is sent by mail, addressed to the correct official of the Internal Revenue Service, it is deemed timely filed, even though actually received after the period for filing has expired, if (1) it was registered prior to the deadline or (2) it bears a postmark dated within the statutory period.[140]

Where and How To File Claims for Refund

Claims for refund should be filed with the office of the District Director of Internal Revenue for the district in which the tax in question was paid.[141] Even when the tax paid with the return is sent to a Regional Service Center the taxpayer should file his claim with the District Director for his home district.

While there is no prescribed method of filing claims for refund it is recommended that the taxpayer take precautions to insure his ability to prove the fact of, and the date of, filing his claim for refund. A common practice is to ask the District Director's office, either in a registered [142] letter or in person, to stamp an extra copy of the claim for refund with the date of receipt.

If no receipt for a claim for refund is obtained and the limitation period for filing the claim is about to expire, the precaution of filing a duplicate claim should be taken. Where, after the statutory period has expired, a taxpayer ascertains that the Internal Revenue Service has no record of

---

[137] See I.T. 3483, Cum. Bull. 1941–1 p. 397.

[138] IRC § 7503.

[139] The correct official is, under present procedures, the District Director of Internal Revenue for the district in which the taxpayer resides. Treas. Reg. § 301.6402 (a)(2).

[140] IRC § 7502. For mailing requirements, see Treas. Reg. § 301.7502–(1)(c).

[141] Treas. Reg. § 301.6402–2(a)(2).

[142] Registration (not simply mailing) of a letter constitutes prima facie evidence that it, and its contents, was delivered to the addressee. IRC § 7502(c).

receiving his claim for refund, he should immediately gather his proof of timely filing.

In the case of a claim sent by registered mail, proof from the Post Office verifying that the envelope containing the claim was timely registered together with an affidavit or other document establishing that the registered envelope in fact contained the claim for refund would appear adequate to establish the date of mailing, and the registration would constitute prima facie evidence that the claim was delivered to the addressee.[143] Therefore, the taxpayer would receive the benefit of the statute providing that the date of registration is considered to be the date of filing.[144] For a hand-delivered claim the affidavit of the person who delivered the claim to the appropritae office would be required.[145] For claims sent by ordinary mail the taxpayer would have to provide proof of the fact of mailing and of the date the envelope containing the claim was mailed. His proof may, or may not, be held adequate to establish the filing of a claim where the Internal Revenue Service has no record of its receipt.[146] If the taxpayer's affidavits or other proof of filing are not accepted as adequate by the Government, he will have to prove at trial, through testimony and exhibits, the fact that he did file timely claims.[147]

Amended and Successive Claims

Where a taxpayer ascertains that a claim for refund requires "repairs" either to correct possible defects or to state additional grounds for recovery, he should prepare and file an amended or new claim if possible.

If the need for correction or addition to a claim is discovered before the expiration of the period limiting the filing of new claims, the taxpayer has few problems. If the original claim has not yet been rejected, the taxpayer should prepare an amended claim incorporating all the corrections and additions desired and file it before the statutory period expires. The amended claim will stand in place of the originally filed document, and defects or omissions in the first claim will not harm the taxpayer. If the original claim has been rejected, it cannot be amended at all.[148] It has also

---

[143] IRC § 7502(c)(1).

[144] IRC §§ 7502(a), (c).

[145] J. H. Williams & Co. v. United States, 48 F.2d 672, *denying new trial in* 39 F.2d 1019 (Ct. Cl.).

[146] *Compare* Jones v. United States, 226 F.2d 24 (C.A.9th), *reversing* 48 A.F.T.R. 1543 (Wash.) (proof held adequate), *with* Rosengarten v. United States, 181 F. Supp. 275 (Ct. Cl.), *and* Staten Island Ship Bldg. Co. v. United States, 33 F. Supp. 134 (E.D.N.Y.) (proof held inadequate).

[147] See Nyhoff v. Durey, 15 A.F.T.R. 915 (N.D.N.Y.), for an example of taxpayer's proof of filing. See also Charlson Realty Co. v. United States, 20 A.F.T.R.2d 5578 (Ct. Cl.).

[148] United States v. Memphis Cotton Oil Co., 288 U.S. 62, 72.

been held that once a claim has been allowed it cannot be amended.[149] However, in lieu of an amended claim, the taxpayer can file a new corrected claim for the refund of the same payments as those sought in the rejected claim.[150] The newly filed claim, being timely, will be proper and can serve as the jurisdictional basis for a tax refund suit. One *caveat* should be observed. The device of filing successive timely refund claims based on the same grounds cannot be used for the purpose of extending the limitations period on bringing a refund suit. In computing the time within which the taxpayer must file suit, the statutory period commences when the originally filed claim is rejected.[151] However, if the subsequent filed claim presents new grounds not presented in the original claim it is the date of rejection of the subsequent claim that commences the running of the statute for filing suit *with regard to the new grounds* raised in that claim.[152]

Where the necessity for a correction or addition to a claim for refund is discovered after the expiration of the limitations period for filing new claims, serious problems may exist. If the claim has been disallowed, neither amendment nor the filing of a new claim is possible. Any refund suit to be filed must be based upon the originally filed claim, "as is." [153] If the claim has not been rejected, then it may be amended to better state grounds for refund already known to the Internal Revenue Service but not to express new grounds for refund. As the Supreme Court said in the leading case of *United States* v. *Andrews*:

> Where a claim which the Commissioner could have rejected as too general, and as omitting to specify the matters needing investigation has not misled him but has been the basis of an investigation which disclosed facts necessary to his action in making a refund, an amendment which merely makes more definite the matters already within his knowledge, or which, in the course of his investigation, he would naturally have ascertained, is permissible. On the other hand, a claim which demands relief upon one asserted fact situation, and asks an investigation of the elements appropriate to the requested relief, cannot be amended to discard that basis and invoke action requiring examination of other matters not germane to the first claim.[154]

In planning for litigation, all amendments and corrections to claims for refund should be made within the statutory period to avoid difficulties. When, unfortunately, the need for amendment appears after the limitation period has run, it would appear advisable to draft an amended claim if there

[149] New York Trust Co. v. United States, 87 F.2d 889 (C.A.2d), *cert. denied,* 301 U.S. 704.

[150] L.O. 1116, Cum. Bull. III–1 p. 350 (1924).

[151] 18th St. Leader Stores, Inc. v. United States, 142 F.2d 113 (C.A.7th) ; Einson-Freeman Co. v. Corwin, 112 F.2d 683 (C.A.2d.) ; Harvard Trust Co. v. United States, 19 A.F.T.R.2d 180S (Mass.).

[152] W. A. Schemmer Limestone Quarry, Inc. v. United States, 240 F. Supp. 356 (S.D. Iowa).

[153] Tobin v. Tomlinson, 310 F.2d 648 (C.A.5th).

[154] 302 U.S. 517, 524.

is a basis to contend that the rule of *United States* v. *Andrews, supra,* is being met.[155] The amended claim should be drafted carefully so as to show that it constitutes merely a specific statement of grounds for recovery previously made known to the Internal Revenue Service.

In any case in which a question might arise regarding the validity of an amendment to a claim for refund, the precedents on this point will be of particular importance in the taxpayer's choice of the forum for his refund suit.

Government Waiver of Defects in Claims for Refund

Claims that do not comply with all of the formal requirements can still be valid and support the jurisdiction of a tax refund suit provided the defects in the claim have been waived by the government. In discussing formal defects subject to waiver we are referring to the requirements imposed by Treasury Regulations and not those imposed by statute.[156] It is established that the Internal Revenue Service may not waive the statutorily provided limitations regarding the time for filing claims for refund.[157]

The possibility that there has been a waiver of defects is of particular importance to taxpayers such as those relying upon a prematurely filed claim, an informal claim, or a claim (formal or informal) that does not state the grounds for recovery with as much specificity as might be desired. All of the aforementioned defects, and others can be, and have been, waived by the Internal Revenue Service.[158] It is even possible that the government could waive defects in a claim after suit has commenced.[159]

To establish that the government has waived formal defects in a claim, a taxpayer must prove that the merits of the claim were considered notwithstanding its defective form. For the government to be held to have waived defects there must have been an actual waiver, that is "an intentional relinquishment of a known right." [160] The government must have, through its actions, chosen to accept the formally defective claim as if it were valid. Where the Internal Revenue Service has insisted that a taxpayer strictly comply with the formal requirements of the regulations, there has been no waiver.[161]

---

[155] Of course, the application of the Andrews rule to any specific case leaves considerable room for argument. See Smith, *Amendment of Refund Claims,* 51 A.B.A.J. 961 (1965).

[156] Garbutt Oil Co. v. United States, 302 U.S. 528; Tucker v. Alexander, 275 U.S. 228.

[157] *Ibid.* (both references).

[158] See generally 10 Mertens, Law of Federal Income Taxation § 58.19 (Zimet rev., 1964) ; 3 Casey, Federal Tax Practice § 10.34 (1955).

[159] United States v. Henderson Clay Prods., 324 F.2d 7 (C.A.5th).

[160] Johnson v. Zerbst, 304 U.S. 458, 464 (criminal case) ; Smale & Robinson, Inc. v. United States, 123 F. Supp. 457, 462 (S.D. Calif.).

[161] *Cf.* May Seed Nursery Co. v. Commissioner, 242 F.2d 151 (C.A.8th).

The issue of waiver of defects arises in many cases in conjunction with the question of whether there was a formal defect at all. The taxpayer's standard position is that (1) there were no defects, but if there were, then (2) the Government waived them. Apparently, some courts tend to permit evidence of waiver of defects to influence their determination of whether any defects exist at all.[162]

When forced to litigate the waiver question a taxpayer should carefully examine all communications from the Internal Revenue Service to see if there is an indication that his claim or the ground upon which he wishes to rely was considered on its merits. The ultimate determination of whether or not there has been a waiver of formal defects will depend upon the facts and circumstances of the specific case and the precedents in the selected tribunal.

Administrative Procedures

When a claim for refund is filed it is examined by the Internal Revenue Service in much the same manner as a tax return.[163] Moreover, the taxpayer who filed the claim has available to him administrative procedures similar to those afforded taxpayers whose returns are being audited.

When a claim for refund is received by the Internal Revenue Service it is assigned to an Internal Revenue Agent for examination whether or not the claim relates to a deficiency assessed after an audit. Should the Agent propose that the claim be rejected the taxpayer may have an informal conference of the same type as that afforded when a deficiency assessment is proposed during an audit. In lieu of an informal conference, or after one, the taxpayer may request a "thirty-day letter" which will give him the opportunity to file a protest with the Appellate Division. Ultimately a conference can be held at the Appellate Division level. Should the claim for refund be rejected at the Appellate Division level either a formal notice of disallowance will be issued or (if the taxpayer agrees) a waiver of the formal notice will be executed.

The taxpayer should pursue the available administrative procedures only when there is a reasonable chance that the claim for refund will be granted. Normally, this means that it is not a fruitful use of time to have the Internal Revenue Service reconsider the very same issues determined during the procedures that led to the assessment in question. However, if the subject matter of the claim for refund has not previously been reviewed within the Service, it can be worthwhile to try to resolve the controversy prior to bringing a refund suit.[164]

---

[162] *E.g.*, Import Wholesalers Corp. v. United States, 368 F.2d 577 (Ct. Cl.).

[163] Treas. Reg. § 601.105 (e)(2). See p. 1·12 *et seq. supra.*

[164] See generally Pfister, *Tax Refund Claims and District Court Actions,* 1960 TRIAL LAW. GUIDE 273, 290–91.

PREMATURE FILING OF REFUND SUIT

The Internal Revenue Code of 1954 provides,

No suit or proceeding under section 7422(a) for the recovery of any internal revenue tax, penalty, or other sum, shall be begun before the expiration of 6 months from the date of filing the claim required under such section unless the Secretary or his delegate renders a decision thereon within that time. . . .[165]

U. S. TREASURY DEPARTMENT
INTERNAL REVENUE SERVICE
DISTRICT DIRECTOR

IN REPLY REFER TO
Form L—60
Code

CERTIFIED MAIL.

The Vincent Upholstering Company
3015 Oakley Avenue
Cleveland, Ohio   44308

IN RE: CLAIM FOR REFUND OF

$148,456.42

FOR THE PERIOD

Corp-1963

Gentlemen:

In accordance with the provisions of existing internal revenue laws, this notice of disallowance in full of your claim or claims is hereby given.

No suit or proceeding in any court for the recovery of any internal revenue tax, penalty, or other sum which is a part of the claim for which this notice of disallowance is issued, may be begun after the expiration of two years from the date of mailing of this letter.

Very truly yours,

District Director

Form L—60 (4/59)

Fig. 10–2. Notice of Claim Disallowance.

Therefore, after all other administrative prerequisites have been met, a taxpayer must still refrain from filing his tax refund suit until after either (1) six months have elapsed from the date he filed his refund claim or (2) his claim has been disallowed by the Internal Revenue Service.[166]

---

[165] IRC § 6532(a)(1).
[166] Treas. Reg. § 301.6532–1(a).

A suit brought prematurely is properly subject to a motion to dismiss for lack of jurisdiction.[167] A dismissal due to premature filing would be without prejudice, thus enabling the taxpayer to file a new action as soon as the administrative prerequisites have been met.[168]

The simplest and safest action for a taxpayer is to wait six months before filing suit on a claim for refund unless a formal notice of disallowance [169] is received. Figure 10–2 is a typical formal notice of claim disallowance.

It should be noted, however, that the wait may not be absolutely necessary. Prior to receiving a formal notice of disallowance of a claim for refund, a taxpayer receives a "thirty-day letter" [170] advising him that his claims have not been accepted and offering him the right to file a protest or request a conference. It has been held, although the point cannot be considered as settled, that the thirty-day letter constitutes an administrative "decision" on a claim for refund so as to permit the commencement of a tax refund suit.[171] However, the authors recommend that in order to avoid the possibility of litigation on an unimportant point, a taxpayer not rely upon a thirty-day letter as a "decision" permitting the early filing of a tax refund suit. If a taxpayer wishes to bring his suit as rapidly as possible, it is suggested that he accompany his claims for refund with a written request that a notice of disallowance be issued as rapidly as possible.

Having made the required tax payment and filed a proper and timely claim for refund, a taxpayer need wait no longer thn six months to fulfill the administrative requirements for filing a tax refund suit. When his claim has been disallowed or six months have passed from the date of filing his claim, the taxpayer is able to bring his controversy properly before a United States District Court or the United States Court of Claims.

[167] Conway Import Co. v. United States, 17 A.F.T.R.2d 226 (E.D.N.Y.); Woodard v. United States, 232 F. Supp. 831 (E.D. Pa.); Handshoe v. Fox, 1 A.F.T.R.2d 301 (Md.).

[168] *Ibid.* (all three references).

[169] By certified or registered mail. IRC § 6532(a)(1).

[170] See Administrative Practice Form No. 4, page **C·9**, for a sample "30-day letter."

[171] Register Publishing Co. v. United States, 189 F. Supp. 626 (Conn.); Stephens v. United States, 216 F. Supp. 854 (E.D. Ark.).

CHAPTER 11

PLEADINGS IN TAX REFUND SUITS

In this chapter the pleading stage of tax refund suits will be dealt with. At this stage, the procedural rules governing tax refund suits in the district courts are substantially similar to those applicable to Court of Claims actions. Indeed, the present Court of Claims Rules were predicated upon the Federal Rules of Civil Procedure.[1] Accordingly, the pleadings in the two tribunals available to a taxpayer bringing a refund suit can be discussed together.

COMMENCEMENT OF A TAX REFUND SUIT

A tax refund suit is commenced when the taxpayer-plaintiff files either a complaint with a United States District Court or a petition with the United States Court of Claims.[2] Mechanically, all the taxpayer need do is present the correct number of copies of his complaint or petition to the Clerk of the

[1] Rules of the United States Court of Claims, Forward, iii (1964 rev.). All citations to the Court of Claims Rules herein refer to the 1964 revision. The Rules are available from the Court, in Washington, D.C.

[2] Fed. R. Civ. P. 3; Ct. Cl. R. 5(a). United States v. Hardy, 74 F.2d 841 (C.A. 4th).

appropriate court and pay the required filing fee.[3] Service of the taxpayer's pleading on the government will thereafter be effected.[4] However,
it is the date when the complaint or petition is filed and not when service is
effected that is critical in determining whether or not the taxpayer's suit
was commenced within the period of the statute of limitations.[5]

Statute of Limitations for Commencing Tax Refund Suits

As has been seen, a tax refund suit, if commenced prematurely, is subject to a motion to dismiss.[6] However, the dismissal of a case filed too
early will only require the taxpayer to go through the formality of filing a
new suit after the required six months' waiting period has expired or after
a decision has been rendered disallowing his claim for refund.[7] The consequences of a late-filed refund suit are more serious. The taxpayer's complaint will be dismissed with prejudice and his right to a recovery of any
overpayment of taxes will be extinguished regardless of the substantive
merit of his claim.[8]

The Internal Revenue Code of 1954 provides that a tax refund suit may
not be commenced

. . . before the expiration of 6 months from the date of filing the claim [for
refund] unless the Secretary or his delegate renders a decision thereon within
that time, nor after the expiration of 2 years from the date of mailing by
certified mail or registered mail by the Secretary or his delegate to the taxpayer
of a notice of the disallowance of the part of the claim to which the suit or
proceeding relates.[9]

This statute prescribes a condition under which the United States has consented to suit by taxpayers for a refund of taxes. Commencing suit within
the statutory period, therefore, is a jurisdictional prerequisite to a tax
refund suit.[10]

The two-year limitation period commences on the date of mailing of the
formal notice of disallowance of the subject claim.[11] If a claim is never for-

---

[3] A listing of the numbers of copies and methods of duplication required for documents in the Court of Claims can be found in the Appendix, page **B**·1 *infra*.

[4] Fed. R. Civ. P. 4; Ct. Cl. R. 6.

[5] Bates Mfg. Co. v. United States, 303 U.S. 567. See Charlson Realty Co. v. United
States, 20 A.F.T.R.2d 5578 (Ct. Cl.) (extended litigation as to when suit was commenced).

[6] See p. **10**·34 *supra*.

[7] *E.g.*, Handshoe v. Fox, 1 A.F.T.R.2d 301 (Md.).

[8] Root v. United States, 294 F.2d 484 (C.A.9th); Tolerton & Warfield Co. v. United
States, 285 F.2d 124 (Ct. Cl.).

[9] IRC § 6532(a).

[10] Garbutt Oil Co. v. United States, 302 U.S. 528; Bell v. Gray, 287 F.2d 410 (C.A.
6th), *affirming on the decision of the district court* 191 F. Supp. 328 (E.D. Ky.).

[11] See Fig. 10–2, p. **10**·33, for a sample formal notice of disallowance. One court has
alluded to the possibility that a 30-day letter referring to the claim for refund could
constitute a statutory notice of rejection. Register Publishing Co. v. United States,
189 F. Supp. 626 (Conn.), relying on Beardsley v. United States, 126 F. Supp. 775
(Conn.). A reading of the Beardsley opinion, however, indicates that a 30-day letter
would not constitute a statutory notice except under the unusual facts of that case.

mally rejected, the statutory period may never commence running. Hence, the cause of action could theoretically remain alive indefinitely.[12]

The two-year limitation period may begin without the issuance of a formal notice of disallowance provided the taxpayer has filed a written waiver of the requirement of a formal notice (Treasury Form 2297). Figure 11–1 (page **11**·4) illustrates the form of such a waiver. On the day a written waiver of the formal notice requirement is filed, the two-year limitation period for commencing a tax refund suit begins to run.[13]

The two-year statutory period may be extended by agreement between the taxpayer and the Internal Revenue Service. Such an agreement [14] must be signed by the taxpayer or a fiduciary on his behalf and is not effective until signed by a District Director, a Director of an Internal Revenue Service Center, or an Assistant Regional Commissioner of the Internal Revenue Service.[15] Figure 11–2 (page **11**·5) is a sample agreement to extend the statute of limitations.

The statutory period for filing a refund suit cannot be enlarged except by the aforementioned specific agreement with the Internal Revenue Service. Thus, once a formal notice of disallowance has been mailed, further action (such as reconsideration) by the Internal Revenue Service on the claim for refund will not extend the period within which suit may be begun.[16] Therefore, the period of limitations on filing tax refund suits cannot be extended by the device of filing a second or further timely claim for refund raising the same grounds as an earlier filed claim. A notice of disallowance [17] of the first filed claim raising the grounds on which the suit is based will commence the statutory period of limitations. Later rejection, or consideration without rejection, of the second or later-filed claim will not operate to enlarge the time within which suit may be brought.[18]

To summarize, a tax refund suit must be filed no later than two years from the date on which (1) the statutory notice of rejection of the subject claim is appropriately mailed or (2) a waiver of the notice of statutory disallowance has been filed, unless a formal agreement is entered into extending the statutory period.

The determination of the last day for commencing a tax refund suit is made in the same manner as it was with regard to the limitations period

---

[12] See Detroit Trust Co. v. United States, 130 F. Supp. 815 (Ct. Cl.), where suit was timely, though filed almost thirty years after original claim.

[13] IRC § 6532(a)(3). Treas. Reg. § 301.6532–1(c).

[14] Treasury Form 907.

[15] IRC § 6532(a)(2). See Treas. Reg. § 301.6532–1(b), stating the formal requirements for such an agreement.

[16] IRC § 6532(a)(4).

[17] Or a waiver of notice of disallowance.

[18] 18th St. Leader Stores, Inc. v. United States, 142 F.2d 113 (C.A.7th); Einson-Freeman Co. v. Corwin, 112 F.2d 683 (C.A.2d); Cf. W. A. Schemmer Limestone Quarry, Inc. v. United States, 240 F. Supp. 356 (S.D. Iowa) (if the later claim raises new grounds, the date of its disallowance will commence the statutory period).

FORM **2297** (REV. FEB. 1965)	U. S. TREASURY DEPARTMENT · INTERNAL REVENUE SERVICE **WAIVER OF STATUTORY NOTIFICATION OF CLAIM DISALLOWANCE**		
	CLAIM(S)		
TAXABLE YEAR OR PERIOD (a)	TYPE OF TAX (b)	AMOUNT OF CLAIM (c)	AMOUNT OF CLAIM DISALLOWED (d)
1965	Personal income tax	$32,000.00	$32,000.00
1966	Personal income tax	.$15,490.00	$15,490.00

Pursuant to section 6532(a)(3) of the Internal Revenue Code, there is hereby waived the requirement under section 6532(a)(1) that a notice be sent by certified or registered mail of disallowance of the part of the claim(s) for credit or refund shown in column (d) above.

I understand that the filing of this waiver is irrevocable, and it will begin the two-year period provided in section 6532(a)(1) of the Internal Revenue Code for filing suit for refund of the part of the claim(s) disallowed, as though a notice of disallowance had been sent to the taxpayer by certified or registered mail.

NAME AND ADDRESS OF TAXPAYER(S) *(Number, street, city or town, State, ZIP code)*

Meyer and Mildred Rehert
12810 Bartol Avenue
Wheaton, Maryland   20078

SIGNATURE /s/ Meyer Rehert	DATE Jan 8, 1969	Corporate Seal
SIGNATURE /s/ Mildred Rehert	DATE Jan 8, 1969	
BY *(Signature)*	TITLE DATE	

NOTE: The execution and filing of this waiver within six months from the date the claim was filed will not permit filing a suit for refund before the six-month period has elapsed unless a decision is rendered by the Service within that period.

If the waiver is for a year for which a JOINT RETURN OF A HUSBAND AND WIFE was filed, it must be signed by both husband and wife unless one acting under a power of attorney, signs as agent for the other.

If the taxpayer is a corporation, the waiver must be signed with the corporate name followed by the signature and title of the officer(s) duly authorized to sign. It is not necessary that the corporate seal be affixed. The space

provided for the seal is for the convenience of corporations required by charter or by the laws of the jurisdiction in which they are incorporated to affix their corporate seals in the execution of instruments.

The waiver may be executed by the taxpayer's attorney or agent provided such action is specifically authorized by a power of attorney which, if not previously filed, must accompany the form.

If the waiver is executed by a person acting in a fiduciary capacity (such as executor, administrator, trustee, etc.), Form 56, "Notice of Fiduciary Relationship," should, unless previously filed, accompany this form.

U. S. GOVERNMENT PRINTING OFFICE : 1965 O - 108-223   FORM **2297** (REV. 2-65)

FIG. 11–1.

FORM **907** (REV. JANUARY 1965)	U. S. TREASURY DEPARTMENT - INTERNAL REVENUE SERVICE **AGREEMENT TO EXTEND PERIOD OF LIMITATIONS** *(Submit in duplicate)*

NAME OF TAXPAYER
Nathan Warshaw

ADDRESS *(Number, street, city, State, ZIP Code)*
4017 Fairview Avenue, Baltimore, Maryland, 24316

THIS AGREEMENT, made pursuant to section 6532(a)(2) of the Internal Revenue Code, by and between the taxpayer named above, residing or having its principal office or place of business at the address shown, and the District Director or Assistant Regional Commissioner;
WHEREAS, the taxpayer has timely filed the following claims for tax alleged to have been overpaid:

	TAXABLE YEAR	TYPE OF TAX	AMOUNT OF TAX	DATE NOTICE OF DISALLOWANCE MAILED OR WAIVER FILED
REFUND CREDIT	1965	Personal income	$10,000.00	January 5, 1969

AND

such claims have been disallowed in whole or in part, and either a notice of disallowance has been mailed to the taxpayer, OR the taxpayer has waived the requirement of section 6532(a)(3) of the Internal Revenue Code that a notice of disallowance be issued by certified or registered mail;
THIS AGREEMENT WITNESSES, that the taxpayer and the District Director or Assistant Regional Commissioner hereby mutually agree that the period of limitations specified in section 6532 of the Internal Revenue Code, for bringing suit by the taxpayer for recovery of the tax alleged to have been overpaid, is hereby extended for the period named below. The approval by the District Director or Assistant Regional Commissioner shall not be taken to import that he will be bound in the disposition of the taxpayer's case, the subject of this agreement, by the final decision in any cases now in litigation.

PERIOD FOR WHICH EXTENDED

One year from the date of effect of this agreement.

IN WITNESS WHEREOF, the above parties have subscribed their names to these presents.

(Signature)	(Date)	
/s/ Nathan Warshaw	December 23, 1970	
(Signature)	(Date)	
(Signature) (Title)	(Date)	Corporate Seal
By _____		
District Director of Internal Revenue or Assistant Regional Commissioner (Title)	(Date)	
/s/ Irving Machiz Dist. Dir.	January 3, 1971	
(Signature) (Title)	(Date)	
By _____		

IMPORTANT: The taxpayer must submit with this agreement a statement setting forth the issues involved in the claim or claims.
The taxpayer may request in writing that the claim or claims be reopened and reconsidered at any time before expiration of the period set forth in the agreement. The particular circumstances upon which the request is based should be cited therein, and the claim or claims with respect to which the request is made should be identified by stating the amounts claimed, year or years involved, and the date and symbols appearing on the letter

If the taxpayer is a corporation, the agreement must be signed with the corporate name followed by the signature and title of the officer(s) duly authorized to sign. It is not necessary that the corporate seal be affixed. The space provided for the seal is for the convenience of corporations required by charter or by the laws of the jurisdiction in which they are incorporated to affix their corporate seals in the execution of instruments.

in which notice of the disallowance was given or the date the waiver (Form 2297) was filed. A copy of this agreement should be attached to the request.
The agreement will not be effective unless and until it is signed by the District Director or Assistant Regional Commissioner. The taxpayer should therefore be prepared to protect his interests by bringing suit if he cares to do so at any time before the date the District Director or the Assistant Regional Commissioner actually signs the agreement.

The agreement may be executed by the taxpayer's attorney or agent provided such action is specifically authorized by a power of attorney which, if not previously filed, must accompany the form.
If the agreement is executed by a person acting in a fiduciary capacity (such as executor, administrator, trustee, etc.), Form 56, "Notice of Fiduciary Relationship," should, unless previously filed, accompany this form.

GPO-889-228

FORM **907** (REV. 1-65)

FIG. 11–2.

for filing refund claims. The day of the event triggering the statute of limitations (the notice of disallowance or the waiver) is excluded.[19] If the last day for commencing the suit is a Saturday, Sunday, or legal holiday the statutory period does not end until the next day not a Saturday, Sunday, or legal holiday.[20]

TAXPAYER'S COMPLAINT OR PETITION

Proper Party Plaintiff

The rules of both tribunals available for tax refund suits provide that actions must be brought in the name of the real party in interest.[21] In the typical tax refund suit the correct plaintiff is readily determined. He is the taxpayer who filed the subject tax returns, filed the claims on which the suit is based, and now wishes to sue for an overpayment.

Where there has been a change in ownership of the claim for refund the factual situation must be analyzed with reference to the particular law (whether state or federal) that determines the right to sue on claims previously owned by the original claimant. The proper party plaintiff in a tax refund suit is the party who properly filed the claims for refund upon which the suit is based or his successor in interest to the claim.[22] By successor in interest here is meant a party to whom title to the claim for refund has passed by operation of law.[23] Therefore, an executor, for example, can sue on a claim filed by a deceased taxpayer until the estate is closed,[24] a successor corporation can sue on a claim filed by its predecessor,[25] and a statutory trustee can sue on a claim filed by a dissolved corporation.[26] However, a dissolved corporation has not been permitted to bring suit on its own refund claim after the expiration of the state statutory period of its existence.[27]

Care must be taken to file the tax refund suit in the name of the correct party plaintiff, because a tax refund suit brought by an improper plaintiff may not suffice to meet the statute of limitations. If the error is discovered after the statute of limitations has expired the cause of action may be lost. It has been held that the substitution of the correct for an incorrect party

---

[19] Fed. R. Civ. P. 6(a), Ct. Cl. R. 9(a).   [21] Fed. R. Civ. P. 17(a) ; Ct. Cl. R. 24(a).
[20] *Ibid.*   [22] See p. **10·**15 *et seq. supra.*

[23] If title to the claim has passed by voluntary assignment as opposed to operation of law, there has been a violation of the Anti-assignment Statute. 31 U.S.C. § 203. See p. **12·**9–10 *infra.*

[24] After the estate is closed, assignees can sue. Pettengill v. United States, 17 A.F.T.R.2d 598. *Cf.* Lewis v. Fontenot, 110 F.2d 65 (C.A.5th), *cert. denied,* 311 U.S. 621, *motion denied,* 311 U.S. 646, *rehearing denied,* 311 U.S. 727, *rehearing denied,* 311 U.S. 728.

[25] Seaboard Airline Ry. Co. v. United States, 256 U.S. 655; Consolidated Paper Co. v. United States, 59 F.2d 281 (Ct. Cl.), *new trial motion overruled,* 1 F. Supp. 858 (Ct. Cl.), *cert. denied,* 288 U.S. 615.

[26] Signal Gasoline Corp. v. United States, 46 F. Supp. 276 (S.D. Calif.). See also Dayton Engineering Labs. Co. v. United States, 3 F. Supp. 351 (S.D. Ohio).

[27] Zahn v. United States, 6 F. Supp. 317 (Ct. Cl.).

plaintiff in a tax refund suit amounts to the commencement of a new suit.[28] Therefore, the amended but late complaint naming the proper plaintiff as well as the timely complaint brought by an improper plaintiff are both subject to dismissal with prejudice.

Proper Party Defendant

Under present law there is only one proper party defendant in a tax refund suit whether it is brought in the United States Court of Claims or in a United States District Court, *i.e.* the United States of America. Suits against the District Director who collected the subject taxes, formerly permitted in the district courts, have been abolished.[29] Now, however, aliens can sue the United States in the Court of Claims without proof of reciprocity.[29a]

Tax refund suits brought against an improper party defendant are subject to dismissal.[30] However, the statutory amendment that abolished suits against the District Director provides that, in any action in which the District Director is named as defendant, the court should order the pleadings to be amended to substitute the United States as the party defendant.[31]

Venue for Tax Refund Suits in the District Courts

For plaintiffs other than corporations, a tax refund suit may be brought only "in the judicial district where the plaintiff resides." [32] For corporations bringing tax refund suits venue will lie

. . . in the judicial district in which is located the principal place of business or principal office or agency of the corporation; or if it has no principal place of business or principal office or agency in any judicial district (A) in the judicial district in which is located the office to which was made the return of the tax in respect of which the claim is made, or (B) if no return was made, in the judicial district in which lies the District of Columbia.[33]

In considering the venue rules one should note that the pertinent locations are the locations as of the time of bringing the suit and not as of the time of payment of the tax sought to be refunded.

The venue rules are not jurisdictional and may be waived by the government.[34] Moreover, even where the defense of improper venue is

[28] Broadway Petroleum Corp. v. United States, 16 A.F.T.R.2d 5362 (N.D. Ohio). *But see* DeFranco v. United States, 18 F.R.D. 156 (S.D. Calif.), in which additional plaintiffs were permitted to be added to a tax refund suit after the statute of limitations had expired.

[29] IRC § 7422(f)(1) as amended Nov. 2, 1966, P.L. 89–713.

[29a] IRC § 7422(f)(2) as amended Nov. 2, 1966, P.L. 89–713.

[30] Helms v. Caplin, 15 A.F.T.R.2d 610 (W.D. Va.); Baumohl v. Columbia Jewelry Co., 127 F. Supp. 865 (Md.).

[31] IRC § 7422(f)(2) as amended, *supra* note 29.

[32] 28 U.S.C. § 1402(a)(1).

[33] 28 U.S.C. § 1402(a)(2).

[34] Texas Constr. Co. v. United States, 236 F.2d 138 (C.A.5th); Pettengill v. United States, *supra* note 24.

properly raised, a suit need not necessarily be dismissed. In the interest of justice the district court may transfer the case to any district in which the action properly could have been brought.[35] This is normally done where the statute of limitations would prevent the taxpayer from commencing a new action in a proper district.[36]

Finally, it should be noted that if a suit is filed in a proper, but inconvenient, judicial district the parties are not without a possible remedy. As provided by general statute:

For the convenience of parties and witnesses, in the interest of justice, a district court may transfer any civil action to any other district or division where it might have been brought.[37]

By special statute, in the case of corporations bringing tax refund suits against the United States, the district courts

For the convenience of the parties and witnesses, in the interest of justice, may transfer any such action to any other district or division.[38]

Drafting the Complaint or Petition

The Federal Rules of Civil Procedure require a complaint (or any other pleading setting forth a claim for relief) in the district courts to contain

(1) A short and plain statement of the grounds upon which the Court's jurisdiction depends . . .
(2) A short and plain statement of the claim showing that the pleader is entitled to relief, and
(3) A demand for judgment for the relief to which he deems himself entitled.[39]

The Court of Claims requirements for the petition are, in substance, identical.[40] The averments contained in a complaint or petition should be made in separate numbered paragraphs, each of which is limited as far as practicable to a statement of a single set of circumstances.[41]

SAMPLE COMPLAINT AND PETITION. It will be helpful to illustrate this discussion by reference to a sample complaint (Fig. 11–3, pages **11·9**–10) and a sample petition (Fig. 11–4, page **11·11**).[42]

---

[35] 28 U.S.C. § 1406(a).
[36] *E.g.,* Stevenson v. United States, 197 F. Supp. 355 (M.D. Tenn.).
[37] 28 U.S.C. § 1404(a). Also, a case may be transferred from one division to another in the same judicial district. 28 U.S.C. § 1404(b).
[38] 28 U.S.C. § 1402(a)(2).
[39] Fed. R. Civ. P. 8(a).
[40] Ct. Cl. R. 17(a).
[41] Fed. R. Civ. P. 10(b); Ct. Cl. R. 15(b).
[42] See Tax Refund Suit Forms Nos. 7–9, pp. C·77–80, for additional sample complaints and petitions.

IN THE UNITED STATES DISTRICT COURT
FOR THE DISTRICT OF MARYLAND

KENDALL MARVA,

　　　　　Plaintiff,

　　　　　v.　　　　　　Civil No. _____

THE UNITED STATES OF AMERICA,

　　　　　Defendant.

COMPLAINT

1. Plaintiff, Kendall Marva, is a citizen of the United States and resides at 2805 Terrace Drive, Chevy Chase, Maryland.

2. The defendant is the United States of America.

3. This is a suit arising under the internal revenue laws of the United States for the refund of taxes erroneously and illegally assessed against and collected from the plaintiff.

4. Jurisdiction is conferred upon this court by 28 U. S. C., Sec. 1346(a)(1).

COUNT ONE

5. On April 15, 19—, plaintiff filed his individual federal income tax return for the calendar year 19— with the District Director of Internal Revenue, Baltimore, Maryland and paid the sum of $_____ in income taxes reported due on said return.

6. On June 1, 19—, the District Director of Internal Revenue assessed against the plaintiff a deficiency of $_____ in additional taxes plus interest for the calendar year 1964.

7. On June 14, 19—, plaintiff paid to the District Director of Internal Revenue $_____ which was the full amount of the deficiency assessment against him for the calendar year 19—, with interest to the date of payment.

8. The assessment and collection of the deficiency, plus interest, for the calendar year 19___, were erroneous and illegal.

9. On July 1, 19—, plaintiff filed with the District Director of Internal Revenue a claim for refund of the deficiency plus interest, paid by him with respect to the calendar year 19—. A true copy of said claim for refund is attached hereto as Exhibit A.

10. On November 1, 19—, the District Director of Internal Revenue mailed to the plaintiff by certified mail a Notice of Disallowance of his claim for refund with regard to the calendar year 19—.

11. As grounds for recovery, plaintiff incorporates herein by reference the averments contained in his claim for refund for the calendar year 19—, Exhibit A hereto.

12. Plaintiff has overpaid his federal income taxes for the calendar year 19— and is entitled to recover from defendant the sum of $_____ plus interest, no part of which has been repaid to plaintiff.

FIG. 11–3. TAXPAYER'S COMPLAINT

13. Plaintiff is the sole owner of his claim against the defendant and has made no assignment of said claim.

COUNT TWO

14. On April 15, 19—, plaintiff filed his individual federal income tax return for the calendar year 19— with the District Director of Internal Revenue, Baltimore, Maryland and paid the $_____ in income taxes reported due on said return.

15. On June 1, 19—, the District Director of Internal Revenue assessed against the plaintiff a deficiency of $_____ in additional taxes plus interest for the calendar year 19—.

16. On June 14, 19—, plaintiff paid to the District Director of Internal Revenue $_____ which was the full amount of the deficiency assessment against him for calendar year 19—, plus interest, to the date of payment.

17. The assessment and collection of the deficiency, plus interest, for the calendar year 19___, were erroneous and illegal.

18. On July 1, 19—, plaintiff filed with the District Director of Internal Revenue a claim for refund of the deficiencies plus interest paid by him with respect to the calendar year 19—. A true copy of said claim for refund is attached hereto as Exhibit B.

19. On November 1, 19___, the District Director of Internal Revenue mailed to the plaintiff by certified mail a Notice of Disallowance of his claim for refund with regard to the calendar year 19—.

20. Plaintiff herein incorporates by reference the averments contained in his claim for refund for the calendar year 19—, Exhibit B hereto.

21. Plaintiff has overpaid his federal income taxes for the calendar year 19— and is entitled to recover from defendant the sum of $_____, plus interest, no part of which has been repaid to plaintiff.

22. Plaintiff is the sole owner of his claim against the defendant and has made no assignment of said claim.

WHEREFORE, plaintiff prays for judgment against the defendant in the total amount of $_____ together with his costs and interest as provided by law.

Allen L. Schwait
Attorney for Plaintiff
Law Building
Baltimore, Maryland

PLAINTIFF DEMANDS TRIAL BY JURY

FIG. 11–3. (*Continued*).

If the same suit were filed in the Court of Claims, the petition would be, in substance, the same as the complaint illustrated in Fig. 11–3. This sample petition is, therefore, given only in part.

IN THE
UNITED STATES COURT OF CLAIMS

Docket No. _____

KENDALL MARVA, *Plaintiff,*

v.

THE UNITED STATES, *Defendant.*

PETITION

1. Plaintiff Kendall Marva is a citizen of the United States and resides at 2805 Terrace Drive, Chevy Chase, Maryland.

*   *   *

4. Jurisdiction is conferred upon the United States Court of Claims by 28 U. S. C. Section 1491.

*   *   *

WHEREFORE, plaintiff prays for judgment against the defendant in the amount of $_____ together with his costs and interest as provided by law.

> Allen L. Schwait
> Attorney for Plaintiff
> Law Building
> Baltimore, Maryland

FIG. 11–4. PETITION IN THE COURT OF CLAIMS

Caption. The applicable procedural rules require a caption, as illustrated, stating the name of the court, the file or docket number,[43] and a designation of the pleading as a complaint or petition.[44]

In naming the plaintiff or plaintiffs in the complaint or petition all plaintiffs must be listed. In pleadings other than the complaint only the first plaintiff need be named so long as there is an appropriate indication of other parties.[45]

Allegations Establishing Venue and Jurisdiction. At the beginning of the complaint or petition the taxpayer should set forth sufficient allegations to establish that the court has jurisdiction of the controversy and, in district court actions, that venue is proper.

[43] The docket number is not placed on the complaint or petition by counsel when drafting the pleading. The clerk will stamp the appropriate number on the document when it is filed.
[44] Fed. R. Civ. P. 10(a) ; Ct. Cl. R. 15(a).
[45] *Ibid.*

Description of Parties. First, the parties should be described briefly so as to establish the fact that the court has before it the correct plaintiff and defendant and that, in district court actions, venue properly lies in the judicial district where suit was brought.

For an individual, or a husband and wife suing jointly for a tax refund, the illustrated description alleging citizenship and residence is adequate.[46]

If a corporation is the plaintiff, its description should include an allegation of its state of incorporation, its principal place of business, and, in a district court complaint, any additional fact on which venue may be premised. The following description of a corporate plaintiff is customary:

Plaintiff, A.B.C. Upholstering Company is a Maryland corporation having its principal place of business at 1745 Greenmount Avenue, Baltimore, Maryland.

In cases in which the plaintiff is suing on behalf of another, sufficient facts should be pleaded to establish his right to bring the suit. For example, an executor might be described as follows:

1. Plaintiff James Goubeaux is Executor of the Estate of Donald Bright, deceased, pursuant to appointment of the Probate Court of Darke County, Ohio. Plaintiff resides at 312 Enid Street, Greenville, Ohio.

In describing the defendant, the simple statement used in the sample complaint [47] is adequate.

Statement of Nature of the Case. Following the description of the parties there should be a brief statement setting forth the nature of the case as a tax refund suit arising under the internal revenue laws of the United States.[48]

Statement of Statute Giving Court Jurisdiction. Next, the statutory section giving the court jurisdiction of the suit should be identified. For tax refund suits jurisdiction is conferred on the district courts by 28 U. S. C., Section 1346(a), and on the Court of Claims by 28 U. S. C., Section 1491.

Statement of Taxpayer's Substantive Case. Following the basic allegations establishing venue and jurisdiction over the suit, the complaint or petition must contain averments establishing the plaintiff's right to the recovery demanded. The Court of Claims Rules as well as the Federal Rules of Civil Procedure provide that each claim founded upon a separate transaction or occurrence shall be stated in a separate count whenever a separation facilitates the clear presentation of the matters set forth.[49] In an income tax case involving several different taxable years it is good practice to plead the facts as to each year in a separate count as illustrated in the

---

[46] Fig. 11–3, ¶ 1 p. 11·9 *supra;* Fig. 11–4, ¶ 1 p. 11·11.
[47] Fig. 11–3, ¶ 2 p. 11·9 *supra.*
[48] Fig. 11–3, ¶ 3 p. 11·9 *supra.*
[49] Fed. R. Civ. P. 10(b) ; Ct. Cl. R. 15(b).

sample complaint. In suits for refund of "divisible taxes," often involving a large number of taxable periods, the division of the complaint or petition into separate counts is frequently impractical.[50]

Statement of Jurisdictional Prerequisites. In the complaint or petition in a tax refund suit it is essential for the taxpayer to allege that all of the jurisdictional prerequisites to his suit have been met.[51] Thus, as indicated in the sample complaint, the following matters must be pleaded:

1. That payment has been made, on an assessment, of the amount sought to be refunded.[52]
2. That a proper and timely claim for refund has been filed claiming the repayment of the subject taxes.[53]
3. That the Secretary of the Treasury or his delegate, *i.e.*, the District Director of Internal Revenue, has disallowed the claim or that six months has elapsed since the time the claim was filed without action having been taken thereon.[54]

Statement of Grounds for Recovery. In stating the grounds for recovery it is permissible, and recommended, that the taxpayer simply incorporate by reference all averments contained in the claim for refund on which his action is based. Since, in a tax refund suit, the taxpayer's grounds for recovery are limited to those presented in his claim for refund,[55] there is usually no substantial benefit to be gained by restating his points in the body of the complaint. The grounds for refund can be set out in full in the body of the complaint in an attempt to narrow the issues.[56] However, the end of narrowing the issues can better be accomplished through other procedures utilized after government counsel has had a chance to become familiar with the facts of the case so as to be in a position to admit the taxpayer's uncontroversial assertions.

Care must be taken in situations in which a taxpayer has filed more than one claim for refund with respect to any one taxable period. While there is no limit to the number of claims that may be filed for a given taxable period, only one suit may be brought to recover an overpayment of taxes

[50] See Tax Refund Suit Form No. 8, p. **C**·78–79, for an example of a complaint in a multiperiod divisible tax suit.

[51] Vorachek v. United States, 337 F.2d 797 (C.A.8th).

[52] See p. **10**·2 *supra* for a discussion of the full-payment rule. After alleging the fact of assessment and payment, the complaint should state the taxpayer's contention that the assessment and collection of the tax were erroneous and illegal. Fig. 11–3, ¶ 8.

[53] See p. **10**·7 *et seq. supra.* In appropriate excise tax cases, the complaint must contain an allegation that the tax was not passed on to customers or that their consent to the suit was obtained. Etheridge v. United States, 300 F.2d 906, 908. *Cf.* Treas. Reg. § 48.6416(a)–1(b).

[54] See p. **10**·33 *supra.*

[55] See p. **10**·13 *supra.*

[56] See Tax Refund Suit Form No. 9, p. **C**·79–80, for an example of this form of complaint.

for that period.[57] Accordingly, all claims for refund that have been filed with regard to a given taxable period must be incorporated in the taxpayer's cause of action as to that period. Any claims not made a part of the taxpayer's suit cannot later provide the basis for a second cause of action with respect to a taxable period previously litigated.[58] Thus, if a first claim for refund is filed for a given period followed by a second, timely claim supplementing the grounds for recovery previously stated, the taxpayer's complaint should incorporate both claims for refund unless he wishes to abandon those grounds raised by the omitted claim.

Statement of Ultimate Contention. After the taxpayer's grounds for recovery are pleaded, the complaint or petition should allege the ultimate contention in a tax refund suit, *i.e.,* that the taxpayer overpaid his taxes for the period in question and has not received a refund of the overpayment. The authors suggest the following form for this allegation:

Plaintiff has overpaid his federal income taxes for the calendar year 19— and is entitled to recover from the defendant the sum of $_____ plus interest, no part of which has been repaid to plaintiff.

In one form of complaint for a tax refund suit, the draftsman suggested phrasing this allegation as follows:

No portion of the sum of $_____ or interest thereon has been refunded by defendant to plaintiff and no legal offsets or credits exist with respect to the sum.[59]

In the authors' view, however, any allegation regarding an offset or credit, if made at all, should be made by the government.[60]

Statement of Plaintiff's Ownership of Cause of Action. Finally, the complaint or petition should contain an allegation that the cause of action being prosecuted is the property of the plaintiff and has not been assigned.

Demand for Relief. The pleading rules of the tax refund tribunals require the plaintiff to state a demand for the relief to which he considers himself entitled.[61] In a tax refund suit the taxpayer should demand

    1. A refund of the amount of his overpayment

    2. Interest thereon as provided by law [62]

[57] Chicago Junction Rys. v. United States, 10 F. Supp. 156 (Ct. Cl.). *Cf.* Pettengill v. United States, *supra* note 24. See generally 10 MERTENS, LAW OF FEDERAL INCOME TAXATION § 58A.07 (Zimet rev., 1965), and see p. **12 · 12** *et seq. infra* for a discussion of the doctrine of res judicata.

[58] Except for claims arising because of net operating loss carrybacks from a subsequent year. IRC § 6511(d)(2)(B).

[59] See BALTER, TAX FRAUD AND EVASION at 9.10 note 33 (3d ed. 1963), quoting *Handling Federal Tax Litigation,* 1961 CALIFORNIA CONTINUING EDUCATION OF THE BAR at 95.

[60] *Cf.* Routzahn v. Brown, 95 F.2d 766, 771 (C.A.6th).

[61] Fed. R. Civ. P. 8(a) Ct. Cl. R. 17(a).

[62] It has been held that a taxpayer who did not demand interest in his complaint was not entitled to recover interest on his overpayment of taxes. Steiner v. Nelson, 199 F. Supp. 441 (E.D. Wis.).

3. Costs [63]

The taxpayer should not demand additional relief, such as an abatement of the assessment, an injunction, or a writ of mandamus. A request for such relief is subject to a motion to strike or to dismiss.[64]

Signature. In the tax refund forums, pleadings must be signed by at least one attorney of record in the case, and his address must be stated. The attorney's signature constitutes a certification that he has read the pleading and that, to the best of his knowledge and belief, there is good ground to support it and it is not interposed for purposes of delay.[65]

Demand for Jury Trial. If a taxpayer desires a jury trial in a district court tax refund suit he should endorse a demand for trial by jury on his complaint.[66] A demand for trial by jury may also be made, in writing, by a separate document formally served and filed at any time within 10 days after the last pleading is filed.[67]

The taxpayer may, if he believes it will be advantageous, demand a jury trial of some, but not all, of the issues in the case.[68] The government can, however, demand that all of the issues be presented to the jury.[69] If there has been no specification of the issues to be submitted to the jury, a jury demand is deemed to have requested the submission of all issues of fact to the jury.[70] Once a jury demand has been made by either party it cannot be withdrawn without the consent of the adversary.[71]

If neither party has made a timely jury demand the parties have waived their respective rights to trial by jury.[72] However, in its discretion upon motion. the court may order the submission to a jury of any, or all, of the factual issues in the case.[73]

THE GOVERNMENT'S ANSWER

The government must answer the taxpayer's complaint in a district court or his petition in the Court of Claims within 60 days after service.[74] Contrary to its former practices the government at present almost never

---

[63] See p. **16·6** *et seq. infra.*

[64] Etheridge v. United States, 300 F.2d 906 (C.A.D.C.); Poretto v. Usry, 295 F.2d 499 (C.A.5th).

[65] Fed. R. Civ. P. 11; Ct. Cl. R. 16(a), (c).

[66] Fed. R. Civ. P. 38(b). See p. **15·6** *et seq. infra* for a discussion of the factors to consider in deciding whether a trial by jury would be advantageous.

[67] Fed. R. Civ. P. 38(c).

[68] *Ibid.*

[69] *Ibid.*

[70] *Ibid.*

[71] Fed. R. Civ. P. 38(d). See also Fed. R. Civ. P. 39(a).

[72] Fed. R. Civ. P. 38(d).

[73] Fed. R. Civ. P. 39(b).

[74] Fed. R. Civ. P. 12(a); Ct. Cl. R. 20(a)(1).

requests an extension of the time within which it must answer.[75] Nevertheless, the processing of files from the Internal Revenue field offices, through Chief Counsel's office, to the appropriate section of the Tax Division of the Department of Justice still takes an appreciable part of the 60 days allotted the government. Moreover, by the time the case is on the desk of the trial attorney who must prepare the answer the deadline usually is imminent. Accordingly, taxpayers generally will find that the government's answers in tax refund suits will contain admissions only of pleaded facts evidenced by documents in the files of the Internal Revenue Service or of averments that have been verified by the Service during the administrative procedures that preceded the refund suit. Nevertheless, the government's admissions usually will encompass the taxpayer's allegations relating to venue and jurisdiction.

The generally applicable procedural rules of the tax refund tribunals govern the pleading of defenses.[76] Of particular note is the requirement that the government set forth affirmatively the taxpayer's fraud upon which a fraud penalty assessment was made.[77]

Sample Answer

Typically, the government's answer to the sample complaint discussed above would be similar to that shown in Fig. 11–5 (pages **11 · 9**–10). A typical answer to a petition in the Court of Claims would be (with the exception of the caption, the statutory provision giving jurisdiction,[78] and the identity of the government's attorney of record [79]) identical.

Government Counterclaims

In either tax refund tribunal the government may assert a counterclaim against a plaintiff taxpayer.[80] Usually, counterclaims arise in "divisible" tax cases in which the taxpayer has paid only a part of the total assessment in dispute. The government will normally counterclaim for the unpaid balance of the "divisible tax" assessment. A government counterclaim can also arise

---

[75] Annual Report of the Attorney General of the United States for the Fiscal Year Ended June 30, 1965, 298, 304.

[76] Fed. R. Civ. P. 8, 9, 12; Ct. Cl. R. 13, 14, 19, 20. See generally 2 MOORE'S FEDERAL PRACTICE pt. III (2d ed. 1965). Several defenses can be waived unless properly raised in the government's answer or in a motion filed prior to the answer. Fed. R. Civ. P. 12(h); Ct. Cl. R. 20(h). See 2 MOORE'S FEDERAL PRACTICE ¶ 12.23 (2d ed. 1965).

[77] Fed. R. Civ. P. 9(b); Ct. Cl. R. 14(b). Trainer v. United States, 145 F. Supp. 786 (E.D. Pa.)

[78] 28 US.C. § 1491.

[79] The Assistant Attorney General, Tax Division, is the government's attorney of record in tax refund suits in the Court of Claims.

[80] 28 U.S.C. § 1346(c), 1503. See Scott v. United States, 354 F.2d 292 (Ct. Cl.), in which a counterclaim having no relationship to the subject matter of the complaint was permitted against one of several plaintiffs.

IN THE UNITED STATES DISTRICT COURT
FOR THE DISTRICT OF MARYLAND

KENDALL MARVA,

    Plaintiff,

    v.   Civil Action No. 68–123

THE UNITED STATES OF AMERICA,

    Defendant,

ANSWER

Defendant, United States of America, answers plaintiff's complaint as follows:

1. Admits the allegations contained in paragraph 1 of the complaint.

2. Admits the allegations contained in paragraph 2 of the complaint.

3. Denies that any taxes were illegally or erroneously assessed against and collected from the plaintiff.

4. Avers that if jurisdiction exists, it exists by virtue of 28 U. S. C., Section 1346(a)(1).

COUNT ONE

5. Admits the allegations contained in paragraph 5 of the complaint.

6. Admits the allegations contained in paragraph 6 of the complaint.

7. Admits the allegations contained in paragraph 7 of the complaint except avers that the date of payment was June 16, 1967.

8. Denies the allegations contained in paragraph 8 of the complaint.

9. Admits the allegations contained in paragraph 9 of the complaint.

10. Admits the allegations contained in paragraph 10 of the complaint.

11. Denies each and every allegation contained in Exhibit A to the complaint unless otherwise expressly admitted herein.

12. Denies the allegations contained in paragraph 12 of the complaint except admits that no part of the amount claimed has been refunded to plaintiff.

13. Defendant is presently without knowledge or information sufficient to permit it to admit or deny the allegations contained in paragraph 13 of the complaint.

COUNT TWO

*   *   *

WHEREFORE, defendant, having answered fully, prays that judgment be entered dismissing plaintiff's complaint with prejudice and granting defendant its costs.

United States Attorney*

* Although the local United States Attorney is attorney of record, most tax refund cases are handled solely by Tax Division trial attorneys. See p. **14·6,** *infra.*

FIG. 11–5. GOVERNMENT'S ANSWER TO COMPLAINT

IN THE UNITED STATES DISTRICT COURT
FOR THE DISTRICT OF DELAWARE

DONALD R. ANDERSON, *Plaintiff,* *v.* UNITED STATES OF AMERICA, *Defendant.*	Civil Action No. 68–1123

ANSWER

*   *   *   *

COUNTERCLAIM

Defendant, the United States of America, asserts a counterclaim against plaintiff based on the following facts:

1. This counterclaim is asserted at the request of the Commissioner of Internal Revenue and at the direction of the Attorney General.

2. Jurisdiction over this counterclaim is conferred upon this court by 28 U. S. C. § 1346(a)(1).

3. On June 14, 19—, the Commissioner of Internal Revenue assessed against the plaintiff a 100% penalty under Section 6672 of the Internal Revenue Code of 1954 in the total amount of $6,900.00, comprised of the following:

Tax Period Covered	Penalty Assessed
Third quarter of 19—	$3,450.00
Fourth quarter of 19—	3,450.00
	$6,900.00

This penalty was assessed for the third and fourth quarters of 19— for the income taxes and Federal Insurance Contributions Act taxes withheld from the wages of the employees of A. B. C., Inc., a now defunct Delaware corporation.

4. Proper notice and demand for payment of the aforementioned assessment was served on plaintiff.

5. The aforementioned assessment was correctly made in accordance with law.

6. On November 25, 19—, plaintiff paid the sum of $1,000.00 to the defendant on the assessed penalty and has made no further payment.

7. The amount of $5,900.00 plus interest as provided by law remains due and owing the defendant as a result of the aforementioned penalty assessment.

WHEREFORE, defendant, having answered fully, prays that judgment be entered dismissing plaintiff's complaint with prejudice, and further prays for judgment against the plaintiff on defendant's counterclaim in the amount of $5,900.00 together with interest thereon in accordance with law and its costs in this action.

United States Attorney

FIG. 11–6. GOVERNMENT COUNTERCLAIM

as a result of the issuance of a deficiency notice while a tax refund suit is pending.[81]

The government's counterclaim normally is pleaded as a part of its answer to the taxpayer's complaint or petition. A counterclaim may, with permission of the court,[82] be asserted by means of a supplemental pleading or amended answer filed after the original answer.[83]

The sample in Fig. 11–6 (page **11·**18) illustrates a typical government counterclaim pleaded as part of its answer in a district court tax refund suit. A counterclaim pleaded in the Court of Claims would, in substance, be identical.

TAXPAYER'S RESPONSE TO GOVERNMENT'S ANSWER

In a tax refund suit a taxpayer need respond to the government's answer only(1) if the government has raised a counterclaim or, (2) in the Court of Claims, if the government has alleged the taxpayer's fraud.[84] The taxpayer's responsive pleading should only be directed toward the matter as to which a response is required by the rules. As to those issues, however, the taxpayer will be deemed to have admitted any allegation not denied or avoided.[85] Allegations as to which no responsive pleading is required are taken as denied or avoided.[86]

The taxpayer's response to the sample counterclaim would appear as in Fig. 11–7 (page **11·**20).

AMENDMENT OF PLEADINGS

The pleading rules of the tax refund tribunals are liberal in allowing parties to amend their respective pleadings.

In the district courts a pleading may be amended once without permission of the court at any time before a response to the pleading is served. If the pleading to be amended is one for which no responsive pleading is permitted (*e.g.* a typical answer without a counterclaim) it may be amended within 20 days after it is served.[87] In the Court of Claims a pleading may be amended by a party as a matter of right at any time before service on him of a responsive pleading or of a motion to dismiss or for summary

---

[81] IRC § 7422(e). See p. **13·**29 *et seq. infra.*

[82] Note that, in the Court of Claims, procedural matters may be passed upon by the trial commissioner rather than by the Court itself. Ct. Cl. R. 4(c).

[83] Fed. R. Civ. P. 13(e), (f); Ct. Cl. R. 21(d), (e).

[84] Fed. R. Civ. P. 7(a); Ct. Cl. R. 10(a). For time limits on the taxpayer's response to the answer, see Fed. R. Civ. P. 12(a); Ct. Cl. R 20(a)

[85] Fed R. Civ. P. 8(d); Ct. Cl. R. 19(c).

[86] *Ibid.*

[87] Fed. R. Civ. P. 15(a).

IN THE UNITED STATES DISTRICT COURT
FOR THE DISTRICT OF DELAWARE

DONALD R. ANDERSON,

    Plaintiff,

    v.   Civil Action No. 68–1123

UNITED STATES OF AMERICA,

    Defendant.

REPLY TO COUNTERCLAIM

Plaintiff, DONALD R. ANDERSON, responds to the defendant's counterclaim as follows:

1. Admits the allegations contained in paragraph 1 of the counterclaim.
2. Admits the allegations contained in paragraph 2 of the counterclaim.
3. Admits the allegations contained in paragraph 3 of the counterclaim but denies that the assessment was correct.
4. Admits the allegations contained in paragraph 4 of the counterclaim.
5. Denies the allegations contained in paragraph 5 of the counterclaim.
6. Admits the allegations contained in paragraph 6 of the counterclaim.
7. Denies the allegations contained in paragraph 7 of the counterclaim.

WHEREFORE, plaintiff having answered defendant's counterclaim fully prays that judgment be entered in accordance with plaintiff's complaint in this action, dismissing defendant's counterclaim with prejudice and granting plaintiff his costs in this action.

Thomas Field
Suite 611–614
Limestone Building
Wilmington, Delaware

FIG. 11–7. TAXPAYER'S RESPONSE TO COUNTERCLAIM

judgment. If no response is permitted, the pleading may be amended within 30 days after service.[88]

After the time within which amendment is a matter of right has expired, a pleader may amend his pleadings by obtaining either the consent of his adversary or leave of court.[89] The procedural rules of the district courts and the Court of Claims expressly provide that leave to amend "shall be freely given when justice so requires."[90]

[88] Ct. Cl. R. 22(a).
[89] Fed. R. Civ. P. 15(a) ; Ct. Cl. R. 22(a).
[90] *Ibid.*

Amended pleadings stand in the place of the originally filed documents. They require the same type of response as did the original pleadings they replace.[91]

Where a pleading is amended, the rules of both possible tax refund tribunals provide that the amendment "relates back" to the date of the original pleading if the claim or defense asserted in the amendment arose out of the transaction or occurrence set forth (or attempted to be set forth) in the original pleading.[92] This provision is of particular importance where a complaint or petition must be amended after the time for commencing a new tax refund suit has expired. Normally, the amendment to the complaint or petition will relate to the same transactions as were set forth in the original document. Hence, the relation-back rule will normally operate to make the amended pleading timely. However, if the effect of the amendment is to plead a totally new cause of action, for example by substituting a proper party plaintiff for an improper one, there will be no relation back. Hence, the statute of limitations will require dismissal of the action.[93]

Mechanically, it is best to file a complete amended pleading incorporating all changes. However, it is proper to file an amendment to a pleading in which only the amendment and as much of the original document as needed for clarity are included.[94]

THIRD–PARTY PRACTICE IN TAX REFUND SUITS

The procedural rules of the tax refund tribunals provide for third-party practice.[95] As noted by Professor Moore:

> The general purpose of [the rule permitting third-party practice] is to avoid two actions which should be tried together to save the time and cost of a reduplication of evidence [and] to obtain consistent results from identical or similar evidence . . .[96]

The government can be expected to seek to utilize third-party practice to bring additional taxpayers into a refund action whenever the plaintiff taxpayer has taken a position regarding a transaction or relationship that is inconsistent with the position taken by other taxpayers. For example, in a "responsible officer" penalty assessment case the government would seek to join as a party any person whom the plaintiff taxpayer may claim was the real responsible party.[97] In employer's tax cases, where taxpayers fre-

---

[91] *Ibid.*
[92] Fed. R. Civ. P. 15(c) ; Ct. Cl. R. 22(c).
[93] See Broadway Petroleum Corp. v. United States, *supra* note 28.
[94] See Ct. Cl. R. 22(e).
[95] Fed. R. Civ. P. 14 ; Ct. Cl. R. 23.
[96] 3 Moore's Federal Practice ¶ 14.04, at 501 (2d ed. 1966).
[97] *E.g.,* Gardner v. United States, 36 F.R.D. 453 (S.D.N.Y.).

quently allege that their workmen were independent contractors who hired their own helpers, the government would attempt to join the workmen as parties.[98] Even in income-tax controversies there are, on occasion, circumstances in which two or more taxpayers take conflicting views of a significant, taxwise, but factually ambiguous transaction. Typical are questions of whether a contract amounted to a sale or a lease, the proper allocation of a purchase price to various assets sold, and whether payments made by a corporation to a widow were gifts or compensation.

In order for the government to be able to bring an additional taxpayer into a tax refund suit several conditions must be met.

Firstly, suit against the additional taxpayer must be timely, venue must be proper, and there must exist no prohibition against suing him.[99]

Secondly, the additional taxpayer must bear a relationship to the pending tax refund suit such that the procedural rules will permit his joinder. For example, in the district courts the government may bring in, as a third-party defendant, a taxpayer who is or may be liable for all, or part, of the plaintiff's claim against the government.[100] In other words, the government must be able to say "If the plaintiff should recover a refund of the taxes claimed, then the third-party defendant will (or may) be liable for all, or part of the taxes refunded."

To illustrate this point it is helpful to refer to an employer's tax case.[101] Plaintiff was a home improvement company which applied artificial stone to houses. The physical work was done by crews of workmen directed by a crew leader. Plaintiff had met the jurisdictional prerequisites to his tax refund suit by paying the F.I.C.A. and F.U.T.A. taxes assessed against him with respect to a single workman for a single taxable period. In his suit for a refund of the employer's taxes plaintiff contended that he had no employees and that the crew leaders were independent contractors who themselves employed the workmen. The government was allowed to implead, as a third-party defendant, the crew leader who supervised the workman with respect to whom plaintiff paid the tax. The crew leader fit the description of a third-party defendant. If plaintiff had been correct in his assertion, the crew leader and not the plaintiff would be liable for the employer's taxes paid. Accordingly, if plaintiff recovered a refund the third-party defendant might be liable to the government for all, or part, of the taxes refunded.

Only in rare income, estate, or gift tax controversies would the government be able to fit an additional taxpayer into the definition of a third-party defendant contained in the Federal Rules of Civil Procedure. The

---

[98] Silverman v. United States, 18 A.F.T.R.2d 5089 (Md.).
[99] See 3 MOORE'S FEDERAL PRACTICE ¶¶ 14.25–.29 (2d ed. 1966).
[100] Fed. R. Civ. P. 14(a).
[101] Silverman v. United States, *supra* note 98.

Court of Claims Rules provide for the impleader, as third-party defendants, of persons having an interest in the subject matter of a pending suit or against whom the United States may be asserting a claim or contingent claim for the recovery of money paid by the government in respect of the transaction or matter constituting the subject matter of the suit.[102]

It does not appear that either category of permissible third-party defendants can be found in the context of a suit for refund of income, estate, or gift taxes, and the authors are not, at present, aware of a reported case in which the government has attempted to implead a third-party defendant in such a suit.

Finally, allowing the addition of a third-party defendant is discretionary with the court.[103] Even though a third-party complaint may be filed without leave of court, the court retains the authority to dismiss the complaint in its discretion.[104] It appears, however, that most United States District Judges and Court of Claims Commissioners would tend to permit joinder of a third-party defendant. The practical merit of permitting the government to join third-party defendants in tax refund suits was well expressed by Circuit Judge John R. Brown in his concurring opinion in United States v. Egbert:

> The "right" of the Government to have this employer withholding tax refund case tried before a single jury which would simultaneously resolve the inherently conflicting theories of the plaintiff shrimp vessel owners and the impleaded captains-independent contractors is a valuable one in a practical sense. Indeed, it is so valuable that unless tried together, the Government can lose both cases. On the other hand, the "right" of the Taxpayer-Plaintiff to run its own lawsuit before a jury chosen for one case, not two, is equally valuable to them. The fact remains that there is one decisive issue: are the captains and crew members employees of the vessel-owner operator? Or employees of the captain acting as an independent contractor? Despite our ingrained notions of an Article III case and controversy and the traditional notion that litigation is somehow the private domain of the litigants, resolution of this common question under procedures which may likely produce contradictory results is not the search for truth. This is not the quest of justice under law. This is a game.[105]

Where the government cannot implead an additional taxpayer as a third-party defendant it may be able to obtain the benefit of a single trial of several related controversies by other means. For example, the government may be in a position to move to consolidate the trial of several pending

---

[102] Ct. Cl. R. 23(a).

[103] Fed. R. Civ. P. 14(a).

[104] See 3 MOORE'S FEDERAL PRACTICE ¶ 14.05[2] (2d ed. 1966). Ct. Cl. R. 23.

[105] 347 F.2d 987 (C.A.5th). In this case, the trial judge had dismissed the government's third-party complaint in an employer's tax case. The Court of Appeals dismissed the government's appeal on the ground that the trial court's action was not a final judgment subject to appeal. Judge Brown, in concurring with the dismissal of the appeal, discussed the pros and cons of permitting the government to implead third-party defendants in tax refund suits.

tax refund suits.[106] Or, it may be able to commence an independent law suit against the additional taxpayer and then move for consolidation.[107] If, for example, as the result of an allocation of income, taxes were collected from one party to a series of transactions and refunded to another, then suits to recover erroneous refunds may be consolidated with a tax refund suit for a joint trial.[108] Finally, it is possible that the procedural rules allowing the joinder of additional plaintiffs and defendants may be applicable where third-party practice, as such, is not.[109]

[106] Fed. R. Civ. P. 42(a); Ct. Cl. R. 47(a). *E.g.,* Gutterman v. Scanlon, 222 F. Supp. 1007 (E.D.N.Y.)

[107] See Judge Brown's suggestion in United States v. Egbert, *supra* note 105.

[108] *E.g.,* Shaker Apartments, Inc. v. United States, 18 A.F.T.R.2d 5217 (N.D. Ohio).

[109] Fed. R. Civ. P. 19–24; Ct. Cl. R. 25–28.

LEGAL PRINCIPLES OF TAX REFUND SUITS

THEORY OF THE TAXPAYER'S CASE

Tax refund suits have long been recognized in the law [1] as actions in the nature of a suit for money had and received brought by taxpayers against the tax collector.[2] As the Supreme Court put it,

The action, brought to recover a tax erroneously paid, although an action at law, is equitable in its function. It is the lineal successor of the common count in *indebitatus assumpsit* for money had and received.[3]

[1] In this country, tax refund suits were litigated long before the creation of the Internal Revenue Service. *E.g.,* Bend v. Hoyt, 38 U.S. 263 (1839).

[2] Stone v. White, 301 U.S. 532, 534.

[3] *Id.* at 534.

The ultimate issue in a tax refund suit is whether the taxpayer has overpaid his taxes for the period in issue, and it is to this question that judicial inquiry is directed.[4] Unlike a Tax Court case, a tax refund suit is not, strictly speaking, a judicial review of the determination of an administrative agency. Rather, it is a suit in which the taxpayer must establish that the government has money that it should refund to him.[5] Accordingly, in a tax refund suit the taxpayer must not only prove that the Internal Revenue Service was wrong; he must go further and establish the correct amount of his tax liability for the period in suit.[6] It is only when the court can ascertain the amount of taxes the taxpayer should have paid that it can ascertain whether there has been an overpayment of taxes requiring a refund.[7] In sum, in a tax refund suit, the taxpayer's theory is that he can prove that he overpaid his true tax liability for the taxable periods in issue.

GOVERNMENT DEFENSES

Lack of Overpayment

In every tax refund suit the government will prevail unless the evidence discloses that there has been an overpayment of the taxpayer's tax liability for the periods in issue. The government's defense based upon a lack of overpayment can take either, or both, of two lines. Firstly, the government can contend that, with regard to the taxpayer's asserted grounds for recovery, he is incorrect. Secondly, the government can contend that even if the taxpayer should be correct with regard to the grounds on which he relies, there still was no overpayment of taxes because additional offsetting adjustments to the taxpayer's liability should be made.

TAX ADJUSTMENTS RAISED BY THE CLAIMS FOR REFUND. As discussed more fully below,[8] the jurisdictional rules relating to tax refund suits restrict the taxpayer's grounds for recovery to those set forth in his claims for refund. In his claims the taxpayer will contend that one or more tax adjustments (*i.e.* the disallowance of a deduction, the inclusion of an item in income, etc.) were incorrect and caused him to overpay his taxes. In its defense on the adjustments placed in issue by the taxpayer by virtue of his refund claims the government usually is not restricted to any legal or factual theory that the Internal Revenue Service may have adopted during

---

[4] Reinecke v. Spalding, 280 U.S. 227, 232–33.

[5] Taylor v. Commissioner, 70 F.2d 619, 620–21 (C.A.2d), *affirmed sub nom.* Helvering v. Taylor, 293 U.S. 507.

[6] Compton v. United States, 334 F.2d 212, 216 (C.A.4th); Taylor v. Commissioner, *supra* note 5; Forbes v. Hassett, 124 F.2d 925, 928 (C.A.1st).

[7] Decker v. Korth, 219 F.2d 732, 737 (C.A.10th); Hodoh v. United States, 153 F. Supp. 822 (N.D. Ohio).

[8] See p. **12·7** *et seq. infra.*

the administrative procedures preceding suit. If the adjustments were in fact correct, the circumstance that the Internal Revenue Service might have taken an incorrect approach to the case is completely immaterial.[9] To illustrate the point consider the case of a taxpayer who claimed a deduction for the losses of his wholly owned subchapter-S farm corporation.[10] The Internal Revenue Service disallowed the deduction on the theory that the corporation had been acquired for the purpose of avoiding income taxes, hence that Section 269 permitted the disallowance of the deductions. The taxpayer paid the deficiency assessed against him, filed claims for refund on the ground that the disallowance of the deduction was incorrect, and subsequently filed suit. Prior to trial, the government conceded that the disallowance of the deduction based upon Section 269 was incorrect, but alleged that the deduction was still not allowable because the farm operation was not a business conducted for profit. The case then proceeded to trial on the merits of the "business vs. hobby" issue.

"NEW" ADJUSTMENTS—THE DOCTRINE OF *Lewis* v. *Reynolds*. In addition to defending with regard to the tax adjustments put in issue by the taxpayer, the government may place additional items in dispute. Since the taxpayer's recovery depends upon a showing that he overpaid his taxes for the periods in issue, any adjustment affecting his tax liability for these periods may be utilized defensively by the government. These "new" offsetting adjustments may be asserted by the government even though the statute of limitations would bar a further deficiency assessment with respect to the taxable periods in suit in the refund action.[11] As the Supreme Court said in the leading case of *Lewis* v. *Reynolds* [12] (relying heavily upon the opinion of the Tenth Circuit),

[T]he Circuit Court of Appeals said—The above quoted provisions clearly limit refunds to overpayments. It follows that the ultimate question presented for decision, upon a claim for refund, is whether the taxpayer has overpaid his tax. This involves a redetermination of the entire tax liability. While no new assessment can be made, after the bar of the statute has fallen, the taxpayer, nevertheless, is not entitled to a refund unless he has overpaid his tax. The action to recover on a claim for refund is in the nature of an action for money had and received, and it is incumbent upon the claimant to show that the United States has money which belongs to him.

---

[9] Helvering v. Gowran, 302 U.S. 238, 246; Blansett v. United States, 283 F.2d 474, 478–79 (C.A.8th). An exception to this general rule arises in the event it is the actions of the Service which are under consideration. For example, in a § 482 case the theory of the Internal Revenue Service for its allocation may well be important.

[10] DuPont v. United States, 13 A.F.T.R.2d 824 (Del.) (decision on burden of proof), 234 F. Supp. 681 (Del.) (decision on the merits).

[11] Lewis v. Reynolds, 284 U.S. 281, *affirming* 48 F.2d 515 (C.A.10th); Dysart v. United States, 340 F.2d 624 (Ct. Cl.); United States v. Pfister, 205 F.2d 538, 541–42 (C.A.8th); Routzahn v. Brown, 95 F.2d 766, 769 (C.A.6th).

[12] Lewis v. Reynolds, *supra* note 11, at 283.

We agree with the conclusion reached by the courts below.

While the statutes authorizing refunds do not specifically empower the Commissioner to reaudit a return whenever repayment is claimed, authority therefor is necessarily implied. An overpayment must appear before refund is authorized. Although the statute of limitations may have barred the assessment and collection of any additional sum, it does not obliterate the right of the United States to retain payments already received when they do not exceed the amount which might have been properly assessed and demanded.

By virtue of the doctrine of *Lewis* v. *Reynolds* the government can totally or partially defeat a tax refund claim with offsetting adjustments beyond the scope of the taxpayer's claim for refund. And, the government can properly use discovery proceedings to ascertain whether any such defensive adjustment exist. In short, a tax refund suit is not limited to those adjustments that the taxpayer wishes to place in issue. For example, in the previously discussed farm loss case [13] the sole adjustment raised by the taxpayer's claims was the disallowance of a deduction for a farm's operating loss. The court concluded that the taxpayer was entitled to the deduction because the farm was a business. However, the taxpayer's recovery was reduced because the court found that a number of claimed farm expenses, not questioned during the administrative procedure, were not correctly deducted. While it did not occur in this instance, the taxpayer's recovery could have been further reduced or totally eliminated if the court had found that other tax adjustments for the periods in issue, even adjustments having no connection whatsoever with the farm operation, should have been made.

It has been suggested (and it appears logical) that once the government has gone beyond the scope of the refund claims to raise new issues, the taxpayer should be allowed to do so also.[14] This would result in the taxpayer's being able to raise counter offsetting adjustments to reduce the amount of the government's offsets.

Recoupment—Offset of Tax Liability for Statutorily Barred Period

In the tax law the pertinent statutes of limitations are usually strictly applied. In the specific context of tax refunds the Internal Revenue Code provides that the government may not offset against a taxpayer's overpayment of taxes for a given taxable period his underpayment for another period as to which collection or assessment is barred by the statute of limitations. That is, a credit of an overpayment against an asserted tax liability for a period for which assessment or collection is barred by the statute of limitations is void.[15] Thus, for example, a taxpayer who has

---

[13] DuPont v. United States, *supra* note 10.
[14] *E.g.*, CASEY, FEDERAL TAX PRACTICE § 11.15, at 169 (1955).
[15] IRC § 6514(b).

established a $25,000.00 overpayment of his income taxes for 1968 normally is entitled to a full refund even though he may, in fact, have underpaid his income taxes for 1960 (a year as to which assessment and collection is barred) by $50,000.00. However, in very limited situations, where the strict application of the statutes of limitations would enable a party to gain an unfair advantage by assuming inconsistent positions for closed and open taxable periods, an inequitable result will not be permitted. In effect, the law sometimes permits the opening of a closed taxable period in order to make corrections normally barred by the statute of limitations. The narrowly applied judicial doctrine of equitable recoupment provides for relief from a party's attempt to "burn the candle at both ends" of a transaction.

In *Rothensies* v. *Electric Storage Battery Co.*[16] the Supreme Court stated the doctrine of equitable recoupment in the following terms.

> The essence of the doctrine of recoupment is stated in the *Bull* case; "recoupment is in the nature of a defense arising out of some feature of the transaction upon which the plaintiff's action is grounded." 295 U.S. 247, 262. It has never been thought to allow one transaction to be offset against another, but only to permit a transaction which is made the subject of suit by a plaintiff to be examined in all its aspects, and judgment to be rendered that does justice in view of the one transaction as a whole.[17]

This defense, which allows the government an offset against the refund a taxpayer would otherwise be entitled to, is to be distinguished from the defense of lack of overpayment which can also give rise to an offset. In the words of the United States Court of Claims:

> . . . the defense of recoupment in a refund suit should not be confused with the broader and more fundamental defense of lack of overpayment of the particular tax involved in the suit for refund, traceable to the landmark decision by the Supreme Court in Lewis v Reynolds, 284 U.S. 281, 52 S.Ct. 145, 76 L.Ed. 293 (1932). The former involves attempts to set off tax liability from one year against that for another year after the statute of limitations has run or where attempts are made to set off the tax liability of one taxpayer against that of a second taxpayer. This type of defense has been commonly referred to as "equitable recoupment." In these situations where the challenged item arose in a year other than in suit or where different parties are involved, the defense may only be maintained where a single or same transaction is involved.

On the other hand, where both the taxpayer's claim and the government's setoff concern the same tax for the same year by the same taxpayer, the government's right to raise such a defense is unconditional and need not meet the "same transaction" requirement of the equitable recoupment defense. Here the right of the government is based on the broader principle that a taxpayer is not entitled to a refund unless he has in fact overpaid the particular tax, while in "equitable recoupment" the right to raise such a defense is based on the more limited principle that a party should not gain the protection of the statute of

---

[16] 329 U.S. 296.
[17] *Id.* at 299.

limitations where he has given a different tax treatment to the same transaction in different years.[18]

The application of the doctrine of equitable recoupment is illustrated by the case of *Stone* v. *White* [19] in which trustees paid (under protest) taxes that should have been paid by the beneficiary. After the statute of limitations barred collection from the beneficiary the trustees sued for a refund on the ground that income was properly taxable to the beneficiary and not to them. They contended that they were entitled to a refund even though their recovery would be paid over to the beneficiary and the net result would be that no tax at all would be collected on the income in question. The trustees argued that statutory provisions barred the collection of the tax from the beneficiary and also prohibited the government from using an underpayment for a closed year as an offset against an overpayment for an open year. The Supreme Court, relying upon the basically equitable nature of a tax refund suit, answered the trustees' contentions as follows:

> These provisions limit the collection of a tax, and prevent the retention of one paid after it is barred by the statute. They preclude, in a suit by the taxpayer against the collector or the government, reliance on a claim against the taxpayer, barred by statute, as a set-off, or counterclaim. But the demand made upon the trustees was not barred by limitation and it would be an unreasonable construction of the statute, not called for by its words, to hold that it is intended to deprive the government of defenses based on special equities establishing its right to withhold a refund from the demanding taxpayer. The statute does not override a defense based on the estoppel of the taxpayer. *R. H. Stearns Co.* v. *United States,* 291 U. S. 54, 61, 62. The statutory bar to the right of action for the collection of the tax does not prevent reliance upon a defense which is not a set-off or a counterclaim, but is an equitable reason, growing out of the circumstances of the erroneous payment, why petitioners ought not to recover.
>
> Here the defense is not a counter demand on petitioners, but a denial of their equitable right to undo a payment which, though effected by an erroneous procedure, has resulted in no unjust enrichment to the government, and in no injury to petitioners or their beneficiary. The government, by retaining the tax paid by the trustees, is not reviving a stale claim. Its defense, which inheres in the cause of action, is comparable to an equitable recoupment or diminution of petitioners' right to recover. "Such a defense is never barred by the statute of limitations so long as the main action itself **is** timely." *Bull* v. *United States,* 295 U. S. 247, 262; *Williams* v. *Neely,* 134 Fed. 1, 13.[20]

In §§ 1311–1315 of the Internal Revenue Code of 1954 [21] Congress has, in part, codified the doctrine of equitable recoupment and to an extent expanded the ability of the government and taxpayers to avoid the unfair effects that can sometimes result from a strict application of the statutes of

---

[18] Dysart v. United States, 340 F.2d 624, 627 (Ct. Cl.).

[19] 301 U.S. 532.

[20] *Id.* at 538–39.

[21] For a detailed discussion of these mitigation provisions, see 2 MERTENS, LAW OF FEDERAL INCOME TAXATION, c. 14 (Zimet rev., 1961).

limitations. These complex statutory provisions, applicable in specified situations only, will permit adjustments in spite of normally applicable statutes of limitations to correct errors of the following types:

1. Double inclusion of an item of gross income
2. Double allowance of a deduction or credit
3. Double exclusion of an item of gross income
4. Double disallowance of a deduction or credit
5. Correlative deductions and inclusions for trusts or estates and legatees, beneficiaries, or heirs
6. Correlative deductions and credits for related corporations
7. Erroneous basis of property resulting from erroneous treatment of a prior transaction [22]

It has been held that Congress, in establishing the detailed mitigation provisions of §§ 1311–1315 of the Internal Revenue Code of 1954, superseded any common law recoupment remedies formerly available with regard to those categories of situations described in § 1312.[23] When used as a defense in a tax refund suit, the net result of §§ 1311–1315 is that of an equitable recoupment. In effect, the "deficiency" for the closed taxable period is used to eliminate or reduce the refund due as a result of the overpayment for the open taxable period in suit in the refund case.[24] Achieving the net result can require the assessment of an adjustment for the closed years as if it were a deficiency, followed by a credit of the "deficiency" against the overpayment for the open years.[25]

It should be noted that the doctrine of equitable recoupment and the statutory mitigation provisions, although discussed here as defenses for the government, can also be utilized by a taxpayer. Thus they could, in appropriate circumstances, provide the foundation for a refund action.[26]

Variance from Grounds Stated in Claims for Refund

In a tax refund suit the taxpayer's grounds for recovery are limited to those grounds set forth in the claims for refund on which his suit is based.[27] Where, in a refund suit, a taxpayer seeks recovery on grounds not presented in his claims, a so-called "fatal variance" exists, and his action, to the extent it varies from the claims, is subject to dismissal. The jurisdictional prerequisite of a claim for refund will not be met as to the ground not raised in a timely claim for refund.

[22] IRC § 1312.
[23] Gooding v. United States, 326 F.2d 988, 995–96 (Ct. Cl.).
[24] IRC § 1314.
[25] IRC § 1314(b). See MERTENS, LAW OF FEDERAL INCOME TAXATION § 14.20 (Zimet rev., 1961).
[26] *E.g.,* Bull v. United States, 295 U.S. 247; Boyle v. United States, 355 F.2d 233 (C.A.3d).
[27] Real Estate—Land Title & Trust Co. v. United States, 309 U.S. 13; United States v. Andrews, 302 U.S. 517; United States v. Felt & Tarrant Mfg. Co., 283 U.S. 269.

As illustrative of this point consider the case of a bank which, in its claims for refund, asserted that it was entitled to a refund because the Internal Revenue Service erroneously disallowed a deduction for a claimed "loss" due to the bank's having adjusted downward the book value of its furniture and fixtures. In a refund suit based on these claims the bank asserted, as an additional ground for recovery, that it had not been allowed deductions for alleged charitable deductions made during the periods in suit. The government was entitled to a dismissal of the taxpayer's complaint to the extent it claimed a refund based upon charitable deduction grounds.[28] In upholding the government's defense based upon the variance between the taxpayer's grounds at trial and those presented in its claim for refund, the court noted,

> Both the Code and the Regulations require the filing of a refund claim prior to the institution of a civil suit for refund. This procedure is designed to apprise the Commissioner of what subject matter to review and he can take the claim at face value and examine only those grounds to which his attention has been directed. United States v. Garbutt Oil Co., 302 U.S. 528, 58 S.Ct. 320, 82 L.Ed. 405 (1938). As a corollary to this general principle, a taxpayer may not advance one ground or legal theory in his claim filed with the Commissioner and rely upon an entirely different ground or theory in a subsequent suit for refund. United States v. Felt & Tarrant Mfg. Co., 283 U.S. 269, 51 S.Ct. 376, 75 L.Ed. 1025 (1931); Carmack v. Scofield, 201 F.2d 360 (5th Cir. 1953). Neither may a claimant raise a wholly new factual basis for his claim at the later trial. Dascomb v. McCuen, 73 F.2d 417 (2d Cir. 1934), cert. den. Chandler v. McCuen, 295 U.S. 737, 55 S.Ct. 649, 79 L.Ed. 1685 (1934).

> In Nemours Corp. v. United States, 188 F.2d 745 (3rd Cir. 1951), cert. den. 342 U.S. 834, 72 S.Ct. 50, 96 L.Ed. 631 (1951), Judge Goodrich commented:

> "This is hard law, no doubt. Perhaps it is necessarily strict law in view of the scope of the operations of a fiscal system as large as that of the United States. Whether that is so we are not called upon to say. We apply the rule; we do not make it. It is to be observed that recovery of claims against the Government has always been the subject of a strict compliance requirement. The recovery of claims for tax refunds is but an application of this broad and strict rule." Id. at 750.[29]

The determination of whether the taxpayer has, in his refund suit, varied from the grounds stated in his claims for refund depends upon the circumstances of the particular case under consideration. The issue has been stated by Casey in his treatise as follows:

> The question posed . . . is, what is the "ground" of refund relied upon in the claim. It appears that by "ground" of refund is not meant merely the adjustment or item as to which reversal in treatment is desired, but the concept is

---

[28] The Schuykill Haven Trust Co. v. United States, 252 F. Supp. 557, 561–62 (E.D. Pa.).

[29] *Id.* at 561–62.

generally held to include the reasons and theory justifying such reversal. As a result, any departure or variance whatever from such theory may be open to challenge under judicial interpretations of the meaning of "ground" which often seem harshly restrictive.[30]

In sum, it appears that the legal test for variance is analogous to the test utilized to ascertain whether an alleged informal claim is valid to support jurisdiction for a tax refund suit.[31] Was the refund claim (in the context of the case under consideration) adequate to put the Commissioner of Internal Revenue on notice of the grounds for recovery asserted in the refund suit so that in his investigation of the claim he would have been led to a consideration of these grounds?

Assignment of Claim for Refund in Violation of Statute

By statute, assignments of claims against the United States, including tax refund claims, are limited by the "Anti-assignment" Statute.[32] This statute provides,

All transfers and assignments made of any claim upon the United States, or of any part or share thereof, or interest therein, whether absolute or conditional, and whatever may be the consideration therefor, and all powers of attorney, orders, or other authorities for receiving payment of any such claim, or of any part or share thereof, . . . shall be absolutely null and void, unless they are freely made and executed in the presence of at least two attesting witnesses, after the allowance of such a claim, the ascertainment of the amount due, and the issuing of a warrant for the payment thereof.

The statutory ban on assignment of claims does not apply to assignments that take place "by operation of law." [33]

Tax refund suits are, of course, actions to recover on claims against the Unitd States. The tax refund claims on which the suits are based have not been allowed by the government. Accordingly their assignment, other than by operation of law, is prohibited by the Anti-assignment Statute. Where suit on a claim for refund is brought by an assignee, if the assignment should be held void, the action is subject to dismissal for want of the proper plaintiff. For example, consider the situation of an individual who sells all his stock in his wholly owned corporation at a time when it had a claim for refund pending before the Internal Revenue Service. If, as part of the deal, the corporation transferred the pending claim for refund to the seller, the Anti-assignment Statute would be violated. Therefore, a tax

---

[30] 3 CASEY, FEDERAL TAX PRACTICE § 10.32, at 69 (1955). See also Moser, *The Effect of Variations Between Claim for Refund and Trial in Suits for Refund,* N.Y.U. 12th INST. ON FED. TAX. 949 (1954).

[31] See p. **10·8–9** *supra.*

[32] 31 U.S.C. § 203.

[33] United States v. Aetna Surety Co., 338 U.S. 366.

refund suit by the seller (transferee) based on the claim for refund that had been transferred to him would be subject to dismissal.[34]

The exemption from the Anti-assignment Statute of assignments of transfers of claims that take place by operation of law was read into the statute by the courts to prevent manifest unfairness. As noted by Judge Graven:

> Where a just claim against the United States passes by operation of law from the party to whom the claim accrued to another, if the Anti-assignment Statute were to be held to interdict such assignee from bringing action on the claim, then the result would be that a just claim would go unpaid since the party to whom the claim accrued could not bring an action on it because he was no longer the owner of it. The exception was based on the necessity.[35]

The judicially created exception allows transferees to bring actions on claims for refund where they became the owner of the claim by "devolutions of title by force of law." [36] Thus, the personal representative of a deceased taxpayer may pursue his claims for refund,[37] and the trustee of a bankrupt may prosecute his claims.[38] The claims of an estate are considered to pass by operation of law to the beneficiaries upon the final distribution of the assets of the estate.[39] However, an attempt to assign claims owned by an estate prior to final distribution will violate the Anti-assignment Statute.[40] Similarly, transfers of claims from a corporation to its shareholders in connection with the complete liquidation of the business,[41] or assignments by virtue of corporate merger, dissolution, or consolidation are considered to occur by operation of law and do not violate the Anti-assignment Statute.[42]

Estoppel of Taxpayer from Prosecuting Refund Suit by Virtue of a Form 870–AD (or Equivalent) Agreement

The government contends that, in the following context, taxpayers are barred from bringing refund suits as to taxable periods that have been administratively settled pursuant to an agreement on Treasury Form 870–AD [43] or its equivalent. Assume that an Internal Revenue Agent has

---

[34] Lane, *Assignment of Claims for Refund*, 19 J. TAXATION 362 (1963).

[35] Kinney—Lindstrom Foundation, Inc. v. United States, 186 F. Supp. 133, 138 (N.D. Iowa).

[36] *Ibid.*

[37] United States v. Aetna Surety Co., *supra* note 33, at 375; Erwin v. United States, 92 U.S. 392, 397; Kinney—Lindstrom Foundation, Inc. v. United States, *supra* note 35.

[38] Erwin v. United States, *supra* note 37, at 397. *Cf.* United States v. Rochelle, 363 F.2d 225, 233 (C.A.5th).

[39] Pettengill v. United States, 253 F. Supp. 321 (N.D. Ind.).

[40] Kinney—Lindstrom Foundation, Inc. v. United States, *supra* note 35.

[41] Novo Trading Corp. v. Commissioner, 113 F.2d 320 (C.A.2d).

[42] Seaboard Air Line Ry. v. United States, 256 U.S. 656. *Cf.* Western Pac. R.R. v. United States, 268 U.S. 271.

[43] See Fig. 1–4, p. 1·26 *supra*.

contended that deficiencies should be assessed against a taxpayer by virtue of three tax adjustments, for example (1) the disallowance of travel and entertainment expenses, (2) the treatment of income from a sale as ordinary income instead of capital gains, and (3) the reduction of a claimed charitable deduction from $10,000 to $1,000. At the Appellate Division level of the Internal Revenue Service an agreement can be reached whereby the government will concede the two deduction issues and the taxpayer will concede the capital gains issue. At this point the taxpayer submits a proposal on Treasury Form 870–AD whereby he waives the restrictions of Section 6213(a) and consents to the assessment and collection of the deficiency resulting from the capital gains issue. The agreement also provides,

> If this proposal is accepted by or on behalf of the Commissioner, the case shall not be reopened in the absence of fraud, malfeasance, concealment or misrepresentation of material fact, or an important mistake in mathematical calculation; and no claim for refund shall be filed or prosecuted for the year(s) above stated other than for the amounts of overassessments shown above.

The agreement is accepted on behalf of the Commissioner, and the payment called for is made by the taxpayer. The matter rests until the statute of limitations (plus any extensions applicable) on additional assessments expires. Then, the taxpayer, in spite of the words of the agreement, files claims for refund for the period in question alleging that the Internal Revenue Service erroneously treated the sale proceeds as capital gains and, therefore, that there was an overpayment of taxes. Thereafter, a refund suit is filed by the taxpayer based on his claims for refund. The courts are divided upon the question of whether the taxpayer's refund suit is barred by virtue of his actions and therefore subject to dismissal. However, all agree that an agreement under Form 870–AD (or equivalent) does not amount to a statutory settlement of the taxpayer's liability for the periods in question.[44]

Those courts that have held the taxpayer estopped to bring his refund suit have found that the taxpayer has, by delaying the filing of his claims for refund until too late for the government to act,[45] prevented the government from being placed in the position it had before the agreement was executed.[46] As Judge Warren L. Jones, speaking for the Fifth Circuit, put it,[47] "The Government, relying upon the representations that no refund would be claimed and no suit to recover would be brought, lost its right to

---

[44] Botany Worsted Mills v. United States, 278 U.S. 282, 288–89; Daugette v. Patterson, 250 F.2d 753, 755–56 (C.A.5th); Uinta Livestock Corp. v. United States, 355 F.2d 761, 765 (C.A.10th).

[45] Presumably, if the taxpayer submits claims for refund sufficiently before the statute of limitations on assessments expires, even those courts will find no estoppel.

[46] Cain v. United States, 255 F.2d 193 (C.A.8th); Daugette v. Patterson, *supra* note 44; Schneider v. United States, 119 F.2d 215 (C.A.6th); Guggenheim v. United States, 77 F. Supp. 186 (Ct. Cl.); Lowe v. United States, 223 F. Supp. 948 (Mont.). *Cf.* Monge v. Smith, 229 F.2d 361 (C.A.9th), *cert. denied,* 335 U.S. 908.

[47] Daugette v. Patterson, *supra* note 44, at 756.

assess deficiencies." Therefore, it has been held that the doctrine of equitable estoppel bars the taxpayer from prosecuting his tax refund suit.

Other courts, however, have not considered the taxpayer prohibited from pursuing his refund claims in the absence of the classic elements of estoppel, *i.e.,* (1) a false representation or wrongful misleading silence (2) arising out of a statement of fact (3) as to which the person claiming estoppel was ignorant of the true facts and (4) adversely affected by the false statements or misleading silence.[48] These tribunals have failed to find any false representation or misleading conduct on the taxpayer's part. Nor do they find that the government was justified in relying upon an "agreement" that it should have known did not meet the statutory requirements for a settlement of the taxpayer's liability and which was, therefore, not binding upon the parties. Several courts have also concluded that equitable estoppel is not appropriate because the government is free to assert the statutorily barred deficiencies as offsets against any recovery by the taxpayer.[49]

Res Judicata and Collateral Estoppel

In considering the application of res judicata and collateral estoppel to federal tax controversies, it is helpful to begin by differentiating between the two doctrines. As the Supreme Court has stated the distinction,

> . . . under the doctrine of *res judicata,* a judgment "on the merits" in a prior suit involving the same parties or their privies bars a second suit based on the same cause of action. Under the doctrine of collateral estoppel, on the other hand, such a judgment precludes relitigation of issues actually litigated and determined in the prior suit, regardless of whether it was based on the same cause of action as the second suit.[50]

And, as the Court said in the leading case of *Commissioner* v. *Sunnen,*

> These same concepts are applicable in the federal income tax field. Income taxes are levied on an annual basis. Each year is the origin of a new liability and of a separate cause of action. Thus if a claim of liability or non-liability relating to a particular tax year is litigated, a judgment on the merits is *res judicata* as to any subsequent proceeding involving the same claim and the same tax year. But if the later proceeding is concerned with a similar or unlike claim relating to a different tax year, the prior judgment acts as a collateral estoppel only as to those matters in the second proceeding which were actually

---

[48] Uinta Livestock Corp. v. United States, *supra* note 44; United States v. Prince, 348 F.2d 746 (C.A.2d) ; Van Antwerp v. United States, 92 F.2d 871 (C.A.9th) ; Morris White Fashions, Inc. v. United States, 176 F. Supp. 760 (S.D.N.Y.). *Cf.* Joyce v. Gentsch, 141 F.2d 891 (C.A.6th) ; Bank of N.Y. v. United States, 170 F.2d 20 (C.A. 3d).

[49] *E.g.,* Uinta Livestock Corp. v. United States, *supra* note 44; Morris White Fashions, Inc. v. United States, *supra* note 48. *Cf.* Cuba R.R. v. United States, 254 F.2d 280 (C.A.2d). For a discussion of offsets, see p. **12**·3 *et seq. supra.*

[50] Lawlor v. National Screen Serv. Corp., 349 U.S. 322, 326.

presented and determined in the first suit. Collateral estoppel operates, in other words, to relieve the government and the taxpayer of "redundant litigation of the identical question of the statute's application to the taxpayer's status." Tait v. Western Md. R. Co., 289 U.S. 620, 624, 53 S.Ct. 706, 707, 77 L.Ed. 1405.[51]

The judgment to which reference is made is a final judgment.[52]

IDENTITY-OF-PARTY REQUIREMENT IN TAX CASES. It should be noted that, for purposes of the identity of party requirements of the doctrines of res judicata and collateral estoppel, the Commissioner of Internal Revenue, the District Director of Internal Revenue, and the United States of America are considered to be identical parties.[53] Accordingly, a difference in the nominal identity of the governmental party will not affect the applicability of these doctrines.

As to the taxpayer, the normally applicable rules are utilized to determine whether the party in a pending suit is the same, or in privity with, a corresponding party in a decided case so as to permit the application of the doctrines of res judicata and collateral estoppel.[54]

APPLICATION OF RES JUDICATA TO TAX CASES. In tax suits [55] the doctrine of res judicata bars a refund action by a taxpayer with regard to his tax liability for a taxable period that has been the subject of a prior suit.[56] Hence, if a taxpayer has litigated his income tax liability for the taxable year 1966 in either the Tax Court or a tax refund forum he cannot, thereafter, bring an action with respect to his 1966 income tax liability.[57] He is barred from suing even though he may, in his new suit, raise issues totally different from those considered in the prior action. The reason for the prohibition against a second suit is that a court of competent jurisdiction had, in the first suit, established the correct amount of his 1966 income tax liability. This liability, once established, cannot be the subject of a new action between the same parties.[58]

---

[51] 333 U.S. 591, 598–99.

[52] For a detailed discussion of res judicata and collateral estoppel, see 1B MOORE'S FEDERAL PRACTICE ¶¶ 0.405–.448 (2d ed. 1965).

[53] IRC § 7422(c). Tait v. Western Md. Ry., 289 U.S. 620, 626–27.

[54] See generally 1B MOORE'S FEDERAL PRACTICE ¶¶ 0.411, 0.422[3] (2d ed. 1965).

[55] The doctrine of res judicata is applicable to Tax Court cases as well as tax refund suits. However, in the context of a Tax Court case, the doctrine would normally be utilized by a taxpayer who would allege that the government is asserting a deficiency for a taxable period that has already been the subject of concluded litigation. Since a deficiency notice must precede a taxpayer's petition, it seems unlikely that the Commissioner could successfully argue that the taxable period is "closed" by res judicata if he has issued a deficiency notice based upon its being "open."

[56] Commissioner v. Sunnen, 333 U.S. 591, 598–99.

[57] Except for certain exceptional circumstances specified by statute, *e.g.*, a net operating loss carryback that offsets the taxpayer's liability for the already litigated taxable period. IRC § 6511(d)(2)(B)(i). See p. **10·**24–25 *supra*.

[58] Guettel v. United States, 95 F.2d 229 (C.A.8th), *cert. denied,* 305 U.S. 603 (estate tax case).

APPLICATION OF COLLATERAL ESTOPPEL TO TAX CASES. In tax suits,[59] the doctrine of collateral estoppel, when applicable, acts to prohibit the relitigation of an issue that has been determined between the parties in a prior suit, even though the prior suit is not res judicata as to the issues in the second suit.[60] For example, consider a taxpayer who litigated (whether in the Tax Court or a refund forum) his right to deduct support payments to his wife for the taxable years 1963 and 1964. If he lost his case, collateral estoppel would prevent his litigating in a second suit his right to deduct the same type of payments under the same agreement for 1965 and 1966. Assuming no pertinent changes in the circumstances, the issue regarding the deductibility of the payments would have been determined in the first suit. Collateral estoppel can also operate to the advantage of the taxpayer. Hence, a favorable determination may bar the government from relitigating decided issues for other taxable periods.[61]

The applicability of the doctrine of collateral estoppel is strictly limited to situations in which the precise question at issue in the pending case was decided in a prior controversy. If the prior court did not actually decide the issue (for example if it had been stipulated) collateral estoppel would not be applicable.[62] There must have been no intervening change in the facts or law pertinent to the issue previously litigated. As the Supreme Court stated in the leading case of *Commissioner* v. *Sunnen,*

[Collateral estoppel] is designed to prevent repetitious lawsuits over matters which have once been decided and which have remained substantially static, factually and legally. It is not meant to create vested rights in decisions that have become obsolete or erroneous with time, thereby causing inequities among taxpayers.

And so where two cases involve income taxes in different taxable years, collateral estopped must be used with its limitations carefully in mind so as to avoid injustice. It must be confined to situations where the matter raised in the second suit is identical in all respects with that decided in the first proceeding and where the controlling facts and applicable legal rules remain unchanged. Tait v. Western Md. R. Co., supra. If the legal matters determined in the earlier case differ from those raised in the second case, collateral estoppel has no bearing on the situation. See Travelers Ins. Co. v. Commissioner, 2 Cir., 161 F.2d 93. And where the situation is vitally altered between the time of the first judgment and the second, the prior determination is not conclusive. See State Farm Ins. Co. v. Duel, 324 U.S. 154, 162, 65 S.Ct. 573, 577, 89 L.Ed. 812; 2 Freeman on Judgments, 5th Ed. 1925, § 713. As demonstrated by Blair v. Commissioner, 300 U.S. 5, 9, 57 S.Ct. 330, 331, 81 L.Ed. 465, a judicial declaration intervening between the two proceedings may so change the legal atmosphere as to render the rule of collateral estoppel inapplicable. But the interven-

---

[59] The doctrine of collateral estoppel is applicable to Tax Court cases as well as tax refund suits.

[60] Commissioner v. Sunnen, *supra* note 56.

[61] *E.g.,* Staffilino v. United States, 18 A.F.T.R.2d 5882 (N.D. Ohio) ; Harold's Club v. United States, 18 A.F.T.R.2d 5394 (Nev.).

[62] Food Mach. & Chemical Corp. v. United States, 366 F.2d 1007 (Ct. Cl.).

ing decision need not necessarily be that of a state court, as it was in the Blair case. While such a state court decision may be considered as having changed the facts for federal tax litigation purposes, a modification or growth in legal principles as enunciated in intervening decisions of this Court may also effect a significant change in the situation. Tax inequality can result as readily from neglecting legal modulations by this Court as from disregarding factual changes wrought by state courts. In either event, the supervening decision cannot justly be ignored by blind reliance upon the rule of collateral estoppel. Henricksen v. Seward, 9 Cir., 135 F.2d 986, 988, 989, 150 A.L.R. 1; Pelham Hall Co. v. Hassett, 1 Cir., 147 F.2d 63, 68, 69; Commissioner v. Arundel-Brooks Concrete Corp., 4 Cir., 152 F.2d 225, 227, 162, A.L.R. 1200; Corrigan v. Commissioner, 6 Cir., 155 F.2d 164, 165; and see West Coast Life Ins. Co. v. Merced Irr. Dist., 9 Cir., 114 F.2d 654, 661, 662; contra: Commissioner v. Western Union Tel. Co., 2 Cir., 141 F.2d 774, 778. It naturally follows that an interposed alteration in the pertinent statutory provisions or Treasury regulations can make the use of that rule unwarranted.   Tait v. Western Md. R. Co., supra, 625 of 289 U.S., 53 S.Ct. 706.

Of course, where a question of fact essential to the judgment is actually litigated and determined in the first tax proceeding, the parties are bound by that determination in a subsequent proceeding even though the cause of action is different. See Evergreens v. Nunan, 2 Cir., 141 F.2d 927. And if the very same facts and no others are involved in the second case, a case relating to a different tax year, the prior judgment will be conclusive as to the same legal issues which appear, assuming no intervening doctrinal change. But if the relevant facts in the two cases are separable, even though they be similar or identical, collateral estoppel does not govern the legal issues which recur in the second case. Thus the second proceeding may involve an instrument or transaction identical with, but in a form separable from, the one dealt with in the first proceeding. In that situation, a court is free in the second proceeding to make an independent examination of the legal matters at issue. It may then reach a different result or, if consistency in decision is considered just and desirable, reliance may be placed upon the ordinary rule of *stare decisis*. Before a party can invoke the collateral estoppel doctrine in these circumstances, the legal matter raised in the second proceeding must involve the same set of events or documents and the same bundle of legal principles that contributed to the rendering of the first judgment. Tait v. Western Maryland R. Co., supra. And see Griswold, "Res Judicata in Federal Tax Cases," 46 Yale L.J. 1320; Paul and Zimet, "Res Judicata in Federal Taxation," appearing in Paul, Selected Studies in Federal Taxation, 2d series, 1938, p. 104.[63]

A peculiar situation exists with regard to the application of collateral estoppel in civil fraud penalty cases that follow criminal prosecutions of the taxpayer. If the taxpayer was acquitted in the criminal case collateral estoppel does not apply to bar the government from asserting a civil fraud penalty for the same taxable periods.[64] In the criminal case the government had to sustain the burden of proving the taxpayer's fraud beyond a reasonable doubt. In the civil case, however, the government need only present evidence sufficient to show the taxpayer's fraud by clear and con-

[63] Commissioner v. Sunnen, *supra* note 56.
[64] Helvering v. Mitchell, 303 U.S. 391.

vincing evidence. Accordingly, a finding that the government failed to sustain its burden in the criminal case does not preclude its being able to sustain the lighter burden in a civil case.

If a taxpayer pleads *nolo contendere* in a criminal case, collateral estoppel will not operate to prohibit his denying liability for a civil fraud penalty.[65] His plea does not constitute an admission of guilt, and he is therefore free to deny his fraud in a later civil case.

If a taxpayer is convicted in a criminal case, however, whether because of a plea of guilty or as the result of trial on the merits, the doctrine of collateral estoppel will operate in favor of the Government in the absence of a "tainted" conviction.[66] In a subsequent civil case the taxpayer is estopped to deny his fraud with respect to the taxable periods for which he was convicted. He is not estopped, however, to contest the amount of his tax liability for those periods since the determination of the exact amount of tax liability was not essential to his conviction. Nor is the government estopped to establish a larger tax deficiency than it asserted in the criminal case.[67]

BURDEN OF PROOF IN TAX REFUND SUITS

Taxpayer's Burden To Prove Overpayment of Taxes

In a tax refund suit the burden of proving that he is entitled to a refund, *i.e.,* that there was an overpayment of taxes, rests upon the taxpayer. Hence the taxpayer must sustain what is commonly referred to as a "double burden of proof." As in a Tax Court case the taxpayer must prove that the Commissioner's assessment was erroneous. Then, he must go further and prove his correct tax liability for the period in suit so that the court may find that there has been an overpayment and the amount thereof.

The taxpayer's burden of proof in a tax refund action, as distinguished from his burden in a Tax Court proceeding, was well stated by the United

[65] Mickler v. Fahs, 243 F.2d 515 (C.A.5th) (forbidding even the use of the taxpayer's plea for impeachment purposes before a jury) ; Masters v. Commissioner, 243 F.2d 335 (C.A.3d), *affirming* 25 T.C. 1093 (allowing use of taxpayer's plea for impeachment purposes before Tax Court). *Cf.* Lott v. United States, 367 U.S. 421, 427.

[66] Moore v. United States, 360 F.2d 353, *modified,* 360 F.2d 357 (C.A.4th) (husband convicted in trial estopped to deny fraud, no estoppel of wife, who signed joint return) ; Tomlinson v. Lefkowitz, 334 F.2d 262 (C.A.5th), *cert. denied,* 379 U.S. 962 (husband and wife estopped) ; Armstrong v. United States, 354 F.2d 274, 290–91 (Ct. Cl.) ; Amos v. Commissioner, 43 T.C. 50, *affirmed,* 360 F.2d 358 (C.A.4th) (overruling earlier Tax Court holdings to the contrary in Safra v. Commissioner, 30 T.C. 1026, and Vasallo v. Commissioner, 23 T.C. 656) ; Arctic Ice Cream Co. v. Commissioner, 43 T.C. 68 (taxpayer convicted by virtue of guilty plea estopped to deny fraud). ¶ *But see* Worcester v. Commissioner, 370 F.2d 713 (C.A.1st), where a conviction at a "tainted" criminal trial did not estop the taxpayer.

[67] Moore v. United States, *supra* note 66, at 356–57, *reversing on other grounds but affirming on this point* 235 F. Supp. 387, 391–92 (W.D. Va.).

States Court of Appeals for the Fourth Circuit in *Compton* v. *United States*:[68]

It is a well established principle that in every case, whether in a proceeding in the Tax Court to contest a deficiency assessment or in a District Court in a suit for refund, the assessment of the Commissioner is presumed to be correct.[69] To be sure, this presumption is not evidence in itself and may be rebutted by competent evidence. It operates merely to place upon the opposing party the burden of going forward with the evidence. However, to prevail in an action for refund, the taxpayer must not only overcome this presumption but must assume and discharge the added burden of demonstrating the correct amount of the tax due or that he owes no tax at all. See Helvering v. Taylor, 293 U.S. 507, 55 S.Ct. 287, 79 L.Ed. 623 (1935); Commissioner of Int. Rev. v. R. J. Reynolds Tobacco Co., 260 F.2d 9, 14 (4 Cir. 1958); Clinton Cotton Mills v. Commissioner of Internal Revenue, 78 F.2d 292 (4 Cir. 1935); 9 Mertens, Federal Income Taxation, § 50.65 (Zimmet Rev. 1958).

An action for refund of taxes paid is in the nature of an action of assumpsit for money had and received and the plaintiff's right to recover must be measured by equitable standards.[70] Here, taxpayer's entire liability is at issue and if, under any state of facts, the Government is entitled to the money claimed, she cannot prevail. Consequently, it is not enough merely to show that the assessment was invalid or that the Commissioner erred; the plaintiff must go further and produce evidence from which another and proper determination can be made.[71] The extent of the taxpayer's burden in a refund action was aptly stated by Judge Learned Hand in Taylor v. Commissioner, 70 F.2d 619, 620 (2 Cir. 1934), aff'd sub. nom. 293 U.S. 507, 55 S.Ct. 287, 79 L.Ed. 623 (1935):

"* * * If the burden of proof goes so far as to demand not only that the taxpayer show that the deficiency assessed against him is wrong, but what is the proper deficiency, or that there should be none at all, the decision was right, even though we know that the tax is too high. In an action to recover taxes unlawfully collected the burden does go so far. * * * But the reason for this is obvious; a plaintiff, seeking an affirmative judgment measured in dollars, must prove how much is due. His claim is for money paid and he must show that every dollar he recovers is unjustly withheld. So it is not enough merely to prove that the tax as a whole was unlawful; some of the dollars he paid may nevertheless have been due. * * *"

To put it another way, the ultimate question in a suit for refund is not whether the Government was wrong, but whether the plaintiff can establish that

---

[68] 334 F.2d 212, 216 (C.A.4th). See also Maroosis v. Smyth, 187 F.2d 228, 231–32 (C.A.9th).

[69] See *e.g.*, Helvering v. Taylor, 293 U.S. 507, 55 S.Ct. 287, 79 L.Ed. 623 (1935); Veino v. Fahs, 257 F.2d 364 (5 Cir. 1958). See generally 9 MERTENS, FEDERAL INCOME TAXATION § 50.71 (Zimmet Rev. 1958).

[70] *E.g.*, Stone v. White, 301 U.S. 532, 57 S.Ct. 851, 81 L.Ed. 1265 (1937); Lewis v. Reynolds, 284 U.S. 281, 52 S.Ct. 145, 76 L.Ed. 293 (1932); United States v. Pfister, 205 F.2d 538 (8 Cir. 1953); Western Maryland Ry. Co. v. United States, 131 F. Supp. 873 (D. Md. 1955), *aff'd per curiam*, 227 F.2d 576 (4 Cir. 1955), *cert. denied*, 351 U.S. 907, 76 S.Ct. 696, 100 L.Ed. 1443 (1956).

[71] Helvering v. Taylor, *supra* note [69]; United States v. Pfister, *supra* note [70]; United States v. Harris, 216 F.2d 690 (5 Cir. 1954); 10 Mertens op. cit. supra note [69] § 58A. 35. But cf. United States v. Hover, 268 F.2d 657 (9 Cir. 1959).

taxes were in fact overpaid. The plaintiff, to prevail, must establish the exact amount which she is entitled to recover. [Footnotes in original renumbered.]

Burden of Proof on Government's Offsets

As previously noted, in a tax refund suit the government may assert that it is entitled to offsets against the taxpayer's recovery with regard to matters not raised in his claims for refund.[72] When defending on the basis of an offsetting adjustment the government is injecting into the tax refund case a new issue for the Court's consideration. Under the Tax Court Rules the government would be required to sustain the burden of proof with regard to the new matter it brought into the case.[73] However, in a tax refund suit the situation is different, with the burden of proof depending upon the nature of the offsetting adjustment raised.

The allocation of the burden of proof with regard to offsets in tax refund suits was resolved by the Court of Claims in a special decision on this issue alone.[74] The Court said, [75]

The defense of a setoff can be raised by the government in several factual situations. The differences among them, we think, are material to the ultimate issue we are called to decide. It appears that a setoff can be raised by the government in a refund suit with respect to the tax treatment accorded an item found (1) in the same tax year involving the same type of tax for which a refund is sought, (2) in the same year involving a different type of tax which, however, is related and ultimately affects the amount of tax liability involved in the suit for refund, (3) in the same year involving a different type of tax which is independent of and unrelated to the tax involved in the suit for refund, (4) in another year involving any type of tax whether related or unrelated.

. . . .

When a suit is brought for the recovery of taxes, the taxpayer must affirmatively show that he has overpaid his taxes since "[a]n overpayment must appear before refund is authorized." Lewis v. Reynolds, supra, 284 U.S. at 283, 52 S.Ct. at 146. In other words, the taxpayer has the burden of proving the exact dollar amount to which he is entitled.[76] See Helvering v. Taylor, 293 U.S. 507, 155 S.Ct. 287, 79 L.Ed. 623 (1935). This of necessity puts in issue every credit or deduction found in the particular tax return for which refund is sought or in a related tax return. However, this does not involve a redetermination of taxpayer's tax liability under unrelated tax returns for that year.

---

[72] See p. **12·3** *et seq. supra.*
[73] Tax Ct. R. 32. See p. **8·5** *supra.*
[74] Missouri Pac. R.R. v. United States, 338 F.2d 668 (Ct. Cl.).
[75] *Id.* at 670–71.
[76] This is to be contrasted to the situation present in the Tax Court where the taxpayer merely has the burden of proving that the Commissioner's assessment is wrong since the proceedings before that court are in the nature of a review of the Commissioner's assessment. See Taylor v. Commissioner of Internal Revenue, 70 F.2d 619 (2d Cir. 1934). The government has the burden of proof as to "new matter" pleaded in the answer to taxpayer's petition. (Tax Court Rule 32.)

We view the taxpayer's tax liabilities as a series of obligations arising from each tax imposed.[77] Thus, when the government by way of a setoff challenges the validity of the tax treatment accorded an item found in the same tax return or in a related and dependent tax return (situations (1) and (2) outlined above), we think that the burden of proving the correctness of the challenged item is ultimately on the taxpayer. When the challenged item is found in an unrelated tax return (situations (3) and (4)), we think that the burden of proof remains on the government throughout the entire proceedings.[78] We say this because under the former situation, the challenged item is directly involved with the final computation of taxpayer's taxes under which refund is sought, while in the latter situation the challenged items in no way affect taxpayer's tax liability under the return connected with the suit for refund. [Footnotes in original renumbered.]

The decision of the Court of Claims with regard to the allocation of the burden of proof is consistent with the law as expressed by the other courts that have passed upon the issue.[79] It should also be noted that the Court of Claims (consistent with the practice in the district courts) does not require the taxpayer to produce evidence pertaining to an offset affecting the tax liability in question (cases (1) and (2) in its *Missouri Pacific* opinion) merely upon the government's bare assertion that an offset existed. Rather, initially the burden is on the government to present some concrete evidence supporting its claimed offset before the taxpayer will be required to proceed with his proof on the issue.[80] However, the burden of proof with regard to offsets can be particularly onerous, since it can require evidence regarding transactions that the taxpayer had assumed to be closed long before his tax refund suit was commenced. In one case the taxpayer had to prove the details of a transaction that originated more than forty years prior to trial.[81]

[77] This concept follows the conventional view of other subject matter upon which civil actions are based; viz., contracts. See Atchison, Topeka & Santa Fe Ry. Co. v. United States, 94 F. Supp. 677, 118 Ct. Cl. 194 (1951).

[78] We recognize that the right of the government to challenge items found in unrelated tax returns (situations (3) and (4)) is not present in every case. See Rothensies v. Electric Storage Battery Co., 329 U.S. 296, 301, 67 S.Ct. 271, 91 L.Ed. 296 (1946). We are concerned in this case only with establishing who has the burden of proof once it is determined that the government can properly challenge the item by way of a setoff defense.

[79] Roybark v. United States, 218 F.2d 164 (C.A.9th), *affirming* 104 F. Supp. 759 (S.D. Calif.); duPont v. United States, 13 A.F.T.R.2d 824 (Del.) (special decision on burden of proof); Western Md. Ry. v. United States, 131 F. Supp. 873, 889–90 (Md.), *affirmed,* 227 F.2d 576 (C.A.4th), *cert. denied,* 351 U.S. 907. *Contra,* Service Life Ins. Co. v. United States, 189 F. Supp. 282 (Neb.), *affirmed without discussion of this point,* 293 F.2d 72 (C.A.8th) (holding erroneously based on Tax Court procedural precedents); Massingale v. United States, 3 A.F.T.R.2d 995 (Ariz.) (holding erroneously based on Tax Court procedure and inexplicably fails to cite contrary Ninth Circuit decision in Roybark v. United States, *supra,* written by same judge).

[80] Missouri Pac. R.R. v. United States, *supra* note 74, at 671–72; Routzahn v. Brown, 95 F.2d 766, 769–71 (C.A.6th); Budd Co. v. United States, 19 F.R.D. 346 (E.D. Pa.); Western Md. Ry. v. United States, *supra* note 79, 131 F. Supp. at 890.

[81] Dysart v. United States, 340 F.2d 624 (Ct. Cl.).

Burden of Proof on Government's Counterclaims

In considering the burden of proof in tax refund suits with regard to the government's counterclaims, it is important to distinguish between the two types of counterclaims that can be asserted.

COUNTERCLAIMS BASED ON NEWLY ISSUED DEFICIENCY NOTICE. If, during the pendency of a tax refund suit, the Internal Revenue Service issues to the taxpayer a deficiency notice with respect to the taxes at issue in the case, the court proceedings are automatically suspended.[82] At this point, the taxpayer may elect to have the subject matter of the deficiency notice presented to the Tax Court. However, if the taxpayer does not petition the Tax Court for review of the new deficiency notice then the government may assert a counterclaim in the refund suit based upon the subject matter of the deficiency notice. The allocation of the burden of proof on a counterclaim of this type is expressly stated by the Internal Revenue Code:

The taxpayer shall have the burden of proof with respect to the issues raised by such counterclaim . . . except as to the issue of whether the taxpayer has been guilty of fraud with intent to evade tax.[83]

COUNTERCLAIMS TO RECOVER UNPAID PORTIONS OF ASSESSMENTS OF DIVISIBLE TAXES. In most cases involving divisible taxes such as excise taxes and employer and responsible officer [84] assessments, taxpayers will bring a refund suit in which their complaint places in issue only a small part of the total tax assessment involved in the case.[85] The government will usually give the court jurisdiction over the entire tax assessment by asserting a counterclaim for the unpaid portion of the total assessment. Accordingly, in a case in which a "responsible officer" had a $5,186.47 assessment made against him,[86] he was able to pay only $50.00 (the assessment as to one individual employee) and satisfy the full-payment rule. Thereafter, he filed a claim for refund of the $50.00 and ultimately gave a court jurisdiction of a refund suit for its recovery. The government then, in order to get its full assessment before the Court, counterclaimed for the unpaid balance.

The courts have had difficulties in allocating the burden of proof on the government's counterclaims for the unpaid portion of a divisible tax assessment. As in a tax collection action, the government on its counterclaim is a plaintiff seeking a positive recovery and would traditionally be required to

[82] IRC § 7422(e) ; United States v. Joe Graham Post No. 119, Am. Legion, 340 F.2d 474 (C.A.5th) ; Cole v. Bookwalter, 170 F. Supp. 527 (W.D. Mo.). See p. **13·29** *et seq. infra.*

[83] IRC § 7422(e).

[84] IRC § 6672.

[85] See p. **10·4** *et seq. supra* for a discussion of the full-payment rule as applied to divisible taxes.

[86] Steele v. United States, 280 F.2d 89 (C.A.8th).

prove its claim. Yet, it is undoubted that to the extent a taxpayer has prepaid his taxes and sues for a refund he must bear the burden of proving an overpayment, and it does not appear logical to reward a taxpayer with a lighter burden of proof insofar as he has not paid in advance. In working out a solution, the courts have considered that the overall burden of proving its claim rests on the government but that the burden of producing evidence shifts from party to party.[87] Initially, the burden is on the government to produce evidence to persuade the court that the taxpayer has a liability. This burden it can meet by proving that an assessment was duly made against the taxpayer. The taxpayer then has the burden of proving, by a preponderance of the evidence, that the assessment was erroneous. If the taxpayer successfully challenges the assessment then the government, in order to recover, must establish that the taxpayer does owe it taxes for the period in issue, although his liability may be different from the amount originally assessed.

The application of the burden of proof rules can be illustrated by a cabaret excise tax case [88] in which an assessment of $195,181.26 for a ten-year period was made. The taxpayers paid $1,767.57, the assessment as to one taxable period (a quarter), and sued for its refund. The government counterclaimed for the unpaid balance. As to the prepaid quarter the normal burden of proof rule was applicable, and the taxpayers had to prove an overpayment in order to recover. With regard to the remaining taxable periods the government established that the assessment was made in a procedurally proper manner. The taxpayers established, however, that as to some quarters the assessment was erroneous because it had been based on an unreasonable estimate that 95% of gross receipts was subject to tax. Thus, the taxpayers had sustained their burden of proof and had successfully challenged the assessment. However, the court found that, from all the evidence, the government had carried its burden of establishing that the taxpayers did have a cabaret excise tax liability although in a smaller amount than that assessed. Accordingly, the court held for the government on its counterclaim in the lesser amount it found due from the taxpayers.

Burden of Proof in Fraud Cases

There is an exception to the generally applicable burden of proof rules in tax refund suits involving an assessment of a fraud penalty. The government must sustain the burden of proving the taxpayer's fraud.[89]

[87] Lesser v. United States, 368 F.2d 306 (C.A.2d) ; United States v. Lease, 346 F.2d 696 (C.A.2d) ; United States v. Molitor, 337 F.2d 917 (C.A.9th) ; Spivak v. United States, 254 F. Supp. 517, 525 (S.D.N.Y.).

[88] Sitnick v. United States, 244 F. Supp. 656 (Md.), *affirmed,* 367 F.2d 282 (C.A. 4th).

[89] Klassie v. United States, 289 F.2d 96, 99 (C.A.8th) ; Paddock v. United States, 280 F.2d 563 (C.A.2d).

Moreover, the government will not satisfy its burden merely by proving fraud by a preponderance of the evidence. Rather, it is the government's obligation to establish the taxpayer's fraud by clear and convincing evidence.[90]

It should be noted that, in a fraud case, it is only the burden of proof with respect to the fraud issue that is imposed on the government. The taxpayer retains his normal obligation in connection with the underlying alleged tax deficiency. Therefore, in tax refund suits involving a fraud penalty the burden of proof is allocated between the parties as follows:

1. In order to be entitled to a refund of taxes (excluding the fraud penalty) the taxpayer must, by a preponderance of the evidence, prove what his correct tax liability was for the period in issue so that the court can determine that there was an overpayment.[91]
2. In order to sustain its fraud penalty assessment [92] the government must, by clear and convincing evidence, prove that the taxpayer committed fraud with intent to evade tax.

In some fraud cases, particularly those in which a criminal prosecution is being considered, the Internal Revenue Service will delay making an assessment. This delay often results in the making of an assessment after the normally applicable limitations period for assessments [93] has run. Thus, unless the taxpayer has committed fraud, the assessment will be untimely and a full refund will be required.[94] In these cases the government's ability to sustain its burden of proof on the fraud issue will often be the sole point of contention in the suit.[95]

TAXPAYER'S SUIT BASED ON THEORY OF ACCOUNT STATED

A discussion of tax refund suits would not be complete without some reference to the related taxpayer's action on the theory of an account stated. This theory, in essence, is that there exists an implied contract be-

---

[90] Breland v. United States, 323 F.2d 492, 497 (C.A.5th); Putman v. United States, 301 F.2d 751 (C.A.6th).

[91] Of course, any reduction of the tax deficiency will necessarily reduce the amount of any fraud penalty applicable.

[92] And thus avoid a refund of the fraud penalty collected.

[93] IRC § 6501(a).

[94] If the taxpayer has committed fraud, there is no limitation on the time for an assessment. IRC §§ 6501(c)(1), (2).

[95] See, *e.g.*, Toledano v. Commissioner, 362 F.2d 243 (C.A.5th), and Benes v. Commissioner, 42 T.C. 358, *affirmed per curiam*, 355 F.2d 929 (C.A.6th), as examples of the many cases in which the validity of assessments has depended upon a finding of fraud.

tween the Government and the taxpayer whereby a stipulated refund is to be made to the taxpayer.[96]

Usually, a suit on an account stated arises in a context in which a taxpayer has not met the jurisdictional prerequisites to a tax refund suit but can contend that the government has agreed to make a refund to him. If there was, in fact, an account stated the taxpayer would be able to recover on contractual grounds without having to satisfy the stringent prerequisites to the bringing of a tax refund suit.

Legal Theory of Suit on Account Stated

A suit on the theory of an account stated does not arise out of the Internal Revenue Code; it is a judicial addition thereto.[97] The cause of action is based upon the common law concept that an implied contract arises when a debtor submits to a creditor a statement of the final balance due on an account and the creditor agrees to accept the proposed balance to close the account.[98] As the Supreme Court said in *Toland* v. *Sprague,*

The mere rendering an account does not make it a stated one; but . . . if the other party receives the account, admits the correctness of the items, claims the balance, or offers to pay it as may be in his favor or against him; then it becomes a stated account.[99]

In the context of tax controversies, the account stated is considered to arise when all three of the following have occurred:

1. The government and the taxpayer have agreed that the taxpayer has overpaid his taxes for a given taxable period.
2. Accord has been reached with regard to the amount of the overpayment.
3. The government has proposed, and the taxpayer has agreed, that a refund of the stated amount will be made and accepted to close the account.

The courts require plain evidence that all of the elements of an account stated exist before they will permit the normally applicable requirements for a recovery of taxes to be superseded. As the Supreme Court noted, its ruling in the leading *Bonwit Teller* case is "not to be extended through an enlargement of the concept of an account stated by latitudinarian construction." [100]

[96] Bonwit Teller & Co. v. United States, 283 U.S. 258.
[97] Note, *Account Stated as a Theory of Action for Recovering Federal Tax Overpayments*, 56 HARV. L. REV. 115, 120 (1942).
[98] Bonwit Teller & Co. v. United States, *supra* note 96; R. H. Stearns Co. v. United States, 291 U.S. 54, 65; Daube v. United States, 289 U.S. 367, 370; Hoon Kwan Young v. United States, 110 F. Supp. 237 (Hawaii).
[99] 37 U.S. 300, 335. See also Nutt v. United States, 125 U.S. 650, 655.
[100] Daube v. United States, *supra* note 98, at 372–73.

Administrative Action Creating Account Stated

Under the Internal Revenue Service procedures followed at the time the leading Supreme Court cases in this area of the law were decided, the critical document in an account stated case was a Certificate of Overassessment. This certificate was issued by the Commissioner of Internal Revenue. Where this document was issued and the circumstances of its issuance and acceptance amounted to an implied contract an account stated was considered to exist.[101]

Under present Internal Revenue Service procedures the power to allow a refund has been delegated to the respective District Directors of Internal Revenue.[102] Functionally, the Commissioner's Certificate has been replaced by the District Director's Notice of Adjustment [103] which is used to advise the taxpayer that an overassessment has been determined with regard to his tax liability. The Notice discloses the amount of the overassessment determined by the District Director and his disposition of it, *i.e.* the amount to be credited to outstanding liabilities of the taxpayer and the amount to be refunded.[104] By analogy to the precedents under the former procedure it appears that now the Notice of Adjustment is the critical document in an account stated case. Accordingly, if the Notice were delivered to the taxpayer in a context in which there could be implied a contract in accordance with the terms of the document, an account stated would exist.

Absence of Requirement for Claim for Refund

A suit on an account stated is one in which the taxpayer's cause of action is based upon the government's promise to make a payment. As such, it is not an action for the recovery of an overpayment of taxes under the Internal Revenue Code. Hence, as the United States Court of Appeals for the Third Circuit has noted, "in an action of this kind which is not for a tax refund, a claim for refund is, of course, not a condition precedent." [105]

Tribunals Available for Suit on Account Stated

Since a taxpayer's action on an account stated is not a suit for the recovery of taxes pursuant to the Internal Revenue Code, the jurisdictional provisions of the United States Code with respect to tax refund suits [106]

---

[101] United States v. Swift, 282 U.S. 468; Bonwit Teller & Co. v. United States, *supra* note 96; R. H. Stearns & Co. v. United States, *supra* note 98; Daube v. United States, *supra* note 98.

[102] Treas. Reg. § 301.6402.

[103] Treasury Form 1331, Tax Refund Form No. 6, p. **C**·76.

[104] Pursuant to IRC § 6402.

[105] Wm. J. Friday & Co. v. United States, 61 F.2d 370, 373 (C.A.3d).

[106] 28 U.S.C. § 1346(a)(1) gives the district courts original jurisdiction, concurrent with the Court of Claims, over tax refund suits.

are not applicable. Jurisdiction over suits on the theory of an account stated is based solely upon the statutes by means of which the United States has consented to be sued on contractual claims.[107] Accordingly, if the taxpayer's claim is not in excess of $10,000 he may bring his action in either the United States Courts of Claims or a United States District Court,[108] since these forums have concurrent jurisdiction over contract claims up to that amount.[109] However, if his claim is in excess of the aforementioned amount his action can only be brought in the United States Court of Claims.[110]

Statute of Limitations Applicable to Suits on Theory of Account Stated

Since a suit on the theory of an account stated is based upon an implied contract, the pertinent statute of limitations is the provision generally applicable to suits against the United States. Therefore, the taxpayer's action must be commenced within six years after the cause of action "first accrues." [111] The cause of action "first accrues" when the implied contract first comes into existence. This will occur when the critical document, the Notice of Adjustment, is delivered to the taxpayer and he accepts it.[112] Should there be continued disagreement regarding the proposed overpayment after the delivery of the Notice, an account stated does not arise and the statutory period does not commence running until agreement is reached.[113]

---

[107] 28 U.S.C. §§ 1346(a)(2), 1491.

[108] Venue for district court suits lies only in the district in which the taxpayer resides. 28 U.S.C. § 1402(a)(1). A corporate taxpayer does not have the benefit of the broader venue provision available in tax refund suits. Compare 28 U.S.C. § 1402(a)(2), and see p. 11·8 *supra.*

[109] 28 U.S.C. § 1346(a)(2).

[110] *Cf.* Uptagrafft v. United States, 315 F.2d 200 (C.A.4th) (non-tax case), *cert. denied,* 375 U.S. 818. See also 10 MERTENS, LAW OF FEDERAL INCOME TAXATION § 58A. 13, at note 95.1 (Zimet rev., 1964).

[111] 28 U.S.C. §§ 2401, 2501.

[112] Bonwit Teller & Co. v. United States, *supra* note 96.

[113] Midpoint Realty Co. v. United States, 42 F. Supp. 76 (Ct. Cl.).

PROCEEDINGS PRIOR TO TRIAL OF TAX REFUND SUITS

In this chapter we will discuss the most important procedures available to the parties in civil suits in the district courts and the Court of Claims. Primary emphasis will be placed upon the utilization of these procedures in tax refund litigation.

DISPOSITIVE MOTIONS

Both tax refund tribunals provide for motions by means of which a party can attempt to obtain a resolution of the case prior to a trial hearing.

Government's Motion To Dismiss Complaint or Petition

The tax refund forums afford the government the first opportunity to utilize a dispositive motion. Upon receipt of the taxpayer's complaint or petition the government may file a motion to dismiss based upon procedural grounds or upon the taxpayer's failure to state a claim upon which relief can be granted.[1]

In deciding a motion to dismiss, the court will consider solely the taxpayer's complaint (together with any amendments [2] that may properly have been made).[3] For purposes of the motion the material facts alleged in the complaint are taken to be true in determining whether, as a matter of law, the defendant is entitled to dismissal of plaintiff's complaint.[4]

In tax refund suits the following grounds are those most commonly raised by the government in support of a motion to dismiss:

1. Expiration of statutory period for bringing tax refund suit [5]
2. Prematurely brought suit [6]
3. Failure to meet the prerequisites to bringing a tax refund suit [7]
4. Variance between grounds for recovery stated in complaint and grounds presented by claims for refund [8]
5. Legal insufficiency of alleged grounds for recovery to support a judgment for taxpayer [9]

Motion for Judgment on the Pleadings

After the pleadings are closed, but not so late as to interfere with a trial of the case, either party to a tax refund suit may file a motion for judgment on the pleadings.[10]

In considering this motion the court will have before it solely the pleadings in the case plus facts of which the court may take judicial notice.[11] For purposes of a motion for judgment on the pleadings all allegations of fact contained in the opposing party's pleadings are taken as true, and all denied

---

[1] Fed. R. Civ. P. 12(b); Ct. Cl. R. 20(b).

[2] A complaint or petition may be amended to eliminate defects, even after a motion to dismiss is filed, pursuant to the normally applicable rules pertaining to amendments of pleading. See 11·19 *et seq. supra.*

[3] If, on a motion to dismiss for failure to state a claim upon which relief can be granted, matters outside the pleadings are presented to the court, and not excluded, the motion is treated as one for summary judgment. Thereafter, each party will be given a chance to present materials pertinent to such a motion. Fed. R. Civ. P. 12(b); Ct. Cl. R. 20(b).

[4] See generally 2 MOORE'S FEDERAL PRACTICE ¶ 12.08 (2d ed. 1965).

[5] See p. 11·2 *et seq. supra.*

[6] See p. 10·33 *supra.*

[7] See p. 10·2 *supra;* and see Chap. 2, generally.

[8] See p. 12·7 *et seq. supra.*

[9] This ground is the classic demurrer testing the legal sufficiency of the plaintiff's allegations.

[10] Fed. R. Civ. P. 12(c); Ct. Cl. R. 20(c). See Tax Refund Suit Form No. 10, p. C·81, for a sample motion for judgment on the pleadings.

[11] Should either party on a motion for judgment on the pleadings present matters outside the pleadings, the court may either exclude the extraneous materials and decide solely upon the pleadings or treat the motion as one for summary judgment. In the latter circumstance, each party will be given an opportunity to submit appropriate additional materials. Fed. R. Civ. P. 12(c); Ct. Cl. R. 20(c).

factual allegations of the moving party are deemed to be false.[12] On the facts thus before the court, judgment will be granted only if the movant is clearly entitled to judgment as a matter of law.

It should be noted that the government will only rarely admit sufficient facts in its answer to permit the taxpayer to succeed on a motion for judgment on the pleadings. However, if it should appear reasonable to expect the answer to contain significant admissions, the taxpayer's complaint should be drafted with a view toward a motion for judgment on the pleadings. Instead of incorporating by reference the grounds for recovery stated in the claim for refund, the taxpayer should set out the essential facts in the complaint.[13]

Motion for Summary Judgment

Either party to a tax refund suit may file a motion for summary judgment at (with minor exceptions) any time prior to the trial.[14] Moreover, if matters outside the pleadings are presented (and not excluded) on a motion for judgment on the pleadings or a motion to dismiss for failure to state a claim, then the pending motion is treated as a motion for summary judgment.[15] Where appropriate, partial summary judgment can be granted, eliminating from trial some, but not all, of the issues in a case.

A motion for summary judgment will be granted if, from the materials before the court, there exists no genuine issue of material fact and the movant is entitled to a judgment as a matter of law.[16]

In tax refund suits, the taxpayer should consider a motion for summary judgment as a "target" in the developmental stages of the case. Where it would be possible, and advantageous, to have the case resolved without a trial, the taxpayer should attempt to place on record sufficient materials to support a summary judgment motion. Even if the motion is unsuccessful because the government is able to raise a genuine issue of fact, at least the taxpayer will have succeeded in "smoking out" those facts that his adversary contends are really in dispute.

CROSS-MOTION FOR SUMMARY JUDGMENT. It should be noted that a party on whom a motion for summary judgment is served may serve a cross-motion requesting summary judgment for himself.[17] There is author-

---

[12] See generally 2 MOORE'S FEDERAL PRACTICE ¶ 12.15 (2d ed. 1965).

[13] See p. 11·13 *supra.* See Tax Refund Suit Form No. 9, p. C·79–80, for an example of a complaint of this type.

[14] Fed. R. Civ. P. 56(a), (b) ; Ct. Cl. R. 64(a), (b). See Tax Refund Suit Form No. 11, p. C·81, for a sample motion for summary judgment.

[15] Fed. R. Civ. P. 12(b), (c) ; Ct. Cl. R. 20(b), (c).

[16] Fed. R. Civ. P. 56(c) ; Ct. Cl. R. 64(d). See generally 6 MOORE'S FEDERAL PRACTICE ¶¶ 56.15, 56.17 [63] (2d ed. 1965).

[17] Fed. R. Civ. P. 56(a). In the Court of Claims, leave of court must be obtained in order to file a cross-motion for summary judgment after the prospective cross-movant has responded to the adversary's motion. Ct. Cl. R. 64(c).

ity that will support the court's granting summary judgment to the opposing party even without a formal cross-motion.[18] However, it is recommended that a party served with a motion for summary judgment who feels that he himself, may be entitled to summary judgment take the precautionary step of filing a formal cross-motion.[19]

FINDINGS WHERE MOTION NOT GRANTED.   The procedural rules of both tax refund forums expressly provide that, even if a motion for summary judgment is not granted, the court may ascertain the extent to which there exist material facts in dispute and enter an appropriate order in accordance with its findings.[20] This determination can be made by examination of the materials before the court and by interrogating counsel at a hearing on the motion.[21]

MATERIALS CONSIDERED ON SUMMARY JUDGMENT MOTION.   The materials that the court may consider in deciding a motion for summary judgment include the following materials of record:

1. The pleadings
2. Depositions
3. Answers to interrogatories in the district courts
4. Responses to calls in the Court of Claims
5. Responses to requests for admissions
6. Stipulations
7. Affidavits on file with the court [22]

When a motion for summary judgment (with or without supporting affidavits) is filed, the adversary is given an opportunity to file affidavits in support of his opposition to the motion. Moreover, the adversary may be able to persuade the court to delay consideration of the motion until after discovery has been completed so that further material bearing upon the motion may be filed.[23]

AFFIDAVITS IN SUPPORT OF MOTION.   The value to the taxpayer of the right to file affidavits in support of a motion for summary judgment cannot be overestimated. As to any material fact that the taxpayer feels should not be in dispute but that will not be admitted by the government, the taxpayer can effectively utilize his own or a witness' affidavit.

---

[18] *E.g.,* Proctor & Gamble Independent Union of Port Ivory, N.Y. v. Proctor & Gamble Mfg. Co., 312 F.2d 181 (C.A.2d), *cert. denied,* 374 U.S. 830; Kent v. United States, 228 F. Supp. 929 (S.D.N.Y.). See also cases cited in 2 MOORE'S FEDERAL PRACTICE ¶ 5612, at 2241–43 (2d ed. 1965).

[19] See Tax Refund Suit Form No. 12, p. C·81, for a sample cross-motion for summary judgment.

[20] Fed. R. Civ. P. 56(d) ; Ct. Cl. R. 64(e).

[21] *Ibid.*

[22] Fed. R. Civ. P. 56(c) ; Ct. Cl. R. 64(d). See generally 6 MOORE'S FEDERAL PRACTICE ¶ 56.11 (2d ed. 1965).

[23] Fed. R. Civ. P. 56(f) ; Ct. Cl. R. 64(g).

An affidavit in support of a motion for summary judgment must be made on the personal knowledge of the affiant, must disclose that he is competent to testify to the matters contained in the affidavit, and must set forth facts that would be admissible in evidence.[24]

Usually, the taxpayer will have a relatively easy time in obtaining affidavits establishing the material facts regarding which there should be no genuine dispute. Due to the nature of tax litigation, the typical case involves solely an inquiry into the actions of the taxpayer and/or those with whom he has had business dealings. Often the potential witnesses to the case are readily accessible to the taxpayer and may be willing to provide an affidavit for him. In fact, most witnesses are happy to sign a statement if it may help them avoid the inconvenience of testifying at a trial.

As a matter of tactics, affidavits should be submitted only when, and to the extent that, there is a real chance that summary judgment will be granted. Gratuitously provided affidavits can often be extremely helpful to the adversary in its development of the case.

AFFIDAVITS IN OPPOSITION TO MOTION.   An affidavit opposing a motion for summary judgment must meet the same requirements as a supporting one. Moreover, the affidavit must set forth specific facts showing that there exists a genuine issue of material fact in the case.[25]

An opposing affidavit can be used to present reasons why the opposing party is unable to present affidavits essential to justify his opposition to the motion for summary judgment.[26] Often, in tax refund suits, the government's counsel will present such an affidavit and request the court to delay consideration of the pending motion until after discovery has been completed. The court may refuse to grant judgment for the movant, grant a continuance of the pending motion to permit discovery, or issue any other order to justly handle the matter.[27]

RECORD REQUIRED FOR TAXPAYER'S MOTION.   As previously noted, the taxpayer's record for summary judgment can be made through the pleadings, formal discovery, stipulations, and affidavits. In general terms, the matters placed before the court on the motion should establish the following three elements:

1. All the jurisdictional prerequisites to suit have been met.
2. There exists no material issue of fact in connection with the ground for recovery raised by the taxpayer's claim for refund.
3. If the taxpayer is correct with regard to the grounds raised by the claim for refund, then he has overpaid his taxes in an ascertainable amount.

[24] Fed. R. Civ. P. 56(e) ; Ct. Cl. R. 64(f). Certified copies of documents to which reference is made should be attached to the affidavit.

[25] *Ibid.*

[26] Fed. R. Civ. P. 56(f) ; Ct. Cl. R. 64(g).

[27] *Ibid.*

With respect to the jurisdictional prerequisites for suit the taxpayer must be certain that the record contains each of the following elements:

1. The full payment rule was satisfied (*i.e.* that payment was made on an assessment of the appropriate amount of taxes).[28]
2. Proper and timely claims for refund were filed with respect to the taxes sought to be refunded.[29]
3. The claimant was the proper party to file the claims for refund.[30]
4. The claims were disallowed or at least six months had expired between the time the claims were filed and the time the suit was commenced.[31]
5. Suit was commenced within the statutory period.[32]
6. The parties to the suit are proper.[33]
7. The grounds for refund asserted in the complaint (and by the motion for summary judgment) do not vary from those raised in the claims for refund.[34]

Normally, all of the jurisdictional elements will be established by the pleadings. However, it is always advisable for the taxpayer to check off the listed items in considering his motion for summary judgment so that any that have not been conceded by the government can be placed on the record prior to filing his motion.

The nature of the taxpayer's substantive case will govern the essential facts required to establish that there exists no factual issue with respect to the grounds raised in his claim for refund. It is helpful to prepare a checklist of essential facts (like the list that should be prepared prior to any trial) and to check off each basic fact as it is placed on the record for summary judgment. If, and when, all of the determinative facts are properly before the court, the case is ripe for a summary judgment motion.

The final element of the taxpayer's case, that if he is correct with respect to the grounds raised in his claims for refund he is entitled to a refund in an ascertainable amount, is sometimes overlooked. If this is omitted from the record a complete summary judgment for the taxpayer would not be possible. It is, however, easily placed on the record. The taxpayer should place before the court (typically by stipulation or in response to a request for admissions) the tax returns he filed for the periods in issue and a description of any adjustments to those tax returns not in issue in the suit. With these matters on the record, the court, if it holds for the taxpayer with regard to his grounds for recovery, will have before it an adequate record

[28] See p. **10 · 2** *et seq. supra.*
[29] See p. **10 · 7** *et seq. supra.*
[30] See p. **10 · 15** *et seq. supra.*
[31] See p. **10 · 33** *supra.*
[32] See p. **11 · 2** *et seq. supra.*
[33] See p. **11 · 6–7** *supra.*
[34] See p. **12 · 7** *et seq. supra.*

upon which it can ascertain that the taxpayer has, in fact, overpaid his taxes and the amount of the overpayment.

It is important to note, at this point, that the government has the right to contend that any item in the subject returns is incorrectly reported and that it is entitled to an offset against the taxpayer's recovery.[35] If the government should raise such an offsetting adjustment in response to the taxpayer's motion for summary judgment a genuine issue of fact may be raised. In this event, the taxpayer would be entitled to, at most, partial summary judgment with regard to the grounds raised in his claim for refund. The issues raised by the government's offsets would remain in controversy and could require a trial for their resolution. However, the authors do not believe that the taxpayer has the burden of placing on the record, in the first instance, facts establishing that no possible offset exists. And it appears that if the government has not raised any offset in response to the taxpayer's motion, the court should take the taxpayer's returns (as adjusted) to be correct for purposes of determining the existence and amount of his overpayment of taxes.[36]

Procedure on Dispositive Motions

In both tax refund forums dispositive motions are properly made in writing and filed together with such additional materials and briefs as may be appropriate. Because of the basic difference between the two forums, however, the process by means of which a dispositive motion is considered is different.

DISTRICT COURT PROCEDURE.   In the district courts a dispositive motion is simply assigned to a judge for decision. Depending upon the district, the deciding judge may be the "motion" judge, a judge to whom the case was assigned when filed, or a judge assigned the particular motion pursuant to other local procedures. The extent to which oral argument on the motion is permitted, or required, and the time when any hearing will be held depends upon the particular court in which the case is pending. Upon consideration of the appropriate materials, and the parties' respective contentions, the judge will decide the motion.

COURT OF CLAIMS PROCEDURE.   In the Court of Claims a case, when filed, is referred to a trial commissioner who will handle the development and trial of the case.[37] However, the filing of a dispositive motion suspends the reference of the case for purposes of the particular motion.[38] The court may, and usually does, refer the dispositive motion by order to the commis-

---

[35] See p. **12·3** *et seq. supra.*
[36] *Cf.* Missouri Pac. R.R. v. United States, 338 F.2d 668 (Ct. Cl.).
[37] Ct. Cl. R. 52(b), 53(a).
[38] Ct. Cl. R. 53(b)(2).

sioner for his recommendations of conclusions of law thereon.[39] With regard to all dispositive motions the opposing party has an opportunity to file an objection or response, and the movant can file a reply brief thereto.[40]

Motion Not Referred to Trial Commissioner. If the court has not referred a dispositive motion to the trial commissioner, it will decide the matter without his recommendations. After all documents have been filed in connection with the motion, the court may have the matter set on the calendar for argument.[41] In the court's discretion, however, a dispositive motion may be acted upon without argument.[42]

Motion Referred to Trial Commissioner. In connection with a referred dispositive motion the commissioner may take any action requisite to his determination including requesting additional information, calling a conference, or scheduling a hearing.[43] After consideration, the commissioner will file his recommendation for conclusions of law, and each party will receive notice of his action.[44]

A party dissatisfied with the commissioner's recommendation may file a request for review by the court.[45] He can, on review, either file a statement indicating that he will rely upon previously filed papers or submit an additional brief specifying with particularity the matters he wishes the court to consider in the review and discussing the issues involved.[46] If the latter course is selected the adverse party may file an answering brief.[47] When a timely request for review is filed, the motion is placed on the calendar for argument before the court.[48] Where no request for review is timely filed, the dispositive motion is decided by the court without argument.[49]

FORMAL DISCOVERY PROCEDURES

In both tax refund forums there is available a variety of formal discovery devices that can be utilized for two not totally distinct purposes. Perhaps of primary importance in most tax cases is the use of discovery devices evidentiarily, *i.e.* to obtain evidence that can be presented to the court on a motion for summary judgment, in an agreed submission of the case, or as

[39] Ct. Cl. R. 54(b).
[40] Ct. Cl. R. 12.
[41] Ct. Cl. R. 65(b)(1).
[42] Ct. Cl. R. 65(b)(2).
[43] Ct. Cl. R. 54(d).
[44] Ct. Cl. R. 55(b)(1), (2).
[45] Ct. Cl. R. 55(b)(3)(i).
[46] *Ibid.*
[47] *Ibid.*
[48] Ct. Cl. R. 55(b)(3)(ii).
[49] Ct. Cl. R. 55(b)(3)(iii).

part of the trial proof. Also significant in appropriate cases is the use of discovery procedures for purely discovery purposes, *i.e.* to obtain leads for further discovery or investigation, to obtain the testimony of the adversary's witnesses prior to trial, to obtain access to material documents, etc. The discovery devices available in the two tax refund forums are quite similar.[50] However, in the district courts, with one exception (the motion for production [51]), discovery can be carried out without the need to obtain the permission of the court. The court gets involved in discovery solely when there are problems regarding discovery that one party or the other wishes to submit to the court for resolution. In the Court of Claims, on the other hand, the use of any formal discovery device must be preceded by obtaining leave of court, *i.e.* leave of the trial commissioner assigned to the case.

Scope of Discovery Permitted

In the district courts and the Court of Claims the scope of permissible discovery is relatively broad. Generally speaking, discovery is allowed if it is being used either to obtain admissible evidence or if it is "reasonably calculated to lead to the discovery of admissible evidence." [52]

DISCOVERY BY THE GOVERNMENT. The government's possible range of discovery from the taxpayer in tax refund suits is a broad one. Since the issue in the case is whether the taxpayer has overpaid his taxes for the periods in question, every matter on the subject tax returns (as well as possible recoupment items) is open to discovery that will yield evidence or is reasonably calculated to lead to admissible evidence. Of course, all defenses to discovery available in any civil case may be raised against the government in a tax refund suit.[53]

DISCOVERY BY THE TAXPAYER. The government is not, in any sense, immune from discovery in tax refund suits or in other civil actions.[54]

Government Has Available All Defenses Usable by Private Litigant. With respect to discovery the government is, and should be, no worse off than a private litigant in a civil case. Thus the government may object to attempted discovery on the ground that it seeks the attorney's work product, or it seeks information that is irrelevant, immaterial, incompetent, or otherwise improper. Moreover, such matters as the identity of witnesses, copies of their statements or reports, trial exhibits, and the like are

---

[50] The Court of Claims Rules were comprehensively revised in 1951 to make them similar to the Federal Rules of Civil Procedure. Foreword, Court of Claims Rules (revised April 1, 1964).

[51] Fed. R. Civ. P. 34.

[52] Fed. R. Civ. P. 26(b), 33, 34; Ct. Cl. R. 30(g), 38(a), 39(b), 40(b).

[53] See generally 4 MOORE'S FEDERAL PRACTICE ¶¶ 26.15–.24, 33.10–.22, 34.09–.17 (2d ed. 1966).

[54] United States v. Proctor & Gamble Co., 356 U.S. 677, 681.

not subject to discovery to any greater extent than they are from private litigants.[55]

It should be noted that even the normally available defenses to discovery arise in a slightly unusual context when the government raises them. As stated in a comprehensive article regarding discovery against the government, "Familiar objections, such as work product, may take on a special flavor [because the executive branch of the Government is involved]." [56]

Discovery To Obtain Theories, Opinions, Recommendations, or Conclusions of Government Personnel. A difficult problem in tax refund suits arises when taxpayers seek to inquire beyond the facts of the case into the process by means of which the Internal Revenue Service reached its determination regarding the taxpayer's liability.

The issue in a tax refund suit is whether the taxpayer has overpaid his taxes for the period in issue. In the typical case it is totally immaterial what any Internal Revenue Service employee thought or recommended regarding the case. Nor are the reasons why the Service made an assessment normally pertinent, since, in a tax refund suit, the government is not limited to the reasoning used by the Internal Revenue Service in its administrative process.[57] While taxpayers might like to know how their adversary has analyzed the case, normally this information is not available to them. As noted by Judge Thornton:

> The most that plaintiff can gain from the matters it seeks is an idea of defendant's theory as to why Section 531 has application to it. We do not conceive that this is information to which plaintiff is entitled. If plaintiff proves its case *for* the retention of net profits what difference does it make what theory defendant has to the contrary? [58]

However, in exceptional circumstances inquiry into the government's theories is permissible. Thus, inquiry into the reasoning of the Internal Revenue Service has been permitted in appropriate circumstances.[59] However it must appear that a legitimate reason exists for the discovery sought.[60] Nevertheless the "limitation" on discovery of the reasons why the Internal Revenue Service acted by no means bars discovery of evidence, or facts that could reasonably be calculated to lead to evidence, in the possession of the government. Moreover, it can be hoped that future tests of the

---

[55] See textual material cited in note 53 *supra*.

[56] Taubeneck and Sexton, *Executive Privilege and the Court's Right To Know*, 48 Geo. L. Rev. 486 (1960).

[57] Blansett v. United States, 283 F.2d 474, 478 (C.A.8th). See also Compton v. United States, 334 F.2d 212, 216 (C.A.4th).

[58] Unistrut Corp. v. United States, 37 F.R.D. 478, 479 (E.D. Mich.).

[59] Timken Roller Bearing Co. v. United States, 38 F.R.D. 57 (N.D. Ohio).

[60] In Conway Import Co. v. United States, 40 F.R.D. 5 (E.D.N.Y.), the court distinguished *Timken* on the ground that, in *Conway*, there was no "mystery" as to the reasons for the assessment in question.

limits of discovery against the government will change the present one-sided nature of tax litigation discovery. If the taxpayer must disclose his grounds for recovery or be barred from suit it seems only fair that the government reveal its grounds for denying his claims.

Government May Assert Executive Privilege as Defense to Discovery. In addition to the ordinary defenses against discovery, the government may assert that the inquired matters are protected by the executive privilege.

For there to be an effective claim of executive privilege it must formally be made by the head of the executive agency involved, upon his personal consideration.[61] In tax refund suits the Commissioner of Internal Revenue usually is the appropriate agency head to assert the privilege, since it is usually access to Internal Revenue documents that is sought.[62] Where the materials in question are part of the files of another agency (*e.g.* the Department of Justice) the head of that agency must assert the privilege.[63]

Although the Commissioner of Internal Revenue may claim executive privilege, the power and responsibility for evaluating the claim rests with the court before which the controversy is pending.[64]

With regard to discovery of such matters as military and state secrets,[65] identity of informers,[66] and grand jury proceedings [67] the privilege is more or less absolute.[68] As to other matters more pertinent to tax refund suits, the taxpayer's right to discovery depends upon a balancing of his need for the information against the government's interest in maintaining the security of its files.[69] In tax refund suits, the bulk of litigation involving the executive privilege has involved access to documents of the Internal Revenue Service such as reports, opinions, and the like. The courts have both permitted and denied discovery on the facts and circumstances of the particular case.[70] The only safe generalization is that the taxpayer must demonstrate a real need (not merely a desire) to pursue the discovery in question.

[61] United States v. Reynolds, 345 U.S. 1, 7–8.

[62] Cenname v. Bingler, 7 A.F.T.R.2d 1886 (W.D. Pa.).

[63] See, *e.g.,* United States v. Gates, 35 F.R.D. 524 (Col.), where the Attorney General claimed privilege with regard to materials gathered in connection with a suit by the government to recover an allegedly erroneous refund.

[64] United States v. Reynolds, *supra* note 61, 345 U.S. at 8.

[65] United States v. Reynolds, *supra* note 61, 345 U.S. at 6–7; Totten v. United States, 92 U.S. 105.

[66] Roviaro v. United States, 353 U.S. 53; Scher v. United States, 305 U.S. 251.

[67] United States v. Pittsburgh Plate Glass Co., 360 U.S. 395; United States v. Proctor & Gamble Co., *supra* note 54.

[68] In all of these instances, except perhaps where military or state secrets are involved, the government's privilege may give way to the court's "need to know" in appropriate circumstances. See cases cited in notes 65–67 *supra.*

[69] Kaiser Aluminum & Chem. Corp. v. United States, 157 F. Supp. 939 (Ct. Cl.) (decision by Supreme Court Justice Reed, sitting by designation).

[70] See p. **13·21** *infra* for a listing of types of Internal Revenue Service documents that have been the subject of taxpayers' motions for production in reported cases.

The Freedom of Information Act [71] (effective July 4, 1967) makes public some previously undisclosed governmental materials. However, it specifically exempts, *inter alia,* privileged or confidential financial information as well as "inter-agency or intra-agency memorandums or letters which would not be available by law to a private party in litigation with the agency [having such materials]." Accordingly, it is debatable whether this Act will have any effect upon the scope of discovery afforded taxpayers in tax refund litigation.

Depositions

The rules of both available tax refund forums provide for depositions upon oral examination or upon written interrogatories.[72] In the vast majority of cases the oral procedure is utilized, and deponents are examined and cross examined by attorneys for all parties to the suit. The most noteworthy features of oral depositions include the opportunities they afford to

1. Question the witness directly without, as with other discovery devices, having the question and answer filter through opposing counsel
2. Observe the deponent so as to be able to estimate the type of witness he will make at trial
3. Inquire in detail about "intangible" facts such as the witness' intent, belief, or other pertinent state of mind
4. Obtain, prior to trial, the testimony the witness would give if called as a witness
5. Use the give-and-take of an oral proceeding to clarify questions and answers that if presented in writing would be difficult to communicate without undue correspondence
6. "Size up" opposing counsel

In tax litigation, the government has the opportunity to take the deposition of the opposing party, *i.e.,* the taxpayer himself or an officer, director, or managing agent of a taxpayer-corporation. On the other hand, a taxpayer cannot examine the government, as such, in a deposition. A taxpayer can take depositions of appropriate Internal Revenue Service employees, but, normally, their answers to questions will not constitute admissions of a party.

EVIDENTIARY DEPOSITIONS. In certain circumstances the transcript of a deposition can be placed in evidence at trial, and it will constitute the testimony of the deponent. Parties frequently take evidentiary depositions of witnesses in the following situations:

1. When the witness' age or state of health makes it probable that he will not be able to testify at trial

[71] 5 U.S.C. § 1002 (as amended, July 4, 1966, 80 Stat. 250).
[72] Fed. R. Civ. P. 26–32; Ct. Cl. R. 30–36.

2. When the witness anticipates that he will be absent from the trial
3. When the witness resides, or will reside at trial time, sufficiently far from the place of hearing that his attendance at trial cannot be obtained or would be unduly inconvenient
4. When the deposition transcript can be used as part of the record upon which a motion for summary judgment can be based
5. When the parties agree to the presentation of the witness' testimony by deposition. (This is commonly done where a case is to be submitted for decision upon depositions and other materials of record without a formal trial hearing.)

Two factors in particular should be considered when deciding whether it would be advantageous to take evidentiary depositions during the developmental stage of the case. First, the evidentiary deposition taken by the proponent of the witness will give the adversary, well in advance of trial, notice of the precise tack the proponent will take in presenting his evidence. Second, when it is possible to choose between presenting a witness through a deposition or bringing him to the trial hearing, the extra cost of producing the witness at trial should be balanced against the possibility that his tesimony might be given greater weight if presented in person rather than through a "cold record."

DISCOVERY DEPOSITIONS. From the government's point of view discovery, or investigative, depositions are of particular value in tax refund suits. Normally, in cases involving questions of fact, the government will take the depositions of the taxpayer and his employees and business associates who have knowledge of the transactions in issue. The government can also be expected to take depositions of anticipated key witnesses for the taxpayer and of other persons whose records it wishes to have available or to inspect as part of its trial investigation.

For the taxpayer, who is normally on the "inside" of the transactions in issue, discovery depositions are usually less valuable than they are to the government. However, in appropriate circumstances they can be useful indeed. Firstly, the depositions of anticipated fact witnesses to be produced by the government can be taken. Secondly, where the taxpayer needs access to third-party records and they are not voluntarily made available to him, he can serve a subpoena *duces tecum* upon the custodian of the records and compel their production at a deposition. Finally, where appropriate, Internal Revenue employees, particularly those who are expected to be called as witnesses at trial, can be questioned at a deposition and pertinent documents can be subpoenaed. One important point should be noted when considering taking depositions of Internal Revenue Service employees in tax refund suits. Discovery from the government is not unlimited, and objections will be raised at any attempt to go beyond the government's view of permissible discovery. Nevertheless, in some cases, depositions of government personnel may properly be used by the taxpayer. For example, where the assessment in question was made as the result of an Agent's estimate, details of his method of estimation would be subject to deposition inquiry.[73] Also, to the extent that an Internal Revenue Agent could testify to facts (for example, statements made by the taxpayer or the Agent's observations of material facts) he would properly be subject to questioning at a deposition.[74]

DISTRICT COURT DEPOSITION PROCEDURES. In the district courts a party may take the deposition of any person without leave of court.[75] For a deposition upon oral examination (the usual procedure) the party need only give reasonable notice in writing to each party and secure the presence of the witness either by consent or through the use of a subpoena.[76] By means of a subpoena *duces tecum* the witness can be compelled to bring documents or other materials to the deposition.[77]

Whether a deposition was originally taken for discovery or evidentiary purposes, the transcript may, in the district courts, be used in the same manner.

Prior to trial the transcript is a part of the record in the case and can be used by either party in connection with a motion for summary judgment.[78] At trial the deposition transcript of any deponent can be used to impeach or contradict him as a witness.[79] Moreover, all or part of the deposition transcript of a party (or of an officer, director, or managing agent of a party) can be used as an admission against the party, *i.e.*, as positive evidence for the deponent's adversary without regard to the availability of the deponent.[80]

A deposition transcript may be placed in evidence and will constitute the testimony of the witness if at the time of trial the witness

1. Is deceased
2. Is more than 100 miles from the place of trial or out of the country

[73] *Cf.* Shippen v. Commissioner, 274 F.2d 860 (C.A.5th).

[74] Campbell v. Eastland, 307 F.2d 478, 489 (C.A.5th) ; Brewer v. Hassett, 2 F.R.D. 222 (Mass.). *Cf.* O'Keefe v. Shaughnessy, 95 F. Supp. 900 (N.D.N.Y.).

[75] Fed. R. Civ. P. 26(a). By motion, either a party or a deponent can request the court to order that the deposition not be taken or that any other suitable action be taken with regard to the deposition for the protection of the parties or the deponent. Fed. R. Civ. P. 30(b).

[76] Fed. R. Civ. P. 26, 30, 45. See also Rules 27–32 for the detailed provisions relating to deposition procedures. Typically, counsel are able to agree upon convenient times and places for all depositions.

[77] Fed. R. Civ. P. 45(d).

[78] Fed. R. Civ. P. 26(d), 56(c).

[79] Fed. R. Civ. P. 26(d)(1).

[80] Fed. R. Civ. P. 26(d)(2). Community Counselling Serv., Inc. v. Reilly, 317 F.2d 239, 243 (C.A.4th) ; Pursche v. Atlas Scraper & Engineering Co., 300 F.2d 467, 488 (C.A.9th).

3. Is unable to testify due to age, ill health, or imprisonment
4. Cannot be brought to court by the proponent through use of a subpoena

or if

5. The court determines that such exceptional circumstances exist as to permit the use of the deposition in lieu of the witness' testimony in court [81]

COURT OF CLAIMS DEPOSITION PROCEDURES. In the Court of Claims depositions may be taken only after leave of court is obtained upon a formal motion.[82] The motion must specify whether the deposition is to be taken (1) for discovery, (2) for use as evidence, or (3) to supplement or oppose a motion for summary judgment and must set forth good cause for the granting of leave.[83] The adverse party normally is given an opportunity to respond to the motion prior to action being taken thereon.[84] Leave to take an evidentiary deposition will be granted only upon a finding that it will be impracticable for the trial commissioner to hear the testimony of the proposed deponent.[85]

The attendance of a witness at a deposition can be compelled by means of a subpoena.[86] The deponent can be required to produce documents and other items by virtue of a subpoena *duces tecum* only if permission for the use of such a subpoena has expressly been given upon a showing that the specific items to be produced are needed and that the production of these items is feasible.[87]

Normally, the times and places for depositions are set by agreement once permission for their taking has been obtained. Court of Claims depositions are taken in the same manner as district court and Tax Court depositions.[88]

Prior to trial in the Court of Claims all deposition transcripts are on file and thus part of the record to which reference can be made in connection with a motion for summary judgment.[89]

At trial, any deposition can be used to impeach or contradict the testimony of the deponent as a witness.[90] Also, admissions made in the depo-

---

[81] Fed. R. Civ. P. 26(d)(3).
[82] Ct. Cl. R. 30(a).
[83] Ct. Cl. R. 30(b).
[84] Ct. Cl. R. 30(c). Where leave is granted for the taking of a deposition, an appropriate order may be entered imposing conditions for the protection of the parties or of the witness. Ct. Cl. R. 30(d)(3).
[85] Ct. Cl. R. 30(d)(2).
[86] Ct. Cl. R. 30(e), 51.
[87] *Ibid.*
[88] See Ct. Cl. R. 30–36 for the detailed provisions relating to deposition procedures.
[89] Ct. Cl. R. 64(d).
[90] Ct. Cl. R. 34(a)(4).

sition of a deponent who is a party or an officer, agent, or employee of a party testifying within the scope of his authority may be used as evidence by the adverse party.[91]

In the Court of Claims an evidentiary deposition is admissible at trial to the same extent and with the same effect as if the deponent were present and testifying in court.[92] A discovery deposition is admissible in evidence only if at the time of trial the witness

1. Is deceased
2. Is resident overseas for an indefinite period
3. Is unable to testify due to age, ill health, or imprisonment
4. Cannot be brought to court by the proponent through the use of a subpoena
5. There is a finding that such exceptional circumstances exist as to permit the use of the deposition in lieu of the witness' testimony in court.[93]

Interrogatories in the District Courts

Under the Federal Rules of Civil Procedure a party may serve upon an adversary written interrogatories to be answered under oath.[94] Sets of interrogatories may be served without leave of court. Answers to interrogatories must be provided not only from personal knowledge but also from information available to the party.[95] Answers to interrogatories are matters of record in the case and may be utilized in connection with a motion for summary judgment as well as at trial as admissions of an adverse party.[96] A party may not, however, place in evidence his own self-serving answers to interrogatories.[97]

Answers to the government's interrogatories must be signed under oath by the taxpayer if an individual or by an officer or agent of a corporate or other non-individual taxpayer.[98] Answers to interrogatories served upon the government by the taxpayer will be prepared and attested to by the trial attorney in charge of the case.[99]

---

[91] Ct. Cl. R. 34(a)(5).

[92] Ct. Cl. R. 34(b).

[93] Ct. Cl. R. 34(c). See also Ct. Cl. R. 34(a)(4), (5), (6).

[94] Fed. R. Civ. P. 33.

[95] *Ibid.* Answers are required to all interrogatories (within fifteen days after service unless a longer period is specified) unless formal objections are made and sustained. Only the answers to interrogatories to which objections have been made may be delayed until the objections are ruled upon.

[96] Fed. R. Civ. P. 33, 56(c).

[97] Lobel v. American Airlines, 192 F.2d 217 (C.A.2d).

[98] Fed. R. Civ. P. 33.

[99] *Ibid.* Van Horne v. Hines, 31 F. Supp. 346 (D.C.) (response to request for admissions signed by an assistant United States Attorney). *Cf.* United States v. 42 Jars, More or Less, Etc., 264 F.2d 666, 670 (C.A.3d).

GOVERNMENT INTERROGATORIES. The government normally will serve a set of interrogatories (often quite extensive) upon the taxpayer shortly after filing its answer. These interrogatories will usually be designed to ascertain the "solid" facts in the case and to discover leads for further discovery or investigation. Typically, the government's interrogatories will inquire into the following areas:

1. The identity of officers, directors, and shareholders in corporations or other entities involved in the suit
2. Detailed data that can be provided from books and records
3. Names and addresses of persons who had contact with the transactions involved in the suit and who are potential witnesses
4. The identity and location of documents material to the controversy
5. Other information of record available to the taxpayer

The government generally will not, by interrogatories, inquire about such "soft" facts as intent, belief, and the like which are best inquired into at a deposition upon oral examination.

TAXPAYER'S INTERROGATORIES. As part of the development of his case in a tax refund suit taxpayer's counsel should consider the desirability of directing interrogatories to the government.[100] Among others, the following areas of inquiry should be investigated:

1. The jurisdictional facts that were not admitted in the answer, *i.e.* such matters as dates of filing key documents, rejection of claims, amounts and dates of tax payments, etc.
2. The identity of Internal Revenue or other government personnel who might be subject to deposition questioning (This would include agents who made estimates upon which an assessment was based, agents having knowledge of facts material to the case, and agents who interviewed potential witnesses.)
3. The identity of government documents that might be subject to a motion for production (The answers to interrogatories calling for this information will enable the taxpayer to describe with reasonable specificity the documents he will seek on a formal motion for production. Of particular importance is the identity of all statements pertaining to the case that were submitted to the Service by the taxpayer or potential witnesses and documents that may constitute evidence at trial.)
4. Relevant financial or other detailed data material to the case that is in the possession of the government (This would normally include details of computations by means of which the amounts of assessments were determined.)
5. In connection with facts that the taxpayer feels should not be in dispute, but that are not admitted in the government's answer, what the government says these facts are

[100] See Tax Refund Suit Form No. 13, p. **C**·82, for an example of the form of interrogatories.

6. The identity of the entries (if any) on the subject tax returns that the government contends were not correctly reported and the government's contention as to how the entry should have been reported (An inquiry into this area will reveal any offsets the government may raise sufficiently early for the taxpayer to be able to prepare his proof on the "new issues.")

7. To the extent possible the identity of potential witnesses to the case.[101]

The authors' list of possible areas of inquiry cannot, of course, be complete since every case will present its own peculiar discovery needs. Moreover, the list does not constitute the authors' opinion regarding areas of questioning that are either necessary or permissible in every case.

As with all discovery devices, interrogatories should be used with discretion and only when they will genuinely aid the party in preparing his case. In drafting interrogatories the taxpayer should be careful to limit the scope of the questions to an area susceptible of a meaningful answer. As a horrible example consider the taxpayer transit company that asked the government to list the names of "all persons having knowledge of plaintiff's operations." In its sustained objection, the government noted that an answer to the interrogatory would have as its starting point the city telephone directory. On the other hand, the taxpayer should be sure to make his interrogatories "continuing" so that any requested information that may become available to the government after the answers are filed will be supplied to the taxpayer in a supplemental answer to the interrogatories. This is accomplished by inserting a "continuing" clause in the preamble to the set of interrogatories.[102]

Calls in the Court of Claims

The Court of Claims Rules do not provide for interrogatories to parties as do the Federal Rules of Civil Procedure. The Court of Claims Rules do provide for the taking of depositions upon written interrogatories.[103] However, this procedure is extremely awkward when compared to interrogatories to parties pursuant to the Federal Rules of Civil Procedure.[104] However, some of the ends achieved by interrogatories in the district courts can be accomplished through calls in the Court of Claims.

---

[101] See generally 4 MOORE'S FEDERAL PRACTICE ¶ 26.19 (2d ed. 1966) for a discussion of the ability to discover the identity of witnesses.

[102] See Tax Refund Suit Form No. 13, p. C·82, for a sample clause of this type. Wolf v. Dickinson, 16 F.R.D. 250 (E.D. Pa.). See also Smith v Acacia Overseas Freighters, Ltd., 120 F. Supp. 192 (E.D. Pa.) (admiralty case), indicating that interrogatories are continuing in nature even in the absence of such a clause.

[103] Ct. Cl. R. 32.

[104] See Miller, *Tax Refund Litigation in the Court of Claims,* 55 GEO. L.J. 454, 465 (1966–67).

Upon motion of a party [105] the court or commissioner can order a party to file with the clerk

1. Documents or other identified materials relevant to the case
2. Information relating to the identity and location of persons having knowledge of the relevant facts or of documents and other materials pertinent to the case [106]

The motion for a call must state (with reasonable particularity) the identity of the documents or other materials desired, the respect in which they are proper objects of discovery, and that they are not already in the possession of the moving party.[107] In lieu of filing called documents or materials a party can produce them for inspection and copying by the moving party.[108]

The Court of Claims Rules provide that a response to call is not considered evidence unless and until offered and received in evidence at trial, or upon the hearing of a motion, or by express direction of the court.[109] Unlike interrogatories in the district courts, calls cannot be used to obtain detailed information. Responses to calls merely give the moving party access to the materials containing the information and/or the identity of the persons who have knowledge of the information and access to documents containing the data sought. With this limitation, calls can be utilized for the same purposes as interrogatories in the district courts.[110]

Motions for Production of Documents and Materials

In both the district courts and the Court of Claims a party may seek an order compelling the adversary to produce and permit copying and inspection of any designated documents or other tangible objections (not privileged) in his possession, custody, or control.[111] Similarly, the right to enter upon property in the possession of control of an adverse party may be obtained by motion.[112]

GOVERNMENT'S MOTION FOR PRODUCTION. Normally, the government will wish to inspect the following types of materials as part of its preparation for trial:

1. The taxpayer's business records relating to the period and transactions in question

[105] Ct. Cl. R. 39(b). Or on the trial commissioner's own motion (against the government). Ct. Cl. R. 39(a). See Tax Refund Suit Form No. 14, p. **C**·82–83, for a sample motion for a call.
[106] Ct. Cl. R. 39(b).
[107] Ct. Cl. R. 39(d).
[108] Ct. Cl. R. 39(c).
[109] Ct. Cl. R. 39(e).
[110] See p. **13**·17–18 *supra* for areas of inquiry that should be considered.
[111] Fed. R. Civ. P. 34; Ct. Cl. R. 40. See Tax Refund Suit Form No. 15, p. **C**·83, for a sample motion for production.
[112] Fed. R. Civ. P. 34; Ct. Cl. R. 40.

2. All original documents pertaining to the transactions in question, *i.e.* wills, contracts, etc.
3. In cases involving questions of intent, materials revealing tax advice received by the taxpayer from others than lawyers.[113]
4. Other materials of evidentiary value in the particular case

The government's right to access to these materials is tested under the rules normally applied in civil litigation, *i.e.* will the produced documents constitute admissible evidence or lead to such evidence? [114]

TAXPAYER'S MOTION FOR PRODUCTION. In the course of developing his case the taxpayer should consider whether he needs access to any of the following general categories of materials in the possession of the government:

1. Formal documents such as tax returns, claims for refund, etc., filed by the taxpayer with the Internal Revenue Service of which copies were not retained
2. Correspondence and informal documents submitted by the taxpayer to the Internal Revenue Service and transcripts (or equivalent) of oral statements made by the taxpayer to Internal Revenue employees
3. Documents material to the transactions at issue (*e.g.* contracts) of which the taxpayer does not have copies
4. Copies or secondary evidence of records inspected by the Internal Revenue Service and no longer available to the taxpayer
5. Witness' statements, trial exhibits, and similar items
6. Internal documents of the Internal Revenue Service

Except with regard to the last listed category a motion for production of these documents in a tax refund suit raises no novel issues. The first four types of items are normally produced as a matter of course. The fifth category raises the "work-product" issue common to all civil litigation.[115] A motion for the production of internal government documents, however, raises unique problems. In sum, the court must balance against the taxpayer's need (if any) for the materials, the government's interest in keeping its files confidential.[116]

The following is a list of Internal Revenue Service documents and materials that have been the subject of motions for production in tax refund suits. It can be seen that access to substantially similar government docu-

---

[113] In federal tax litigation, no privilege protects from discovery tax advice given taxpayers by accountants or other tax advisers who are not lawyers. Lustman v. Commissioner, 322 F.2d 253, 258 (C.A.3d). See also Katsoris, *Confidential Communications: The Accountant's Dilemma*, 35 FORDHAM L. REV. 51 (1966).

[114] Fed. R. Civ. P. 26(b), 34; Ct. Cl. R. 40. See generally 4 MOORE'S FEDERAL PRACTICE ¶ 34.09–.18 (2d ed. 1966).

[115] Hickman v. Taylor, 329 U.S. 497. See generally 4 MOORE'S FEDERAL PRACTICE ¶ 26.23 (2d ed. 1966).

[116] See p. **13·9** *et seq. supra.*

ments has been both granted and denied by the courts after consideration of the peculiar circumstances of the individual case.

Type of Document	*Production Order*	
Internal Revenue Agent's and Special Agent's reports and transmittal memoranda, reports of Internal Revenue Service engineers, etc.	Granted [117]	Denied [118]
Reports and memoranda of review level personnel of the Internal Revenue Service (e.g., Appellate Division Technical Adviser's reports and supporting statements).	Granted [119]	Denied [120]
Materials collected by Internal Revenue Service relative to a case, and analysis of the materials.	Granted [121]	Denied [122]
Internal Revenue Service intra-agency communications (e.g., memoranda between Appellate Division and Audit).	Granted [123]	Denied [124]
Miscellaneous documents such as control cards, third-party tax returns, etc.	Granted [125]	Denied [126]

PROCEDURE ON MOTIONS FOR PRODUCTION. In both tax refund tribunals a party seeking the production of documents must, by a formal motion, show good cause for the issuance of an order for production.[127] The motion must designate with reasonable specificity the materials sought. Accordingly, it is advisable to utilize other formal discovery procedures (normally interrogatories or calls) prior to the motion to produce in order to obtain a description adequate to identify the documents to be demanded.

[117] Timken Roller Bearing Co. v. United States, 38 F.R.D. 58 (N.D. Ohio); United States v. San Antonio Portland Cement Co., 33 F.R.D. 513 (W.D. Tex.) (erroneous refund suit by government); Frazier v. Phinney, 24 F.R.D. 406 (S.D. Tex.); United States v. Gates, 35 F.R.D. 524 (Colo.) (erroneous refund suit by government).

[118] Conway Import Co. v. United States, 40 F.R.D. 5 (E.D.N.Y.); Unistrut Corp. v. United States, 37 F.R.D. 478 (E.D. Mich.); Cenname v. Bingler, 7 A.F.T.R. 2d 1886 (W.D. Pa.). Cf. Campbell v. Eastland, 307 F2d 478 (C.A.5th), cert. denied, 371 U.S. 955.

[119] Timken Roller Bearing Co. v. United States, supra note 117; United States v. San Antonio Portland Cement Co., supra note 117. United States v. Gates, supra note 117.

[120] Conway Import Co. v. United States, supra note 118; Unistrut Corp. v. United States, supra note 118; Cenname, v. Bingler, supra note 118.

[121] United States v. Gates, 35 F.R.D. 524 (Colo.) (erroneous refund suit by government). Timken Roller Bearing Co. v. United States, supra note 117 (communications from third parties to be inspected in camera prior to ruling on existence of informer privilege).

[122] Conway Import Co. v. United States, supra note 118 (reports of conferences between government and taxpayer representatives). Cf. Campbell v. Eastland, supra note 118.

[123] Timken Roller Bearing Co. v. United States, supra note 117; United States v. San Antonio Portland Cement Co., supra note 117.

[124] E. W. Bliss Co. v. United States, 203 F. Supp. 175 (N.D. Ohio).

[125] Timken Roller Bearing Co. v. United States, supra note 117; United States v. Gates, supra note 117.

[126] Conway Import Co. v. United States, supra note 118.

[127] Fed. R. Civ. P. 34; Ct. Cl. R. 40(a).

After considering any objections to the motion the district court (or trial commissioner in the Court of Claims) will rule. The order (if issued) will specify the materials to be produced and may also designate the time, place, and other conditions of the production.[128] Usually the parties are able to agree upon the details of production once an order has been issued specifying the materials to be made available.

Requests for Admissions

In the tax refund forums a party has the opportunity to obtain from the adversary formal admissions of (1) the truth of relevant facts and (2) the genuineness of relevant documents.[129] Requests for admissions are utilized to make part of the record to be relied upon on a motion for summary judgment or to reduce the amount of proof that must be presented at a trial through witnesses.

In most cases the taxpayer should attempt to work out a set of stipulations of undisputed facts with the government before drafting a set of requests for admissions. The give and take of stipulation negotiations frequently yields more agreed facts than the formal procedure for obtaining admissions. However, where stipulation is not possible or is impractical, resort should be had to formal requests for admissions.

In drafting a set of requests for admissions for submission to the government the taxpayer should verify that the facts to be asserted are true, and he should see to it that they are not subject to a good faith denial by the government. It may be necessary to provide the government with information, or documents, or access to records that will enable it to verify the truth of the statements made. The taxpayer should be at least neutral in wording the admissions. The purpose of the draftsman is to prepare statements with which the opponent cannot disagree. Arguments, legal conclusions, and deductions to be made from the facts should be omitted from requests for admissions.[130]

DISTRICT COURT REQUEST FOR ADMISSIONS PROCEDURES. After commencement of a district court refund suit either party may serve on the other a written request for admissions of facts and the genuineness of documents (copies of which are provided).[131] The requests are deemed admitted unless, within the required time, the party requested to admit serves on the requesting party (1) A sworn statement specifically denying all or some of the requested items or stating in detail why he cannot truthfully admit or deny the items or (2) written objections to some or all of the

---

[128] Fed. R. Civ. P. 34; Ct. Cl. R. 40(c).
[129] Fed. R. Civ. P. 36; Ct. Cl. R. 42.
[130] See Tax Refund Suit Form No. 16, p. C·83, for a sample set of requests for admissions.
[131] Fed. R. Civ. P. 36.

requested admissions on the ground that they are irrelevant, privileged, or otherwise improper.[132] The Federal Rules of Civil Procedure expressly call for a party to respond in good faith to requests for admissions. Hence, a denial should fairly meet the substance of the requested admission. Also, when only part or a qualification of a request is denied, the responding party should indicate the part of the statement that is true and deny only the remainder.

COURT OF CLAIMS REQUEST FOR ADMISSIONS PROCEDURE.   In the Court of Claims, once the government has responded to the taxpayer's petition, either party may, by motion, apply for leave to serve a request for admissions.[133] The rules provide that leave shall freely be granted to promote discovery, to eliminate surprise, and to shorten trial.[134]

In the Court of Claims a request for admissions must contain

1. A statement of material facts believed to be undisputed with a request that the opponent admit their truth
2. A list of documents that are relied upon and are to be offered in evidence, and a request that the adversary consent to their admission in evidence [135]

Copies of any documents listed in the request for admissions must be served with the request unless the adversary already has the originals or copies of the documents.[136]

The party upon whom the requests are served must file a timely response which contains

1. A statement admitting, denying, or specifying the reason why he cannot admit or deny the factual propositions contained in the request for admissions, or objecting on the grounds that some or all of the requested admissions are privileged, plainly irrelevant, or otherwise improper
2. A statement consenting to or stating objection to the admission of the documents listed in the request [137]

To the extent that there is no proper response to a request for admissions, the statements of fact are deemed admitted and the listed documents deemed unobjecionable.[138]

---

[132] *Ibid.* The response must be served within the time stated in the request for admissions, not less than ten days after service, unless otherwise set by the court.

[133] Ct. Cl. R. 42(a). A copy of the proposed set of requests for admissions must accompany the motion.

[134] Ct. Cl. R. 42(c).

[135] Ct. Cl. R. 42(b).

[136] *Ibid.*

[137] Ct. Cl. R. 42(d). The response must be served within thirty days after the service of the request unless some other period is set by the trial commissioner or the court.

[138] Ct. Cl. R. 42(d)(3).

As in the district courts, a party in the Court of Claims is expressly required to respond in good faith to a request for admissions.[139]

STIPULATIONS

Characteristically, tax refund suits are heavily stipulated. Taxpayers tend to wish to stipulate to the extent possible in order to reduce the expense of producing formal proof of facts at trial. The government's policy toward stipulation is one of cooperation. As stated by one high ranking official of the Tax Division:

> If you believe we know facts, or should know some we have denied, a good procedure is to draw up a proposed stipulation and submit it for approval. The sooner this is done the better, for it gives the Department a chance to have the Revenue Service verify any facts contained in the stipulation which are not coupled by files furnished us by the Service. However, don't ask us to stipulate the Government out of Court.[140]

Regardless of the government's willingness to stipulate the taxpayer should always be careful not to agree to too much. To the extent his case can more effectively and meaningfully be presented to the trier of fact through live testimony he should decline to stipulate. All too often important facts that could be presented tellingly at a trial (particularly a jury trial) are lost in the midst of an extensive stipulation.

Negotiations for Stipulations

The taxpayer should commence negotiations for stipulations early in the development stage of the case. An early start will allow time for the working out of problems and, when necessary, for the taxpayer to gather his formal proof should the Government not agree to stipulate to the extent the taxpayer might wish.

It is best for the taxpayer's counsel to commence stipulation negotiations by preparing a draft of a proposed set for submission to the government. The preparation of this draft often yields the side benefit of a checklist of essential facts that can be used in planning for trial and for a motion for summary judgment. The taxpayer's proposed stipulations should be neutrally worded so that the government's objections can be limited to matters of substance.

The taxpayer's proposed set of stipulations should be sent to the government's attorney for his consideration. In addition, supporting information

---

[139] Ct. Cl. R. 42(d) (2).

[140] Roberts, *Tips on Refund Suits,* 37 TAXES 493, 494 (1959). Mr. Roberts, then chief of the Compromise Section, subsequently has been Second Assistant for the Tax Division as well as Acting Assistant Attorney General.

and/or documents that will aid the Government in verifying the facts stated in the stipulations should be made available. Usually, where a mass of records or materials must be examined, the taxpayer will advise the government of their location and keep them accessible for inspection. Copies of documents of particular importance to the case are normally made part of a proposed set of stipulations.

Within a reasonable time the government's trial attorney will contact taxpayer's counsel indicating the areas of agreement and disagreement and suggesting any further stipulation he may wish to add to taxpayer's proposal. On occasion, the government will feel that further discovery is necessary before a stipulation can be entered into.

Frequently it is helpful for taxpayer's counsel to meet with his governmental counterpart to discuss the proposals and counterproposals for stipulations. Normally a letter or telephone call to government counsel will suffice to set up a meeting on the Tax Division attorney's next trip to the taxpayer's city.

One point of particular importance to tax litigation should be noted with respect to stipulation negotiations. If it should appear that agreement can be reached with government counsel regarding some, but not all, of the points in dispute it is advisable to reduce the area of agreement to writing in a formal stipulation. In this way the taxpayer can be protected against the possibility that a turnover of government personnel would result in the assignment of his case to a new attorney with whom negotiations would have to be started from scratch.

Finally, it is important to bear in mind that a court may relieve a party from a stipulation where justice so requires.[141]

Contents of Set of Stipulations

The aim in preparing a set of stipulations is to obtain a single document that states all of the pertinent matters in the case as to which agreement has been reached.[142] Therefore, facts that have been admitted in the pleading should be included.

JURISDICTIONAL FACTS. The stipulation should commence with a recitation of the jurisdictional facts establishing that the taxpayer is properly before the court. Normally, this portion of the stipulation will consist of paragraphs of the taxpayer's complaint that the government has already admitted.

SUBSTANTIVE FACTS. The agreed substantive facts should be set out in as logical a fashion as possible. Pertinent documents (such as tax

[141] *E.g.*, Logan Lumber Co. v. Commissioner, 365 F.2d 846 (C.A.5th); Stavroudis v. United States, 309 F.2d 480 (C.A.2d).

[142] See Tax Refund Suit Form No. 18, p. **C·**85, for a sample set of stipulations illustrating the form of the types of stipulations discussed below.

returns, claims for refund, contracts, etc.) and schedules showing important financial data should be made exhibits to the stipulation.

ALLEGEDLY INADMISSIBLE FACTS. A question often arises regarding true and provable statements that one party feels are inadmissible in evidence. Some attorneys are reluctant to stipulate to a fact they believe is not admissible.[143] However, a more cooperative attitude is recommended, except in the case of a fact so prejudicial that its being brought to the attention of the court would materially affect the case. It is advisable to place all propositions believed by one party or the other to be inadmissible in a supplemental stipulation, the preamble of which states the evidentiary disputes.[144] In this manner the court, on reading the stipulations, will be on notice of which facts the parties agree are admissible and which are in dispute.

MATTERS OF TRIAL PROCEDURE. If agreement can be reached that will expedite and reduce the expense of the trial, it should be made part of the set of stipulations. Typically, these agreements relate to the use of copies of documents in lieu of originals and the presentation of part of the proof in an informal manner. For example, it can be agreed that an affidavit, memorandum, letter, or even a publication would be accepted as the testimony of the writer or that the depositions of certain witnesses, who otherwise would have to be called at trial, may be considered to be their trial testimony. While all stipulations regarding the "informal" presentation of evidence should be approved by the district court (or trial commissioner) it can be expected that virtually any agreement that will shorten trial time will be welcomed by the trier.

ISSUES IN THE CASE. If agreement can be obtained from the government, the stipulation should state the issues in the case, *e.g.,* what specific tax adjustments are in issue. If government counsel will agree, it is helpful to stipulate that all items in the subject tax returns (as adjusted by the Internal Revenue Service), with specified exceptions, are taken to be correct for purposes of the case. If he will not agree, formal discovery should be used to ascertain precisely what items are in issue.

COMPUTATION OF JUDGMENT. The stipulations in a tax refund suit ordinarily will include an agreement regarding the manner in which any judgment in the case will be computed. The following terms are commonly used:

It is agreed that any computation necessary as a result of the decision of the Court in this case shall initially be made by the defendant. The defendant's

---

[143] In the Tax Court, the alleged inadmissibility of a proposed stipulation is not considered an adequate ground for a refusal to stipulate. Tax Ct. R. 31(b)(5). See **p. 6·21**, n. 80 *supra*.

[144] See Tax Refund Suit Form No. 19, p. **C·85–86** *infra*, for an illustration of the **form** of stipulations of allegedly inadmissible facts.

computation shall be submitted to the plaintiff for his approval. In the event the parties are unable to agree upon the computation then the issue shall be resolved by a procedure to be set by the Court.

In jury trials the government usually will either defer the computation stipulation until after an adverse verdict is a rendered, or will include, as part of the stipulation, an agreement that the computation stipulation shall not be brought to the attention of the jury.

STIPULATION OF SUBMISSION WITHOUT TRIAL. In every non-jury tax refund suit the parties should consider whether the controversy can be submitted for decision without a formal trial hearing. The record for decision would consist of the stipulations of fact as well as other matters that the parties can stipulate. These will constitute evidence in the case. Like the Tax Court, the refund tribunals favor submissions without trial because of the great savings in judicial time and litigant's expense that they accomplish.

In deciding whether or not to agree to submit a case for decision without trial, the taxpayer should consider whether

1. *The case is of a type susceptible to decision on a cold record.* Obviously, cases which, after discovery and good faith stipulations of fact, boil down to questions of law should be submitted without trial. In fact, once the record is made, either party can move for summary judgment and, in effect, submit the case for decision. Even in cases that have sufficient issues of fact to prevent a summary judgment's being granted, a trial may not be necessary. Thus, in factual cases involving the tax effects of admitted actions where the credibility of witnesses is not really in dispute, depositions can often be adequately substituted for testimony at a trial. For example, in a "debt vs. equity" case where the issue is whether shareholder advances to a closely held corporation constitute loans or invested capital, a case can often be presented solely through the use of corporate records and the depositions of the shareholders. However, cases in which credibility of witnesses is a pertinent factor or explanatory or expert testimony is required normally cannot be presented adequately without giving the trier of fact the opportunity to observe the witnesses under examination.

2. *The agreed record for decision contains all the evidence the taxpayer wishes to present.* It should be noted that the government's agreement to submit a case for decision on an agreed record does not constitute an admission that the record makes out a prima facie case for the taxpayer. Therefore, the taxpayer's first check of the record should be made to determine the bare legal sufficiency of the case to support a decision in his favor. Beyond this, however, the taxpayer should ascertain whether evidence that the government will not incorporate in the agreed record will materially aid his case. If there is such proof and the expense of presentation will not outweigh its value, a trial should be held.

3. The taxpayer's case can be more persuasively presented at a trial hearing. Even though a case could be submitted on a cold record, and the government would agree to the taxpayer's desired proof, it is sometimes advantageous for a taxpayer to present some live testimony in the case. In complex cases, for example, the parties may not be able to anticipate all of the problems that might arise in a judge's mind, and the calling of a witness who can be questioned by the court can be of value. In other cases, counsel may feel that the trier should see the taxpayer and hear his testimony in order fully to appreciate his case.

THE FORMAL PRETRIAL CONFERENCE

Both the Federal Rules of Civil Procedure and the Court of Claims Rules, in virtually identical terms, provide for a formal pretrial conference to be utilized at the discretion of the court (or trial commissioner in the Court of Claims).[145] The Rules state that the following matters can be considered at the pretrial conference as well as any others that would aid in the handling of the case:

1. Simplication of the issues
2. Amendments to the pleadings
3. Reduction of necessary formal proof through admissions of facts and of the genuineness and admissibility of documents
4. Limitation of the number of expert witnesses [146]
5. In the district courts, the possibility of utilizing a master

While not expressly stated in the rules, a principal item of discussion at the pretrial conference is frequently the possibility of settlement of the controversy.

Although their use is discretionary, some form of pretrial conference is utilized by just about every district court and trial commissioner in the Court of Claims. The precise format and procedure for the pretrial conference varies considerably depending upon the particular district court or commissioner before whom the case is pending. Accordingly, only a few comments of general applicability to tax refund suit pretrial conferences are appropriate.

For maximum effectiveness, a very short brief should be submitted prior to the pretrial conference whether or not required by local rule or pretrial order. In some cases a pretrial order may be issued requiring the parties to submit extensive amounts of information prior to the pretrial conference.[147] Except where more is required by rule or order, the pretrial

---

[145] Fed. R. Civ. P. 16; Ct. Cl. R. 44. See generally *Seminar on Practice and Procedure, Pretrial Conference Procedure,* 28 F.R.D. 37, 137–72 (1962).

[146] The Court of Claims Rules mention the possibility of a pretrial exchange of written statements constituting the direct examination of expert witnesses. Ct. Cl. R. 42(a)(4).

[147] See Ct. Cl. R. 43(e) as an illustration of the possible scope of such an order.

conference brief usually should do no more than set the scene of the case. The essential facts should be stated in summary and nonargumentative fashion. The pertinent statutes and one or two leading cases should be cited in order to provide a general background for the pretrial conference discussion.[148]

At the pretrial conference itself, the parties can expect the question of settlement to be raised. While taxpayer's counsel may have full authority to settle the case on the spot, the government's attorney will not. He may only make a recommendation regarding settlement once an offer is submitted in accordance with the normal formal settlement procedures.[149] However, his recommendation memorandum will include a summary of the court's comments regarding settlement. As might be expected, these comments are given considerable weight in the evaluation of a settlement proposal.

In addition to settlement, another item of particular importance to tax refund suits is commonly discussed at pretrial conferences. This is the subject of the issues in the case. In tax refund suits, of course, the government's defense need not be consistent with the position taken by the Internal Revenue Service during the administrative procedures that preceded the suit. Also, totally new adjustments can be raised as defenses in the case. At the pretrial conference the taxpayer should be careful to do everything possible to have the issues in the case narrowed. The matter should be raised in the pretrial conference discussion and a request should be made that the issues be stated, in writing, either in a formal order, a stipulation, or other document. The taxpayer should request that, at the least, the government should specify at, or shortly after, the conference which items in the subject returns are accepted as correct and which are not.

After the pretrial conference most courts and trial commissioners will issue an order reflecting the action taken at the conference as well as such rulings as have been made to govern the further conduct of the case.[150]

STAY OF TAX REFUND SUIT DUE TO ISSUANCE OF DEFICIENCY NOTICE

If, at any time prior to the trial of a tax refund suit involving income, estate, or gift taxes,[151] the Internal Revenue Service issues a deficiency notice to the taxpayer with regard to the taxes that are the subject matter

---

[148] See Tax Refund Suit Form No. 17, p. **C·84**, for a sample unsolicited pretrial conference memorandum.

[149] See Chapter 14 *infra* for a discussion of the settlement of tax refund suits.

[150] Fed. R. Civ. P. 16; Ct. Cl. R. 45. *See* Peter Pan Seafoods, Inc. v. United States, 20 A.F.T.R.2d 5080 (W.D. Wash.) in which the government was allowed to raise a § 269 defense not specifically set forth in the pretrial order.

[151] Or any penalty relating to such taxes.

of the action, the proceeding is interrupted. At this point the taxpayer has the option to petition the Tax Court for a redetermination of the asserted deficiency, and the tax refund suit is automatically stayed for the period during which the taxpayer may petition the Tax Court and for 60 days thereafter, *i.e.* usually a total of 150 days.[152]

If the taxpayer files a petition with the Tax Court the refund tribunal loses jurisdiction of the case to the extent the Tax Court obtains jurisdiction over the controversy.[153] To illustrate the situation, consider the case of a taxpayer who filed a suit for refund of income taxes for the calendar years 1964, 1965, and 1966 and received a deficiency notice asserting additional taxes were due for calendar year 1966. If the taxpayer petitioned the Tax Court as to calendar year 1966, the refund tribunal would lose jurisdiction of the refund action insofar as it pertained to that year.[154]

If a taxpayer does not petition the Tax Court within the time permitted, the newly asserted deficiency can be contested in the refund suit. The government may assert a counterclaim at any time during the period the refund suit is stayed.[155]

---

[152] IRC § 7422(e).

[153] *Ibid.* United States v Joe Graham Post No. 119, Am. Legion, 340 F.2d 474 (C.A.5th), *cert. denied,* 382 U.S. 824; Cole v. Bookwalter, 170 F. Supp. 527 (W.D. Mo.).

[154] S. Rep. No. 1622, 83d Cong., 2d Sess. 610–11 (1954), U.S. Code Cong. & Adm. News, 83d Cong., 2d Sess. (1954), vol. 3, at 5261. *But cf.* Rosamond Gifford Charitable Corp. v. United States, 170 F. Supp. 239 (N.D.N.Y.) (questionable decision on this point).

[155] IRC § 7422(e). Bar L Ranch, Inc. v. Phinney, 20 A.F.T.R.2d 5062 (S.D. Tex.).

CHAPTER **14**

SETTLEMENT OF TAX REFUND SUITS

All tax cases commence with a dispute between the taxpayer and the Internal Revenue Service. Most are settled with the Service at some point during the administrative process. However, once a complaint or petition is filed in a tax refund suit, the controversy (from the government's point of view) comes within the jurisdiction of the United States Department of Justice.[1] The Department, primarily through its Tax Division, controls the course of litigation for the government. Also, the Attorney General, and those to whom he has delegated authority, have the power to settle tax refund suits.[2]

[1] Executive Order No. 6166 (June 10, 1933).
[2] *Ibid.* 38 Ops. Atty.-Gen. 98 & 124 (1934), IRC § 7122(a).

14 · 1

Upon receipt of every complaint or petition in a tax refund suit the Tax Division dispatches a letter to taxpayer's counsel inviting him to consider at least the possibility of settlement of his case.[3] Virtually every taxpayer does, during the course of a tax refund suit, seriously consider compromise, and almost two-thirds are able to arrive at a mutually acceptable settlement with the government.[4]

This chapter discusses the government personnel with whom taxpayer's counsel may have contact during the course of trying or settling a tax refund suit and the process by which a settlement may be reached.

GOVERNMENT PERSONNEL INVOLVED IN TAX REFUND LITIGATION

It is helpful to begin the discussion of the settlement of tax refund suits with a survey of the tax department of the government's "law firm" and its mode of operation. Fig. 14–1 (page **14 · 3**) illustrates the organization of the Tax Division of the Department of Justice, which is primarily responsible for handling all tax litigation in the federal courts.[5]

Refund Trial Sections

The Refund Trial Sections of the Tax Division are in charge of the conduct of tax refund suits in the United States District Courts as well as the Court of Claims. In all Court of Claims cases, and in most district court cases, all work done in preparing and defending tax refund suits for the government is performed by Tax Division trial attorneys stationed in Washington, D.C. Even where the trial work is performed by the tax section of a United States Attorney's office [6] or a Tax Division field office,[7] the government attorney handling the tax refund litigation is subject to the general supervision of the geographically appropriate Refund Trial Section, and settlement offers are processed through the Tax Division. Throughout the book the term "trial attorney" is used to describe both an attorney employed by the Tax Division and an Assistant United States Attorney handling a tax refund suit.

[3] And inclosing a copy of the Tax Division's "General Information Concerning the Settlement of Tax Refund Suits." Tax Refund Suit Form No. 20, p. **C·**86–87.

[4] Annual Report of the Attorney General of the United States for the fiscal year ended June 30, 1966, 325, 357.

[5] Litigation in the Tax Court is handled for the government by the Internal Revenue Service Regional Counsel's offices.

[6] At this writing, Assistant United States Attorneys handle most tax refund suits in the Southern District of New York and the California districts.

[7] At this writing, the Tax Division maintains a field office in Fort Worth, Texas, which handles tax refund litigation in Texas, Arkansas, New Mexico, Oklahoma, and Louisiana.

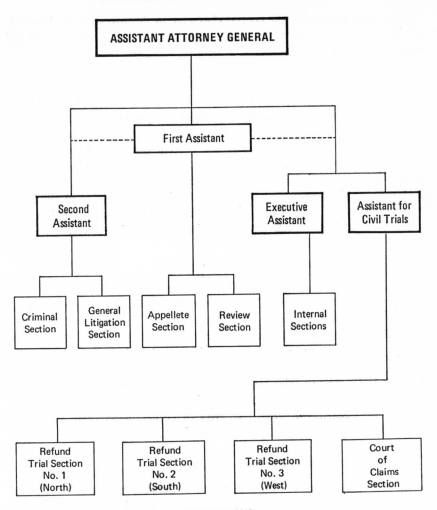

JURISDICTIONS

Refund Trial Section No. 1 (North): Connecticut, Delaware, Illinois, Indiana, Iowa, Kentucky, Maine, Maryland, Massachusetts, Michigan, Minnesota, New Hampshire, New Jersey, New York, Ohio, Pennsylvania, Rhode Island, Vermont, Wisconsin, Puerto Rico, Virgin Islands.

Refund Trial Section No. 2 (South): Alabama, Arkansas, District of Columbia, Florida, Georgia, Louisiana, Mississippi, New Mexico, North Carolina, Oklahoma, South Carolina, Tennessee, Texas, Virginia, West Virginia, Canal Zone.

Refund Trial Section No. 3 (West): Alaska, Arizona, California, Colorado, Hawaii, Idaho, Kansas, Missouri, Montana, Nebraska, Nevada, North Dakota, Oregon, South Dakota, Utah, Washington, Wyoming, Guam.

Court of Claims Section: No geographical limitation; all Court of Claims tax refund suits.

Fig. 14–1. Organization of Tax Division, U.S. Department of Justice.

The trial attorney is the central character in the government's handling of the case. Almost every tax refund suit, when received, will be assigned to a single trial attorney who will have responsibility for the controversy until it is closed.[8] While assistance and advice are available to him, the trial attorney assigned to a case is given wide discretion in the preparation and presentation of the government's defense. Moreover, the trial attorney is responsible for the negotiation of settlement proposals for the government and for making the first recommendations on any offer submitted.

Letters from the Tax Division are written over the signature of the Assistant Attorney General and a Section Chief. These men normally have little personal knowledge of the case. The name of the trial attorney responsible for the taxpayer's case usually can be ascertained from any letter sent to taxpayer's counsel from the Tax Division after an answer has been filed. Each such letter will contain, in the upper left hand corner, a reference which will appear as follows:

UV:WXY:JADoe:jmg
5–57–5288

The first two letters will be the initials of the Assistant Attorney General, Tax Division. The next set of initials are those of the Chief of the Refund Trial Section in whose jurisdiction the case is pending. The third item, containing a complete surname, refers to the actual author of the letter who normally will be the trial attorney assigned to the case. The final initials identify the secretary who typed the letter. The number represents the Department of Justice identification number of the case, *i.e.*, 5 (type of case —tax), 57 (district—Northern District of Ohio), 5288 (case identity— Department of Justice, not court, case number).

Chief Counsel, Internal Revenue Service

The Chief Counsel, Internal Revenue Service, through his Refund Litigation Division, acts as "house counsel" for the Internal Revenue Service in tax refund suits.

When a complaint is filed in a tax refund suit, Chief Counsel, while collecting the pertinent files for the Tax Division, will also prepare a memorandum commonly called a "defense letter," summarizing the facts as they appear from the Internal Revenue files, stating the more pertinent legal authorities bearing upon the case, and recommending either defense or concession by the government. Utilizing the "RIRA" system,[9] Chief Counsel's

---

[8] See Smith, *The Civil Trial Function of the Tax Division,* 52 A.B.A.J. 255 (1966).

[9] "RIRA" is the Reports and Information Retrieval Activity of the Internal Revenue Service, which maintains a system whereby pending and decided cases are indexed by legal issues presented.

staff will also coordinate the government's defense in the refund suit under consideration with its position in other pending tax litigation involving the same or related issues. Perhaps most important from the point of view of the taxpayer who wishes to settle his case, Chief Counsel will classify the controversy as "Prime," "Standard," or "S.O.P." [10]

"S.O.P." or Settlement Option Procedure cases are suits in which only factual issues are presented and relatively small amounts of money are in suit. Normally, a case that presents an issue of a continuing nature, or the resolution of which will affect the liability of nonparty taxpayers, will not be classified as "S.O.P." The principal feature of an "S.O.P." classification is the abbreviated procedure that will be followed by the government in passing upon a proposed settlement. Offers submitted, provided they do not involve tax years beyond those in suit, are not referred to Chief Counsel for the views of the Internal Revenue Service. Accordingly, the time within which an offer can be acted upon by the government is substantially reduced.

"Prime" cases are, generally speaking, cases that either have a large amount of money directly in issue or present legal issues of particular importance to the Internal Revenue Service in its administration of the tax laws. These cases are given particularly careful attention throughout the course of litigation.

"Standard" cases are those that are too large, have moderately important legal issues, or are too entangled with periods or persons not in suit to be classified as "S.O.P." but not of sufficient size or legal importance to be "prime."

During the course of a tax refund suit, Chief Counsel's staff will aid the Tax Division's liaison with the field offices and other branches of the Internal Revenue Service. Chief Counsel will also advise the Justice Department of the Service's position regarding settlement proposals (except in "S.O.P." cases) and will make recommendations regarding the advisability of appeal from an adverse decision.

As a practical matter, the contact between the government's trial attorney and his counterpart in Chief Counsel's Refund Litigation Division is frequent and informal. Taxpayer's counsel, however, is unlikely to meet a member of Chief Counsel's staff during the course of a refund suit.

Internal Revenue Service Field Offices

The Internal Revenue Service field offices will assist the government's trial attorney in the same manner as a corporate client's internal counsel assists outside trial counsel. Where appropriate, an Internal Revenue Agent will conduct a supplemental investigation for the Department of

[10] Smith, *op. cit., supra* note 8, at 257 (1966).

Justice. Also, an Agent, or sometimes a Special Agent, may work directly with a trial attorney in developing the case for trial.

In most cases the local Internal Revenue Offices (including the Appellate Division) will have nothing to do with the settlement of a tax refund suit. However, where a settlement proposal encompasses periods not directly in issue in the refund suit, or where referral is otherwise appropriate, the views of the local Internal Revenue Service office will be obtained before final action is taken upon an offer.

Regional Counsel, Internal Revenue Service

On occasion a tax refund suit will be connected with a pending Tax Court suit. In this event the Tax Division trial attorney will work with the Assistant Regional Counsel in developing the government's position in the two cases. Normally, settlement of the connected cases will be coordinated through Chief Counsel.

United States Attorney

In all tax refund suits in the district courts the local United States Attorney will be attorney of record for the government. In a few instances an Assistant United States Attorney will act as the government's trial attorney in tax refund suits. However, in most cases the United States Attorney's role in a tax refund suit is primarily ministerial. His staff will see to the filing of documents and handle routine procedural matters while the Tax Division trial attorney assigned to the case will control the litigation for the government.

Review Section of Tax Division

The Review Section of the Tax Division passes on all settlement proposals in tax refund suits as well as in other types of tax litigation even though ultimate authority to act on a particular offer may not lie within the Section. Accordingly, the Section will have contact with a refund suit when an offer to settle is submitted. Review Section attorneys review settlement recommendations from the Tax Division's trial sections and Chief Counsel, Internal Revenue Service, and write their own memoranda regarding the acceptability of offers. The Chief of the Section takes final action on offers within the scope of his authority and makes recommendations on those that must be acted upon at a higher level. Normally, taxpayer's counsel will deal directly with Review Section attorneys only if he has requested a settlement conference in Washington or if, after the submission of an offer, clarification or further negotiation is necessary.

Appellate Section of Tax Division

Appellate proceedings in tax refund cases (as well as Tax Court suits and other tax litigation) are handled by attorneys of the Appellate Section of the Tax Division. Moreover, where the Government has lost a case in a trial court the Appellate Section will make recommendations regarding the advisability of the Government's seeking appellate review.[11] In tax refund litigation, taxpayer's counsel will first come in contact with the Appellate Section when a tax refund suit is on appeal.

It should be noted that a tax case can be settled while it is pending on appeal. A settlement can be negotiated with the appellate attorney handling the appeal who will (like the trial attorney in a case at the trial level) prepare a recommendation on any offer submitted. Usually, the trial attorney who tried the case will be asked to state his views regarding any proposal of settlement even though he is no longer responsible for the conduct of litigation.

Criminal Section of Tax Division

The Criminal Section handles matters involving alleged criminal violations of almost all internal revenue laws.[12] Its attorneys make recommendations regarding proposed prosecutions, aid in the development of cases in which prosecution is authorized, and give aid to United States Attorneys in criminal tax cases presented to grand juries or tried. On occasion a tax refund suit will be connected with a potential or pending criminal prosecution. This occurs most frequently when a taxpayer, while a criminal prosecution is pending, seeks to institute a civil refund suit in order to utilize the discovery provisions of the Federal Rules of Civil Procedure.[13] In this event the refund trial attorney asgned to the civil suit will cooperate with the Criminal Section in order that the refund action interfere as little as possible with the connected criminal matter.

General Litigation Section of Tax Division

The General Litigation Section handles all civil tax litigation except tax refund suits. Principally, its attorneys (and the United States Attorneys in cooperation with this Section) represent the government in collection matters, lien foreclosures, bankruptcies, injunction and mandamus actions,

[11] Final authority to decide whether or not the government will appeal from an adverse decision is vested, outside the Tax Division, in the Solicitor General of the United States.

[12] The Criminal Division, and not the Tax Division, handles alcohol, narcotics, wagering, gaming, and amusement tax prosecutions.

[13] *E.g.*, Farnsworth & Chambers Co. v. Phinney, 279 F.2d 538 (C.A.5th), *affirming* 178 F. Supp. 330 (S.D. Tex.).

and government suits for erroneous refunds. The Section is divided into several units, each responsible for work arising in a separate geographical area. It is not uncommon for a tax refund suit to be integrally related to a matter being handled by the General Litigation Section. In this event, all connected cases usually will be assigned to a single attorney in the section with predominant responsibility for the controversy as a whole.

Internal Sections of Tax Division

The Executive Assistant exercises supervisory control over the "housekeeping" sections of the Tax Division, which include the Administrative Section, the Research and Digest Unit, the Legislative History Unit, and the Litigation Control Unit. In tax refund litigation a taxpayer may have contact with the last group after judgment is entered since the Litigation Control Unit is responsible for expediting the payment of refund checks due as a result of decisions or settlements.

THE PROCESS OF SETTLING A TAX REFUND SUIT

As in all civil litigation, counsel in a tax refund suit should attempt to evaluate the suit for settlement purposes prior to negotiating a compromise with the adversary. Settlement evaluation has two facets. First, it is necessary to ascertain the minimum amount that the taxpayer will accept. Second, it is necessary to attempt to predict the maximum amount that the government will concede. To the extent the two areas overlap, settlement is possible.

Evaluation of the Case

In evaluating a tax refund suit for settlement purposes the taxpayer should, first of all, seek to balance all of the factors normally taken into account in any civil suit. Hence, among other things, he should weigh

1. The strength of his case in view of the probable proof and the applicable precedents
2. The additional expenses that will be incurred in trying (and possibly in appealing) the case rather than settling it
3. The adverse effects (if any) that would result from even a successful trial, for example, possible bad publicity, strain on the taxpayer, disruption of business activities due to trial preparation, etc.

In tax litigation additional factors, not usually present in other forms of disputes, must be taken into account. It is always necessary for the taxpayer to analyze carefully the precise effect that resolution (by trial or settlement) of the tax refund suit at issue will have on his total tax picture.

A taxpayer can only rarely walk away from a refund suit with a refund check and, like the plaintiff in the typical negligence action, close the case. The legal and practical effects of a settlement will often be felt in future years. For example, resolution of a continuing issue (the recognition *vel non* of a family partnership) may well affect the taxpayer's tax liability and tax planning for the foreseeable future. Even a case that does not (strictly speaking) present continuing issues will frequently have substantial effects on future tax liability. For example, future auditing Agents may be led to an issue by virtue of the taxpayer's having conceded all, or part, of a similar issue in prior years.

In evaluating a tax case, then, the following types of considerations must be taken into account:

1. To what extent does the taxpayer desire (or need) a resolution of the issues in dispute upon which he can rely for future planning?
2. Can a resolution of continuing issues be obtained by settlement? If not, can the taxpayer afford to settle the case and face a subsequent dispute on the same matters?
3. What will be the overall effect of any contemplated settlement of the case?

The government will approach the settlement of a tax refund suit in much the same manner as the taxpayer. Its counsel will go through the same sort of analysis in order to arrive at a settlement position. However, due to the nature of the government as the litigant charged with the overall administration of the tax laws, its settlement policies will not always be based solely upon the circumstances of the particular case under consideration. For example, if the issue presented is a particularly important one that requires judicial resolution the government may decide to try a relatively small case or reject an offer in order to obtain a needed precedent. On the other hand the government may concede or "undersell" a case where its position, if adopted by the court, might make bad law. In view of the great volume of cases handled, the government has tended to adopt several general settlement policies to expedite its job. Thus, the government normally will not settle cases at the extremes of the settlement spectrum. For example, the government will not make a nuisance value refund to a taxpayer with a meritless case. On the other hand, where the government's case is so weak that its chances are speculative at best, it will make an administrative settlement (*i.e.* full concession) rather than attempt to eke out a small concession from the taxpayer.

Negotiation of Settlement

As noted by a former Tax Division Assistant for Civil Trials: "Taxpayer's counsel should assume that the Government attorney will apply the same basic rule in approaching settlement as himself, *i.e.,* 'Is it in the best interest of the client?' " [14]

Typically, negotiations regarding the settlement of the dispute between the taxpayer and the government have been engaged in during the administrative procedure preceding the filing of the refund suit. Those attempts to settle have, of course, failed. With the filing of a tax refund suit responsibility and authority to compromise the case pass to the Department of Justice, and settlement can be discussed from a relatively fresh start. The Tax Division will have the files of the Internal Revenue Service relating to the case. Hence, it will be aware of the settlement negotiations that have taken place within the Service. However, the Tax Division does not consider itself bound by the Service's settlement position.

Settlement negotiations are usually commenced, and concluded, with the trial attorney handling the case for the government. In dealing with the trial attorney it is important to note that his authority regarding settlement is limited. He may only make a recommendation regarding the acceptability of an offer, which is subject to review at several levels within the Tax Division. Nevertheless, in most cases the trial attorney can make a pretty good estimate of the chances that a given offer will ultimately be accepted. Moreover, while not the *sine qua non* for acceptance, the trial attorney's recommendation (particularly in cases involving factual issues alone) is an important step in the taxpayer's attempt to get his proposal accepted by the government.

The Tax Division, upon request, will normally afford a taxpayer the opportunity to confer in Washington regarding the settlement of a tax refund suit.[15] These conferences are not the rule. Rather, settlement negotiations are usually conducted with the trial attorney alone when he is in the taxpayer's city. However, in unusual cases, where the amount involved and the nature of the issues warrant, a taxpayer may find it helpful to obtain a Washington conference. The principal possible advantage of a Washington conference is that the taxpayer can discuss settlement directly with review level personnel who may or may not indicate their probable recommendations regarding a proposed offer. However, settlement will still proceed formally, with an offer being submitted by the taxpayer and recommendations being made just as if the offer had been negotiated by the trial attorney alone.

In tax cases, as in all civil litigation, the process of settlement negotiation is one of "horsetrading" for the best bargain. The normal rules (or, rather, lack of rules) apply. A few points are worthy of particular note in connection with tax refund suits, however. Unlike the Tax Court Rules,

---

[14] Smith, *loc. cit., supra* note 8.

[15] See "General Information Concerning the Settlement of Tax Refund Suits," ¶ 3, Tax Refund Suit Form No. 20, p. **C**·86.

the procedural rules of the tax refund tribunals provide for liberal discovery. Therefore, the taxpayer can expect that most of his case will become known to the Government prior to trial. Accordingly, there is little advantage to be gained from hesitating to divulge prospective trial evidence (whether favorable or unfavorable). Second, the government will not negotiate (as do most civil litigants) through an offer-counteroffer process. Hence, negotiations should aim toward an agreement (at least with the trial attorney) on the best offer the Government is likely to accept. Third, and perhaps most important, settlement offers in tax cases are processed in accordance with a formal procedure. This processing takes time. In fact, the average time taken to process a settlement offer in a recent year was in excess of two months.[16] Of course, the average includes a number of unusual cases that might take as long as six months to consider. Settlement of tax refund suits cannot be accomplished on the steps to the courthouse. Negotiations should be undertaken, and the taxpayer's best offer submitted, well before he will have to incur the expense of final preparation for trial.

Taxpayer's Offer To Settle

Whether settlement negotiations are conducted with the trial attorney alone or with review level personnel at a Washington conference, they (it is to be hoped) will conclude with a meeting of the minds of the negotiators regarding a basis for disposing of the case. With this "agreement," or without it, the taxpayer must submit an offer to the government in order to get the case settled. While no particular form is required for submitting an offer in a tax refund suit, it must be in writing. Normally an offer is made in the form of a letter from taxpayer's counsel to the Assistant Attorney General in charge of the Tax Division.

Necessary Contents of Taxpayer's Offer

In making an·offer to settle a case [17] the taxpayer should be sure to cover all of the following elements in addition to any others that might be pertinent to the particular case : [18]

1. The disposition of taxpayer's case, *i.e.,* that he will dismiss his complaint with prejudice
2. The substantive resolution of the controversy, *i.e.,* the amount to be refunded and any other agreement regarding the substantive issues
3. The amount of any refund to be allocated to assessed deficiency tax (and thus not income to the taxpayer) and the amount allocable to assessed interest (and therefore taxable income)

[16] Attorney General's Report, *supra* note 4, at 363.
[17] See Tax Refund Suit Form No. 21, p. c·87, for a sample letter submitting an offer to compromise a tax refund suit.
[18] Roberts, *Tips on a Refund Suit in the District Courts,* 37 Taxes 493 (1959).

4. The extent to which interest will run on the principal amount of the refund called for by the offer (Normally it is agreed that interest will run "as provided by law," *i.e.,* at 6% per annum from the date of overpayment.)[19]

Bases of Settlement of Tax Refund Suits

In view of the nature of tax litigation there is considerable flexibility with regard to the bases upon which cases can be compromised. While some cases can be settled upon the basis of a refund of a portion of the amount of taxes in issue, others will require a more elaborate agreement in order for the parties to reach a mutually acceptable settlement. In this discussion we shall describe the most common types of tax refund suit settlements. It should be noted, however, that the government has no rigid policy regarding the basis for settling a case. So long as the government and the taxpayer can reach agreement any type of settlement can be achieved.

THE FLAT CASH REFUND SETTLEMENT. The simplest, and most common, basis for settlement of a tax refund case is to call for a cash payment from the government to the taxpayer (or vice versa where a counterclaim is present). A proposal of this sort would simply spell out the amount of money to be refunded (or paid), and the components (deficiency tax and assessed interest) of the principal amount.

A sample proposal of this type would be

Taxpayer will dismiss his complaint with prejudice in return for a refund of the principal amount of $5,000.00 plus interest thereon as provided by law. The principal amount of $5,000.00 shall consist of $4,127.00 in assessed deficiency tax and $883.00 in assessed interest.

This type of offer is also frequently made on a percentage basis, as follows:

Taxpayer will dismiss his complaint with prejudice in return for a refund of 50% of the amount claimed in his complaint, plus interest on said amount as provided by law. The principal amount of the refund shall consist of 50% of the amount of taxes claimed and 50% of the amount of assessed interest claimed.

THE FORMULA OR ISSUE-BY-ISSUE SETTLEMENT. In some cases the nature of the controversy requires a settlement based upon a formula or an issue-by-issue compromise. In an estate tax case, for example, a formula is often needed since the exact amount refundable cannot be determined until after the case is settled and additional deductions resulting from the suit itself (*e.g.* attorneys' fees) are taken into account. In cases involving other types of taxes also, it is often desirable to have the settlement agreement spell out the precise treatment afforded each item in dispute. This is particu-

---

[19] IRC § 6611.

larly true where the tax basis of assets will be affected by a resolution of the case.

A sample proposal of the formula type is the following:

Taxpayer will dismiss his complaint with prejudice in return for a refund of the overpayment of estate tax and assessed interest resulting from (1) the inclusion in decedent's gross estate of only $500,000.00 of the gift of November 24, 1966 as a gift in contemplation of death (2) the allowance of such additional deductions for allowable administrative expenses that have been incurred in connection with the prosecution of this tax refund suit. Interest is to run on the principal amount of the refund as provided by law.

An issue-by-issue offer would appear as follows:

Taxpayer will dismiss his complaint with prejudice in return for a refund of the overpayment of taxes and assessed interest resulting from the treatment of the proceeds of sale of the A.B.C. Building as ordinary income and the treatment of the proceeds of sale of the D.E.F. Building as ordinary income. Interest is to run on the principal amount of the refund as provided by law.

CONTINUING ISSUE SETTLEMENT—SETTLEMENT OF YEARS UNDER REVIEW BY INTERNAL REVENUE SERVICE. Where an issue in a tax refund suit is repeated in years subsequent to those in suit, it is possible to settle the issue once and for all. Such a settlement is not absolutely mandatory. However, in some cases the government (or the taxpayer) may decide that settlement can only be reached if the problem is ironed out for all years in which the issue is pending before the Internal Revenue Service.

A continuing issue proposal would appear as follows:

Taxpayer proposes to settle the case on the following basis:
  (1) Taxpayer will dismiss his complaint with prejudice,
  (2) With regard to the years in suit the government will refund the principal amount of $9,000.00 (80% to be deficiency tax and 20% assessed interest) plus interest thereon as provided by law,
  (3) For the years 1964 through 1967, inclusive, 50% of the alimony paid to taxpayer's first wife, shall be deductible and 50% shall not be.

CLOSING AGREEMENT—PERMANENT SETTLEMENT OF CONTINUING ISSUES. If the taxpayer seeks a settlement that will bind the Commissioner of Internal Revenue for future years as to which no returns have yet been filed it is necessary to enter into a formal closing agreement with the Commissioner.[20]

An offer of this type would appear as follows:

Taxpayer proposes to settle this case on the following basis:
  (1) Taxpayer will dismiss its complaint with prejudice,
  (2) For years up to and including calendar year 1967 the income received by the A.B.C. Bank as Trustee under the Will of John Doe will be taxed as if a single trust were created by said Will,

[20] IRC § 7121.

(3) For all years subsequent to calendar year 1967 the income received by the A.B.C. Bank as Trustee under the Will of John Doe will be taxed as if four trusts were created by said Will.

SETTLEMENT BASED UPON COLLECTIBILITY. In tax refund suits in which the government has asserted a counterclaim the taxpayer may seek a settlement based upon his inability to pay the judgment sought by the government. In such a case the taxpayer is, in effect, making an "offer in compromise" as that term is used in Internal Revenue Service procedures. As with an Internal Revenue Service offer in compromise, he must submit a formal financial statement [21] and collateral agreement [22] to the Justice Department as part of his proposal. An offer based on collectibility would appear as follows:

Taxpayer offers to settle this case upon the following basis:

(1) Taxpayer will dismiss his complaint with prejudice.
(2) Taxpayer will consent to the entry of a judgment against him on the government's counterclaim in the amount of $10,000.00 with interest thereon to run according to law.
(3) In satisfaction of the judgment taxpayer will pay the Government $1,000.00 within 30 days of notification of acceptance of this offer and will make further payments in accordance with the terms of the collateral agreement (Treasury Form 2261) enclosed herewith.
(4) A financial statement (Treasury Form 433) is enclosed herewith and submitted as part of this offer.

Figure 14–2 (pages **14·**15–16) is a sample of the collateral agreement (Treasury Form 2261) to be submitted with an offer based upon collectibility.

ADMINISTRATIVE SETTLEMENT—100 PER CENT REFUND. In appropriate cases the government will make an "administrative settlement" in a tax refund suit by tendering to the taxpayer a check for the full amount claimed. If a taxpayer believes that his case is so overwhelming that a full refund is appropriate he can suggest an administrative refund to the trial attorney. Often the government will make such a disposition of the case without any outside suggestion. And, normally, the fact that government has not volunteered an administrative refund indicates that it will not make one if prodded.

On occasion a taxpayer does not wish to accept an administrative settlement if it means that his complaint is dismissed as moot. Rather, he wants an adjudication on the merits of his case. This most frequently occurs where the taxpayer has more of an interest in the principle to be established by the case than in the amount of money in suit. There have been disputes

---

[21] Treasury Form 433. This is an eight-page form on which the taxpayer must set forth (under oath) extremely detailed information regarding his financial condition.

[22] Treasury Form 2261. See Fig. 14–2, pp. **14·**15–16.

FORM **2261** (REV. SEPT. 1963)	U. S. TREASURY DEPARTMENT - INTERNAL REVENUE SERVICE **COLLATERAL AGREEMENT** FUTURE INCOME—INDIVIDUAL

TO: COMMISIONER OF INTERNAL REVENUE

The undersigned taxpayer has submitted an offer dated July 7, 19-- in the amount of $ 1,000.00

to compromise unpaid_____personal income_____tax liability, including additions to the tax, for the

year(s)_____19--

The purpose of this collateral agreement (hereinafter referred to as this agreement) is to provide additional consideration for acceptance of the above-described offer in compromise. It is understood and agreed:

1. That in addition to the payment of the aforesaid sum of $ 1,000.00 the taxpayer will pay out of

   annual income for the years 19-- to 19-- , inclusive

   (a) Nothing with respect to the first $ 5,000.00 of annual income.

   (b) 20 % of annual income in excess of $ 5,000.00 and not in excess of $ 7,000.00 .

   (c) 30 % of annual income in excess of $ 7,000.00 and not in excess of $ 10,000.00 .

   (d) 50 % of annual income in excess of $ 10,000.00 .

2. That the term "annual income" as used herein means adjusted gross income as defined in section 62 of the Internal Revenue Code of 1954, (except that losses from sales or exchange of property and the deduction allowed by section 1202 for long-term capital gains shall not be allowed) plus all nontaxable income, profits, or gains from any source whatsoever (including the fair market value of gifts, bequests, devises, or inheritances) minus (a) the Federal income tax due for the year in question and paid, and (b) any payment made on the offer in compromise itself (Form 656) for the year in which such payment is made. The "annual income" shall not be reduced by net operating losses incurred prior or subsequent to the period covered by this agreement. However, a net operating loss for any year during such period may be deducted from the "annual income" of the following year only. It is also agreed that "annual income" shall include all income, gains or profits of the undersigned, regardless of whether these amounts are community income under State law.

3. In the event the undersigned taxpayer is or becomes a stockholder in a close corporation, the computation of "annual income" shall include his proportionate share of "corporate annual income" in excess of $5,000.00. The term "corporate annual income" as used in this paragraph means the taxable income of the corporation before net operating loss deduction and special deductions (except that in computing such "corporate annual income" the losses from sales or exchange of property shall not be allowed), plus all nontaxable income not included therein and minus (a) dividends paid, and (b) Federal income tax due for the year in question and paid. For this purpose, the "corporate annual income" shall not be reduced by any net operating loss incurred prior or subsequent to the periods covered by this agreement, but a net operating loss for any year during such period may be deducted from the "corporate annual income" for the following year only. The provisions of this paragraph shall also be applicable in the event the undersigned taxpayer has an interest in a proprietorship or partnership, which elects to be taxed as a corporation under the provisions of section 1361 of the 1954 Code.

4. That the annual payments provided for in this agreement, (including interest at 6% per annum on delinquent payments computed from the due date for such payment as provided in this paragraph) shall be paid to the District Director, without notice from him, on or before the fifteenth day of the fourth month next following the close of the calendar or fiscal year, such payments to be accompanied by a sworn statement and a copy of the

---

(Over)   FORM **2261** (REV. 9-63)

FIG. 14–2.

Federal income tax return. The statement shall refer to this agreement and set forth the "annual income" computed in accordance with paragraphs numbered 2 and 3. In the event the "annual income" for any year covered by this agreement is insufficient to require a payment under the terms of this agreement, the taxpayer shall nevertheless furnish the District Director with a sworn statement of such "annual income", together with a copy of the Federal income tax return. All books, records, and accounts shall be open at all reasonable times for inspection to verify the "annual income" set forth in the statement. The payments, if any, the sworn statement and a copy of the Federal income tax return shall be transmitted to:

District Director, Internal Revenue Service; Collection Division (Offer In Compromise)

Address: _____

5. That the aggregate amount paid in accordance with the terms of the offer and the additional amounts paid under the terms of this agreement shall not exceed an amount equivalent to the liability covered by the offer in compromise plus accrued interest that would have become due in the absence of the compromise.

6. That upon notice to the taxpayer of the acceptance of the offer in compromise of the liability aforesaid, the taxpayer shall have no right, in the event of default in payment of any installment of principal or interest due under the terms of the offer and this agreement, or in the event any other provision of this agreement is not carried out in accordance with its terms, to contest in court or otherwise the amount of the liability sought to be compromised; and that in the event of such default or non-compliance, or in the event the taxpayer becomes the subject of any proceeding under the Bankruptcy Act, or the subject of any proceeding whereby the affairs of the taxpayer are placed under the control and jurisdiction of a court or other party, the Commissioner or his delegate at his option, (a) may proceed immediately by suit to collect the entire unpaid balance of the offer and this agreement, or (b) may proceed immediately by suit to collect as liquidated damages an amount equal to the tax liability sought to be compromised minus any payments already received under the terms of the offer in compromise and this agreement, with interest at the rate of 6% per annum from the date of default, or (c) may disregard the amount of such offer and this agreement, and apply all amounts previously paid thereunder against the amount of the liability sought to be compromised and may, without further notice of any kind, assess and/or collect by levy or suit (the restrictions against assessment and/or collection being specifically waived) the balance of such liability.

7. That the taxpayer waives the benefit of any statute of limitations applicable to the assessment and/or collection of the liability sought to be compromised, and agrees to the suspension of the running of the statutory period of limitations on assessment and/or collection for the period during which the offer and this agreement are pending or the period during which any installment under the offer and/or this agreement remains unpaid or any provision of this agreement is not carried out in accordance with its terms, and for one year thereafter.

8. That when all sums, including interest, due under the terms of the offer in compromise and this agreement, except those sums which may become due and payable under the provisions of paragraph numbered 1 of this agreement, have been paid in full, then and in that event only, all Federal tax liens at that time securing the tax liabilities which are the subject of the said offer shall be immediately released. However, if, at the time consideration is being given to the release of the Federal tax liens, there are any sums due and payable under the terms of paragraph numbered 1 of this agreement, they must also be paid prior to the release of such liens.

This agreement shall be of no force or effect unless the offer in compromise is accepted.

Waiver of statutory period of limitations is hereby accepted.	SIGNATURE *(Taxpayer)*
SIGNATURE *(District Director)*	/s/ John Jones
BY *(Signature and Title)*	DATE	DATE

887-079   U.S. GOVERNMENT PRINTING OFFICE : 1964 O—199-176   FORM **2261** (REV. 3-63)

FIG. 14–2 (*Continued*).

as to the government's right to have taxpayers' complaints dismissed after they have tendered a check for the full amount claimed.[23] The issue is not free from doubt.

A proposal for an administrative settlement, whether initiated upon the request of the taxpayer or within the government, is processed in the same manner as an offer to settle the case.

Submission of Materials in Support of an Offer

The government will give consideration to any materials the taxpayer may wish to submit in support of an offer to settle a case. However, it usually is not advantageous to submit anything unless requested to do so by the trial attorney handling the case. If the trial attorney recommends acceptance of the offer his memorandum will state, as persuasively as possible, the reasons why it should be accepted. Any supporting data needed by the trial attorney will be requested. Usually, the taxpayer's gratuitously provided memorandum in support of an offer will be at best superfluous. At worst, it may give someone reviewing the offer a target on which to base his recommendation for rejection.

Where the taxpayer expects the trial attorney to recommend rejection, his supporting materials may be helpful. He may be able, through a memorandum in support of an offer, to persuade the reviewing officials that the trial attorney's recommendation should be overruled. However, his efforts can better be spent trying to convince the trial attorney to change his view of the case.

Government Processing of Offers To Settle Tax Refund Suits

When an offer to settle a tax refund suit is received by the Tax Division it is processed in accordance with a formal settlement procedure. The taxpayer will, usually, have no direct contact with the settlement process between the time he has submitted his offer and the time that final action is taken. However, it is possible that he will be contacted by a government attorney (either the trial attorney or a review level attorney) in order to clarify the offer or renegotiate a provision in the proposal.

REFUND TRIAL SECTION ACTION. Upon receipt, an offer to settle a tax refund suit is referred to the trial attorney assigned to the case. He will, first of all, write a letter to taxpayer's counsel acknowledging receipt of the offer and stating the government's interpretation of the offer. If any of the elements of the offer have not explicitly been stated by the taxpayer the trial attorney will either (1) ask for a clarification or (2) set forth his

---

[23] *E.g.,* Regina v. United States, 208 F. Supp. 137 (W.D. Pa.). *Cf.* California v. San Pablo R.R., 149 U.S. 308.

version of how the omitted elements are to be treated. For example, where an offer does not state the manner in which interest would be computed on the refund the trial attorney would normally state his understanding that interest is to run in accordance with law. A prompt response by taxpayer's counsel to any misinterpretation of his offer is essential in order to avoid problems regarding the precise terms being considered by the government.

After acknowledgement of the offer the trial attorney will (except in S.O.P. cases) refer the proposal to Chief Counsel, Internal Revenue Service, for the Service's views. He will also prepare his own "compromise memorandum." The trial attorney's memorandum will contain (1) a statement of the facts in the case, (2) a discussion of the applicable law, (3) a discussion of all of the factors he believes to bear upon the acceptability of the offer, and (4) his recommendation regarding the action that should be taken on the offer. Of particular note is the inclusion in every compromise memorandum of a summary of any statements that may have been made by the court (or trial commissioner) bearing upon settlement. The compromise memorandum written by the trial attorney, along with the concurrence or dissent of the Chief of his Section, is forwarded to the Review Section of the Tax Division.

INTERNAL REVENUE SERVICE ACTION. Offers to settle tax refund suits are referred to the Internal Revenue Service for its recommendation except where the Chief Counsel, Internal Revenue Service, has indicated that reference is unnecessary. Reference is not necessary when a refund suit is initially classified by the Internal Revenue Service as a "Settlement Option Procedure" case or when a prior offer has been referred to Chief Counsel who has already advised the Justice Department of the Service's settlement position in the case.

The Refund Litigation Division of the Chief Counsel's office will prepare the Internal Revenue Service recommendation regarding the subject offer. In appropriate cases, Chief Counsel will refer the offer to the District Director's office for his comments. This is usually done where years other than those in suit are the subject of the offer. When Chief Counsel's recommendation on the offer is received by the Justice Department, it is sent to the Review Section of the Tax Division and is considered along with the recommendation of the Refund Trial Section.

REVIEW LEVEL ACTION IN THE TAX DIVISION. Upon receipt of the respective recommendations of the Trial Section trial attorney and the Chief Counsel, Internal Revenue Service, along with the pertinent files in the case, the Chief of the Review Section will assign the offer to an attorney in his section. The Review Section attorney will then review the files and memoranda and recommend action to be taken on the offer. From that point on the taxpayer's offer will wend its way upward through the Department of Justice until it reaches the person who has authority to take final action. At each step up the ladder an additional recommendation will be made until the proposal finally reaches the person with authority to act on the offer.

Authority to take final action on offers to settle tax refund suits is vested in the Attorney General of the United States or his delegate. By delegation of authority to the Assistant Attorney General for the Tax Division and redelegation by him of a portion of his authority final action may be taken by lower level Tax Division personnel.

The authority of Tax Division personnel to take final action on offers to settle tax refund suits is spelled out in Tax Division Directive No. 10 (1967),[24] as follows:

(A) The chiefs of the trial sections and the Appellate Section can reject any offer if the Internal Revenue Service agrees.

(B) The Chief of the Review Section can, in cases with unanimous Internal Revenue Service and trial section recommendations,

(1) Accept offers and approve administrative settlements requiring refunds up to $50,000.

(2) Reject any offer.

(C) The First Assistant, Second Assistant and Assistant for Civil Trials can,

(1) Accept offers and approve administrative settlements requiring refunds up to $250,000. If the Internal Revenue Service objects or the case must be referred to the Joint Committee on Internal Revenue Taxation (see below) the limiting amount is lowered to $100,000.

(2) Reject any offer.

The Directive further provides:

(A) If the proposed action will control or adversely influence the disposition of other claims totaling more than the amounts specified in the Directive, the total involved shall govern.

(B) If the person otherwise authorized to act feels that, for any reason, a proposed disposition requires higher level review, the case will be forwarded for such review.

(C) Confession of error and administrative refunds in cases on appeal are excepted from the redelegation of authority.

[24] 28 C.F.R. app. to subpt. W.

Offers that cannot be acted upon by lower level Tax Division personnel are referred to the Assistant Attorney General for the Tax Division who makes the final recommendation for the Division. The offer is then forwarded to the Attorney General who will take final action thereon. In statutorily required instances the Attorney General will delay action on the offer until the matter has been referred to the Joint Committee for Internal Revenue Taxation and its comments have been received.

Each year approximately 1,700 offers in civil tax cases are processed through the Tax Division.[25] Of these, approximately 70% ultimately are accepted.[26] Relatively few offers, however, reach the Assistant Attorney General and less than 10% are acted upon by the Attorney General. In the fiscal year ended June 30, 1965, the following action was taken by the persons authorized to act upon offers in civil tax cases:[27]

Final Action	Accepted	Rejected	Total
Attorney General	132	—	132
Assistant Attorney General	202	122	324
Chief, Review Section	913	299	1,212
Total	1,247	421	1,668

It is interesting to note that the Attorney General rejected no offers. This is a strong indication of the careful screening done by the Tax Division before any offer is submitted to the Attorney General for his decision.

The average time that elapses between the submission of an offer to settle a tax case and final action by the government is slightly over two months.[28] However, in relatively small cases (particularly those that need not be referred to the Internal Revenue Service) this time can be reduced to a month or less.

REFERRAL OF OFFERS TO THE JOINT COMMITTEE. When an offer to settle a tax refund suit calls for the refund of more than $100,000.00 in income, estate, or gift taxes,[29] the Attorney General, by statute, must refer the proposal to the Joint Committee on Internal Revenue Taxation.[30] The Joint Committee, through its staff, will comment upon the acceptability of the offer. Upon receipt of the Joint Committee's comments, and after any necessary conferences with its staff, final action on the offer will be taken by the Attorney General.

---

[25] Attorney General's Report, *supra* note 4, at 357. This amount includes offers in all civil tax cases, not just in tax refund suits.

[26] *Id.* at 357.

[27] *Id.* at 332.

[28] *Id.* at 304.

[29] Also war profits and excess profits taxes.

[30] IRC § 6405.

Final Action on Offer

By letter (or telegram) from the Tax Division, taxpayer's counsel will be advised whether his offer has been accepted or rejected, or has evoked a counteroffer from the government.

STEPS AFTER OFFER IS REJECTED. The rejection of an offer by the Justice Department is not an invitation to the taxpayer to commence haggling to "split the difference" between his position and the government's. He may, if he still wishes to settle, negotiate further with the trial attorney assigned to the case. However, unless some significant change has taken place in the circumstances of the case, the taxpayer will normally be wasting his time in submitting a new offer that does not substantially differ from the proposal already considered and rejected by the Department.

STEPS AFTER COUNTEROFFER IS RECEIVED. On occasion the government will, in rejecting a taxpayer's proposal for settlement, make a counteroffer. The government's counteroffer often, but not always, is conditioned upon acceptance within a stated period of time after receipt.

One point is particularly important in considering whether or not to accept a counteroffer proposed by the government in a tax refund suit. The government is not, by any means, suggesting that the taxpayer commence haggling in the area between the original offer and the counteroffer. The Tax Division will have carefully considered the settlement potential of the case prior to making its proposal. In the absence of a substantial change in the circumstances of the case it will not budge from its counterproposal. Accordingly, counteroffers are made on a "take it or leave it" basis.

A letter from taxpayer's counsel stating that the government's counteroffer has been accepted is sufficient to settle the case. Thereafter, the same steps will be taken as in a case where the government accepts an offer from the taxpayer.

STEPS AFTER OFFER IS ACCEPTED. In the letter advising the taxpayer of acceptance of his offer, the steps to be taken will be spelled out. In the normal case, where settlement results in a refund to the taxpayer, a check for the amount refundable pursuant to the settlement offer will be sent to the United States Attorney for the district in which the case is pending or to the Tax Division in Court of Claims cases. Upon execution of the customary stipulation of dismissal,[31] the check will be given to the taxpayer. The average time taken between acceptance of an offer and the issuance of a check to the taxpayer is about six weeks.[32]

[31] Tax Refund Form No. 22, p. **C**·88.
[32] Attorney General's Report, *supra* note 4, at 363. It should be noted that the computation of the interest payable by virtue of a settlement is made by the local District Director of Internal Revenue.

CHAPTER 15

TRIAL PROCEDURES IN TAX REFUND SUITS

This chapter discusses the three types of trial procedures available in tax refund suits, *i.e.* trial to a judge, trial to a jury, and trial to a commissioner subject to review by a quasi-appellate court. In discussing each form of trial the authors place emphasis on matters of particular note in tax cases as distinguished from the general run of civil cases tried by the respective tax refund forums.

DISTRICT COURT TRIALS

The United States District Courts are the most popular tax refund tribunals, handling approximately 90% of all suits.[1]

Scheduling of Case for Trial

Tax refund suits in most districts are placed on the general civil calendar and called for trial in accordance with the particular practice

---

[1] Annual Report of the Attorney General of the United States for the fiscal year ended June 30, 1966, 325, 368.

adopted by the district. In several districts the Tax Division and the local tax bar have succeeded in persuading the local United States District Court to establish a tax docket.[2] Where a tax docket has been accepted, once or twice a year all tax refund suits (and sometimes tax collection suits as well) are called on a special calendar, normally for a pretrial conference. Cases ready for trial are tried immediately or at a special trial docket set by the court to the extent the court has set aside time to hear tax matters. Cases not then ready for trial are usually deferred until the next tax docket. Typically, tax dockets are set so as not to interfere either with the "tax season" or a docket of the Tax Court.

Rules of Evidence Applied in District Courts

In the United States District Courts evidence is admissible under either (1) the statutes of the United States, (2) the rules of evidence applied in federal district courts prior to the adoption of the Federal Rules of Civil Procedure, or (3) the rules of evidence applied in the courts of general jurisdiction of the state in which the district court is located.[3] In any case, the statute or rule that favors the reception of evidence governs.

Subpoenas for Trial

In tax refund suits subpoenas are issued and served as in other civil cases in the district courts. Therefore, the parties do not have the benefit of the nationwide subpoena range afforded by the Tax Court Rules [4] and, in effect, available under the Court of Claims Rules.[5]

Upon request of either party the Clerk of the district court will issue subpoenas (including subpoenas *duces tecum*) to compel witnesses to attend the trial of a case (and to bring designated materials).[6] Subpoenas may be served by a Deputy United States Marshal or any other person not a party to the action.[7] A subpoena may be served at any place within the district in which the case is pending or at any place outside the district that is within 100 miles of the place of the hearing or trial specified in the subpoena.[8]

---

[2] Attorney General's Report, *supra* note 1, at 366; Smith, *The Civil Trial Function of the Tax Division*, 52 A.B.A.J. 255, 256 (1966).

[3] Fed. R. Civ. P. 43(a). See 28 U.S.C. §§ 1731–45. The competence of witnesses to testify is determined in like manner.

[4] See p. **8·7** *et seq. supra.*

[5] The Court of Claims Rules generally limit the place of service to a place within 100 miles of the place of the hearing. Ct. Cl. R. 51(b). However, the trial commissioner may authorize service anywhere. *Ibid.* Moreover, the trial commissioner may set trial hearings at two or more locations in the United States to bring a witness within normal subpoena range. Ct. Cl. R. 48(b).

[6] Fed. R. Civ. P. 45(a), (b).

[7] Fed. R. Civ. P. 45(c).

[8] Fed. R. Civ. P. 45(e)(1).

Trial to the Court Without a Jury

PRETRIAL BRIEF. Whether or not it is required by local rule or pretrial order [9] it is good practice to file a pretrial brief in a tax refund suit. Every judge will appreciate a short and to-the-point pretrial memorandum that will acquaint him with the pertinent facts and give him an insight into the law involved in the case he is about to hear.

The approach in writing the pretrial brief will depend upon the circumstances of the particular case. Where the case involves questions of fact in a frequently litigated area of the law (e.g. a "contemplation of death" [10] case or a "reasonable compensation" [11] case) it is normally advisable to present only a brief discussion of the law with citations to a few leading or particularly pertinent authorities.

Where the legal questions are significant, correspondingly more detail is needed in the pretrial brief. However, it is important not to overlook the introductory nature of the pretrial memorandum. It should not constitute an exhaustive argument of the law unless the court should request one. In any event, anticipated evidentiary disputes (particularly objections to the government's evidence) should be discussed in the pretrial brief. In discussing expected evidence in any brief that must be exchanged with the adversary,[12] a line must be drawn between too much pretrial disclosure of evidence to the opposing party and too little to the court.

OPENING STATEMENT. Most, but not all, district judges permit opening statements in trials to the court. Prior to the hearing of any evidence the party who will present his case first (usually the taxpayer) will be afforded the opportunity to make his opening statement. This should be as concise as possible, making reference to the pretrial brief in which the background law and facts have been set out. Depending upon local practice, the opening statement of the second party (typically the government) will be presented either immediately after the adversary's address or at the conclusion of the adversary's case in chief.

ORDER OF PROOF. In tax refund suits the taxpayer, usually having the burden of proof, almost always presents his evidence first. Then the government presents its case followed by rebuttal evidence to the extent necessary. It is conceivable that a district court would, in a fraud case, require

---

[9] In many districts, a pretrial brief is expressly required by local rule or court order, and sometimes its contents are strictly prescribed.

[10] IRC § 2035.

[11] Was the salary paid a corporate officer excessive? E.g., Savko Bros. Co. v. Commissioner, P-H Tax Ct. Memo ¶ 63,203, aff'd, 338 F.2d 956 (C.A.6th).

[12] In some districts, pretrial briefs are not exchanged with the adversary and are treated as confidential by the court.

the government to present its evidence first since it has the burden of proving taxpayer's fraud. However, even in cases involving a fraud penalty assessment most courts will follow the customary order of proof and require the plaintiff (taxpayer) to proceed first.

PRESENTATION OF PROOF ESTABLISHED PRIOR TO TRIAL. In tax refund suits, a good deal of the proof usually will be made through stipulations of facts and the use of depositions or other discovery devices. It is good practice for the taxpayer to commence his proof by formally offering all stipulations and other matters of record that are going to be placed in evidence. The offer of proof and its reception by the court are needed in order to make the material evidence in the case. Moreover, the practice of presenting the evidence at the beginning of the case will avoid oversights during the presentation of "live" evidence. In a trial to the court the consideration by the judge of evidence offered "out of sequence" can conveniently be deferred until the necessary background facts have been proved.

TAXPAYER'S CASE. Having placed in evidence the stipulations and other proof made prior to trial, the taxpayer will proceed to present the remainder of his evidence as in any civil case.

The essential elements of the taxpayer's case in a tax refund suit are the following:

1. All of the jurisdictional prerequisites to the suit have been met.
2. The taxpayer is correct with regard to the substantive grounds for recovery set forth in his claim for refund.
3. The taxpayer has overpaid his taxes for the period in suit and establishes the amount of the overpayment.

Typically, proof of the jurisdictional prerequisites is made by stipulation prior to trial and offered in evidence at the commencement of the trial. However, any jurisdictional element not already established must be proved at trial, or the taxpayer will fail in his proof.

Proof regarding the taxpayer's grounds for recovery, *i.e.,* the specific tax adjustments in dispute by virtue of the claims for refund, normally constitutes the principal focus of the evidence in the case. As in any civil action the taxpayer must present proof disclosing that he is correct and the government wrong with regard to the substantive issues involved in the case.

The final element of the taxpayer's case should not be overlooked. He must place in evidence proof from which a determination of his correct liability for the periods in suit can be made. To do this he should place in evidence his tax returns for the subject taxable periods. It is best to place on the record, along with the returns, a concession by the government that, except for specifically enumerated items, the return is accepted as correct. This concession can be obtained by stipulation, through discovery proceedings against the government, or as a response to a pretrial order. However, it appears that, even without a formal concession by the government, its failure to raise a specific issue regarding the correctness of the items reported on the return would bar it from claiming (after trial) that the taxpayer did not establish his case by offering proof of the correctness of each and every item on the return.[13] It should be noted that where the government does raise an offset contending that additional items on the subject tax returns were erroneously reported, the taxpayer must carry the burden of proving that the government's contentions are erroneous.[14]

Government's Case. By the time the taxpayer has concluded his case in chief a portion (and frequently a substantial part) of the government's evidence will have been presented through cross-examination of the taxpayer's witnesses. The government will, of course, present witnesses and exhibits to the extent the facts and circumstances of the case require.

It is important to note one point in particular when seeking to anticipate the government's proof. In just about every tax refund suit the government can be expected to place in evidence some portion of the taxpayer's responses to discovery—usually all or part of a deposition transcript. This material is, of course, admissible as positive proof of the statements contained therein without regard to the availability of the taxpayer to testify.[15] Where only part of his deposition transcript has been introduced in evidence by the government the taxpayer can require the government to introduce all of it that is relevant to the part introduced.[16] Moreover, the taxpayer may, and should prepare to, present evidence on rebuttal regarding any of his statements that require explanation or amplification.

Rebuttal Evidence. At the close of the government's case the taxpayer may present evidence to rebut the government's proof but not (without leave of court) to present new matters. The most frequent use of rebuttal evidence is to explain or clarify the taxpayer's statements or responses to discovery that the government has placed in evidence.

Posttrial Argument and Briefs. Most district courts will not hear arguments of counsel immediately after the close of evidence in a tax refund suit. The most common practice is for the court to set a briefing schedule commencing after the parties receive their copies of the official trial transcript, and for any oral argument to be set after the court has had an oppor-

---

[13] Missouri Pac. R.R. v. United States, 337 F.2d 637 (Ct. Cl.).

[14] See p. **12·18** et seq. supra.

[15] Community Counselling Serv., Inc. v. Reilly, 317 F.2d 239 (C.A.4th) ; Pursche v. Atlas Scraper & Engineering Co., 300 F.2d 467, 488 (C.A.9th).

[16] Fed. R. Civ. P. 26(d)(4).

tunity to study the parties' respective briefs and requested findings of facts and conclusions of law. Posttrial briefs in tax cases differ only in substantive content from those submitted in other civil cases. The aim is to present a persuasive, adequately supported argument for the client's position. Requested findings of fact and conclusions of law should present a logical and orderly statement of the case with references to the portions of the record on which the findings are based.

In the tax law it is not uncommon for a significant legal development (such as a decision in a comparable case) to occur after briefs and arguments have been presented but before decision has been reached. It is helpful to advise the court of any newly available precedent by means of a letter enclosing a copy of the opinion and a very short discussion of the bearing it has upon the case under consideration. Where appropriate, permission to submit a supplemental brief or to present additional argument can be requested.

DECISION. Upon consideration of the evidence and oral and written arguments the court will issue its decision in the case. The Federal Rules of Civil Procedure require the trial judge to either state separately his findings of fact and conclusions of law in the case or write an opinion or memorandum of decision containing his findings and conclusions.[17] Judgment will be entered in accordance with the court's decision. In tax refund suits, in which a computation is necessary to determine the amount of recovery called for by the decision, the preparation of the judgment is normally delegated to the parties to the suit.

Trial by Jury

The trial of any complicated factual issue to a jury presents problems for the court as well as the parties to the case. Tax refund suits are no exception. As stated by Judge Timbers [18] for the United States Court of Appeals for the Second Circuit, "Every District Judge shudders at the prospect of presiding over the trial of a tax refund suit with a jury." [19] Nevertheless, every tax refund suit filed in a district court can result in a jury trial upon the demand of either the taxpayer or the government.[20]

FACTORS TO CONSIDER IN ELECTING TRIAL BY JURY. The first and most important step in a jury trial is the election to have the case presented to a jury rather than a judge. In tax litigation the taxpayer, initially, has the ability completely to block a jury trial by choosing to test his tax liability in either the Court of Claims or the Tax Court. Once suit has been filed

---

[17] Fed. R. Civ. P. 52(a).

[18] Chief Judge, District of Connecticut, sitting by designation.

[19] Lifetime Siding, Inc. v. United States, 359 F.2d 657 (C.A.2d), *cert. denied,* 385 U.S. 921.

[20] 28 U.S.C. § 2402.

in a district court, however, the government as well as the taxpayer has the right to demand a trial by jury.[21]

Of course, it is impossible to list exhaustively the factors that should be taken into account in deciding whether it would be advantageous to present a tax refund suit to a jury. Nevertheless, there are a number of guidelines that can be useful in trying to see the case, and the taxpayer, from the point of view of a prospective jury.

The taxpayer should try to visualize himself as the jury will see him. Is the taxpayer a person with whom a cross section of the community will naturally sympathize? And, how is the United States government likely to be treated by a jury in the taxpayer's home district?[22] Is the taxpayer engaged in a business that would tend to cause laymen to trust or distrust him? Will the jury like the taxpayer? In short, does the taxpayer have the elusive characteristic called "jury appeal?"

As important as the nature of the taxpayer is the nature of the case in which a jury demand is contemplated. Tax attorneys are significantly aided in considering whether or not to seek a trial by jury by the practice of the tax services in regularly reporting jury instructions and verdicts. One can easily ascertain from standard tax references the number of cases of a particular type that have been tried to juries and the verdicts rendered. Often a comparison of the decisions reached by judges and juries on comparable evidence can serve as a guide to the desirability of a trial by jury. Sometimes the precedents will contain cases of such factual similarity to the taxpayer's that his preference for a jury or judge trial will turn solely upon whether or not he wishes the trier of fact to be aware of the previously decided cases.

There is a general feeling among tax litigators (both private and government) that a jury trial of certain issues in the tax law will be very advantageous to one party or the other. For example, taxpayers will very often seek to present to juries "contemplation of death"[23] cases or "family partnership"[24] cases. Accumulated earnings tax cases[25] are, by some, believed to be excellent jury cases for taxpayers.[26] However, the government has been successful before juries in the 531 area.[27] Employer's tax cases involving the question of whether workmen are employees of a

---

[21] See p. 11·15 *supra* for a discussion of the manner in which a jury trial may be obtained.

[22] Statistics indicate that the government does far worse before juries in the southern states than in the rest of the country. Walston, *The Use of Juries in Federal Civil Income Tax Cases,* 39 TAXES 144 (1961).

[23] IRC § 2035.

[24] *E.g.,* Ballou v. United States, 15 A.F.T.R.2d 886 (S.D. Ohio) (rare government victory before a jury).

[25] IRC § 531.

[26] Cole, *Special Problems in Trying the 531 Case to a Judy,* 1964 J. TAXATION 141.

[27] *E.g.,* Churchill Constr. Co. v. United States, 17 A.F.T.R.2d 45 (N.D. Ohio); Stevenson v. United States, 17 A.F.T.R.2d 170 (S.D.N.Y.).

taxpayer or independent contractor are often tried to juries upon the government's demand.[28]

In addition to considering the precedents one must also try to take into account the facts and circumstances of the particular case. Among other things, one should ponder the following considerations:

1. To a jury the issue presented will be fresh regardless of the number of similar cases that may clog the reports. Does the taxpayer wish a fresh approach to the question presented or would he rather present his case to a trier of facts who will be familiar with the results of comparable cases?

2. On nearly every jury one can expect to have one or more businessmen. Is the taxpayer's plight one that he can expect a businessman to understand? Does the taxpayer want the trier of fact to include one or more members who have a business background?

3. Was a transaction structured in a special form in order to save taxes? This may strike a jury as an unreasonable tax "gimmick" and thus be subject to great suspicion.

4. Did the taxpayer act as a typical person believes he would have in the circumstances of the case?

5. Does anyone other than the Government stand to lose if the taxpayer should win his case? Are there potential third-party defendants whose presence before a jury would be undesirable for the taxpayer?

No discussion of the factors to be considered or the weight to be accorded them in the determination of the desirability of a trial by jury can be complete or definitive. One can only take advantage of the opportunity to see how judges and juries have decided similar cases, read what various authors have suggested regarding jury trials in tax refund cases,[29] and attempt to consider all the pertinent factors. The net result can only be an educated guess regarding the expected reaction of a jury to the evidence that will be produced at trial. Taxpayer's counsel can rest assured, however, that his government counterpart will make his own estimate should suit be filed in a district court. Accordingly, whether he likes it or not, a taxpayer who has filed a tax refund suit in a district court may find himself preparing for a trial by jury.

PRETRIAL BRIEF. The pretrial brief is even more important in a jury trial than in a trial to the court. The trial judge cannot, as he might when

---

[28] *Compare* Service Trucking Co. v. United States, 14 A.F.T.R.2d 5488 (Md.), *aff'd*, 347 F.2d 671 (C.A.4th) (jury verdict holding truck unloaders employees), *with* Bonney Motor Express, Inc. v. United States, 206 F. Supp. 22 (E.D. Va.) (court decision holding truck unloaders not employees). See also Silverman v. United States, 18 A.F.T.R.2d 5089 (Md.).

[29] *E.g.*, Holzman, *Should You Demand a Jury in a Refund Case?*, 26 TAXES 301 (1958); Cole, *op. cit., supra* note 26; Walston, *op. cit., supra* note 22.

sitting without a jury, postpone difficult and important rulings until after the presentation of evidence. Rather, he must, during the course of the trial, (1) limit the scope of the evidence to the matters pertinent to the substantive tax dispute being presented, (2) prepare his instructions for the jury and rule upon the requested charges presented by the parties, (3) draft or approve a form of verdict for submitting the case to the jury, and (4) rule upon motions for directed verdict. Accordingly, the pretrial brief in a jury trial must, to a greater extent than in a court trial, advise the judge of the applicable law, the expected proof, and the anticipated evidentiary disputes.

REQUESTED JURY INSTRUCTIONS. Some judges require, and all appreciate, the parties' submitting their requested jury instructions prior to the commencement of trial. Of course, any additional instructions needed as a result of developments at trial can be submitted when their need becomes known.

It is customary to submit the requested instructions together with a motion asking the court to advise counsel of the ruling upon the requests prior to the presentation of final argument.[30] In form, each requested instruction is typed on a separate page which includes the body of the requested charge and citations of authority in support of the request. The following sample request illustrates the usual form:

PLAINTIFFS' REQUESTED INSTRUCTION NO. 10

You are instructed that the Internal Revenue law permits the plaintiffs, Mr. and Mrs. Clarence Gillis, to have a deduction equal to the difference between the fair market value of their residence immediately before the hurricane of September 7, 1967, and its fair market value immediately after the hurricane.

Section 165(c)(3), Internal Revenue Code of 1954
Walton v. Commissioner, P-H Memo TC, ¶ 61, 130.

In drafting a set of requested instructions the aim is to present a complete explanation of the party's view of the law in terms that will be understood by a group of laymen. To the extent possible ordinary, and not legal, language should be used. Where proper, the specific persons or events involved in the case should be used in lieu of abstract or general designations. Thus, instead of "the plaintiffs" one should use "Mr. and Mrs. Taxpayer"; instead of "lessor" and "lessee" the more familiar terms "landlord" and "tenant" would be used. Excessive and blatant advocacy should be omitted from requested charges. They should be drafted so that they can be accepted and given by the judge as written.

[30] Fed. R. Civ. P. 51. See Tax Refund Suit Forms Nos. 24, 25, pp. C·89–92, for a sample motion and set of requested jury instructions.

It is extremely important that a set of requested jury instructions include a request for a charge on every point of law that the proponent wants given. A valid objection cannot be made to the court's failure to instruct the jury on a point unless such a charge has been requested by the objecting party.[31] For example, in a "farm hobby loss" case a taxpayer may contend that if his farm was not a business he still is entitled to deduct the operating loss under Section 212 as an expense of maintaining land held for the production of income. Should he fail to request an instruction on his alternate theory and lose the case, he cannot contend that the court's failure to instruct regarding his alternative ground constituted reversible error. On the other hand, a party cannot cite as error the giving of a jury instruction that he requested be given.[32]

A requested charge must provide an adequate explanation of the point of law involved. It has been held error for a court to give a charge on a complex point of tax law, central to a case, which amounted to no more than a repetition of the pertinent section of the Internal Revenue Code.[33]

There are valuable research tools available to the draftsmen of jury instructions in tax refund suits. The tax reporters regularly publish jury charges given in tax cases. Thus, in addition to reported decisions stating the law, the parties will have access to the charges that have been given to juries in substantially similar cases. Jury instructions are indexed in the Prentice-Hall and Commerce Clearing House tax services together with the decisions on the substantive tax issue under consideration. Good sources of "boiler plate" instructions (*i.e.,* those of general applicability to all cases) include Mathes and Devitt, Federal Jury Practice and Instructions (1965), and the periodically published suggested civil jury instructions found in the West System's Federal Rules Decisions series.[34]

SELECTION OF JURY. The first step in a jury trial is the selection of the jury that will hear the case. While the precise mechanics of jury selection vary from district to district, in every court there will be an examination of the prospective jurors (commonly known as a voir dire examination) followed by the parties' respective exercise of peremptory challenges and challenges for cause.[35]

Several days prior to trial, the taxpayer's attorney should request the Clerk of the district court to permit him to inspect the information customarily made available in that district to counsel regarding the panel of

[31] Fed. R. Civ. P. 51. Kane v. American Tankers Corp. of Del., 219 F.2d 637, 640 (C.A.2d).

[32] Detroit T. & I. R. Co. v. Hahn, 47 F.2d 59, 60, *cert. denied,* 283 U.S. 842.

[33] Lesser v. United States, 368 F.2d 306 (C.A. 2d).

[34] *E.g.* 28 F.R.D. 401 (1962) ; 22 F.R.D. 127 (1958).

[35] Fed. R. Civ. P. 47(a). For a brief discussion of the process of selecting a jury in one district court, see *Seminar on Practice and Procedure, Empaneling a Jury,* 28 F.R.D. 37, 185–89.

jurors from which his jury will be selected. The data available can range (depending upon local practice) from a list of the jurors with their occupations to the relatively detailed questionaires used by the court in determining their qualification for jury duty.

Also prior to trial, counsel should prepare voir dire questions to be asked of the prospective jurors.[36] In most districts the requested questions are submitted to the judge, in writing, immediately prior to the voir dire. The judge then asks the prospective jurors (known as veniremen) his own standard questions as well as those requested by the parties that he decides are appropriate. In drafting proposed questions for voir dire examination it is important to exercise both restraint and tact. Restraint is needed because the court, with wide discretionary power in the voir dire examination,[37] will reject a question that is too argumentative or prejudicial (*e.g.,* Have you, or any members of your immediate family, had, like Mr. and Mrs. Stoll, your home and bank account taken by the Internal Revenue Service in collecting a tax you didn't feel was owed?). Tact is necessary to avoid offending the jurors (*e.g.,* Have you, or any members of your immediate family, been indicted or investigated for tax evasion?).

While every judge can be expected to make the standard inquiries to ascertain whether the jurors know the attorneys, the parties, or the facts of the case, less common questions are often helpful in obtaining an impartial jury in a tax refund suit. Taxpayer's counsel will usually wish to be aware of

1. All present and former Federal employees and their close relatives
2. All present and former employees of state and local governments (particularly law enforcement agencies) and their close relatives
3. All persons who have had unpleasant contacts with the taxpayer or with persons in businesses similar to that of the taxpayer

The government will usually seek to find out about:

1. Controversies that members of the panel or their close relatives have had with the United States government
2. Contacts that the members of the panel and their close relatives have had with the Internal Revenue Service
3. Whether the members of the panel or their close relatives are engaged in the business of preparing tax returns
4. Whether the prospective jurors are in the taxpayer's business or a related one.

At the conclusion of the voir dire examination the parties are given the opportunity to challenge prospective jurors. The procedure for exercising

---

[36] See Tax Refund Form No. 23, p. **C**·88, for a sample set of requested voir dire questions.

[37] Goosman v. A. Duie Pyle, Inc., 320 F.2d 45, 49–50 (C.A.4th) ; *cf.* Stone v. United States, 324 F.2d 804 (C.A.5th), *cert. denied,* 376 U.S. 938.

these challenges varies so much from district to district that no general statement can be made regarding the practice.

Each party has the right to challenge any number of prospective jurors "for cause or favor." [38] Generally speaking a juror is subject to such a challenge only where his inability to decide the case fairly has been shown.[39] However, many district judges will utilize their discretion to exclude from the jury a number of categories of persons who might possibly be unable to be completely impartial in a tax case. For example, accountants, tax advisors, employees of the United States, employees of state and local governmental taxing or law enforcement agencies, persons whose tax returns are presently under audit, etc., are sometimes excused even though, strictly speaking, grounds for a challenge for cause would not exist.

Each party also has the right to exercise three peremptory challenges.[40] The use of these challenges requires a consideration of all responses to voir dire questions, background information available about the jurors, counsel's and taxpayer's feeling about the particular jurors, whether any juror has been unsuccessfully challenged for cause, and the possibility that any peremptorily challenged juror will be replaced by another less desirable.[41]

After the panel of twelve jurors is selected, one or more alternates may be chosen by an analogous procedure.[42] In addition, or in lieu of alternative jurors, the court may ask the parties to stipulate that they will accept the decision of a jury or less than twelve members should one or more jurors become incapacitated during trial.[43]

In the United States District Courts the voir dire process is quite rapid —usually it is completed within an hour. Accordingly, advance preparation for jury selection is extremely important.

OPENING STATEMENT. In a jury trial the taxpayer's opening statement is of far more importance than in a trial to the court. It provides him with the invaluable opportunity to introduce to the jury the facts of the case from his point of view before the government has had a chance to state its case. The opening statement should be well prepared, relatively concise, clear, and explicit; it should subtly put across the taxpayer's case and, above all, make the case interesting. Argument (as opposed to a statement of what the evidence will prove) is objectionable and should be avoided.

---

[38] 28 U.S.C. § 1870. Kempe v. United States, 160 F.2d 406 (C.A.8th), *cert. denied*, 331 U.S. 843.

[39] *E.g.*, Irvin v. Dowd, 366 U.S. 717; United States v. Wood, 299 U.S. 123 (government employees not disqualified from jury in criminal case); Lusich v. Bloomfield S.S. Co., 355 F.2d 770, 775 (C.A.5th).

[40] 28 U.S.C. § 1870.

[41] For a comprehensive discussion of many authors' views regarding the desirability of various types of jurors, see Comment, *The Jury Voir Dire*, 11 S.D.L. REV. 306 (1966).

[42] Fed. R. Civ. P. 47(b).

[43] Fed. R. Civ. P. 48.

In preparing the opening statement to the jury, several points in particular should be kept in mind:

1. Unlike other types of cases, most tax refund suits arise in a context outside the common experience of most jurors. Therefore, they need an introduction to the background of the case so that the importance of evidence to be presented will be meaningful.
2. In addition to general background information the jury needs an introduction to the persons and specific events pertinent to the case. An effective "foreword" to the taxpayer's case can add considerably to the persuasive effect of his evidence.
3. The taxpayer's case should not be overstated. When counsel tells the jury what the evidence will show he should be prepared to prove it. If he does not, he can expect government counsel to point out the failure of the taxpayer to deliver his promised proof.

In most districts the government will deliver its opening statement immediately after the taxpayer has completed his.[44]

ORDER OF PROOF. The order of proof in tax refund jury trials is the same as that in tax cases tried to the court.[45] Thus, usually the taxpayer will proceed first with his proof followed by the government's case. Rebuttal evidence, to the extent appropriate, will be permitted thereafter.

PRESENTATION OF EVIDENCE. The presentation of the taxpayer's and the government's cases will generally proceed in a jury trial as they would in a trial to the court.[46] The presence of the jury will influence the manner rather than the substance of the proof. While a separate volume would be needed to discuss fully the presentation of proof to juries it is helpful here to mention the following principal differences between jury and court trials:

1. The rules of evidence are most strictly applied. In a judge trial close evidentiary questions frequently are resolved in favor of admission "for what it is worth" or admission subject to posttrial ruling. In jury trials evidentiary rulings must be made "under the gun."

2. More background evidence is needed in jury trials. A jury, usually unfamiliar with the context of a tax dispute, must be educated to enable it to understand the controversy. To a greater extent than in a court trial, evidence must be presented to provide a setting for the transactions in dispute.

3. More demonstrative evidence is needed. The specific financial and organizational data pertinent to the case must be presented to the jury in an understandable form—usually by means of visual aids. Thus, corporate

---

[44] In some districts, a defendant may not make his opening statement until after the plaintiff has completed the presentation of his case in chief.
[45] See p. **15 · 3**–4 *supra.*
[46] See p. **15 · 4** *et seq. supra.*

relationships must be placed on a diagram and financial data must be summarized and, where appropriate, presented in the form of a graph or chart.

4. Usually, more live witnesses are needed. Two factors combine to make it the rule that more witnesses are called in a jury trial than would be called if the same case were tried to a judge. First, it is easier to draft neutrally worded stipulations for a judge than for a jury. Second, to a considerable extent, lawyers believe that a jury is more readily persuaded by a live witness than by a stipulation or document alone on a significant point.

In addition, the factors that persuaded one, or both, of the parties to elect to have a trial by jury will influence the approach taken in presenting the evidence. Hence, the "human" side of the controversy will normally be emphasized in a jury trial.

PRESENTATION OF PROOF ESTABLISHED PRIOR TO TRIAL. In a jury trial, as in a trial to the court, it is necessary to offer in evidence at the trial all matters to be considered as evidence in the case, including materials put on the court's record prior to trial. The stipulation of agreed facts should usually be offered at the beginning of the case so that the jury can be acquainted with the undisputed facts before hearing evidence relating to the controverted issues. With regard to discovery responses and evidentiary depositions, it is usually better to offer them in their logical place during the course of the trial rather than at the beginning.

There are two standard means used for presenting a deposition (or part thereof) to a jury at trial. The best method is, for the offering party to have a person actually take the witness stand and testify in place of the deponent. The deposition is then used as a script with counsel reading the questions and the "witness" reading the answers as they were given at the deposition. The presentation of evidence in this manner should be rehearsed so that the "witness" becomes familiar with all exhibits used in the deposition and is able to utilize them as did the deponent. The alternative method, faster but less likely to hold the interest of the jury, is to have one person (usually counsel) read both the questions and answers.

MOTIONS FOR DIRECTED VERDICT. During the course of a trial by jury the parties may make a motion for directed verdict at the close of the adversary's case and/or at the close of all of the evidence.[47] The motion for directed verdict is critically important, for failure to make it constitutes a waiver of any right to a judgment notwithstanding an adverse jury verdict (commonly called a "judgment n.o.v.").[48]

[47] Fed. R. Civ. P. 50. Also, there is authority indicating that a motion for directed verdict may be granted after the opening statements if the statements clearly indicate that the movant is entitled to judgment as a matter of law. See generally 5 MOORE'S FEDERAL PRACTICE ¶ 50.04, at 2338 (2d ed. 1966).

[48] See 5 MOORE'S FEDERAL PRACTICE ¶¶ 50.05, 50.08, 50.11 (2d ed. 1966).

In a tax refund suit, the government normally will make a motion for directed verdict (usually in writing) at the close of the taxpayer's case. To the extent the motion is granted the trial is over and judgment will be entered accordingly. Thus, in a two-issue case, the motion may be granted as to one issue, requiring the government to proceed with its proof solely as to the remaining issue in the case. To the extent the motion is denied the government will proceed with its proof.[49] However, the government must renew the motion at the close of all the evidence to protect its right to a possible judgment n.o.v.[50]

At the close of all the evidence in the case, the government will renew its directed verdict motion and the taxpayer should make his. The motion should be made out of the hearing of the jury so that a denial of the motion will not appear to be a ruling by the court on the strength of the taxpayer's case. The motion should always be made in order to protect taxpayer's right to a possible judgment n.o.v. However, argument on the motion should be requested only if there appears to be a substantial chance that the motion will be granted.

The motion for directed verdict must state the specific grounds upon which it is based. Moreover, the grounds stated in the motion for directed verdict will limit the grounds upon which the moving party can base a post-trial motion for judgment notwithstanding the verdict.[51] However, "Technical precision is not necessary in stating grounds for the motion so long as the trial court is aware of the movant's position." [52]

In close cases most district judges will not grant a motion for directed verdict. As stated by Professor Moore:

Where the Court has any doubt as to whether to grant a motion for a directed verdict the better practice is for the trial judge not to direct a verdict but to reserve decision and let the jury bring in a verdict. Then the trial judge is in a position to consider a post verdict motion under Rule 50(b) and upon such motion he can set the verdict aside, if he thinks it improper, and grant judgment notwithstanding the verdict. Furthermore, the appellate court is also then in a position to reinstate the verdict, if it disagrees with the trial judge's disposition of the motion under Rule 50(b) and thus another trial may be avoided.[53]

The Federal Rules of Civil Procedure provide that

Whenever a motion for a directed verdict made at the close of all the evidence is denied or for any reason not granted, the court is deemed to have submitted the action to the jury subject to a later determination of the legal questions raised by the motion.[54]

[49] Fed. R. Civ. P. 50(a).
[50] 5 Moore's Federal Practice ¶ 50.05, at 2322 (2d ed. 1966).
[51] United States v. Fenix & Scisson, Inc., 360 F.2d 260, 265 (C.A.10th).
[52] Id. at 266.
[53] 5 Moore's Federal Practice ¶ 50.03, at 2320 (2d ed. 1966).
[54] Fed. R. Civ. P. 50(b).

Accordingly, the taxpayer's motion for directed verdict at the close of all of the evidence will fully protect his right to move for a judgment notwithstanding the verdict.

SUMMATIONS TO THE JURY. After the close of the evidence the parties will present their summations to the jury. The taxpayer, having the burden of proof, will be able to make the closing argument.[55] In some districts the taxpayer may also present an initial summation, with the government's argument sandwiched between the taxpayer's opening and closing. Time alloted for argument is set by the trial judge depending upon the length and complexity of the case.

In tax refund suits the old adage, "your final argument is your case," is particularly apt. The jury has sat through a tax trial in which the facts arose in an unfamiliar context, and the distinctions upon which the case turns may not be completely clear to them. They expect, and need, counsel to bring together the fragments of evidence, to clarify the issues, and to show them why the respective parties contend they are entitled to a verdict.

In addition to the considerations that enter into the presentation of final argument in the typical civil case, the following are of particular importance to the taxpayer in a tax refund suit tried to a jury:

1. Argument should anticipate the judge's instruction. Pursuant to the Federal Rules of Civil Procedure the judge will advise the parties of his proposed action on requested jury instructions prior to final argument.[56] The anticipated charge should be taken into account in final argument. Of course, no statement should be made in argument that will be contradicted by the judge. Moreover, the jury should be shown how the facts of the case, under the law to be stated in the court's instructions will entitle the taxpayer to a verdict.

2. Argument should be directed to the verdict requested. Almost every tax case tried to a jury is decided by a special verdict. In argument the jury's attention should be directed to the specific special interrogatories that the jury will answer.[57] As to each interrogatory the jury should be advised of the taxpayer's position and the reasons why they should answer the questions as he desires.

3. The complex facts of the case must be clarified. Tax cases are complicated and can bewilder a jury if not clearly presented. In final argument the case must be made understandable so that an accurate verdict can be rendered. The demonstrative evidence used by witnesses in the court at trial should be incorporated into the final argument in clarifying the case

[55] Some courts may give the government the right to make the closing argument on issues, such as fraud, on which it has the burden of proof.

[56] Fed. R. Civ. P. 51.

[57] See p. 15·17–18 *infra* for a discussion of special interrogatories for the jury.

and issues. Also, any misleading or erroneous aspects of the adversary's demonstrative evidence should be carefully explained.

4. The taxpayer must effectively rebut the government's final argument. The taxpayer's principal advantage in presenting jury argument lies in his opportunity to have the last word. The opportunity should not be wasted. Government counsel can be expected to present an effective summation on behalf of his client. The taxpayer should, to the extent possible, anticipate the government's principal arguments and be prepared with a strong rebuttal. Taxpayer's counsel should also be thoroughly familiar with the case and flexible in his thinking so that any errors made by opposing counsel can be fully exposed to the jury and any unexpected arguments can be answered convincingly.

SPECIAL VERDICTS.   In almost every tax refund suit it is impractical to request the jury to return a general verdict for the taxpayer in a given amount of money. A general verdict in a multi-issue or evaluation-type case is likely to require a tax computation in order to ascertain the taxpayer's recovery. Even single-issue cases will usually present a variety of alternative findings.

The Federal Rules of Civil Procedure provide that the trial judge, in his discretion, may require the jury to return a special verdict in the form of answers to written questions or in other form.[58] This discretion is normally exercised in tax refund suits. Typically, the judge will ask the parties at the commencement of trial either to prepare an agreed form of special verdict or to submit their respective requested special verdict forms for resolution by the court.

The aim in drafting a special verdict form is to present a clear and neutrally worded series of questions by means of which the jury can indicate its decision in the case. For the taxpayer, care should be taken to include every possible alternative finding in his favor in the special verdict (preferably with a separate question for each finding). Suggestions for special verdicts can be found in the standard tax reporting services which publish the jury instructions (and special verdicts rendered) in tax cases.

The sample in Fig. 15–1 (page **15·**18) illustrates a relatively simple special verdict for use in a tax refund suit.[59]

Even an uncomplicated farm loss case, however, can present a burdensome number of questions for resolution by the jury. In one case,[60] for example, the jury had to find separately the correct amount of each of eighteen claimed deductions (including depreciation).

---

[58] Fed. R. Civ. P. 49(a).

[59] See Tax Refund Suit Form No. 26, p. **C·**93, for an additional form of special interrogatories for the jury.

[60] Dubose v. Ross, 18 A.F.T.R.2d 5708 (N.D. Ga.).

SPECIAL VERDICT

1. Did Kendall Marva, in 1966, operate Crawness Farm as a business?

Yes or No

If you answer "Yes," answer no further questions.
If you answer "No," go on to question 2.

2. What part, if any, of Kendall Marva's expenditures for operating Crawness Farm in 1966 were made in order to maintain property held for the production of income?

Answer All, None, or give
the dollar amount up to
$35,621.00.

FOREMAN

Fig. 15–1.

COURT'S CHARGE TO JURY AND OBJECTIONS. After final arguments have been completed the court will charge the jury.[61] The judge will include in the instructions the requested charges he has decided to adopt or modify as well as those he believes should be included regardless of any specific request. In addition, the judge may, in his discretion, comment on the evidence to assist the jury in arriving at a just conclusion so long as he makes it clear that the ultimate determinations of fact are left to the jury.[62]

As an example of a forceful, but proper, judicial comment on the evidence, consider the following remarks by Judge Wyzanski in his charge in a farm loss (hobby vs. business) case:

Now let me put to you a question that you do not have to think is relevant. Suppose that the dairy and poultry operations had been in Lexington or Concord, and over a dozen years had not once returned a profit. In spite of the diversity of Mr. Clark's operations, why has he shown a tendency to hold on for as long as a dozen years to an operation that does not make a profit and wait out the market for that long? You do not have to believe that is a relevant question. But, as I have been thinking about the problem, it seems to me to be relevant.[63]

[61] Fed. R. Civ. P. 51.
[62] See 5 MOORE'S FEDERAL PRACTICE ¶ 51.07 (2d ed. 1966).
[63] Clark v. United States, 17 A.F.T.R.2d 459, 461 (Mass.) (jury verdict for taxpayer), *rev'd on another issue*, 358 F.2d 892 (C.A.1st), *cert. denied*, 365 U.S. 817.

During the course of the court's charge to the jury it is mandatory that counsel note any possible objections to the charge. The Federal Rules of Civil Procedure provide that

No party may assign as error the giving or the failure to give an instruction unless he objects thereto before the jury retires to consider its verdict, stating distinctly the matter to which he objects and the grounds of his objection.[64]

The Rules require the court to give the parties an opportunity to make objections to the charge out of the hearing of the jury. However, should the court not expressly advise the parties regarding this matter at the conclusion of his instructions, it is important for counsel to request a bench conference so that the Rules may be followed.[65]

Objection should be made to the court's failure to give requested instructions as well as to any allegedly incorrect matter included in the charge.[66] In phrasing objections to instruction, care should be taken to spell out the reasons for the objections. Moreover, the court should be advised as to how the objecting party believes an alleged error can be corrected. In the absence of an objection, the court's charge to the jury is not reviewable on appeal except where an error was so fundamental that it warrants disregard of the procedural rules.[67]

The following illustrates the form of making objections (here by government counsel) at the conclusion of the court's charge to the jury:

Gentlemen, are there any particular requests?
Taxpayers' Counsel: No, your Honor.
Govt. Counsel: May we approach the Bench, your Honor?
(The following took place at the Bench out of the hearing of the jury:)
Govt. Counsel: Your Honor, I object to the charge in that you have failed to include as an element for the plaintiffs' recovery a fact which they must establish in order to be entitled to recovery, and that is the fact that the payments in question were not made by Mr. Finkelmeier pursuant to his personal obligation.
I believe your Honor's charge stated that if the payments were made by Mr. Finkelmeier personally the jury could still find for the plaintiffs. I respectfully submit that the charge should be corrected by requiring the jury in order to find for the plaintiffs to find that the payments were not made by Mr. Finkelmeier personally on account of a personal obligation of Mr. Finkelmeier.[68]

After the jury has retired, it is possible that additional instructions may be necessary to answer questions asked by the jury. In this event the

---

[64] Fed. R. Civ. P. 51.
[65] It is unwise to object to the court's instructions in the presence of the jury, as the objections themselves tend to emphasize the very points believed to be incorrect.
[66] Even if an objection was made before the charge, it should be made again after the instructions and before the jury retires. The court usually will permit the earlier objections to be made by reference to the earlier statement by counsel.
[67] 5 MOORE'S FEDERAL PRACTICE ¶ 51.04 (2d ed. 1966).
[68] Finkelmeier v. United States, 17 A.F.T.R.2d 112, 114 (S.D. Ohio).

judge, after consulting with counsel and considering any arguments that may be appropriate, will answer the jury's question. Also, it is possible that a jury may deliberate so long that the judge considers it appropriate to give a charge, commonly called a "dynamite" or "Allen" charge.[69] This is an instruction in which, in substance, the jury is told that each juror should consider the arguments and opinions of the others, that a minority juror should consider whether the majority may not be correct, and that every effort should be made to arrive at a decision if the jurors can conscientiously do so in order to avoid the necessity of a new trial.[70] Supplemental charges are handled in the same way as the original instructions.

RENDERING OF VERDICT. After the jury has deliberated and reached its verdict, they will advise the Deputy Marshal of this fact, and court will be opened for the rendering of the verdict. The verdict will be announced in open court by either the foreman of the jury or the Clerk. The losing party may request that the jury be polled and that each individual juror be asked if the verdict rendered is in accordance with his decision.[71] If the verdict does represent the unanimous decision of the jury, it stands, in the absence of extremely rare circumstances that may justify its impeachment.[72] Thereafter, judgment will be entered in accordance with the verdict.[73]

POSTVERDICT MOTIONS FOR JUDGMENT NOTWITHSTANDING VERDICT AND FOR NEW TRIAL. After receiving an adverse verdict, a party who feels that the jury's decision was either unsupported by proof or against the weight of the evidence must file motions with the district court in order to protect his rights. The key postverdict motions in jury trials are

1. The motion for judgment notwithstanding the verdict (commonly called "judgment n.o.v.") [74]

2. The motion for new trial [75]

The motion for judgment n.o.v. is based upon the legal insufficiency of the evidence to support the verdict against the movant.[76] The motion for new trial is addressed to the discretion of the trial judge and, in effect, is an assertion that in spite of the bare legal sufficiency of the adversary's case the verdict was against the weight of the evidence, or that other circum-

---

[69] Named after Allen v. United States, 164 U.S. 492.

[70] Allen v. United States, *supra* note 69; Muldrow v. Daly, 329 F.2d 886, 890 (C.A.D.C.); Wilson v. Southern Farm Bureau Cas. Corp., 275 F.2d 819 (C.A.5th), *cert. denied,* 364 U.S. 817.

[71] Humphries v. District of Columbia, 174 U.S. 190. 5 MOORE'S FEDERAL PRACTICE ¶ 49.07 (2d ed. 1966).

[72] See 6 MOORE'S FEDERAL PRACTICE ¶ 59.08[4] (2d ed. 1965).

[73] See p. **16 · 1** *et seq. infra.*

[74] Fed. R. Civ. P. 50(b)

[75] Fed. R. Civ. P. 59. See p. **16 · 8–9** *infra.*

[76] United States v. Simmons, 346 F.2d 213, 215 (C.A.5th).

stances exist justifying the granting of a new trial.[77] The two motions were compared by Judge Sobeloff in the following terms:

There is a difference in the function of the judge when he is ruling on a motion for directed verdict [or for judgement n.o.v.] and when he passes on a motion for a new trial. In the former instance, it is his duty to accept the [prevailing party's] version as true for the purposes of the motion, notwithstanding the existence of strong testimony to the contrary; the judge is not concerned with the weight of the evidence. On a motion for new trial, however, he has wider, though not unlimited latitude and he may set the verdict aside where it is against the weight of the evidence or to prevent injustice. The two situations should not be confused.[78]

The motion for judgment notwithstanding, the verdict is critical because it provides the basis for the trial court's or an appellate court's entering a judgment for the movant. If the motion is not made, the trial court and an appellate court are empowered only to grant a new trial even though they may conclude that the recipient of the adverse verdict was substantively entitled to a judgment in his favor without the need for a new trial.[79] Accordingly, a taxpayer who feels that an adverse jury verdict lacks evidentiary support must file a motion for judgment n.o.v.[80]

A motion for judgment notwithstanding the verdict may be made only if the movant had moved for a directed verdict at the close of all the evidence at trial.[81] Furthermore, the grounds asserted in the motion for directed verdict cannot be enlarged or added to (although they can be clarified) in the post-verdict motion for judgment n.o.v.[82]

A motion for new trial may be filed with the motion for judgment n.o.v., or in the latter motion itself a new trial may be requested in the alternative.[83]

COURT OF CLAIMS TRIALS

The "trial" of a case in the United States Court of Claims is a bipartite procedure. Evidence is taken, and recommended firdings of fact and con-

---

[77] See generally 6 MOORE'S FEDERAL PRACTICE ¶ 59.07, 59.08 (2d ed. 1965).

[78] McCracken v. Richmond, Fredericksburg & Potomac R.R., 240 F.2d 484, 488 (C.A.4th).

[79] Johnson v. New York, New Haven & Hartford R.R., 344 U.S. 48. See generally 5 MOORE'S FEDERAL PRACTICE ¶ 50.11, at 2333 (2d ed. 1966).

[80] Arguments are available that might persuade a court that a trial judge, if not an appellate court, can enter judgment for a party in the absence of a posttrial motion for judgment n.o.v. See 5 MOORE'S FEDERAL PRACTICE ¶ 59.11, at 2339 (Supp. 1965). However, it is highly advisable to file the motion rather than face the strong possibility that available relief would be limited.

[81] Fed. R. Civ. P. 50(b). See p. 15·14 *et seq. supra.*

[82] United States v. Fenix & Scisson, Inc., *supra* note 51.

[83] Fed. R. Civ. P. 50(b). See Tax Refund Suit Form No. 28, p. C·93, for a sample motion for judgment n.o.v. requesting, in the alternative, a new trial.

clusions of law are made by a trial commissioner. Thereafter the parties present their respective contentions to the judges of the Court of Claims in a quasi-appellate proceeding.

Rules of Evidence Applied in the Court of Claims

In the United States Court of Claims such evidence is admissible as is admissible under the statutes of the United States or under the rules of evidence applied in the United States District Court for the District of Columbia.[84] In any case of conflict, the rule that favors the reception of offered evidence governs. Accordingly, as in the Tax Court,[85] statutory sources of the law of evidence in the Court of Claims include the evidentiary provisions of the United States Code [86] and the District of Columbia Code.[87]

Procedures Before the Trial Commissioner

When filed, a case in the Court of Claims is referred to a trial commissioner whose function is that of a trial judge in the case.[88] He will

1. Handle all matters prior to the trial hearing including the pretrial conference
2. Preside over the presentation of evidence
3. Make and report findings of fact in the case
4. If so directed by the court, submit recommended conclusions of law [89]

All rulings and orders of the trial commissioner are subject to review by the court.[90] Moreover, even though the trial commissioner hears the evidence and reports his findings of fact, it is the Court of Claims (and not its commissioners) that has the responsibility for making ultimate determinations both of fact and law.[91]

SCHEDULING OF CASE FOR TRIAL. The rules of the Court of Claims provide that the taking of evidence shall be begun as expeditiously as possible.[92] The actual amount of time that will expire between the filing of the taxpayer's petition and the commencement of the trial itself will vary

[84] Ct. Cl. R. 49(a). The competence of witnesses to testify is determined in like manner.
[85] Tax Ct. R. 31(a). See p. **8·6** *supra*.
[86] 28 U.S.C. §§ 1731–45. See Appendix A *infra*.
[87] Title 14, D.C. Code. See Appendix A *infra*.
[88] Ct. Cl. R. 53.
[89] Ct. Cl. R. 52(a), (b). By general order of September 23, 1964, the Court of Claims has directed its trial commissioners to submit recommendations for conclusions of law in all cases in which they make findings of fact.
[90] Ct. Cl. R. 52(c).
[91] Bringwald, Inc. v. United States, 334 F.2d 639, 643 (Ct. Cl.).
[92] Ct. Cl. R. 48(b)(1).

considerably, depending upon such factors as the nature of the case, the amount of time the trial commissioner feels the parties need to complete the pretrial procedures (including discovery), and the schedules of the parties, counsel, and the commissioner.

The place (or places) of trial will be fixed by the trial commissioner with, in the words of the rules,

. . . due regard to (i) the places of residence of the claimant and the witnesses, and (ii) the degree of convenience of all concerned to be served by convening at some central place.[93]

Whenever practical the trial will be scheduled for one continuous session or a series of continuous sessions. However, it is not uncommon for a single trial to require several separate trial hearings at one or more different locations. In fact, this flexibility of hearing procedures is one of the important factors tending to make the Court of Claims a desirable tribunal for a case in which the witnesses are widely dispersed or where conditions require a significant time lag between witnesses.

SUBPOENAS FOR TRIAL. In the Court of Claims a party may request the Clerk to issue subpoenas (including subpoenas *duces tecum*) to compel witnesses to attend the trial of a case (and to bring designated materials).[94] Also, subpoenas may be issued to the trial commissioner who may order service on his own motion or release the subpoenas to the parties for service.[95]

Subpoenas may be served by a Deputy United States Marshal or any other person not a party to the action.[96] A subpoena requiring the attendance of a witness at a trial may be served at any place within 100 miles (by the shortest usual means of travel) of the place of trial.[97] The trial commissioner, may, upon good cause shown, authorize the service of a subpoena at a place farther than 100 miles from the place of trial.[98]

PRESENTATION OF EVIDENCE. The presentation of evidence to a trial commissioner of the Court of Claims will proceed in the same manner as in a case to a United States District Judge sitting without a jury.[99] More frequently than a district judge a trial commissioner will dispense with opening statements, relying upon the parties' submissions prior to trial (including any pretrial briefs submitted) for an introduction to the dispute.

Order of Proof. The normal order of proof in the Court of Claims is the same as that in the district courts, *i.e.* the taxpayer will present his evi-

[93] Ct. Cl. R. 48(b)(2).
[94] Ct. Cl. R. 51(a), (b), (c).
[95] Ct. Cl. R. 56(e).
[96] Ct. Cl. R. 51(e). A person serving a subpoena may not be less than eighteen years of age.
[97] Ct. Cl. R. 51(b).
[98] *Ibid.*
[99] See p. **15·3** *et seq. supra.*

dence, followed by the government's case and such rebuttal as may be necessary. However, in the Court of Claims there is considerable flexibility in this regard. Inasmuch as trial hearings may be set at two or more widely separated places, it is not uncommon for geographical considerations to outweigh the customary order of proof. Hence, the trial commissioner is likely to hear all the witnesses in one geographical area before adjourning for a separate hearing in another city. Also, trial commissioners tend to be liberal in permitting a party to take witnesses out of order where necessity or convenience dictates, and to interrupt the testimony of a witness with a continuance where circumstances warrant this procedure.

Presentation of Proof Established Prior to Trial. Where part of a party's case has been made of record prior to the trial (*i.e.* in the form of evidentiary depositions or through formal discovery procedures) he must offer the material at trial in order to make it part of the record in the case. The Court of Claims Rules expressly provide that depositions, as well as information, documents, or objects filed in response to calls, are not considered part of the evidence in the case until they are offered and received in evidence at trial.[100] The rules are not explicit with regard to such items as stipulations and formally obtained admissions.[101] Nevertheless, it appears good practice, if not absolutely essential, to make a formal offer of proof in this form at the trial hearing.

POSTHEARING PROCEDURES BEFORE TRIAL COMMISSIONER. Afer the taking of evidence has been completed the trial commissioner will file a notice of the closing of evidence. This document triggers the formal post hearing procedures.[102]

First, the taxpayer will file, within the time provided, requested findings of fact and a brief on the law.[103] Thereafter,[104] the government will file its requested findings of fact, objections to the taxpayer's requested findings, and a brief.[105] Finally, the taxpayer will respond with his objections to the government's requested findings of fact and a reply brief (if necessary).[106]

The Court of Claims Rules specifically require that requested findings of fact be in separate numbered paragraphs so written that each one can be

---

[100] Ct. Cl. R. 34(a)(1), 39(e).

[101] See Ct. Cl. R. 42(d)(4), stating that formally obtained admissions are "conclusively established."

[102] Ct. Cl. R. 57(b).

[103] These must be filed within thirty days from the filing of the commissioner's notice of closing of the evidence unless otherwise provided. Ct. Cl. R. 57(b)(1).

[104] The commissioner may, at his discretion, require the parties to file the documents simultaneously rather than seriatim.

[105] These must be filed within thirty days after the filing of the taxpayer's documents. Ct. Cl. R. 57(b)(2).

[106] These must be filed within twenty days after the filing of the government's documents. Ct. Cl. R. 57(b)(3).

considered separately from the others.[107] The requested findings must be supported with citations to the portions of the record on which they are based.[108] Objections to requested findings must state with particularity the reasons for objection to each unacceptable proposed finding.[109] Failure to request a significant finding of fact or to object to a requested finding made by the adversary may have serious consequences. The court may refuse to consider a party's exception (1) to the trial commissioner's failure to make a finding not requested or (2) to the trial commissioner's finding a fact where the excepting party did not object to his adversary's request.[110]

Normally, no oral argument is presented to the trial commissioner after the post hearing documents are submitted.

TRIAL COMMISSIONER'S REPORT. Upon consideration of the evidence presented and the documents submitted by the parties the trial commissioner will arrive at his decision. He will then file with the Clerk a report containing his findings of fact and recommendations for conclusions of law.[111] Commissioner's reports in Court of Claims tax refund suits have (since 1966) been reported in the standard tax reporting services.[112]

Procedures Before the Court

The post hearing procedures before the Court of Claims itself, while in the nature of an appeal, are not, strictly speaking, an appellate review of the trial commissioner's decision. As the Court of Claims has put it,

While the findings [of fact] and opinion of a trial commissioner are entitled to much consideration and weight, yet under our rules and procedure the court has the ultimate responsibility for determining these matters.[113]

Nevertheless, the procedures followed in the Court of Claims after the trial commissioner has filed his report have the flavor of an appeal.

NOTICE OF INTENTION TO EXCEPT TO COMMISSIONER'S REPORT. In virtually every tax refund suit the trial commissioner's report will contain both findings of fact and recommendations for conclusions of law.[114] A party dissatisfied with the commissioner's report must file a timely notice

---

[107] Ct. Cl. R. 57(c) (1).
[108] *Ibid.*
[109] Ct. Cl. R. 57(c) (2).
[110] Ct. Cl. R. 57(f) (1), (2), (3).
[111] C. Cl. R. 57(a).
[112] 6 P–H 1966. Fed. Tax Serv. ¶ 58,000; 7 CCH 1966 Stand. Fed. Tax. Rep. ¶ 8150.
[113] Bringwald, Inc. v. United States, *supra* note 91, at 643.
[114] Even before the general order of September 23, 1964, requiring the commissioners to recommend conclusions of law in all cases, they were almost always directed to do so in tax cases.

of intention to except.[115] Where no such notice has been filed the parties will be deemed to have accepted the trial commissioner's report as the basis for judgment in the case.[116]

EXCEPTIONS AND BRIEFS. If the taxpayer alone or both parties have filed a notice of intention to except to the trial commissioner's report, the taxpayer must file his brief and exceptions within forty-five days after the report is filed.[117] Thereafter, the government must file its brief and exceptions (if any).[118] Finally, the taxpayer may file a reply brief.[119] In a case in which the government is the only party to file a notice of intention to except, the order of filing documents to the court is reversed.[120]

The Court of Claims Rules, in addition to requiring briefs to be compact, concise, logically arranged, and free from improper matter,[121] specify that the first brief filed with the court must contain

1. A table of contents
2. A table of authorities cited
3. A succinct statement of the questions presented
4. A concise statement of the case
5. Argument on the facts and law
6. A conclusion stating the relief sought [122]

Subsequent briefs filed with the court must have the same contents except for the statement of questions presented and the statement of the case.[123] These items need be included only if the briefing party is dissatisfied with the adversary's statements of these points. Briefs that do not comply with the rule prescribing their contents may be disregarded by the court.[124]

SUBMISSION OF CASE WITHOUT EXCEPTIONS AND BRIEF. A party who is completely satisfied with the commissioner's findings of facts and recommended conclusions of law may elect to submit the case to the court solely upon the commissioner's report.[125] This choice, made by filing a statement of election, does not prevent the adversary from submitting his exceptions

---

[115] Ct. Cl. R. 59. The notice must be filed within thirty days after the filing of the report.

[116] Ct. Cl. R. 59, 65(a).

[117] Ct. Cl. R. 58(b)(1)(i). The parties may stipulate to extend this time as well as the others applicable to exceptions and briefs. Ct. Cl. R. 58(b)(4).

[118] These must be filed within thirty days after the taxpayer's documents are filed. Ct. Cl. R. 58 (b)(1)(ii).

[119] The reply brief must be filed within twenty days after the government's documents are filed. Ct. Cl. R. 58(b)(1)(iii).

[120] Ct. Cl. R. 58(b)(3).

[121] Ct. Cl. R. 60(d).

[122] Ct. Cl. R. 60(a).

[123] Ct. Cl. R. 60(b), (c).

[124] Ct. Cl. R. 60(d).

[125] Ct. Cl. R. 62.

and briefs pursuant to the normally applicable rules.[126] Moreover, the election may eliminate any opportunity for the electing party to offer arguments in his favor. Hence, where a taxpayer has made the election he may file a reply to the government's brief only by leave of court for good cause shown.[127] Moreover, the court may order that no argument be had in the case or that argument may be presented only by the government.[128]

ARGUMENT TO THE COURT OF CLAIMS.   After a case has been tried (or submitted on stipulated facts) and the time for filing documents to the court has expired it will be placed on a monthly argument calendar.[129] Reasonable notice of the date of argument will be given the parties.[130] The parties can stipulate that no oral argument will be presented.[131]

All arguments are held at the United States Court of Claims in Washington, D.C. Argument may be presented to the full Court of Claims *en banc* or to a division of the three judges of the Court.[132] Where argument is presented to a division, a rehearing *en banc* may be granted.

Unless the time for argument is otherwise prescribed each party will have thirty minutes to present its contentions.[133] The party who filed the first brief to the court (normally the taxpayer) has the right to divide his time between an opening and closing argument.[134] The adversary's argument is sandwiched between the first party's opening and closing address.

Argument itself will proceed in the same manner as in an appellate court. As a practical matter one party will usually be attacking, and the other defending, the trial commissioner's report as if it were the decision of a lower court being reviewed.

DECISION.   The Court of Claims Rules provide,

In all actions tried on the facts, the court will find the facts and state separately its conclusions of law, and will direct the entry of an appropriate judgment.[135]

Once argument has been held the court will reach its decision through its internal decisional process. As in the United States Supreme Court

[126] Ct. Cl. R. (62(b), (c).

[127] Ct. Cl. R. 62(c).

[128] *Ibid.*

[129] Ct. Cl. R. 65(a).

[130] Ct. Cl. R. 65(c). In practice, one day a month is customarily set aside for arguments in cases to be argued by counsel located outside of Washington, D.C.

[131] This stipulation, which must be approved by the court, may be made by a written waiver of argument filed with the Clerk or stated orally in open court when the case is called. Ct. Cl. R. 65(e).

[132] The statute providing for the addition of two judges to the Court of Claims directs the court to sit in divisions of three judges unless the court orders a hearing (or rehearing) *en banc*. Act of May 11, 1966, P.L. 89–425, 89th Cong. 2d Sess., 80 Stat. 139, amending 28 U.S.C. §§ 171, 175.

[133] Ct. Cl. R. 65(d).

[134] Ct. Cl. R. 65(a).

[135] Ct. Cl. R. 66.

and the Courts of Appeals this process of decision will include conferences, votes by the judges, the drafting of opinions and dissents, and, finally, a formal decision with or without dissenting opinions.

In a tax refund suit the court will normally decide only the taxpayer's right to a recovery. The case will be referred back to the trial commissioner for a determination of the amount of recovery called for by the court's resolution of the case. However, judgment will be entered upon the court's determination of the right to a recovery.[136]

---

[136] See p. **16·5–6** *infra*.

CHAPTER 16

POSTDECISION PROCEDURES IN
TAX REFUND SUITS

JUDGMENTS IN TAX REFUND SUITS

District Court Judgments

In the district courts a judgment is a document, separate from the decision or verdict on which it is based, that sets forth the parties' respective rights to recovery and the amounts of recovery to which they are entitled.[1]

---

[1] Fed. R. Civ. P. 54(a), 58. Note 3 to Fed. R. Civ. P., Official Forms Nos. 31 and 32. 6 MOORE'S FEDERAL PRACTICE ¶ 58.01[8] at 3504 (2d ed. 1965 Supp.).

Therefore, in the district courts judgment is not entered and times measured from the entry of judgment cannot commence running until after the amount of any recovery is computed and made a part of the judgment.

COMPUTATION OF AMOUNT OF RECOVERY. Except in a case in which the taxpayer's complaint is dismissed completely, the decision or verdict in a tax refund suit must be translated into dollars and cents of recovery through a tax computation. Since these computations can be complex, the courts normally depart from their usual practice [2] and place the primary burden for preparing the computation on the parties.

It has become customary for the parties in tax refund suits to follow a procedure analogous to that prescribed by Tax Court Rule 50 [3] in computing the amount of recovery. Typically, the procedure is embodied in a stipulation in the following terms:

It is agreed that any computation necessary as a result of the decision of the court in this case shall initially be made by the defendant. The defendant's computation shall be submitted to the plaintiff for his approval. In the event the parties are unable to agree upon the computation then the issue shall be resolved by a procedure to be set by the Court.

Pursuant to this standard stipulation the Tax Division, upon receipt of a decision or verdict requiring a computation, will forward the necessary materials to Chief Counsel, Internal Revenue Service. The computation will then be prepared by the Service and returned to the Tax Division. At this point the computation, and a proposed judgment based upon the computation, will be forwarded to taxpayer's counsel for his agreement or comments. It is rare for any dispute regarding the amount of recovery to survive a conference between taxpayer's counsel and the government's trial attorney. However, where there are irreconcilable differences the matter is presented to the court for resolution. Generally, even the disputed matters turn upon questions of law rather than complex computational issues. Nevertheless, it is not unknown for a dispute regarding a computation to become so entangled that a master must be appointed to unscramble the omelet.

PREPARATION OF THE JUDGMENT. In a tax refund suit the judgment document usually is prepared in a manner analogous to that used for computing the amount of recovery. Hence, the government (while computing the amount of recovery) will also draft a proposed judgment and submit it to taxpayer's counsel for agreement or comments. The body of the judg-

---

[2] The Federal Rules of Civil Procedure provide that the parties shall not be directed to submit forms of judgment as a matter of course. Fed. R. Civ. P. 58. However, the courts generally recognize that tax refund suits are an exception to the general practice prescribed by the Rules.

[3] See p. **9·**10 *et seq. supra* for a discussion of Rule 50 practice in the Tax Court.

ment in a tax refund suit in which the taxpayer has recovered will be worded more or less as follows: [4]

It is ordered and adjudged—

> that the plaintiff, John Taxpayer, recover of the defendant, the United States of America, the sum of $5,467.98 with interest thereon as provided by law together with his costs in this action.[5]

Where no computation is necessary, *i.e.,* where the taxpayer has completely lost a refund suit, the court may enter judgment without directing the parties to submit a form of judgment. The body of such a judgment will be worded, in substance, as follows:

It is ordered and adjudged—

> that the plaintiff, John Taxpayer, take nothing, that the action be dismissed on the merits, and that the defendant, the United States of America recover of the plaintiff John Taxpayer its costs in this action.[6]

Upon receipt of a proposed judgment taxpayer's counsel will endorse his approval as to form unless there should be some disagreement. Disagreements usually relate to the computation or to the allowance or disallowance of costs. All disputes are resolved by the court.

ENTRY OF JUDGMENT. After a judgment has been prepared and any disagreements have been resolved by the court, the judgment will be filed and entered. Since many time limits are triggered by the entry of judgment it is important to clarify this term. In the Federal Rules of Civil Procedure it is provided that a judgment is effective only when entered by the Clerk on the civil docket.[7] Therefore, a judgment signed by the court, received by the Clerk, and marked "filed" as of the date of receipt is not yet entered.[8] However, a judgment is usually entered on the civil docket on the day it is filed by the court. Moreover, because a district court judgment must reflect the amount of any recovery awarded, it will not be entered (or prepared) until after the computational process has been completed.

JUDGMENT AGAINST DISTRICT DIRECTOR (SUITS COMMENCED UNDER PRIOR LAW). Under prior law a taxpayer had the right to name as the defendant in a tax refund suit the District Director who collected the tax in

---

[4] See Tax Refund Suit Forms No. 27, p. C·93, and No. 29, p. C·94, for sample judgments.

[5] The last phrase of the judgment might be "the parties to bear their own costs," reflecting a decision not to award costs.

[6] See note 5, *supra.*

[7] Fed. R. Civ. P. 58, 79(a).

[8] Fed. R. Civ. P. 79(a). See 6 MOORE'S FEDERAL PRACTICE ¶ 58.02 (2d ed. 1965 Supp.).

issue.[9] Many of these suits are presently pending and some can reasonably be expected to result in judgments against the District Director. Such judgments must be, in effect, converted into judgments against the United States in order for the taxpayer to obtain payment from the government.

The United States Code provides,

Execution shall not issue against [a District Director] on a final judgment in any proceeding against him for . . . the recovery of any money . . . paid to him and subsequently paid into the Treasury, in performing his official duties, if the court certifies that:

(1) probable cause existed; or
(2) [he] acted under the direction of the Secretary of the Treasury or other proper Government officer.

When such certificate has been issued, the amount of the judgment will be paid out of the proper appropriation by the Treasury.[10]

It should also be noted that the government will indemnify a District Director for any costs a taxpayer may be awarded in a tax refund suit.[11]

A "certificate of probable cause," as the document is commonly called, should be prepared and submitted to the court along with the judgment in a tax refund suit against a District Director. It appears that, in virtually every tax refund suit, the court would be required to issue the certificate.[12] In practice the government will prepare the certificate when a decision is received against a District Director, often making the certification a part of the judgment.[13]

The court's issuance of a certificate of probable cause affects only the ultimate payment of the judgment. The United States is neither substituted for nor added as a party defendant in the suit. Nor does the certificate in any way limit the defendant's rights with regard to appellate review of the judgment entered. On the other hand, the amount of recovery called for by the judgment is subject to any credit that may be available to the government to the same extent as if the judgment were one entered against the United States.[14]

---

[9] Tax refund suits against the District Director have been abolished. IRC § 7422(f), as amended Nov. 2, 1966, P.L. 89–713 (applicable to suits commenced ninety or more days after passage of the amendment).

[10] 28 U.S.C. § 2006.

[11] IRC § 7423.

[12] Geo. Moore Ice Cream Co. v. Rose, 289 U.S. 373. *But see* Toledo Edison Co. v. McMaken, 103 F.2d 72 (C.A.6th), *cert. denied,* 308 U.S. 569, where the certificate was withheld when the representative of a deceased collector waived the statute of limitations.

[13] *E.g.,* Associated Arkansas Newspapers, Inc. v. Johnson, 18 A.F.T.R.2d 5894, 5897 (E.D. Ark.).

[14] See Blair v. United States, 6 F.2d 484 (C.A.D.C.).

Court of Claims Judgments

In the Court of Claims the court will direct the entry of a judgment solely upon the parties' respective rights to the recovery.[15] Thereafter, where there is a recovery a separate judgment with regard to the amount of recovery (a "money judgment") will be entered. Accordingly, in a Court of Claims case time measured from the entry of judgment commences running even before the amount of recovery is ascertained.

COMPUTATION OF AMOUNT OF RECOVERY. The Court of Claims will normally conclude a decision holding for the taxpayer in a tax refund suit with a statement to the following effect:

. . . the plaintiff is entitled to recover . . . . Judgment is entered to that effect. The amount of recovery will be determined under Rule 47(c).[16]

Under Rule 47(c) the matter of computation of the amount recoverable pursuant to the court's decision is referred to the trial commissioner. In practice, the same procedure will be followed in the Court of Claims as in a district court suit.[17] Hence, analogously to Rule 50 practice in the Tax Court, the government will prepare a proposed computation subject to the taxpayer's approval or disapproval. Any disputes that cannot be resolved by the parties will be decided by the trial commissioner or, ultimately, the court. The court will issue an order stating the amount recoverable pursuant to its decision and the Clerk will enter judgment accordingly.

PREPARATION OF JUDGMENT. In the Court of Claims the parties to the action do not normally have any part in the preparation of the judgment document. Judgment as to the right to recovery is entered by the Clerk on the court's docket directly from the court's decision or from an order reflecting its decision. When the amount of recovery is determined, judgment is entered by the Clerk from an order of the court reflecting the amount recoverable pursuant to its decision.

ENTRY OF JUDGMENT. The court's decision will normally state "judgment is entered," and the day the decision is handed down the Clerk will make an appropriate notation on the court's docket.[18] The Clerk immediately thereafter will notify the parties of the entry of judgment.[19] The judgment on the right to recovery is a final judgment [20] of the Court of Claims which

---

[15] Ct. Cl. R. 47(c).

[16] *E.g.,* International Business Machs. Corp. v. United States, 343 F.2d 914, 925 (Ct. Cl.).

[17] See p. **16·2** *supra.*

[18] Ct. Cl. R. 72(a).

[19] Ct. Cl. R. 72(b).

[20] Subject to postdecision proceedings under Rules 68 and 69.

starts the running of post decision time limits under the Court of Claims Rules.[21]

After the amount of recovery is determined pursuant to Rule 47(c) a separate "money judgment" will be entered pursuant to an order of the court.[22] This judgment may be entered several months after the entry of judgment on the right to recovery. However, any post decision motions addressed to the court's determination of the right to recovery should be filed within the specified time after the entry of the judgment on the right to recovery. Motions addressed to the "money judgment" should be filed within the appropriate times after the entry of that judgment.

COSTS IN TAX REFUND SUITS

In tax refund suits, a district court or the Court of Claims may, in its discretion, award costs to the prevailing party. The awarding of costs will be reflected in the judgment which will indicate either (1) that the prevailing party shall recover costs from the adversary or (2) that each party shall bear its own costs. However, the judgment itself will not indicate the amount of costs awarded, and its entry will not be delayed for the taxing of costs or the resolution of any dispute regarding costs.[23]

Allowable Costs in Suits Commenced After July 18, 1966

The United States Code provides that, as to tax refund suits commenced after July 18, 1966,

Except as otherwise specifically provided by statute, a judgment for costs, as enumerated in section 1920 of this title but not including the fees and expenses of attorneys or expert witnesses, may be awarded to the prevailing party in any action brought by or against the United States or any agency or official of the United States or any agency or official of the United States acting in his official capacity, in any court having jurisdiction of such action. A judgment for costs when taxed against the Government shall, in an amount established by statute or court rule or order, be limited to reimbursing in whole or in part the prevailing party for the costs incurred by him in the litigation. Payment of a judgment for costs shall be as provided in section 2414 of this title for the payment of judgments against the United States.[24]

Hence costs are allowable to the prevailing party in a tax refund suit to just about the same extent as to the prevailing party in ordinary civil litigation. The allowable costs as enumerated by statute [25] include

---

[21] Ct. Cl. R. 47(c)(2).

[22] See Peartree, *Statistical Analysis of the Court of Claims,* 55 Geo. L.J. 541, 545–47 (1966–67).

[23] Fed. R. Civ. P. 58.

[24] 28 U.S.C. § 2412, as amended July 18, 1966, P.L. 89–507.

[25] 28 U.S.C. § 1920. See generally, as to costs, 6 MOORE'S FEDERAL PRACTICE ¶ 54.77 (2d ed. 1965).

(1) Fees of the clerk and marshal;
(2) Fees of the Court Reporter for all or part of the stenographic transcript necessarily obtained for use in the case;
(3) Fees and disbursements for printing and witnesses;[26]
(4) Fees for exemplification and copies of papers necessarily obtained for use in the case;
(5) Docket fees under [28 U.S.C. 1923].

It should be noted that allowable costs in a tax case can be considerable, sometimes amounting to several thousand dollars.[27] One should not overlook the possibility that the government, as well as the taxpayer, may be awarded costs.

Allowable Costs in Suits Commenced Before July 19, 1966

In tax refund suits filed prior to the date of amendment of 28 U.S.C. § 2412 the extent to which costs are allowable depends upon whether the United States or the District Director was named as the defendant.

In a tax refund suit filed against the United States on or before July 18, 1966 the costs allowable to the prevailing party are quite limited. The United States Code provides,

In a [tax refund suit against the United States] if the United States puts in issue plaintiff's right to recover, the district court or Court of Claims may allow costs to the prevailing party from the time of joining such issue. Such costs shall include only those actually incurred for witnesses and fees paid to the clerk.[28]

Under this statute not even the filing fee is an allowable cost since it is paid prior to the time suit is commenced.[29]

In tax refund suits filed against a District Director the special statute limiting costs allowable against the United States has been held inapplicable.[30] Accordingly, in suits against a District Director, whether filed before or after the amendment of 28 U.S.C. § 2412, costs are allowable to the same extent as in civil litigation between private parties.[31]

[26] Fees and disbursements for witnesses are limited to those allowable by general statute, *i.e.,* a prescribed travel allowance plus a statutorily fixed subsistence allowance. 28 U.S.C. § 1821. E. W. Bliss Co. v. United States, 226 F. Supp. 382 (N.D. Ohio), *aff'd specifically on this point,* 351 F.2d 449, 451 (C.A.6th) ; see also United States v. Portland and Cement Co. of Utah, 338 F.2d 798, 803 (C.A.10th).
[27] *E.g.,* Mayer v. Donnelly, 5 A.F.T.R2d 1014 (E.D. La.) (costs of $2,898.98 allowed to the taxpayer).
[28] U.S.C. § 2412 (before amendment of July 18, 1966).
[29] United States v. Mohr, 274 F.2d 803 (C.A.4th), *reversing* 168 F. Supp. 734 (E.D. Va.).
[30] Williams v. Patterson, 289 F.2d 485 (C.A.5th) ; Lichter Foundation, Inc. v. Welch, 269 F.2d 142 (C.A.6th).
[31] It should be noted that tax refund suits against the District Director are no longer permitted. See note 9 *supra.*

Procedure for Obtaining Costs

A party awarded costs must present to the Clerk of the court a bill of costs and an affidavit verifying (1) that each item set forth in the bill is correct and (2) that the expenses listed have actually been incurred as a necessary part of the case.[32] In the district courts the procedural rules provide that the Clerk will tax costs subject to review by the court.[33] The Court of Claims Rules do not expressly provide for a procedure relating to costs.[34] However, it would appear that the submission to the Clerk of a bill of costs and affidavit would be sufficient to obtain costs if they are awarded.

It is recommended that a prevailing taxpayer prepare his proposed bill of costs and provide it to the government during the time the tax computation on his right to recovery is being carried out. Frequently disputes regarding costs can be ironed out amicably rather than through formal procedures which may cost more than the amount in dispute.[35]

POST DECISION MOTIONS

In both tax refund tribunals the procedural rules provide for post decision motions by means of which the trial court can, in effect, review its own actions. In district court jury trials the failure to make a postverdict motion will result in a party's losing his right to a judgment notwithstanding an adverse verdict.[36] The available motions, and the grounds for granting them, are the same in tax cases as in all civil litigation in the refund tribunals. Accordingly, we shall here simply describe the more important of these motions.

Motion for New Trial

A total, or partial, new trial may be granted on the court's own motion or on the timely [37] motion of a party.[38] The procedural rules of the refund tribunals provide that the traditional grounds for new trials shall be avail-

[32] 28 U.S.C. § 1924. See Tax Refund Suit Form No. 30, p. **c**·94–95, for a sample bill of costs with affidavit.

[33] Fed. R. Civ. P. 54(d).

[34] However, by statute, the Court is authorized, and directed in some instances, to tax costs, and the Clerk is directed to report to Congress the costs taxed in Court of Claims cases. 28 U.S.C. §§ 791(c), 2412, 2520(d).

[35] *E.g.,* United States v. Mohr, *supra,* note 29, in which the taxpayer's right to recover the $15 filing fee was litigated through the Court of Appeals.

[36] See p. **15**·14 *et seq. supra.*

[37] Ten days after the entry of judgment in the district court and thirty days after the entry of judgment in the Court of Claims. Fed. R. Civ. P. 59(b) ; Ct. Cl. R. 68(c).

[38] Fed. R. Civ. P. 59(a) ; Ct. Cl. R. 68(a).

able in the district courts and the Court of Claims.[39] The most common grounds asserted are (1) that the court in its decision made a manifest error of law or fact and (2) that newly discovered evidence would change the court's opinion in the case.[40] A rehearing in the Court of Claims, or reargument to a district court, can sometimes be requested where there has been a significant development in the law subsequent to the court's decision. In jury trials in the district courts the most commonly asserted grounds for a new trial are (1) that the verdict was against the weight of the evidence, (2) that the court erred in its charge to the jury, and (3) that the court erred in its evidentiary rulings.[41]

The granting of a new trial is within the discretion of the trial court.[42] In allowing a new trial the court may open a judgment that has been entered, hear such additional evidence as may be required, and amend or change previous findings of fact.[43]

Motion To Alter or Amend Judgment

A party may, within specified time limits,[44] file a motion to alter or amend a judgment entered against him.[45] This motion is most commonly used to change a judgment based upon an erroneous tax computation, to change an order of dismissal with prejudice to one without prejudice, to vacate a dismissal on jurisdictional or procedural grounds if the defect can be remedied, etc.[46] In some instances it may be difficult to determine whether a motion is actually one for a new trial or for an alteration or amendment of the judgment. The movant will not be bound by his choice of caption, however, provided he had clearly stated the grounds for his motion. Regardless of the label put on the motion the party will receive any relief to which he may be entitled.[47]

Motion for Relief from Judgment

A party may move for relief from a judgment entered against him within specified times after the entry of the judgment.[48] The rules of the tax re-

---

[39] *Ibid.*

[40] See 6 MOORE'S FEDERAL PRACTICE ¶ 59.07 (2d ed. 1965).

[41] See 6 MOORE'S FEDERAL PRACTICE ¶ 59.08 (2d ed. 1965).

[42] *E.g.,* McCracken v. Richmond, Fredericksburg & Potomac R.R., 240 F.2d 484, 488 (C.A.4th).

[43] Fed. R. Civ. P. 59(a) ; Ct. Cl. R. 68(b).

[44] Ten days after the entry of judgment in the district courts and thirty days after the entry of judgment in the Court of Claims. Fed. R. Civ. P. 59(e) ; Ct. Cl. R. 68(c).

[45] Fed. R. Civ. P. 59(e) ; Ct. Cl. R. 68(a).

[46] See generally 6 MOORE'S FEDERAL PRACTICE ¶ 58.12[1] (2d ed. 1965).

[47] Hutches v. Renfroe, 200 F.2d 337, 340–41 (C.A.5th).

[48] Fed. R. Civ. P. 60; Ct. Cl. R. 69. The time limit for filing the motion is set forth in the cited rules.

fund tribunals set forth, among others, the following grounds for a motion for relief from judgment:

1. Clerical mistakes
2. Mistake, inadvertence, or excusable neglect
3. Newly discovered evidence not discoverable in time to move for a new trial
4. Fraud, misrepresentation, or misconduct of an adverse party
5. Any other reason justifying relief from the operation of a judgment [49]

The adequacy of the grounds asserted for relief from judgment in a tax refund suit will be tested by the same standards applied in ordinary civil litigation.[50]

APPELLATE REVIEW

Upon receipt of a totally, or partially, adverse decision of a trial court a party must decide whether or not to seek appellate review of the determination. In substance this decision will be made by balancing the chances of obtaining a reversal (or remand) on appeal, the expense likely to be incurred in prosecuting an appeal plus any further proceedings in the trial court required as a result of the appellate decision, and the importance (in terms of money or other considerations) of seeing the trial court's decision reversed. The government, in reaching its decision regarding an appeal, will give considerable weight to the probable effect of the trial court's decision and of an appellate court's determination upon the overall administration of the tax laws.

Government Procedure for Deciding Whether To Seek Appellate Review

Upon receipt of a decision or jury verdict partially or totally adverse to the government in a tax refund suit, the Tax Division trial attorney will initiate a procedure analogous to that used for processing settlement proposals. Ultimate decision regarding the government's appeal or petition for certiorari will be made by the Solicitor General of the United States.

First, the trial attorney will request the views of Chief Counsel, Internal Revenue Service, regarding appeal.[51] Chief Counsel's views will normally

[49] For additional specified grounds, see Fed. R. Civ. P. 60(b)(4), (5) and Ct. Cl. R. 69(b)(4), (5).

[50] See generally 6 MOORE'S FEDERAL PRACTICE, c. 60 (2d ed. 1965); 7 MOORE'S FEDERAL PRACTICE c. 60 (2d ed. 1966).

[51] Normally, this is done at the time the trial attorney requests the Internal Revenue Service to prepare a computation of the amount refundable under the adverse decision.

include his opinion of the importance of the question presented by the case in terms of the overall administration of the tax laws. The trial attorney will also prepare his own special memorandum containing his own recommendations. The trial attorney's memorandum (along with the comments of the Chief of the Trial Section) and the Chief Counsel's recommendation will be forwarded to the Appellate Section of the Tax Division.

From, and after, the time the case is before the Appellate Section of the Tax Division the precise procedure utilized will vary depending upon the importance of the particular case. One or more attorneys in the Appellate Section will study the matter and make recommendations regarding appeal. Conferences may be held at which representatives of the Internal Revenue Service, the Solicitor General's office, and the Tax Division present their views and suggestions regarding appeal. The matter may be considered by the senior officers of the Tax Division, including the First Assistant and the Assistant Attorney General himself. Finally, a formal recommendation from the Tax Division will be forwarded to the Solicitor General. Upon consideration of the case and recommendations (including the views of his staff attorney assigned to the case) the Solicitor General will decide whether or not the government will appeal.

The taxpayer, normally, will have no contact with the government's processing of the case until he is notified [52] of the Solicitor General's decision.

Appeal from a District Court Judgment

A losing party has the right to appeal from an adverse judgment of a United States District Court.[53] As in all district court cases venue for the appeal lies in the United States Court of Appeals for the circuit embracing the district in which the case was tried.[54]

PERFECTING TAXPAYER'S APPEAL. The filing of a timely [55] notice of appeal [56] is a prerequisite to the jurisdiction of the appellate court over the appeal.[57]

---

[52] By letter or telegram.
[53] 28 U.S.C. § 1291.
[54] 28 U.S.C. § 1294.
[55] The taxpayer must file his notice of appeal prior to the later of
1. Sixty days after the entry of judgment
2. Sixty days after the court acts upon a timely motion for judgment, notwithstanding the verdict, to amend or make additional findings of fact or to alter or amend the judgment, or after it denies a motion for a new trial
28 U.S.C. § 2107. Fed. R. Civ. P. 73(a).
The aforementioned time limits can be extended by the district court for up to thirty days upon a showing of excusable neglect. Fed. R. Civ. P. 73(a).
[56] See Tax Refund Suit Form No. 31, p. C·95, for a sample notice of appeal.
[57] United States v. Molitor, 337 F.2d 917 (C.A.9th).

The notice of appeal must specify the party seeking appeal, the judgment or part thereof appealed from, and the name of the court to which appeal is taken.[58]

Following the filing of his notice of appeal the appellant must see that the record on appeal is filed with the court of appeals and the appeal is docketed.[59] This must be accomplished within 40 days after the notice of appeal is filed or within a longer period that district court may set.[60]

The record on appeal consists of

1. The original papers and exhibits filed in the district court
2. The transcript of proceedings [61]
3. A certified copy of the docket entries prepared by the Clerk.[62]

The rules provide that the Clerk shall file the record within the time required, although it is the appellant's duty to take all steps necessary to aid the Clerk in assembling and transmitting the record—*e.g.* appellant must order the required transcript, etc.[63]

The appeal record will be filed and the appeal docketed when the Clerk of the court of appeals receives the record on appeal from the Clerk of the district court and the docket fee from the appellant.[64]

Once a tax case is properly docketed in a United States Court of Appeals it is handled as is any other appellate case.[65]

TAXPAYER'S STEPS WHERE GOVERNMENT FILES NOTICE OF APPEAL. The government's filing a notice of appeal in a tax refund suit does not necessarily indicate that it has decided to prosecute an appeal. As previously noted, the government has established an often time-consuming procedure for processing recommendations regarding appeal. Frequently a notice of appeal is filed by the government solely as a precaution in order to protect its right to appellate review should the Solicitor General decide in favor of appeal. Nevertheless, upon receipt of the government's notice of appeal the

---

[58] Fed. R. Civ. P. 73(b).

[59] Fed. R. Civ. P. 73(g).

[60] Fed. R. Civ. P. 73(g). The district court, however, is not authorized to extend the time to a day more than ninety days after the date on which the notice of appeal, or the first of several notices of appeal, is filed. See 7 MOORE'S FEDERAL PRACTICE ¶ 73.29 (2d ed. 1966).

[61] Within ten days after the notice of appeal is filed, the appellant must order a transcript of those parts of the proceedings not already on file that he feels should be included in the record. He must also serve on the appellee a description of these parts so that the appellant may complete the record to the extent he wishes. Fed. R. Civ. P. 75 (b).

[62] Fed. R. Civ. P. 75(a). By stipulation, the parties can agree that designated parts of the record need not be transmitted to the Court of Appeals unless the court, or a party, later requests their transmission. Fed. R. Civ. P. 75(a), (e), (f), 76.

[63] Fed. R. Civ. P. 75(e), (f).

[64] Fed. R. Civ. P. 73(g).

[65] See generally Tucker, *Suggestions to Attorneys Concerning Appellate Rules and Practice,* 23 F.R.D. 47 (1959). For a detailed guide to appellate procedures, see WIENER, BRIEFING AND ARGUING FEDERAL APPEALS (1961).

taxpayer should consider taking the precaution of filing his own notice of appeal [66] in order to protect his right to a cross-appeal from any portion of the trial court's decision that was adverse to him. Should the government withdraw its appeal the taxpayer would have the option to drop his cross-appeal or to proceed as an appellant.

Appeal from a Court of Claims Judgment

A losing party has no right to appellate review of a decision of the United States Court of Claims. He may only petition the Supreme Court to issue a writ of certiorari to review the judgment of the Court of Claims.[67] And the Court does not often grant the writ.[68] As stated in the Rules of the United States Supreme Court:

A review on writ of certiorari is not a matter of right, but of sound judicial discretion, and will be granted only where there are special and important reasons therefor.[69]

COURT OF CLAIMS PROCEDURE FOR WRIT OF CERTIORARI. If a losing party wishes to petition the Supreme Court for a writ of certiorari to the Court of Claims he must initially proceed in the trial tribunal. At least 20 days before the petition is due to be filed in the Supreme Court [70] the petitioner must file a written application with the Clerk of the Court of Claims stating that he intends to file a petition for a writ of certiorari and requesting a certified transcript of the record in the case.[71] Unless the petitioner designates for inclusion in the certified transcript the complete record and all the proceedings and evidence in the case, he must accompany his application with (1) a concise statement of the points on which he intends to rely and (2) a designation of the portions of the record to be incorporated into the transcript.[72] The adversary may thereafter request that additional materials be incorporated in the certified transcript.[73]

---

[66] This notice of appeal, which will have the same contents as one he would file as an appellant, must be filed within the period of the two following that terminates later:

  1. The time in which the taxpayer could have filed an initial notice of appeal
  2. Fourteen days after the government files its notice of appeal

Fed. R. Civ. P. 73(a).

[67] 28 U.S.C. § 1255. It is also possible, although even rarer than the granting of a writ of certiorari, for the Court of Claims to certify a question of law and request the Supreme Court to give binding instruction. *Ibid.*

[68] The Supreme Court granted a writ of certiorari in only three tax cases decided by the Court of Claims in the five and one-half years from January, 1961, through July, 1966, Miller, *Tax Litigation in the United States Court of Claims* 55 GEO. L.R. 454, 458 (1966–67).

[69] S. Ct. R. 19.

[70] *I.e.,* seventy days after judgment is entered by the Court of Claims. 28 U.S.C. § 2101(c).

[71] Ct. Cl. R. 71(a).

[72] *Ibid.*

[73] Ct. Cl. R. 71(b). Instead of filing formal designations, the parties may stipulate to the contents of the certified transcript. Ct. Cl. R. 71(c).

The Clerk will prepare and certify the pleadings, commissioner's report, findings of fact, conclusions of law, and judgment and opinion of the court.[74] The party requesting certification of additional parts of the record must file an original and one copy of such materials (usually the transcript of proceedings) with the Clerk for certification.[75]

SUPREME COURT PROCEDURE ON PETITION FOR WRIT OF CERTIORARI. The petition for writ of certiorari to the Court of Claims and a certified transcript of the record must be filed with the Clerk of the Supreme Court within ninety days after judgment [76] is entered in the Court of Claims.[77] The contents of the petition and the procedure to be followed in presenting it to the Court are prescribed by the Supreme Court Rules.[78]

The Supreme Court's denial of certiorari will terminate the case. If the Supreme Court decides to grant certiorari, the certified transcript of the record of Court of Claims proceedings already filed is treated as though it had been sent up in response to a formal writ.[79] Thereafter the case will be presented to the Supreme Court in accordance with its procedural rules.[80]

AMOUNT REFUNDED TO PREVAILING TAXPAYER

A judgment in favor of a taxpayer in a tax refund suit becomes "final" and subject to payment after the government has either (1) exhausted all possible appellate remedies or (2) decided not to prosecute an appeal.[81] Payment to the prevailing taxpayer is made "on settlement" by the General Accounting Office.[82] In sum, without having to file any further claim [83] the prevailing taxpayer will receive from the government a check for the amount of his overpayment as determined by the court, plus interest thereon as provided by law less any setoffs against collection to which the government may be entitled.

[74] Ct. Cl. R. 71 (d).

[75] *Ibid.*

[76] It appears that the petition will be timely if filed within ninety days after the entry of either a judgment on the right to recover or a "money judgment." See Peartree, *op. cit., supra* note 22, at 547, note 38.

[77] 28 U.S.C. § 210(c). S. Ct. R. 21, 22(3).

[78] S. Ct. R. 23, 24.

[79] S. Ct. R. 25(1).

[80] For a detailed guide to procedures in the United States Supreme Court, see STERN & GRESSMAN, SUPREME COURT PRACTICE (3d ed. 1962).

[81] 28 U.S.C. § 2414.

[82] *Ibid.* Court of Claims judgments in tax refund suits are paid pursuant to the same procedures as district court judgments. Compare 28 U.S.C. § 2517. *Cf.* Peartree, *op. cit., supra* note 22, at 546.

[83] T.D. 6219, 1956–2 CUM. BULL. 1371, relieved taxpayers from having to file claims for refund to recover on tax refund suit judgments.

The amount of the taxpayer's overpayment is determined by the court and is reflected in the judgment in the taxpayer's favor. In the following paragraphs we discuss the interest added to, and the setoffs that may be subtratcted from the overpayment of taxes in arriving at the amount of the refund check that the prevailing taxpayer will receive.

Interest on Taxpayer's Overpayment

The United States Code provides that, in a judgment in any tax refund suit, "interest shall be allowed at the rate of 6 per centum per annum upon the amount of the overpayment." [84] Interest runs from the date the taxpayer made the overpayment of taxes until a date preceding the issuance of the refund check by not more than thirty days.[85] Usually, this right to interest is stated in the judgment as simply "interest in accordance with law."

It should be noted that the taxpayer is not entitled to a compounding of interest from the date of judgment on the interest that accrued prior to that date.[86] Interest simply runs continuously from the date of overpayment, through the date of judgment, until the date statutorily provided for its termination. Interest does run, however, on any overpayment of assessed interest.[87]

It is helpful to consider the running of interest in connection with the following illustration:

Date	Event
January 31, 1966	Taxpayer pays $5,500.00, consisting of $5,000.00 in deficiency tax and $500,000 assessed interest.
January 31, 1968	Taxpayer wins refund suit, judgment entered for refund of the $5,500.00 payment plus "interest as provided by law."
August 30, 1968	Taxpayer receives refund check for $6,325.00 (interest to July 31, 1968) in satisfaction of judgment.

The amount received by the taxpayer consists of

Refund of overpayment of taxes	$5,000.00
Refund of overpayment of assessed interest	500.00
Interest for 2½ years on overpayment of tax	750.00
Interest for 2½ years on overpayment of assessed interest	75.00
Total refund check in satisfaction of judgment	$6,325.00

At any time after judgment for the taxpayer becomes final the Commissioner can stop the running of interest by tendering a check for payment of the judgment with interest to date.[88]

---

[84] 28 U.S.C. § 2411. See also IRC § 6611. For a general discussion of interest on overpayments of taxes, see 10 MERTENS, LAW OF FEDERAL INCOME TAXATION §§ 58.44–54, 58A.43–45 (Zimet rev., 1964).

[85] *Ibid.* (all three references).

[86] Whayne v. Glenn, 245 F.2d 237 (C.A.6th), *reversing per curiam on this point* 51 A.F.T.R. 1740 (W.D. Ky.). Rev. Rul. 57–271, 1957–1 CUM. BULL. 453.

[87] Treas. Reg. § 301.6611–1(c), Example (2).

[88] 28 U.S.C. § 2411.

Internal Revenue Service Offsets Against Taxpayer's Recovery

The Internal Revenue Code provides that the Commissioner of Internal Revenue,

within the applicable period of limitations may credit the amount of [any] overpayment including any interest allowed thereon, against any liability in respect of an internal revenue tax on the part of the person who made the overpayment and shall refund any balance to such person.[89]

Hence, any outstanding tax liability of a prevailing taxpayer will be used to reduce the amount refunded to him in satisfaction of his judgment. Moreover, the Commissioner of Internal Revenue may defer a refund pending determination of a tax deficiency asserted but not yet established.[90] While the Internal Revenue Service may not raise an offset based upon a non-tax debt due the government from the taxpayer, the General Accounting Office may.

Non-tax Offsets Against Taxpayer's Recovery

The government's payment in satisfaction of a judgment in a tax refund suit must be approved by the General Accounting Office.[91] This agency will, prior to approving the refund, offset against the taxpayer's recovery any claim the United States may have against the taxpayer.[92] Only after all possible offsets have been made will the balance be paid to the taxpayer. However, should the General Accounting Office invalidly offset a claim against the taxpayer's recovery, the taxpayer will be entitled to additional interest on the amount erroneously withheld from him.[93]

---

[89] IRC § 6402(a). See generally 10 Mertens, Law of Federal Income Taxation § 58A.41 (Zimet rev., 1964).

[90] United States *ex rel.* New River Co. v. Morgenthau, 105 F.2d 50 (C.A.D. C.), *cert. denied,* 308 U.S. 577; United States *ex rel.* Cole v. Helvering, 73 F.2d 852 (C.A.D.C.).

[91] 31 U.S.C. §§ 71, 227.

[92] *Ibid.* United States v. Rochelle, 363 F.2d 225, 233 (C.A.5th). 10 Mertens, Law of Federal Income Taxation § 58A.41 (Zimet rev., 1964). *Cf.* Cherry Cotton Mills v. United States, 327 U.S. 536.

[93] Rev. Rul. 57–82, 1957–1 Cum. Bull. 451.

Appendixes

EVIDENTIARY STATUTES APPLICABLE TO TAX CASES

Title 28. United States Code

Title 14. District of Columbia Code

1. EVIDENTIARY PROVISIONS OF THE UNITED STATES CODE APPLICABLE TO ALL TAX LITIGATION [1] —TITLE 28. UNITED STATES CODE—

§ 1731.　Handwriting

The admitted or proved handwriting of any person shall be admissible, for purposes of comparison, to determine genuineness of other handwriting attributed to such person.

§ 1732.　Record made in regular course of business; photographic copies

(a) In any court of the United States and in any court established by Act of Congress, any writing or record, whether in the form of an entry in a book or otherwise, made as a memorandum or record of any act, trans-action, occurrence, or event, shall be admissible as evidence of such act, transaction, occurrence, or event, if made in regular course of any business,

---

[1] Tax Ct. R. 31(a) ; Fed. R. Civ. P. 43(a) ; Ct. Cl. R. 49(a).

and if it was the regular course of such business to make such memorandum or record at the time of such act, transaction, occurrence, or event or within a reasonable time thereafter.

All other circumstances of the making of such writing or record, including lack of personal knowledge by the entrant or maker, may be shown to affect its weight, but such circumstances shall not affect its admissibility.

The term "business," as used in this section, includes business, profession, occupation, and calling of every kind.

(b) If any business, institution, member of a profession or calling, or any department or agency of government, in the regular course of business or activity has kept or recorded any memorandum, writing, entry, print, representation or combination thereof, of any act transaction, occurrence, or event, and in the regular course of business has caused any or all of the same to be recorded, copied, or reproduced by any photographic, photostatic, microfilm, micro-card, miniature photographic, or other process which accurately reproduces or forms a durable medium for so reproducing the original, the original may be destroyed in the regular course of business unless its preservation is required by law. Such reproduction, when satisfactorily identified, is as admissible in evidence as the original itself in any judicial or administrative proceeding whether the original is in existence or not an enlargement or facsimile of such reproduction is likewise admissible in evidence if the original reproduction is in existence and available for inspection under direction of court. The introduction of a reproduced record, enlargement, or facsimile does not preclude admission of the original. This subsection shall not be construed to exclude from evidence any document or copy thereof which is otherwise admissible under the rules of evidence. As amended Aug. 28, 1951, c. 351, §§ 1, 3, 65 Stat. 206; Aug. 30, 1961, Pub.L. 87–183, 75 Stat. 413.

§ 1733. Government records and papers; copies

(a) Books or records of account or minutes of proceedings of any department or agency of the United States shall be admissible to prove the act, transaction or occurrence as a memorandum of which the same were made or kept.

(b) Properly authenticated copies or transcripts of any books, records, papers or documents of any department or agency of the United States shall be admitted in evidence equally with the originals thereof.

§ 1734. Court record lost or destroyed, generally

(a) A lost or destroyed record of any proceeding in any court of the United States may be supplied on application of any interested party not at fault, by substituting a copy certified by the clerk of any court in which an authentic copy is lodged.

(b) Where a certified copy is not available, any interested person not at fault may file in such court a verified application for an order establishing the lost or destroyed record.

Every other interested person shall be served personally with a copy of the application and with notice of hearing on a day stated, not less than sixty days after service. Service may be made on any nonresident of the district anywhere within the jurisdication of the United States or in any foreign country.

Proof of service in a foreign country shall be certified by a minister or consul of the United States in such country, under his official seal.

If, after the hearing, the court is satisfied that the statements contained in the application are true, it shall enter an order reciting the substance and effect of the lost or destroyed record. Such order, subject to intervening rights of third persons, shall have the same effect as the original record.

§ 1735. Court record lost or destroyed where United States interested

(a) When the record of any case or matter in any court of the United States to which the United States is a party, is lost or destroyed, a certified copy of any official paper of a United States attorney, United States marshal or clerk or other certifying or recording officer of any such court, made pursuant to law, on file in any department or agency of the United States and relating to such case or matter, shall, on being filed in the court to which it relates, have the same effect as an original paper filed in such court. If the copy so filed discloses the date and amount of a judgment or decree and the names of the parties thereto, the court may enforce the judgment or decree as though the original record had not been lost or destroyed.

(b) Whenever the United States is interested in any lost or destroyed records or files of a court of the United States, the clerk of such court and the United States attorney for the district shall take the steps necessary to restore such records or files, under the direction of the judges of such court.

§ 1736. Congressional Journals

Extracts from the Journals of the Senate and the House of Representatives, and from the Executive Journal of the Senate when the injunction of secrecy is removed, certified by the Secretary of the Senate or the Clerk of the House of Representatives shall be received in evidence with the same effect as the originals would have.

§ 1737. Copy of officer's bond

Any person to whose custody the bond of any officer of the United States has been committed shall, on proper request and payment of the fee allowed by any Act of Congress, furnish certified copies thereof, which shall be prima facie evidence in any court of the execution, filing and contents of the bond.

§ 1738. State and Territorial statutes and judicial proceedings; full faith and credit

The Acts of the legislature of any State, Territory, or Possession of the United States, or copies thereof, shall be authenticated by affixing the seal of such State, Territory or Possession thereto.

The records and judicial proceedings of any court of any such State, Territory or Possession, or copies thereof, shall be proved or admitted in other courts within the United States and its Territories and Possessions by the attestation of the clerk and seal of the court annexed, if a seal exists, together with a certificate of a judge of the court that the said attestation is in proper form.

Such Acts, records and judicial proceedings or copies thereof, so authenticated, shall have the same full faith and credit in every court within the United States and its Territories and Possessions as they have by law or usage in the courts of such State, Territory or Possession from which they are taken.

§ 1739. State and Territorial nonjudicial records; full faith and credit

All nonjudicial records or books kept in any public office of any State, Territory, or Possession of the United States, or copies thereof, shall be proved or admitted in any court or office in any other State, Territory, or Possession by the attestation of the custodian of such records or books, and the seal of his office annexed, if there be a seal, together with a certificate of a judge of a court of record of the county, parish, or district in which each office may be kept, or of the Governor, or secretary of state, the chancellor or keeper of the great seal, of the State, Territory, or Possession that the said attestation is in due form and by the proper officers.

If the certificate is given by a judge, it shall be further authenticated by the clerk or prothonotary of the court, who shall certify, under his hand and the seal of his office, that such judge is duly commissioned and qualified; or, if given by such Governor, secretary, chancellor, or keeper of the great seal, it shall be under the great seal of the State, Territory, or Possession in which it is made.

Such records or books, or copies thereof, so authenticated, shall have the same full faith and credit in every court and office within the United States and its Territories and Possessions as they have by law or usage in the courts or offices of the State, Territory, or Possession from which they are taken.

§ 1740. Copies of consular papers

Copies of all official documents and papers in the office of any consul or vice consul of the United States, and of all official entries in the books or records of any such office, authenticated by the consul or vice consul, shall be admissible equally with the originals.

§ 1741. Foreign official documents

An official record or document of a foreign country may be evidenced by a copy, summary, or excerpt authenticated as provided in the Federal Rules of Civil Procedure. As amended Oct. 3, 1964, Pub.L. 88–619, § 5(a), 78 Stat. 996.

§ 1743. Demand on postmaster

The certificate of the Postmaster General or the General Accounting Office of the mailing to a postmaster of a statement of his account and that payment of the balance stated has not been received shall be sufficient evidence of a demand notwithstanding any allowances or credits subsequently made. A copy of such statement shall be attached to the certificate.

*   *   *   *   *

§ 1744. Copies of Patent Office documents, generally

Copies of letters patent or of any records, books, papers, or drawings belonging to the Patent Office and relating to patents, authenticated under the seal of the Patent Office and certified by the Commissioner of Patents, or by another officer of the Patent Office authorized to do so by the Commissioner, shall be admissible in evidence with the same effect as the originals.

Any person making application and paying the required fee may obtain such certified copies. As amended May 24, 1949, c. 139, § 92(c), 63 Stat. 103.

§ 1745. Copies of foreign patent documents

Copies of the specifications and drawings of foreign letters patent, or applications for foreign letters patent, and copies of excerpts of the official journals and other official publications of foreign patent offices belonging to the United States Patent Office, certified in the manner provided by section 1744 of this title are prima facie evidence of their contents and of the dates indicated on their face. Formerly § 1746. Renumbered § 1745, May, 24, 1949, c. 139, § 92(e), 63 Stat. 103, amended Oct. 3, 1964, Pub.L. 88–619, § 7(a), 78 Stat. 996.

*   *   *   *   *

§ 1781. Transmittal of letter rogatory or request

(a) The Department of State has power, directly, or through suitable channels—

(1) to receive a letter rogatory issued, or requested made, by a foreign or international tribunal, to transmit it to the tribunal, officer, or agency in the United States to whom it is addressed, and to receive and return it after execution; and

(2) to receive a letter rogatory issued, or request made, by a tribunal in the United States, to transmit it to the foreign or international tribunal, officer, or agency to whom it is addressed, and to receive and return it after execution.

(b) This section does not preclude—

(1) the transmittal of a letter rogatory or request directly from a foreign or international tribunal to the tribunal, officer, or agency in the United States to whom it is addressed and its return in the same manner; or

(2) the transmittal of a letter rogatory or request directly from a tribunal in the United States to the foreign or international tribunal, officer, or agency to whom it is addressed and its return in the same manner.

As amended Oct. 3, 1964, Pub.L. 88–619, § 8(a), 78 Stat. 996.

§ 1782. Assistance to foreign and international tribunals and to litigants before such tribunals

(a) The district court of the district in which a person resides or is found may order him to give his testimony or statement or to produce a document or other thing for use in a proceeding in a foreign or international tribunal. The order may be made pursuant to a letter rogatory issued, or request made, by a foreign or international tribunal or upon the application of any interested person and may direct that the testimony or statement be given, or the document or other thing be produced, before a person appointed by the court. By virtue of his appointment, the person appointed has power to administer any necessary oath and take the testimony or statement. The order may prescribe the practice and procedure, which may be in whole or part the practice and procedure of the foreign country or the international tribunal, for taking the testimony or statement or producing the document or other thing. To the extent that the order does not prescribe otherwise, the testimony or statement shall be taken, and the document or other thing produced, in accordance with the Federal Rules of Civil Procedure.

A person may not be compelled to give his testimony or statement or to produce a document or other thing in violation of any legally applicable privilege.

(b) This chapter does not preclude a person within the United States from voluntarily giving his testimony or statement, or producing a document or other thing, for use in a proceeding in a foreign or international tribunal before any person and in any manner acceptable to him. As amended Oct. 3, 1964, Pub.L. 88–619, § 9(a); 78 Stat. 997.

§ 1783. Subpoena of person in foreign country

(a) A court of the United States may order the issuance of a subpoena requiring the appearance as a witness before it, or before a person or body designated by it, of a national or resident of the United States who is in a foreign country, or requiring the production of a specified document or other thing by him, if the court finds that particular testimony or the production of the document or other thing by him is necessary in the interest of justice, and, in other than a criminal action or proceeding, if the court finds, in addition, that it is not possible to obtain his testimony in admissible form without his personal appearance or to obtain the production of the document or other thing in any other manner.

(b) The subpoena shall designate the time and place for the appearance or for the production of the document or other thing. Service of the subpoena and any order to to show cause, rule, judgment, or decree authorized by this section or by section 1789 of this title shall be effected in accordance with the provisions of the Federal Rules of Civil Procedure relating to service of process on a person in a foreign country. The person serving the subpoena shall tender to the person to whom the subpoena is addressed his estimated necessary travel and attendance expenses, the amount of which shall be determined by the court and stated in the order directing the issuance of the subpoena. As amended Oct. 3, 1964, Pub.L. 88–619, § 10(a), 78 Stat. 997.

§ 1784. Contempt

(a) The court of the United States which has issued a subpoena served in a foreign country may order the person who has failed to appear or who has failed to produce a document or other thing as directed therein to show cause before it at a designated time why he should not be punished for contempt.

(b) The court, in the order to show cause, may direct that any of the person's property within the United States be levied upon or seized, in the manner provided by law or court rules governing levy or seizure under execution, and held to satisfy any judgment that may be rendered against him pursuant to subsection (d) of this section if adequate security, in such amount as the court may direct in the order, be given for any damage that he might suffer should he not be found in contempt. Security under this subsection may not be required of the United States.

(c) A copy of the order to show cause shall be served on the person in accordance with section 1783 (b) of this title.

(d) On the return day of the order to show cause or any later day to which the hearing may be continued, proof shall be taken. If the person is found in contempt, the court, notwithstanding any limitation upon its power generally to punish for contempt, may fine him not more than $100,000 and direct that the fine and costs of the proceedings be satisfied by a sale of the property levied upon or seized, conducted upon the notice required and in the manner provided for sales upon execution. As amended Oct. 3, 1964, Pub.L. 88–619, § 11, 78 Stat. 998.

*   *   *   *   *

§ 1821. Per diem and mileage generally; subsistence

A witness attending in any court of the United States, or before a United States commissioner, or before any person authorized to take his deposition pursuant to any rule or order of a court of the United States, shall receive $4 for each day's attendance and for the time necessarily occupied in going to and returning from the same, and 8 cents per mile for going from and returning to his place of residence. Regardless of the mode of travel employed by the witness, computation of mileage under this section shall be made on the basis of a uniform table of distances adopted by the Attorney General. Witnesses who are not salaried employees of the Government and who are not in custody and who attend at points so far removed from their respective residence as to prohibit return thereto from day to day shall be entitled to an additional allowance of $8 per day for expenses of subsistence including the time necessarily occupied in going to and returning from the place of attendance: *Provided,* That in lieu of the mileage allowance provided for herein, witnesses who are required to travel between the Territories and possessions, or to and from the continental United States, shall be entitled to the actual expenses of travel at the lowest first-class rate available at the time of reservation for passage, by means of transportation employed: *Provided further,* That this section shall not apply to Alaska.

When a witness is detained in prison for want of security for his appearance, he shall be entitled, in addition to his subsistence, to a compensation of $1 per day. As amended May 10, 1949, c. 96, 63 Stat. 65; May 24, 1949, c. 139, § 94, 63 Stat. 103; Oct. 31, 1951, c. 655, § 51(a), 65 Stat. 727; Sept. 3, 1954, c. 1263, § 45, 68 Stat. 1242; Aug. 1, 1956, c. 826, 70 Stat. 798.

§ 1822. Competency of interested persons; share of penalties payable

Any person interested in a share of any fine, penalty or forfeiture incurred under any Act of Congress, may be examined as a witness in any proceeding for the recovery of such fine, penalty or forfeiture by any party thereto. Such examination shall not deprive the witness of his share.

§ 1823. United States officers and employees

(a) Any officer or employee of the United States or any agency thereof, summoned as a witness on behalf of the United States, shall be paid his necessary expenses incident to travel by common carrier, or, if travel is made by privately owned automobile, at a rate not to exceed that prescribed in section 4 of the Travel Expense Act of 1949, together with a per diem allowance in lieu of subsistence not to exceed the rates of per diem described in, or established pursuant to, section 3 thereof under regulations prescribed by the Attorney General. Such expenses for appearing as a witness in any case involving the activity in connection with which such person is employed shall be payable from the appropriation otherwise available for travel expenses of such officer of the department or agency concerned. In any case which does not involve its activity, any department or agency may advance or pay the travel expenses and per diem allowance of its officer or employee, summoned as a witness on behalf of the United States, and later obtain reimbursements from the department or agency properly chargeable with such witness' travel expenses.

(b) Employees of the United States or an agency thereof in active service called as witnesses on behalf of the District of Columbia in any judicial proceeding in which the government of the District of Columbia is a party, and employees of such government called as witnesses on behalf of the United States or the District of Columbia in any judicial proceeding in which the United States or the government of the District of Columbia is a party, shall not be paid witness fees, but the period of such service shall be without loss of salary or compensation and shall not be deducted from any authorized leave of absence with pay.

(c) No officer of any court of the United States located in any State, Territory or the District of Columbia shall be entitled to witness fees for attendance before any court or commissioner where he is officiating. As amended May 24, 1949, c. 139, § 95, 63 Stat. 103; Oct. 5, 1949, c. 601, 63

Stat. 704; July 7, 1952, c. 581, 66 Stat. 439; July 28, 1955, c. 424, § 3, 69 Stat. 394.

§ 1824. Mileage fees under summons as both witness and juror

No constructive or double mileage fees shall be allowed by reason of any person being summoned both as a witness and a juror.

§ 1825. Payment of fees

In any case wherein the United States or an officer or agency thereof, is a party, the United States marshal for the district shall pay all fees of witnesses on the certificate of the United States Attorney or Assistant United States Attorney, and in the proceedings before a United States Commissioner, on the certificate of such commissioner.

In all proceedings, in forma pauperis, for a writ of habeas corpus or in proceedings under section 2255 of this title, the United States marshal for the district shall pay all fees of witnesses for the party authorized to proceed in forma pauperis, on the certificate of the district judge.

Fees and mileage need not be tendered to the witness upon service of a subpoena issued in behalf of the United States or an officer or agency thereof, or upon service of a subpoena issued in behalf of a party, authorized to proceed in forma pauperis, where the payment thereof is to be made by the United States marshal as authorized in this section. As amended Sept. 2, 1965, Pub.L. 89–162, 79 Stat. 618.

2. EVIDENTIARY PROVISIONS OF THE DISTRICT OF COLUMBIA CODE APPLICABLE TO LITIGATION IN THE TAX COURT AND THE COURT OF CLAIMS [2] —TITLE 14. DISTRICT OF COLUMBIA CODE—

§ 14–101. Evidence under oath—Affirmation in lieu of oath—Perjury

(a) All evidence shall be given under oath according to the forms of the common law.

(b) A witness who has conscientious scruples against taking an oath, may, in lieu thereof, solemnly, sincerely, and truly declare and affirm. Where an application, statement, or declaration is required to be supported or verified by an oath, the affirmation is the equivalent of an oath.

(c) Whoever swears, affirms, declares, or gives testimony in any form, where an oath is authorized by law, is lawfully sworn, and is guilty of perjury in a case where he would be guilty of that crime if sworn according to

[2] Tax Ct. R. 31(a) ; Ct. Cl. R. 49(a).

the forms of the common law. (Dec. 23, 1963, 77 Stat. 517, Pub.L. 88–241, § 1.)

§ 14–102. Impeachment of own witness—Surprise

When the court is satisfied that the party producing a witness has been taken by surprise by the testimony of the witness, it may allow the party to prove, for the purpose only of affecting the credibility of the witness, that the witness has made to the party or to his attorney statements substantially variant from his sworn testimony about material facts in the cause. Before such proof is given, the circumstances of the supposed statement sufficient to designate the particular occasion must be mentioned to the witness, and he must be asked whether or not he made the statements and if so allowed to explain them. (Des. 23, 1963, 77 Stat. 518, Pub. L. 88–241, § 1.)

*   *   *   *   *

§ 14–301. Parties and other interested persons generally

Except as otherwise provided by law, a person is not incompetent to testify in a civil action or proceeding by reason of his being a party thereto or interested in the result thereof. If otherwise competent to testify, he is competent to give evidence on his own behalf and competent and compellable to give evidence on behalf of any other party to the action or proceeding. (Dec. 23, 1963, 77 Stat. 518, Pub. L. 88–241, § 1).

§ 14–302. Testimony against deceased or incapable person

(a) In a civil action against:

    (1) a person who, from any cause, is legally incapable of testifying, or

    (2) the committee, trustee, executor, administrator, heir, legatee, devisee, assignee, or other representative of a deceased person or of a person so incapable of testifying,

a judgment or decree may not be rendered in favor of the plaintiff founded on the uncorroborated testimony of the plaintiff or of the agent, servant, or employee of the plaintiff as to any transaction with, or action, declaration or admission of, the deceased or incapable person.

(b) In an action specified by subsection (a) of this section, if the plaintiff or his agent, servant, or employee, testifies as to any transaction with, or action, declaration, or admission of, the deceased or incapable person, an entry, memorandum, or declaration, oral or written, by the deceased or incapable person, made while he was capable and upon his personal knowledge, may not be excluded as hearsay. (Dec. 23, 1963, 77 Stat. 519, Pub. L. 88–241, § 1.)

§ 14–303. Testimony of deceased or incapable person

When a party, after having testified at a time while he was competent to do so, dies or becomes incapable of testifying, his testimony may be given in evidence in any trial or hearing in relation to the same subject-matter between the same parties or their legal representatives, as the case may be; and in such a case the opposite party may testify in opposition thereto. (Dec. 23, 1963, 77 Stat. 519, Pub. L. 88–241, § 1.)

§ 14–304. Death or incapacity of partner or other interested person

Where any of the original parties to a contract or transaction which is the subject of investigation are partners or other joint contractors, or jointly entitled or liable, and some of them have died or become incapable of testifying, any others with whom the contract or transaction was personally made or had, or in whose presence or with whose privity it was made or had, or admissions in relation to the same were made, are not, nor is the adverse party, incompetent to testify because some of the parties or joint contractors, or those jointly entitled or liable, have died or become incapable of testifying. (Dec. 23, 1963, 77 Stat. 519. Pub. L. 88–241, § 1.)

§ 14–305. Conviction of crime

A person is not incompetent to testify, in either civil or criminal proceedings, by reason of his having been convicted of crime. The fact of conviction may be given in evidence to affect his credibility as a witness, either upon the cross-examination of the witness or by evidence aliunde; and the party cross-examining him is not bound by his answers as to such matters. To prove the conviction of crime the certificate, under seal, of the clerk of the court wherein proceedings containing the conviction were had, stating the fact of the conviction and for what cause, is sufficient. (Dec. 23, 1963, 77 Stat. 519, Pub. L. 88–241, § 1.)

§ 14–306. Husband and wife

(a) In civil and criminal proceedings, a husband or his wife is competent but not compellable to testify for or against the other.

(b) In civil and criminal proceedings, a husband or his wife is not competent to testify as to any confidential communications made by one to the other during the marriage. (Dec. 23, 1963, 77 Stat. 519, Pub. L. 88–241, § 1.)

§ 14–307. Physicians

(a) In the courts of the District of Columbia a physician or surgeon may not be permitted, without the consent of the person afflicted, or of his legal representative, to disclose any information, confidential in its nature, that he has acquired in attending a patient in a professional capacity and that was necessary to enable him to act in that capacity, whether the informtion was obtained from the patient or from his family or from the person or persons in charge of him.

(b) This section does not apply to:

(1) evidence in criminal cases where the accused is charged with causing the death of, or inflicting injuries upon, a human being, and disclosure is required in the interests of public justice; or

(2) evidence relating to the mental competency or sanity of an accused in criminal trials where the accused raises the defense of insanity, or in the pretrial or posttrial proceedings involving a criminal case where a question arises concerning the mental condition of an accused or convicted person.

(Dec. 23, 1963, 77 Stat. 519, Pub. L. 88–241, § 1.)

*   *   *   *   *

§ 14–309. Clergy

A priest, clergyman, rabbi, or other duly licensed, ordained, or consecrated minister of a religion authorized to perform a marriage ceremony in the District of Columbia or duly accredited practitioner of Christian Science may not be examined in any civil or criminal proceedings in the courts of the District of Columbia with respect to any—

(1) confession, or communication, made to him, in his professional capacity in the course of discipline enjoined by the church or other religious body to which he belongs, without the consent of the person making the confession or communication; or

(2) communication made to him, in his professional capacity in the course of giving religious or spiritual advice, without the consent of the person seeking the advice; or

(3) communication made to him, in his professional capacity, by either spouse, in connection with an effort to reconcile estranged spouses, without the consent of the spouse making the communication.

(Dec. 23, 1963, 77 Stat. 520, Pub. L. 88–241, § 1.)

*   *   *   *   *

§ 14–501. Proof of record

An exemplification of a record under the hand of the keeper of the record, and the seal of the court or office where the record is made, is good and sufficient evidence to prove a record made or entered in any State, territory, commonwealth or possession of the United States. The certificate of the person purporting to be the keeper of the record, accompanied by the seal, is prima facie evidence of that fact. (Dec. 23, 1963, 77 Stat. 520, Pub. L. 88—241, § 1.)

§ 14–502. Records of deeds, instruments, and wills

Under the hands of the keeper of a record and the seal of the court or office in which the record was made:

(1) a copy of the record of a deed, or other written instrument not of a testamentary character, where the laws of the State, territory, commonwealth, possession or country where it was recorded require such a record, and that has been recorded agreeably to those laws; and

(2) a copy of a will that the laws require to be admitted to probate and record by judicial decree, and of the decree of the court admitting the will to probate and record—

are good and sufficient prima facie evidence to prove the existence and contents of the deed, will, or other written instrument, and that it was executed as it purports to have been executed.
(Dec. 23, 1963, 77 Stat. 521, Pub. L. 88–241, § 1.)

§ 14–503. Record of will as prima facie evidence of contents and execution

A record of a will or codicil recorded in the office of the Register of Wills of the District of Columbia, that has been admitted to probate by the United States District Court for the District of Columbia, or by the former orphans' court of the District, or a record of the transcript of the record and probate of a will or codicil elsewhere, or of a certified copy thereof filed in the office of the Register of Wills, is prima facie evidence of the contents and due execution of the will or codicil. (Dec. 23, 1963, 77 Stat. 521, Pub. L. 88–24, § 1.)

*   *   *   *   *

§ 14–506. Certified mail return receipts as prima facie evidence of delivery

Return receipts for the delivery of certified mail which is utilized under any provision of law shall be received in the courts as prima facie evidence of delivery to the same extent as return receipts for registered mail. (Dec. 23, 1963, 77 Stat. 521, Pub. L. 88–241, § 1.)

§ 14–507. Other methods of proof

This chapter does not prevent the proof of records or other documents by any method authorized by other laws or rules of court. (Dec. 23, 1963, 77 Stat. 521, Pub. L. 88–241, § 1.)

*   *   *   *   *

§ 14–701. Presumption of death

If a person leaves his domicile without a known intention of changing it, and does not return or is not heard from for seven years from the time of his so leaving, he shall be presumed to be dead in any case where his death is in question, unless proof is made that he was alive within that time. (Dec. 23, 1963, 77 Stat. 522, Pub. L. 88–241, § 1.)

§ 14–702. Person presumed dead found living

If the person presumed to be dead pursuant to section 14–701 is found to be living, a person injured by the presumption shall be restored to the rights of which he was deprived by reason of the presumption. (Dec. 23, 1963, 77 Stat. 522, Pub. L. 88–241, § 1.)

B

REQUIRED NUMBER OF COPIES AND METHODS OF DUPLICATION OF FORMAL DOCUMENTS IN THE COURT OF CLAIMS [1]

REQUIRED NUMBER OF COPIES AND METHODS OF DUPLICATION

Description	Copies and Method	Rule	Page †
Petition	25 printed	82(a)	95
Answer	25 printed	82(b)	96
Reply	25 printed	82(b)	96
Motions, dispositive:			
Dismiss petition, to	16 mimeographed*	82(d)	97
Judgment on pleadings, for	16 mimeographed*	82(d)	97
Request for review, for	16 mimeographed*	82(d)	97
Summary judgment, for	16 mimeographed*	82(d)	97
Motions, procedural:			
Call and discovery, for	6 typewritten	82(c)	96
Response to	2 typewritten	39(b)	43
All others, for	4 typewritten	82(c, i)	96, 98
Request for review, for	4 typewritten	82(c)	96
Motions for rehearing, etc.	7 typewritten	82(e)	97
Briefs and exceptions to commissioner's report	25 printed	82(g, h)	98
Certiorari, request for record in	4 typewritten	71(a) 82(i)	86 98
Depositions:			
Interrogatories	4 typewritten	32(a)	35
Notice of	4 typewritten	31(a)	32
Objection to	4 typewritten	35(d)	39
Findings and brief, request for	4 typewritten	82(f)	98
Miscellaneous	4 typewritten	82(i)	98
Transfers from District Court	25 printed	93(b)	109

* May be typewritten if not more than 5 pages in length.

† Page references refer to pages of the Official Rules of the Court of Claims.

NOTES: See Rule 81 as to form and size. Above requirements relative to number of copies apply in two-party cases. Additional copies will be required where additional parties represented by other counsel are present. See Rules 79–82 as to requirements.

[1] Index, Official Rules of the United States Court of Claims (April 1, 1964 rev.).

C

PRACTICE FORMS

1 Administrative Practice Forms

2 Tax Court Forms

1. ADMINISTRATIVE PRACTICE FORMS

ADMINISTRATIVE PRACTICE FORM 1. GENERAL POWER OF ATTORNEY
(FORM 2848)

FORM **2848**
(Rev. September 1967)
U.S. Treasury Department
Internal Revenue Service

Power of Attorney
(See Separate Instructions)

Name, address including ZIP code, and identifying number of taxpayer(s)

KAREN RISA - 060-29-0288
48 West 12th Street
New York, N. Y. 10011

hereby appoints (name, address including ZIP code, and telephone number of appointee(s))

FANNIE COOPER, ESQ.
605 Third Avenue
New York, N. Y. 10016
986-6833

as attorney(s)-in-fact to represent the taxpayer(s) before any office of the Internal Revenue Service with respect to (specify Internal Revenue tax matters and years or periods):

Income Tax 1966
Income Tax 1967

Said attorney(s)-in-fact (or either of them) shall, subject to revocation, have authority to receive confidential information and full power to perform on behalf of the taxpayer(s) the following acts with respect to the above tax matters:

(Strike through any of the following which are not granted.)

To receive, but not to endorse and collect, checks in payment of any refund of Internal Revenue taxes, penalties, or interest.
To execute waivers (including offers of waivers) of restrictions on assessment or collection of deficiencies in tax and waivers of notice of disallowance of a claim for credit or refund.
To execute consents extending the statutory period for assessment or collection of taxes.
To execute closing agreements under section 7121 of the Internal Revenue Code.
To delegate authority or to substitute another representative.
Other acts (specify) ....NONE..

Copies of notices and other written communications addressed to the taxpayer(s) in proceedings involving the above matters should be sent to (Name, address including ZIP code, and telephone number):

KAREN RISA:, 48 West 12th Street, New York, N. Y. 10011 -- WA 9 -6695

and

FANNIE COOPER, ESQ., 605 Third Avenue, New York, N. Y. 10016 -- 986-6833

This power of attorney revokes all prior powers of attorney and tax information authorizations on file with the same Internal Revenue office with respect to the same matters and years or periods covered by this instrument, except the following:

....
(Specify to whom granted, date, and address including ZIP code, or refer to attached copies of prior powers and authorizations)

Signature of or for taxpayer(s)

If signed by a corporate officer, partner, or fiduciary on behalf of the taxpayer, I certify that I have the authority to execute this power of attorney on behalf of the taxpayer.

/S/ KAREN RISA   12-2-1967

  (Signature)   (Title, if applicable)   (Date)

  (Signature)   (Title, if applicable)   (Date)

FORM **2848** (Rev. 9–67)

ADMINISTRATIVE PRACTICE FORM 1 (*Concluded*)

If the power of attorney is granted to an attorney, certified public accountant, or enrolled agent, this declaration must be completed.

I declare that I am not currently under suspension or disbarment from practice before the Internal Revenue Service. and that:

I am a member in good standing of the bar of the highest court of the jurisdiction indicated below; or

~~I am duly qualified to practice as a certified public accountant in the jurisdiction indicated below; or~~

~~I am enrolled as an agent pursuant to the requirements of Treasury Department Circular No. 230.~~

Designation (Attorney, C.P.A., or Agent)	Jurisdiction (State, etc.) or Enrollment Card Number	Signature	Date
Attorney	New York	/S/ FANNIE COOPER	12-4-67

If the power of attorney is granted to a person other than an attorney, certified public accountant, or enrolled agent, it must be witnessed or notarized below.

The person(s) signing as or for the taxpayer(s):   (Check and complete one.)

☐ is/are known to and signed in the presence of the two disinterested witnesses whose signatures appear here:

_____   _____
(Signature of Witness)   (Date)

_____   _____
(Signature of Witness)   (Date)

☐ appeared this day before a notary public and acknowledged this power of attorney as his/her/their voluntary act and deed.

_____   _____   NOTARIAL SEAL
(Signature of Notary)   (Date)   (If required)

U.S. GOVERNMENT PRINTING OFFICE : 1967—O-238-932

FORM **2848** (Rev. 9–67)

ADMINISTRATIVE PRACTICE FORM 2. LIMITED POWER OF ATTORNEY
(FORM 2848–A)

Form **2848–D** (September 1967) U.S. Treasury Department Internal Revenue Service	**Authorization and Declaration** (See Separate Instructions)

Part I—TAX INFORMATION AUTHORIZATION

Name, address including ZIP code, and identifying number of taxpayer(s)

Mr. William Ferris
220 Highland Road
Forest Hills, New York, 10087

hereby authorizes (Name, address including ZIP code, and telephone number)

John Jones
28 Broadway
New York City, N. Y., 10009

344-6950

to receive from or inspect confidential tax information in any office of the Internal Revenue Service with respect to (Specify Internal Revenue tax matters and years or periods):

Income Tax-1966
Income Tax-1967

Copies of notices and other written communications addressed to the taxpayer(s) in proceedings involving the above matters should be sent to (Name, address including ZIP code, and telephone number):

Mr. William Ferris
220 Highland Road, Forest Hills, N. Y., 10087   BO 3 7854

and John Jones
28 Broadway, New York City, N. Y., 10009   344-6950

This tax information authorization revokes all prior tax information authorizations on file with the same Internal Revenue office with respect to the same matters and years or periods covered by this instrument, except the following:

....
(Specify to whom granted, date, and address including ZIP code, or refer to attached copies of prior authorizations)

~~This tax information authorization revokes all prior tax information authorizations on file with the same Internal Revenue office with respect to the same matters and years or periods covered by this instrument, except the following:~~

....
(Specify to whom granted, date, and address including ZIP code)

Signature of or for taxpayer(s)

If signed by a corporate officer, partner, or fiduciary on behalf of the taxpayer, I certify that I have the authority to execute this tax information authorization on behalf of the taxpayer.

/s/   William Ferris   12-1-67
           (Signature)   (Title, if applicable)   (Date)

....
           (Signature)   (Title, if applicable)   (Date)

                                              Form **2848–D** (9–67)

ADMINISTRATIVE PRACTICE FORM 2 (*Concluded*)

Part II—DECLARATION BY ATTORNEY, CERTIFIED PUBLIC ACCOUNTANT, OR ENROLLED AGENT

Name, address including ZIP code, and telephone number of representative(s) (not required if stated in Part I)

I declare that I am not currently under suspension or disbarment from practice before the Internal Revenue Service, that I am a member in good standing of the bar of the highest court of the jurisdiction indicated below; or

~~that I am duly qualified to practice as a certified public accountant in the jurisdiction indicated below; or~~

~~that I am enrolled as an agent pursuant to the requirements of the Treasury Department Circular No. 230.~~

And that I am authorized to represent ...... Mr. William Ferris ....

Designation (Attorney, C.P.A. or Agent)	Jurisdiction (State, etc.) or Enrollment Card Number	Signature	Date
Attorney	New York	/s/ John Jones	12/2/67

U.S. GOVERNMENT PRINTING OFFICE ; 1967—O-216-915   Form **2848—D** (9–67)

ADMINISTRATIVE PRACTICE FORM 3. ADMINISTRATIVE SUMMONS

FORM **2039** (REV. SEPT. 1961)	U. S. TREASURY DEPARTMENT - INTERNAL REVENUE SERVICE # SUMMONS

In the matter of the tax liability of

Monroe Pharmacy Corporation
1567 Monroe Street
Baltimore, Maryland

Internal Revenue District of   Maryland

PERIOD(S)
Fiscal years ended June 30, 19--, 19-- and 19--.

THE COMMISSIONER OF INTERNAL REVENUE

TO: Stanley G. Chupnick, C,P.A.

AT: One Charles Center, Baltimore, Maryland

GREETING:

You are hereby summoned and required to appear before ___Francis O'Brien___ ,
an officer of the Internal Revenue Service, to give testimony relating to the tax liability and/or the
collection of the tax liability of the above named person for the period(s) designated and to bring with
you and produce for examination the following books, records, and papers at the time and place hereinafter set forth:

All the following in your custody, possession or control:

(1) All books, records, correspondence and memoranda of communications

relating or pertaining to the receipts and expenditures of the Monroe

Pharmacy Corporation for the above-stated fiscal years.

(2) All your workpapers relating or pertaining to the corporate income tax

liability of the Monroe Pharmacy Corporation for the above-stated fiscal

years.

Place and time for appearance:

At_____ Room 1313, Federal Building, Post Office Square, Baltimore, Maryland _____

_____ on the _____ twenty-fifth _____ day of _____ August _____

19--, at ___two___ o'clock ___P.___ M.

**Failure to comply with this summons will render you liable to proceedings in the district court
of the United States or before a United States Commissioner to enforce obedience to the requirements of this summons, and to punish default or disobedience.**

Issued under authority of Section 7602, Internal Revenue Code of 1954

this _____ eighteenth _____ day of _____ August _____ , 19--

ORIGINAL

SIGNATURE:...........................   Francis O'Brien

TITLE :...........................   Internal Revenue Agent

ADMINISTRATIVE PRACTICE FORM 3 (*Concluded*)

CERTIFICATE OF SERVICE OF SUMMONS
(Pursuant to Section 7603, Internal Revenue Code of 1954)

I hereby certify that I served the summons on the reverse hereof

DATE SUMMONS SERVED *(Day, month, year)*	TIME

HOW SUM- MONS WAS SERVED *(Check one)*

☐ I handed an attested copy thereof to the person to whom it was directed,

☐ I left an attested copy thereof with the following person at the last and usual place of abode of the person to whom it is directed,

SIGNATURE	TITLE

Sec. 7603. Service of Summons. — A summons issued under section 7602 shall be served by the Secretary or his delegate, by an attested copy delivered in hand to the person to whom it is directed, or left at his last and usual place of abode; and the certificate of service signed by the person serving the summons shall be evidence of the facts it states on the hearing of an application for the enforcement of the summons. When the summons requires the production of books, papers, records, or other data, it shall be sufficient if such books, papers, records, or other data are described with reasonable certainty.

FORM **2039** (REV. 9-61)

ADMINISTRATIVE PRACTICE FORM 4. 30-DAY LETTER (FORM L–191A)

U. S. TREASURY DEPARTMENT
INTERNAL REVENUE SERVICE
DISTRICT DIRECTOR
P. O. BOX 3100
NEW YORK, N. Y. 10015

IN REPLY REFER TO
Form L-191A

January 16, 1967

Ricar Corporation
3540 Fifth Avenue
New York, New York 10017

Gentlemen:

Enclosed is your copy of an examination report explaining adjustments to your tax liability for the years shown. We have carefully reviewed this report.

If you accept the findings, please sign and return the enclosed Waiver Form. If additional tax is due, you may prefer to make payment at this time. See paragraph 1 of the enclosed instructions for details.

If you do not accept the findings, we recommend that you request a conference to discuss the proposed adjustments with a member of our Conference Staff. Most cases considered at a conference are brought to a satisfactory conclusion.

If you do not desire a District conference, you may request a hearing with the Appellate Division of the Regional Commissioner's Office.

Your request for either a District conference or an Appellate hearing must be accompanied by a written protest. If a hearing is requested, we will forward your protest to the Appellate Division. That Division will contact you to arrange a hearing. See paragraphs 2, 3 and 4 of the enclosed instructions for details concerning a District conference, preparation of a protest and representation.

If you do not respond within 30 days from the date of this letter, we will process your case on the basis of the adjustments shown in the examination report.

Important: Please send all communications concerning your case to the above address using the symbols in the upper right corner of this letter.

Very truly yours,

District Director

Enclosures - 3:
Examination report
Waiver Form
Instructions - Unagreed Income, Estate, or Gift Tax Cases

FORM L-191A (8-64)

U. S. TREASURY DEPARTMENT
INTERNAL REVENUE SERVICE
DISTRICT DIRECTOR
P. O. BOX 3100
NEW YORK, N. Y. 10015

IN REPLY REFER TO
Form L-191B

January 17, 1967

Mr. Richard Crane and
Mrs. Ellen Crane
89 Lexington Avenue
New York, New York 10054

Dear Mr. and Mrs. Crane:

Enclosed is your copy of an examination report explaining adjustments to your tax liability for the years shown. We have carefully reviewed this report.

If you accept the findings, please sign and return the enclosed Waiver Form. If additional tax is due, you may prefer to make payment at this time. See paragraph 1 of the enclosed instructions for details.

If you do not accept the findings, you may request a hearing with the Appellate Division of the Regional Commissioner's Office. We recommend this course of action in your case.

However, if you prefer, you may request a conference to discuss the proposed adjustments with a member of our Conference Staff.

Your request for either an Appellate hearing or a District conference must be accompanied by a written protest. If a hearing is requested, we will forward your protest to the Appellate Division. That Division will contact you to arrange a hearing. See paragraphs 2, 3 and 4 of the enclosed instructions for details concerning a District conference, preparation of a protest and representation.

If you do not respond within 30 days from the date of this letter, we will process your case on the basis of the adjustments shown in the examination report.

Important: Please send all communications concerning your case to the above address using the symbols in the upper right corner of this letter.

Very truly yours,

District Director

Enclosures - 3:
Examination report
Waiver Form
Instructions - Unagreed Income, Estate, or Gift Tax Cases

FORM L-191B (8-64)

ADMINISTRATIVE PRACTICE FORM 6. INSTRUCTIONS—UNAGREED INCOME, ESTATE, OR GIFT TAX CASES (PUB. NO. 5, REV. 8–64)

INSTRUCTIONS—*Unagreed Income, Estate, or Gift Tax Cases*

Reasonable people can and do sometimes disagree on tax issues. For this reason the Internal Revenue Service maintains a system of appeals. This system has been remarkably successful in that a great majority of the disputed tax cases are settled without trial.

1. If, However, You Now Agree and Desire to Pay Without Waiting for a Bill—Your remittance should be made payable to the INTERNAL REVENUE SERVICE and should include interest on the additional tax (but not interest on penalties, if any) at 6% a year from the due date of the return to the date of payment. Please do not send cash—use a check or money order.

2. District Conference—Your first right of appeal is a District conference; more than half of all the cases considered at conferences are brought to a satisfactory conclusion at this point. If you request, we will arrange for a District conference at a mutually convenient time and place. You may appear personally or be represented by an attorney or agent, and bring anyone to the conference *as a witness* who has knowledge of the facts and can furnish evidence to support your position. To avoid the time and expense of further conferences, you or your representative should come prepared to discuss all the issues at one conference. If agreement is not reached at a conference, you may request consideration of your case by the Appellate Division of the Regional Commissioner's Office.

3. How to Prepare a Protest—The protest must be filed in duplicate and should contain:

A. Your name and address (individuals should show the residence address and corporations the address of the principal office or place of business);

B. The date and symbols on the letter which transmitted the proposed adjustments or findings covered in the protest;

C. The taxable year (s) involved;

D. A statement that you desire a District conference; or,

E. If a District conference is not desired, a statement that you desire consideration of your case by the Appellate Division of the Regional Commissioner's Office;

F. An itemized schedule of the adjustments or findings to which you take exception;

G. A statement of the facts upon which you rely concerning each contested issue where the facts are in dispute. Such statement and all evidence submitted, except that of a supplementary or incidental character, must be declared true under penalties of perjury. This requirement may be satisfied by adding to the protest the following statement signed by the taxpayer (by an authorized officer in the case of a corporation):

"Under the penalties of perjury, I declare that the statement of facts presented in this protest and in any accompanying schedules and statements has been examined by me and to the best of my knowledge and belief is true, correct, and complete."

H. A statement outlining the law or other authority upon which you rely (generally, this statement is not required in Offer in Compromise cases); and

I. If the protest is prepared or filed by your attorney or agent, it should contain, in addition to the declaration required in G above, a statement signed by such attorney or agent indicating:

1. Whether he prepared the protest.

2. Whether he knows of his own knowledge that the information contained therein is true.

4. If You Plan to Be Represented by an Attorney or Agent—Your representative must qualify to practice before the Internal Revenue Service either by enrollment or under the provisions of section 10.7 of Treasury Department Circular No. 230, (Revised). In addition, if you are not present at a conference which your qualified representative attends, a true copy of a power of attorney, specifically authorizing him to act for you, must be filed for each taxable year on or before the date of the conference. .

5. Further Right of Appeal—If agreement is not reached at a District conference, or if such a conference is not desired, you may request consideration of your case by the Appellate Division of the Regional Commissioner's Office. If agreement cannot be reached with the Appellate Division[1] and your case involves a deficiency, a statutory notice of deficiency will be sent to you; you are given 90 days[2] within which to file a petition with the Tax Court of the United States. A statutory notice of deficiency is a final statement of intent by the Internal Revenue Service to adjust your tax liability.

If a petition is filed and docketed, the Appellate Division will give you an opportunity to settle your case without the necessity of a trial before the Tax Court. If a settlement cannot be reached, your case will be scheduled for trial before the Tax Court.

Appeal from the decision of the Tax Court may be made to the appropriate U. S. Court of Appeals.

If an overassessment only is proposed, the procedure is the same as above except that your appellate rights do not extend beyond the Appellate Division unless the case involves a claim for refund disallowed in whole or in part. In such case, you may file suit with the appropriate United States District Court or the United States Court of Claims.

IMPORTANT: If you wish to exercise your rights of appeal in the Internal Revenue Service, you must, within 30 days[3] from the date of the letter which enclosed these instructions, use one of the options of appeal presented in that letter.

---

[1] In *Offer in Compromise* cases, your rights of appeal do not extend beyond the Appellate Division of the Regional Commissioner's Office.

[2] 150 Days if addressed to a person outside the United States.

[3] 60 Days if addressed to a person outside the United States.

U. S. TREASURY DEPARTMENT—INTERNAL REVENUE SERVICE   Publication No. 5 (Rev. 8–64)

U. S. GOVERNMENT PRINTING OFFICE : 1964 O - 108-034

ADMINISTRATIVE PRACTICE FORM 7. AGREEMENT AS TO FINAL DETERMINATION OF TAX LIABILITY (FORM 866)

FORM 866
(Rev. Nov. 1964)

.ORIGINAL
NATIONAL OFFICE COPY

U.S. TREASURY DEPARTMENT—Internal Revenue Service

AGREEMENT AS TO FINAL DETERMINATION OF TAX LIABILITY

THIS AGREEMENT, made in triplicate under and in pursuance of Section 7121 of the Internal Revenue Code of 1954, by and between ___ Mr. John Jones and Mrs. Jane Jones   1421 East 15th Street ___
(Name   of taxpayer   and address   )
___ Brooklyn, New York ___
and the Assistant Commissioner of Internal Revenue;

WHEREAS, there has been a determination of the tax liability of said taxpayer   in respect of internal revenue tax   , exclusive of any penalty or interest properly applicable thereto as provided by law, in the sum   and for the taxable period   indicated below:

Period	Character of Tax	Chapter Number and Subchapter Letter of I.R.C.	Total Amount of Tax
Cal. Yr. 1963	Income	1A, I.R.C. (1954)	$2,980.29

NOW, THIS AGREEMENT WITNESSETH, that the said taxpayer   and said Assistant Commissioner of Internal Revenue hereby mutually agree that such liability so determined shall be final and conclusive subject, however, to the provisions of Sections 1311 to 1315, inclusive, of the Internal Revenue Code of 1954.

IN WITNESS WHEREOF, the above parties have subscribed their names to these presents in triplicate.

Signed this ___ Fifteenth ___ day of ___ February ___ 19 67.

[SEAL]

(Do not write in this space)

/s/ John Jones
(See instructions)   Taxpayer.

/s/ Jane Jones

By ___

___
Assistant Commissioner of Internal Revenue.

___
(Date)

(See reverse)

ADMINISTRATIVE PRACTICE FORM 7 (*Concluded*)

INSTRUCTIONS

(1) The agreement must be executed and filed in triplicate; (2) the original and copies of the agreement must be identical; (3) the name of the taxpayer must be stated accurately; (4) the agreement may relate to one or more years; (5) the liability must be segregated as to taxable periods and character of taxes, together with the Chapter Number and Subchapter Letter of the Internal Revenue Code of 1939 or 1954, under which each tax covered was imposed, as illustrated in the following examples:

Period	Character of Tax	Chapter Number and Subchapter Letter of I.R.C.	Total Amount of Tax
F.Y. ended June 30, 1946	Income	1B, I.R.C.	$9,000.00
F.Y. ended June 30, 1946	Excess-profits	2E, I.R.C.	5,000.00
F.Y. ended June 30, 1946	Dec. Val. Excess-profits	2B, I.R.C.	200.00
F.Y. ended June 30, 1946	Surtax, Sec. 500	2A, I.R.C.	6,000.00
Cal. Yr. 1950	Income	1B, I.R.C. (1939)	6,000.00
Cal. Yr. 1950	Excess-profits	1D, I.R.C.	3,000.00
Cal. Yr. 1950	Surtax, Sec. 500	2A, I.R.C.	4,000.00
F.Y. ended July 31, 1951	Income	1B, I.R.C.	8,000.00
F.Y. ended July 31, 1951	Excess-profits	1D, I.R.C.	1,000.00
F.Y. ended July 31, 1951	Surtax, Sec. 500	2A, I.R.C.	6,000.00
Cal. Yr. 1954	Income	1A, I.R.C. (1954)	3,000.00
Cal. Yr. 1954	Personal Holding Co.	1G, I.R.C.	6,000.00

If the agreement is executed by an attorney or agent on behalf of the taxpayer, the original or a true copy of the power of attorney authorizing such agent or attorney to sign the agreement on behalf of the taxpayer must accompany the agreement. If the agreement is executed with respect to a year for which a joint income tax return was filed by a husband and wife, it should be signed by both spouses, except that one spouse may sign as agent for the other, provided the original or a true copy of the document specifically authorizing such agent to act in that capacity has been submitted.

If the agreement is signed by the fiduciary on behalf of a decedent or estate, an attested copy of the letters testamentary or the order of the court vesting such person with authority so to act, together with a certificate to the effect that such authority remains in full force and effect, should be submitted with the agreement. If signed by a trustee, there should be submitted a certified copy of the trust instrument or a certified copy of extracts from that instrument showing:

(1) Date of instrument.

(2) That it is or is not of record in any court.

(3) The beneficiaries.

(4) The appointment of the trustee, the authority granted, and such other information as may be necessary to show that such authority extends to Federal tax matters.

(5) That the trust has not been terminated, and that the trustee appointed therein is still acting.

Where the taxpayer is a corporation, the agreement must be dated and signed with the corporate name, followed by the signature and title of an authorized officer, or officers, or by the signature of an authorized attorney or agent. It is not necessary that the corporate seal be affixed.

U.S. GOVERNMENT PRINTING OFFICE : 1964—O-748-620   FORM 866 (Rev. 11-64)

ADMINISTRATIVE PRACTICE FORM 8. CLOSING AGREEMENT AS TO FINAL DETERMINATION COVERING SPECIFIC MATTERS (FORM 906)

FORM 906
(Rev. June 1966)

U.S. TREASURY DEPARTMENT—Internal Revenue Service

ORIGINAL

CLOSING AGREEMENT AS TO FINAL DETERMINATION COVERING SPECIFIC MATTERS

THIS AGREEMENT, made in triplicate under and in pursuance of Section 7121 of the Internal Revenue Code of 1954 by and

between _____ James H. Baroff, 12345 Academy Way, Rockville, Maryland _____
(Name   of taxpayer   and address   from which return was or will be filed)

and the Commissioner of Internal Revenue:

WHEREAS.

(1) On June 15, 1967, James Harley Baroff made a gift of 30,000 shares of Applied Mathematics, Inc. common stock to Angela Baroff,

(2) On June 15, 1967 the mean traded price of Applied Mathematics, Inc. common stock on the New York Stock Exchange was $30.00 per share, and

(3) On June 15, 1967, there were outstanding 345,000 shares of Applied Mathematics, Inc. common stock.

It is agreed that James H. Baroff should, for gift tax purposes,

be allowed a blockage discount on the value of Applied Mathe-

matics, Inc. stock equal to $1.25 per share with respect to the

gift of June 15, ·1967.

WHEREAS, this determination is hereby agreed to by said taxpayer

NOW, THIS AGREEMENT WITNESSETH, that said taxpayer   and said Commissioner of Internal Revenue hereby mutually agree that the matter   so determined shall be final and conclusive (subject, however, to the provisions of Sections 1311 to 1315, inclusive, of the Internal Revenue Code of 1954), except that if this agreement relates to any taxable period ending subsequent to the date of this agreement, it is subject to any change in or modification of the law enacted subsequent to said date and applicable to such taxable period.

IN WITNESS WHEREOF, the above parties have subscribed their names to these presents in triplicate.

[SEAL]

Signed this _____ 30th _____ day of _____ August _____, 19 68

(Do not write in this space)

/s/ James H. Baroff
(See instructions)   Taxpayer.

By _____

(Title)
Commissioner of Internal Revenue

By _____ Robert Bachedler

Reg. Comm.
(Title)

Date _____

(See reverse)

ADMINISTRATIVE PRACTICE FORM 8 (*Concluded*)

INSTRUCTIONS

(1) The agreement must be executed and filed in triplicate; (2) the original and copies of the agreement must be identical; (3) the agreement may relate to one or more years; and (4) the determination clause should contain an accurate and concise statement of the determination made, preceded by one or more WHEREAS clauses containing the premises supporting, and information identifying the matters covered in, the determination.

If the agreement is executed by an attorney or agent on behalf of the taxpayer, the original or a true copy of the power of attorney authorizing such agent or attorney to sign the agreement on behalf of the taxpayer must accompany the agreement. If the agreement is executed with respect to a year for which a joint income tax return was filed by a husband and wife, it should be signed by both spouses, except that one spouse may sign as agent for the other, provided the original or a true copy of the document specifically authorizing such agent to act in that capacity has been submitted.

If the agreement is signed by the fiduciary on behalf of a decedent or estate, an attested copy of the letters testamentary or the order of the court vesting such person with authority so to act, together with a certificate to the effect that such authority remains in full force and effect, should be submitted with the agreement. If signed by a trustee, there should be submitted a certified copy of the trust instrument or a certified copy of extracts from that instrument showing:

(1) Date of instrument.

(2) That it is or is not of record in any court.

(3) The beneficiaries.

(4) The appointment of the trustee, the authority granted, and such other information as may be necessary to show that such authority extends to Federal tax matters.

(5) That the trust has not been terminated, and that the trustee appointed therein is still acting.

Where the taxpayer is a corporation, the agreement must be dated and signed with the corporate name, followed by the signature and title of an authorized officer, or officers, or by the signature of an authorized attorney or agent. It is not necessary that the corporate seal be affixed.

U.S. GOVERNMENT PRINTING OFFICE : 1966—O-222-244   FORM 906 (Rev. 6-66)

ADMINISTRATIVE PRACTICE FORM 9. STATEMENT ACCOMPANYING
90-DAY LETTER

STATEMENT

Excelsior Construction Company, Inc.
1970 Third Avenue
New York, New York, 10034

INCOME TAX

Taxable Year Ended	Deficiency
December 31, 1965	$13,309.34
December 31, 1966	18,385.39
Total	$31,694.73

It is held that you were availed of for the purpose of avoiding income tax with respect to your shareholders by permitting earnings and profits in the respective amounts of $26,199.21 and $35,793.71 for the taxable years 1965 and 1966 to accumulated instead of being distributed.

Taxable Year Ended December 31, 1965

ADJUSTMENT TO INCOME

Taxable income as disclosed by return	$14,1367.9
Unallowable deductions and additional income:	
(a) Compensation and Pension Plan Contribution	16,431.93
Taxable income as corrected	$30,568.72

EXPLANATION OF ADJUSTMENT

(a) The deduction of $17,831.93 claimed in each of the taxable years 1965 and 1966 for compensation of Arnold Johnson and pension plan contributions on his account has been disallowed to the extent of $16,431.93 because it has not been established that the amount in excess of $1,400.00 constitutes an ordinary and necessary business expense incurred during the taxable year and is reasonable in amount.

COMPUTATION OF ACCUMULATED EARNINGS TAX

Taxable income per return	$14,136.79	
Add: Special deductions (Section 535 (b)(3))	31.06	
Income adjustments herein	16,431.93	$30,599.78
Less: Federal income tax per return	$ 4,229.64	
Long term capital gain on return less tax applicable thereto	170.93	4,400.57
Accumulated taxable income as corrected		$26,199.21
Accumulated earnings tax $26,199.21 at 27½%		$ 7,204.78

COMPUTATION OF ALTERNATIVE TAX

Taxable income as corrected	$30,568.72
Less: Net long-term capital gain reduced by net short-term capital loss	227.91
Balance	$30,340.81
Tax on $30,340.81 — 52% less $5,500.00	$10,277.22
Partial tax	$10,277.22
Add: 25% of $227.91	56.98
Alternative tax	$10,334.20

COMPUTATION OF INCOME TAX

Taxable income as corrected	$30,568.72
Tax at 52% less $5,500.00	$19,395.73
Alternative tax, the lesser	$10,334.20
Plus: Accumulated earnings tax	7,204.78
Income tax liability as corrected	$17,538.98
Income tax liability disclosed by return	4,229.64
Deficiency	$13,309.34

ADJUSTMENT TO INCOME

Taxable income as disclosed by return	$28,835.62
Unallowable deductions and additional income:	
(a) Compensation and Pension Plan Contribution	16,431.93
Taxable income as corrected	$45,267.55

EXPLANATION OF ADJUSTMENT

(a) See explanation for similar item with respect to the taxable year ended December 31, 1965.

COMPUTATION OF ACCUMULATED EARNINGS TAX

Taxable income per return	$28,835.62	
Add: Special deduction (Section 535(b)(3))	27.59	
Income adjustment herein	16,431.93	$45,295.14
Less: Federal income tax per return	$ 9,494.52	
Long term capital gain on return		
less tax applicable thereto	6.91	9,501.43
Accumulated taxable income as corrected		$35,793.71
Accumulated earnings tax $35,793.71 at 27½%		$ 9,843.27

ADMINISTRATIVE PRACTICE FORM 9 (*Concluded*)

COMPUTATION OF ALTERNATIVE TAX

Taxable income as corrected	$45,267.55
Less: Net long-term capital gain reduced by net short-term capital loss	9.22
Balance	$45,258.33
Tax on $45,258.33 — 52% less $5,500.00	$18,034.33
Partial tax	$18,034.33
Add: 25% of $9.22	2.31
Alternative tax	$18,036.64

COMPUTATION OF INCOME TAX

Taxable income as corrected	$45,267.55
Tax at 52% less $5,500.00	$18,039.13
Alternative tax, the lesser	$18,036.64
Plus: Accumulated earnings tax	9,843.27
Income tax liability as corrected	$27,879.91
Income tax liability disclosed by return	9,494.52
Deficiency	$18,385.39

ADMINISTRATIVE PRACTICE FORM 10. 90-DAY LETTER (FORM L-21) AND
ACCOMPANYING STATEMENT

U. S. TREASURY DEPARTMENT
INTERNAL REVENUE SERVICE
DISTRICT DIRECTOR
P. O. BOX 6901
CLEVELAND, OHIO, 44101

IN REPLY REFER TO
Form L-21

August 13, 1966

Code 430: 90–D

Mr. Stephen Mitchell
600 East 59th Street
New York, New York 10034

Dear Mr. Mitchell:

	TAXABLE YEAR ENDED	DEFICIENCY
	12/31/60 Tax	$5,819.47
	Fraud Penalty Section 6653 (b)	$2,927.45

In accordance with the provisions of existing internal revenue laws, notice is given that the determination of your income tax liability discloses a deficiency or deficiencies in the amounts and for the taxable years shown above. The enclosed statement shows the computation of the deficiency or deficiencies.

If you do not intend to contest this determination in the Tax Court of the United States, please sign the enclosed Waiver, Form 870, and return it promptly in the enclosed envelope. This will permit early assessment of the deficiency or deficiencies and limit accumulation of interest.

If you do not sign and return the Waiver, the deficiency or deficiencies will be assessed for collection, as required by law, upon the expiration of 90 days (150 days if you are outside the States of the Union and the District of Columbia) from the date of this letter, unless within that time you contest this determination in the Tax Court of the United States by filing a petition with that Court in accordance with its rules. A copy of the rules of the Court may be obtained by writing to the Clerk, Tax Court of the United States, Box 70, Washington, D. C. 20044.

Very truly yours,

Commissioner

By

District Director

Enclosures - 3:
Statement
Waiver, Form 870
Return envelope

FORM L-21 (REV. 12-65)

ADMINISTRATIVE PRACTICE FORM 10 (*Continued*)

STATEMENT

Mr. Stephen Mitchell
600 East 59th Street
New York, New York 10034

INCOME TAX

Taxable Year Ended	Deficiency	Penalty Section 6653(b)
December 31, 1960	$5,819.47	$2,927.45

The 50% penalty has been asserted for the year 1960 under the provisions of section 6653(b) of the Internal Revenue Code of 1954.

A copy of this letter and statement has been mailed to your representative, Mr. Edward Roth, 169 Broadway, New York, New York 10006, in accordance with the authority contained in the power of attorney executed by you.

ADJUSTMENT TO INCOME

Taxable income as disclosed by return		$12,192.15
Unallowable deductions and additional income:		
(a) Dividend income	$12,000.00	
(b) Depreciation	80.00	
(c) Medical deduction	362.40	12,442.40
Taxable income as corrected		$24,634.55

EXPLANATION OF ADJUSTMENTS

(a) It has been determined that you received additional dividend income in 1960 of $12,000.00 as follows:

Funds diverted from XYZ Engineering Company, Inc. in 1960	$10,000.00
Disallowed expenses of XYZ Engineering Company, Inc. in 1960 which inured to your personal benefit	2,000.00
Total	$12,000.00

(b) It has been determined and previously agreed that the depreciation deduction relating to the horse, Light Foot, claimed on the return was subject to an adjustment computed as follows:

Cost of Light Foot—1959	$4,000.00
Section 179 depreciation allowed in 1959	800.00
Balance	$3,200.00
Allowable depreciation—10% of $3,200.00	$ 320.00
Depreciation claimed	400.00
Adjustment	$ 80.00

ADMINISTRATIVE PRACTICE FORM 10 (*Concluded*)

(c) The deduction for medical expenses is decreased in the amount of $362.40 (3% of $12,080.00) by reason of the increase in adjusted gross income occasioned by adjustments (a) and (b), supra.

COMPUTATION OF ALTERNATIVE TAX

Taxable income as corrected	$24,634.55
Less: 50% of excess of total net long-term capital gain over total net short-term capital loss	1,298.55
Balance	$23,336.00
Partial tax	$ 9,168.24
Add: 50% of $1,298.55	649.28
Alternative tax	$ 9,817.52

COMPUTATION OF INCOME TAX

Taxable income as corrected		$24,634.55
Combined normal tax and surtax—single person		$ 9,934.38
Alternative tax, if applicable		$ 9,817.52
Less: Dividends received credit 4% of $16,375.00		655.00
Income tax liability as corrected		$ 9,162.52
Income tax liability disclosed by return	$3,307.62	
Add: Additional assessment,		
Account No. D 43933, July 6, 1962	35.43	3,343.05
Deficiency		$ 5,819.47
Section 6653(b) penalty—50% of $5,854.90		$ 2,927.45

FORM **656** (REV. 7-57)	U. S. TREASURY DEPARTMENT - INTERNAL REVENUE SERVICE **OFFER IN COMPROMISE**	To be filed in duplicate with District Director

NAME(S) AND ADDRESS OF TAXPAYER(S)

William and Mary Burke
1234 Erie Lane
Hazleton, Pennsylvania

FOR USE OF DISTRICT DIRECTOR

INDICATE WHETHER OFFER IS - *(Check applicable box)*
☐ CASH *(Paid in full)*
☒ DEFERRED PAYMENT

SERIAL NUMBER

(Cashier's stamp)

AMOUNT PAID $

TO COMMISSIONER OF INTERNAL REVENUE
Through the District Director
DATE

1. This offer is submitted by the undersigned to compromise a liability resulting from alleged violation(s) of law or failure to pay an internal revenue liability as follows: Unpaid personal income tax liability as follows;

(State specifically the violation of law involved and/or the kind and total amount of
Calendar year 19**, income tax $xxxxxx, assessed interest $xxxx

unpaid tax, ad valorem penalty and any assessed interest by periods and each period involved)
Calendar year 19**, income tax $xxxxxx, assessed interest $xxxx;

2. The total sum of $ 10,000.00 paid in full or payable on the deferred payment basis as follows 1/:

(See footnote 1/ on reverse)

$5,000.00 deposited with this offer, $500.00 to be paid on each of the following dates: March 15, 19**, June 15, 19**, September 15, 19**, December 15, 19**, and on the anniversary of each of these dates until the compromised liability plus interest is satisfied in full.

together with interest at the rate of 6 percent per annum on the deferred payments, if any, from the date the offer is accepted until the respective payments are made in full, is hereby tendered voluntarily with the request that it be accepted in compromise of the above described liability (plus any accrued interest on the liability covered by this offer) of the taxpayer aforesaid.

3. In making this offer, and as a part consideration thereof, the proponent agrees (a) that all payments and other credits heretofore made to the account(s) for the period(s) covered by this offer shall be retained by the United States; and (b) that any and all amounts of money to which the proponent may be entitled under the internal revenue laws, due through overpayments of any tax or other liability, including interest and penalties, made for periods ending prior to or during the calendar year in which this offer is accepted, as are not in excess of the difference between the liability sought to be compromised and the amount herein offered, shall also be retained by the United States. Any such refund received after the filing of this offer will be returned immediately to the office of the District Director.

4. It is further agreed that upon notice of the acceptance of this offer in compromise of the liability aforesaid, the proponent shall have no right to contest in court or otherwise the amount of the liability sought to be compromised; and that in the event this offer is a deferred payment offer and there is a default in payment of any installment of principal or interest due under the terms of the offer, the Commissioner of Internal Revenue (or his delegate), at his option, (a) may proceed immediately by suit to collect the entire unpaid balance of the offer, or (b) may proceed immediately by suit to collect as liquidated damages an amount equal to the liability sought to be compromised, minus any deposits already received under the terms of the offer in compromise, with interest on the unpaid balance at the rate of 6 percent per annum from the date of default, or (c) may disregard the amount of such offer and apply all amounts previously deposited thereunder against the amount of the liability sought to be compromised and may, without further notice of any kind, assess and/or collect by levy or suit the balance of such liability, the right of appeal to the Tax Court of the United States and the restrictions against assessment and/or collection being hereby waived.

5. The following facts and reasons are submitted as grounds for acceptance of this offer: As shown on our financial statement (Form 433) we are unable to satisfy the full amount of the liability. Any more rapid rate of payment could not be made.

(If space is insufficient attach supporting statement)

6. The undersigned proponent waives the benefit of any statute of limitations applicable to the assessment and/or collection of the liability sought to be compromised, and agrees to the suspension of the running of the statutory period of limitations on assessment and/or collection for the period during which this offer is pending, or the period during which any installment remains unpaid, and for 1 year thereafter.

7. It is understood that this offer will be considered and acted upon in due course and that it does not afford relief from the liability sought to be compromised unless and until it is actually accepted in writing by the Commissioner or his duly authorized representative, and the terms of the offer have been fully complied with.

Waiver of statutory period of limitations is hereby accepted by the undersigned:	I declare under the penalties of perjury that this offer (including any accompanying schedules and statements) has been examined by me and to the best of my knowledge and belief is true and correct.
DISTRICT DIRECTOR OF INTERNAL REVENUE *(Enter name)*	SIGNATURE(S) OF PROPONENT(S) /s/ William Burke /s/ Mary Burke
BY *(Signature and title)* DATE	

U. S. GOVERNMENT PRINTING OFFICE: 1958 O - 108499 - B

C · 22

2. TAX COURT FORMS

TAX COURT FORM 1.   PETITION (INDIVIDUALS, HUSBAND AND WIFE)

TAX COURT OF THE UNITED STATES

JOHN DOE

                              and

JANE DOE,

                    Petitioners,   Docket No.

                        v.

COMMSSIONER OF INTERNAL REVENUE,
                    Respondent.

PETITION

The above-named petitioners hereby petition for a redetermination of the deficiency set forth by the Commissioner of Internal Revenue in his notice of deficiency (correspondence symbols Ap :NY :AB :XYZ) dated October 29, 1966, and, as a basis of their case, allege as follows:

1. The petitioners, John Doe and Jane Doe, are individuals and are married to each other. The petitioners reside at 60 West 19th Street, New York, New York. The petitioners filed joint tax returns (for individuals) for the calendar years 1960 and 1961, the years in controversy, with the District Director of Internal Revenue at 484 Lexington Avenue, New York, New York.

2. The statutory notice (a copy of which is attached and marked Exhibit A) was mailed to the petitioners on October 29, 1966.

3. (a) The deficiency as determined by the Commissioner is in respect of income tax for the calendar year 1960 in the sum of $22,417.18, of which sum the amount of $21,878.69 is in dispute.

3. (b) The overassessment as determined by the Commissioner is in respect of income tax for the calendar year 1961 in the sum of $13,037.88, of which the entire amount is in dispute.

4. The determination of tax or overassessment set forth in the statutory notice is based upon the following errors:

(a) In determining the taxable income of the petitioners for the year 1960, the Commissioner erroneously included, in the determination of the said taxable income, realized capital gain in the total amount of $85,518.00 (before capital gain deductions), that sum representing the capital gain that would have been realized upon the liquidation of Doe Realty Corp. had Jane Doe been a shareholder at the time of liquidation. The Commissioner erroneously contends that Jane Doe was a shareholder at the time of liquidation of Doe Realty Corp.

(b) In determining the taxable income of the petitioners for the year 1960, the Commissioner erroneously eliminated from taxable income the sum reported by the taxpayers as a capital gain (before capital gain deduction) the amount realized, on the installment method, from the sale of the stock of the Doe Realty Corp. by Jane Doe.

(c) In determining the taxable income of the petitioners for the year 1960, the Commissioner erroneously disallowed deductible interest expense in the total amount of $13,298.31.

*　　　*　　　*　　　*　　　*

5. The facts upon which the petitioners rely as the basis of this case are as follows:

(a) The taxpayers, John Doe and Jane Doe, are husband and wife, and filed joint tax returns for the calendar years 1960 and 1961, and later filed amended tax returns for 1960 and 1961.

(b) On November 8, 1955, a Certificate of Incorporation of the Doe Realty Corp. was filed with the Department of State of the State of New York.

(c) On December 31, 1955, Jane Doe was issued one (1) share of the capital stock of the aforesaid corporation, represented by certificate number "1".

(d) Jane Doe subscribed to the aforesaid one share at a price of $15,000.00, which sum was paid to the corporation.

(e) On January 6, 1960, Jane Doe sold her one share, representing a 100% interest in the stock of the Doe Realty Corp., to Eleanor Ricks.

(f) Jane Doe sold her stock interest, as aforesaid, at a gross selling price of $68,000.00.

(g) The purchase price was payable as follows: the sum of $5,000.00 in the year of sale (1960), and the balance of $63,000.00 represented by a series of ten (10) promissory notes, each in the amount of $6,300.00, the first note payable on January 6, 1961, and the remaining notes annually thereafter, with the final note due January 6, 1970.

(h) The ten (10) notes above referred to bore interest at the rate of 4½% per annum.

(i) Taxpayer has elected, in proper fashion, to report the gain on the installment basis and so reported such gain on the installment basis.

(j) Taxpayers have a daughter, born Eleanor Doe, who was and is married to one Edward Ricks.

*　　　*　　　*　　　*　　　*

WHEREFORE, the petitioners pray that this Court may hear the case and determine that there is only a deficiency of $538.49 due from the petitioners for the year 1960, and

WHEREFORE, the petitioners further pray that this Court determine that there is no overassessment as respects the petitioners for the year 1961, and

Tax Court Form 1 (*Continued*)

WHEREFORE, the petitioners further pray that this Court determine that there is a deficiency of $578.18 due from the petitioners for the year 1961, and

WHEREFORE, the petitioners further pray that this Court may grant such other and further relief as may seem just and proper to this Honorable Court.

DATED, January 15, 1967

s/   (John Jones)
Counsel for Petitioners
Jones & Smith
1 Park Avenue
New York, New York

STATE OF NEW YORK }
COUNTY OF NEW YORK } SS.:

JOHN DOE, being duly sworn, says that he is one of the petitioners above named; that he has read the foregoing Petition, or had the same read to him, and is familiar with the statements contained therein, and that the statements contained therein are true, except those stated to be upon information and belief, and that those he believes to be true.

s/   (Jane Doe)
JOHN DOE

Subscribed and sworn to before me
this 15th day of January 1967.

STATE OF NEW YORK }
COUNTY OF NEW YORK } SS.:

JANE DOE, being duly sworn, says she is one of the petitioners above named; that she has read the foregoing Petition, or had the same read to her, and is familiar with the statements contained therein, and that the statements conained therein are true, except those stated to be upon informaion and belief, and that those she believes to be true.

s/   (Jane Doe)
JANE DOE

Subscribed and sworn to before me
this 15th day of January 1967.

Tax Court Form 1 *(Concluded)*

U. S. TREASURY DEPARTMENT
INTERNAL REVENUE SERVICE
DISTRICT DIRECTOR
P. O. BOX 6901
CLEVELAND, OHIO **44101**

IN REPLY REFER TO
Form L-50
Code 430; 90–D

OCT 29 1965

Mr. John Doe and
Mrs. Jane Doe
(Husband and Wife)
40 East 9th Street
New York, New York

Dear Mr. and Mrs. Doe:

In accordance with the provisions of existing internal revenue
laws, notice is hereby given that the determination of your income tax liability discloses a deficiency for the taxable year
ended December 31, 1960, in the amount of $22,417.18 and an
overassessment for the taxable year ended December 31, 1961,
in the amount of $13,037.88. The attached statement shows the
computation of the deficiency and overassessment.

If you do not intend to contest this determination in the Tax Court of the United States, please
sign the enclosed Waiver and return it promptly in the enclosed envelope. This will permit early
assessment of the deficiency or deficiencies and limit accumulation of interest.

If you do not sign and return the Waiver, the deficiency or deficiencies will be assessed for collection, as required by law, upon the expiration of 90 days (150 days if you are outside the States
of the Union and the District of Columbia) from the date of this letter, unless within that time you
contest this determination in the Tax Court of the United States by filing a petition with that
Court in accordance with its rules. A copy of the rules of the Court may be obtained by writing to
the Clerk, Tax Court of the United States, Box 70, Washington, D. C. 20044.

Very truly yours,

Commissioner

By

District Director

Enclosures - 3:
Statement
Waiver
Return envelope
Form 443

(Exhibit A – Page A)

FORM L-50 (REV. 12-65)

TAX COURT FORM 2. ANSWER (USUAL FORM)

TAX COURT OF THE UNITED STATES

JOHN DOE AND JANE DOE,
              Petitioners,

                   v.   } Docket No.

COMMISSIONER OF INTERNAL REVENUE,
              Respondent.

ANSWER

THE RESPONDENT, in answer to the petition filed in the above-entitled case, admits, denies and alleges as follows:

1. Admits the allegations in the first and second sentences of paragraph 1 of the petition. Denies the remaining allegations of paragraph 1 of the petition. Alleges that the petitioners filed original and amended joint income tax returns for 1960 and for 1961 with the District Director, Manhattan, New York.

2. Admits the allegations of paragraph 2 of the petition.

3. (a) Admits that the Commissioner determined a deficiency in income tax for the year 1960 in the sum of $22,417.18. Further admits that the entire amount is not in dispute. Denies the remaining allegations of subparagraph (a) of paragraph 3 of the petition.

(b) Denies the allegations of subparagraph (b) of paragraph 3 of the petition.

4. (a) to (f), inclusive. Denies the allegations of error of subparagraphs (a) to (f), inclusive, of paragraph 4 of the petition.

5. (a) Admits the allegations of subparagraphs (a) of paragraph 5 of the petition.

(b) Denies the allegations of subparagraph (b) of paragraph 5 of the petition.

(c) Admits that Jane Doe was issued one (1) share of the capital stock of Doe Realty Corp., represented by certificate number "1". Denies the remaining allegations of subparagraph (c) of paragraph 5 of the petition.

(d) Admits that Jane Doe paid $15,000.00 for the aforesaid share. Denies the remaining allegations of subparagraph (d) of paragraph 5 of the petition.

(e) to (i), inclusive. Denies the allegations of subparagraphs (e) to (i), inclusive, of paragraph 5 of the petition.

(j) and (k) Admits the allegations of subparagraphs (j) and (k] of paragraph 5 of the petition.

(1) to (x), inclusive. Denies the allegations of subparagraphs (1) to (x), inclusive, of paragraph 5 of the petition.

TAX COURT FORM 2 (*Concluded*)

6. Denies generally each and every allegation of the petition not hereinbefore specifically admitted, qualified or denied.

WHEREFORE, it is prayed that the deficiency determined by the respondent be in all respects approved.

A. G. REED
Chief Counsel
Internal Revenue Service

OF COUNSEL:
  M. E. HOVING
    Regional Counsel
  P. H. FERRIS
    Attorney
  Internal Revenue Service
  30 Church Street
  New York, New York 10007

TAX COURT FORM 3. PETITION (CORPORATION, NOTICE OF DEFICIENCY ANNEXED)

TAX COURT OF THE UNITED STATES

ABC, INC.,

Petitioner,

v.

COMMISSIONER OF INTERNAL REVENUE,

Respondent.

Docket No.

PETITION

The above-named petitioner hereby petitions for a redetermination of the deficiency set forth by the Commissioner of Internal Revenue in the notice of deficiency (Symbols AU:X:90Y) dated March 7, 1966, and as a basis for its case alleges as follows:

(1) The petitioner is a corporation which was organized on April 3, 1938 under the laws of the State of New York, having a business address at 12 West 44th Street, New York, New York. The return for the period here involved was filed with the District Director of Internal Revenue, Lower Manhattan, New York, New York.

(2) The notice of deficiency (a copy of which is attached and marked as Exhibit A) was mailed to the petitioner on March 7, 1966.

(3) The deficiency, as determined by the Commissioner, is in income tax for the calendar year 1959 in the amount of $36,380.33, all of which is in dispute.

(4) The assessment and collection of the deficiency in tax set forth in the notice of deficiency is barred by application of Section 6501(a) of the Internal Revenue Code of 1954 in that:

(a) A Federal Income Tax Return (Form 1120) was filed by ABC, Inc. for the calendar year 1959 on or about March 13, 1960;

(b) No agreement or waiver extending the statutory period for the assessment of tax for the year 1959 was executed by or on behalf of ABC, Inc.; and

(c) More than three years had expired after said return for the year 1959 was filed by ABC, Inc. when the notice of deficiency, dated March 7, 1966, was mailed to the petitioner herein.

(5) The Federal Income Tax Return filed by the petitioner for the calendar year 1959 was examined by an Agent of the Internal Revenue Service during the year 1961. The Revenue Agent's Report, dated November 4, 1961, proposed no change in the income tax as reported and paid by the petitioner for the year 1959.

Tax Court Form 3 (*Continued*)

(6) The petitioner has not requested a re-examination of its Federal Income Tax Return for the calendar year 1959 and, to its knowledge, neither the Secretary of the Treasury nor his delegate, after investigation, has notified the petitioner in writing that an additional inspection of its 1959 return is necessary.

(7) Alternatively, the determination of tax set forth in the notice of deficiency is based upon the following further error:

The respondent erred in his determination that The XYZ Company, a partnership, is not a valid partnership for income tax purposes and that the net income of $97,513.53 of the partnership for the taxable period ending January 31, 1959, is additional net income of ABC, Inc., a corporation.

(8) The facts on which the petitioner relies as a basis of this proceeding under paragraph 7 are as follows:

(a) ABC, Inc., was incorporated on April 3, 1938, pursuant to the laws of the State of New York.

(b) At all times material herein, all the issued and outstanding stock of ABC, Inc., was held by Arnold Sanders, and he was the President and operating head of the corporation.

(c) From its incorporation, ABC, Inc. has engaged in the business of originating and importing on order ceramic gift and tableware from Japan.

(d) The XYZ Company is a partnership formed in 1952, the partners being Arnold Sanders, the Trust Estate for John Sanders and the Trust Estate for James Sanders, each partner having a one-third interest in the partnership.

(e) The trustees for both the Trust Estate for John Sanders and the Trust Estate for James Sanders are Henrietta Sanders and N. P. Kant.

(f) The two Trust Estate partners have during times material herein contributed substantial amounts of capital to The XYZ Company partnership, and Arnold Sanders has contributed substantial services and capital to the partnership.

(g) From its formation. The XYZ Company has engaged in the business of buying ceramic goods imported from Japan and selling them to retail stores and wholesale jobbers in the United States.

(h) During the year 1959, ABC, Inc. sold ceramic goods imported into the United States to The XYZ Company, and placed orders for ceramic goods in Japan on a commission basis for the MNO Company, Ltd., a Canadian corporation.

(i) The dealings between ABC, Inc. and The XYZ Company were at all times at arm's length, and the prices paid by The XYZ Company to ABC, Inc. for imported ceramic goods represented fair market value.

(j) The petitioner herein has never owned any interest, either directly or indirectly, in the MNO Company, Ltd.

(k) ABC, Inc. and The XYZ Company each have valid business reasons for existence, are owned and controlled by different interests, are operated separately, engage in separate and different businesses, have different employees, maintain separate books and records and have separate lines of credit.

TAX COURT FORM 3 (*Continued*)

WHEREFORE, the petitioner prays that the Court may hear the case and determine that no deficiency is due in this proceeding for the year 1959 pursuant to the considerations set forth above, and that this Court may grant such other and further relief as it may deem proper under the circumstances.

s/   (Fannie Cooper)
FANNIE COOPER
605 Third Avenue
New York City, New York

COUNSEL FOR PETITIONER

STATE OF NEW YORK   } ss.:
COUNTY OF NEW YORK }

ARNOLD SANDERS, being duly sworn, says that he is the President of ABC, INC., petitioner above named, and that he is duly authorized to verify the foregoing petition; that he has read the foregoing petition and is familiar with the statements contained therein and that the statements contained therein are true.

s/ (Arnold Sanders)
ARNOLD SANDERS

Subscribed and Sworn to
before me this 25th day
of May, 1966.

s/   (Helen Shine)
Notary Public in and for
said County and State

My Commission expires:

HELEN SHINE
Notary Public, State of New York
No.
Qualified in Queens County
Term Expires March 30, 1968

TAX COURT FORM 3 (*Continued*)

U. S. TREASURY DEPARTMENT
INTERNAL REVENUE SERVICE
DISTRICT DIRECTOR
P. O. BOX 6901
CLEVELAND, OHIO 44101

IN REPLY REFER TO
Form L-21

Mar 7 1966

Code 430: 90–D

ABC, Inc.
10 Fifth Avenue
New York, New York

TAXABLE YEAR ENDED	DEFICIENCY
Dec. 31, 1959	
Tax	$36,380.33

In accordance with the provisions of existing internal revenue laws, notice is given that the determination of your income tax liability discloses a deficiency or deficiencies in the amounts and for the taxable years shown above. The enclosed statement shows the computation of the deficiency or deficiencies.

If you do not intend to contest this determination in the Tax Court of the United States, please sign the enclosed Waiver, Form 870, and return it promptly in the enclosed envelope. This will permit early assessment of the deficiency or deficiencies and limit accumulation of interest.

If you do not sign and return the Waiver, the deficiency or deficiencies will be assessed for collection, as required by law, upon the expiration of 90 days (150 days if you are outside the States of the Union and the District of Columbia) from the date of this letter, unless within that time you contest this determination in the Tax Court of the United States by filing a petition with that Court in accordance with its rules. A copy of the rules of the Court may be obtained by writing to the Clerk, Tax Court of the United States, Box 70, Washington, D. C. 20044.

Very truly yours,

Commissioner

By

District Director

Enclosures - 3:
Statement
Waiver, Form 870
Return envelope

(Exhibit A)

FORM L-21 (REV. 12-65)

TAX COURT FORM 3 (*Concluded*)

STATEMENT

ABC, Inc.
10 Fifth Avenue
New York, New York

TAX LIABILITY FOR THE TAXABLE YEAR ENDED
December 31, 1959

Income Tax

Liability	Assessed	Deficiency
$42,071.20	$5,690.87	$36,380.33

ADJUSTMENTS TO TAXABLE INCOME

Taxable income disclosed in the return	$18,969.55
Additional income and unallowable deductions:	
(a) Redistribution of The XYZ Company income	97,513.53
Total	$116,483.08
Non-taxable income and additional deductions:	
(b) Officer's salary	25,000.00
Taxable income as adjusted	$91,483.08

EXPLANATION OF ADJUSTMENTS

(a) It has been determined that the partnership, The XYZ Company, is not a valid partnership for income tax purposes and the net income of $97,513.53 of the partnership for the taxable period ending January 31, 1959, is held to be additional net taxable income of the corporation, ABC, Inc.

(b) It has been determined that a deduction for the additional salary of $25,000.00 to Arnold Sanders, the controlling shareholder of ABC, Inc. is ordinary, necessary, and allowable.

COMPUTATION OF THE TAX

Taxable income as adjusted	$91,483.08
Income tax liability	42,071.20
Liability disclosed in the return	5,690.87
Deficiency in income tax	$36,380.33

TAX COURT FORM 4. ANSWER (WITH AFFIRMATIVE ALLEGATIONS)

TAX COURT OF THE UNITED STATES

ABC, INC.,

     Petitioner,

      v.   Docket No.

COMMISSIONER OF INTERNAL REVENUE,

     Respondent.

ANSWER

THE RESPONDENT, in answer to the petition filed in the above-entitled case, admits, denies, avers and alleges as follows:

(1) Admits that the petitioner is a corporation organized on April 3, 1938, under the laws of the State of New York. That the return for the period here involved was filed with the District Director of Internal Revenue, Lower Manhattan, New York, New York. Denies the remaining allegations contained in paragraph (1) of the petition. Avers that the address shown on the income tax return as filed and as shown on the statutory notice of deficiency mailed to this petitioner was 10 Fifth Avenue, New York 1, N. Y.

(2) and (3). Admits the allegations contained in paragraphs (2) and (3) of the petition.

(4)(a), (b) and (c). Denies the allegations of error contained in subparagraphs (a), (b) and (c) of paragraph (4) of the petition.

(5) Admits the allegations contained in paragraph (5) of the petition.

(6) Denies the allegations contained in paragraph (6) of the petition.

(7) Denies the allegations of error contained in paragraph (7) of the petition.

(8)(a). Admits the allegations contained in subparagraph (a) of paragraph (8) of the petition.

(b) Admits that all of the issued and outstanding stock of ABC, Inc. was held by Arnold Sanders and he was its president. Denies the remaining allegations contained in subparagraph (b) of paragraph (8) of the petition.

(c) Denies for lack of information the allegations contained in subparagraph (c) of paragraph (8) of the petition.

(d) Denies the allegations contained in subparagraph (d) of paragraph (8) of the petition.

(e) Denies for lack of information the allegations contained in subparagraph (e) of paragraph (8) of the petition.

(f), (g), (h) and (i). Denies the allegations contained in subparagraphs (f), (g), (h) and (i), of paragraph (8) of the petition.

(j) Denies for lack of information the allegations contained in subparagraph (j) of paragraph (8) of the petition.

Tax Court Form 4 (*Concluded*)

(k) Denies the allegations contained in subparagraph (k) of paragraph (8) of the petition.

(9) Denies generally and specifically each and every allegation contained in the petition not heretofore admitted, qualified or denied.

(10) Further answering the petition, respondent alleges affirmatively as follows:

(11) That pursuant to section 6501 (a) of the Internal Revenue Code of 1954, the period of limitation upon the assessment and collection of the deficiency herein asserted against the petitioner for the calendar year 1959 has not expired. In support thereof, the respondent relies upon the following:

(a) The statutory notice of deficiency from which the present appeal was filed was sent to the petitioner by mail on March 7, 1966.

(b) The petitioner filed its Federal income tax return for the calendar year 1959 with the District Director of Internal Revenue, Lower Manhattan, on or about March 15, 1960.

(c) The amount of gross income reported in petitioner's income tax return for the calendar year 1959 was $582,709.49.

(d) The amount which was omitted from gross income for said year but which was properly includible therein was $778,870.47.

(e) In said return for the year 1959 petitioner omitted from gross income an amount properly includible therein which was in excess of 25% of the amount of gross income stated in the return.

(f) The statutory notice of deficiency covering the calendar year 1959 was mailed to the petitioner within six years after the return for said year was filed.

WHEREFORE, it is prayed that the deficiency determined by the respondent be in all respects approved.

C. C. CALDWELL
Chief Counsel
Internal Revenue Service.

OF COUNSEL
    W. X. ADLER
    Regional Counsel
    RICHARD D. CONWAY
    Attorney
Internal Revenue Service
30 Church Street
New York 7, New York.

TAX COURT FORM 5. REPLY TO ANSWER

TAX COURT OF THE UNITED STATES

ABC, INC.,

Petitioner,

v.

COMMISSIONER OF INTERNAL REVENUE,

Respondent.

Docket No. 696

REPLY

Petitioner in reply to the answer filed in the above-entitled case, admits and denies as follows:

1. In reply to the last sentence of paragraph 1 of the Commissioner's answer, admits that the address shown on the petitioner's income tax return as filed and as shown on the notice of deficiency mailed to the petitioner was 10 Fifth Avenue, New York 1, N. Y., and in all other respects denies the affirmative allegations contained in paragraph 1 of the answer.

*   *   *   *   *

11. Denies that the period of limitation upon the assessment or collection of the alleged deficiency herein asserted against the petitioner for the calendar year 1959 has not expired or that said deficiency may lawfully be assessed or collected, and in further reply to paragraph 11 answers as follows:

(a) Admits that the notice of deficiency from which the present appeal is filed was sent to the petitioner by mail on March 7, 1966, and in all other respects denies the allegations contained in paragraph 11(a) of the answer.

(b) Admits that the petitioner filed its Federal income tax return for the calendar year 1959, with the District Director of Internal Revenue, Lower Manhattan, on or about March 13, 1960, and in all other respects denies the allegations contained in paragraph 11 (b) of the answer.

(c) Denies the allegations in paragraph 11(c) of the answer.

(d) Denies the allegations in paragraph 11(d) of the answer.

(e) Denies the allegations in paragraph 11(e) of the answer.

(f) Admits that the notice of deficiency covering the calendar year 1959 was mailed to the petitioner on March 7, 1966 and within six years after the return for said year was filed, and in all other respects denies the allegations contained in paragraph 11(f) of the answer.

WHEREFORE, the petitioner prays that this Court may hear the case and determine that no deficiency is due in this proceeding for the year 1959 pursuant to the considerations set forth above and in the petition, and that this Court may grant such other and further relief as it may deem proper under the circumstances.

s/   (Fannie Cooper)
FANNIE COOPER

TAX COURT FORM 6. PETITION (WITH CLAIM FOR OVERPAYMENT)

TAX COURT OF THE UNITED STATES

JOHN SMITH AND JOAN SMITH,
     Petitioners,

     v.   Docket No.

COMMISSIONER OF INTERNAL REVENUE,
     Respondent.

PETITION

The above-named petitioners hereby petition for a redetermination of the deficiency set forth by the Commissioner of Internal Revenue in his notice of deficiency dated August 30, 1966, and determination that petitioner has made overpayment of income tax in the year here included, and as a basis for this proceeding alleges as follows:

1. The petitioners are John Smith and Joan Smith who reside at 15 West 24th Street, New York, New York. The joint return of the petitioners for the period here involved was filed with the District Director of Internal Revenue, Lower Manhattan, New York, New York.

2. The notice of deficiency (a copy of which is attached and marked Exhibit A) was mailed to the petitioners on August 30, 1966.

3. The deficiency, as determined by the Commissioner, is for income taxes of the petitioners for the calendar year 1960 in the amount of $70,341.81, substantially all of which amount is in dispute.

4. The determination of taxes set forth in said notice of deficiency is based upon the following errors:

(a) The respondent erred in his determination that petitioners realized additional taxable income from capital gain in the amount of $125,000.

(b) The respondent erred in his determination that petitioners were not entitled to deduct losses in the amount of $20,359.72 sustained by petitioners in 1960 from the worthlessness of stock owned by them.

(c) The respondent erred in his determination that petitioners received a constructive dividend of $4,854.79 in 1960.

(d) The respondent erred in his determination that petitioners' medical expense deduction should be reduced in accordance with respondent's determination increasing the adjusted gross income of the petitioners.

5. The facts upon which the petitioners rely as the basis of the error alleged in paragraph 4(a) are as follows:

Tax Court Form 6 (*Continued*)

(a) During 1960 petitioners John Smith and Joan Smith each owned 12½% of the outstanding stock of RP Corp., a New York corporation, each petitioner being the owner of 25 shares out of 200 outstanding shares of common stock of the corporation.

(b) On June 30, 1960, RP Corp. as part of the complete liquidation of the corporation distributed to its shareholders as tenants in common title to a parcel of real estate containing a factory building located at 10 West 40th Street, New York City, N.Y., known on the Tax Map of the City of New York as Section 20, Block 2850, lot 40. Title to the land and building was distributed by RP Corp. subject to an existing net lease to Harder, Inc., which expires on December 31, 1989.

(c) On the basis of independent appraisals obtained by RP Corp., the property distributed by the corporation was valued at $1,200,000 by the petitioners. Petitioners John Smith and Joan Smith, having each received a one-eighth undivided interest in the property as a tenant in common with the other former shareholders of the RP Corp., reported in their 1960 joint income tax return, as a liquidating distribution from RP Corp., receipt of two one-eighth undivided interests in the property valued in the aggregate at $300,000.

(d) The respondent determined that there was a deficiency in the income taxes paid by the petitioners on the ground that the property distributed by RP Corp. to its shareholders should have been valued at $2,200,000 rather than the $1,200,000 at which it had been appraised by an independent appraiser and valued by the petitioners. Thus, respondent determined that the petitioners should have reported on their joint income tax return receipt of interests in real estate worth in the aggregate $550,000 instead of $300,000.

6. The facts upon which the petitioners rely as the basis of the error alleged in paragraph 4(b) are as follows:

(a) During 1960 petitioners owned stock of certain corporations. The number of shares owned by petitioners, the name of the corporation and the basis of such stock to the petitioners being as follows:

*   *   *   *   *

(b) The stocks listed in paragraph 6(a) were capital assets of the petitioners.

(c) During 1960 petitioners' investment in each of the stocks listed in paragraph 6(a) became wholly worthless.

7. The facts upon which the petitioners rely as the basis of the error alleged in paragraph 4(c) are as follows:

(a) During all of 1960, petitioner John Smith was employed by Harder, Inc. in the capacity of vice-president of the corporation.

(b) During 1960, Harder, Inc. purchased for $4,850.79 an automobile which it permitted said petitioner to use in connection with the business of the corporation. At all times, the automobile was owned by Harder, Inc.

(c) Petitioner John Smith during 1960 owned 16¼ shares of common stock (constituting approximately 1% of the common stock) and 20 shares of preferred stock (constituting less than 6% of the total preferred stock) of Harder, Inc.

(d) Respondent determined that the entire cost of the automobile purchased by Harder, Inc. and used by petitioner John Smith was a constructive dividend from the corporation to him.

8. The facts upon which the petitioners rely as the basis of the error alleged in paragraph 4(d) are as follows:

(a) During 1960, petitioners incurred and paid medical expenses in the amount of $5,904.84. All of these expenses were of the type which were deductible under Section 213 of the Internal Revenue Code.

(b) In accordance with Section 213(a) of the Internal Revenue Code, petitioners deducted on their 1960 joint income tax return the excess of their allowable medical expenses over 3% of their adjusted gross income as shown on their joint return.

(c) Respondent has determined that petitioners' adjusted gross income for 1960 should be increased as indicated in Exhibit A hereto and has disallowed the portion of petitioners' medical expense deduction not in excess of 3% of their adjusted gross income as so determined to reflect this adjustment.

9. The facts upon which petitioners rely as the basis of their claim for refund of overpayments of income tax are as follows:

(a) Petitioner John Smith acquired the land and building located at 550 Madison Avenue, New York, New York, in 1956 in a tax free exchange under Section 1031 of the Internal Revenue Code of 1954.

(b) On January 31, 1958 said petitioner sold the property to XYZ Corporation commencing January 1, 1990 for $71,261.70. Petitioner retained ownership and possession of the property for the term of years ending December 31, 1989.

(c) Petitioner allocated his basis in the property on January 1, 1958 between the retained term of years and the conveyed future interest in proportion to the value of these two interests, allocating to the conveyed future interest a basis of $140,461.80.

(d) Petitioner claimed a loss of $69,197.10 on his 1958 income tax return on the sale of the future interest.

(e) The loss on the sale of the future interest having been disallowed, petitioner claims he is entitled to allocate the portion of his basis in the property as to which loss was not recognized to his retained term of years and to amortize such basis over the life of the retained term of years.

(f) Petitioner claims a deduction in the amount of $2,096.88 in the year 1960, which is the year covered by the notice of deficiency attached as Exhibit A, as amortization of the portion of the basis of the said property to which no loss was recognized.

WHEREFORE, the petitioners pray that this Court may try this case and determine that:

(a) no deficiency is due for the year 1960;

(b) petitioners have made an overpayment of income tax and are entitled to a refund of tax in the year in issue as alleged in paragraph 9; and

TAX COURT FORM 6 (*Concluded*)

(c) petitioners are entitled to such other and further relief herein as is proper in the circumstances.

s/   (Benjamin H. Oremland)
         BENJAMIN H. OREMLAND

BENJAMIN H. OREMLAND
385 Fifth Avenue
New York, New York
COUNSEL FOR THE PETITIONERS

STATE OF NEW YORK   ⎱
COUNTY OF   ⎰ ss.:

JOHN SMITH, being duly sworn, says that he is one of the petitioners above named; that he has read the foregoing petition, or had the same read to him, and is familiar with the statements contained therein, and that the statements contained therein are true

s/   (John Smith)
       JOHN SMITH

Subscribed and sworn to before
me the   day of November, 1966.

Notary Public

STATE OF NEW YORK   ⎱
COUNTY OF   ⎰ ss.:

JOAN SMITH, being duly sworn, says that she is one of the petitioners above named; that she has read the foregoing petition, or had the same read to her, and is familiar with the statements contained therein, and that the statements contained therein are true.

s/   (Jane Smith)
       JANE SMITH

Sworn to and subscribed before me
the   day of November, 1966.

Notary Public

TAX COURT FORM 7. REQUEST FOR DESIGNATION OF PLACE OF TRIAL

TAX COURT OF THE UNITED STATES

MORTON LIEB AND
  MARCIA LIEB
 	
       Petitioners,
 	
       v.
 	
COMMISSIONER OF INTERNAL REVENUE,
       Respondent.
	Docket No.

REQUEST FOR DESIGNATION OF PLACE OF TRIAL

Petitioners, by their attorney, Marvin L. Olshan, in accordance with Rule 26 of the Court's Rules of Practice, respectfully request that the Court designate that the trial of the above entitled case be held at New York, New York, in order to afford the respective parties an opportunity to produce evidence at the trial with a minimum of expense.

Dated: November   , 1966.   s/   Marvin L. Olshan
                                                MARVIN L. OLSHAN

                                                MARVIN L. OLSHAN
                                                605 Third Avenue
                                                New York, New York

TAX COURT FORM 8. MOTION TO DISMISS FOR LACK OF JURISDICTION
(IMPROPER PETITIONER)

TAX COURT OF THE UNITED STATES

JOHN JONES,

on behalf of

JANE ROE,

Petitioner,

v.

COMMISSIONER OF INTERNAL REVENUE,
Respondent.

Docket No.

MOTION TO DISMISS FOR LACK OF JURISDICTION

THE RESPONDENT MOVES that the above-entitled case be dismissed for lack of jurisdiction because the petition filed herein was neither signed nor verified by the proper party as required by Rules 6 and 7 of the Tax Court Rules of Practice.

IN SUPPORT THEREOF, the respondent respectfully shows unto the Court:

1. The notice of deficiency involved herein, a copy of which is attached to the petition, was mailed to Mrs. Jane Roe on April 14, 1965.

2. Paragraph 1 of the petition alleges that the petitioner is John Jones. Subparagraph (a) of Paragraph 1 of the petition states that Mr. Jones is the "Co-Executor under the Last Will and Testament of Edward Roe, Deceased, former husband of Jane Roe from whom she was divorced at the time of his death." The unnumbered paragraph immediately above Paragraph 1 of the petition states that Mr. Jones is petitioning "for a delay for the redetermination of the deficiency" determined against Jane Roe in the notice dated April 14, 1965.

3. The petition is signed by John Jones. At the bottom of Page 3 of the petition he signed a verification wherein he states that he is "the petitioner and fiduciary on behalf of Jane Roe." Jane Roe has neither signed the petition nor verified it.

4. Rule 6 of the Tax Court Rules of Practice provides in pertinent part:

"A case in the Tax Court shall be brought by and in the name of the person against whom the Commissioner determined the deficiency . . . or by and in the full descriptive name of the fiduciary legally entitled to institute a case on behalf of such person."

5. Rule 7(c)(4)(D) of the Tax Court Rules of Practice provides in pertinent part:

"Verifications by fiduciaries shall contain a statement that the fiduciaries signing and verifying have authority to act for the taxpayer."

6. John Jones alleged status as Co-Executor of the Estate of Edward Roe does not qualify him as a fiduciary for Jane Roe. The petition alleges no other

Tax Court Form 8 (*Concluded*)

basis for Mr. Jones to assert that he is Jane Roe's fiduciary. Mr. Jones is not an attorney and he does not state that he is admitted to practice before this Court.

7. It does not appear that a petition has been filed in the above-entitled case, either by the taxpayer to whom the notice of deficiency was directed or by a fiduciary authorized to act on the taxpayer's behalf, during the ninety-day period contemplated by § 6213(a) of the Internal Revenue Code of 1954. The respondent submits that neither an amended petition nor an amendment to the petition could now confer jurisdiction on this Court. *Soren J. Hoj,* 26 T.C. 1074 (1956).

WHEREFORE, it is prayed that this notion be granted.

O. PAUL GREEN
Chief Counsel
Internal Revenue Service

OF COUNSEL:
  EDW. A. EAMES
    Regional Counsel
  GEORGE GREENBERG
    Attorney
  Internal Revenue Service
  30 Church St., New York, New York 10007.

TAX COURT FORM 9. MOTION TO DISMISS FOR LACK OF JURISDICTION
(LATE FILING)

TAX COURT OF THE UNITED STATES

PETER SAND AND JUDITH SAND,
    Petitioners,

      v.   Docket No.

COMMISSIONER OF INTERNAL REVENUE,
    Respondent.

MOTION TO DISMISS FOR LACK OF JURISDICTION

THE RESPONDENT MOVES that the above-entitled case be dismissed for lack of jurisdiction for failure of the petitioners to file a petition within the period prescribed by the applicable provisions of the Internal Revenue Code of 1954.

IN SUPPORT THEREOF respondent respectfully shows unto the Court:

1. THAT duplicate originals of the statutory notice of deficiency, upon which notice this case is based, were sent to the petitioners at their last known address, 10 East 8 Street, New York, New York, by certified mail on April 10, 1966, as shown by the postmark date stamped on respondent's receipt of certified mail, United States Post Office Department's Form 3877, a copy of which is attached hereto as Exhibit A (copies of the duplicate originals of the statutory notice of deficiency are attached hereto and marked Exhibits B and C) ;

2. THAT the 90-day period for filing a timely petition with this Court from said notice of deficiency expired on Thursday, July 9, 1966, which date was not a legal holiday in the District of Columbia;

3. THAT a one-sentence "application to desist," bearing a July 9, 1966 postmark date, was filed with the Tax Court on July 10, 1966;

4. THAT the one-sentence "application to desist" is not a petition within the meaning of Section 6213(a) of Internal Revenue Code of 1954 because it does not request a redetermination of a deficiency determined by the Commissioner and it does not assign any errors to the Commissioner's determination (See *I. J. Rosenberg,* 32 B.T.A. 618 (1935) and *Estate of Bliss Stebbins,* 40 B.T.A. 613 (1939), affirmed, 121 F.2d 892, 27 A.F.T.R. 753 (D.C. Cir. 1941) ;

5. THAT the failure of the one-sentence "application to desist" to qualify as a petition within the meaning of Section 6213(a) of the Internal Revenue Code of 1954 is ground for this case to be dismissed for lack of jurisdiction; and

6. THAT the petitioners have failed to file with the Tax Court a petition within the period of time prescribed by Sections 6213(a) and 7502(a) of the Internal Revenue Code of 1954.

TAX COURT FORM 9 (*Concluded*)

WHEREFORE, it is prayed that this motion be granted.

LAWRENCE BLACK
Chief Counsel
Internal Revenue Service

OF COUNSEL:
D. W. KROMARIK
  Regional Counsel
ALVIN SANDS
  Attorney
Internal Revenue Service
Office of Regional Counsel
30 Church Street
New York, New York

Tax Court Form 10. Motion for Consolidation (No Objection Endorsed)

TAX COURT OF THE UNITED STATES

JOSEPH SMITH AND
HARRIET SMITH,

        Petitioners,

        v.

COMMISSIONER OF INTERNAL REVENUE,
        Respondent.

} Docket No. 1573–67

SMITH, INC.,

        Petitioner,

        v.

COMMISSIONER OF INTERNAL REVENUE,
        Respondent.

} Docket No. 1574–67

MOTION FOR CONSOLIDATION OF CASES

The above named petitioners by their counsel, Jerome Kretchmer, hereby move for an order by the Court to consolidate the two cases, Docket Nos. 1573–67 and 1574–67, for the reason that, although each petition is by different taxpayers, both petitions are based upon deficiency notices involving the same years and similar and related issues of law and fact.

s/ (Jerome Kretchmer)
JEROME KRETCHMER
605 Third Avenue
New York, New York

NO OBJECTION

s/ W. Gibbs McKenney
Chief Counsel
Internal Revenue Service

TAX COURT FORM 11. MOTION FOR CONTINUANCE

TAX COURT OF THE UNITED STATES

ARNOLD SANDERS, AND
HENRIETTA SANDERS,
        Petitioners,

        v.   } Docket No.

COMMISSIONER OF INTERNAL REVENUE,
        Respondent.

ABC, INC.,
        Petitioner,

        v.   } Docket No.

COMMISSIONER OF INTERNAL REVENUE,
        Respondent.

MOTION FOR CONTINUANCE

The above-named petitioners, by their counsel, Niel Grundman, hereby move pursuant to this Court's Rule 27(c) for a continuance of trial in the above-captioned consolidated cases for the purpose of avoiding a multiplicity of suits as more fully shown below:

The petitions in the above-captioned cases were both filed on May 31, 1963, and involve alleged deficiencies in income tax for the year 1957. By order of this Court, dated October 3, 1965, the two cases were consolidated for the purpose of trial. The cases are presently set for trial in the City of New York on April 29, 1964. No continuance of trial has been previously granted herein.

The two cases are based on a determination by the Commissioner of Internal Revenue that XYZ Company, a family partnership, is invalid for purposes of the income tax, that the net income of the partnership is additional net income of ABC, Inc., and that all of the distributable income of the partnership is dividend income to Arnold Sanders from the ABC, Inc. The petitioners herein allege that the Commissioner's determination is erroneous, and in addition plead the three-year statute of limitations and related defenses.

We have been advised by the Internal Revenue Service that notices of deficiency for the years 1958, 1959 and 1960, raising the same issues as are involved in the instant consolidated cases, are being prepared and will shortly be sent to the Sanders and ABC, Inc. The six-year statute of limitations for the year 1958 will expire on April 15, 1964, just two weeks prior to the date of trial. Thus, it appears that no later than April 15, 1964, notices of deficiency for the years 1958, 1959 and 1960 will be received by the petitioners.

Tax Court Form 11 (*Concluded*)

Both of the petitioners herein intend to file petitions to this Court as to the Commissioner's determination of a deficiency in tax for the years 1958, 1959 and 1960. Once the cases are at issue, both petitioners intend to file a motion to consolidate all of the cases for trial, including the cases for the year 1957, since all the petitions will involve related issues of law and fact. The cases for the years 1958, 1959 and 1960 will require petitions, answers and replies, and will not be at issue prior to April 29, 1964, the present trial date.

Trial will take at least a day, and the petitioners will have to call two witnesses who live in Pittsburgh, Pennsylvania. The petitioners herein respectfully request a continuance of the present date for trial so that all of the related cases for the years 1957 through 1960 may be tried together, and so that an undue burden will not be placed upon either this Court or the litigants.

Respectfully submitted,

s/   (Niel Grundman)
_____
Niel Grundman
Counsel for Petitioners
605 Third Avenue
New York, New York

TAX COURT FORM 12. SUBPOENA

𝕿𝖆𝖝 𝕮𝖔𝖚𝖗𝖙 𝖔𝖋 𝖙𝖍𝖊 𝖀𝖓𝖎𝖙𝖊𝖉 𝕾𝖙𝖆𝖙𝖊𝖘

WASHINGTON, D. C.

Howard Johnson

_____ Petitioner,

_v._

COMMISSIONER OF INTERNAL REVENUE, Respondent.

Docket No. 9918-66

SUBPOENA

To _____ Dolley Madison _____

_____

YOU ARE HEREBY COMMANDED to appear before the Tax Court of the United States

(or the name and official title of a person authorized to take depositions)

at _9:30 a.m._ on the ____ fifteenth ____ day of ____ March 1967 ____
  (Time)   (Date)   (Month)

at ____ 220 East 42nd Street   New York, New York ____
                                        (Place)

then and there to testify on behalf of ____ Petitioner ____ in the above-entitled case,
                                    (Petitioner) or (Respondent)

and to bring with you ____ All canceled checks and checkbook stubs for _____

____ the period commencing August 10, 1964 and ending on December 31, 1964. ____

(Use reverse if necessary)

and not to depart without leave of the Court.

Date ____ March 1, 1967 ____

Richard Miles, Esq. _____
    Attorney for (Petitioner) (Respondent)

HOWARD F. _____

By _____ Deputy Clerk.

RETURN ON SERVICE

The above-named witness was summoned on the ____ 3rd ____ day of ____ March ____, 19_67_
at ____ 10 West 42 Street, N.Y.C. ____ by delivering a copy of this subpoena to her ____ and, if a witness for the petitioner, by tendering fees and mileage to her ____ pursuant to Rule 60 of the Rules of Practice of the Tax Court.

Dated ____ March 3, 1967 ____   Signed ____ Van Illa ____

Subscribed and sworn to before me this ____ 3rd ____ day of ____ March ____, 19_67_.

FORM 4
June 1957

____ Mark Custard, Notary Public ____
                (Name and Title)

[SEAL]

☆ U. S. GOVERNMENT PRINTING OFFICE: 1959 O - 498497

TAX COURT FORM 13. APPLICATION FOR ORDER TO TAKE DEPOSITIONS

TAX COURT OF THE UNITED STATES

JOHN SMITH
....
Petitioner,

v.

COMMISSIONER OF INTERNAL REVENUE,
Respondent.

Docket No.   5201-67

APPLICATION FOR ORDER TO TAKE DEPOSITIONS*

To the Tax Court of the United States:

1. Application is hereby made by the above-named................ John Smith
for an order to take the deposition... of the following-named person...:   (Petitioner or respondent)

Name of witness	Post-office address
(a) Barbara Cooper	510 Fifth Avenue New York, New York
(b)	
(c)	
(d)	

2. It is desired to take the depositions of the persons above named and each of them for the following reasons:

(a) Barbara Cooper, a medical doctor .... will testify to the following material matters:
(Set forth briefly the matter upon which said witness will be called to testify)

The petitioner's illness and the medical treatment required
by the petitioner.

(b) .... will testify to the following material matters:

(c) .... will testify to the following material matters:

(d) .... will testify to the following material matters:

---

*Applications must be filed at least 30 days prior to the date set for trial. When the applicant seeks to take depositions upon written interrogatories the title of the application shall so indicate and the application shall be accompanied by an original and five copies of the proposed interrogatories. The taking of depositions upon written interrogatories is not favored, except when the depositions are to be taken in foreign countries, in which latter case any depositions taken must be upon written interrogatories, except as otherwise directed by the Court for cause shown. (See Rule 46.) If the parties so stipulate depositions may be taken without application to the Court. (See Rule 45 (e).)

10—0050-4   (OVER)

Form 5-A
Rev. Apr. 1954

3. The reasons why ____petitioner____ desires to take the testimony of the above-named persons rather than have them appear personally and testify before the Court are as follows: (State specifically reasons for each witness.)

Barbara Cooper, the petitioner's physician, intends to leave the country to live abroad during the next year. Accordingly, she will be unable to appear and testify at the hearing of this case.

4. It is desired to take the testimony of ____Barbara Cooper____
(Names of witnesses)

on the __29th__ day* of __July__, 19_67_, at the hour of __10__ o'clock __a.__ m. before __Robert Bander__
*(A date sufficiently in advance of the day set for hearing of the proceedings to enable the deposition to be completed and filed with the Court at least 10 days prior to the hearing)   (State name and title of official)

____Notary Public____ in the city of ____New York____, State of ____New York____

at room __22, 450 Fifth Avenue__
(Give number of room, street number, and name of building)

5. That ____Robert Bander____ is a ____Notary Public____, who has
(Name of official before whom depositions are to be taken)   (Give official title)

authority to administer oaths but has no office connection or business employment with the petitioner or his counsel.

Dated __May 5,__, 19_67_

(Signed) _/s/ Jerome Kretchmer, Esq._
(Petitioner or counsel)

__450 Fifth Avenue__
(Post-office address)

STATE OF ____New York____ } ss:
COUNTY OF ____New York____

____Jerome Kretchmer, Esq.____, being duly sworn, says that the foregoing application for order to take depositions is made in good faith and for the reasons therein stated and that the same is not made for purposes of delay.

(Signed) ____

Subscribed and sworn to before me this ____ day of ____ , 19____

(Signed) ____
(Official title)

[SEAL]   U.S. GOVERNMENT PRINTING OFFICE : 1962 O—628880

TAX COURT FORM 14. STIPULATION OF FACTS

TAX COURT OF THE UNITED STATES

MICHAEL RICHARDSON,

       Petitioner,

       —against—   Docket No. 590–66

COMMISSIONER OF INTERNAL REVENUE,

       Respondent.

STIPULATION OF FACTS

It is hereby stipulated with respect to the above-entitled proceeding that the following statements may be accepted as facts and that this stipulation shall be without prejudice to the right of either party to introduce other and further evidence at the trial of this case not inconsistent with the facts herein stipulated and without prejudice to the right of either party to object to the admission of such facts solely upon the grounds of relevancy and materiality.

1. For the taxable years here involved, namely, 1960, 1961 and 1962, Michael Richardson (herein called "Richardson") filed federal income tax returns in which he reported the amounts received by him as referred to in Paragraph 14 below, to be proceeds of the sale of a capital asset, i.e., his interest in the partnership "Art Life Productions."

2. On or about October 3, 1957, Richardson and Wilde executed a partnership agreement, a photostatic copy of which is annexed as a part of this stipulation and marked Exhibit 1–A.

3. On or about October 1, 1957, Richardson doing business as "Richardson Productions" entered into a radio package show contract with ABC, Inc., an advertising agency acting on behalf of XYZ, Inc. Such radio package show contract was modified by letter agreement of October 4, 1957. A photostatic copy of the contract is annexed as a part of this stipulation and marked Exhibit 4–D. A photostatic copy of the modification is annexed as a part of this stipulation and marked Exhibit 5–E. The radio package show contract was assigned to, and assumed by, the partnership known as "Richardson-Wilde Productions" by the partnership agreement dated October 3, 1957 hereinabove referred to as Exhibit 1–A.

*   *   *   *   *

10. On or about May 26, 1960, MNO, Inc. submitted to Richardson and Wilde a written bid. A photostatic copy of said bid is annexed as a part of this stipulation and is marked Exhibit 11–K.

*   *   *   *   *

14. Pursuant to the terms of such contracts (Exhibits 14–N and 15–O), Richardson received payments of $10,000 in the calendar year 1960, $74,000 in the calendar year 1961, and $74,000 in the calendar year 1962.

*   *   *   *   *

Tax Court Form 14 (*Concluded*)

18. Annexed as part of this stipulation are the income tax returns filed by the petitioner for the taxable years in issue. Said returns are marked as Exhibit 21–U being the return for the taxable year 1960; 22–V being the return for the taxable year 1961; 23–W being the return for the taxable year 1962.

19. Annexed as part of this stipulation as Exhibit 27–AA is the final partnership return of the "Richardson-Wilde Productions."

s/   (Theodore R. Shrier)
_____
THEODORE R. SHRIER
COUNSEL FOR PETITIONER

s/   _____
COUNSEL FOR RESPONDENT

TAX COURT OF THE UNITED STATES

DON KANE AND RUTH KANE,

    Petitioners,

      v.   Docket No. 1019–66

COMMISSIONER OF INTERNAL REVENUE,

    Respondent,

ARTIC, INC.,

    Petitioner,

      v.   Docket No. 1020–66

COMMISSIONER OF INTERNAL REVENUE,

    Respondent.

STIPULATION OF FACTS

IT IS HEREBY STIPULATED AND AGREED by and between counsel for the parties hereto that the following statements shall be accepted as facts for the purpose of these cases and all exhibits referred to herein and attached hereto are incorporated in this stipulation and made a part hereof, provided, however, that either party may introduce other and further evidence not inconsistent with the facts herein stipulated, and further reserving to either party the right to object to the admission of said facts in evidence on the ground that said facts are immaterial and irrelevant.

1. It is agreed that the use in this stipulation of specific terms of description or designation, including but not limited to such terms as taxpayer, partnership, partner and other similar descriptive terms shall be without prejudice to the right of either party to show or contend that these terms are not always determinative as they might otherwise be if the parties were not at issue in a case such as this.

2. Don Kane and Ruth Kane, the petitioners in Docket No. 1019–66, are husband and wife residing at 30 West 75th Street, New York, New York.

3. Don Kane and Ruth Kane filed joint U. S. individual income tax returns (Form 1040) on the following dates:

> On or before April 16, 1960 for the calendar year 1959;
> On or before April 15, 1961 for the calendar year 1960;
> On or before April 15, 1962 for the calendar year 1961;
> On or before April 15, 1963 for the calendar year 1962.

A true copy of said returns are attached hereto as Joint Exhibits 1–A, 2–B, 3–C and 4–D, respectively.

4. The notice of deficiency in tax for the calendar year 1959 directed to Don Kane and Ruth Kane was mailed to Don Kane and Ruth Kane on March 7,

TAX COURT FORM 15 (*Continued*)

1962, a true copy of said notice of deficiency being attached to the petition in Docket No. 1019–66.

*   *   *   *   *

6. No agreement or waiver extending the statutory period for the assessment of Federal income tax for the calendar years 1959, 1960, 1961 or 1962 was executed by, or on behalf of, Don Kane and/or Ruth Kane.

7. The deficiencies against Don Kane and Ruth Kane, as determined by the Commissioner of Internal Revenue, are in income tax for the calendar years 1959, 1960, 1961 and 1962, in the respective amounts of $29,747.26, $37,975.18, $27,753.28 and $26,915.96, all of which amounts are in dispute.

8. Peter Kane and Pat Kane are the minor children of Don Kane and Ruth Kane.

9. A true copy of a document entitled "Voluntary Trust Agreement" dated June 28, 1958, is attached hereto as Joint Exhibit 5–E.

10. On or about April 13, 1958, the Trust Estate for Peter Kane filed its first U. S. fiduciary income tax return (Form 1041), a return for the calendar year 1957, a true copy of said return being attached hereto as Joint Exhibit 6–F.

*   *   *   *   *

25. Artic, Inc. filed its income tax return on a calendar year basis and in accordance with an accrual method of accounting.

26. During the calendar years 1959 through 1962 all the issued and outstanding stock of Artic, Inc. was held by Don Kane, and he was the president of the corporation.

*   *   *   *   *

44. Attached hereto as Joint Exhibit 44–RR is a true copy of a letter, dated August 18, 1964, from the District Director of Internal Revenue, New York, N. Y. to Artic, Inc. and the report of Internal Revenue agent Julius Isaacs to the taxpayer, dated August 4, 1964, attached to said letter.

51. Attached hereto as Joint Exhibit 51–YY are true copies of balance sheets and profit and loss statements of Artic, Inc. from Edward Jones & Co., certified public accountants, for Artic, Inc.'s fiscal years ended January 31, 1958 through January 31, 1962.

*   *   *   *   *

53. Attached hereto as Joint Exhibit 53–AAA are true copies of "Account No. 52, Purchases-Merchandise" and "Account No. 21, Artic, Inc." for the fiscal year ended January 31, 1957 taken from the General Ledger of The XYZ Company.

54. The record of cash disbursements of The XYZ Company for the fiscal year beginning February 1, 1966 and ending January 31, 1959 show cash disbursements by The XYZ Company to Artic, Inc. as set forth on the schedule attached hereto as Joint Exhibit 54–BBB.

55. The XYZ Company maintained one bank account during the fiscal year beginning February 1, 1956 and ending January 31, 1957, said account being

Tax Court Form 15 (*Concluded*)

with the First National Bank. Attached hereto as Joint Exhibit 55–CCC is a true copy of "Account No. 1, Cash in Bank—First National Bank" for the fiscal year ended January 31, 1957 taken from the General Ledger of The XYZ Company. Attached hereto as Joint Exhibit 56–DDD is a true copy of page 1 of the General Journal of The Shafford Company.

     *   *   *   *   *

57. Gross Sales, miscellaneous income, sales discounts and allowances, and sales returns of The XYZ Company on an annualized basis for the calendar years 1959 through 1962, as shown by the General Ledger accounts of The XYZ Company for the fiscal years ended January 31, 1959 through January 31, 1963, are as follows:

Year	Sales	Miscellaneous Income	Sales Discounts and Allowances	Sales Returns
1959	$778,870.47	$ 79.27	$6,588.56	$23,624.53
1960	944,591.74	7.68	9,674.65	10,639.48
1961	952,361.49	478.00	9,062.84	13,263.08
1962	911,032.39	2,796.72	7,802.70	7,290.48

     *   *   *   *   *

s/   (Donald Bright)
DONALD BRIGHT

s/   (Harvey Kaufman)
HARVEY KAUFMAN

s/   (Kenneth Semmel)
KENNETH SEMMEL
(COUNSEL FOR PETITIONERS)

s/   (R. P. Hertzog)
R. P. HERTZOG
(ACTING CHIEF COUNSEL
INTERNAL REVENUE SERVICE)

TAX COURT FORM 16. STIPULATION OF FACTS

TAX COURT OF THE UNITED STATES

MORTON LIEB AND MARCIA LIEB,

    Petitioners,

      v.   Docket No. 5173–67

COMMISSIONER OF INTERNAL REVENUE,

    Respondent.

STIPULATION OF FACTS

It is hereby stipulated that, for the purposes of this case, the following statements are accepted as facts, subject to the right of either party to object to the admission in evidence of such facts on the grounds of materiality and relevancy, and all exhibits referred to herein and attached hereto are incorporated in this stipulation and made a part hereof; provided, however, that either party may introduce other and further evidence not inconsistent with the facts herein stipulated.

1. Morton Lieb and Marcia Lieb (hereinafter sometimes referred to as the petitioners) are husband and wife. They reside at 1050 Fifth Avenue, New York, New York. They filed a joint 1965 income tax return (a copy of which it attached hereto as Exhibit 1) and a joint 1966 income tax return (a copy of which is attached hereto as Exhibit 2) with the District Director, Lower Manhattan, New York. The petitioners are on the cash method of accounting.

2. At all times relevant petitioner Morton Lieb held the majority interest in the partnership Lieb & Co. (sometimes referred to hereinafter as the partnership). Attached as Exhibit 3 is a copy of the 1966 Form 1065, U. S. Partnership Return of Income, for Lieb & Co., which was filed with the District Director of Internal Revenue, New York, New York.

3. Lieb & Co. was organized on October 14, 1960 in the State of New York to carry on, as a partnership, the business of "stock brokers."

4. Attached as Exhibit 4 is a copy of Lieb & Co.'s amended partnership agreement, dated July 1, 1965. Pursuant to this agreement, the partnership was to commence business on July 1, 1965 with a total capital of $650,000.00, which was contributed as follows:

Morton Lieb	$500,000.00
John Morris	100,000.00
Arthur Miles	50,000.00

Pursuant to said agreement, the net profits, if any, or the net losses, if any, of the partnership were to be shared as follows:

Morton Lieb	60%
John Morris	20%
Arthur Miles	20%

TAX COURT FORM 16 (*Concluded*)

---

5. On June 30, 1966, Mr. Miles, after having given timely notice of his intention to withdraw from the partnership, did, by mutual consent, withdraw from Lieb & Co. As of June 30, 1966, Mr. Miles' combined personal and capital account reflected a debit balance as follows:

*   *   *   *   *

9. After Mr. Miles' withdrawal from the partnership, the remaining partners (Messrs. Lieb and Morris), through the firm's attorney, requested payment of the $260,092.37. Mr. Miles refused to make said payment.

10. On July 2, 1966, Morton Lieb and John Morris entered into an agreement with John E. Williams. A copy of that agreement is attached as Exhibit 5.

11. After prolonged negotiations between Messrs. Lieb and Morris and Mr. Miles, they agreed to settle their dispute by having Mr. Miles pay $80,000 to the partnership in settlement of the indebtedness shown in his capital and personal account as of June 30, 1966. Attached as Exhibit 6 is a copy of their agreement, dated September 17, 1966.

12. The petitioners content that the partnership suffered a loss on this settlement, and they reported a "Loss on Settlement of former partner's accounts" of this amount on the partnership's 1966 income tax return (Exhibit 3 of this stipulation).

13. When the partnership closed its 1966 books, 75% of the aforementioned amount was apportioned by the partnership to Petitioner Morton Lieb and 25% was apportioned to John Morris. Mr. Lieb included the claimed loss from the partnership for the year 1966 on his personal income tax return for that year (Exhibit 2 of this stipulation).

14. The respondent determined that the partnership did not suffer a deductible loss, as claimed.

15. By notice of deficiency dated July 24, 1967, the respondent determined a deficiency in the petitioners' 1966 income tax aggregating $70,403.63.

16. The only adjustment in that notice of deficiency which is in dispute in this case is the disallowance, as not deductible, of the loss claimed by the petitioners for 1966.

s/   (Kurt Kamm)
COUNSEL FOR PETITIONERS

CHIEF COUNSEL
INTERNAL REVENUE SERVICE

TAX COURT FORM 17. ORDER FOR TRIAL STATUS REPORT

TAX COURT OF THE UNITED STATES
WASHINGTON, D.C.

April 26, 1963   EDWARD PETERSON;
                                  Docket No(s): 1259-65

⌐

  Thomas Mason, Esq.
  1 Chase Manhattan Plaza
  New York 5, N.Y.

∟

ORDER FOR TRIAL STATUS REPORT

You are hereby notified that the above-entitled case(s) has been reached for trial and will be calendared for the Session of the Court at ___New York, N.Y.___ on ___Nov. 4, 1966___ unless there are cogent reasons for passing it at that time. The parties are so informed at this date to allow time for mutual collaboration, conferences or negotiations regarding possibilities of disposition of this case without trial in order that complete report may be made to the Court as to the status of this case for trial, if necessary. The same information has been requested from respondent for that purpose. Accordingly,

BY ORDER OF THE COURT, the following report shall, not earlier than 75 days, nor later than 80 days, after the date of this Order, be submitted to the Court by use of the enclosed copy of this Order, using reverse for response if necessary:

1. Has basis for settlement of this case been reached between the parties? _____ or is it expected that this case must be tried?___X___.

2. If this case must be tried, will it be ready for trial, without later request for continuance, at the session indicated? ___Yes___. If the answer is "No" or if trial at that session is not appropriate, state why. (If awaiting outcome of other litigation, state name of case and court.) _____

3. Give the best present estimate of trial time for this case with full compliance with Rule 31(b)(1) and (b)(2) relating to stipulation of facts which are not, or fairly should not be, in dispute. ___8___ hours.

If this case is settled between the parties prior to return of the response, that fact should be indicated in item 1 in the response. If the case is reported as settled or the report is that a basis of settlement has been reached between the parties, this case will be calendared at a Washington, D.C., Motions Session for settlement purposes. If the settlement stipulation is not filed by the specified date, the Court may add this case to the calendar for the session indicated above.

THIS IS NOT A NOTICE OF TRIAL. The Court will not prepare the calendar for the session indicated until expiration of the time allowed for trial status responses. If this case is calendared for trial at that session, a "Notice of Trial" will be sent to petitioner approximately 90 days prior to the first day of that session.

Date reply prepared: _____

Signed: _/s/ Thomas Mason_____
      (Counsel for Petitioner)   Louis J. Lewis
      Thomas Mason   **Clerk of the Court.**

Form 30 (Rev. Apr. 1965)

TAX COURT FORM 18. NOTICE SETTING CASE FOR TRIAL

TAX COURT OF THE UNITED STATES
WASHINGTON

GERALD CARSON	Docket No.: 127-66
Petitioner,	
v.	Trial On: April 29, 1967
COMMISSIONER OF INTERNAL REVENUE,	Trial At: Courtroom No. 1
Respondent.	Rm 820, News Bldg.
	220 E. 42nd St.
	New York, N.Y.

NOTICE SETTING CASE FOR TRIAL

TAKE NOTICE that the above-entitled case is set for trial before a Division of the Tax Court of the United States as indicated above.

The calendar for that Session will be called at 10:00 A.M. on the date indicated and you will be expected to answer the call at that time and be prepared when the case is reached for trial. Failure to appear will be taken as cause for dismissal in accordance with Rule 27(c)(3) of the Court's Rules of Practice.

You are expected to be familiar with the Court's Rules of Practice in all other respects.

Your attention is called particularly to Rule 31(b) which requires that the parties stipulate facts and evidence to the fullest possible extent prior to the call of the calendar. You should confer with your adversary promptly in order to comply with that rule.

Ex parte motions for continuance of trial, filed 30 days or less prior to the first day of the Session, will be calendared for hearing at calendar call at the Session unless the Court, in its discretion, directs otherwise in exceptional circumstances.

Clerk of the Court.

To: Thomas Mason, Esq.   To: Counsel for Respondent
1 Chase Manhattan Plaza
New York 5, New York

GPO 16—75579-3

Form 40
(Rev. Feb. 1963)

THE TAX COURT OF THE UNITED STATES

Charles Kane,

           Petitioner,

         v.   Docket No.

Commissioner of Internal Revenue,

           Respondent.

MOTION FOR LEAVE TO FILE AMENDMENTS TO ANSWERS TO CONFORM PLEADINGS TO PROOF IN THE RECORD

Comes now the respondent and moves for leave to file amendments to his answer in the above docketed case in order to conform his pleadings to the proof in the record. Said amendments are hereby attached to and incorporated within this motion.

For cause respondent states as follows:

(1). The case was tried on the New York calendar of October 1, 1966.

(2). In due course the transcript of the record was received by respondent and preparation of his brief was commenced. The briefs were seriatum and petitioner's brief was received on December 31, 1966.

(3). In the course of the review of the aforesaid transcript, respondent became aware of testimony in the record which established that the critical date for the sale of the partnership interests and/or assets in issue was May 27, 1960 instead of July 26, 1960, the date of the signing of the contracts. Upon receipt of petitioners' brief this fact was confirmed by petitioners' requested findings numbered 24 and 25.

(4). In the light of this fact it becomes important to argue the question of the holding period of the partnership interests involved, because if these interests were not held for longer than six months, then irrespective of other issues in these cases, the petitioners are not entitled to long-term capital gain treatment upon the income involved.

(5). Respondent has not been dilatory in the filing of this motion, but to the contrary, only became aware of such after the transcript was received and petitioner's brief was received. The testimony in these cases was voluminous, and lasted for four days. The particular testimony involved could not be properly evaluated during the course of the day-by-day trial.

(6). This amendment will not prejudice the petitioner, for the facts are in the record and will not require a re-opening of the case. In addition, petitioner has the benefit of a reply brief to argue his analysis of such facts.

(7). In the interests of justice to the respondent, since the tax liabilities are still before the Court, these amendments are necessary in order that the Court may properly determine the true tax liability of the petitioner.

(8). This motion is covered by Rule 19(b) of the Rules of Practice Before The Tax Court of the United States.

TAX COURT FORM 19 (*Concluded*)

WHEREFORE, it is prayed that this motion be granted.

s/   R. THOMAS REILLY
ACTING CHIEF COUNSEL
INTERNAL REVENUE SERVICE

OF COUNSEL:
  CARL EDELWEISS
    Regional Counsel
  HARRY J. MCCRACKEN
    Assistant Regional Counsel
  JOSEPH ST. ONGE
    Special Attorney
    Internal Revenue Service

THE TAX COURT OF THE UNITED STATES

CHARLES KANE,

    Petitioner,

      v.   Docket No.

COMMISSIONER OF INTERNAL REVENUE,

    Respondent.

AMENDMENT TO ANSWER

8. Respondent asserts that the petitioner, Charles Kane, did not hold his partnership interest in the partnership "Camaron Company" for a period longer than six months as is required by Section 117(a)(1) of the Internal Revenue Code of 1939.

WHEREFORE, it is prayed that the appeal of the petitioner herein be denied; and further that by reason of the allegations set forth in paragraphs 7 and 8, the Court determine the deficiency due from the petitioner to be in such increased amount as will be reflected by a computation under Rul 50 of the Rules of Practice Before The Tax Court of the United States.

s/   R. THOMAS REILLY
ACTING CHIEF COUNSEL
INTERNAL REVENUE SERVICE

OF COUNSEL:
  CARL EDELWEISS
    Regional Counsel
  HARRY J. MCCRACKEN
    Assistant Regional Counsel
  JOSEPH ST.ONGE
    Special Attorney
    Internal Revenue Service

TAX COURT FORM 20. MOTION TO EXTEND TIME FOR FILING BRIEF

THE TAX COURT OF THE UNITED STATES

CHARLES KANE,

Petitioner,

v.   } Docket No.

COMMISSIONER OF INTERNAL REVENUE,

Respondent.

MOTION

COMES NOW the Commissioner of Internal Revenue, by his attorney, Nelson P. Rose, Chief Counsel, Internal Revenue Service, and moves the Court to extend the time within which his brief in the above-entitled case may be filed to April 19, 1967.

In support of this motion, it is respectfully shown that respondent's brief is due April 4, 1967; that the brief has been prepared but review thereof has not been completed and that the additional time herein requested is required to adequately complete a review of the brief.

WHEREFORE, it is prayed that this motion be granted.

s/ REGINALD OLDS
Chief Counsel
Internal Revenue Service

OF COUNSEL:
  CARL EDELWEISS
    Regional Counsel
  HARRY J. MCCRACKEN
    Assistant Regional Counsel
  JOSEPH ST. ONGE
  CHARLES E. S. WEND
    Special Attorneys
    Internal Revenue Service

THE TAX COURT OF THE UNITED STATES

DAVID NOONAN,

        Petitioner,

        v.   Docket No.

COMMISSIONER OF INTERNAL REVENUE,

        Respondent.

MOTION FOR REVIEW BY THE ENTIRE COURT

THE RESPONDENT MOVES that the above-entitled case in which an opinion was filed on October 23, 1966, be reviewed by the entire Court.

In support of this motion, the respondent shows as follows:

1. The opinion in this case states that "Aside from irrelevant factual dissimilarities, this case presents essentially the same question as was decided by the Court in *Jack Benny*, 25 T.C. 197 (1955)" and rests its conclusion upon that case, whereas the dissimilarities in the two cases are relevant and the *Jack Benny, supra,* case, is not support for a determination in these cases.

2. The burden of proof as to value was upon the petitioner in this case, and the opinion of the Court did not reflect a determination that such a burden was sustained. Further, the opinion of the Court apparently places that burden upon the respondent (note 1 page 22), and hence incorrectly evaluates the burden of proof rule.

3. The Court in its opinion summarily dismisses respondent's arguments to the effect (1) that the partnership interests did not include the literary property, (2) that partnership assets not interests were sold, and (3) that the literary property was not a capital asset. No reason is given for the rejection of arguments (2) and (3) other than failure of burden of proof. However, all the facts to evaluate the arguments are in the record, and the rejection of these arguments must be on the merits not a failure of proof. With respect to argument (1) the Court rejects the argument on the basis of the wording of the contracts of sale, whereas, these contracts were later in date to the partnership agreement upon which a determination of this argument must be based.

4. With respect to the arguments set forth in paragraph 3, *supra,* the Court made no specific findings of fact.

In further support of this motion for review by the full Court, respondent alleges as follows:

5. The failure of the trial judge to adequately consider the defects set forth in paragraphs 1 to 4, *supra.*

6. This case is of great importance in the administration of the tax laws and involves a substantial question which should be considered by the whole Court.

7. The trial judge placed reliance upon the *Jack Benny* (25 T.C. 197) case. That case was revised by the whole Court and resulted in three dissents. The

TAX COURT FORM 21 *(Concluded)*

---

judges who dissented are still on the present Court. In view of these dissents, the reliance by the Court on the *Jack Benny, supra,* case, and the arguments made in respondent's brief on the facts in this case, the whole Court should have an opportunity to review the issue.

WHEREFORE, it is prayed that this motion be granted.

OF COUNSEL:
 CARL EDELWEISS, Regional Counsel,
 WM. O. FORD, Special Attorney,
 Internal Revenue Service.

s/   REGINALD OLDS
Chief Counsel,
Internal Revenue Service

TAX COURT FORM 22. RESPONDENT'S COMPUTATION FOR ENTRY OF
DECISION

TAX COURT OF THE UNITED STATES

RICHARD SILVER,

        Petitioner,

           v.   Docket No. 2591

COMMISSIONER OF INTERNAL REVENUE,

        Respondent.

RESPONDENT'S COMPUTATION FOR ENTRY OF DECISION

The attached computations reflecting no deficiencies in income tax for the taxable years 1960 through 1962 are submitted on behalf of the respondent in compliance with the opinion of the Court determining the issues in this case.

The computations are submitted without prejudice to the respondent's right to contest the correctness of the decision entered herein by the Court pursuant to the statute in such cases made and provided.

OF COUNSEL:
  CARL EDELWEISS
    Regional Counsel
  JOSEPH ST. ONGE
    Special Attorney
  Internal Revenue Service

                       REGINALD OLDS
                       Chief Counsel
                       Internal Revenue Service

Without prejudice to the right of appeal, it is agreed that the attached computations are in accordance with the opinion of the Tax Court in the above-entitled case.

                      s/   (Kurt Kamm)
                      —————————————
                      KURT KAMM
                      COUNSEL FOR PETITIONER

AUDIT STATEMENT

In re: Richard Silver
260 West 20 Street
New York, N.Y.
Docket No. 2591

Tax Liability for the Taxable Years Ended
December 31, 1960
December 31, 1961
December 31, 1962

TAX COURT FORM 22 (*Continued*)

Richard Silver   Audit Statement

INCOME TAX

Year	Deficiency
1960	$ None
1961	None
1962	None

Recomputation of tax liability prepared in accordance with the Opinion of The Tax Court of the United States filed October 23, 1967 (16 T.C. No. 13).

Taxable Year Ended December 31, 1960

ADJUSTMENTS TO NET INCOME

Net income shown in deficiency letter dated May 20, 1965	$132,769.39
Addition:	
(a) Net long term capital gain	3,750.00
Total	$136,519.39
Deduction:	
(b) Compensation for personal services decreased	7,500.00
Net income as corrected	$129,019.39

Taxable Year Ended December 31, 1960

EXPLANATION OF ADJUSTMENTS

(a) and (b) Adjustments (a) and (c) of the deficiency letter have been reversed, inasmuch as The Court held that the amount received by the petitioner as his share from the sale of a partnership interest is taxable as a capital gain. (See pages 21 and 25 of The Tax Court's Opinion).

COMPUTATION OF ALTERNATIVE TAX

Income subject to tentative tax		$127,819.39
Less: Excess of net long term capital gain over net short term capital loss		8,081.45
Balance subject to tentative tax		$119,737.94
Tentative tax		$ 84,886.77
Tax Reduction: $ 400.00 at 13%	$ 52.00	
84,486.77 at 9%	7,603.81	
Total tax reduction		7,655.81
Combined partial normal tax and surtax		$77,230.96
Add: 50% of excess of net long term capital gain over net short term capital loss $8,081.45		$ 4,040.73
Alternative tax		$81,271.69

TAX COURT FORM 22 (*Continued*)

Richard Silver   Audit Statement

COMPUTATION OF INCOME TAX

Net income as corrected	$129,019.39
Less: Exemptions (2) × $600.	1,200.00
Income subject to tentative tax	$127,819.39
Tentative tax	$92,079.26

Taxable Year Ended December 31, 1960

Tax Reduction:	$ 400.00 at 13%	$ 52.00	
	91,679.26 at 9%	8,251.13	
Total tax reduction			8,303.13
Combined normal tax and surtax			$ 83,776.13
Alternative tax			$ 81,271.69
Less: Income tax payments to a foreign country			30.00
Corrected income tax liability			$ 81,241.69
Income tax liability disclosed by return a/c #3256104		$79,137.06	
Additional assessment, Feb. 18, 1964 list, a/c #2–510765		2,104.63	81,241.69
Deficiency of income tax			$ None

Taxable Year Ended December 31, 1961

ADJUSTMENTS TO NET INCOME

Net income shown in deficiency letter dated May 20, 1965	$273,758.27
Addition:	
(a) Net long term capital gain	27,749.98
Total	$301,508.25
Deduction:	
(b) Compensation for personal services decreased	55,500.00
Net income as corrected	$246,008.25

EXPLANATION OF ADJUSTMENTS

(a) and (b) See explanation of similar adjustments to net income for the year 1969.

TAX COURT FORM 22 (*Continued*)

Richard Silver   Audit Statement

Taxable Year Ended December 31, 1961

COMPUTATION OF ALTERNATIVE TAX

Income subject to tax	$244,808.25
Less: Excess of net long term capital gain over net short term capital loss	51,356.52
Balance subject to partial tax	$193,451.73
Combined partial normal tax and surtax	$151,402.56
Add: 50% of excess of net long term capital gain over net short term capital loss, $51,356.52	25,678.26
Alternative tax	$177.080.82

COMPUTATION OF INCOME TAX

Net income as corrected		$246,008.25
Less: Exemptions (2) × $600.		1,200.00
Income subject to tax		$244,808.25
Tax on $244,808.25		$198.071.51
Alternative tax		$177,080.82
Less: Income tax payments to a foreign country		102.15
Corrected income tax liability		$176,978.67
Income tax liability disclosed by return, a/c #271007416	$173,954.52	
Additional assessment, Feb. 16, 1964, list, a/c #2–510766	3,024.15	176,978.67
Deficiency of income tax		$ None

Taxable Year Ended December 31, 1962

ADJUSTMENTS TO NET INCOME

Net income shown in deficiency letter dated May 20, 1965	$219,659.49
Addition:	
(a) Net long term capital gain	27,749.99
Total	$247,409.48
Deduction:	
(b) Compensation for personal services decreased	55,500.00
Net income as corrected	$191,909.48

Tax Court Form 22 (*Concluded*)

Richard Silver   Audit Statement

Taxable Year Ended December 31, 1962

EXPLANATION OF ADJUSTMENTS

(a) and (b) See explanation of similar adjustments to net income for the year 1960.

COMPUTATION OF ALTERNATIVE TAX

Income subject to tax if separate return; or one-half of such income if joint return	$190,709.48
Less: Excess of net long term capital gain over net short term capital loss	42,460.14
Balance subject to partial tax	$148,249.34
Combined partial normal tax and surtax (Head of Household)	$105,023.94
Add: 52% of excess of net long term capital gain over net short term capital loss, $42,460.14	22,079.27
Alternative tax	$127,103.21

COMPUTATION OF INCOME TAX

Net income as corrected		$191,909.48
Less: Exemptions (2) × $600.		1,200.00
Income subject to tax		$190,709.48
Tax on $190,709.48 (Head of Household)		$142,336.34
Alternative tax		$127,103.21
Less: Income tax payments to a foreign country		91.34
Corrected income tax liability		$127,011.87
Income tax liability disclosed by return, a/c #243001317	$124,514.14	
Income		
Additional assessment, March 19, 1965 list, a/c #3–510414	2,497.73	127,011.87
Deficiency of income tax		$ None

TAX COURT FORM 23. PETITION FOR APPELLATE REVIEW

IN THE UNITED STATES COURT OF APPEALS
FOR THE SECOND CIRCUIT

NEWARK BOLT CO.,

          Petitioner,

     —*against*—   T. C. Docket No. 61364

COMMISSIONER OF INTERNAL REVENUE,

          Respondent.

PETITION FOR REVIEW

Newark Bolt Co., the petitioner in this cause, by Richard M. Frome, Counsel, hereby files its petition for review by the United States Court of Appeals for the Second Circuit of the decision by the Tax Court of the United States entered on February 25, 1966, 46 T. C. No. 108, determining deficiencies in the petitioner's Federal income and excess profits taxes for the calendar years 1960 and 1961 in the respective amounts of $153,959.75 and $402,847.03, and respectfully shows:

I.

The petitioner, Newark Bolt Co., is a corporation duly organized and existing under and by virtue of the laws of the State of New Jersey, with its principal office in the City of New York, State of New York. Petitioner's Federal income tax returns for the years 1960 and 1961 were filed with the Director of Internal Revenue, Upper Manhattan District of New York. By reason of Section 7482 (b) (1) of the Internal Revenue Code of 1954, the aforesaid decision of the Tax Court of the United States may be reviewed by the United States Court of Appeals for the Second Circuit.

II.

Nature of the Controversy

The controversy involves the proper determination of the petitioner's liability for Federal income and excess profits taxes for the calendar years 1960 and 1961.

The petitioner owned and operated at all times material herein a mill at Rutherford, New Jersey, the principal products of which are nuts and bolts. The petitioner's mill operation is complete from raw metal to finished product.

Petitioner began a major capital improvements program to meet increasing demand for its products. New machinery was installed and other machinery was rebuilt and reconditioned during the years 1956 through 1958 for the purpose of increasing the capacity of the mill. The total cost of petitioner's capital improvements and additions exceeded $11,000,000. As a result, petitioner's

Tax Court Form 23 (*Concluded*)

production increased from 131,494 tons in 1956 to 138,768 tons in 1957 to 157,993 tons in 1958 to 160,647 tons in 1959 to 180,210 tons in 1960 to 186,357 tons in 1961.

In the operation of its mill facilities, petitioner relies upon electric power. As a result of its increased capacity, petitioner's normal requirements for power to operate its mill increased from an average of about 21,400 kilowatts of power in early 1967 to an average of about 26,600 kilowatts by May, 1958.

The Power Company supplies mainly hydroelectric power and a small amount of hydromechanical power, the production of which is entirely dependent upon the flow of water in the Hackensack River. Under average river flow conditions, representing a flow of approximately 2400 cubic feet per second, the power system was capable of producing enough hydroelectric and hydromechanical power to meet the average demands on the system.

Commencing in the summer of 1957, the entire State of New Jersey suffered a severe drought. The drought became worse during the latter half of that year and continued, except for a very brief spring runoff of winter snows, through the year 1958. As a result, the great reduction of flow of the river caused a substantial reduction in the generating capacity of the Power Company and in the amount of power available to the petitioner. As a direct result of this prolonged and drastic shortage of power, the petitioner experienced an interruption and diminution in nuts and bolts production and higher mill costs for its operations.

Every step which could possibly be taken to overcome the loss of electric power or to minimize the resulting losses of production was adopted by the petitioner. Nevertheless, the available power was insufficient to keep the taxpayer's machines going full time, and some of the machines were shut down for various periods during the years 1957 and 1958. Moreover, this enforced idleness occurred in times when the demand for the petitioner's products far exceeded its productive capacity.

*   *   *   *   *

III.

The said Newark Bolt Co., being aggrieved by the findings of fact and conclusions of law contained in the said findings and opinion of the Tax Court of the United States, and by its decision entered pursuant thereto, desires to obtain a review thereof by the United States Court of Appeals for the Second Circuit.

s/ (Richard M. Frome)

RICHARD M. FROME
Counsel for Petitioner
375 Park Avenue
New York, New York

3. TAX REFUND SUIT FORMS

TAX REFUND SUIT FORM 1. CLAIM FOR REFUND (INCOME TAX)

| FORM **843** (Rev. July 1965) | U.S. TREASURY DEPARTMENT - INTERNAL REVENUE SERVICE
CLAIM
TO BE FILED WITH THE DISTRICT DIRECTOR WHERE
ASSESSMENT WAS MADE OR TAX PAID | District Director's Stamp (Date Received) |

The District Director will indicate in the block below the kind of claim filed, and fill in, where required.

- [X] Refund of Taxes Illegally, Erroneously, or Excessively Collected.
- [ ] Refund of Amount Paid for Stamps Unused, or Used in Error or Excess.
- [ ] Abatement of Tax Assessed (not applicable to estate, gift, or income taxes).

PLEASE TYPE OR PRINT PLAINLY

Name of taxpayer or purchaser of stamps
Casper & Gail Pelczynski

| Number and street
6102 Moorefield Road | City, town, State, Postal ZIP Code
Baltimore, Maryland   31328 |

Fill in applicable items—Attach letter size sheets if space is not sufficient

a. Your social security number	Wife's number, if joint return	b. If an employer, enter employer identification number
123 45 678	234 56 789	

c. District in which return (if any) was filed	d. Name and address shown on return, if different from above
Maryland	Same

e. Period—if for tax reported on annual basis, prepare separate form for each taxable year	f. Kind of tax
From January 1 1967 , To December 31 1967	Personal income tax

| g. Amount of assessment
$ 2,154.00 | Dates of payment
July 2, 1969 |

| h. Date stamps were purchased from Government | i. Amount to be refunded (If income tax, complete computation below)
$ 2,154.00 | j. Amount to be abated (not applicable to income, estate, or gift taxes)
$ |

k. The claimant believes that this claim should be allowed for the following reasons:

The District Director of Internal Revenue erroneously disallowed claimed

deductions amounting to $_____ which represented the total of

Mr. Pelczynski's living expenses while away from home on a temporary job

assignment. Mr. Pelczynski spent the entire calender year 1967 in Abidjan, The

Ivory Coast, performing consultant services for the African Fruit & Vegetable

Corporation. However, Mr. Pelczynski's home, for tax purposes, remained in Baltimore.

COMPUTATION OF INCOME TAX REFUND	Income Tax
1. Tax withheld.	$ 4,000.00
2. Estimated tax paid.	1,000.00
3. Tax paid with original return	700.00
4. Any additional income tax paid	2,154.00
5. Total tax paid (Add lines 1–4).	7,854.00
6. Less: Your computation of correct tax.	5,700.00
7. Amount of overpayment.	2,154.00
8. Amount previously refunded.	–
9. Net overpayment (Enter in item i above).	2,154.00

Under penalties of perjury, I declare that this claim, including any accompanying schedules and statements, has been examined by me and to the best of my knowledge and belief it is true and correct.

Signed /s/ Casper Joseph Pelczynski

Dated August 23 , 19 69 /s/ Gail Cashen Pelczynski

SEE INSTRUCTIONS ON REVERSE

FORM 843 (Rev. 7–65)

TAX REFUND SUIT FORM 1 (*Concluded*)

INSTRUCTIONS

1. The claim must set forth in detail each ground upon which it is made and facts sufficient to apprise the Service of the exact basis thereof.

2. If a joint income tax return was filed for the year for which this claim is filed, social security numbers, if any, of both husband and wife must be entered and each must sign this claim even though only one had income. If the taxpayer has been assigned an employer identification number, it must be entered on the form.

3. The claim may be executed by an agent of the taxpayer, but the original or a true copy of a power of attorney must accompany the claim.

4. If a return is filed by an individual and a refund claim is thereafter filed by a legal representative of the deceased, certified copies of the letters testamentary, letters of administration, or similar evidence must be annexed to the claim, to show the authority of the executor, administrator, or other fiduciary

by whom the claim is filed. If an executor, administrator, guardian, trustee, receiver, or other fiduciary files a return and thereafter refund claim is filed by the same fiduciary, documentary evidence to establish the legal authority of the fiduciary need not accompany the claim, provided a statement is made on the claim showing that the return was filed by the fiduciary and that the latter is still acting.

5. Where the taxpayer is a corporation, the claim will be signed with the corporate name, followed by the signature and title of the officer having authority to sign for the corporation.

6. If claim is for excess social security (F.I.C.A.) tax withheld as a result of having had more than one employer during a calendar year, include the names and addresses of your employers, and the amount of wages received and F.I.C.A. employee tax withheld by each as part of your explanation in item k. Do not claim tax withheld if you have claimed the excess withholding on your individual income tax return.

TAX REFUND SUIT FORM 2. STATEMENT OF GROUNDS FOR REFUND
(ESTATE TAX)

The claimant believes that this claim should be allowed for the following reasons:

(1) The District Director of Internal Revenue erroneously determined the value of decedent's residence, as of the date of his death, to be $250,000.00. The actual fair market value of decedent's residence as of the date of death was not more than $150,000.00.

(2) The District Director of Internal Revenue erroneously included in decedent's estate, for estate tax purposes, the amount of $1,500,000.00, representing the fair market value as of decedent's date of death, of 30,000 shares of D.E.F. Company, Inc. Said shares, however had been transferred to decedent's three daughters (in equal shares) on December 25, 1966 as Christmas gifts and for other reasons. The District Director erroneously considered the gifts to have been in contemplation of death as that term is used in Section 2035 of the Internal Revenue Code of 1954.

TAX REFUND SUIT FORM 3. STATEMENT OF GROUNDS FOR REFUND
(GIFT TAX)

The claimant believes that this claim should be allowed for the following reasons:

John J. Taxpayer made a gift of 25,000 shares of common stock of the X.Y.Z. Corporation on April 4, 1967. The mean price of X.Y.Z. stock traded on the New York Stock Exchange on April 4, 1967 was $40.00 per share. The District Director erroneously used $40.00 per share as the value of the gift for

TAX REFUND SUIT FORM 3 (*Concluded*)

---

gift tax purposes. The District Director should have reduced the value of the gift by at least $3.00 per share in order to take into account the size of the block of stock being valued.

TAX REFUND SUIT FORM 4. STATEMENT OF GROUNDS FOR REFUND
(EMPLOYER'S TAX)

The claimant believes that this claim should be allowed for the following reasons:

The District Director of Internal Revenue erroneously assessed and collected from Taxpayer Home Improvement Company the sum of $25,000.00 representing F.I.C.A. employer's taxes for the period July 1, 1965 through June 30, 1967. The assessment was made on the basis of the company's having had employees who performed services for the company in the home improvement field. The names of the workmen with respect to whom taxes were assessed may be found on the list attached hereto as Exhibit A. However, none of the workmen was an employee of Taxpayer Home Improvement Company at any time during the aforementioned period. The workmen were either independent contractors or employees of independent contractors. The relationship between Taxpayer Home Improvement Company and the workmen in question is the same as that which existed in the case of United States v. Thorson, 282 F.2d 157 (C.A.1st). In that case the United States Court of Appeals held that the workmen were not employees of the home improvement company. A refund should be made.

TAX REFUND SUIT FORM 5. STATEMENT OF GROUNDS FOR REFUND
(RESPONSIBLE OFFICER PENALTY)

The claimant believes that this claim should be allowed for the following reasons:

The District Director of Internal Revenue has assessed against John Officer a 100% penalty in the total amount of $7,500.00 representing withholding taxes allegedly unpaid by the Insolvent Company, Inc., with respect to wages paid during the first and second quarters in 1966. John Officer has paid the sum of $56.75, representing the assessment with respect to one employee (Able Adamac) for the first quarter of 1966. The assessment was erroneous and illegal because John Officer was not a "responsible person" as that term is used in Sections 6671 and 6672 of the Internal Revenue Code of 1954. The amount which John Officer has paid with respect to said assessment should be refunded (together with interest) and the remainder of the assessment should be abated.

Tax Refund Suit Form 6. Notice of Adjustment

Form 1331 (3-Part Set) (REV. JULY, 1964) Form approved by Comptroller General, U. S. September 28, 1942	U. S. TREASURY DEPARTMENT – INTERNAL REVENUE SERVICE		SCHEDULE NO. 67-1,876
	NOTICE OF ADJUSTMENT		DATE CERTIFIED 10-15-67
			SERIAL NO. 1

YOUR TAX RETURN FORM NO. 1040	◀	Your tax liability for the taxable period shown has been reduced. All amounts previously charged and all previous reductions are shown in Section I below. The amount of this reduction has been adjusted for (1) abatement, (2) credits, or (3) refund, as explained in Section II.
TAXABLE PERIOD 1964		

NAME AND ADDRESS OF TAXPAYER

⌈ William Wier ⌉
321 Cynwood Terrace
Wilmington, Delaware   19807

$ **$18,480.00**

Amount of Check if
Check is Enclosed

SECTION I - COMPUTATION OF OVERASSESSMENTS

ITEM	TAX	PENALTY	INTEREST
1. TAX WITHHELD	$ 10,000.00		
2. PAID ON ESTIMATED TAX	4,000.00		
3. TAX DUE PER RETURN	14,000.00	$	$
4. ADDITIONAL TAX CHARGED-ACCOUNT NUMBER	18,000.00		900.00
5. TOTAL TAX PREVIOUSLY CHARGED	32,000.00		900.00
6. LESS CORRECT TAX	16,000.00		100.00
7. OVERCHARGE	16,000.00		800.00
8. LESS AMOUNTS PREVIOUSLY REFUNDED OR CREDITED TO OTHER ACCOUNTS			
9. NET OVERCHARGE	$ 16,000.00	$	$ 800.00

10. REASON FOR ADJUSTMENT	DATE
☐ EXPLAINED IN EXAMINER'S REPORT. COPY OF WHICH WAS FURNISHED TO YOU ☐ OTHER *(Specify)*	
☒ CLAIM ☐ AMENDED RETURN	PREPARED BY

SECTION II - DISPOSITION OF OVERASSESSMENT AND INTEREST ALLOWED ON OVERPAYMENT

ADJUSTMENT OF OVERCHARGE	TAX PERIOD ACCOUNT NUMBER	AMOUNT	ALLOWABLE INT. COMPUTED TO	TOTAL PAID
REFUND	D-329876-64	$ 16,800.00	10/15/67	$ 18,480.00
ALLOWABLE INTEREST PAID		$ 1,680.00		
ABATEMENT (AMOUNT ASSESSED — NOT PAID — NOT DUE)				Interest allowed on any overpayment is taxable income. If your income is reported on the cash basis, the amount is income in the year in which received; if on the accrual basis, see Revenue Ruling 62-160, C. B. 1962 - 2-139. An overpayment due to a decrease in interest previously assessed is taxable income for the year received to the extent a deduction claimed in a prior year for such interest reduced the tax for that year. (See Income Tax Regulations section 1.111-1.)
CREDIT (AMOUNT OVERPAID) APPLIED AS CREDIT TO TAX (T), PENALTY (P), AND INTEREST (I) DUE ON OTHER OUTSTANDING ACCOUNTS				
TOTAL OVERCHARGE ABATED AND CREDITED				$
INTEREST ALLOWED APPLIED AS CREDIT		$ $		$
TOTAL ABATED AND CREDITED				$

DISTRICT Delaware	DISTRICT DIRECTOR OF INTERNAL REVENUE Frank Smallwood	COMPLETED BY AND DATE JDG 10-13-67

Part 1 - Taxpayer's Copy   Form 1331 (3 Part Set) (Rev. 7-64)

Tax Refund Suit Form 7. Complaint (Usual Form)

1. Plaintiffs, John and Jane Taxpayer are citizens of the United States who reside at 5432 Elmwood Drive, Wilmington, Delaware.

2. The defendant is the United States of America.

3. This is a suit arising under the internal revenue laws of the United States for the refund of taxes erroneously and illegally assessed against and collected from the plaintiffs.

4. Jurisdiction is conferred upon this court by virtue of 28 U.S.C. Sec. 1346(a)(1).

COUNT ONE

5. On April 15, 1965 plaintiffs filed their joint federal income tax return for the calendar year 1964 with the Internal Revenue Service at the Regional Service Center in Philadelphia, Pennsylvania and paid the sum of $_____ in income taxes reported due on said return.

6. On July 2, 1967 the District Director of Internal Revenue for the Delaware District assessed against plaintiffs a deficiency of $_____ in additional taxes plus interest for the calendar year 1964.

7. On July 25, 1967 plaintiffs paid to the District Director the sum of $_____ which was the full amount of the deficiency plus interest assessed against them for the calendar year 1964, together with interest to the date of payment.

8. The assessment and collection of the deficiency plus interest for the calendar year 1964 was erroneous and illegal.

9. On August 3, 1967 plaintiffs filed with the District Director a claim for refund of the deficiency plus interest paid by them with respect to the calendar year 1964. A true copy of said claim for refund is attached hereto as Exhibit A.

10. On November 21, 1967 the District Director mailed to the plaintiffs, by certified mail, a formal notice of disallowance of their claim for refund with regard to the calendar year 1964.

11. As grounds for recovery plaintiffs incorporate herein by reference the averments contained in their claim for refund for the calendar year 1964, Exhibit A hereto.

12. Plaintiffs have overpaid their federal income taxes for the calendar year 1964 and are entitled to recover from defendant the sum of $_____ plus interest, no part of which has been repaid to plaintiffs.

13. Plaintiffs are the sole owners of their claim against the defendant and have made no assignment of said claim.

COUNT TWO

14. On April 15, 1966 plaintiffs filed their joint federal income tax return for the calendar year 1965 with the Internal Revenue Service at the Regional Service Center in Philadelphia, Pennsylvania and paid the sum of $_____ in income taxes reported due on said return.

Tax Refund Suit Form 7 (*Concluded*)

---

15. On November 5, 1967 the District Director of Internal Revenue for the Delaware District assessed against plaintiffs a deficiency of $_____ in additional taxes plus interest for the calendar year 1965.

16. On November 23, 1967 plaintiffs paid to the District Director the sum of $_____ which was the full amount of the deficiency plus interest assessed against them for the calendar year 1965, together with interest to the date of payment.

17. The assessment and collection of the deficiency plus interest for the calendar year 1965 was erroneous and illegal.

18. On December 5, 1967 plaintiffs filed with the District Director a claim for refund of the deficiency plus interest paid by them with respect to the calendar year 1965. A true copy of said claim for refund is attached hereto as Exhibit B.

19. On February 7, 1968 the District Director mailed to the plaintiffs, by certified mail, a formal notice of disallowance of their claim for refund with regard to the calendar year 1965.

20. As grounds for recovery plaintiffs incorporate herein by reference the averments contained in their claim for refund for the calendar year 1965, Exhibit B hereto.

21. Plaintiffs have overpaid their federal income taxes for the calendar year 1965 and are entitled to recover from defendant the sum of $_____ plus interest, no part of which has been repaid to plaintiffs.

22. Plaintiffs are the sole owners of their claim against the defendant and have made no assignment of said claim.

WHEREFORE, plaintiffs pray for judgment against the defendant in the total amount of $_____ together with their costs and interest as provided by law.

THOMAS FIELD
Limestone Building
Wilmington, Delaware
Attorney for plaintiffs

PLAINTIFFS DEMAND TRIAL BY JURY *

---

* Consult local rules for requirements regarding location of jury demand on pleadings.

Tax Refund Suit Form 8. Complaint (Multiperiod Divisible Tax)

---

1. Plaintiff Taxpayer Home Improvement Company, Inc., is a New York corporation having its principal place of business at 32 West Street, Syracuse, New York.

2. The defendant is the United States of America.

3. This is a suit arising under the internal revenue laws of the United States for the refund of taxes erroneously and illegally assessed against and collected from the plaintiff.

TAX REFUND SUIT FORM 8 (*Concluded*)

4. Jurisdiction is conferred upon this court by virtue of 28 U.S.C. Sec. 1346(a)(1).

5. On March 23, 1965 the District Director of Internal Revenue, Buffalo, New York assessed against plaintiff F.I.C.A. taxes with respect to the period July 1, 1961 to June 30, 1964, inclusive, in the total amount of $_____ together with interest thereon.

6. On July 6, 1965 plaintiff paid the F.I.C.A. tax assessment, together with interest thereon, for one employee (Able Adamac) with respect to the third quarter of 1961 in the total amount of $_____.

7. On August 8, 1966 plaintiff filed a claim for refund of said payment with the District Director. A copy of the claim for refund of F.I.C.A. taxes is attached hereto as Exhibit A.

8. On December 3, 1966 the District Director mailed to the plaintiff, by registered mail, a formal notice of disallowance of its claim for refund of F.I.C.A. taxes.

9. As grounds for recovery plaintiff incorporates herein by reference the averments contained in its claim for refund of F.I.C.A. taxes, Exhibit A hereto.

10. The assessment and collection of F.I.C.A. taxes was erroneous and illegal.

11. Plaintiff has overpaid its liability for F.I.C.A. taxes for the third quarter of 1961 and is entitled to recover from the defendant the sum of $_____ plus interest, no part of which has been repaid to plaintiff.

12. Plaintiff is the sole owner of its claim against the defendant and has made no assignment of said claim.

WHEREFORE, plaintiff prays for judgment against the defendant in the amount of $_____ together with its costs and interest as provided by law.

> BURTON LIPSKY
> 6700 University Building
> Syracuse, New York
> Attorney for plaintiff

TAX REFUND SUIT FORM 9. COMPLAINT (FORM SEEKING ADMISSIONS)

---

1. Plaintiff Thomas Trustworthy is Executor of the Estate of John Decedent, deceased, pursuant to appointment of the Probate Court of Montgomery County, Ohio. Plaintiff resides at 345 Elder Street, Dayton, Ohio.

2. The defendant is the United States of America.

3. This is a suit arising under the internal revenue laws of the United States for the refund of taxes erroneously and illegally assessed against, and collected from, the estate of John Decedent.

4. Jurisdiction is conferred upon this court by virtue of 28 U.S.C. Sec. 1346(a)(1).

TAX REFUND SUIT FORM 9 (*Concluded*)

5. John Decedent died on March 30, 1964, leaving a will. Attached hereto as Exhibit A is a true copy of the last will of John Decedent.

6. On June 14, 1965 plaintiff timely filed a Federal estate tax return on behalf of the estate of John Decedent with the District Director of Internal Revenue in Cincinnati, Ohio and paid the sum of $_____ in estate taxes shown due on said return.

7. On December 17, 1965 the District Director of Internal Revenue assessed against the estate of John Decedent the sum of $_____ representing an asserted deficiency in estate tax plus interest thereon.

8. Said deficiency assessment was based upon the District Director's determination that bequest set forth in paragraph FOURTH of the will of John Decedent (Exhibit A hereto) did not qualify for the marital deduction.

9. On January 23, 1966 the estate of John Decedent paid to the District Director the sum of $_____ which was the full amount of the deficiency plus interest assessed against the estate together with interest to the date of payment.

10. The assessment and collection of the deficiency plus interest was erroneous and illegal.

11. On February 4, 1966 plaintiff, on behalf of the estate of John Decedent, filed with the District Director a claim for refund of the deficiency plus interest paid. A true copy of said claim for refund is attached hereto as Exhibit B.

12. The ground for recovery raised by said claim for refund was that the bequest set forth in paragraph FOURTH of the will of John Decedent did qualify for the marital deduction.

13. On July 6, 1966 the District Director mailed to plaintiff, by certified mail, a formal notice of disallowance of the claim for refund.

14. Plaintiff avers that the bequest set forth in paragraph FOURTH of the will of John Decedent did qualify for the marital deduction.

15. The estate of John Decedent has overpaid its federal estate taxes and plaintiff is entitled to recover from the defendant the sum of $_____ plus interest, no part of which has been repaid to plaintiff or the estate of John Decedent.

16. The estate of John Decedent is entitled to an additional refund of estate taxes which will result from the deduction of additional allowable administration expenses incurred, and to be incurred, in prosecuting the estate's claim for refund of estate taxes.

17. The estate of John Decedent is the sole owner of its claim against the defendant and has made no assignment of said claim.

WHEREFORE, plaintiff prays for judgment against the defendant in the sum of $_____ or such greater amount as may be refundable, together with his costs and interest as provided by law.

> JAMES J. GOUBEAUX
> 123 Main Street
> Greenville, Ohio
> Attorney for plaintiff

TAX REFUND SUIT FORM 10. MOTION FOR JUDGMENT ON THE PLEADINGS

Pursuant to Rule 12(c) of the Federal Rules of Civil Procedure [Rule 20(c) of the Court of Claims Rules] plaintiff, Taxpayer, Inc., respectfully moves this Court for judgment on the pleadings. The grounds for this motion, as more fully stated in plaintiff's Brief in Support of Motion for Judgment on the Pleadings are that, from the pleadings in this action, it is apparent that

(1) There is no genuine issue as to any material fact in this case, and

(2) The plaintiff is entitled to judgment as a matter of law.

s/ (Robert F. Sama)
_____
Attorney for Plaintiff

TAX REFUND SUIT FORM 11. MOTION FOR SUMMARY JUDGMENT

Plaintiff, Taxpayer, Inc., respectfully moves this Court pursuant to Rule 56 of the Federal Rules of Civil Procedure [Rule 64 of the Court of Claims Rules] for summary judgment against the defendant United States of America. The grounds for this motion, as more fully stated in plaintiff's Brief in Support of Motion for Summary Judgment filed herewith are:

(1) There is no genuine issue as to any material fact in this case, and

(2) The plaintiff is entitled to judgment as a matter of law based upon the record before this court.

s/ (Edward J. Snyder)
_____
Attorney for Plaintiff

TAX REFUND SUIT FORM 12. CROSS-MOTION FOR SUMMARY JUDGMENT

Plaintiff, Taxpayer, Inc., respectfully moves this Court pursuant to Rule 56 of the Federal Rules of Civil Procedure [Rule 64 of the Court of Claims Rules] to deny defendant's pending motion for summary judgment and to grant summary judgment in favor of the plaintiff. The grounds for this motion, as more fully stated in the Brief in Opposition to Defendant's Motion for Summary Judgment and in Support of Plaintiff's Cross-Motion for Summary Judgment, filed herewith, are:

(1) There is no genuine issue as to any material fact in this case, and

(2) The plaintiff, and not the defendant, is entitled to a judgment as a matter of law.

s/ (Daniel J. Dinan)
_____
Attorney for Plaintiff

Tax Refund Suit Form 13. Interrogatories

Pursuant to Rule 33 of the Federal Rules of Civil Procedure plaintiff, Taxpayer, Inc., requests the defendant, the United States of America, from information available to it, to answer the following interrogatories and to serve a copy upon the undersigned counsel for the plaintiff within twenty days after service hereof. If any part of the following interrogatories cannot be answered in full, please answer to the extent possible, specifying the reason for defendant's failure to answer the remainder.

These interrogatories shall be deemed continuing so as to require supplemental answers if defendant obtains further information between the time answers are served and the trial of this case.

1. Set forth a description adequate to identify each and every report prepared by Internal Revenue Agent Able Baker relating or pertaining to statements made to the Agent by any officer or director of plaintiff regarding plaintiff's corporate income tax liability for the calendar year 1965.

2. State the name and address of every employee of the Internal Revenue Service who made an analysis of plaintiff's financial records and made a recommendation to the Internal Revenue Service regarding the allowable deduction for plaintiff's depreciation in 1965.

*   *   *   *   *

s/ (John G. Milano)
———————————————
Attorney for Plaintiff

Tax Refund Suit Form 14. Motion for Call in the Court of Claims

Plaintiff, Taxpayer, Inc., respectfully moves this Court, pursuant to Rule 39 of the Court of Claims Rules, to issue a call upon the defendant, and to order the Internal Revenue Service to either file with the clerk or produce for inspection by the plaintiff the following:

(1) A list setting forth a description adequate to identify each and every report, memorandum and similar document reflecting any statements made by the plaintiff to any employee of the Internal Revenue Service relating or pertaining to plaintiff's federal income tax liability for calendar years 1959, 1960 and 1961.

(2) A list setting forth the name and address of each present or former employee of the Internal Revenue Service who made any report described in paragraph (1) or who was present at any interview or conversation described in a report described in paragraph (1).

(3) A copy of each document described in paragraph (1).

*   *   *   *   *

The materials requested by this motion, as more fully appears in plaintiff's Memorandum in Support of Motion for Call, filed herewith, are relevant to

TAX REFUND SUIT FORM 14 (*Concluded*)

---

the subject matter of this suit and are needed by the plaintiff in order adequately to prepare his case. All of the requested information and materials are in the possession of the defendant and not in the possession of the plaintiff.

s/   (Arthur L. Stern, III)
Attorney for Plaintiffs

TAX REFUND SUIT FORM 15. MOTION FOR PRODUCTION

Plaintiff, Taxpayer, Inc., respectfully moves this Court pursuant to Rule 34 of the Federal Rules of Civil Procedure [Rule 40 of the Court of Claims Rules] for an order requiring the defendant to produce and to permit the plaintiff to inspect and copy all of the following documents in its custody, possession or control;

(1) Interview memorandum of June 3, 1966 prepared by Internal Revenue Agent Adam Baker.

(2) Special Agent's Report of October 5, 1966 prepared by Special Agent Charles Dalton, and all exhibits thereto.

(3) All workpapers and reports prepared by Internal Revenue Agent Adam Baker. Special Agent Charles Dalton or any other employee of the Internal Revenue Service utilized in the defendant's estimation of plaintiff's gross receipts for the calendar year 1964.

*   *   *   *   *

s/   (Barry Fink)
Attorney for Plaintiff

TAX REFUND SUIT FORM 16. REQUEST FOR ADMISSIONS *

Plaintiff, John Taxpayer, pursuant to Rule 36 of the Federal Rules of Civil Procedure, requests defendant, the United States of America, within ten days after service of this request, to make the following admissions for purposes of this action only and subject to all pertinent objections to admissibility which may be raised:

1. Exhibit A hereto is a true copy of the claim for refund filed by plaintiff with the District Director of Internal Revenue in Baltimore, Maryland on June 14, 1965.

2. Exhibit B hereto is a true copy of the contract of employment between John Taxpayer and A.B.C. Upholstering Company of Baltimore, Maryland which was in effect during the calendar year 1964.

* In the Court of Claims, a motion is required in order for a party to obtain leave to serve a set of requests for admissions. See p. **13·23** *supra* and Ct. Cl. R. 40.

Tax Refund Suit Form 16 (*Concluded*)

3. With the exception of plaintiff's claimed deduction of $10,000.00 for travel and entertainment expenses not reimbursed by his employer, all other entries on plaintiff's 1964 federal income tax return were correctly made.

*   *   *   *   *

s/   (John S. Stephan)

Attorney for Plaintiff

Tax Refund Suit Form 17. Pretrial Conference Memorandum (Unsolicited)

Issue

Was a gift of 35,000 share of X.Y.Z. Company made by decedent John Richman, on December 25, 1964 a gift "in contemplation of death" as that terms is used in the estate tax law?

Summary Statement and Contentions

On December 25, 1964 decedent John Richman made a gift to his only child, Percy Richman, of 35,000 shares of X.Y.Z. Company common stock. The total value of this gift was approximately one million dollars. John Richman died almost one year later on December 20, 1965.

Section 2035 of the Internal Revenue Code of 1954 provides that gifts made within three years of a decedent's death are deemed to have been made "in contemplation of death" unless the contrary is shown. Gifts "in contemplation of death" are included in the estate of the donor for federal estate tax purposes.

Plaintiff contends that the evidence in this case will establish that the gift was not in contemplation of death but was made with normal life motives. The Government contends that the gift was made in contemplation of death. Resolution of this factual issue will require consideration of the many factors relevant to contemplation of death controversies. An introduction to this area of the law is afforded by the case of United States v. Wells, 283 U.S. 102.

Conclusion

This pretrial conference memorandum is submitted by the plaintiff in order to introduce the Court to the issues presented by this case.

Respectfully submitted,

Moshe Schuldinger

605 Third Avenue

New York, New York

Tax Refund Suit Form 18. Stipulation

The parties to this law suit hereby stipulate the following for purposes of this case only:

1. Plaintiff, Subchapter S Corporation, Inc. was, at all times pertinent to this law suit, an Ohio corporation with its principal place of business in Cincinnati, Ohio.

      *   *   *   *   *

5. On October 2, 1961 the shareholders of Subchapter S Corporation, Inc. entered into a voting trust agreement. Exhibit A to this set of stipulations is a true copy of said voting trust agreement.

      *   *   *   *   *

8. Exhibit C to this set of stipulations is a true copy of a letter written by Joseph Adams on December 13, 1966. It is agreed that said letter shall constitute the testimony of Mr. Adams in this case with the same force and effect as if Mr. Adams were to appear at the trial hearing of this case to make the statements contained in the letter.

      *   *   *   *   *

10. All items of income and expense reported on the Form 1120-s filed by Subchapter S Corporation, Inc. for the calendar year 1961 are accepted as correct by the defendant. This stipulation does not constitute an admission, however, that said corporation was a qualified small business corporation entitled to file a Form 1120-s as opposed to a Form 1120.

11. It is agreed that any computation necessary as a result of the decision of the Court in this case shall initially be made by the defendant. The defendant's computation shall be submitted to the plaintiff for approval. In the event the parties are unable to agree upon the computation the issue shall be resolved by a procedure to be set by the Court.

s/   (Gerald G. Fain)
———————————————
Attorney for Plaintiff

s/   (Daniel L. Power)
———————————————
Attorney for Defendant

Tax Refund Suit Form 19. Supplemental Stipulation (Allegedly Inadmissible Facts)

In addition to the facts stated in the Stipulation in this case, the parties hereby stipulate that the following statements are to be taken as true for purposes of this case. However, the respective parties expressly reserve the right

TAX REFUND FORM 19 (*Concluded*)

to contend that the following statements (or any of them) have no relevancy to or bearing upon the issues before the Court in this case.

1. After October 1, 1961, the stock transfer records of the Subchapter S Corporation, Inc. continued to show William and Mary Taxpayer to be the owners of record of all of the stock of said corporation.

2. After October 2, 1961, and throughout the period in suit, William Taxpayer, as voting trustee, exercised all voting rights for all the shares of the corporation.

     *   *   *   *   *

s/   (Herbert E. Grossman)
Attorney for Plaintiff

s/   (Michael Marr)
Attorney for Defendant

TAX REFUND SUIT FORM 20. TAX DIVISION SETTLEMENT INFORMATION MEMORANDUM

GENERAL INFORMATION CONCERNING THE SETTLEMENT OF TAX REFUND SUITS

1. An offer in compromise of a tax case need not follow any particular form —a letter addressed to the Assistant Attorney General in charge of the Tax Division will suffice. The offer should set forth clearly the proposed terms of settlement, including provisions for the assessed taxes, penalties and interest to be refunded, and the statutory interest to be paid thereon. Statutory interest is computed in accordance with law (usually Section 6611, I.R.C. 1954) unless the settlement agreement provides for a lesser amount.

2. Prior to taking action on an offer in compromise the Department, as a matter of policy, obtains the recommendation of the Chief Counsel, Internal Revenue Service, on the specific offer, unless the latter has previously placed the case in the category in which he considers further reference to him to be unnecessary.

3. Upon timely request on behalf of the plaintiff, the Tax Division customarily affords the taxpayer and/or his counsel of record the opportunity to confer informally in Washington concerning the settlement of a pending case. At these conferences the Government is represented by one or more attorneys of the Tax Division, and, in appropriate cases, by one or more representatives of the Internal Revenue Service. Requests for conferences are denied in a few instances, e.g., request not timely, case not susceptible of settlement, pendency of a related criminal matter, etc.

TAX REFUND SUIT FORM 20 (*Concluded*)

4. Tax settlements require the final approval of the Attorney General, or certain officials of the Department specifically designated by him. See Code of Federal Regulations, Title 28, Chap. I, Subpart W, and Appendix. Neither the United States Attorney nor the trial attorney for the Government has such authority. The Government is not bound by any compromise until a formal notice of approval is sent by the Department to the proponent.

5. If a settlement is consummated, it is the policy of the Department to enter a stipulation for terminating the case by dismissal (instead of by judgment) in terms substantially as follows: "It is hereby stipulated and agreed that the above-entitled action be dismissed with prejudice, each party to bear its own costs." The terms of settlement are not included in the stipulation.

6. Section 6402, I.R.C. 1954, authorizes the crediting of the overpayment resulting from the settlement against any outstanding liability of the taxpayer for any internal revenue tax.

7. Additional information concerning settlement procedures may be obtained from the attorney in the Tax Division assigned to handle the case.

September, 1967.

TAX REFUND SUIT FORM 21. OFFER TO SETTLE TAX REFUND SUIT

Honorable _____ _____
Assistant Attorney General
Tax Division
United States Department of Justice
Washington, D.C. 20530

> In Re: Delaware National Bank v. United States,
> Civil No. 1432 (D. Delaware)
>
> Your ref: UV:WXY:MSchuldinger 5-15-1234

Dear Mr. _____:

Plaintiff, Delaware National Bank, hereby offers to compromise the above-entitled tax refund suit. Plaintiff will dismiss its complaint with prejudice in return for a refund of $90,000.00 plus interest thereon as provided by law. The principal amount of the refund shall consist of $80,000.00 in overpaid corporate income tax for the calendar year 19— and $10,000.00 in overpaid assessed interest with respect to the same tax.

> Sincerely yours,
>
> JEROME H. FRIDKIN

cc: _____
    United States Attorney
    Wilmington, Delaware

TAX REFUND SUIT FORM 22. STIPULATION OF DISMISSAL AFTER
SETTLEMENT

It is hereby stipulated that plaintiff's complaint shall be dismissed with prejudice, the parties to bear their respective costs.

s/   (Mark S. Rothman)
<u>Attorney for Plaintiff</u>

s/   (Larry J. Ross, Jr.)
<u>Attorney for Defendant</u>

APPROVED:

s/   (Daniel P. Mallarky)
<u>United States District Judge</u>

TAX REFUND SUIT FORM 23. REQUESTED QUESTIONS FOR VOIR DIRE
EXAMINATION OF PROSPECTIVE JURORS

Plaintiff, Taxpayer Liquor Supply Company, respectfully requests the Court to ask the prospective jurors in this case the following questions upon voir dire:

1. Are any of you, or are any members of your immediate family, employees of the United States Government? (If any juror answers "Yes" the Court is requested to inquire as to the nature of the juror's or his relative's employment.)

2. Do any of you have personal convictions (whether due to religious belief or other cause) against persons or companies engaged in the sale of alcoholic beverages? (Plaintiff submits that any juror who answers this question in the affirmative should be dismissed for cause.)

3. Are any of you, or are any members of your immediate family, employees of any State or local law enforcement agency? (If any juror answers "yes" the Court is requested to inquire as to the nature of the juror's or his relative's employment.)

4. In this case testimony will be given for the Government by accountants who are employed by the Internal Revenue Service and for the plaintiff by Certified Public Accountants in private practice in this city. Do any of you feel that the testimony of an accountant who works for the Government is necessarily entitled to greater weight than that of an accountant engaged in private practice?

*   *   *   *   *

HENRY G. ZAPRUDER
1700 J Street, N.W.
Washington, D.C.
Attorney for Plaintiff

TAX REFUND SUIT FORM 24. MOTION ACCOMPANYING REQUESTED JURY INSTRUCTIONS

Pursuant to Rule 51 of the Federal Rules of Civil Procedure plaintiffs, John and Joan Taxpayer, respectfully request the Court to instruct the jury by giving the following instructions, attached hereto, and to advise counsel prior to argument which of the requested instructions will be given and which will not.

s/ (Peter J. Ciano)

Attorney for Plaintiffs

TAX REFUND SUIT FORM 25. SET OF REQUESTED JURY INSTRUCTIONS

PLAINTIFFS' REQUESTED INTRUCTION NO. 1

MEMBERS OF THE JURY:

Now that you have heard the evidence and the arguments of counsel, the time has come to instruct you as to the law governing this case.

Although you as jurors are the sole judges of the facts, you are duty bound to follow the law as stated in the instructions of the Court and to apply the law so given to the facts as you find them from the evidence before you.

You are not to be concerned with the wisdom of any rule of law. Regardless of any opinion you may have as to what the law ought to be, it would be a violation of your sworn duty to base a verdict upon any view of the law other than that given you in the Court's instructions.

Jury Instructions and Forms—Civil
Civ. 1.01, (Modified) 28 F.R.D. 401, 413.

PLAINTIFFS' REQUESTED INSTRUCTION NO. 2

This is a civil tax suit brought by Harry and Mary Homeowner against the United States for a refund of income taxes which they have paid. The fact that Mr. and Mrs. Homeowner have already paid the taxes in dispute in no way indicates that they at any time believed that they owed any tax deficiency. The law required them to make the payment in order to be able to bring their case in this Court upon a suit for its refund.

Flora v. United States, 362 U.S. 145

PLAINTIFFS' REQUESTED INSTRUCTION NO. 3

The fact that the plaintiffs, Mr. and Mrs. Homeowner are private citizens and the defendant is the Government should not enter into or affect your verdict. All parties are equal before the law and should be given the same fair treatment by you. You are to decide this case on the evidence presented to you during the trial of this case and you are to be guided by the law as I state it to you.

PLAINTIFFS' REQUESTED JURY INSTRUCTION NO. 4

In this case the burden of proof is on the plaintiffs, Harry and Mary Home-owner, to prove every essential element of their case by a preponderance of the evidence.

To "establish by a preponderance of the evidence" means to prove that something is more likely so than not so. In other words, a preponderance of the evidence means such evidence as, when considered and compared with that opposed to it, has more convincing force and produces in your minds belief that what is sought to be proved is more likely true than not true. In this case, therefore, the plaintiffs, Harry and Mary Homeowner do not have to prove their case beyond a reasonable doubt but merely have to persuade you that their assertions are more likely than not to have been true.

Jury Instructions and Forms—Civil
Civ. 2.01 (modified) 28 F.R.D. 401, 415

PLAINTIFFS' REQUESTED JURY INSTRUCTION NO. 5

The evidence in this case consists of the sworn testimony of the witnesses, all exhibits which have been received in evidence, all facts which have been admitted or stipulated, all facts and events which have been judicially noticed, and all applicable presumptions stated in these instructions.

You are to consider only the evidence in the case. But in your consideration of the evidence you are not limited to the bald statements of the witnesses. On the contrary, you are permitted to draw, from facts which you find have been proved, such reasonable inferences as seem justified in the light of your own experience.

Suggested Civil Forms, Form Civ. 5
(Modified) 22 F.R.D. 127, 134.

PLAINTIFFS' REQUESTED INSTRUCTION NO. 6

It is the duty of attorneys on each side of a case to object when the other side offers testimony or other evidence which counsel believes is not properly admissible.

When the Court has sustained an objection to a question, the jury are to disregard the question, and may draw no inference from the wording of it or speculate as to what the witness would have said if permitted to answer.

Upon allowing testimony or other evidence to be introduced over the objection of counsel, the Court does not, unless expressly stated, indicate any opinion as to the weight or effect of such evidence.

Jury Instructions and Forms—Civil
Civ. 9.04, 28 F.R.D. 401, 450.

TAX REFUND SUIT FORM 25 (*Continued*)

PLAINTIFFS' REQUESTED INSTRUCTION NO. 7

The issues which you are to decide in this case center around Mr. and Mrs. Homeowner's claim that they sustained a "casualty loss" as the result of a landslide which occurred on May 5, 19— during the construction of their residence. You will first have to ascertain whether there was, in fact, a casualty as that term will be defined to you. Then you will have to determine the amount of the casualty loss deduction, if any, to which Mr. and Mrs. Homeowner were entitled on their 19— income tax return.

PLAINTIFFS' REQUESTED INSTRUCTION NO. 8

In the Internal Revenue Code of 1954, which is the law governing this suit, taxpayers are entitled to a deduction for a loss which arises from a fire, storm, shipwreck or other casualty.
Section 165 (c), Internal Revenue Code of 1954, 26 U.S.C.

PLAINTIFFS' REQUESTED INTRUCTION NO. 9

For an event to constitute a casualty under the tax law it need not be a fire, storm or shipwreck. It need only possess the characteristic of suddenness common to such events. Accordingly, if you find that the landslide of May 5, 19— was caused by the sudden, unexpected operation of a hostile force then it constitutes a casualty.

Denton v. Bingler, 12 AFTR 2d 5735 (W.D.Pa.)
Fay v. Helvering, 120 F.2d 263 (C.A.3d)

PLAINTIFFS' REQUESTED INSTRUCTION NO. 10

If you should find that the landslide of May 5, 19— was an ordinary incident of construction of their residence then it was not a casualty loss and Mr. and Mrs. Homeowner would not be entitled to a casualty loss deduction. However, if you should find that the landslide was an unusual and unexpected event occurring during the construction of the residence then it did constitute a casualty loss and Mr. and Mrs. Homeowner are entitled to the deduction which they have claimed.

Jones v. Smith, 193 F. 2d 381,384 (C.A. 10th)
Kipp v. Bingler, 14 A.F.T.R. 2d 5735 (W.D.Pa.)

PLAINTIFFS' REQUESTED INSTRUCTION NO. 11

If you find that Mr. and Mrs. Homeowner are entitled to a casualty loss deduction then you should ascertain the amount of their deduction.

I instruct you that the amount of the Homeowners' casualty loss deduction is the difference between the fair market value of their residence immediately before the landslide and the fair market value of their residence immediately after the landslide.

Walton v. Commissioner, P–H Memo T.C. ¶ 61,130
du Pont v. United States, 19 A.F.T.R. 2d 791 (Del.)

PLAINTIFFS' REQUESTED INSTRUCTION NO. 12

With regard to the amount of the casualty loss deduction to which Mr. and Mrs. Homeowner are entitled, each side has presented the testimony of an expert witness. Mr. Lowman, testifying for the Government, stated that he felt that the loss sustained was not more than $1,000.00. Mr. Highman, testifying for Mr. and Mrs. Homeowner, stated that he felt that the loss sustained was not less than $25,000.00.

Both of these men were what is called expert witnesses. The rules of evidence ordinarily do not permit a witness to testify as to his opinions or conclusions. An expert witness is an exception to this general rule. A person who has become expert in any art, science, profession or calling may be permitted to state his opinion as to a matter in which he is versed and may also state the reasons for his opinion. You should consider the expert testimony received in evidence in this case and give it such weight as you think it deserves. You may reject entirely the testimony of any expert witness if you feel that the reasons given in support of his opinion are unsound.

Suggested Civil Forms, Civ. 19
22 F.R.D. 127,137

PLAINTIFFS' REQUESTED INSTRUCTION No. 13

Your verdict in this case will be rendered in response to two questions which are called special interrogatories. You will be given a written form on which to provide your answers to these questions.

The first question is "Did Mr. and Mrs. Homeowner, on May 5, 19— sustain a casualty loss?" If you find that there was no casualty loss as I have defined that term to you then you should answer "No," and terminate your deliberations. If you find there was a casualty loss then you should answer the question "Yes," and proceed to the next question.

The second question is "What was the amount of the casualty loss deduction to which Mr. and Mrs. Homeowner are entitled as a result of the casualty loss of May 5, 196–?" You should answer this question by stating the dollar amount of the deduction to which you find Mr. and Mrs. Homeowner are entitled pursuant to my instructions. The answer will be expressed in a dollar amount which can range from $1,000.00, as contended by the Government, to $25,000.00, as contended by Mr. and Mrs. Homeowner.

TAX REFUND SUIT FORM 26. SPECIAL INTERROGATORIES FOR THE JURY

---

1. Did Mr. and Mrs. Homeowner, on May 5, 196–, sustain a casualty loss?

Answer "Yes" or "No."

If your answer to question No. 1 was "No" do not answer question No. 2.
If your answer to question No. 2 was "Yes" please answer question No. 2.

2. What is the amount of the casualty loss deduction to which Mr. and Mrs. Homeowner are entitled as a result of the casualty loss of May 5, 196–?

Answer with a dollar amount
from $1,000.00 to $25,000.00

Foreman

TAX REFUND SUIT FORM 27. JUDGMENT ORDER ON JURY VERDICT

This action, having been duly tried before the Court and a jury, Honorable Myron S. Stoll, District Judge, presiding, and the jury having duly rendered its verdict,

It is Ordered and Adjudged:

that the plaintiff, Taxpayer Corporation, recover of the defendant, the United States of America, the sum of $_____ together with interest thereon at the rate of six per cent per annum as provided by law and that [the parties shall bear their own respective costs] plaintiff, Taxpayer Corporation, shall recover its costs from the defendant the United States of America.

s/   (Myron S. Stoll)
United States District Judge

TAX REFUND SUIT FORM 28. MOTION FOR JUDGMENT N.O.V. AND ALTERNATIVELY FOR NEW TRIAL

Plaintiffs, John and Joan Taxpayer, respectfully move this Court to set aside the verdict returned on March 24, 1965 and the judgment entered in accordance therewith on March 25, 1965 and to enter judgment for the plaintiffs in accordance with their motion for directed verdict made at the close of all the evidence in this case. This motion should be granted because, as more fully stated in plaintiffs' brief in support of this motion filed herewith, the evidence in this case established that plaintiffs were entitled to judgment as a matter of law and the verdict should have been directed in their favor.

In the alternative, plaintiffs respectfully move this Court to grant a new trial because the jury's vedict was against the weight of the evidence.

s/   (Gene A. Castleberry)
Attorney for Plaintiffs

TAX REFUND SUIT FORM 29. JUDGMENT ORDER ON DECISION
BY THE COURT

This action, having been duly tried before the Court, Honorable Daniel B. Davis, District Judge, presiding and a decision having been duly rendered,

It is Ordered and Adjudged:

that the plaintiffs, John and Joan Taxpayer, recover of the defendant, the United States of America, the sum of $_____ together with interest thereon at the rate of six per cent per annum as provided by law and that [the parties shall bear their own respective costs] plaintiffs, John and Joan Taxpayer, shall recover their costs of the defendant, the United States of America.

s/   (Daniel B. Davis)
United States District Judge

TAX REFUND SUIT FORM 30. BILL OF COSTS WITH AFFIDAVIT

Plaintiff, Taxpayer Corporation, submits the following list of recoverable costs incurred in the above-entitled suit. Pursuant to the judgment of this Court, entered March 24, 1965, plaintiffs request that these costs be taxed against the defendant, the United States of America.

Docket fee	$_____
Marshal's fee	_____
Witness' fees	_____
Cost of transcripts of depositions placed in evidence	_____
Total	$_____

District of_____ } ss

AFFIDAVIT OF LEVON KASARJIAN, JR.

I, Levon Kasarjian, Jr., being duly sworn, hereby depose and state that:
(1) I am counsel for plaintiff, Taxpayer Corporation in the above-entitled case, and I have personally inspected the attached bill of costs,
(2) Each item on the attached bill of costs is correctly stated,
(3) The costs stated were actually incurred as a necessary part of the case, and
(4) The services for which charges have been made in the bill of costs have actually been performed

LEVON KASARJIAN, JR.

Tax Refund Suit Form 30 (*Concluded*)

Sworn to before me this ⸻
day of ⸻, 19⸺.

⸻
John Doe, Notary Public

Tax Refund Suit Form 31. Notice of Appeal

Notice is hereby given that plaintiffs, John and Joan Taxpayer hereby appeal to the United States Court of Appeals for the Second Circuit from the judgment entered on March 24, 1965 dismissing their complaint with prejudice.

s/   (Michael B. Arkin)
⸻
Attorney for Plaintiffs

D

TABLE OF RULES OF THE COURTS

(Boldface numbers refer to chapters; lightface numbers following dots refer to pages.)

FEDERAL RULES OF CIVIL PROCEDURE
(United States District Courts)

SUPREME COURT RULES

TAX COURT RULES

E

TABLES OF LAW AND REGULATIONS

(Boldface numbers refer to chapters; lightface numbers following dots refer to pages.)

* All references herein are to the Internal Revenue Code of 1954.

E · 1

TREASURY REGULATIONS *

* All references herein are to Treasury Regulations promulgated under the Internal Revenue Code of 1954.

F

TABLE OF CASES

G

GENERAL INDEX

(Boldface numbers refer to chapters; lightface numbers following dots refer to pages.)

Appellate Division; *see* Administrative procedures

Appellate review (refund suits)
Court of Claims
procedure on petition for certiorari, **16·**13–14
right to petition for certiorari, **16·**13
Supreme Court procedure, **16·**14
district courts
appellate procedure, **16·**12
cross-appeal, **16·**12–13
notice of appeal, **16·**11–12, **C·**95
procedures on government appeal, **16·**12–13
procedures on taxpayer appeal, **16·**11–12
right to appeal, **16·**11
venue, **16·**11
government procedure on adverse decision, **16·**10–11
whether to appeal, **16·**10

Appellate review (Tax Court)
bond required, **9·**19
form of petition for review, **C·**71–72
government procedure on adverse decision, **9·**17
procedure for, **9·**18–19
right to appeal, **9·**17
scope of review, **9·**17–18
venue, **9·**18
whether to appeal, **9·**17

Assessment of tax
jeopardy; *see* Jeopardy assessment
limitations; *see* Limitations on assessment
penalties, **3·**4
prohibited by issuance deficiency notice, **3·**2
prohibited after Tax Court petition filed, **3·**2, **4·**1
refund suit jurisdictional prerequisite, **10·**3
time for assessment; *see* Limitations on assessment

Assignments of error; *see* Pleadings (Tax Court)

Audit of tax returns, 1·2
conduct of, **1·**6–9
extensions of assessment period, **1·**10–12
field audit, **1·**6–7
limitation on number of examinations, **1·**8
office audit, **1·**6
preparation for audit, **1·**4–6
scope, **1·**8–9
selection of returns, **1·**2–4
special agent's presence, **1·**7

Automatic Data Processing, 1·2, **1·**4

Bankruptcy and receivership, effect on deficiency notice requirement, 4·2

Bond; *see* Appeal bond (Tax Court)

Briefs; *see* Trial procedure (Court of Claims), Trial procedure (district courts), *and* Trial procedure (Tax Court)

Burden of proof (refund suits)
counterclaims, **12·**20–21
divisible taxes, **12·**20–21
fraud, **12·**21–22
general rule, **12·**16–18
new deficiency notice, **12·**20
new issues, **12·**18–19, **12·**20
offsets, **12·**18–19
overpayment of taxes, **12·**16–18
Tax Court compared, **2·**12–13

Burden of proof (Tax Court)
accumulated earnings tax, **2·**13, **8·**6
extension of limitations, **4·**10, **8·**6
fraud, **8·**5
general rule, **8·**4–5
new issues, **8·**5
refund suit compared, **2·**12–13
transferee cases, **8·**5

Business records, proof of, statute, A·2–3

Calls, discovery device (Court of Claims)
described, **13·**18–19
motion for, **13·**19, **C·**82–83
use of response, **13·**19, **15·**24; *see also* Discovery (refund suits)

Certificate of probable cause, 16·4

Certiorari; *see* Appellate review (refund suits)

Claim for abatement; *see* Abatement of assessment

Claim for refund
administrative procedures on, **10·**32
amended tax return as claim, **10·**8
amendment, **10·**29–31, **12·**7–9
amount refundable
limit to; *see* Limitations on claim for refund
statement on claim, **10·**12–13
claimant; *see* party to file, *infra*
contents of claim, **10·**9–15
date deemed filed, **10·**28
defects, waiver of, **10·**31–32
definition of claim, **10·**8
disallowance
notice of disallowance, **10·**33–34
prerequisite to suit, **10·**33–34
thirty-day letter as notice, **10·**34
waiver of notice of disallowance, **11·**3, **11·**4
drafting claim, **10·**9–15

Fraud cases (*Cont.*)
collateral estoppel, **12**·15–16
limitations on assessment, extended, **4**·10
pleadings (refund suits), **11**·16, **11**·19
pleadings (Tax Court), **5**·16, **5**·27
"Freedom of Information" Act, 6·14, **13**·12
Full-payment rule, 10·2
amelioration of rule, **10**·3–4
amount to pay, **10**·6–7
assessment required, **10**·3
divisible taxes, **10**·4–5
employers' taxes, **10**·5–6
excise taxes, **10**·5
occupational taxes, **10**·6
penalty for failure to collect and pay over, **10**·5–6
"responsible officer" penalty, **10**·5–6
stamp taxes, **10**·6
estate tax, **10**·4
general rule, **10**·2
gift tax, **10**·4
income tax, **10**·3–4
interest on tax, **10**·2
selection of payment to make, **10**·6–7

Gift tax payment; *see* Full-payment rule
Government defenses (refund suits)
assignment, improper, **12**·9–10
collateral estoppel, **12**·12–16
equitable recoupment, **12**·4–7
estoppel by agreement, **1**·24–27, **12**·10–12
lack of overpayment, **12**·2–7
offsetting adjustments, **12**·3–4
recoupment, **12**·4–7
res judicata, **12**·12–16
variance, **10**·30–31, **12**·7–9
Government employees; *see* Witnesses
Government personnel in refund litigation
Appellate Section, Tax Division, **14**·7
Chief Counsel, Internal Revenue Service, **14**·4–5
Criminal Section, Tax Division, **14**·7
General Litigation Section, Tax Division, **14**·7
Internal Revenue Service field offices, **14**·5–6
internal sections, Tax Division, **14**·8
Litigation Control Unit, Tax Division, **14**·8
Regional Counsel, Internal Revenue Service, **14**·6
Refund Trial Sections, Tax Division, **14**·2–4
Review Section, Tax Division, **14**·6
United States Attorney, **14**·6

Government records
discovery, **13**·20–21
evidence, statutes on, **A**·3–7, **A**·14–15

Income tax payment; *see* Full-payment rule
Increased deficiency by Tax Court, 3·2, **3**·6
Injunction, assessment and collection, 4·8
Interest on deficiencies, 2·8
Interest on refunds, 2·8, **16**·15
Internal Revenue Code (specific sections); *see* Appendix E
Internal Revenue Service documents (discovery), **13**·20–21
Interrogatories (refund suits)
answers to, preparation of, **13**·16
Court of Claims, not available, **13**·8
form of interrogatories, **C**·82
government interrogatories, **13**·17
taxpayer interrogatories, **13**·17–18
use of answers at trial, **13**·16, **15**·4, **15**·14; *see also* Discovery (refund suits)

Jeopardy assessment
effect on Tax Court jurisdiction, **3**·5
Joint Committee on Internal Revenue Taxation
administrative procedures, **1**·14
refund suit settlements, **14**·20
Tax Court settlements, **7**·9
Judgment (refund suits)
Court of Claims judgments, **16**·5
computation of amount, **16**·5
costs; *see* Costs (refund suits)
entry of judgment, **16**·5–6
"money" judgment, **16**·6
preparation of judgment, **16**·5
district court judgments, **16**·1–2
certificate of probable cause, **16**·3–4
computation of amount, **16**·2
contents, **16**·2–3
costs; *see* Costs (refund suits)
definition, **16**·1–2
District Director as defendant, **16**·3–4
entry of judgment, **16**·3
forms of judgment, **C**·93, **C**·94
preparation of judgment, **16**·2–3
Judgment (Tax Court); *see* Entry of decision (Tax Court)
Jurisdiction (refund suits), **10**·1–2
assessment requirement, **10**·3
claim requirement; *see* Claim for refund
deficiency notice while suit pending, effect, **2**·15, **13**·29–30
disallowance of claim, **10**·33–34
extent of jurisdiction acquired, **10**·6–7